presented to

_____

by

_____

on the occasion of

_____

date

_____

The grass withers
and the flowers fade,
but the word of our
God stands forever.

ISAIAH 40:8

new believer's
BIBLE
new testament

first steps for new christians
GREG LAURIE, GENERAL EDITOR

New Living
Translation®
SECOND EDITION

Tyndale House Publishers, Inc.
Carol Stream, Illinois

Contributors

Greg Laurie, General Editor
Karen Dagher, Harvest Ministries Editor
Danny Bond, Harvest Ministries Assistant Editor
Steve Benson, Tyndale House Editor
Ron Kaufmann and Timothy R. Botts, Graphic Designers

Greg Laurie is not only an evangelist, author, and pastor but is the president of Harvest Ministries as well. Harvest Ministries sponsors Harvest Crusades. These crusades are public evangelistic events intended to present the message of Jesus Christ to people in a nonreligious environment. Begun in 1990, Harvest Crusades are known for their informal atmosphere, contemporary music, and simple, straightforward messages by Greg Laurie. If you would like more information on Harvest Ministries and/or their crusades, write to Harvest Ministries, P.O. Box 4000, Riverside, CA 92514-4000. Or call (951) 687-6595. On the Internet, type http://www.harvest.org.

Photographs: pages 137, 171, and 231 copyright © by Photodisc; pages 97 and 181 copyright © by BrandX; pages 135 and 193 copyright © by Getty Images; page 169 copyright © by Dex Images; page 277 copyright © by Digital Vision; page 309 copyright © by Alamy. All rights reserved.

Photograph on page 63 courtesy of Phil Comfort. All rights reserved.

This Bible is typeset in the typeface *Lucerna,* designed by Brian Sooy & Co. exclusively for Tyndale House Publishers, Inc. All rights reserved.

ISBN 978-1-4143-1219-4 Softcover (BAC ed.)
ISBN 978-1-4143-1306-1 How to Find God (BAC ed.)
ISBN 978-1-4143-1653-6 Set Free (BAC ed.)

www.biblesatcost.com

Printed in the United States of America

17   16   15   14   13   12
17   16   15   14   13   12

Tyndale House Publishers and Wycliffe Bible Translators share the vision for an understandable, accurate translation of the Bible for every person in the world. Each sale of the *Holy Bible,* New Living Translation, benefits Wycliffe Bible Translators. Wycliffe is working with partners around the world to accomplish Vision 2025—an initiative to start a Bible translation program in every language group that needs it by the year 2025.

Congratulations! You are holding in your hands the best-selling book in the history of humanity—the Bible. It was given to us by God thousands of years ago. Although the Bible has been around for some time, the wisdom and knowledge contained within are still relevant today. In fact, everything you need to know about God and life is found in the pages of this book. It is the "user's manual of life" that we all have been searching for.

The Bible does not just teach us about life, though. It also shows us how to come into a *personal* relationship with the very God who inspired this book. This particular Bible contains features that have been specially designed to help you understand, discover, and deepen the personal relationship that God wants to have with you.

Perhaps you are not yet a believer in Jesus Christ, but you want to know more about Christianity. You may even want to be a believer, but you just don't know how to become one. In the *New Believer's Bible New Testament,* you will find a section titled "How You Can Know God" (page A11). Here, you will learn how to establish a life-changing relationship with Jesus.

Maybe you have just started in the Christian faith. You are a new believer. Here you will find out how to lay a good foundation for your faith and walk with God in the years ahead.

You may even be a believer who is mature in the faith. Here you will be refreshed and reminded of the essentials of the Christian faith and life.

THE MAIN FEATURES
The *New Believer's Bible New Testament* contains four reading tracks: Cornerstones, First Steps, Off and Running, and Big Questions. Each reading track (except "Big Questions") is composed of two kinds of notes: *up-front* and *in-text*. The up-front notes appear before the Bible text and are made up of one to two paragraphs and two to eight numbered points that refer you to Scripture passages and their accompanying in-text notes. (Big Questions is composed of an up-front list of questions and the page numbers you can find them on, and the in-text notes that answer those questions.)

Reading Track One: Cornerstones: Cornerstones—blocks of stone—were traditionally used to start a building's foundation. Likewise, the Cornerstones reading track helps you to begin to lay a solid foundation for your faith. Here you will learn about God's character, Jesus' life, and the Holy Spirit's role in the lives of believers. Cornerstones also contains notes on the essential Christian character traits that are developed and nurtured by a personal relationship with Jesus Christ. Some of those traits are love, forgiveness, purity, honesty, wisdom, peace, and joy.

Reading Track Two: First Steps: The phrase *first steps* brings to mind the image of a young child taking his or her first unassisted steps. Like this young child, new believers in Christ need to learn how to walk all over again, so to speak. That is because the Christian life for most people is a completely new way of living. To help you learn to live this new life, the First Steps reading track gives you valuable building blocks for growing in your faith. Here you will discover the importance and "how to" of studying the Bible, praying, finding the right church, resisting temptation, and seeking God's will for your life.

Reading Track Three: Off and Running: "How does God's Word apply to my everyday life?" This is one of the most widely asked questions about the Bible today. The Off and Running reading track answers this question. Here you will discover how to put your faith into action. You will see what the Bible has to say about important topics like marriage, parenting, priorities, conversation, and job performance. By helping you apply biblical principles to these aspects of your life, Off and Running takes you to the next level of the Christian life—living it day to day.

Reading Track Four: Big Questions: Life often presents us with difficult situations that cause us to ask hard questions. For instance, you may wonder how a good God could let something bad—like cancer—happen to you. Or you may wonder why Jesus Christ is the only way to God. Aren't other religions just as good? In the Big Questions reading track, you will find out what the Bible has to say about tough issues. Everything from alternative lifestyles to the second coming of Christ is covered here.

ADDITIONAL FEATURES

At the front and back of the *New Believer's Bible New Testament* you will find several features that will help you understand the Bible and your faith better. These features are:

- *How to Study the Bible*—a practical way for you to read through the New Testament of the Bible and a list of questions to ask yourself as you read.

- *23 Great Bible Stories*—a list of well-known Bible stories from the New Testament, where you can find them, and the main lesson you can get out of them.

- *Memory Verses*—a list of key Bible verses from the New Testament to commit to memory.

- *Prophecies about Jesus*—a list of Old Testament passages that contain prophecies about Jesus and the New Testament references that record his fulfillment of those prophecies.

- *Glossary of Christian Terms*—a quick-reference guide to help you understand the meanings of words like *atonement, justification, redemption,* and *sanctification.*

HOW TO USE THE READING TRACKS

The *New Believer's Bible New Testament* is easy to use. Simply turn to page A23 and begin reading the "Who Is God?" up-front note in the Cornerstones reading track. Look up the Scripture passages and in-text notes referred to at the end of the up-front note. After you have read all the Scripture passages and in-text notes for "Who Is God?" move on to the next up-front note ("Who Is Jesus?") and begin the process over again.

You can read one up-front note and its Scripture passages and in-text notes a day. Or, if you prefer, browse through the table of contents and choose the topic(s) that interests you the most for your daily reading.

Colossians 3:16 says, "Let the message about Christ, in all its richness, fill your lives." God wants his Word to permeate every area of your life—your home, your business, your play time as well as your prayer time. So open your Bible and your heart, and God will speak to you from these pages. Don't let anything keep you from spending time each day in God's Word.

Greg Laurie

what is missing in our lives?

Purpose, meaning, a reason for living—these are all things we desire and search for in life. Despite steps each one of us takes to find purpose and meaning in life, we still feel empty, unfulfilled. That is because there is a spiritual emptiness in each of our lives. We each have a hole in our heart, a spiritual vacuum deep within our soul—a "God-shaped blank." Possessions won't fill this hole, nor will success. Relationships alone cannot satisfy this emptiness, and morality, in and of itself, falls miserably short of occupying this space. In fact, even religion cannot fill the void in our heart.

There is only one way to effectively fill that void. This way will not only help us to have a life that is full and rich on this earth, but—more important—will give us the absolute hope of spending eternity in the presence of God. Before we can truly appreciate this good news, though, we need to understand the bad news, which is a serious problem we all have.

the problem: sin The Bible clearly identifies our serious problem as sin. Sin is not just an act but the actual nature of our being. In other words, we are not sinners because we sin. Rather, we sin because we are sinners! We are born with a nature to do wrong. King David, an Old Testament Israelite ruler, wrote, "For I was born a sinner—yes, from the moment my mother conceived me" (Psalm 51:5). Because we are born sinners, sinning comes to all of us naturally. That is why it is futile to think that the answer to all of life's problems comes from "within." According to the Bible, the *problem* is within! Scripture tells us, "The human heart is the most deceitful of all things, and desperately wicked. Who really knows how bad it is?" (Jeremiah 17:9).

We are not basically good—we are basically sinful. This sinfulness spills out into everything we do. Every problem we experience in our society today can be traced back to our refusal to live God's way. Clear back to the Garden of Eden, Adam made his choice, and he suffered the consequences of it, setting the pattern that all humanity would follow. The Bible explains, "When Adam sinned, sin entered the entire world. Adam's sin brought death, so death spread to everyone, for everyone sinned. . . . Yes, Adam's one sin brings condemnation for everyone" (Romans 5:12, 18).

"That's not fair!" you may protest. Why should we suffer because of what someone else has done? Yet, given the opportunity, each one of us would have done the same thing as Adam. In fact, not a single day passes that we do not face the same test that was set before Adam. God has given us the freedom to choose between two separate paths: the path that leads to life and the path that leads to death. The Bible says, "Today, I have given you the choice between life and death, between blessings and curses. Now I call on heaven and earth to witness the choice you make. Oh, that you would choose life, so that you and your descendants might live!" (Deuteronomy 30:19).

without a leg to stand on Someone may say, "But I live a good life. I try to be kind and considerate to others. I live by the Ten Commandments." But the truth of the matter is that the Ten Commandments, or the law, as they are called in the Bible, were not given to make us good but to show us how bad we are. The Bible tells us, "No one can ever be made right with God by doing what the law commands. The law simply shows us how sinful we are" (Romans 3:20). The purpose of the law is to make us realize how sinful we are. You might say that God's law was given to "shut our mouths" and show us that we desperately need his help and forgiveness for our terminal condition as sinners.

Look at the passages below to get a better understanding of the nature and seriousness of sin.

1. We Have All Missed the Mark (see Romans 3:23, page 170). Romans 3:23 says, we have *all* sinned. For those who would claim to be the sole exception to this eternal truth, verse ten of this chapter plainly says, "No one is righteous—not even one" (Romans 3:10). Another word for *righteous* is *good*. The word *righteous* means, "One who is as he or she ought to be." When the Bible says that no one is righteous, or good, it is not so much refer- ring to behavior but to inner character.

What exactly is "God's glorious standard" that Romans 3:23 says we have failed to meet? God's "glorious standard" is absolute perfection. Jesus said, "But you are to be perfect, even as your Father in heaven is perfect" (Matthew 5:48). In other words, anyone who is not as good as God is not acceptable to him.

One definition of *sin*, derived from the Greek word *hamartia*, is to "miss the mark." As far as the mark of perfection goes, we miss it by a mile. Although our sinful nature makes it impossible for us to live up to God's standard, we cannot blame sin on our nature alone. Sin is also a deliberate act.

2. *Sin Is a Deliberate Act* (see Ephesians 2:1-3, page 228). Another word for *sin* in Ephesians 2:1 is *transgressions* or *trespasses*. This word speaks of a lapse or deviation from truth. In contrast to simply "missing the mark," this is a deliberate action. Because sin is a deliberate action, we cannot blame our sin on our society or our environment or our mental or physical state. Everyone has chosen to do what was wrong. If we protest this point, "we are only fooling ourselves and not living in the truth" (1 John 1:8).

3. *The Ultimate Penalty for Sin Is Death* (see Romans 6:23, page 175). According to the Bible, we have offended a Holy God. We have not done this once or twice, but so many times that we are unable to keep count. Romans 6:23 says, "The *wages* of sin is death. . . ." Wages are something that you are paid for work rendered. In other words, you earn your wages. Because we have all repeatedly sinned, we have earned the penalty of death, which is eternal torment and punishment in a place called hell.

Amid all this talk about sin and death, there is some good news. God has given us a way to escape the penalty of our sin. He has made it possible for us to have a relationship with him and enjoy the hope of eternal life without punishment.

the solution: Jesus Christ

God understood our problem and knew that we could do nothing about it. Because God loves us, he sent his own Son, Jesus Christ, to earth to bridge the chasm of sin that separates us from him.

why Jesus can bridge the gap There has never been anyone like Jesus. For starters, Jesus was not conceived in the womb of his mother through natural means. Rather, he was supernaturally conceived in the womb of a young virgin named Mary. Because of his supernatural conception, Jesus, who is wholly God, also became wholly human.

Though Jesus is God, he chose to lay aside the privileges of his deity to live on earth as a man. The Bible, describing the sacrifice Christ made in becoming a man, says that Jesus "gave up his divine privileges; he took the humble position of a slave and was born as a human being. When he appeared in human form, he humbled himself in obedience to God and died a criminal's death on a cross" (Philippians 2:7-8). It is extremely important to note that Jesus did not cease to be God when he came to earth. He simply laid aside his divine privileges and walked the earth as a man. In doing so, he was personally able to experience the gamut of human emotions, ranging from happiness to deep sorrow. He felt what it was like to be tired, cold, and hungry.

Moreover, he came to this earth with a clear objective in mind: to bridge that gap between us and God.

When the Israelites of the Old Testament sinned, they would have the high priest go into the Temple and offer an animal sacrifice to God to atone for their sins. In a symbolic sense, this was a way of putting one's sins on the animal, which stood in the place of the guilty person. The Bible teaches, "Without the shedding of blood, there is no forgiveness of sins" (Hebrews 9:22).

The sacrificial rituals carried out by the Israelites in the Old Testament foreshadowed what Jesus would do when he came to this earth. He took the sin of the world upon himself when he hung on the cross so many years ago.

Numerous Old Testament prophecies pointed not only to his birth and life but also to his death, including the way in which he would die.

Jesus knew from the beginning that he had come expressly to die for the sins of humanity. He also knew that this sacrifice would be made on a Roman cross. He began his final journey to the cross of Calvary at a place called Caesarea Philippi, and he often spoke of his impending death with his disciples. Scripture records, "From then on Jesus began to tell his disciples plainly that it was necessary for him to go to Jerusalem, and that he would suffer many terrible things at the hands of the elders, the leading priests, and the teachers of religious law. He would be killed, but on the third day he would be raised from the dead" (Matthew 16:21).

He was eventually arrested on false charges after Judas Iscariot, one of his own disciples, betrayed him. But it was no accident. If humanity was going to be put in touch with God and have the barrier that separated them removed, something drastic had to be done. In essence, with one hand Jesus took hold of a Holy God, and with the other hand he took hold of the sinful human race. As crude nails were pounded into his hands, he bridged the gap for us!

We must not forget, however, that three days after his crucifixion, Jesus rose from the dead! If it is true that "you can't keep a good man down," then it is even truer that you can't keep the "God-man" down.

we put Jesus on the cross

The necessity of the death of Jesus Christ on the cross shows just how radical our situation was as fallen people. It's been said that you can tell the depth of a well by how much rope is lowered. When we look at "how much rope was lowered" from heaven, we realize how grave our situation really was.

For that reason, don't blame the people of that day for putting Jesus on the cross. We are just as guilty as they. In reality, it was not the Roman soldiers who put him on the cross, nor was it the Jewish leaders: it was our sins that made it necessary for Jesus to volunteer for this torturous and humiliating death.

Read the verses and notes below to see exactly what Jesus did for us.

1. *The Greatest Demonstration of Love* (see Romans 5:6-8, page 173). Jesus did not die for us while we were his friends, but while we were his enemies, opposing him by our sinfulness. Yet, in spite of all of this, God demonstrated his love for us by dying on the cross. In this verse, the apostle Paul explains that Jesus did not simply die for humanity as a whole, but that he died for us as individuals. Elsewhere, Paul writes, "[Christ] loved me and gave himself for me" (Galatians 2:20).

Whenever you are tempted to doubt God's love for you, take a long look at the cross on which Jesus died. Then realize that, for all practical purposes, it was not nails that held him to the cross, but love.

2. *Forsaken That We Might Be Forgiven* (see Luke 23:32-49, page 99). Many of us have heard this story at some point in our lives. Yet the significance behind this heartwrenching scene is often missed or misunderstood. This was not simply some "good teacher" being crucified for his beliefs. It was God in human form who hung on that cross, bridging the gap between sinful people and a holy God.

Matthew's Gospel tells us that when Jesus hung on that cross, he cried out, "My God, my God, why have you abandoned me?" (Matthew 27:46). Many Bible scholars believe that those words marked the precise moment at which God placed the sins of the world upon his Son. The Bible, speaking of God, says, "You are of purer eyes than to behold evil, and cannot look on wickedness" (Habakkuk 1:13, NKJV). For that reason, the holy Father had to "turn his face" and pour out his wrath upon his own Son. On the cross, Jesus received the wages that were due us. He was not heard that we might be heard. The ear of God was closed to Jesus for a time that it might never be closed to us.

3. *Christ, the Sole Mediator* (see 1 Timothy 2:5-6, page 260). Why is there only one mediator who is qualified to bridge the gap between God and people? Haven't there been other religious leaders who have claimed to have *the* way to God? Haven't some of them also died as a result of their message?

While the answers to these questions may be yes, the truth is that not one of these other leaders was fully God and fully human. That is why Jesus is uniquely qualified to deal with sin. Jesus said, "I am the way, the truth, and the life. No one can come to the Father except through me" (John 14:6). Acts 4:12 tells us, "There is salvation in no one else! God has given no other name under heaven by which we must be saved." And, most important, Jesus Christ rose from the dead!

Though it is true that you must believe Jesus died on the cross for your sins in order to receive eternal life and be a true Christian, there is still something else you must do.

the response: accept God's offer

To know Jesus Christ personally and have your sins forgiven, you must believe that you are a sinner separated from God and that your only hope is Jesus Christ, the Son of God, who came and died for your sins. To stop here, however, would be to stop short of salvation.

There are two things you must now do to enter into a relationship with the God from whom you have been separated.

1. *Turn From Your Sins.* As Jesus began his public ministry, his first message was "Repent of your sins" (Mark 1:15). In essence, Jesus was telling the people to repent—to acknowledge their sinning, change their minds, and change the direction of their lives.

Look at it this way. In the past, we have been blinded by our sins, causing us to run from God. As we repent, we do a "U-turn" and start running toward him. It is not enough just to be sorry for our sins. We must also change our lifestyle, for the Bible teaches that "the kind of sorrow God wants us to experience leads us away from sin" (2 Corinthians 7:10). In other words, if you are really sorry for something, it will result in a change in your actions.

The apostle Paul summed up this change succinctly when he quoted Jesus, who had said that people must "turn from darkness to light, and from the power of Satan to God. Then they will receive forgiveness for their sins and be given a place among God's people, who are set apart by faith in me" (Acts 26:18).

You see, there are some things only God can do and some things only you can do. Only God can remove your sins and give you the gift of eternal life, but only you can turn from your sins and receive Jesus as your Savior. That brings up the second thing you must do to respond to God's offer.

2. *Believe in Jesus Christ and Receive Him into Your Life.* Having seen the enormity of your sin and decided to turn from it, you then must believe in and receive Jesus Christ as your Lord and Savior. Becoming a Christian, however, is far more than following a creed or trying to live by certain standards. Jesus said that you must be "born again," or more literally, "born from above" (John 3:3). This spiritual rebirth happens when we personally believe in Jesus Christ, receive him by inviting him into our lives, and turn from our sins. In other words, we ask Jesus to come and take residence in our lives, making the changes he deems necessary. A person must take this all-important step in order to become a child of God.

Notice that this offer is yours for the asking, and it is free. You don't have to work for it, trying to clean up your life before you make this life-changing decision. The Bible says, "The free gift of God is eternal life through Christ Jesus our Lord" (Romans 6:23).

Being a Christian also means having a relationship with the living God. In Revelation 3:20, Jesus said, "Look! I stand at the door and knock. If you hear my voice and open the door, I will come in, and we will share a meal together as friends." To better understand the meaning of this verse, it is important to understand the culture at the time it was written. Eating together in Bible times was a long, drawn-out affair. People would not sit on chairs behind tables in a formal setting as we do, but they would sit on the floor, reclining on pillows around a low table. The relaxed atmosphere made meals a time when you would not only satisfy your appetite but also receive a gratifying

HOW YOU CAN KNOW GOD

serving of enjoyable table conversation. You would share your heart and life with those who sat beside you.

Consequently, when Jesus says that he will "share a meal" with us, it implies intimacy, closeness, and friendship. He offers this to us, but we must first "hear him calling" us.

To hear God calling us, we must know how he speaks. One way in which God speaks to us is described in the Bible as a "still, small voice." This could be described in another way as that tug you might have felt on your heart from the Holy Spirit showing you your need for Jesus. He may even be speaking to you right now! It is at that point that you must "open the door." Only you can do that. Jesus will not force his way in.

Receiving Jesus Christ into Your Heart. If you are ready to turn from your sins and believe in Jesus Christ so that you can receive the forgiveness of sin and the hope of eternal life, then take a moment to bow your head and pray a prayer like this one right now:

> *God, I'm sorry for my sin. I turn from it right now. I thank you for sending Jesus Christ to die on the cross for my sin.*
>
> *Jesus, I ask you to come into my heart and life right now. Be my Lord, Savior, and friend. Help me to follow you all the days of my life as your disciple.*
>
> *Thank you for forgiving and receiving me right now. Thank you that my sin is forgiven and that I am going to heaven. In Jesus' name I pray, amen.*

Rededicating Your Life to Jesus Christ. Perhaps you are already a Christian but you have strayed from Jesus Christ. You have been a prodigal son or daughter. God will forgive you right now if you will return to him. He tells us in Scripture, "My wayward children . . . come back to me, and I will heal your wayward hearts" (Jeremiah 3:22). If you would like to return to God and rededicate your life to him right now, you may want to pray something like this:

> *God, I am sorry for my sin. I am sorry that I have strayed from you. I ask you to forgive me now as I repent of my sin. I don't want to live like a prodigal any longer.*
>
> *Renew and revive me as I once again follow you as my God. Thank you for your forgiveness. In Jesus' name I pray, amen.*

Whether you prayed to make a first time commitment or a recommitment, you have made the right decision. God has forgiven and received you if you really meant it. Know that your relationship with Jesus Christ will bring radical and dramatic changes in your life. Describing this, the Bible says, "Anyone who belongs to Christ has become a new person. The old life is gone; a new life has begun!" (2 Corinthians 5:17). Now that is good news! But more importantly, God has changed your eternal destiny. Instead of fearing an eternal punishment in a place called hell, you will spend peaceful eternity in his presence in heaven.

Read the next section to see what else God has done for you now that you have taken this step.

what God has done for you

What actually happens when Jesus Christ comes into your life? First, he saves you from your sins and the punishment you deserve as a result of them—eternity in hell. This is called salvation, or regeneration, and has to do with what takes place in your heart: God gives you new life.

Second, he justifies you. Justification has to do with your standing before God and includes the complete removal and forgiveness of your sins. Think about it! When you receive Jesus Christ into your life, you are completely forgiven. God's Word tells us, "Brothers, listen! We are here to proclaim that through this man Jesus there is forgiveness for your sins! Everyone who believes in him is declared right with God [justified]—something the law of Moses could never do" (Acts 13:38-39). Speaking of our sins, God says, "I will never again remember [your] sins and lawless deeds" (Hebrews 10:17). What a wonderful promise!

Justification, however, is more than just the forgiveness and removal of the guilt and condemnation that accompany sin. While God has removed your sins and forgiven you of them, he has also placed the perfect righteousness of Jesus Christ "into your account," so to speak. You don't have to earn it or try to achieve it. It is yours as a gracious gift from the God who loves you. To understand justification more fully, read the following Scripture passages and notes below.

1. God Promises Us His Gracious Forgiveness (see 1 John 1:9, page 305).
The word *confess* means "to say the same thing as another" or "to agree with." To confess means that we are agreeing with God about our sin. We are seeing it as he does. We know that God hates sin. Therefore, to truly confess our sin means that we essentially feel the same way God feels about what we have

done. After committing that sin, we will be determined to put it out of our lives and never do it again. That is true confession in the biblical sense. The reason many believers are not experiencing the forgiveness and joy they desire is because they have not yet truly confessed! Once we have met God's conditions, however, we will know his gracious forgiveness. We may not "feel" forgiven, but we are. We have his word on it.

2. **God Has Balanced Our Moral and Spiritual Budget** (see Romans 5:1-2, page 173). When God makes us right in his sight, he does so by placing all of the righteousness of Christ to our credit. This balances the moral and spiritual budget for us. We now have sufficient "capital of character" to get on with the business of living.

   Up to this point, salvation has been God's responsibility. From this point on, it continues to be his responsibility except that we are responsible for the wise investment of our "capital of character"—that is, we are responsible for living as God desires us to. It is as if your checking account were empty, but then someone made a $100,000 deposit. What you do with that money is up to you.

3. **God Calls Us His Children** (see Luke 15:11-32, page 86). This incredible story illustrates what happens when a person turns from sin and returns to God. First, notice that the father in the story did not give this prodigal son what he deserved—banishment. In the same way, we do not receive from God what we deserve—punishment for sin. Second, the young man was given what he did not deserve—the rights and privileges of full sonship. Likewise, although we are not worthy to be called children of God, he calls us sons and daughters. In summary, he doesn't give us what we deserve (judgment). He gives us what we don't deserve (forgiveness and justification).

Speaking of sons and daughters, read on to see how God has adopted you into his family.

adopted and assured

We have looked at what happens when we are regenerated (when Christ comes into our lives) and when we are justified (when God forgives our sin and puts his righteousness in its place). Now let us look at another incredible thing God has done for us. He has adopted us into his family as his children!

Adoption means "to be given the rights of a son." In essence, you have been given the full rights of sonship in the family of God as though you were born that way. The story of the Prodigal Son illustrates this (Luke 15:11-32). The wayward son thought that after leaving home, he would no longer be considered a son but would instead be treated as a hired servant. Much to his surprise, when he made the long journey home, his father welcomed him and smothered him with kisses. He then gave orders to bring out the best robe and to put a ring on his finger, signifying full rights as a son. That is exactly what God has done for you! Take some time now to examine three Scripture passages that assure you of your adoption into God's family.

1. *God Disciplines His Children* (see Hebrews 12:5-9, page 286). Recognizing you are now a child of God is not some distant hope but a present reality. One of the ways God will remind you of this is by correcting you and bringing you back into line like a loving father when you stray away from him.

   Before we were believers, we may have felt no sense of guilt for certain things we did or did not do. But now that we are Christians, God's Holy Spirit shows us the way to live, which includes correcting us. He does this not because he hates us, but because he loves us as his own dear children. Understanding this truth should help us in the way we behave.

2. *You Have an Approachable Father* (see Galatians 4:6, page 224). The Aramaic word translated "dear Father" is *abba*, which is a word of affection that a young child would use endearingly toward his or her father. A Western equivalent of that phrase would be "papa" or "daddy." God does not want to be viewed as some distant, uninterested father, but as a loving, approachable father to whom you can turn at any time because you are his child.

3. *His Promises Are Not Based upon Your Feelings* (see 1 John 5:11-13, page 311). There will be times as a Christian when you may not "feel" God's presence. You may even be tempted to doubt that he has come into your life. But 1 John 5:13 does not say, "I write this to you who believe in the Son of God so that you may *feel* you have eternal life." This is because feelings come and go. They fluctuate. Nor does the Bible say, "I write this so that you may *hope*—if God is in a really good mood—that you have eternal life." It says, "so that you may *know*. . . ." Eternal life is yours! Stand on God's promise to you. You are forgiven, justified, adopted into his family, and assured of salvation. Now that is reason to rejoice!

To find out more about God, turn to "Who Is God?" on the next page in the Cornerstones section.

who is God?

Thousands of years ago, Pharaoh, the Egyptian ruler, posed a question people are still asking today: "Who is the LORD that I should listen to him?" That's a good question, but it is not an easy subject to tackle. It is difficult for our limited minds to grasp the limitless, eternal God. It has been said, "If God were small enough for your minds, he wouldn't be big enough for your needs." For that reason, don't be exasperated if you can't fully understand who God is or why he does certain things. One day, Scripture promises, everything about God and his character will be made perfectly clear to us (1 Corinthians 13:12). But until then, we will find everything we need to know about him in his Word. Look up the following notes and passages to find out who God is.

1. *God Is All-Knowing, Ever Present, and All-Powerful.* The Creator of the Universe knows every intimate detail of his creation (see Matthew 10:29-31, page 13).

2. *God Is Holy.* God's incomparable holiness merits our worship (see Revelation 15:2-4, page 330.

3. *God Is Loving and Just.* God's justice is tempered by his love (see feature on 2 Peter 3:3-9, page 302).

4. *God Is Personal.* This characteristic of God sets him apart from the so-called "gods" of other religions (see feature on Acts 17:22-31, page 156).

5. *God Is in Control.* It is important to remember that God is still in control, even if things around us seem to be in chaos (see Romans 11:33-36, pages 182-183).

6. *The God of the Bible Is the One True God.* While some insist on the existence of many gods, only the God of the Bible is the true, living God, worthy of our devotion (see 1 Corinthians 8:4-6, page 198).

who is Jesus?

Throughout history many people have attempted to answer this question. Some have done so accurately, but many have not. Our best source for answering this question is—once again—God's own Word. The Bible presents us with some inescapable truths about Jesus that demand a response. Anyone who seriously studies Scripture to learn more about Jesus must answer two probing questions: (1) What do you think of Jesus Christ? and (2) Who is he? The writer C. S. Lewis made this observation: "You must make your choice. Either this man was, and is, the Son of God: or else a madman or something worse. You can shut Him up for a fool, you can spit at Him and kill Him as a demon; or you can fall at His feet and call Him Lord and God. But let us not come with any patronising nonsense about His being a great human teacher. He has not left that open to us. He did not intend to" (*Mere Christianity*, rev. ed. [New York: Macmillan, 1952], 41).

Jesus was not just a good man. He was—and is—the God-man. Let's examine what the Bible has to say about Jesus.

1. ***Jesus Is Human.*** Jesus became our supreme example as God in human form (see feature on Philippians 2:5-11, page 238).
2. ***Jesus Is Divine.*** Even though Jesus became human, he still remained God (see feature on Colossians 1:15-20, page 244).
3. ***Jesus Had a Specific Mission to Accomplish.*** Jesus came to save humankind from sin (see feature on Luke 4:16-21, page 68).
4. ***Jesus Made the Ultimate Sacrifice.*** Jesus endured tremendous pain so that we could enjoy eternity with him (see 1 Peter 2:24, page 297).
5. ***Jesus Has Great Power to Transform People.*** Jesus can change the most unlikely person into one of the most powerful witnesses on his behalf (see feature on Acts 4:13, page 134).
6. ***Jesus Has an Eternal Dominion.*** Jesus' Kingdom extends beyond the boundaries of space and time (see feature on Revelation 1:4-8, page 320).

who is the Holy Spirit?

The Holy Spirit is the most mysterious member of the Trinity, which includes God the Father, God the Son (Jesus Christ), and God the Spirit (or the Holy Spirit). Many struggle with the idea of God being three persons, yet one. Quite honestly, we will never fully grasp the concept this side of heaven.

Some, however, have wrongly thought of the Holy Spirit as more of an "it" than a "he." That is probably due in part to biblical descriptions of him as being like the wind or coming upon Jesus in the form of a dove, among other comparisons.

Yet these descriptions must be balanced with the descriptions of the other members of the Trinity. For instance, Jesus referred to himself as "the bread of life" and "the good shepherd." In the same way, God the Father is referred to as "a refuge" and "a consuming fire." Does this mean that Jesus is a loaf of bread or a sheep farmer, or that the Father is a pile of rocks or a blast furnace? Of course not! These are simply metaphors used in Scripture to help communicate God's character. Likewise, the unique descriptions attributed to the Holy Spirit do not imply that the Holy Spirit is merely some "force" or "power." Jesus said this about the Holy Spirit: "When the Spirit of truth comes, he will guide you into all truth. . . . He will tell you about the future" (John 16:13). Note the use of the pronoun *he*. The Holy Spirit has a distinct personality, and he also has specific work that he wants to do in our lives as followers of Jesus Christ. Explore what the Bible says about him.

1. ***Who the Holy Spirit Helps.*** The Holy Spirit strengthens and empowers followers of Christ (see feature on Acts 2:1-41, page 132).
2. ***How the Holy Spirit Works with the Father and the Son.*** The Holy Spirit works alongside God the Father and Jesus, God's Son, to make our lives pleasing to God (see feature on 1 Peter 1:2, page 296).
3. ***Why God Gives Us the Holy Spirit.*** The Holy Spirit's presence in our lives is God's mark of ownership (see feature on Ephesians 1:13-14, page 228).
4. ***How the Holy Spirit Works in Our Lives.*** The Holy Spirit draws us to Christ, enters our lives at conversion, and empowers us as we allow him to work in our lives (see feature on John 14:15-17, page 120).
5. ***When the Holy Spirit Can Be Sinned Against.*** There are six specific ways we can sin against the Holy Spirit (see feature on Acts 5:1-10, page 138).
6. ***Why Christians Need the Holy Spirit.*** Living the Christian life is impossible without the Holy Spirit's help (see feature on Galatians 5:16-26, page 222).

who is the devil?

What is the devil like? Does he really look like the red-suited, pitchfork-holding cartoon caricature seated on a throne in hell? Or does he roam through the earth disguised as an angel of light?

Unfortunately, far too many people do not have an accurate view of who the devil is. Many underestimate him and his prowess, even going so far as to doubt his very existence. Someone once asked the great evangelist Charles Finney, "Mr. Finney, do you believe in a literal devil?" Finney replied, "You try opposing him for a while, and you see if he's literal or not." You will find out how literal the devil is the moment you make a commitment to Jesus Christ.

The Bible clearly shows us just how active and conniving the devil really is. At the same time, Scripture also lets us know about the devil's limitations and ultimate demise. The more we understand the tactics of this intelligent spirit being, the better equipped we will be to ward off his attacks. Below are some key passages of Scripture that answer some of the most commonly asked questions about the devil—who is also referred to as Satan.

1. **Where Did Satan Come From?** Satan's pride led to his fall from heaven (see Revelation 12:7-9, page 327).
2. **What Are Satan's Abilities?** Satan does have the power and access to do certain things in this world (see feature on 2 Corinthians 4:3-4, page 212).
3. **What Are Satan's Limitations?** While we should not underestimate Satan's power, we should realize that it is limited (see 2 Timothy 4:18, page 268).
4. **How Does Satan Attack People?** Satan masterfully uses manipulation and distortion to deceive people (see 2 Corinthians 11:13-15, page 218).
5. **Who Can Thwart Satan's Agenda?** Those who lay down their lives for Christ will defeat this evil foe (see feature on Revelation 12:10-12, page 328).

what are angels?

According to recent surveys, most people believe in the existence of angels. A glut of books on the subject fills bookstore shelves. Still, our only reliable source on angels and their activity is the Bible. Just who are these mysterious creatures? What do they look like? Do they wear long, flowing robes and have large birdlike wings? And what is their purpose?

You might call angels "God's secret agents." They basically work undercover. Most of the time these secret agents remain invisible—except on those special occasions when God allows people to see them. No doubt God realized that if we were allowed to see them all of the time, they would become an object of our worship, which is to be reserved for God alone. Let's take some time to see what the Bible has to say about angels and their role in this world.

1. **Why Did God Create Angels?** God created angels as unique spiritual beings who worship Christ and care for his followers (see feature on Hebrews 1:4-14, page 276).
2. **What Do Angels Do in the Life of a Christian?** God has ordered the angels to protect his followers and keep them from harm (see Acts 27:23-24, page 165).
3. **How Are Angels Involved in Our Prayers?** Our prayers can trigger spiritual warfare (see Luke 22:42-44, page 96).

4. What Role Will Angels Play in the End Times? Angels will play a strategic role in spreading the everlasting gospel (see feature on Revelation 14:6-7, page 330).

what are demons?

Just as there are angels who look out for your welfare, there are angels who are bent upon your destruction. The Bible teaches that when Satan fell from heaven, he took one-third of the angels with him (Revelation 12:4). Although we do not know their exact number, Scripture tells us there are multitudes (Luke 2:13) and legions (Matthew 26:53) of angels. So Satan has a sizable, highly organized force under his control. These fallen angels, also known as demons, help Satan accomplish his purpose, which, in the words of Christ, is to steal, kill, and destroy. While the Bible does not give us specific details as to how demons work, we can be confident that everything we need to know about them is found in Scripture. We do not need to look elsewhere for insights into the spiritual world. See what God's Word has to say about these evil agents.

1. What Do Demons Believe? Strange as it may seem, demons acknowledge that there is only one God (see feature on James 2:19, page 294).

2. Can Demons Personally Harm You? Those people who have a true relationship with Christ cannot be overcome by demons; those who do not are "fair game" for these servants of Satan (see feature on Acts 19:13-20, page 158).

3. What Makes Demons Powerless? The name of Jesus used by the followers of Jesus makes the demons tremble (see feature on Luke 10:1-20, page 78).

what is heaven?

The Bible gives us wonderful, vivid descriptions of heaven. From Scripture we know that heaven's streets are made of gold, and that pain, fear, and sorrow are not present there. But even with all of this detail, we still fall short of understanding "the big picture." That is because it is difficult for us to grasp the absolute perfection and glory of heaven.

All splendor aside, though, what truly makes heaven spectacular is that we will be forever in God's presence. As the psalmist so poignantly expressed,

"You will show me the way of life, granting me the joy of your presence and the pleasures of living with you forever" (Psalm 16:11).

While we may not be able to have all of our questions about heaven answered here on earth, the Bible does answer some of our most probing questions.

1. **Who Will Enter Heaven?** Heaven is a place for those who have received Jesus Christ as Lord (see feature on John 14:2-6, page 118).

2. **When Does a Christian Enter Heaven?** When we take our last breath on earth, we will take our first breath in heaven (see feature on 2 Corinthians 5:6-9, page 214).

3. **Will We Recognize People in Heaven?** While our heavenly bodies may resemble our earthly bodies, we will in some ways be like the angels (see feature on Matthew 22:23-33, page 30).

4. **What Will Life in Heaven Be Like?** Our lives in heaven will no longer be consumed by the cares of this life, but we will be filled with joy being in the presence of our heavenly Father (see feature on Revelation 7:13-17, page 324).

what is hell?

According to the Bible, you have two options to choose from when it comes to deciding where you will spend your life after death. One option is heaven. The other is hell. Interestingly enough, while there seems to be an increased belief in a place called hell, most people don't believe they are headed there. Instead, they believe that hell is reserved for only the most hardened of criminals and other "evil" elements of our society. But God's Word judges people by a different set of criteria. You are not sent to hell for being a bad person any more than you are sent to heaven for being a good person. We all deserve to spend eternity in hell (Romans 3:22-23).

While God clearly says that those who reject the salvation offered through his Son, Jesus Christ, will spend eternity in this place of torment, he repeatedly gives each person ample opportunity to choose life—abundant life on earth and eternal life in heaven (2 Peter 3:9). If you haven't made that choice yet, or if you have decided and want a better understanding of what your nonbelieving friends will have to face, consider these facts about hell from the pages of Scripture.

1. **What Is Hell Like?** Hell is a place of unending, isolated torment (see feature on Luke 16:19-31, page 88).

2. **Who Will Go to Hell?** Those whose names do not appear in the Book of Life are destined to everlasting punishment (see feature on Revelation 20:11-15, page 334).

3. **What Is the Worst Punishment of Hell?** Hell's worst punishment is everlasting separation from God's presence (see feature on 2 Thessalonians 1:7-10, page 256).

love

On one occasion Jesus was asked what commandment was the most important. He replied, "The most important commandment is this: "Listen, O Israel! The LORD our God is the one and only LORD. And you must love the LORD your God with all your heart, all your soul, all your mind, and all your strength.' The second is equally important: "Love your neighbor as yourself'" (Mark 12:29-31).

These are the two most important commandments because if you truly love God with all your heart, soul, mind, and strength, you will want to do what pleases him. In the same way, if you really love others as much as you love yourself, you will be concerned for their welfare and will treat them accordingly. Before you can effectively love God, however, you must first realize how much he loves you.

Scripture explains that God showed his great love for us by sending Christ to die for us while we were still sinners who had no relationship with him (Romans 5:8). The more we realize this wonderful truth, the more our love for God will grow. The Bible correctly recognizes that our love for God comes as a result of his loving us first (1 John 4:19). These Scripture passages explore some different facets of the love we should have for God and for others.

1. *God Should Be the Greatest Love of Our Lives.* Before we can fully love one another, however, we must fully love God and understand his love for us (see Matthew 22:37-38, page 29).

2. *Christ's Love Sets the Standard.* Our love for others should model Christ's love for us (see feature on Ephesians 5:1-2, page 234).

3. *Love Surpasses All Spiritual Gifts.* A Christian who understands what love truly means and shows love in his or her life is the greatest testimony to others (see feature on 1 Corinthians 13:1-13, page 206).

4. *Our Love for God Prepares Us for Service.* The depth of our love for God directly affects our ability to minister to others (see feature on John 21:15-17, page 126).

5. *Our Love for Others Mirrors the Condition of Our Heart.* The love we have for those around us is an indication of the strength of our Christian walk (see feature on 1 John 2:9-11, page 306).

6. *Our Love Should Grow.* The closer we grow to God, the more our love for others should increase (see feature on 1 Thessalonians 3:12-13, page 250).

forgiveness

One of the great principles of the Christian life is forgiveness. Jesus modeled this principle for us when he hung on the cross and prayed for the very people who had put him there (see Luke 23:34, page 99). His words were so powerful and unexpected that they brought about the conversion of one of the thieves hanging on a cross next to him.

Because Jesus completely forgave us, he wants us to follow his example by forgiving others. As Scripture says: "Be kind to each other, tenderhearted, forgiving one another, just as God through Christ has forgiven you. Imitate God, therefore, in everything you do, because you are his dear children" (Ephesians 4:32–5:1). The Bible gives us several important characteristics of the forgiveness we should have for others.

1. ***Forgiveness First Comes from God.*** Our forgiving of others should flow from God's forgiving us (see feature on Mark 11:25, page 54).
2. ***Forgiveness Knows No Limits.*** For a Christian, no wrong is too great or too small to forgive (see feature on Matthew 18:21-35, page 26).
3. ***Forgiveness Is Not Selective.*** You can't choose to forgive some people and not forgive others (see feature on Matthew 5:43-48, page 8).
4. ***Forgiveness Breaks Down Walls.*** When you choose to forgive, you experience true freedom (see Colossians 3:12-15, page 247).

purity

Purity is a quality we hear too little about today. Usually when we do hear something about purity, it is in reference to sexual purity. But purity goes beyond this to include wholesome thoughts, a sincere desire to do what is right, and a commitment to obey God's Word. Jesus alluded to the importance of purity by promising that those whose hearts were pure would see God (Matthew 5:8). In using the word heart, Jesus was saying that the center of our being—our will, our emotions, and our thought processes—needs to be cleansed of sin. The Bible texts below examine the idea of purity and how it affects us as followers of Jesus Christ.

1. ***Don't Place Yourself in the Way of Unnecessary Temptation.*** Know your moral weaknesses and avoid situations where the temptation to sin would be irresistible (see James 1:14-15, page 289).
2. ***Guard the Content of Your Thoughts.*** Don't fill your mind with the world's moral filth (see feature on 2 Timothy 2:22, page 266).
3. ***Beware of the Sins of the Heart.*** The person who commits adultery in his heart is just as guilty as the person who actually carries it out (see feature on Matthew 5:27-30, page 6).

4. *Avoid Adulterous Relationships.* God specifically warns us against living in immoral relationships (see feature on 1 Thessalonians 4:1-8, page 252).

5. *If You Fall, Ask God to Forgive You and Purify Your Heart and Desires.* Only God can forgive you, restore your joy, and fill you with the right desires (see 1 John 1:9, page 305).

6. *Keep an Eternal Perspective.* Don't waste your time chasing after earthly pleasures (see feature on 2 Peter 3:10-11, page 304).

7. *Live to Please God.* Surrendering your life to the leading of the Holy Spirit is the only way to live a life that is pleasing to God (see feature on Romans 8:5-8, page 174).

perseverance

There will be times in your Christian walk when you will feel emotionally "down." You may think that God has forgotten about you. Or you might become discouraged as you see others who have professed faith in Jesus Christ lose interest in spiritual things and fall away. You may begin to wonder whether you are next on the devil's "hit list." But God will not allow you to be hit with more than you can handle spiritually. In fact, it is during times of trouble that you will actually be strengthened, not weakened.

As you read your Bible, you will come across words like *endurance* and *perseverance*. These words are often used when the Bible compares the Christian life to a race. The race referred to is a marathon, not a fifty-yard dash. Because the Christian life is a long-distance run, you need to pace yourself, to persevere, and most of all, to *finish* the race. Look up the following passages that describe how and why you need to persevere through the inevitable struggles of life.

1. *Perseverance Produces Results.* As you steadily grow in your understanding of God's Word and apply it to your life, you will win others to the Lord (see feature on Luke 8:15, page 74).

2. *Life's Trials Will Make You Stronger.* You shouldn't view difficulties as obstacles to your faith, but as opportunities for spiritual growth (see feature on James 1:2-4, page 290).

3. *Christ Endured Great Pain for Us.* Jesus modeled the ultimate in endurance so that we would be encouraged to keep our faith strong in the race of life (see feature on Hebrews 12:1-3, page 284).

4. *God Honors Those Who Persevere.* A wholehearted commitment to God will enable you to "finish well" with your faith intact (see 2 Timothy 4:7-8, page 268).

honesty and integrity

Honesty and integrity seem to be in short supply these days. Yet the Bible tells us that they are a part of the godly person's life. Unfortunately, the world tends to gloss over that aspect of the Christian life. It wants to characterize Christians as people who are out of touch with reality. But the Christian is simply someone who allows God to influence every aspect of his or her life—down to the practical, everyday dealings of business, finances, and relationships. The following passages examine how honesty and integrity should characterize our lives.

1. ***We Should Be above Criticism.*** A faithful and honest lifestyle will cause others to be more receptive to our message (see 2 Corinthians 7:2, page 214).
2. ***Our Conduct Should Cause Others to Glorify Christ.*** Living a good, honest life around our unbelieving neighbors will ultimately bring glory to God (see feature on 1 Peter 2:9-12, page 300).
3. ***We Need to Set an Example for Others.*** We must seriously pursue a life of integrity in order to be a solid example for our fellow Christians (see feature on Titus 2:6-8, page 270).

faith and works

When a person truly comes to Jesus Christ, this relationship will dramatically transform his or her life. We may see this transformation more immediately in the lives of some than others. For those whose lives are characterized by pronounced bad habits and blatant immoral living, the change in lifestyle will show others that something profound has indeed happened within that person's life. For others who may not be known for blatantly sinful living, the change may not be as outwardly pronounced, but it is just as significant. Remember, all of us were separated from God by sin, which was dealt with and atoned for at the cross of Jesus.

Our conversion will show itself in both fruit and works. This concept of "bearing fruit" is used often in Scripture to describe the results of someone's commitment to Jesus Christ. If we do not bear fruit, then it is apparent we have not really come to know Jesus Christ as Lord and Savior. Bearing fruit is not an option. It is the natural result of a person coming into union with God. Sometimes there is confusion in this area of fruit bearing, or works. See what the Bible has to say about the issue.

1. ***Our Lives Should Show That God Is at Work in Our Hearts.*** God desires that we demonstrate our spiritual growth through our outward actions (see feature on Romans 7:4, page 172).

2. ***We Must Live Out Our Faith.*** Faith without deeds is incomplete (see feature on James 2:14-18, page 292).

3. ***God Saved Us for a Purpose.*** While God himself gave us salvation, he planned that our salvation would lead to good works (see feature on Ephesians 2:10, page 230).

4. ***Our Walk Should Match Our Talk.*** God isn't as concerned with what we *say* we believe as with how we *live* what we believe (see feature on Matthew 7:21-23, page 10).

discernment

An inspector who worked for Scotland Yard in the counterfeit department was once asked if he spent a lot of time handling counterfeit money. He said, "No." He then explained that he spent so much time handling the "real thing" that he could immediately detect the counterfeit. In the same way, as we become knowledgeable about God's Word, we, too, will be able to detect teachings and concepts that are contrary to Scripture. Make no mistake—counterfeit "truth" is out there in force. Look at the following Scripture passages to find out how you can keep from falling prey to false teachings.

1. ***Beware of Satan's Clever Imitations.*** Satan's work and agents may appear godly, but in the end they will be exposed for what they really are (see feature on Matthew 13:24-30, page 18).

2. ***Recognize Satan's Strategies.*** Lies and deceit are Satan's two main strategies to lead people away from the truth (see feature on 1 Timothy 4:1-2, page 260).

3. ***Understand the Difference between the True Gospel and a False Gospel.*** Scripture provides us with a "litmus test" to distinguish between truth and error (see feature on 1 John 4:1-3, page 308).

4. ***Use God's Word to Evaluate Someone's Teachings.*** The best way to detect a counterfeit is to become more familiar with the "real thing" (see feature on Acts 17:11, page 154).

peace

Peace of mind—it seems elusive in a day when murders are commonplace, job security is nonexistent, and the moral fabric of society is tearing apart at the seams. Yet Jesus has promised that each one of us can experience true peace:

"I am leaving you with a gift—peace of mind and heart. And the peace I give is a gift the world cannot give. So don't be troubled or afraid" (John 14:27).

Unfortunately, some people are so caught up in the "pursuit of peace" that they have forgotten that Jesus has already given it to them. They have simply left that gift "unopened." And we cannot find peace outside of the parameters God has given us. As Augustine said many years ago, "Our souls are restless until they find their rest in God." Begin to "unwrap" this precious gift by examining what God's Word has to say about it.

1. ***Peace Begins When We Relinquish Control of Our Lives to God.***
When we give Jesus our burdens and allow him to guide us, we find rest (see feature on Matthew 11:28-30, page 14).

2. ***Perfect Peace Builds upon Total Trust.*** As God becomes a regular part of our daily lives, our worries begin to disappear (see John 16:33, page 121).

3. ***Our Peace Continues As We Follow the Holy Spirit.*** We must stop allowing our old, sinful nature to control us before we can really experience peace (see feature on Romans 8:5-8, page 180).

4. ***God's Peace Needs to Rule in Our Hearts.*** We must constantly keep other things from crowding out God's peace in our lives (see feature on Colossians 3:15, page 246).

joy

One noticeable change that takes place in a new believer's life is the inner joy he or she receives. In fact, joy is listed as part of the "fruit of the Spirit" that should be evident in a believer's life (see Galatians 5:22). But this joy is different from the fleeting and temporary "happiness" that is usually dependent upon "good things" happening in someone's life. While sorrows will come a believer's way, the Holy Spirit gives him or her an inner joy and peace that cannot be taken away. Below are some of the ways in which you can experience God's joy in your life.

1. ***Studying God's Word Helps Us to Experience His Joy.*** As we study God's Word and honor God with our lives, we experience his joy in our lives (see 1 Thessalonians 1:6, page 249).

2. ***Knowing and Trusting God Is the Source of Inexpressible Joy.*** The greatest joy we can experience comes only from a personal relationship with Jesus Christ (see feature on 1 Peter 1:8, page 298).

3. *Sharing Your Faith Results in Joy.* While laboring to introduce people to Jesus is difficult work, the end result will give you much to celebrate (see John 4:36, page 105).

4. *Overlooking Petty Issues Frees Us to Experience Joy.* God wants us to experience his joy in our lives and to avoid those things that could hamper that joy (see feature on 1 Corinthians 1:10-17, page 190).

5. *Knowing Whom You Belong to and What the Future Holds Brings True Joy.* Realizing that you are a child of God and that you will spend eternity in heaven with him will bring you joy (see feature on Romans 15:13, page 188).

accountability

Once you receive Jesus Christ into your life as your personal Lord and Savior, not only do you obtain the privileged gift of eternal life, but you immediately acquire a great responsibility. You have been entrusted with the message of the gospel and are responsible for what you do with it in your life. In the end, we know that what we have done on this earth for Christ will be examined before almighty God and displayed before the rest of the world. The question we must all ask is this: Will what I am doing for Christ and his Kingdom stand the test of time? Those who have done much with what God has given them will be greatly rewarded. Take some time to see what God's Word has to say on this subject.

1. *The More We Know, the Greater Our Responsibility Will Be.* The Lord holds those who have been given positions of spiritual leadership to a higher accountability for what they do (see feature on Luke 12:48, page 84).

2. *We Are Responsible for Our Own Sins and Mistakes.* We cannot pass blame onto others for our own failings (see Romans 3:23, page 170).

3. *We Need to Invest Our Abilities and Resources in God's Kingdom.* God has graciously given us abilities and resources to invest in the expansion of his Kingdom (see feature on Luke 19:11-26, page 92).

4. *The Value of Our Work on Earth Will Be Tested.* On Judgment Day, the quality of our faith and the work we have done for Jesus Christ will be revealed and rewarded accordingly (see feature on 1 Corinthians 3:10-15, page 192).

study the Bible

You might say that the Bible is the "user's manual of life" we have all been searching for. Everything we need to know about God and living a life that pleases him is found in its pages.

Tragically, some of us go through life without so much as picking up this amazing book, whose words were inspired by God. Yet success or failure in the Christian life is determined by how much of the Bible we get into our hearts and minds and how obedient we are to the principles and teachings found within it. Just as we need to continually breathe oxygen to survive, we need to regularly study the Bible to grow and flourish spiritually. Here is an important reason why we need to spend time in this life-changing book.

1. ***Studying the Bible Is Necessary for Our Spiritual Growth.*** The Bible performs three functions to help us mature spiritually (see feature on 2 Timothy 3:16-17, page 267).

2. ***Studying the Bible Keeps Us Spiritually Strong.*** The more we get into this book and apply its teachings, the more we will be able to stand our ground in the storms and trials of life (see Matthew 7:24-27, page 10).

3. ***Studying the Bible Makes Scripture a Central Part of Our Lives.*** God desires that we make the Bible an integral part of our lives (see Colossians 3:16, page 247).

4. ***Studying the Bible Helps Us Apply Its Truth to Our Lives.*** We will notice positive changes in our lives as we apply what we read in Scripture (see 2 Timothy 3:16-17, page 267).

pray

The idea of talking to God can be intimidating. But it doesn't have to be. In fact, prayer can be a wonderful experience if we know how to do it God's way. Fortunately, we have God's Word to teach us how to pray. The Bible instructs us to pray at all times, in any posture, in any place, for any reason. In addition, it does not matter whether you pray in King James English or the most contemporary jargon. God only desires that you pray from a pure and sincere heart.

The disciples observed the profound effect prayer had in Jesus' life and ministry. They witnessed how Jesus would often go off by himself to spend time in prayer with his heavenly Father. They saw the power, peace, and tranquillity that emanated from his life, giving him the ability to stay calm in troubled circumstances. Jesus' prayer life so impressed these men that they asked him to teach them to pray (Luke 11:1-13). Certainly if the perfect Son of God often took time to pray during his life here on earth, how much more do we, mere men and women, need to pray?

Because prayer is an essential ingredient to walking with Jesus Christ, we need to examine its elements found in God's Word.

1. *Prayer Was Modeled for Us by Christ.* Jesus took the time to show his followers how to pray (see feature on Matthew 6:5-15, page 7).
2. *Prayer Is Not a Solitary Experience.* God has given us his Holy Spirit to aid us in prayer, even when we do not know what to pray (see feature on Romans 8:26-27, page 175).
3. *Prayer Allows Us to Voice Our Requests to God.* Prayer is God's appointed way for us to relate our concerns and present our needs to him (see feature on James 4:2-3, page 291).
4. *Prayer Enables Us to Seek Forgiveness.* When we pray sincerely for forgiveness, God will hear our prayers and restore us (see James 5:15-16, page 294).
5. *Prayer Helps Us Overcome Worry.* In the midst of troubles, we can receive God's peace through prayer (see feature on Philippians 4:6-7, page 241).
6. *Prayer Increases Our Spiritual Knowledge and Maturity.* God will give us greater spiritual understanding through prayer (see Colossians 1:9, page 243).

look for and attend the right church

One of the essential building blocks of spiritual growth is fellowship with other believers by becoming part of a local church. The church (meaning the entire body of Christians) is not really an organization so much as an organism. It thrives by keeping its members spiritually active and well fed. The church provides you with spiritual instruction from God's Word, allows you to worship God with other believers, enables you to use your God-given gifts and abilities as God intended, and makes you accountable to spiritual leadership.

Some people think they can get enough spiritual input from Christian television, radio programs, and books. While those things do have value, nothing can replace the need to become an active member of a church. Think about it—if joining in fellowship with other believers was not important, why did Jesus establish the church? (See Matthew 16:18.) The Bible has plenty to say about the characteristics of a healthy, vibrant church and the necessity of Christian fellowship. There are four helpful insights from God's Word on looking for and attending the right church.

1. **What to Look for in a Church.** You should look for a church that has the qualities and characteristics of the first-century church (see feature on Acts 2:42, 44-47, page 133).

2. **Why We Need Fellowship with Other Believers.** Fellowship with other Christians sharpens our spiritual discernment and prepares us for Christ's return (see feature on Hebrews 10:25, page 283).

3. **Why the Church Needs You.** Not only will you benefit from the church, but the church will benefit from you and your God-given abilities (see feature on Ephesians 4:11-16, page 229).

4. **You Have a Place in the Church.** God has given each one of us a unique role to play in our place of fellowship (see feature on 1 Corinthians 12:12-31, page 205).

obey God

The real evidence of a true Christian is a changed life. The great British preacher Charles Haddon Spurgeon once said, "Of what value is the grace I profess to receive if it does not dramatically change the way that I live? If it doesn't change the way that I live, it will never change my eternal destiny."

A changed life begins with obedience to God. This means that you will have to stop doing certain things and start doing others. While God begins to change your heart and desires once you have surrendered your life to him, he still gives you the freedom to decide just how much of your life you will let him control. But know this: Whatever you give up to follow Jesus Christ will pale in comparison to what he will give you in return. For example, when you give up sinful behaviors for God, he will replace your sin with forgiveness and a clear conscience. With this incentive for obedience, look at six specific ways the Bible instructs us to obey God.

1. ***Recognize That You Are a New Creation.*** When you understand what God has done in your life, obedience becomes more of a desire than a mere duty (see feature on 2 Corinthians 5:14-17, page 215).

2. ***Follow God Wholeheartedly.*** When you follow God completely, you will finish the race of life well (see Hebrews 12:1-3, pages 285-286).

3. ***Offer God More than Lip Service.*** God looks at your heart more than your religious actions (see Matthew 23:25-28, page 31).

4. ***Live in God's Love.*** Discover the secret of true and lasting joy (see feature on John 15:9-11, page 121).

5. ***Put On God's Armor.*** Obedience prepares you for the battles of life (see feature on Romans 13:11-14, page 183).

6. ***Let God Occupy Your Thoughts.*** Your thoughts will affect your actions (see feature on Colossians 3:2-4, page 245).

resist temptation

Now that you are a follower of Jesus Christ, Satan is going to try to draw you away by tempting you to disobey God's Word. It is not a sin to be tempted—even Jesus was tempted (see Luke 4:1-13, pages 66-67). We sin when we give in to that temptation. The good news is that God will never let a temptation become so strong that we can't handle it. In addition, he has given us specific ways to handle temptation. Here are four things to remember when dealing with temptation.

1. ***Realize Who Is Tempting You.*** Satan is the mastermind behind all of your temptations (see feature on Ephesians 6:10-12, page 233).

2. ***Resist the Devil.*** The Bible says that if you resist Satan's enticements, he will flee from you (see feature on James 4:7-8, page 293).

3. ***Rejoice Because Victory Is Yours in Christ Jesus.*** God promises that he will always provide a way of escape (see feature on 1 Corinthians 10:13, page 201).

live in God's power

Some people look at the Christian life and say, "I couldn't begin to live that way and hold to those standards. It is too hard!" This is true. It is not hard to be a Christian—it is impossible (that is, without the help of the Holy Spirit). You see, God has given you power to live the Christian life. The moment you asked Jesus Christ into your heart, he gave you the gift of his Holy Spirit (see "Who Is the Holy Spirit?" page A24).

The Holy Spirit not only takes up residence in your heart, but he empowers you to live a holy life and to be an effective witness for Jesus Christ. The Holy Spirit's power is much like an investment. You need to draw upon his power daily to live out your faith. To find out more about how the Holy Spirit can empower and strengthen your Christian walk, look up the following passages of Scripture.

1. **God's Spirit Will Guide You.** The Holy Spirit will help you understand the truths of Scripture and the character of God (see feature on John 16:13-15, page 123).

2. **God's Spirit Will Empower Your Witness.** The Holy Spirit will give you greater courage and an increased ability to share your faith (see feature on Acts 1:8, page 131).

3. **God's Spirit Will Encourage You to Be Obedient.** You will have a Holy Spirit-inspired desire to obey God's commands (see Romans 8:13-14, page 176).

4. **God's Spirit Will Help You Overcome Sin.** Sin will no longer have the power over you it had before you accepted Christ into your life (see feature on Romans 8:9-14, page 173).

share your faith

Next to personally knowing Jesus and walking with him, one of the greatest blessings of the Christian life is to lead someone else to Jesus Christ. The good news is that God wants to use you—not just pastors, missionaries, and evangelists—as his instrument to speak to others.

Jesus gave us this very commission in Mark 16:15, where he says, "Go into all the world and preach the Good News to everyone." This wonderful charge is known as the "great commission." But the way some Christians follow it, you would think it was the "great suggestion." Sharing our faith, however, is something that Jesus wants—and commands—us to do! How do we do this? First Peter 3:15-16 tells us to be ready to give an answer to anyone who asks us about the hope we have in Jesus. Here are four passages from God's Word that will help you to share your faith.

1. **You Don't Need Any Training to Share.** A changed heart is all you need to begin sharing your faith with others (see feature on John 9:1-41, page 113).

2. **Be Open to God's Leading.** Effectively sharing your faith begins with a willing heart (see feature on Acts 8:4-8, 26-38, page 143).

3. **Understand the Simplicity of the Gospel.** The message of the gospel is simple yet powerful (see feature on 1 Corinthians 2:1-5, page 191).

4. **Share Your Own Story.** Never underestimate the strength of your personal testimony (see feature on Acts 26:1-23, page 163).

seek God's will

Have you ever wondered about the future? Have you pondered the answers to such important, life-changing decisions as whom you should marry or what career path you should pursue? More than likely, most of us have asked these questions and wondered if God has a definite plan or opinion on the matter. With that in mind, here is some good news: God is vitally interested in your life, and he does want to lead you in your decisions.

Jesus called his followers friends (see John 15:15). As God's friend, you already have an "inside track" in discovering God's will for your life. It is called the Bible. There you will find God's general will for your life (such as putting God first in all you do and following God's guidelines for marriage), as well as some principles to follow when seeking his specific direction for your life. In the end, finding God's will comes down to living out what you read in the Bible and then living by faith. Here are five steps you can take as you seek God's will.

1. **Unconditionally Surrender Your Life.** Certain conditions must be met if you want to know God's will for your life (see feature on Romans 12:1-2, page 177).

2. **Realize That God Has a Plan for Your Life.** Your life has purpose and meaning, and God wants to reveal it to you (see Ephesians 1:7-9, page 227)

3. **Act upon What God Has Already Revealed in Scripture.** God has already given us some specific guidelines to follow in his Word (see feature on 1 Thessalonians 4:1-8, page 251).

4. **Trust God Completely.** There is nothing more reassuring than entrusting an unknown future to a known God (see Philippians 4:6-7, page 240).

5. **Listen for God's Voice.** Sometimes God speaks to us in a quiet voice (see John 10:27, page 112).

live as a disciple

When you hear the word *disciple,* do you immediately think of the Twelve who followed Jesus during his ministry on earth? Many people do not realize that Jesus still has disciples in this day and age. While every disciple is a believer,

not every believer is necessarily a disciple. A disciple is someone who has
made a wholehearted commitment to follow Jesus Christ as Savior and Lord.
In one sense, you might call discipleship "radical Christian living." When
you truly make a commitment to be Christ's disciple, you will be living the
Christian life as it was meant to be lived. Anything short of discipleship is settling for less than what God desires. Here are four passages from the Bible that
explain what it means to truly be a disciple of Jesus.

1. ***A Disciple Takes Up His or Her Cross and Follows Christ.*** Being
   a disciple takes work and commitment (see feature on Luke 9:23-25,
   page 77).
2. ***A Disciple Counts the Cost.*** Jesus' disciples are willing to give up
   everything to follow him (see feature on Luke 14:25-33, page 87).
3. ***A Disciple Abides in Christ.*** The source of a disciple's strength comes
   from his or her closeness to Christ (see feature on John 15:1-17, page 119).
4. ***A Disciple Walks as Jesus Walked.*** Disciples pattern their lives after Jesus,
   the ultimate example of how to live (see feature on 1 John 2:3-6, page 307).

give to God

Money is such an important topic in the Bible that it is the main subject of
nearly *half* the parables Jesus told. In addition, one out of every seven verses
in the New Testament deals with the topic. To give you an idea of how this
compares with other topics, Scripture offers about five hundred verses on
prayer and fewer than five hundred on faith, while there are more than *two
thousand* verses on money!

You may be wondering what money has to do with your faith. Now that Jesus
Christ has come into your life, he wants to be Lord (to be in command) of every aspect of it. That includes your finances. Martin Luther astutely observed, "There are
three conversions necessary: the conversion of the heart, the mind, and the purse
[or wallet]." When we experience this "conversion of the purse" and give freely of
our finances to the Lord's work (to our church, a missionary, or a ministry), we will
make the best investment possible—an investment with eternal dividends. With
that in mind, here are five questions to consider about wealth and giving.

1. ***Why Should You Give a Portion of Your Financial Resources to
   God?*** God wants to prove his faithfulness through your regular giving, or
   tithes (see 2 Corinthians 9:6-11, pages 216-217).
2. ***How Much Should You Give?*** God encourages us to give sacrificially (see
   feature on Mark 12:41-44, page 55).

3. **What Happens When You Give?** When you give with the right motives, you will experience joy and God's generous blessings (see feature on 2 Corinthians 9:6-14, page 219).

4. **How Should You View Material Wealth?** Accumulating wealth should never be a high priority because it is eternally worthless (see feature on Matthew 6:19-34, page 9).

5. **Can You Enjoy Wealth?** God may bless you materially, but you are responsible for using your material blessings wisely (see feature on 1 Timothy 6:17-19, page 261).

have courage in trials

Many Christians have the mistaken idea that once they make a commitment to Jesus Christ, life will be smooth sailing from that day forward. This is certainly not the case. While it is true that walking with Christ will help us avoid many of the problems we used to face, we are still going to experience what the Bible calls "trials."

Trials may come in the form of a crisis, a sudden illness, the loss of a loved one, or some drastic change in your life. You may go through a difficult time when you don't feel God's presence, when church may not be as exciting as it once was for you, or your prayers seem to go no higher than the ceiling. This may cause you to wonder if you have angered God or if he has left you. But God does not allow us to experience trials because he wants to see us suffer. Rather, he allows these difficulties into our lives to help us grow spiritually—to learn to live by faith, not by feelings. Look up the following passages to see the role trials play in our lives. Notice also God's promise to be with us during these times of trouble.

1. **Trials Sharpen Our Faith.** Hardships develop our character and purify our faith (see feature on 1 Peter 1:3-7, page 297).

2. **Trials Help Us Comfort Others.** Experiencing suffering deepens our compassion for others who suffer (see feature on 2 Corinthians 1:3-7, page 211).

3. **Trials Are Survivable.** We must keep our eternal perspective through the tough times (see feature on 2 Corinthians 4:7-18, page 213).

4. **Trials Test Our Foundation.** When we ground our lives in Christ, we can weather any storm (see feature on Luke 6:47-49, page 73).

5. **Jesus Is with Us in Life's Storms.** We are never outside of God's watchful eye and his abiding presence (see feature on Mark 4:35-41, page 43).

6. **God Gives Hope to Our Troubled Hearts.** We can have peace of mind in the middle of our greatest trials (see feature on John 14:1-7, page 117).

marriage

How many times have you heard the cliché, "They have a marriage made in heaven"? This statement implies that some marriages are destined to be good, while others are destined to be bad. Such thinking assumes that marriage has a life of its own, and the only way to find out if you are to have a "good" one or a "bad" one is to "give it a shot." What most people don't seem to understand, though, is that marriage is like a mirror. It reflects what it sees. If a marriage is strong, it is because the husband and wife have put a lot of hard work into it. If a marriage is weak, it is because the husband or wife or both have neglected it.

God never intended for anyone to have a weak marriage. His design for marriage is a lifelong, fulfilling companionship. For a couple's marriage to thrive within his design, the couple must obey God and his Word and lay aside this world's distorted and perverse concept of marriage. The Bible contains truths that will not only help keep a couple together but will also keep their marriage strong. In fact, the lessons the Bible gives on marriage should serve as the foundation of every Christian couple's relationship. Whether you are married or single, the following verses will give you a godly perspective on marriage relationships.

1. **God Created Marriage.** We can learn more about God's marriage ideal from the world's first husband and wife (see Matthew 19:4-6, page 25).

2. **Husbands and Wives Have Distinct Roles in Marriage.** A marriage works when a couple follows God's specific design for the husband and the wife (see feature on Ephesians 5:21-33, page 232).

3. **The Boundaries of Marriage Are to Be Honored and Enjoyed.** Sexual intimacy is meant to be enjoyed only within the bounds of the marriage relationship (see Hebrews 13:4, page 287).

4. *Keeping Your Marriage Strong.* God promises punishment to those who commit adultery or lead immoral lives (see feature on Hebrews 13:4, page 286).

5. *Divorce Is Not Part of God's Plan.* Jesus teaches that marriage is meant to be a lifelong commitment (see feature on Mark 10:2-12, page 50).

6. *A Christian Should Not Leave a Non-Christian Spouse.* An unbelieving husband or wife should not be abandoned, but loved (see feature on 1 Corinthians 7:12-16, page 198).

7. *Marriage Is Not for Everyone.* Although God blesses many with marriage, some are given a calling or ability to remain single (see feature on 1 Corinthians 7:1-40, page 196).

8. *There Is an Intimacy in Marriage That Can Be Found Nowhere Else.* God wants you to have a fulfilling, enjoyable sex life within the parameters of marriage (see 1 Corinthians 7:3-5, page 196).

children

God's plan is to build, strengthen, and protect the family. Satan's plan is to undermine, weaken, and destroy it. Make no mistake: Satan has declared war on the family. Tragically, many of us have been willing accomplices. Why? Because the bulk of the problems in our culture today can be directly traced to the breakdown of the family or to homes in which biblical principles are ignored or disobeyed. This not only includes husbands and wives splitting apart, but also "alternative families," such as homosexual marriages and "live-in" lovers. Such relationships will never be blessed or honored by God, for they are clearly outside the parameters of his will. It has been said, "A family can survive without a country, but a country cannot survive without the family."

Fortunately, there is hope. The Bible gives us specific guidelines to follow when it comes to parenting. If they are put into practice, we will see amazing results. See what the Bible has to say about raising children who love and revere the Lord in a world that is often hostile to God and his values.

1. *Children Are Never Too Young to Learn about God.* Teaching your children to love the Lord in their early years will help them stay true to the Lord later in life (see Galatians 6:7-9, page 226).

2. *Make Sure Your Children Hear the Gospel Message.* The gospel must first be preached in the home (see feature on Acts 16:29-34, page 152).

3. *Encourage Your Children's Spiritual Growth.* As the apostle Paul suggests, a loving father encourages his children to live a life pleasing to God (see feature on 1 Thessalonians 2:11-12, page 250).

4. *Watch the Legacy You Leave.* Your devotion to God—or lack of it—will make a resounding impression on the next generation (see Acts 21:5, page 157).

5. *Discipline Your Children.* Parents who love their chlidren and want them to grow up into young men and women of character will discipline them (see Hebrews 12:5-11, page 286).

6. *Avoid Aggravating Your Children.* Your discipline must be tempered with love so that your children do not become resentful (see feature on Colossians 3:20-21, page 246).

priorities

As a Christian, one of the most dramatic changes in your life will be the way you spend your time. Your pursuits and ambitions in life will be different. After all, you are no longer living for yourself but for God. It may be a difficult transition at first, but here are a few pointers we can glean from God's Word.

1. *Place Christ before All Else.* To be a true follower of Jesus Christ, you need to be wholly devoted to him and let nothing else get in the way of your devotion (see feature on Philippians 3:4-11, page 240).

2. *Balance Christian Service with Worship.* Don't get so caught up in "serving" the Lord that you forget to worship him and get to know him better (see feature on Luke 10:38-42, page 80).

3. *Don't Waste Time Pursuing Things That Won't Last.* Your time on earth is short. Ask God to help you spend it on things that count (see 2 Timothy 4:5-8, page 268).

4. *Spend Time Feeding Your Soul.* God offers blessings to you if you choose to spend time with him rather than to devote your life to the pursuit of temporary satisfaction (see 1 Peter 2:1-3, page 296).

3. *Keep Your Spiritual Zeal Alive.* Work hard to keep that "fire" in your heart burning brightly as you serve the Lord (see feature on Romans 12:11, page 178).

prayer time

Before you became a Christian, you may have prayed before meals, on holidays, or perhaps during times of crisis. As a believer, however, prayer should become second nature. Prayer is no longer an option but should become part of all you do.

As you integrate prayer into every aspect of your life, you will not always see your prayers answered the way you would like them to be. When this happens, it is easy to grow discouraged and give up praying. But Jesus implored us to pray and never give up (Luke 18:1). Paul also instructed believers to "never stop praying" (1 Thessalonians 5:17). When we fail to pray, we miss out on one of the greatest blessings of the Christian life—fellowship with God himself, our power source for living. In addition, we are going against what God has instructed us to do.

The Bible gives us some perspective on how to experience the power of prayer in our lives. The following is a partial list of what should characterize your prayers as a believer.

1. **Pray Regularly.** God wants to hear our prayers throughout the day—not just in times of crisis or before meals (see Acts 10:2, page 143).

2. **Pray without Hindrance.** Sins and other distractions can negatively affect your prayer life (see Luke 22:39-46, page 96).

3. **Pray Expecting to Get Answers.** The Bible gives us guidelines to follow so that our prayers will be answered (see feature on 1 John 5:14-15, page 310).

4. **Pray Effectively.** Prayer can work powerfully in the face of a crisis when God's people come together and call out to him (see feature on Acts 12:1-17, page 146).

5. **Pray Persistently.** God honors persistent prayer (see feature on Luke 18:1-8, page 90).

conversation

As a Christian, it is extremely important to remember that you are a representative of Jesus Christ. One of the more visible ways you represent him is through your speech or conversations. It has been said that every person speaks about thirty thousand words in an average day. That is a considerable amount of "representation time"—especially when you consider the power of the spoken word. With our mouths we have the power to build up or destroy. This should give you even greater motivation to weigh your words before you speak them.

The Bible shares some practical advice when it comes to controlling the tongue. Below are a few passages of Scripture to guide you in this area.

1. **Think before You Speak.** You demonstrate great wisdom and care when you weigh your words (see 1 Timothy 4:12, page 262).

2. **Control Your Tongue.** As you learn to control your tongue, you will be able to control other aspects of your life (see feature on James 3:1-12, page 292).

3. **Refrain from Idle Talk.** We will be held accountable for every idle word we speak (see feature on Matthew 12:35-37, page 16).

4. *Make a Habit of Talking about the Lord.* When we talk about the Lord and his blessings with one another, God is pleased (see Acts 11:20, page 145).

5. *Keep Your Conversation Gracious.* We should speak gently and sensibly as we share our faith with others (see feature on Colossians 4:6, page 248).

6. *Never Use Vulgar Speech.* Our conversations need to reflect God's goodness, not the world's coarseness (see feature on 1 Peter 3:10, page 298).

7. *Think of Ways to Encourage, Praise, and Build Up Others.* As a Christian, you should use your speech constructively (see feature on 1 Thessalonians 5:11, page 254).

relationships

The people we associate with on a regular basis can either help or hinder our spiritual growth. For that reason God has given us some invaluable advice and strong warnings when it comes to choosing our friends. Look at the following Scripture passages to see what to pursue and what to avoid in your relationships with others.

1. *Find a Close Christian Friend.* A true Christian friend will help you get through times of trouble and temptation (see feature on Galatians 6:1-3, page 224).

2. *Don't Associate with Those Who Mock God.* God and his Word should be the focus of praise—not mockery—in your friendships (see 2 Timothy 3:1-5, page 267).

3. *Avoid Relationships That Could Cause You to Sin.* Bad company corrupts good character (see feature on 2 Corinthians 6:14–7:1, page 216).

4. *Make Sure Your Friendships Honor God.* Seek the friendship of those who live as Christ intended (see feature on 1 John 1:7, page 306).

responsibility

A common question that many new Christians have is, "Can I be a Christian and still do . . . ?" Some questions of "Christian liberty" can be answered easily, because the Bible directly addresses these questions. For instance, if someone asks, "Is it OK, as a Christian, to get drunk?" The answer is clearly no. The Bible says, "Don't be drunk with wine, because that will ruin your life. Instead, be filled with the Holy Spirit" (Ephesians 5:18). However, questions like, "Can I be a Christian and still drink alcoholic beverages?" or "Can I listen to any kind of music?" or "Can I go to any movie?" are not answered so easily. They are among the many "gray" areas of the Christian life that do not necessarily have a "chapter and verse" answer.

When you face a situation that the Bible does not directly address, you must consider whether or not your actions will please God. Here is a "litmus test" you can apply to those uncertain areas of life.

1. ***Does This Activity Build Me Up Spiritually?*** You need to avoid anything that has the potential to dull your spiritual senses and take away your hunger for God and his Word (see feature on 1 Corinthians 10:23, page 202).

2. ***Does This Activity Bring Me under Its Power?*** As a Christian, you only want to be controlled by the power of Jesus Christ (see feature on 1 Corinthians 6:12, page 194).

3. ***Do I Have an Uneasy Conscience about This Activity?*** You must be obedient to what God has told you to do, not swayed by what others are doing (see feature on Romans 14:23, page 186).

4. ***Could This Activity Cause Other Christians to Stumble in Their Faith?*** Stay away from things that could negatively influence other Christians around you (see feature on Romans 14:3-21, page 184).

job performance

Some of the greatest challenges you may ever face as a Christian will come from the workplace. Perhaps you work in an unethical, morally questionable environment. Maybe you find it difficult to respect your supervisors. You might find your job tedious or meaningless. You might even wonder if you are making an impact on your coworkers for Christ. Whatever your vocation, your work can become more fulfilling and rewarding when you follow what the Bible has to say about your attitude toward your job or responsibilities. Take these biblical pointers to heart, and see what a difference they will make!

1. ***Work As If You Are Working for the Lord.*** Keep in mind that you are ultimately serving the Lord, not just people (see feature on Colossians 3:22-24, page 248).

2. ***Create a Spiritual Hunger in Those around You.*** Your godly example can help increase your coworkers' desire to know more about Jesus (see feature on Titus 2:9-10, page 270).

3. ***Strive to Be Responsible.*** People will respect you and your message when you can prove that you are responsible (see feature on 1 Thessalonians 4:11-12, page 252).

4. ***Honor Christ with Your Hard Work.*** Don't allow nonbelievers to criticize the Lord because of your poor witness (see 1 Thessalonians 4:11-12, page 253).

5. ***Don't Neglect Your Spiritual Health.*** Never place your desire for material wealth above your spiritual welfare (see feature on Luke 12:15-21, page 82).

attitude toward self

Many are on a quest today to find personal happiness. They will do whatever is necessary to "find themselves." They are told that the answer is "within," so they search in all the wrong places trying to find meaning and purpose in life. The Bible, however, does not teach that the answer is within us. Rather, it teaches that the *problem* is within us. Jeremiah 17:9 tells us, "The human heart is the most deceitful of all things, and desperately wicked. Who really knows how bad it is?" For that reason, all attempts to reform or improve ourselves will meet with failure. We do not need self-esteem as much as we need a realistic view of who we are and who God is. Once we honestly assess our own sinful condition and come to grips with our built-in weakness and vulnerability to sin, then we will be able to appreciate God's solution. In a nutshell, the way to true happiness comes not from seeking *it* but from seeking *God*. Here's what God's Word has to say about how we can be happy, fulfilled people.

1. ***We Need to Recognize Our True Condition.*** As we humble ourselves before a holy God, we will be blessed (see feature on Matthew 5:3-5, page 4).

2. ***Our Needs Must Come Last.*** Jesus gave us the ultimate example of what it means to be a servant (see feature on Hebrews 13:11-13, page 288).

3. ***We Will Find Happiness in Loving God and Serving Others.*** Loving God and others gives us real purpose and meaning in life (see feature on Matthew 22:37-40, page 32).

4. ***We Must Surrender Our Dreams and Seek God's Will.*** True followers of Christ entrust their future into God's hands, because he knows what is best for us (see feature on Matthew 16:24-26, page 22).

big questions
what the Bible has to say about
some of life's troubling issues

This list not only gives you twenty-three Bible stories you should be familiar with as a Christian, but it also provides an interesting reading plan as well. Using the list below, you can read through one great Bible story a week for almost a whole year.

1. Jesus' Birth

Matthew 1:18-25, page 1-2; Luke 1:26-38, pages 61-62; Luke 2:1-7, page 64
In the most humble and amazing circumstances, the Savior of the world is born.

2. Jesus Visits the Temple as a Boy

Luke 2:41-52, page 65
As Jesus' parents return home from the Passover feast in Jerusalem, they notice that Jesus is not with them. Where they find him and what they find him doing astonish them.

3. Jesus' Baptism

Matthew 3:13-17, page 3; Mark 1:9-11, page 39; Luke 3:21-22, page 66; John 1:29-34, page 102
At Jesus' baptism, God expresses his pleasure in his Son and calls him to public ministry.

4. Satan Tempts Jesus

Matthew 4:1-11, page 3; Mark 1:12-13, page 39; Luke 4:1-13, pages 66-67
Jesus withstands temptation from the devil himself, giving his followers a model to follow when they encounter temptation.

5. Jesus Clears the Temple

Matthew 21:12-17, page 27; Mark 11:15-19, pages 52-53; Luke 19:45-48, page 93
In one bold act, Jesus shows his zeal for God's house, making bitter enemies in the process.

6. Jesus and the Miraculous Catch of Fish

Luke 5:1-11, pages 68-69

Jesus' disciples reap great dividends when they follow Jesus' unusual advice.

7. Jesus and the Samaritan Woman

John 4:1-26, page 104

A woman who has spent her life looking for love finds true fulfillment and joy in Jesus Christ.

8. Jesus Calms the Storm at Sea

Matthew 8:23-27, page 11; Mark 4:35-41, page 43; Luke 8:22-25, page 74

The disciples discover that although life can be unpredictable, Jesus can calm the storms.

9. Jesus Heals a Lame Man

John 5:1-15, page 105

A lame man who had been waiting for healing for more than thirty years receives immediate healing when he follows Jesus' instructions.

10. Jesus Feeds Five Thousand

Matthew 14:13-21, pages 19-20; Mark 6:30-44, pages 45-46; Luke 9:10-17, pages 75-76; John 6:1-15, pages 106-107

A little boy's lunch becomes the focal point of one of Jesus' greatest recorded miracles.

11. The Parable of the Good Samaritan

Luke 10:25-37, page 79

Our "neighbor," or friend, may not be the person we expect, as this parable explains.

12. Jesus Heals a Blind Man

John 9:1-41, pages 111-112

This man not only receives his physical sight but also his spiritual sight, as he sees Jesus for who he is.

13. Jesus Raises Lazarus from the Dead

John 11:1-44, pages 113-114

While Lazarus' sisters expected Jesus to perform a healing, Jesus chooses to do something far greater.

14. The Prodigal Son

Luke 15:11-32, page 86

Jesus illustrates God's mercy and forgiveness in this parable of a wayward son and shows us how to get right with God.

15. Zacchaeus Climbs a Sycamore Tree

Luke 19:1-10, page 91

A lonely and despised man finds love and forgiveness in Jesus.

16. The Last Supper

Matthew 26:20-30, page 35; Mark 14:17-26, pages 56-57; Luke 22:14-30, pages 95-96; John 13:1-30, pages 116-117

Jesus uses some of his last moments with his disciples to teach them important lessons about servanthood and the meaning of his impending sacrifice.

17. Jesus' Crucifixion

Matthew 27:15-66, pages 36-38; Mark 15:2-47, pages 58-59; Luke 23:1-56, pages 98-99; John 18:28–19:42, pages 123-25

The Son of God shows his tremendous love for people by enduring the most humiliating torture and execution befitting the worst criminal.

18. Jesus' Resurrection

Matthew 28:1-7, page 38; Mark 16:1-8, page 59; Luke 24:1-12, pages 99-100; John 20:1-9, page 125

Christ's death seems to be a hopeless situation. But what his followers do not know is that he will rise from the dead and break sin's hold on humankind.

19. Peter's First Sermon

Acts 2:14-41, pages 130-131

A once dejected and disloyal follower, Peter shows his love for Jesus by preaching a powerful sermon through which many come to faith in Christ.

20. Saul's Conversion

Acts 9:1-19, pages 141-142

One of the earliest persecutors of Christians becomes a believer while he is on his way to arrest Christians in Damascus.

21. An Angel Rescues Peter from Prison

Acts 12:1-19, pages 145-146

A prayer meeting receives a dramatic answer in the middle of the night.

22. *Paul and Silas in Prison*

Acts 16:16-40, page 151

Paul and Silas rise above their circumstances by praising God for his goodness through their trials.

23. *Paul's Journey to Rome*

Acts 27:1–28:16, pages 163-165

A seemingly hopeless situation turns into a tremendous witnessing opportunity for the apostle Paul.

Memorizing Scripture is not really a difficult thing to do. You already have quite a bit in your memory bank: a few key phone numbers, your address, a relative's birthday, and many more essential pieces of information. So you *do* have the ability to memorize. The good news is that Scripture memorization is a refreshing exercise that the Lord will use to bless your life. As his Word says, "But if you look carefully into the perfect law that sets you free, and if you do what it says and don't forget what you heard, then God will *bless you for doing it*" (James 1:25, italics added).

Below are a few suggestions that may make memorizing God's Word easier for you:

1. When you pick a text to memorize, take time to read the verses surrounding the text so you can better understand the context of the verse. This will help you determine what the verse means.
2. Read the verse(s) several times aloud, and be sure to include the verse reference.
3. Think about the main idea of the verse and how it applies to you personally.
4. You may want to write down the verse several times. You may even choose to write the verse on little cards you can place on your bathroom mirror, in your car, on your refrigerator door, or any other place you frequently find yourself.
5. Review the verse frequently. As someone has said, you memorize a telephone number by dialing, Dialing, DIALING. You can memorize Scripture by reviewing, Reviewing, REVIEWING!
6. Finally, pray over the selected text throughout the day, asking God to help you comprehend its meaning as well as its significance in your own life.

As the verse in James attests, the more you memorize God's Word, the more you will find yourself doing what it says. In effect, filling your mind with Scripture is one of the strongest deterrents for temptation. That is because the more God's Word fills your heart and mind, the less likely you are to want to disregard his commands and displease him. In addition, making the Bible such a central focus of your day will "fill your lives" (Colossians 3:16).

Considering the benefits of Scripture memorization, here are some key verses to help you get started in this practice. The following verses have been selected to help you understand the message of salvation, encourage your spiritual growth, and remind you of God's promises as you journey through life.

GOD'S PLAN OF SALVATION

▶ **We must acknowledge that we are sinners.**

ROMANS 3:23. Every person is guilty of sin and has fallen short of God's standard. *page 170*

JAMES 2:10. Breaking one of God's laws makes us as guilty as someone who has broken all of God's laws. *page 290*

ROMANS 3:10. No one can claim innocence before God. *page 170*

▶ **We must understand the penalty for our sins.**

ROMANS 6:23. The wages of sin is death. *page 175*

▶ **We must confess and repent of our sins.**

1 JOHN 1:9. God promises to forgive our sins when we confess them. *page 305*

ACTS 20:21. We must turn from our sin and turn to God. *page 157*

▶ **We must believe that Christ is the only way of salvation.**

JOHN 14:6. Jesus Christ alone leads you to God. *page 117*

ACTS 4:12. Salvation can be found through no one other than Christ. *page 134*

ROMANS 5:8. Christ's death demonstrates God's unconditional love. *page 173*

1 PETER 3:18. Christ, who never sinned, took the punishment for our sins on the cross of Calvary to bring us to God. *page 299*

ROMANS 10:9-10. Belief in Jesus' death and resurrection is essential to salvation. *page 180*

▶ **We must receive Christ into our lives to obtain forgiveness and eternal life.**

JOHN 3:3. We must be spiritually "reborn." *page 103*

JOHN 3:16. We are promised salvation by believing in Jesus Christ, God's Son. *page 103*

JOHN 10:9. Christ is the gate to salvation. *page 112*

REVELATION 3:20. Jesus waits for an invitation into our lives. *page 322*

EPHESIANS 2:8-9. We can only receive salvation through faith in Christ, not through our good works. *page 228*

TITUS 3:5. The salvation God extends washes away our sins and brings true joy. *page 271*

▶ **We have the assurance of our salvation.**

JOHN 1:12. We become a child of God by receiving his free gift of salvation. *page 101*

GALATIANS 2:20. We have been given a "new" life in Jesus Christ. *page 223*

ROMANS 8:1. We no longer have to fear condemnation. *page 176*

1 PETER 1:3-4. God has reserved for us the priceless gift of eternal life. *page 295*

1 PETER 1:23. Our new life comes from the living God, not from mortal man. *page 296*

JOHN 10:27-28. The Lord personally guards our salvation. *page 112*

1 JOHN 5:13. Our assurance is based upon faith, not feeling. *page 311*

2 CORINTHIANS 1:22. God has placed the Holy Spirit in our hearts as proof that we belong to him. *page 210*

GALATIANS 4:6-7. We have all the privileges and rights that come from being God's children. *page 224*

GOD'S WORK IN OUR LIVES

▶ **God has a plan and purpose for us.**

ROMANS 8:28. Everything he allows in our lives is for our ultimate good. *page 177*

2 TIMOTHY 1:9. He has chosen us to lead holy lives. *page 265*

1 CORINTHIANS 2:9. He has prepared wonderful things for those who love him. *page 191*

▶ **God will change us from the inside out.**

2 CORINTHIANS 5:17. The moment we accept Christ into our lives, we become an altogether "new" person. *pages 212-213*

COLOSSIANS 1:27. Jesus Christ has taken residence inside our hearts. *pages 244-245*

COLOSSIANS 3:10. We are being conformed to Christ's likeness. *page 247*

PHILIPPIANS 1:6. God will complete the work he has started in our lives. *page 237*

PHILIPPIANS 2:13. God will instill in you the desire to obey him. *page 239*

2 CORINTHIANS 4:16. God will spiritually renew us every day. *page 211*

▶ **He will direct our lives.**

1 THESSALONIANS 5:23-24. God will help to keep us devoted to him. *page 254*

JOHN 16:13. The Holy Spirit will guide us into all truth. *page 120*

JUDE 1:24-25. God is able to keep us from slipping and falling. *page 318*

OUR RESPONSE TO GOD'S GOODNESS

▶ **We should honor God with our lives.**

1 CORINTHIANS 6:19-20. We must remember that our body is the home of the Holy Spirit. *page 196*

ROMANS 12:1-2. We must not let this world squeeze us into its mold. *page 183*

EPHESIANS 2:10. We should spend our lives helping others. *page 228*

2 TIMOTHY 2:22. We should pursue righteousness, faith, love, and peace. *page 266*

ROMANS 6:13-14. We need to give ourselves completely to God. *page 175*

EPHESIANS 5:18. Our lives need to be controlled by the Holy Spirit. *page 233*

GALATIANS 5:22-23. Our lives should display the fruit of the Holy Spirit. *page 226*

▶ **We should grow in our knowledge and love of God.**

COLOSSIANS 3:16. We need to allow Christ's words to enrich our lives. *page 247*

2 PETER 1:2-4. We need to get better acquainted with the Lord in order to lead a godly life. *page 301*

MARK 12:30. We need to love God with all of our heart, soul, mind, and strength. *page 54*

JOHN 14:21. We need to follow God's commands. *page 118*

EPHESIANS 3:17-19. We need to make God more at home in our hearts to better comprehend his love for us. *pages 229-230*

JAMES 4:8. As we draw close to God, he will draw close to us. *page 293*

▶ **We should talk to God regularly.**

1 THESSALONIANS 5:17-18. We should pray continually, throughout the day. *page 254*

MATTHEW 18:20. We should make a point to pray with other believers. *page 24*

MATTHEW 26:41. We should pray so that we can resist temptation. *page 35*

MARK 11:24. We should pray, believing God will answer. *page 53*

LUKE 11:9. We should pray persistently. *page 79*

▶ **We should become an active part of God's family.**

HEBREWS 10:24-25. We need to attend church regularly and spend time with other Christians. *page 283*

ROMANS 12:4-5. God has given each of us a distinct role to play in the church. *page 183*

EPHESIANS 5:19. We spiritually encourage one another by praising God in our conversations. *page 233*

1 JOHN 1:7. The closer we walk with God, the more joyful our relationship with other Christians will be. *page 305*

PHILIPPIANS 1:2. Love and unity should characterize our Christian fellowship. *page 237*

▶ **We should serve God wholeheartedly.**

COLOSSIANS 3:23-24. We must work for the Lord, not just for men. *page 247*

HEBREWS 12:2-3. We need to keep our eyes on Jesus to keep from getting discouraged. *pages 285-286*

1 CORINTHIANS 15:58. Nothing we do for the Lord is a wasted effort. *page 207*

GALATIANS 6:9. We will see positive results if we do not give up. *page 226*

▶ **We should share our faith in Christ with others.**

MATTHEW 4:19. Jesus wants us to be "fishers" of men and women. *page 4*

1 CORINTHIANS 9:22. We should lovingly and tactfully share our faith. *page 199*

1 PETER 3:15. We should always be prepared to witness to others. *page 298*

ROMANS 1:16. Those who help bring many to the Lord will be blessed. *page 167*

▶ **We should persevere in our faith.**

PHILIPPIANS 3:13-14. We need to focus our sights on the final "prize" of this spiritual race. *page 240*

EPHESIANS 6:10. We must rely upon God as the source of our strength. *page 235*

HEBREWS 12:1. We must rid ourselves of anything that would slow us down. *page 285*

2 TIMOTHY 4:7-8. We must make it our ambition to finish well. *page 268*

GOD'S PROMISES TO US

▶ **We are precious in God's sight.**

JOHN 15:15. We are friends of Christ. *page 119*

ROMANS 8:38-39. Nothing can separate us from his love. *page 178*

1 JOHN 5:14-15. He hears our prayers. *page 311*

▶ **God is faithful to us.**

HEBREWS 13:5-6. He will never abandon us. *page 287*

2 THESSALONIANS 3:3. He will make us spiritually strong and keep us from evil. *page 256*

1 PETER 3:12. He watches us and hears our prayers. *page 298*

▶ **God watches over us.**

1 PETER 5:7. We can trust him with all of our worries and cares. *page 300*

▶ **God will give us peace.**

JOHN 14:27. God gives us a lasting peace, not a fragile peace. *page 118*

PHILIPPIANS 4:6-7. Trusting God leads to rest and peace. *page 240*

COLOSSIANS 3:15. It is up to us to allow God's peace to control our lives. *page 247*

▶ **God will give us strength to face life's challenges.**

JOHN 15:5. We draw our strength from Christ. *page 119*

2 CORINTHIANS 3:5. Our competence comes from God. *page 210*

2 CORINTHIANS 12:9. God displays his strength in our weaknesses. *page 219*

1 CORINTHIANS 10:13. God will never allow you to go through more than you can handle. *page 200*

PHILIPPIANS 4:13. We can do everything through Christ. *page 241*

HEBREWS 13:6. We do not have to fear what people may do to us. *page 287*

▶ **God promises forgiveness.**

HEBREWS 8:12. He will not only forgive our sins but will also forget them. *page 281*

1 JOHN 2:1. Jesus will stand as our defense before the Father when we ask for forgiveness. *page 305*

▶ **God will empower us for his service.**

PHILIPPIANS 4:13. We can do everything God asks with the help of Christ. *page 241*

2 TIMOTHY 1:7. The Holy Spirit will give us boldness as we share our faith. *page 265*

▶ **God's Word is our infallible guide.**

MARK 13:31. God's Word lasts forever. *page 56*

2 TIMOTHY 3:16. All Scripture is inspired by God and will equip us with all we need to know in this life. *page 267*

HEBREWS 4:12. God's Word reveals who we really are. *page 278*

Matthew

AUTHOR: **MATTHEW (Levi)** | DATE WRITTEN: **A.D. 60–65** | GENRE: **GOSPEL**

This Gospel was written with the Jewish people in mind and therefore has many references to Old Testament prophecies that Jesus fulfilled. It contains at least 129 quotations or allusions to the Old Testament. Matthew's objective was to show the Jewish people that Jesus was indeed their long-awaited Messiah.

CHAPTER 1

The Ancestors of Jesus the Messiah

This is a record of the ancestors of Jesus the Messiah, a descendant of David* and of Abraham:

2 Abraham was the father of Isaac.
Isaac was the father of Jacob.
Jacob was the father of Judah and his brothers.

3 Judah was the father of Perez and Zerah (whose mother was Tamar).
Perez was the father of Hezron.
Hezron was the father of Ram.*

4 Ram was the father of Amminadab.
Amminadab was the father of Nahshon.
Nahshon was the father of Salmon.

5 Salmon was the father of Boaz (whose mother was Rahab).
Boaz was the father of Obed (whose mother was Ruth).
Obed was the father of Jesse.

6 Jesse was the father of King David.
David was the father of Solomon (whose mother was Bathsheba, the widow of Uriah).

7 Solomon was the father of Rehoboam.
Rehoboam was the father of Abijah.
Abijah was the father of Asa.*

8 Asa was the father of Jehoshaphat.
Jehoshaphat was the father of Jehoram.*
Jehoram was the father* of Uzziah.

9 Uzziah was the father of Jotham.
Jotham was the father of Ahaz.
Ahaz was the father of Hezekiah.

10 Hezekiah was the father of Manasseh.
Manasseh was the father of Amon.*
Amon was the father of Josiah.

11 Josiah was the father of Jehoiachin* and his brothers (born at the time of the exile to Babylon).

12 After the Babylonian exile:
Jehoiachin was the father of Shealtiel.
Shealtiel was the father of Zerubbabel.

13 Zerubbabel was the father of Abiud.
Abiud was the father of Eliakim.
Eliakim was the father of Azor.

14 Azor was the father of Zadok.
Zadok was the father of Akim.
Akim was the father of Eliud.

15 Eliud was the father of Eleazar.
Eleazar was the father of Matthan.
Matthan was the father of Jacob.

16 Jacob was the father of Joseph, the husband of Mary.
Mary gave birth to Jesus, who is called the Messiah.

17 All those listed above include fourteen generations from Abraham to David, fourteen from David to the Babylonian exile, and fourteen from the Babylonian exile to the Messiah.

The Birth of Jesus the Messiah

18 This is how Jesus the Messiah was born. His mother, Mary, was engaged to be married to Joseph. But before the marriage took place, while she was still a virgin, she became pregnant through the power of the Holy Spirit. 19 Joseph, her fiancé, was a good man and did not want to

---

1:1 Greek *Jesus the Messiah, son of David*. 1:3 Greek *Aram*, a variant spelling of Ram; also in 1:4. See 1 Chr 2:9-10. 1:7 Greek *Asaph*, a variant spelling of Asa; also in 1:8. See 1 Chr 3:10. 1:8a Greek *Joram*, a variant spelling of Jehoram; also in 1:8b. See 1 Kgs 22:50 and note at 1 Chr 3:11. 1:8b Or *ancestor;* also in 1:11. 1:10 Greek *Amos*, a variant spelling of Amon; also in 1:10b. See 1 Chr 3:14. 1:11 Greek *Jeconiah*, a variant spelling of Jehoiachin; also in 1:12. See 2 Kgs 24:6.

disgrace her publicly, so he decided to break the engagement* quietly.

[20] As he considered this, an angel of the Lord appeared to him in a dream. "Joseph, son of David," the angel said, "do not be afraid to take Mary as your wife. For the child within her was conceived by the Holy Spirit. [21] And she will have a son, and you are to name him Jesus,* for he will save his people from their sins."

[22] All of this occurred to fulfill the Lord's message through his prophet:

[23] "Look! The virgin will conceive a child!
   She will give birth to a son,
and they will call him Immanuel,*
   which means 'God is with us.'"

[24] When Joseph woke up, he did as the angel of the Lord commanded and took Mary as his wife. [25] But he did not have sexual relations with her until her son was born. And Joseph named him Jesus.

CHAPTER 2

Visitors from the East

Jesus was born in Bethlehem in Judea, during the reign of King Herod. About that time some wise men* from eastern lands arrived in Jerusalem, asking, [2] "Where is the newborn king of the Jews? We saw his star as it rose,* and we have come to worship him."

[3] King Herod was deeply disturbed when he heard this, as was everyone in Jerusalem. [4] He called a meeting of the leading priests and teachers of religious law and asked, "Where is the Messiah supposed to be born?"

[5] "In Bethlehem in Judea," they said, "for this is what the prophet wrote:

[6] 'And you, O Bethlehem in the land of Judah,
   are not least among the ruling cities* of
      Judah,
for a ruler will come from you
   who will be the shepherd for my people
      Israel.'*"

[7] Then Herod called for a private meeting with the wise men, and he learned from them the time when the star first appeared. [8] Then he told them, "Go to Bethlehem and search carefully for the child. And when you find him, come back and tell me so that I can go and worship him, too!"

[9] After this interview the wise men went their way. And the star they had seen in the east guided them to Bethlehem. It went ahead of them and stopped over the place where the child was. [10] When they saw the star, they were filled with joy! [11] They entered the house and saw the child with his mother, Mary, and they bowed down and worshiped him. Then they opened their treasure chests and gave him gifts of gold, frankincense, and myrrh.

[12] When it was time to leave, they returned to their own country by another route, for God had warned them in a dream not to return to Herod.

The Escape to Egypt

[13] After the wise men were gone, an angel of the Lord appeared to Joseph in a dream. "Get up! Flee to Egypt with the child and his mother," the angel said. "Stay there until I tell you to return, because Herod is going to search for the child to kill him."

[14] That night Joseph left for Egypt with the child and Mary, his mother, [15] and they stayed there until Herod's death. This fulfilled what the Lord had spoken through the prophet: "I called my Son out of Egypt."*

[16] Herod was furious when he realized that the wise men had outwitted him. He sent soldiers to kill all the boys in and around Bethlehem who were two years old and under, based on the wise men's report of the star's first appearance. [17] Herod's brutal action fulfilled what God had spoken through the prophet Jeremiah:

[18] "A cry was heard in Ramah—
   weeping and great mourning.
Rachel weeps for her children,
   refusing to be comforted,
      for they are dead."*

The Return to Nazareth

[19] When Herod died, an angel of the Lord appeared in a dream to Joseph in Egypt. [20] "Get up!" the angel said. "Take the child and his mother back to the land of Israel, because those who were trying to kill the child are dead."

[21] So Joseph got up and returned to the land of Israel with Jesus and his mother. [22] But when he learned that the new ruler of Judea was Herod's son Archelaus, he was afraid to go there. Then, after being warned in a dream, he left for the region of Galilee. [23] So the family went and lived in a town called Nazareth. This fulfilled what the prophets had said: "He will be called a Nazarene."

CHAPTER 3

John the Baptist Prepares the Way

In those days John the Baptist came to the Judean wilderness and began preaching. His mes-

---

1:19 Greek *to divorce her.*   1:21 *Jesus* means "The LORD saves."   1:23 Isa 7:14; 8:8, 10 (Greek version).   2:1 Or *royal astrologers*; Greek reads *magi*; also in 2:7, 16.   2:2 Or *star in the east.*   2:6a Greek *the rulers.*   2:6b Mic 5:2; 2 Sam 5:2.   2:15 Hos 11:1.   2:18 Jer 31:15.

sage was, [2]"Repent of your sins and turn to God, for the Kingdom of Heaven is near.*" [3]The prophet Isaiah was speaking about John when he said,

"He is a voice shouting in the wilderness,
'Prepare the way for the LORD's coming!
Clear the road for him!'"*

[4]John's clothes were woven from coarse camel hair, and he wore a leather belt around his waist. For food he ate locusts and wild honey. [5]People from Jerusalem and from all of Judea and all over the Jordan Valley went out to see and hear John. [6]And when they confessed their sins, he baptized them in the Jordan River.

[7]But when he saw many Pharisees and Sadducees coming to watch him baptize,* he denounced them. "You brood of snakes!" he exclaimed. "Who warned you to flee God's coming wrath? [8]Prove by the way you live that you have repented of your sins and turned to God. [9]Don't just say to each other, 'We're safe, for we are descendants of Abraham.' That means nothing, for I tell you, God can create children of Abraham from these very stones. [10]Even now the ax of God's judgment is poised, ready to sever the roots of the trees. Yes, every tree that does not produce good fruit will be chopped down and thrown into the fire.

[11]"I baptize with* water those who repent of their sins and turn to God. But someone is coming soon who is greater than I am—so much greater that I'm not worthy even to be his slave and carry his sandals. He will baptize you with the Holy Spirit and with fire.* [12]He is ready to separate the chaff from the wheat with his winnowing fork. Then he will clean up the threshing area, gathering the wheat into his barn but burning the chaff with never-ending fire."

The Baptism of Jesus

[13]Then Jesus went from Galilee to the Jordan River to be baptized by John. [14]But John tried to talk him out of it. "I am the one who needs to be baptized by you," he said, "so why are you coming to me?"

[15]But Jesus said, "It should be done, for we must carry out all that God requires.*" So John agreed to baptize him.

[16]After his baptism, as Jesus came up out of the water, the heavens were opened* and he saw the Spirit of God descending like a dove and settling on him. [17]And a voice from heaven said, "This is my dearly loved Son, who brings me great joy."

CHAPTER **4**

The Temptation of Jesus

Then Jesus was led by the Spirit into the wilderness to be tempted there by the devil. [2]For forty days and forty nights he fasted and became very hungry.

[3]During that time the devil* came and said to him, "If you are the Son of God, tell these stones to become loaves of bread."

[4]But Jesus told him, "No! The Scriptures say,

'People do not live by bread alone,
but by every word that comes from the mouth of God.'* "

[5]Then the devil took him to the holy city, Jerusalem, to the highest point of the Temple, [6]and said, "If you are the Son of God, jump off! For the Scriptures say,

'He will order his angels to protect you.
And they will hold you up with their hands
so you won't even hurt your foot on a stone.'*"

[7]Jesus responded, "The Scriptures also say, 'You must not test the LORD your God.'* "

[8]Next the devil took him to the peak of a very high mountain and showed him all the kingdoms of the world and their glory. [9]"I will give it all to you," he said, "if you will kneel down and worship me."

[10]"Get out of here, Satan," Jesus told him. "For the Scriptures say,

'You must worship the LORD your God
and serve only him.'* "

[11]Then the devil went away, and angels came and took care of Jesus.

The Ministry of Jesus Begins

[12]When Jesus heard that John had been arrested, he left Judea and returned to Galilee. [13]He went first to Nazareth, then left there and moved to Capernaum, beside the Sea of Galilee, in the region of Zebulun and Naphtali. [14]This fulfilled what God said through the prophet Isaiah:

[15] "In the land of Zebulun and of Naphtali,
beside the sea, beyond the Jordan River,
in Galilee where so many
Gentiles live,
[16] the people who sat in darkness
have seen a great light.
And for those who lived in the land
where death casts its shadow,
a light has shined."*

3:2 Or *has come,* or *is coming soon.*   3:3 Isa 40:3 (Greek version).   3:7 Or *coming to be baptized.*   3:11a Or *in.*   3:11b Or *in the Holy Spirit and in fire.*   3:15 Or *for we must fulfill all righteousness.*   3:16 Some manuscripts read *opened to him.* 4:3 Greek *the tempter.*   4:4 Deut 8:3.   4:6 Ps 91:11-12.   4:7 Deut 6:16.   4:10 Deut 6:13.   4:15-16 Isa 9:1-2 (Greek version).

¹⁷From then on Jesus began to preach, "Repent of your sins and turn to God, for the Kingdom of Heaven is near.*"

The First Disciples

¹⁸One day as Jesus was walking along the shore of the Sea of Galilee, he saw two brothers—Simon, also called Peter, and Andrew—throwing a net into the water, for they fished for a living. ¹⁹Jesus called out to them, "Come, follow me, and I will show you how to fish for people!" ²⁰And they left their nets at once and followed him.

²¹A little farther up the shore he saw two other brothers, James and John, sitting in a boat with their father, Zebedee, repairing their nets. And he called them to come, too. ²²They immediately followed him, leaving the boat and their father behind.

Crowds Follow Jesus

²³Jesus traveled throughout the region of Galilee, teaching in the synagogues and announcing the Good News about the Kingdom. And he healed every kind of disease and illness. ²⁴News about him spread as far as Syria, and people soon began bringing to him all who were sick. And whatever their sickness or disease, or if they were demon possessed or epileptic or paralyzed—he healed them all. ²⁵Large crowds followed him wherever he went—people from Galilee, the Ten Towns,* Jerusalem, from all over Judea, and from east of the Jordan River.

4:17 Or *has come,* or *is coming soon.*   **4:25** Greek *Decapolis.*   **5:3** Greek *poor in spirit.*   **5:6** Or *for righteousness.*
5:11 Some manuscripts do not include *and lie about you.*

CHAPTER 5
The Sermon on the Mount

One day as he saw the crowds gathering, Jesus went up on the mountainside and sat down. His disciples gathered around him, ²and he began to teach them.

The Beatitudes

³ "God blesses those who are poor and realize
　　their need for him,*
　　for the Kingdom of Heaven is theirs.
⁴ God blesses those who mourn,
　　for they will be comforted.
⁵ God blesses those who are humble,
　　for they will inherit the whole earth.
⁶ God blesses those who hunger and thirst
　　for justice,*
　　for they will be satisfied.
⁷ God blesses those who are merciful,
　　for they will be shown mercy.
⁸ God blesses those whose hearts are pure,
　　for they will see God.
⁹ God blesses those who work
　　for peace,
　　for they will be called
　　the children of God.
¹⁰ God blesses those who are persecuted
　　for doing right,
　　for the Kingdom of Heaven is theirs.

¹¹"God blesses you when people mock you and persecute you and lie about you* and say all sorts of evil things against you because you are my followers. ¹²Be happy about it! Be very glad! For a great reward awaits you in heaven.

---

off and running
WE NEED TO RECOGNIZE OUR TRUE CONDITION
Read MATTHEW 5:3-5

Jesus shows us the way to true happiness in this text. And believe it or not it has nothing to do with personal fulfillment. Here Jesus gives us a three-step prescription to spiritual health and happiness:

1. See Yourself as You Really Are. When you realize your need for God (verse 3), you see yourself as you really are: a sinner, in desperate need of God's forgiveness. This is the first step. The phrase "need for [God]" in this verse comes from a verb meaning "to shrink, cower, or cringe." It speaks of someone who is destitute and completely dependent on others. Therefore, to realize your need for God is to admit that you are spiritually destitute apart from God.

2. Take Action. Another way to translate verse 4 is "happy are the unhappy." Because we see ourselves as we really are, we mourn over our condition. This

And remember, the ancient prophets were persecuted in the same way.

Teaching about Salt and Light

13 "You are the salt of the earth. But what good is salt if it has lost its flavor? Can you make it salty again? It will be thrown out and trampled underfoot as worthless.

14 "You are the light of the world—like a city on a hilltop that cannot be hidden. 15 No one lights a lamp and then puts it under a basket. Instead, a lamp is placed on a stand, where it gives light to everyone in the house. 16 In the same way, let your good deeds shine out for all to see, so that everyone will praise your heavenly Father.

Teaching about the Law

17 "Don't misunderstand why I have come. I did not come to abolish the law of Moses or the writings of the prophets. No, I came to accomplish their purpose. 18 I tell you the truth, until heaven and earth disappear, not even the smallest detail of God's law will disappear until its purpose is achieved. 19 So if you ignore the least commandment and teach others to do the same, you will be called the least in the Kingdom of Heaven. But anyone who obeys God's laws and teaches them will be called great in the Kingdom of Heaven.

20 "But I warn you—unless your righteousness is better than the righteousness of the teachers of religious law and the Pharisees, you will never enter the Kingdom of Heaven!

Teaching about Anger

21 "You have heard that our ancestors were told, 'You must not murder. If you commit murder, you are subject to judgment.'* 22 But I say, if you are even angry with someone,* you are subject to judgment! If you call someone an idiot,* you are in danger of being brought before the court. And if you curse someone,* you are in danger of the fires of hell.*

23 "So if you are presenting a sacrifice* at the altar in the Temple and you suddenly remember that someone has something against you, 24 leave your sacrifice there at the altar. Go and be reconciled to that person. Then come and offer your sacrifice to God.

25 "When you are on the way to court with your adversary, settle your differences quickly. Otherwise, your accuser may hand you over to the judge, who will hand you over to an officer, and you will be thrown into prison. 26 And if that happens, you surely won't be free again until you have paid the last penny.*

Teaching about Adultery

27 "You have heard the commandment that says, 'You must not commit adultery.'* 28 But I say, anyone who even looks at a woman with lust has already committed adultery with her in his heart. 29 So if your eye—even your good eye*—causes you to lust, gouge it out and throw it away. It is better for you to lose one part of your body than for your whole body to be thrown into hell. 30 And if your hand—even your stronger hand*—causes you to sin, cut it

5:21 Exod 20:13; Deut 5:17. 5:22a Some manuscripts add *without cause*. 5:22b Greek uses an Aramaic term of contempt: *If you say to your brother, 'Raca.'* 5:22c Greek *if you say, 'You fool.'* 5:22d Greek *Gehenna;* also in 5:29, 30. 5:23 Greek *gift;* also in 5:24. 5:26 Greek *the last kodrantes* [i.e., quadrans]. 5:27 Exod 20:14; Deut 5:18. 5:29 Greek *your right eye*. 5:30 Greek *your right hand*.

---

leads us to begin making changes in our lives. Scripture tells us, "For the kind of sorrow God wants us to experience leads us away from sin and results in salvation. There's no regret for that kind of sorrow. But worldly sorrow, which lacks repentance, results in spiritual death" (2 Corinthians 7:10). Our true sorrow will lead to joy—salvation in Jesus Christ.

3. Pursue Meekness. Seeing ourselves as we really are produces two vital spiritual qualities: gentleness and lowliness (verse 5). We have an accurate and honest assessment of ourselves that, in turn, affects how we approach others. This contradicts the world's way of thinking, which advocates standing up for your rights and asserting yourself in order to get what you deserve. The meekness Jesus describes here is not weakness or cowardice, but rather power under constraint, much like a powerful stallion submitting to the control of the bit.

The more we humble ourselves and admit our weaknesses, the more we will rely on God's grace—and the happier we will be with ourselves and others.

For the next note on "Attitude toward Self," turn to p. 288.

cornerstones
BEWARE OF THE SINS OF THE HEART
Read MATTHEW 5:27-30

Some people have the mistaken notion that unless you commit the act of adultery, you have not really sinned. They think it is OK to fantasize about or look at someone, so long as you don't become involved with that person. But Jesus cuts straight to the core. He lets us know that even a lustful glance is as sinful as committing the act of adultery.

In the original Greek, one of the meanings for the word Jesus uses for "look" is intentional and repeated gazing. Jesus' remedy for someone who has a problem in this area seems rather harsh, but you really have to look at the context and the culture of the day to understand this radical but important statement.

In the Jewish culture, the right eye represented one's best vision and the right hand represented one's best skills. In essence, Jesus is saying that you should be willing to give up whatever is necessary to keep you from falling into this sin. That may mean terminating a relationship, canceling cable or a magazine subscription, or changing how or where you spend your spare time. Remove yourself from those things that can have a spiritually destructive effect on your life. Then take practical steps to fill your mind with the things of God: "Fix your thoughts on what is true, and honorable, and right, and pure, and lovely, and admirable. Think about things that are excellent and worthy of praise" (Philippians 4:8).

For the next note on "Purity," turn to p. 252.

---

off and throw it away. It is better for you to lose one part of your body than for your whole body to be thrown into hell.

Teaching about Divorce
31 "You have heard the law that says, 'A man can divorce his wife by merely giving her a written notice of divorce.'* 32 But I say that a man who divorces his wife, unless she has been unfaithful, causes her to commit adultery. And anyone who marries a divorced woman also commits adultery.

Teaching about Vows
33 "You have also heard that our ancestors were told, 'You must not break your vows; you must carry out the vows you make to the LORD.'* 34 But I say, do not make any vows! Do not say, 'By heaven!' because heaven is God's throne. 35 And do not say, 'By the earth!' because the earth is his footstool. And do not say, 'By Jerusalem!' for Jerusalem is the city of the great King. 36 Do not even say, 'By my head!' for you can't turn one hair white or black. 37 Just say a simple, 'Yes, I will,' or 'No, I won't.' Anything beyond this is from the evil one.

Teaching about Revenge
38 "You have heard the law that says the punishment must match the injury: 'An eye for an eye, and a tooth for a tooth.'* 39 But I say, do not resist an evil person! If someone slaps you on the right cheek, offer the other cheek also. 40 If you are sued in court and your shirt is taken from you, give your coat, too. 41 If a soldier demands that you carry his gear for a mile,* carry it two miles. 42 Give to those who ask, and don't turn away from those who want to borrow.

Teaching about Love for Enemies
43 "You have heard the law that says, 'Love your neighbor'* and hate your enemy. 44 But I say, love your enemies!* Pray for those who persecute you! 45 In that way, you will be acting as true children of your Father in heaven. For he gives his sunlight to both the evil and the good, and he sends rain on the just and the unjust alike. 46 If you love only those who love you, what reward is there for that? Even corrupt tax collectors do that much. 47 If you are kind only to your friends,* how are you different from anyone else? Even pagans do that. 48 But you are to be perfect, even as your Father in heaven is perfect.

CHAPTER 6
Teaching about Giving to the Needy
"Watch out! Don't do your good deeds publicly, to be admired by others, for you will lose the reward from your Father in heaven. 2 When you

5:31 Deut 24:1.   **5:33** Num 30:2.   **5:38** Greek *the law that says: 'An eye for an eye and a tooth for a tooth.'* Exod 21:24; Lev 24:20; Deut 19:21. • **5:41** Greek *milion* [4,854 feet or 1,478 meters].   **5:43** Lev 19:18.   **5:44** Some manuscripts add *Bless those who curse you. Do good to those who hate you.* Compare Luke 6:27-28.   **5:47** Greek *your brothers.*

give to someone in need, don't do as the hypocrites do—blowing trumpets in the synagogues and streets to call attention to their acts of charity! I tell you the truth, they have received all the reward they will ever get. ³But when you give to someone in need, don't let your left hand know what your right hand is doing. ⁴Give your gifts in private, and your Father, who sees everything, will reward you.

Teaching about Prayer and Fasting

⁵"When you pray, don't be like the hypocrites who love to pray publicly on street corners and in the synagogues where everyone can see them. I tell you the truth, that is all the reward they will ever get. ⁶But when you pray, go away by yourself, shut the door behind you, and pray to your Father in private. Then your Father, who sees everything, will reward you.

⁷"When you pray, don't babble on and on as people of other religions do. They think their prayers are answered merely by repeating their words again and again. ⁸Don't be like them, for your Father knows exactly what you need even before you ask him! ⁹Pray like this:

Our Father in heaven,
    may your name be kept holy.
¹⁰ May your Kingdom come soon.
May your will be done on earth,
    as it is in heaven.
¹¹ Give us today the food we need,*
¹² and forgive us our sins,
    as we have forgiven those who sin
      against us.
¹³ And don't let us yield to temptation,*
    but rescue us from the evil one.*

¹⁴"If you forgive those who sin against you, your heavenly Father will forgive you. ¹⁵But if you refuse to forgive others, your Father will not forgive your sins.

¹⁶"And when you fast, don't make it obvious, as the hypocrites do, for they try to look miserable and disheveled so people will admire them for their fasting. I tell you the truth, that is the only reward they will ever get. ¹⁷But when you fast, comb your hair and wash your face. ¹⁸Then no one will notice that you are fasting, except your Father, who knows what you do in private. And your Father, who sees everything, will reward you.

Teaching about Money and Possessions

¹⁹"Don't store up treasures here on earth, where moths eat them and rust destroys them,

---

6:11 Or *Give us today our food for the day;* or *Give us today our food for tomorrow.*   6:13a Or *And keep us from being tested.*   6:13b Or *from evil.* Some manuscripts add *For yours is the kingdom and the power and the glory forever. Amen.*

first steps

PRAYER WAS MODELED FOR US BY CHRIST

Read MATTHEW 6:5-15

You have probably heard of "the Lord's Prayer." Jesus gave us this prayer to show us *how* to pray. Incidentally, just because we call this prayer "the Lord's Prayer" does not mean that Jesus prayed it for himself. He had never sinned. It is more accurate to call this prayer "the Disciples' Prayer," because Jesus gave it to his disciples in response to their request, "Lord, teach us to pray." To better understand this prayer, we can break it down into two sets of petitions:

The first three petitions focus on the glory of God.

- "Our Father in heaven": Recognize that you are addressing a holy God who sees you as his child.
- "May your name be kept holy": Begin your prayers with reverence and praise for who God is. This will enable you to put your needs or problems in their proper perspective.
- "May your Kingdom come soon. May your will be done on earth, as it is in heaven": Ask God for his will to rule your life. You cannot pray "your Kingdom come" until you pray "my kingdom go."

The second three petitions focus on our personal needs.

- "Give us today the food we need": Tell God your physical and personal needs. Remember, Scripture tells us that God will provide for all of our needs (see Philippians 4:19, p. 241).
- "And forgive us our sins, as we have forgiven those who sin against us": Confess your sins to God. Psalm 66:18 says, "If I had not confessed the sin in my heart, the LORD would not have listened." If you are clinging to some sin, your prayer life will suffer.
- "And don't let us yield to temptation, but rescue us from the evil one": Recognize your inclination to fall into sin, and pray that the opportunity to sin will not lead to committing the sin.

Make it a point to include these important aspects in your personal prayers. By doing so, you will begin to understand how immense your God is and how small your problems are in comparison.

For the next note on "Pray," turn to p. 175.

cornerstones
FORGIVENESS IS NOT SELECTIVE
Read MATTHEW 5:43-48

As one Bible commentator has put it, "To return evil for good is devilish; to return good for good is human. To return good for evil is divine." Although we are not divine, we do not have the liberty to choose whom we will forgive and not forgive. This means that we must not only forgive our enemies, but love them as well.

Loving our enemies is certainly something that does not come easily—or naturally. In fact, if we wait for some feeling of love to suddenly overtake us, it simply won't happen. We must begin to pray for our enemies even before we are conscious of loving them. This is absolutely impossible to do apart from the help of the Holy Spirit. If you feel you fall short in the area of forgiveness, take heart. The Bible is full of examples of that divine ability to forgive, which can only come from the working of the Holy Spirit in our lives:

- God's Spirit enabled Abraham to give the best land to his traveling partner and nephew, Lot (Genesis 13:1-12).
- God's Spirit gave Joseph the ability to embrace and kiss his brothers, who had sold him into slavery (Genesis 45:1-15).
- God's Spirit kept David from taking advantage of an opportunity to kill King Saul, who was seeking David's life (1 Samuel 24).
- God's Spirit caused Stephen (the first Christian martyr) to pray for those who were stoning him to death (see Acts 7:59-60, p. 140).

But the ultimate example of forgiving one's enemies comes from Jesus. While hanging on the cross, he prayed, "Father, forgive these people, for they don't know what they are doing" (see Luke 23:34, p. 99). If the cruel torture of crucifixion would not silence Jesus' prayer for his enemies, what pain, prejudice, or unfair treatment could justify the silencing of our prayers for our enemies? Just as God's Spirit worked in the lives of the individuals above, he will enable you to love, pray, and do good to those who hate and hurt you.

To begin the next topic, turn to p. A30.

and where thieves break in and steal. 20 Store your treasures in heaven, where moths and rust cannot destroy, and thieves do not break in and steal. 21 Wherever your treasure is, there the desires of your heart will also be.

22 "Your eye is a lamp that provides light for your body. When your eye is good, your whole body is filled with light. 23 But when your eye is bad, your whole body is filled with darkness. And if the light you think you have is actually darkness, how deep that darkness is!

24 "No one can serve two masters. For you will hate one and love the other; you will be devoted to one and despise the other. You cannot serve both God and money.

25 "That is why I tell you not to worry about everyday life—whether you have enough food and drink, or enough clothes to wear. Isn't life more than food, and your body more than clothing? 26 Look at the birds. They don't plant or harvest or store food in barns, for your heavenly Father feeds them. And aren't you far more valuable to him than they are? 27 Can all your worries add a single moment to your life?

28 "And why worry about your clothing? Look at the lilies of the field and how they grow. They don't work or make their clothing, 29 yet Solomon in all his glory was not dressed as beautifully as they are. 30 And if God cares so wonderfully for wildflowers that are here today and thrown into the fire tomorrow, he will certainly care for you. Why do you have so little faith?

31 "So don't worry about these things, saying, 'What will we eat? What will we drink? What will we wear?' 32 These things dominate the thoughts of unbelievers, but your heavenly Father already knows all your needs. 33 Seek the Kingdom of God* above all else, and live righteously, and he will give you everything you need.

34 "So don't worry about tomorrow, for tomorrow will bring its own worries. Today's trouble is enough for today.

6:33 Some manuscripts do not include *of God.*

CHAPTER **7**
Do Not Judge Others
"Do not judge others, and you will not be judged. ²For you will be treated as you treat others.* The standard you use in judging is the standard by which you will be judged.*

³"And why worry about a speck in your friend's eye* when you have a log in your own? ⁴How can you think of saying to your friend,* 'Let me help you get rid of that speck in your eye,' when you can't see past the log in your own eye? ⁵Hypocrite! First get rid of the log in your own eye; then you will see well enough to deal with the speck in your friend's eye.

⁶"Don't waste what is holy on people who are unholy.* Don't throw your pearls to pigs! They will trample the pearls, then turn and attack you.

Effective Prayer
⁷"Keep on asking, and you will receive what you ask for. Keep on seeking, and you will find. Keep on knocking, and the door will be opened to you. ⁸For everyone who asks, receives. Everyone who seeks, finds. And to everyone who knocks, the door will be opened.

⁹"You parents—if your children ask for a loaf of bread, do you give them a stone instead? ¹⁰Or if they ask for a fish, do you give them a snake? Of course not! ¹¹So if you sinful people know how to give good gifts to your children, how much more will your heavenly Father give good gifts to those who ask him.

The Golden Rule
¹²"Do to others whatever you would like them to do to you. This is the essence of all that is taught in the law and the prophets.

The Narrow Gate
¹³"You can enter God's Kingdom only through the narrow gate. The highway to hell* is broad, and its gate is wide for the many who choose that way. ¹⁴But the gateway to life is very narrow and the road is difficult, and only a few ever find it.

The Tree and Its Fruit
¹⁵"Beware of false prophets who come disguised as harmless sheep but are really vicious wolves. ¹⁶You can identify them by their fruit, that is, by the way they act. Can you pick grapes from thornbushes, or figs from thistles? ¹⁷A good tree produces good fruit, and a bad tree

7:2a Or *For God will judge you as you judge others.*
7:2b Or *The measure you give will be the measure you get back.*   7:3 Greek *your brother's eye;* also in 7:5.   7:4 Greek *your brother.*   7:6 Greek *Don't give the sacred to dogs.*
7:13 Greek *The road that leads to destruction.*

first steps

HOW SHOULD YOU VIEW MATERIAL WEALTH?
Read MATTHEW 6:19-34

This section of Jesus' famous Sermon on the Mount deals with possibly the greatest distraction to following him wholeheartedly: wealth. This series of verses gives us at least three warnings about wealth and one prescription to overcome its enslaving effects:

1. We Must Watch How and What We Store. Verse 19 says that we should not "store up treasures." The idea here is not simply saving, but stockpiling. Jesus is not condemning saving your resources or providing for your family (Proverbs 6:6, and 1 Timothy 5:8, p. 262). He is condemning the accumulation of possessions in order to impress others. Enjoy what God has given you without making those possessions your primary ambition.

2. We Must Keep Our Vision Clear. While we can enjoy what God gives us, we need to understand that the material things of this world are only temporary. Our possessions can lose their value, be destroyed by natural disasters, get lost, or be stolen. That is the problem with making the accumulation of "things" your life's passion. It is fleeting, unfulfilling, and even enslaving. Without proper perspective, we can easily become ensnared. Then we are no longer serving God but money (verses 22-24).

3. We Should Not Worry about Material Things. Worry is a powerful force that can divide or distract us. You can worry about anything in your life. But Jesus tells you to stop worrying, because God will *always* meet your needs (verses 25-30). Quite simply, worry is a waste of your valuable time as his servant.

4. We Must Put God First in Our Lives. Our main concern should not be acquiring material possessions or prestige. Our primary pursuit should be seeking to put Jesus Christ first in our lives (verses 31-34). It makes a lot of sense to place your temporary needs and worries in the hands of an eternal God.

For the next note on "Give to God," turn to p. 261.

cornerstones

OUR WALK SHOULD MATCH OUR TALK
Read MATTHEW 7:21

In this verse, Jesus gets to the heart of every person's belief. He states that calling him Lord is not enough to get into heaven. That is because anyone can say the word and not mean it. What counts is a changed person living in obedience to God's will.

Regarding the Christian life, it has been said, "It is not how high you can jump that matters, but how straight you can walk when you hit the ground again." You may be able to say all of the right things, but if your faith does not impact the way you live, it is meaningless—even offensive. In truth, you do not have a real relationship with God.

An engraving on a cathedral wall in Germany bears these soul-searching words:

Thus speaketh Christ our Lord to us,
  "You call me Master and obey me not;
  You call me light and see me not;
  You call me the Way and walk me not;
  You call me life and live me not;
  You call me wise and follow me not;
  You call me fair and love me not;
  You call me rich and ask me not;
  You call me eternal and seek me not;
  If I condemn you, blame me not."

The more we learn about what God has done for us, the more we will want to know about how to live for him. Our motives will come from a pure heart, not from selfish ambition. God is looking for genuine believers whose walk matches their talk. Are you one?

To begin the next topic, turn to p. A33.

---

produces bad fruit. [18] A good tree can't produce bad fruit, and a bad tree can't produce good fruit. [19] So every tree that does not produce good fruit is chopped down and thrown into the fire. [20] Yes, just as you can identify a tree by its fruit, so you can identify people by their actions.

True Disciples

[21] "Not everyone who calls out to me, 'Lord! Lord!' will enter the Kingdom of Heaven. Only those who actually do the will of my Father in heaven will enter. [22] On judgment day many will say to me, 'Lord! Lord! We prophesied in your name and cast out demons in your name and performed many miracles in your name.' [23] But I will reply, 'I never knew you. Get away from me, you who break God's laws.'

Building on a Solid Foundation

[24] "Anyone who listens to my teaching and follows it is wise, like a person who builds a house on solid rock. [25] Though the rain comes in torrents and the floodwaters rise and the winds beat against that house, it won't collapse because it is built on bedrock. [26] But anyone who

8:4 See Lev 14:2-32.

hears my teaching and doesn't obey it is foolish, like a person who builds a house on sand. [27] When the rains and floods come and the winds beat against that house, it will collapse with a mighty crash."

[28] When Jesus had finished saying these things, the crowds were amazed at his teaching, [29] for he taught with real authority—quite unlike their teachers of religious law.

CHAPTER **8**

Jesus Heals a Man with Leprosy

Large crowds followed Jesus as he came down the mountainside. [2] Suddenly, a man with leprosy approached him and knelt before him. "Lord," the man said, "if you are willing, you can heal me and make me clean."

[3] Jesus reached out and touched him. "I am willing," he said. "Be healed!" And instantly the leprosy disappeared. [4] Then Jesus said to him, "Don't tell anyone about this. Instead, go to the priest and let him examine you. Take along the offering required in the law of Moses for those who have been healed of leprosy.* This will be a public testimony that you have been cleansed."

The Faith of a Roman Officer

[5] When Jesus returned to Capernaum, a Roman officer* came and pleaded with him, [6] "Lord, my young servant* lies in bed, paralyzed and in terrible pain."

[7] Jesus said, "I will come and heal him."

[8] But the officer said, "Lord, I am not worthy to have you come into my home. Just say the word from where you are, and my servant will be healed. [9] I know this because I am under the authority of my superior officers, and I have authority over my soldiers. I only need to say, 'Go,' and they go, or 'Come,' and they come. And if I say to my slaves, 'Do this,' they do it."

[10] When Jesus heard this, he was amazed. Turning to those who were following him, he said, "I tell you the truth, I haven't seen faith like this in all Israel! [11] And I tell you this, that many Gentiles will come from all over the world—from east and west—and sit down with Abraham, Isaac, and Jacob at the feast in the Kingdom of Heaven. [12] But many Israelites—those for whom the Kingdom was prepared—will be thrown into outer darkness, where there will be weeping and gnashing of teeth."

[13] Then Jesus said to the Roman officer, "Go back home. Because you believed, it has happened." And the young servant was healed that same hour.

Jesus Heals Many People

[14] When Jesus arrived at Peter's house, Peter's mother-in-law was sick in bed with a high fever. [15] But when Jesus touched her hand, the fever left her. Then she got up and prepared a meal for him.

[16] That evening many demon-possessed people were brought to Jesus. He cast out the evil spirits with a simple command, and he healed all the sick. [17] This fulfilled the word of the Lord through the prophet Isaiah, who said,

> "He took our sicknesses
> and removed our diseases."*

The Cost of Following Jesus

[18] When Jesus saw the crowd around him, he instructed his disciples to cross to the other side of the lake.

[19] Then one of the teachers of religious law said to him, "Teacher, I will follow you wherever you go."

[20] But Jesus replied, "Foxes have dens to live in, and birds have nests, but the Son of Man* has no place even to lay his head."

[21] Another of his disciples said, "Lord, first let me return home and bury my father."

[22] But Jesus told him, "Follow me now. Let the spiritually dead bury their own dead.*"

Jesus Calms the Storm

[23] Then Jesus got into the boat and started across the lake with his disciples. [24] Suddenly, a fierce storm struck the lake, with waves breaking into the boat. But Jesus was sleeping. [25] The disciples went and woke him up, shouting, "Lord, save us! We're going to drown!"

[26] Jesus responded, "Why are you afraid? You have so little faith!" Then he got up and rebuked the wind and waves, and suddenly there was a great calm.

[27] The disciples were amazed. "Who is this man?" they asked. "Even the winds and waves obey him!"

Jesus Heals Two Demon-Possessed Men

[28] When Jesus arrived on the other side of the lake, in the region of the Gadarenes,* two men who were possessed by demons met him. They lived in a cemetery and were so violent that no one could go through that area.

[29] They began screaming at him, "Why are you interfering with us, Son of God? Have you come here to torture us before God's appointed time?"

[30] There happened to be a large herd of pigs feeding in the distance. [31] So the demons begged, "If you cast us out, send us into that herd of pigs."

[32] "All right, go!" Jesus commanded them. So the demons came out of the men and entered the pigs, and the whole herd plunged down the steep hillside into the lake and drowned in the water.

[33] The herdsmen fled to the nearby town, telling everyone what happened to the demon-possessed men. [34] Then the entire town came out to meet Jesus, but they begged him to go away and leave them alone.

CHAPTER 9

Jesus Heals a Paralyzed Man

Jesus climbed into a boat and went back across the lake to his own town. [2] Some people brought to him a paralyzed man on a mat. Seeing their faith, Jesus said to the paralyzed man, "Be encouraged, my child! Your sins are forgiven."

[3] But some of the teachers of religious law said to themselves, "That's blasphemy! Does he think he's God?"

8:5 Greek *a centurion;* similarly in 8:8, 13.   **8:6** Or *child;* also in 8:13.   **8:17** Isa 53:4.   **8:20** "Son of Man" is a title Jesus used for himself.   **8:22** Greek *Let the dead bury their own dead.*   **8:28** Other manuscripts read *Gerasenes;* still others read *Gergesenes.* Compare Mark 5:1; Luke 8:26.

[4] Jesus knew* what they were thinking, so he asked them, "Why do you have such evil thoughts in your hearts? [5] Is it easier to say 'Your sins are forgiven,' or 'Stand up and walk'? [6] So I will prove to you that the Son of Man* has the authority on earth to forgive sins." Then Jesus turned to the paralyzed man and said, "Stand up, pick up your mat, and go home!"

[7] And the man jumped up and went home! [8] Fear swept through the crowd as they saw this happen. And they praised God for sending a man with such great authority.*

Jesus Calls Matthew

[9] As Jesus was walking along, he saw a man named Matthew sitting at his tax collector's booth. "Follow me and be my disciple," Jesus said to him. So Matthew got up and followed him.

[10] Later, Matthew invited Jesus and his disciples to his home as dinner guests, along with many tax collectors and other disreputable sinners. [11] But when the Pharisees saw this, they asked his disciples, "Why does your teacher eat with such scum?*"

[12] When Jesus heard this, he said, "Healthy people don't need a doctor—sick people do." [13] Then he added, "Now go and learn the meaning of this Scripture: 'I want you to show mercy, not offer sacrifices.'* For I have come to call not those who think they are righteous, but those who know they are sinners."

A Discussion about Fasting

[14] One day the disciples of John the Baptist came to Jesus and asked him, "Why don't your disciples fast* like we do and the Pharisees do?"

[15] Jesus replied, "Do wedding guests mourn while celebrating with the groom? Of course not. But someday the groom will be taken away from them, and then they will fast.

[16] "Besides, who would patch old clothing with new cloth? For the new patch would shrink and rip away from the old cloth, leaving an even bigger tear than before.

[17] "And no one puts new wine into old wineskins. For the old skins would burst from the pressure, spilling the wine and ruining the skins. New wine is stored in new wineskins so that both are preserved."

Jesus Heals in Response to Faith

[18] As Jesus was saying this, the leader of a synagogue came and knelt before him. "My daughter has just died," he said, "but you can bring her back to life again if you just come and lay your hand on her."

[19] So Jesus and his disciples got up and went with him. [20] Just then a woman who had suffered for twelve years with constant bleeding came up behind him. She touched the fringe of his robe, [21] for she thought, "If I can just touch his robe, I will be healed."

[22] Jesus turned around, and when he saw her he said, "Daughter, be encouraged! Your faith has made you well." And the woman was healed at that moment.

[23] When Jesus arrived at the official's home, he saw the noisy crowd and heard the funeral music. [24] "Get out!" he told them. "The girl isn't dead; she's only asleep." But the crowd laughed at him. [25] After the crowd was put outside, however, Jesus went in and took the girl by the hand, and she stood up! [26] The report of this miracle swept through the entire countryside.

Jesus Heals the Blind

[27] After Jesus left the girl's home, two blind men followed along behind him, shouting, "Son of David, have mercy on us!"

[28] They went right into the house where he was staying, and Jesus asked them, "Do you believe I can make you see?"

"Yes, Lord," they told him, "we do."

[29] Then he touched their eyes and said, "Because of your faith, it will happen." [30] Then their eyes were opened, and they could see! Jesus sternly warned them, "Don't tell anyone about this." [31] But instead, they went out and spread his fame all over the region.

[32] When they left, a demon-possessed man who couldn't speak was brought to Jesus. [33] So Jesus cast out the demon, and then the man began to speak. The crowds were amazed. "Nothing like this has ever happened in Israel!" they exclaimed.

[34] But the Pharisees said, "He can cast out demons because he is empowered by the prince of demons."

The Need for Workers

[35] Jesus traveled through all the towns and villages of that area, teaching in the synagogues and announcing the Good News about the Kingdom. And he healed every kind of disease and illness. [36] When he saw the crowds, he had compassion on them because they were confused and helpless, like sheep without a shepherd. [37] He said to his disciples, "The harvest is great, but the workers are few. [38] So pray to the Lord who is in charge of the harvest; ask him to send more workers into his fields."

9:4 Some manuscripts read *saw.*   9:6 "Son of Man" is a title Jesus used for himself.   9:8 Greek *for giving such authority to human beings.*   9:11 Greek *with tax collectors and sinners?*   9:13 Hos 6:6 (Greek version).   9:14 Some manuscripts read *fast often.*

CHAPTER **10**

Jesus Sends Out the Twelve Apostles

Jesus called his twelve disciples together and gave them authority to cast out evil* spirits and to heal every kind of disease and illness. ²Here are the names of the twelve apostles:

first, Simon (also called Peter),
then Andrew (Peter's brother),
James (son of Zebedee),
John (James's brother),
³ Philip,
Bartholomew,
Thomas,
Matthew (the tax collector),
James (son of Alphaeus),
Thaddaeus,*
⁴ Simon (the zealot*),
Judas Iscariot (who later betrayed him).

⁵Jesus sent out the twelve apostles with these instructions: "Don't go to the Gentiles or the Samaritans, ⁶but only to the people of Israel—God's lost sheep. ⁷Go and announce to them that the Kingdom of Heaven is near.* ⁸Heal the sick, raise the dead, cure those with leprosy, and cast out demons. Give as freely as you have received!

⁹"Don't take any money in your money belts—no gold, silver, or even copper coins. ¹⁰Don't carry a traveler's bag with a change of clothes and sandals or even a walking stick. Don't hesitate to accept hospitality, because those who work deserve to be fed.

¹¹"Whenever you enter a city or village, search for a worthy person and stay in his home until you leave town. ¹²When you enter the home, give it your blessing. ¹³If it turns out to be a worthy home, let your blessing stand; if it is not, take back the blessing. ¹⁴If any household or town refuses to welcome you or listen to your message, shake its dust from your feet as you leave. ¹⁵I tell you the truth, the wicked cities of Sodom and Gomorrah will be better off than such a town on the judgment day.

¹⁶"Look, I am sending you out as sheep among wolves. So be as shrewd as snakes and harmless as doves. ¹⁷But beware! For you will be handed over to the courts and will be flogged with whips in the synagogues. ¹⁸You will stand trial before governors and kings because you are my followers. But this will be your opportunity to tell the rulers and other unbelievers about me.* ¹⁹When you are ar-

rested, don't worry about how to respond or what to say. God will give you the right words at the right time. ²⁰For it is not you who will be speaking—it will be the Spirit of your Father speaking through you.

²¹"A brother will betray his brother to death, a father will betray his own child, and children will rebel against their parents and cause them to be killed. ²²And all nations will hate you because you are my followers.* But everyone who endures to the end will be saved. ²³When you are persecuted in one town, flee to the next. I tell you the truth, the Son of Man* will return before you have reached all the towns of Israel.

²⁴"Students* are not greater than their teacher, and slaves are not greater than their master. ²⁵Students are to be like their teacher, and slaves are to be like their master. And since I, the master of the household, have been called the prince of demons,* the members of my household will be called by even worse names!

²⁶"But don't be afraid of those who threaten you. For the time is coming when everything that is covered will be revealed, and all that is secret will be made known to all. ²⁷What I tell you now in the darkness, shout abroad when daybreak comes. What I whisper in your ear, shout from the housetops for all to hear!

²⁸"Don't be afraid of those who want to kill your body; they cannot touch your soul. Fear only God, who can destroy both soul and body in hell.* ²⁹What is the price of two sparrows—one copper coin*? But not a single sparrow can fall to the ground without your Father knowing it. ³⁰And the very hairs on your head are all numbered. ³¹So don't be afraid; you are more valuable to God than a whole flock of sparrows.

³²"Everyone who acknowledges me publicly here on earth, I will also acknowledge before my Father in heaven. ³³But everyone who denies me here on earth, I will also deny before my Father in heaven.

³⁴"Don't imagine that I came to bring peace to the earth! I came not to bring peace, but a sword.

³⁵ 'I have come to set a man against his father,
      a daughter against her mother,
   and a daughter-in-law against her mother-
      in-law.
³⁶   Your enemies will be right in your own
      household!'*

³⁷"If you love your father or mother more than you love me, you are not worthy of being

---

10:1 Greek *unclean.*   10:3 Other manuscripts read *Lebbaeus;* still others read *Lebbaeus who is called Thaddaeus.*
10:4 Greek *the Cananean,* an Aramaic term for Jewish nationalists.   10:7 Or *has come,* or *is coming soon.*   10:18 Or *But this will be your testimony against the rulers and other unbelievers.*   10:22 Greek *on account of my name.*   10:23 "Son of Man" is a title Jesus used for himself.   10:24 Or *Disciples.*   10:25 Greek *Beelzeboul;* other manuscripts read *Beezeboul;* Latin version reads *Beelzebub.*   10:28 Greek *Gehenna.*   10:29 Greek *one assarion* [i.e., one "as," a Roman coin equal to ¹⁄₁₆ of a denarius].   10:35-36 Mic 7:6.

cornerstones

PEACE BEGINS WHEN WE RELINQUISH CONTROL OF OUR LIVES TO GOD
Read MATTHEW 11:28-30

In this passage, Jesus teaches us three things we must do in order to find true peace. Yet, for some odd reason, we sometimes find these things difficult to do. Make a point of concentrating on practicing these three necessary actions:

1. Come to Christ. If you have already accepted Jesus Christ as Lord and Savior in your life, you have already completed this step. If you are still searching, you might be right at the door. But know this: You will not find peace from anyone or anything else. Sure, you can achieve temporary peace of mind, but when the bottom falls out, what happens then? Only Christ can guarantee you unending peace.

2. Exchange Your Yoke for His Yoke. A yoke is a heavy wooden harness that is placed over the neck of one or more oxen in order to help pull a wagon or any other piece of equipment. It enables a farmer to direct the oxen. Shifting the analogy to humans, our "heavy yoke" could be the weight of guilt, or the burden of trying to please God through our own good works. Jesus wants you to exchange that load for his lighter load—God's grace. You can rest in knowing that you do not have to work for God's favor; you need only to accept his Son.

3. Let Jesus Lead. This is undoubtedly one of the hardest parts of this promise because we want to be in control. But God says that we need to give him the reins so that he can teach us. Are you ready and willing to leave every aspect of your life in God's hands? Then you will experience God's promised "rest" for your soul.

For the next note on "Peace," turn to p. 180.

---

mine; or if you love your son or daughter more than me, you are not worthy of being mine. ³⁸If you refuse to take up your cross and follow me, you are not worthy of being mine. ³⁹If you cling to your life, you will lose it; but if you give up your life for me, you will find it.

⁴⁰"Anyone who receives you receives me, and anyone who receives me receives the Father who sent me. ⁴¹If you receive a prophet as one who speaks for God,* you will be given the same reward as a prophet. And if you receive righteous people because of their righteousness, you will be given a reward like theirs. ⁴²And if you give even a cup of cold water to one of the least of my followers, you will surely be rewarded."

CHAPTER 11
Jesus and John the Baptist
When Jesus had finished giving these instructions to his twelve disciples, he went out to teach and preach in towns throughout the region.

²John the Baptist, who was in prison, heard about all the things the Messiah was doing. So he sent his disciples to ask Jesus, ³"Are you the Messiah we've been expecting,* or should we keep looking for someone else?"

⁴Jesus told them, "Go back to John and tell him what you have heard and seen—⁵the blind see, the lame walk, the lepers are cured, the deaf hear, the dead are raised to life, and the Good News is being preached to the poor. ⁶And tell him, 'God blesses those who do not turn away because of me.*'"

⁷As John's disciples were leaving, Jesus began talking about him to the crowds. "What kind of man did you go into the wilderness to see? Was he a weak reed, swayed by every breath of wind? ⁸Or were you expecting to see a man dressed in expensive clothes? No, people with expensive clothes live in palaces. ⁹Were you looking for a prophet? Yes, and he is more than a prophet. ¹⁰John is the man to whom the Scriptures refer when they say,

'Look, I am sending my messenger ahead of you,
and he will prepare your way before you.'*

¹¹"I tell you the truth, of all who have ever lived, none is greater than John the Baptist. Yet even the least person in the Kingdom of Heaven is greater than he is! ¹²And from the time John the Baptist began preaching until now, the Kingdom of Heaven has been forcefully advancing,* and violent people are attack-

---

10:41 Greek *receive a prophet in the name of a prophet.* **11:3** Greek *Are you the one who is coming?* **11:6** Or *who are not offended by me.* **11:10** Mal 3:1. **11:12** Or *the Kingdom of Heaven has suffered from violence.*

ing it. [13] For before John came, all the prophets and the law of Moses looked forward to this present time. [14] And if you are willing to accept what I say, he is Elijah, the one the prophets said would come.* [15] Anyone with ears to hear should listen and understand!

[16] "To what can I compare this generation? It is like children playing a game in the public square. They complain to their friends,

[17] 'We played wedding songs,
    and you didn't dance,
so we played funeral songs,
    and you didn't mourn.'

[18] For John didn't spend his time eating and drinking, and you say, 'He's possessed by a demon.' [19] The Son of Man,* on the other hand, feasts and drinks, and you say, 'He's a glutton and a drunkard, and a friend of tax collectors and other sinners!' But wisdom is shown to be right by its results."

Judgment for the Unbelievers

[20] Then Jesus began to denounce the towns where he had done so many of his miracles, because they hadn't repented of their sins and turned to God. [21] "What sorrow awaits you, Korazin and Bethsaida! For if the miracles I did in you had been done in wicked Tyre and Sidon, their people would have repented of their sins long ago, clothing themselves in burlap and throwing ashes on their heads to show their remorse. [22] I tell you, Tyre and Sidon will be better off on judgment day than you.

[23] "And you people of Capernaum, will you be honored in heaven? No, you will go down to the place of the dead.* For if the miracles I did for you had been done in wicked Sodom, it would still be here today. [24] I tell you, even Sodom will be better off on judgment day than you."

Jesus' Prayer of Thanksgiving

[25] At that time Jesus prayed this prayer: "O Father, Lord of heaven and earth, thank you for hiding these things from those who think themselves wise and clever, and for revealing them to the childlike. [26] Yes, Father, it pleased you to do it this way!

[27] "My Father has entrusted everything to me. No one truly knows the Son except the Father, and no one truly knows the Father except the Son and those to whom the Son chooses to reveal him."

[28] Then Jesus said, "Come to me, all of you who are weary and carry heavy burdens, and I will give you rest. [29] Take my yoke upon you. Let me teach you, because I am humble and gentle at heart, and you will find rest for your souls. [30] For my yoke is easy to bear, and the burden I give you is light."

CHAPTER 12

A Discussion about the Sabbath

At about that time Jesus was walking through some grainfields on the Sabbath. His disciples were hungry, so they began breaking off some heads of grain and eating them. [2] But some Pharisees saw them do it and protested, "Look, your disciples are breaking the law by harvesting grain on the Sabbath."

[3] Jesus said to them, "Haven't you read in the Scriptures what David did when he and his companions were hungry? [4] He went into the house of God, and he and his companions broke the law by eating the sacred loaves of bread that only the priests are allowed to eat. [5] And haven't you read in the law of Moses that the priests on duty in the Temple may work on the Sabbath? [6] I tell you, there is one here who is even greater than the Temple! [7] But you would not have condemned my innocent disciples if you knew the meaning of this Scripture: 'I want you to show mercy, not offer sacrifices.'* [8] For the Son of Man* is Lord, even over the Sabbath!"

Jesus Heals on the Sabbath

[9] Then Jesus went over to their synagogue, [10] where he noticed a man with a deformed hand. The Pharisees asked Jesus, "Does the law permit a person to work by healing on the Sabbath?" (They were hoping he would say yes, so they could bring charges against him.)

[11] And he answered, "If you had a sheep that fell into a well on the Sabbath, wouldn't you work to pull it out? Of course you would. [12] And how much more valuable is a person than a sheep! Yes, the law permits a person to do good on the Sabbath."

[13] Then he said to the man, "Hold out your hand." So the man held out his hand, and it was restored, just like the other one! [14] Then the Pharisees called a meeting to plot how to kill Jesus.

Jesus, God's Chosen Servant

[15] But Jesus knew what they were planning. So he left that area, and many people followed him. He healed all the sick among them, [16] but he warned them not to reveal who he was. [17] This fulfilled the prophecy of Isaiah concerning him:

[18] "Look at my Servant, whom I have chosen.
    He is my Beloved, who pleases me.

11:14 See Mal 4:5.   11:19 "Son of Man" is a title Jesus used for himself.   11:23 Greek to Hades.   12:7 Hos 6:6 (Greek version).   12:8 "Son of Man" is a title Jesus used for himself.

I will put my Spirit upon him,
  and he will proclaim justice to the
    nations.
[19] He will not fight or shout
  or raise his voice in public.
[20] He will not crush the weakest reed
  or put out a flickering candle.
  Finally he will cause justice to be
    victorious.
[21] And his name will be the hope
  of all the world."*

Jesus and the Prince of Demons

[22] Then a demon-possessed man, who was blind and couldn't speak, was brought to Jesus. He healed the man so that he could both speak and see. [23] The crowd was amazed and asked, "Could it be that Jesus is the Son of David, the Messiah?"

[24] But when the Pharisees heard about the miracle, they said, "No wonder he can cast out demons. He gets his power from Satan,* the prince of demons."

[25] Jesus knew their thoughts and replied, "Any kingdom divided by civil war is doomed. A town or family splintered by feuding will fall apart. [26] And if Satan is casting out Satan, he is divided and fighting against himself. His own kingdom will not survive. [27] And if I am empowered by Satan, what about your own exorcists? They cast out demons, too, so they will condemn you for what you have said. [28] But if I am casting out demons by the Spirit of God, then the Kingdom of God has arrived among you. [29] For who is powerful enough to enter the house of a strong man like Satan and plunder his goods? Only someone even stronger—someone who could tie him up and then plunder his house.

[30] "Anyone who isn't with me opposes me, and anyone who isn't working with me is actually working against me.

[31] "So I tell you, every sin and blasphemy can be forgiven—except blasphemy against the Holy Spirit, which will never be forgiven. [32] Anyone who speaks against the Son of Man can be forgiven, but anyone who speaks against the Holy Spirit will never be forgiven, either in this world or in the world to come.

[33] "A tree is identified by its fruit. If a tree is good, its fruit will be good. If a tree is bad, its fruit will be bad. [34] You brood of snakes! How could evil men like you speak what is good and right? For whatever is in your heart determines what you say. [35] A good person produces good things from the treasury of a good heart, and an evil person produces evil things from the treasury of an evil heart. [36] And I tell you this, you must give an account on judgment day for every idle word you speak. [37] The words you say will either acquit you or condemn you."

The Sign of Jonah

[38] One day some teachers of religious law and Pharisees came to Jesus and said, "Teacher, we want you to show us a miraculous sign to prove your authority."

[39] But Jesus replied, "Only an evil, adulterous generation would demand a miraculous sign; but the only sign I will give them is the sign of the prophet Jonah. [40] For as Jonah was in the belly of the great fish for three days and three nights, so will the Son of Man be in the heart of the earth for three days and three nights.

[41] "The people of Nineveh will stand up against this generation on judgment day and condemn it, for they repented of their sins at the preaching of Jonah. Now someone greater than Jonah is here—but you refuse to repent. [42] The queen of Sheba* will also stand up against this generation on judgment day and condemn it, for she came from a distant land to hear the wisdom of Solomon. Now someone greater than Solomon is here—but you refuse to listen.

12:18-21 Isa 42:1-4 (Greek version for 42:4).   12:24 Greek *Beelzeboul;* also in 12:27. Other manuscripts read *Beezeboul;* Latin version reads *Beelzebub.*   12:42 Greek *The queen of the south.*

off and running

REFRAIN FROM IDLE TALK
Read MATTHEW 12:35-37

The verse preceding this text says, "For whatever is in your heart determines what you say." Your speech mirrors the condition of your heart, which represents your innermost thoughts, desires, and emotions. If your heart is filled with bitterness, your speech will be tainted by it. If it is filled with the love of God, your words will express that love. If we take seriously Jesus' warning about being held accountable for our idle words, then we should not only

43 "When an evil* spirit leaves a person, it goes into the desert, seeking rest but finding none. 44 Then it says, 'I will return to the person I came from.' So it returns and finds its former home empty, swept, and in order. 45 Then the spirit finds seven other spirits more evil than itself, and they all enter the person and live there. And so that person is worse off than before. That will be the experience of this evil generation."

The True Family of Jesus

46 As Jesus was speaking to the crowd, his mother and brothers stood outside, asking to speak to him. 47 Someone told Jesus, "Your mother and your brothers are outside, and they want to speak to you."*

48 Jesus asked, "Who is my mother? Who are my brothers?" 49 Then he pointed to his disciples and said, "Look, these are my mother and brothers. 50 Anyone who does the will of my Father in heaven is my brother and sister and mother!"

CHAPTER **13**

Parable of the Farmer Scattering Seed

Later that same day Jesus left the house and sat beside the lake. 2 A large crowd soon gathered around him, so he got into a boat. Then he sat there and taught as the people stood on the shore. 3 He told many stories in the form of parables, such as this one:

"Listen! A farmer went out to plant some seeds. 4 As he scattered them across his field, some seeds fell on a footpath, and the birds came and ate them. 5 Other seeds fell on shallow soil with underlying rock. The seeds sprouted quickly because the soil was shallow. 6 But the plants soon wilted under the hot sun, and since they didn't have deep roots, they died. 7 Other seeds fell among thorns that grew up and choked out the tender plants. 8 Still other seeds fell on fertile soil, and they produced a crop that was thirty, sixty, and even a hundred times as much as had been planted! 9 Anyone with ears to hear should listen and understand."

10 His disciples came and asked him, "Why do you use parables when you talk to the people?"

11 He replied, "You are permitted to understand the secrets* of the Kingdom of Heaven, but others are not. 12 To those who listen to my teaching, more understanding will be given, and they will have an abundance of knowledge. But for those who are not listening, even what little understanding they have will be taken away from them. 13 That is why I use these parables,

For they look, but they don't really see.
They hear, but they don't really listen or
understand.

14 This fulfills the prophecy of Isaiah that says,

'When you hear what I say,
you will not understand.
When you see what I do,
you will not comprehend.
15 For the hearts of these people are hardened,
and their ears cannot hear,
and they have closed their eyes—
so their eyes cannot see,
and their ears cannot hear,
and their hearts cannot understand,
and they cannot turn to me
and let me heal them.'*

16 "But blessed are your eyes, because they see; and your ears, because they hear. 17 I tell you the truth, many prophets and righteous people longed to see what you see, but they didn't see it. And they longed to hear what you hear, but they didn't hear it.

18 "Now listen to the explanation of the parable about the farmer planting seeds: 19 The

12:43 Greek *unclean.* **12:47** Some manuscripts do not include verse 47. Compare Mark 3:32 and Luke 8:20. **13:11** Greek *the mysteries.* **13:14-15** Isa 6:9-10 (Greek version).

weigh our words, but we should also examine our hearts—the source of our speech. Here is a good rule to apply before you speak: THINK.

T—Is it true?
H—Is it helpful?
I—Is it inspiring?
N—Is it necessary?
K—Is it kind?

If what you want to say doesn't pass this test, you really shouldn't say it. You will have to give an explanation when you stand before the Lord.

For the next note on "Conversation," turn to p. 248.

cornerstones

BEWARE OF SATAN'S CLEVER IMITATIONS

Read MATTHEW 13:24-30

This is known as the parable of the wheat and the tares. Jesus gave this illustration to expose Satan's tactic of imitation and infiltration.

The thistles, or tares, were actually a plant that came from the darnel seed. In the initial stages of growth, this plant looked exactly like wheat. But in time the wild weed would show itself to be a plant that could uproot the wheat if pulled.

In essence, Satan has followed the pattern of the darnel seed in his attacks against the church. He has flooded the market with his imitations. There are numerous examples of this throughout the Bible. In Exodus, the Egyptian magicians imitated some of the miracles God performed through Moses—like turning a rod into a snake, turning the waters of the Nile into blood, and bringing forth a plague of frogs (Exodus 7:1–8:15). In Acts, the sorcerer Simon imitated Philip (see Acts 8:9-24, p. 141).

In fact, whenever the church has experienced a great revival, a false movement has grown up by its side proclaiming half-truths and deceptions.

Satan knows that half-truths are more dangerous than lies. Those who have modified the truth have always injured the truth more than those who have denied it openly. Therefore we must guard against falling for half-truths and gospel imitations at all costs.

For the next note on "Discernment," turn to p. 260.

seed that fell on the footpath represents those who hear the message about the Kingdom and don't understand it. Then the evil one comes and snatches away the seed that was planted in their hearts. [20] The seed on the rocky soil represents those who hear the message and immediately receive it with joy. [21] But since they don't have deep roots, they don't last long. They fall away as soon as they have problems or are persecuted for believing God's word. [22] The seed that fell among the thorns represents those who hear God's word, but all too quickly the message is crowded out by the worries of this life and the lure of wealth, so no fruit is produced. [23] The seed that fell on good soil represents those who truly hear and understand God's word and produce a harvest of thirty, sixty, or even a hundred times as much as had been planted!"

Parable of the Wheat and Weeds

[24] Here is another story Jesus told: "The Kingdom of Heaven is like a farmer who planted good seed in his field. [25] But that night as the workers slept, his enemy came and planted weeds among the wheat, then slipped away. [26] When the crop began to grow and produce grain, the weeds also grew.

[27] "The farmer's workers went to him and said, 'Sir, the field where you planted that good seed is full of weeds! Where did they come from?'

[28] "'An enemy has done this!' the farmer exclaimed.

"'Should we pull out the weeds?' they asked.

[29] "'No,' he replied, 'you'll uproot the wheat if you do. [30] Let both grow together until the harvest. Then I will tell the harvesters to sort out the weeds, tie them into bundles, and burn them, and to put the wheat in the barn.'"

Parable of the Mustard Seed

[31] Here is another illustration Jesus used: "The Kingdom of Heaven is like a mustard seed planted in a field. [32] It is the smallest of all seeds, but it becomes the largest of garden plants; it grows into a tree, and birds come and make nests in its branches."

Parable of the Yeast

[33] Jesus also used this illustration: "The Kingdom of Heaven is like the yeast a woman used in making bread. Even though she put only a little yeast in three measures of flour, it permeated every part of the dough."

[34] Jesus always used stories and illustrations like these when speaking to the crowds. In fact, he never spoke to them without using such parables. [35] This fulfilled what God had spoken through the prophet:

"I will speak to you in parables.
    I will explain things hidden since the creation of the world.*"

13:35 Some manuscripts do not include *of the world.* Ps 78:2.

Parable of the Wheat and Weeds Explained

36 Then, leaving the crowds outside, Jesus went into the house. His disciples said, "Please explain to us the story of the weeds in the field."

37 Jesus replied, "The Son of Man* is the farmer who plants the good seed. 38 The field is the world, and the good seed represents the people of the Kingdom. The weeds are the people who belong to the evil one. 39 The enemy who planted the weeds among the wheat is the devil. The harvest is the end of the world,* and the harvesters are the angels.

40 "Just as the weeds are sorted out and burned in the fire, so it will be at the end of the world. 41 The Son of Man will send his angels, and they will remove from his Kingdom everything that causes sin and all who do evil. 42 And the angels will throw them into the fiery furnace, where there will be weeping and gnashing of teeth. 43 Then the righteous will shine like the sun in their Father's Kingdom. Anyone with ears to hear should listen and understand!

Parables of the Hidden Treasure and the Pearl

44 "The Kingdom of Heaven is like a treasure that a man discovered hidden in a field. In his excitement, he hid it again and sold everything he owned to get enough money to buy the field.

45 "Again, the Kingdom of Heaven is like a merchant on the lookout for choice pearls. 46 When he discovered a pearl of great value, he sold everything he owned and bought it!

Parable of the Fishing Net

47 "Again, the Kingdom of Heaven is like a fishing net that was thrown into the water and caught fish of every kind. 48 When the net was full, they dragged it up onto the shore, sat down, and sorted the good fish into crates, but threw the bad ones away. 49 That is the way it will be at the end of the world. The angels will come and separate the wicked people from the righteous, 50 throwing the wicked into the fiery furnace, where there will be weeping and gnashing of teeth. 51 Do you understand all these things?"

"Yes," they said, "we do."

52 Then he added, "Every teacher of religious law who becomes a disciple in the Kingdom of Heaven is like a homeowner who brings from his storeroom new gems of truth as well as old."

Jesus Rejected at Nazareth

53 When Jesus had finished telling these stories and illustrations, he left that part of the country. 54 He returned to Nazareth, his hometown. When he taught there in the synagogue, everyone was amazed and said, "Where does he get this wisdom and the power to do miracles?" 55 Then they scoffed, "He's just the carpenter's son, and we know Mary, his mother, and his brothers—James, Joseph,* Simon, and Judas. 56 All his sisters live right here among us. Where did he learn all these things?" 57 And they were deeply offended and refused to believe in him.

Then Jesus told them, "A prophet is honored everywhere except in his own hometown and among his own family." 58 And so he did only a few miracles there because of their unbelief.

CHAPTER 14

The Death of John the Baptist

When Herod Antipas, the ruler of Galilee,* heard about Jesus, 2 he said to his advisers, "This must be John the Baptist raised from the dead! That is why he can do such miracles."

3 For Herod had arrested and imprisoned John as a favor to his wife Herodias (the former wife of Herod's brother Philip). 4 John had been telling Herod, "It is against God's law for you to marry her." 5 Herod wanted to kill John, but he was afraid of a riot, because all the people believed John was a prophet.

6 But at a birthday party for Herod, Herodias's daughter performed a dance that greatly pleased him, 7 so he promised with a vow to give her anything she wanted. 8 At her mother's urging, the girl said, "I want the head of John the Baptist on a tray!" 9 Then the king regretted what he had said; but because of the vow he had made in front of his guests, he issued the necessary orders. 10 So John was beheaded in the prison, 11 and his head was brought on a tray and given to the girl, who took it to her mother. 12 Later, John's disciples came for his body and buried it. Then they went and told Jesus what had happened.

Jesus Feeds Five Thousand

13 As soon as Jesus heard the news, he left in a boat to a remote area to be alone. But the crowds heard where he was headed and followed on foot from many towns. 14 Jesus saw the huge crowd as he stepped from the boat, and he had compassion on them and healed their sick.

15 That evening the disciples came to him and said, "This is a remote place, and it's already getting late. Send the crowds away so they can go to the villages and buy food for themselves."

13:37 "Son of Man" is a title Jesus used for himself.   13:39 Or the age; also in 13:40, 49.   13:55 Other manuscripts read Joses; still others read John.   14:1 Greek Herod the tetrarch. Herod Antipas was a son of King Herod and was ruler over Galilee.

[16] But Jesus said, "That isn't necessary—you feed them."

[17] "But we have only five loaves of bread and two fish!" they answered.

[18] "Bring them here," he said. [19] Then he told the people to sit down on the grass. Jesus took the five loaves and two fish, looked up toward heaven, and blessed them. Then, breaking the loaves into pieces, he gave the bread to the disciples, who distributed it to the people. [20] They all ate as much as they wanted, and afterward, the disciples picked up twelve baskets of leftovers. [21] About 5,000 men were fed that day, in addition to all the women and children!

Jesus Walks on Water

[22] Immediately after this, Jesus insisted that his disciples get back into the boat and cross to the other side of the lake, while he sent the people home. [23] After sending them home, he went up into the hills by himself to pray. Night fell while he was there alone.

[24] Meanwhile, the disciples were in trouble far away from land, for a strong wind had risen, and they were fighting heavy waves. [25] About three o'clock in the morning* Jesus came toward them, walking on the water. [26] When the disciples saw him walking on the water, they were terrified. In their fear, they cried out, "It's a ghost!"

[27] But Jesus spoke to them at once. "Don't be afraid," he said. "Take courage. I am here!*"

[28] Then Peter called to him, "Lord, if it's really you, tell me to come to you, walking on the water."

[29] "Yes, come," Jesus said.

So Peter went over the side of the boat and walked on the water toward Jesus. [30] But when he saw the strong* wind and the waves, he was terrified and began to sink. "Save me, Lord!" he shouted.

[31] Jesus immediately reached out and grabbed him. "You have so little faith," Jesus said. "Why did you doubt me?"

[32] When they climbed back into the boat, the wind stopped. [33] Then the disciples worshiped him. "You really are the Son of God!" they exclaimed.

[34] After they had crossed the lake, they landed at Gennesaret. [35] When the people recognized Jesus, the news of his arrival spread quickly throughout the whole area, and soon people were bringing all their sick to be healed. [36] They begged him to let the sick touch at least the fringe of his robe, and all who touched him were healed.

CHAPTER 15

Jesus Teaches about Inner Purity

Some Pharisees and teachers of religious law now arrived from Jerusalem to see Jesus. They asked him, [2] "Why do your disciples disobey our age-old tradition? For they ignore our tradition of ceremonial hand washing before they eat."

[3] Jesus replied, "And why do you, by your traditions, violate the direct commandments of God? [4] For instance, God says, 'Honor your father and mother,'* and 'Anyone who speaks disrespectfully of father or mother must be put to death.'* [5] But you say it is all right for people to say to their parents, 'Sorry, I can't help you. For I have vowed to give to God what I would have given to you.' [6] In this way, you say they don't need to honor their parents.* And so you cancel the word of God for the sake of your own tradition. [7] You hypocrites! Isaiah was right when he prophesied about you, for he wrote,

[8] 'These people honor me with their lips,
  but their hearts are far from me.
[9] Their worship is a farce,
  for they teach man-made ideas as
    commands from God.'* "

[10] Then Jesus called to the crowd to come and hear. "Listen," he said, "and try to understand. [11] It's not what goes into your mouth that defiles you; you are defiled by the words that come out of your mouth."

[12] Then the disciples came to him and asked, "Do you realize you offended the Pharisees by what you just said?"

[13] Jesus replied, "Every plant not planted by my heavenly Father will be uprooted, [14] so ignore them. They are blind guides leading the blind, and if one blind person guides another, they will both fall into a ditch."

[15] Then Peter said to Jesus, "Explain to us the parable that says people aren't defiled by what they eat."

[16] "Don't you understand yet?" Jesus asked. [17] "Anything you eat passes through the stomach and then goes into the sewer. [18] But the words you speak come from the heart—that's what defiles you. [19] For from the heart come evil thoughts, murder, adultery, all sexual immorality, theft, lying, and slander. [20] These are what defile you. Eating with unwashed hands will never defile you."

The Faith of a Gentile Woman

[21] Then Jesus left Galilee and went north to the region of Tyre and Sidon. [22] A Gentile* woman

---

14:25 Greek *In the fourth watch of the night.*   **14:27** Or *The 'I Aм' is here;* Greek reads *I am.* See Exod 3:14.   **14:30** Some manuscripts do not include *strong.*   **15:4a** Exod 20:12; Deut 5:16.   **15:4b** Exod 21:17 (Greek version); Lev 20:9 (Greek version).   **15:6** Greek *their father;* other manuscripts read *their father or their mother.*   **15:8-9** Isa 29:13 (Greek version).
15:22 Greek *Canaanite.*

who lived there came to him, pleading, "Have mercy on me, O Lord, Son of David! For my daughter is possessed by a demon that torments her severely."

23 But Jesus gave her no reply, not even a word. Then his disciples urged him to send her away. "Tell her to go away," they said. "She is bothering us with all her begging."

24 Then Jesus said to the woman, "I was sent only to help God's lost sheep—the people of Israel."

25 But she came and worshiped him, pleading again, "Lord, help me!"

26 Jesus responded, "It isn't right to take food from the children and throw it to the dogs."

27 She replied, "That's true, Lord, but even dogs are allowed to eat the scraps that fall beneath their masters' table."

28 "Dear woman," Jesus said to her, "your faith is great. Your request is granted." And her daughter was instantly healed.

Jesus Heals Many People

29 Jesus returned to the Sea of Galilee and climbed a hill and sat down. 30 A vast crowd brought to him people who were lame, blind, crippled, those who couldn't speak, and many others. They laid them before Jesus, and he healed them all. 31 The crowd was amazed! Those who hadn't been able to speak were talking, the crippled were made well, the lame were walking, and the blind could see again! And they praised the God of Israel.

Jesus Feeds Four Thousand

32 Then Jesus called his disciples and told them, "I feel sorry for these people. They have been here with me for three days, and they have nothing left to eat. I don't want to send them away hungry, or they will faint along the way."

33 The disciples replied, "Where would we get enough food here in the wilderness for such a huge crowd?"

34 Jesus asked, "How much bread do you have?"

They replied, "Seven loaves, and a few small fish."

35 So Jesus told all the people to sit down on the ground. 36 Then he took the seven loaves and the fish, thanked God for them, and broke them into pieces. He gave them to the disciples, who distributed the food to the crowd.

37 They all ate as much as they wanted. Afterward, the disciples picked up seven large baskets of leftover food. 38 There were 4,000 men who were fed that day, in addition to all the women and children. 39 Then Jesus sent the people home, and he got into a boat and crossed over to the region of Magadan.

CHAPTER 16

Leaders Demand a Miraculous Sign

One day the Pharisees and Sadducees came to test Jesus, demanding that he show them a miraculous sign from heaven to prove his authority.

2 He replied, "You know the saying, 'Red sky at night means fair weather tomorrow; 3 red sky in the morning means foul weather all day.' You know how to interpret the weather signs in the sky, but you don't know how to interpret the signs of the times!* 4 Only an evil, adulterous generation would demand a miraculous sign, but the only sign I will give them is the sign of the prophet Jonah.*" Then Jesus left them and went away.

Yeast of the Pharisees and Sadducees

5 Later, after they crossed to the other side of the lake, the disciples discovered they had forgotten to bring any bread. 6 "Watch out!" Jesus warned them. "Beware of the yeast of the Pharisees and Sadducees."

7 At this they began to argue with each other because they hadn't brought any bread. 8 Jesus knew what they were saying, so he said, "You have so little faith! Why are you arguing with each other about having no bread? 9 Don't you understand even yet? Don't you remember the 5,000 I fed with five loaves, and the baskets of leftovers you picked up? 10 Or the 4,000 I fed with seven loaves, and the large baskets of leftovers you picked up? 11 Why can't you understand that I'm not talking about bread? So again I say, 'Beware of the yeast of the Pharisees and Sadducees.' "

12 Then at last they understood that he wasn't speaking about the yeast in bread, but about the deceptive teaching of the Pharisees and Sadducees.

Peter's Declaration about Jesus

13 When Jesus came to the region of Caesarea Philippi, he asked his disciples, "Who do people say that the Son of Man is?"*

14 "Well," they replied, "some say John the Baptist, some say Elijah, and others say Jeremiah or one of the other prophets."

15 Then he asked them, "But who do you say I am?"

16 Simon Peter answered, "You are the Messiah,* the Son of the living God."

16:2-3 Several manuscripts do not include any of the words in 16:2-3 after *He replied.*   **16:4** Greek *the sign of Jonah.*
16:13 "Son of Man" is a title Jesus used for himself.   **16:16** Or *the Christ. Messiah* (a Hebrew term) and *Christ* (a Greek term) both mean "the anointed one."

[17] Jesus replied, "You are blessed, Simon son of John,* because my Father in heaven has revealed this to you. You did not learn this from any human being. [18] Now I say to you that you are Peter (which means 'rock'),* and upon this rock I will build my church, and all the powers of hell* will not conquer it. [19] And I will give you the keys of the Kingdom of Heaven. Whatever you forbid* on earth will be forbidden in heaven, and whatever you permit* on earth will be permitted in heaven."

[20] Then he sternly warned the disciples not to tell anyone that he was the Messiah.

Jesus Predicts His Death

[21] From then on Jesus* began to tell his disciples plainly that it was necessary for him to go to Jerusalem, and that he would suffer many terrible things at the hands of the elders, the leading priests, and the teachers of religious law. He would be killed, but on the third day he would be raised from the dead.

[22] But Peter took him aside and began to reprimand him* for saying such things. "Heaven forbid, Lord," he said. "This will never happen to you!"

[23] Jesus turned to Peter and said, "Get away from me, Satan! You are a dangerous trap to me. You are seeing things merely from a human point of view, not from God's."

[24] Then Jesus said to his disciples, "If any of you wants to be my follower, you must turn from your selfish ways, take up your cross, and follow me. [25] If you try to hang on to your life, you will lose it. But if you give up your life for my sake, you will save it. [26] And what do you benefit if you gain the whole world but lose your own soul?* Is anything worth more than your soul? [27] For the Son of Man will come with his angels in the glory of his Father and will judge all people according to their deeds. [28] And I tell you the truth, some standing here right now will not die before they see the Son of Man coming in his Kingdom."

CHAPTER 17

The Transfiguration

Six days later Jesus took Peter and the two brothers, James and John, and led them up a high mountain to be alone. [2] As the men watched, Jesus' appearance was transformed so that his face shone like the sun, and his clothes became as white as light. [3] Suddenly, Moses and Elijah appeared and began talking with Jesus.

[4] Peter exclaimed, "Lord, it's wonderful for us to be here! If you want, I'll make three shelters as memorials*—one for you, one for Moses, and one for Elijah."

[5] But even as he spoke, a bright cloud overshadowed them, and a voice from the cloud said, "This is my dearly loved Son, who brings me great joy. Listen to him." [6] The disciples were terrified and fell face down on the ground.

[7] Then Jesus came over and touched them. "Get up," he said. "Don't be afraid." [8] And when

---

16:17 Greek *Simon bar-Jonah;* see John 1:42; 21:15-17. 16:18a Greek *that you are Peter.* 16:18b Greek *and the gates of Hades.* 16:19a Or *bind,* or *lock.* 16:19b Or *loose,* or *open.* 16:21 Some manuscripts read *Jesus the Messiah.* 16:22 Or *began to correct him.* 16:26 Or *your self?* also in 16:26b. 17:4 Greek *three tabernacles.*

---

off and running

WE MUST SURRENDER OUR DREAMS AND SEEK GOD'S WILL

Read MATTHEW 16:24-26

Jesus' words in this passage may seem extremely harsh. Yet in reality they are compassionate, because they point the way to real life. Anyone who wants this real life must become a disciple of Jesus. That means obeying Jesus' commands and adopting an attitude of self-denial. This text makes three points on what it means to adopt that attitude and follow Jesus:

1. We Must Lose Our Life. We find life only in coming into proper alignment with God and his plan for us. As you "lose your life," you find it again. This life Jesus speaks of not only includes life after death, but also life during life. Jesus tells us that he came to "give them a rich and satisfying life" (John 10:10). You should never be afraid to trust an unknown future to a known God. God's plan for you is better than any plan you may have for yourself. God tells us in his Word, "For I know the plans I have for you. . . . They are plans for good and not for disaster, to give you a future and a hope" (Jeremiah 29:11).

they looked up, Moses and Elijah were gone, and they saw only Jesus.

[9] As they went back down the mountain, Jesus commanded them, "Don't tell anyone what you have seen until the Son of Man* has been raised from the dead."

[10] Then his disciples asked him, "Why do the teachers of religious law insist that Elijah must return before the Messiah comes?*"

[11] Jesus replied, "Elijah is indeed coming first to get everything ready. [12] But I tell you, Elijah has already come, but he wasn't recognized, and they chose to abuse him. And in the same way they will also make the Son of Man suffer." [13] Then the disciples realized he was talking about John the Baptist.

Jesus Heals a Demon-Possessed Boy

[14] At the foot of the mountain, a large crowd was waiting for them. A man came and knelt before Jesus and said, [15] "Lord, have mercy on my son. He has seizures and suffers terribly. He often falls into the fire or into the water. [16] So I brought him to your disciples, but they couldn't heal him."

[17] Jesus said, "You faithless and corrupt people! How long must I be with you? How long must I put up with you? Bring the boy here to me." [18] Then Jesus rebuked the demon in the boy, and it left him. From that moment the boy was well.

[19] Afterward the disciples asked Jesus privately, "Why couldn't we cast out that demon?"

[20] "You don't have enough faith," Jesus told them. "I tell you the truth, if you had faith even as small as a mustard seed, you could say to this mountain, 'Move from here to there,' and it would move. Nothing would be impossible.*"

Jesus Again Predicts His Death

[22] After they gathered again in Galilee, Jesus told them, "The Son of Man is going to be betrayed into the hands of his enemies. [23] He will be killed, but on the third day he will be raised from the dead." And the disciples were filled with grief.

Payment of the Temple Tax

[24] On their arrival in Capernaum, the collectors of the Temple tax* came to Peter and asked him, "Doesn't your teacher pay the Temple tax?"

[25] "Yes, he does," Peter replied. Then he went into the house.

But before he had a chance to speak, Jesus asked him, "What do you think, Peter?* Do kings tax their own people or the people they have conquered?*"

[26] "They tax the people they have conquered," Peter replied.

"Well, then," Jesus said, "the citizens are free! [27] However, we don't want to offend them, so go down to the lake and throw in a line. Open the mouth of the first fish you catch, and you will find a large silver coin.* Take it and pay the tax for both of us."

17:9 "Son of Man" is a title Jesus used for himself.   **17:10** Greek *that Elijah must come first?*   **17:20** Some manuscripts add verse 21, *But this kind of demon won't leave except by prayer and fasting.* Compare Mark 9:29.   **17:24** Greek *the two-drachma (tax);* also in 17:24b. See Exod 30:13-16; Neh 10:32-33.   **17:25a** Greek *Simon?*   **17:25b** Greek *their sons or others?*   **17:27** Greek *a stater* (a Greek coin equivalent to four drachmas).

---

2. We Must Deny Ourselves. To "deny ourselves" means that we put the will and purposes of God above our own. We discover God's will for our lives as we search, study, and obey God's Word.

3. We Must Take Up Our Cross. This speaks of "dying" to our own will and selfish ambition. But don't let this passage frighten you—it is by dying to ourselves that we find God's plan and purpose for our lives.

The Christian life is not one of misery and hyper self-examination. It is a life of peace and joy as we walk in harmony with God. Paul sums it up perfectly when he writes, "My old self has been crucified with Christ. It is no longer I who live, but Christ lives in me. So I live in this earthly body by trusting in the Son of God, who loved me and gave himself for me" (Galatians 2:20). It is only when the bulb of a tulip goes into the ground and dies that a beautiful flower can grow in its place. Be willing to entrust yourself to God's plan for your life. You won't regret it.

To begin the next reading track, turn to p. A53.

CHAPTER **18**

The Greatest in the Kingdom

About that time the disciples came to Jesus and asked, "Who is greatest in the Kingdom of Heaven?"

2 Jesus called a little child to him and put the child among them. 3 Then he said, "I tell you the truth, unless you turn from your sins and become like little children, you will never get into the Kingdom of Heaven. 4 So anyone who becomes as humble as this little child is the greatest in the Kingdom of Heaven.

5 "And anyone who welcomes a little child like this on my behalf* is welcoming me. 6 But if you cause one of these little ones who trusts in me to fall into sin, it would be better for you to have a large millstone tied around your neck and be drowned in the depths of the sea.

7 "What sorrow awaits the world, because it tempts people to sin. Temptations are inevitable, but what sorrow awaits the person who does the tempting. 8 So if your hand or foot causes you to sin, cut it off and throw it away. It's better to enter eternal life with only one hand or one foot than to be thrown into eternal fire with both of your hands and feet. 9 And if your eye causes you to sin, gouge it out and throw it away. It's better to enter eternal life with only one eye than to have two eyes and be thrown into the fire of hell.*

10 "Beware that you don't look down on any of these little ones. For I tell you that in heaven their angels are always in the presence of my heavenly Father.*

Parable of the Lost Sheep

12 "If a man has a hundred sheep and one of them wanders away, what will he do? Won't he leave the ninety-nine others on the hills and go out to search for the one that is lost? 13 And if he finds it, I tell you the truth, he will rejoice over it more than over the ninety-nine that didn't wander away! 14 In the same way, it is not my heavenly Father's will that even one of these little ones should perish.

Correcting Another Believer

15 "If another believer* sins against you,* go privately and point out the offense. If the other person listens and confesses it, you have won that person back. 16 But if you are unsuccessful, take one or two others with you and go back again, so that everything you say may be confirmed by two or three witnesses. 17 If the per-

son still refuses to listen, take your case to the church. Then if he or she won't accept the church's decision, treat that person as a pagan or a corrupt tax collector.

18 "I tell you the truth, whatever you forbid* on earth will be forbidden in heaven, and whatever you permit* on earth will be permitted in heaven.

19 "I also tell you this: If two of you agree here on earth concerning anything you ask, my Father in heaven will do it for you. 20 For where two or three gather together as my followers,* I am there among them."

Parable of the Unforgiving Debtor

21 Then Peter came to him and asked, "Lord, how often should I forgive someone* who sins against me? Seven times?"

22 "No, not seven times," Jesus replied, "but seventy times seven!*

23 "Therefore, the Kingdom of Heaven can be compared to a king who decided to bring his accounts up to date with servants who had borrowed money from him. 24 In the process, one of his debtors was brought in who owed him millions of dollars.* 25 He couldn't pay, so his master ordered that he be sold—along with his wife, his children, and everything he owned—to pay the debt.

26 "But the man fell down before his master and begged him, 'Please, be patient with me, and I will pay it all.' 27 Then his master was filled with pity for him, and he released him and forgave his debt.

28 "But when the man left the king, he went to a fellow servant who owed him a few thousand dollars.* He grabbed him by the throat and demanded instant payment.

29 "His fellow servant fell down before him and begged for a little more time. 'Be patient with me, and I will pay it,' he pleaded. 30 But his creditor wouldn't wait. He had the man arrested and put in prison until the debt could be paid in full.

31 "When some of the other servants saw this, they were very upset. They went to the king and told him everything that had happened. 32 Then the king called in the man he had forgiven and said, 'You evil servant! I forgave you that tremendous debt because you pleaded with me. 33 Shouldn't you have mercy on your fellow servant, just as I had mercy on you?' 34 Then the angry king sent the man to prison to be tortured until he had paid his entire debt.

18:5 Greek *in my name.*   18:9 Greek *the Gehenna of fire.*   18:10 Some manuscripts add verse 11, *And the Son of Man came to save those who are lost.* Compare Luke 19:10.   18:15a Greek *If your brother.*   18:15b Some manuscripts do not include *against you.*   18:18a Or *bind,* or *lock.*   18:18b Or *loose,* or *open.*   18:20 Greek *gather together in my name.* 18:21 Greek *my brother.*   18:22 Or *seventy-seven times.*   18:24 Greek *10,000 talents* [375 tons or 340 metric tons of silver].   18:28 Greek *100 denarii.* A denarius was equivalent to a laborer's full day's wage.

35 "That's what my heavenly Father will do to you if you refuse to forgive your brothers and sisters* from your heart."

CHAPTER 19

Discussion about Divorce and Marriage

When Jesus had finished saying these things, he left Galilee and went down to the region of Judea east of the Jordan River. 2 Large crowds followed him there, and he healed their sick.

3 Some Pharisees came and tried to trap him with this question: "Should a man be allowed to divorce his wife for just any reason?"

4 "Haven't you read the Scriptures?" Jesus replied. "They record that from the beginning 'God made them male and female.'*" 5 And he said, "'This explains why a man leaves his father and mother and is joined to his wife, and the two are united into one.'* 6 Since they are no longer two but one, let no one split apart what God has joined together."

7 "Then why did Moses say in the law that a man could give his wife a written notice of divorce and send her away?"* they asked.

8 Jesus replied, "Moses permitted divorce only as a concession to your hard hearts, but it was not what God had originally intended. 9 And I tell you this, whoever divorces his wife and marries someone else commits adultery—unless his wife has been unfaithful.*"

10 Jesus' disciples then said to him, "If this is the case, it is better not to marry!"

11 "Not everyone can accept this statement," Jesus said. "Only those whom God helps. 12 Some are born as eunuchs, some have been made eunuchs by others, and some choose not to marry* for the sake of the Kingdom of Heaven. Let anyone accept this who can."

Jesus Blesses the Children

13 One day some parents brought their children to Jesus so he could lay his hands on them and pray for them. But the disciples scolded the parents for bothering him.

14 But Jesus said, "Let the children come to me. Don't stop them! For the Kingdom of Heaven belongs to those who are like these children." 15 And he placed his hands on their heads and blessed them before he left.

The Rich Man

16 Someone came to Jesus with this question: "Teacher,* what good deed must I do to have eternal life?"

17 "Why ask me about what is good?" Jesus replied. "There is only One who is good. But to answer your question—if you want to receive eternal life, keep* the commandments."

18 "Which ones?" the man asked.

And Jesus replied: " 'You must not murder. You must not commit adultery. You must not steal. You must not testify falsely. 19 Honor your father and mother. Love your neighbor as yourself.'* "

20 "I've obeyed all these commandments," the young man replied. "What else must I do?"

21 Jesus told him, "If you want to be perfect, go and sell all your possessions and give the money to the poor, and you will have treasure in heaven. Then come, follow me."

22 But when the young man heard this, he went away sad, for he had many possessions.

23 Then Jesus said to his disciples, "I tell you the truth, it is very hard for a rich person to enter the Kingdom of Heaven. 24 I'll say it again—it is easier for a camel to go through the eye of a needle than for a rich person to enter the Kingdom of God!"

25 The disciples were astounded. "Then who in the world can be saved?" they asked.

26 Jesus looked at them intently and said, "Humanly speaking, it is impossible. But with God everything is possible."

27 Then Peter said to him, "We've given up everything to follow you. What will we get?"

28 Jesus replied, "I assure you that when the world is made new* and the Son of Man* sits upon his glorious throne, you who have been my followers will also sit on twelve thrones, judging the twelve tribes of Israel. 29 And everyone who has given up houses or brothers or sisters or father or mother or children or property, for my sake, will receive a hundred times as much in return and will inherit eternal life. 30 But many who are the greatest now will be least important then, and those who seem least important now will be the greatest then.*

CHAPTER 20

Parable of the Vineyard Workers

"For the Kingdom of Heaven is like the landowner who went out early one morning to hire workers for his vineyard. 2 He agreed to pay the normal daily wage* and sent them out to work.

3 "At nine o'clock in the morning he was passing through the marketplace and saw some people standing around doing nothing. 4 So he hired them, telling them he would pay them

---

18:35 Greek *your brother.* 19:4 Gen 1:27; 5:2. 19:5 Gen 2:24. 19:7 See Deut 24:1. 19:9 Some manuscripts add *And anyone who marries a divorced woman commits adultery.* Compare Matt 5:32. 19:12 Greek *and some make themselves eunuchs.* 19:16 Some manuscripts read *Good Teacher.* 19:17 Some manuscripts read *continue to keep.* 19:18-19 Exod 20:12-16; Deut 5:16-20; Lev 19:18. 19:28a Or *in the regeneration.* 19:28b "Son of Man" is a title Jesus used for himself. 19:30 Greek *But many who are first will be last; and the last, first.* 20:2 Greek *a denarius,* the payment for a full day's labor; similarly in 20:9, 10, 13.

cornerstones

FORGIVENESS KNOWS NO LIMITS
Read MATTHEW 18:21-35

The religious leaders of that day taught that one who had been wronged was to forgive the one who wronged him two to three times—at the most!

But Peter, mustering up as much forgiveness as he could, wondered if forgiving someone seven times would be enough in Jesus' eyes. Imagine Peter's shock when Jesus told him that he should forgive up to "seventy times seven," or *490* times.

So, if someone needed forgiveness after the four-hundred-ninetieth time, should we say no? No! Rather, Jesus was teaching that we should extend unlimited forgiveness to others. He then went on to tell this dramatic story of a man who was forgiven for so much (possibly $10 million), yet was unwilling to even work out terms with a person who owed him far less (around two thousand dollars). The point of Jesus' message is that we, as sinners, have been forgiven much; therefore, we ought to forgive those who have hurt us, no matter how badly we've been hurt. They owe us little compared to what we owe God.

For the next note on "Forgiveness," turn to p. 8.

---

whatever was right at the end of the day. ⁵So they went to work in the vineyard. At noon and again at three o'clock he did the same thing.

⁶"At five o'clock that afternoon he was in town again and saw some more people standing around. He asked them, 'Why haven't you been working today?'

⁷"They replied, 'Because no one hired us.'

"The landowner told them, 'Then go out and join the others in my vineyard.'

⁸"That evening he told the foreman to call the workers in and pay them, beginning with the last workers first. ⁹When those hired at five o'clock were paid, each received a full day's wage. ¹⁰When those hired first came to get their pay, they assumed they would receive more. But they, too, were paid a day's wage. ¹¹When they received their pay, they protested to the owner, ¹²'Those people worked only one hour, and yet you've paid them just as much as you paid us who worked all day in the scorching heat.'

¹³"He answered one of them, 'Friend, I haven't been unfair! Didn't you agree to work all day for the usual wage? ¹⁴Take your money and go. I wanted to pay this last worker the same as you. ¹⁵Is it against the law for me to do what I want with my money? Should you be jealous because I am kind to others?'

¹⁶"So those who are last now will be first then, and those who are first will be last."

Jesus Again Predicts His Death

¹⁷As Jesus was going up to Jerusalem, he took the twelve disciples aside privately and told them what was going to happen to him. ¹⁸"Listen," he said, "we're going up to Jerusalem, where the Son of Man* will be betrayed to the leading priests and the teachers of religious law. They will sentence him to die. ¹⁹Then they will hand him over to the Romans* to be mocked, flogged with a whip, and crucified. But on the third day he will be raised from the dead."

Jesus Teaches about Serving Others

²⁰Then the mother of James and John, the sons of Zebedee, came to Jesus with her sons. She knelt respectfully to ask a favor. ²¹"What is your request?" he asked.

She replied, "In your Kingdom, please let my two sons sit in places of honor next to you, one on your right and the other on your left."

²²But Jesus answered by saying to them, "You don't know what you are asking! Are you able to drink from the bitter cup of suffering I am about to drink?"

"Oh yes," they replied, "we are able!"

²³Jesus told them, "You will indeed drink from my bitter cup. But I have no right to say who will sit on my right or my left. My Father has prepared those places for the ones he has chosen."

²⁴When the ten other disciples heard what James and John had asked, they were indignant. ²⁵But Jesus called them together and said, "You know that the rulers in this world lord it over their people, and officials flaunt their authority over those under them. ²⁶But among you it will be different. Whoever wants to be a leader among you must be your servant, ²⁷and whoever wants to be first among you must become your slave. ²⁸For even the Son of

20:18 "Son of Man" is a title Jesus used for himself.   20:19 Greek *the Gentiles*.

Man came not to be served but to serve others and to give his life as a ransom for many."

Jesus Heals Two Blind Men

²⁹As Jesus and the disciples left the town of Jericho, a large crowd followed behind. ³⁰Two blind men were sitting beside the road. When they heard that Jesus was coming that way, they began shouting, "Lord, Son of David, have mercy on us!"

³¹"Be quiet!" the crowd yelled at them.

But they only shouted louder, "Lord, Son of David, have mercy on us!"

³²When Jesus heard them, he stopped and called, "What do you want me to do for you?"

³³"Lord," they said, "we want to see!" ³⁴Jesus felt sorry for them and touched their eyes. Instantly they could see! Then they followed him.

CHAPTER 21

Jesus' Triumphant Entry

As Jesus and the disciples approached Jerusalem, they came to the town of Bethphage on the Mount of Olives. Jesus sent two of them on ahead. ²"Go into the village over there," he said. "As soon as you enter it, you will see a donkey tied there, with its colt beside it. Untie them and bring them to me. ³If anyone asks what you are doing, just say, 'The Lord needs them,' and he will immediately let you take them."

⁴This took place to fulfill the prophecy that said,

5 "Tell the people of Jerusalem,*
  'Look, your King is coming to you.
He is humble, riding on a donkey—
  riding on a donkey's colt.'"*

⁶The two disciples did as Jesus commanded. ⁷They brought the donkey and the colt to him and threw their garments over the colt, and he sat on it.*

⁸Most of the crowd spread their garments on the road ahead of him, and others cut branches from the trees and spread them on the road. ⁹Jesus was in the center of the procession, and the people all around him were shouting,

"Praise God* for the Son of David!
  Blessings on the one who comes in the
    name of the Lord!
  Praise God in highest heaven!"*

¹⁰The entire city of Jerusalem was in an uproar as he entered. "Who is this?" they asked.

¹¹And the crowds replied, "It's Jesus, the prophet from Nazareth in Galilee."

Jesus Clears the Temple

¹²Jesus entered the Temple and began to drive out all the people buying and selling animals for sacrifice. He knocked over the tables of the money changers and the chairs of those selling doves. ¹³He said to them, "The Scriptures declare, 'My Temple will be called a house of prayer,' but you have turned it into a den of thieves!"*

¹⁴The blind and the lame came to him in the Temple, and he healed them. ¹⁵The leading priests and the teachers of religious law saw these wonderful miracles and heard even the children in the Temple shouting, "Praise God for the Son of David."

But the leaders were indignant. ¹⁶They asked Jesus, "Do you hear what these children are saying?"

"Yes," Jesus replied. "Haven't you ever read the Scriptures? For they say, 'You have taught children and infants to give you praise.'* "

¹⁷Then he returned to Bethany, where he stayed overnight.

Jesus Curses the Fig Tree

¹⁸In the morning, as Jesus was returning to Jerusalem, he was hungry, ¹⁹and he noticed a fig tree beside the road. He went over to see if there were any figs, but there were only leaves. Then he said to it, "May you never bear fruit again!" And immediately the fig tree withered up.

²⁰The disciples were amazed when they saw this and asked, "How did the fig tree wither so quickly?"

²¹Then Jesus told them, "I tell you the truth, if you have faith and don't doubt, you can do things like this and much more. You can even say to this mountain, 'May you be lifted up and thrown into the sea,' and it will happen. ²²You can pray for anything, and if you have faith, you will receive it."

The Authority of Jesus Challenged

²³When Jesus returned to the Temple and began teaching, the leading priests and elders came up to him. They demanded, "By what authority are you doing all these things? Who gave you the right?"

²⁴"I'll tell you by what authority I do these things if you answer one question," Jesus replied. ²⁵"Did John's authority to baptize come from heaven, or was it merely human?"

They talked it over among themselves. "If we say it was from heaven, he will ask us why we didn't believe John. ²⁶But if we say it was merely human, we'll be mobbed because the

21:5a Greek *Tell the daughter of Zion.* Isa 62:11.   21:5b Zech 9:9.   21:7 Greek *over them, and he sat on them.*
21:9a Greek *Hosanna*, an exclamation of praise that literally means "save now"; also in 21:9b, 15.   21:9b Pss 118:25-26; 148:1.   21:13 Isa 56:7; Jer 7:11.   21:16 Ps 8:2.

people believe John was a prophet." ²⁷So they finally replied, "We don't know."

And Jesus responded, "Then I won't tell you by what authority I do these things.

Parable of the Two Sons

²⁸"But what do you think about this? A man with two sons told the older boy, 'Son, go out and work in the vineyard today.' ²⁹The son answered, 'No, I won't go,' but later he changed his mind and went anyway. ³⁰Then the father told the other son, 'You go,' and he said, 'Yes, sir, I will.' But he didn't go.

³¹"Which of the two obeyed his father?"

They replied, "The first."*

Then Jesus explained his meaning: "I tell you the truth, corrupt tax collectors and prostitutes will get into the Kingdom of God before you do. ³²For John the Baptist came and showed you the right way to live, but you didn't believe him, while tax collectors and prostitutes did. And even when you saw this happening, you refused to believe him and repent of your sins.

Parable of the Evil Farmers

³³"Now listen to another story. A certain landowner planted a vineyard, built a wall around it, dug a pit for pressing out the grape juice, and built a lookout tower. Then he leased the vineyard to tenant farmers and moved to another country. ³⁴At the time of the grape harvest, he sent his servants to collect his share of the crop. ³⁵But the farmers grabbed his servants, beat one, killed one, and stoned another. ³⁶So the landowner sent a larger group of his servants to collect for him, but the results were the same.

³⁷"Finally, the owner sent his son, thinking, 'Surely they will respect my son.'

³⁸"But when the tenant farmers saw his son coming, they said to one another, 'Here comes the heir to this estate. Come on, let's kill him and get the estate for ourselves!' ³⁹So they grabbed him, dragged him out of the vineyard, and murdered him.

⁴⁰"When the owner of the vineyard returns," Jesus asked, "what do you think he will do to those farmers?"

⁴¹The religious leaders replied, "He will put the wicked men to a horrible death and lease the vineyard to others who will give him his share of the crop after each harvest."

⁴²Then Jesus asked them, "Didn't you ever read this in the Scriptures?

'The stone that the builders rejected
  has now become the cornerstone.

This is the LORD's doing,
  and it is wonderful to see.'*

⁴³I tell you, the Kingdom of God will be taken away from you and given to a nation that will produce the proper fruit. ⁴⁴Anyone who stumbles over that stone will be broken to pieces, and it will crush anyone it falls on.*"

⁴⁵When the leading priests and Pharisees heard this parable, they realized he was telling the story against them—they were the wicked farmers. ⁴⁶They wanted to arrest him, but they were afraid of the crowds, who considered Jesus to be a prophet.

CHAPTER **22**

Parable of the Great Feast

Jesus also told them other parables. He said, ²"The Kingdom of Heaven can be illustrated by the story of a king who prepared a great wedding feast for his son. ³When the banquet was ready, he sent his servants to notify those who were invited. But they all refused to come!

⁴"So he sent other servants to tell them, 'The feast has been prepared. The bulls and fattened cattle have been killed, and everything is ready. Come to the banquet!' ⁵But the guests he had invited ignored them and went their own way, one to his farm, another to his business. ⁶Others seized his messengers and insulted them and killed them.

⁷"The king was furious, and he sent out his army to destroy the murderers and burn their town. ⁸And he said to his servants, 'The wedding feast is ready, and the guests I invited aren't worthy of the honor. ⁹Now go out to the street corners and invite everyone you see.' ¹⁰So the servants brought in everyone they could find, good and bad alike, and the banquet hall was filled with guests.

¹¹"But when the king came in to meet the guests, he noticed a man who wasn't wearing the proper clothes for a wedding. ¹²'Friend,' he asked, 'how is it that you are here without wedding clothes?' But the man had no reply. ¹³Then the king said to his aides, 'Bind his hands and feet and throw him into the outer darkness, where there will be weeping and gnashing of teeth.'

¹⁴"For many are called, but few are chosen."

Taxes for Caesar

¹⁵Then the Pharisees met together to plot how to trap Jesus into saying something for which he could be arrested. ¹⁶They sent some of their disciples, along with the supporters of Herod, to meet with him. "Teacher," they said, "we

---

21:29-31 Other manuscripts read *"The second."* In still other manuscripts the first son says "Yes" but does nothing, the second son says "No" but then repents and goes, and the answer to Jesus' question is that the second son obeyed his father. **21:42** Ps 118:22-23. **21:44** This verse is not included in some early manuscripts. Compare Luke 20:18.

know how honest you are. You teach the way of God truthfully. You are impartial and don't play favorites. [17]Now tell us what you think about this: Is it right to pay taxes to Caesar or not?"

[18]But Jesus knew their evil motives. "You hypocrites!" he said. "Why are you trying to trap me? [19]Here, show me the coin used for the tax." When they handed him a Roman coin,* [20]he asked, "Whose picture and title are stamped on it?"

[21]"Caesar's," they replied.

"Well, then," he said, "give to Caesar what belongs to Caesar, and give to God what belongs to God."

[22]His reply amazed them, and they went away.

Discussion about Resurrection

[23]That same day Jesus was approached by some Sadducees—religious leaders who say there is no resurrection from the dead. They posed this question: [24]"Teacher, Moses said, 'If a man dies without children, his brother should marry the widow and have a child who will carry on the brother's name.'* [25]Well, suppose there were seven brothers. The oldest one married and then died without children, so his brother married the widow. [26]But the second brother also died, and the third brother married her. This continued with all seven of them. [27]Last of all, the woman also died. [28]So tell us, whose wife will she be in the resurrection? For all seven were married to her."

[29]Jesus replied, "Your mistake is that you don't know the Scriptures, and you don't know the power of God. [30]For when the dead rise, they will neither marry nor be given in marriage. In this respect they will be like the angels in heaven.

[31]"But now, as to whether there will be a resurrection of the dead—haven't you ever read about this in the Scriptures? Long after Abraham, Isaac, and Jacob had died, God said,* [32]'I am the God of Abraham, the God of Isaac, and the God of Jacob.'* So he is the God of the living, not the dead."

[33]When the crowds heard him, they were astounded at his teaching.

The Most Important Commandment

[34]But when the Pharisees heard that he had silenced the Sadducees with his reply, they met together to question him again. [35]One of them, an expert in religious law, tried to trap him with this question: [36]"Teacher, which is the most important commandment in the law of Moses?"

[37]Jesus replied, " 'You must love the LORD your God with all your heart, all your soul, and all your mind.'* [38]This is the first and greatest commandment. [39]A second is equally important: 'Love your neighbor as yourself.'* [40]The entire law and all the demands of the prophets are based on these two commandments."

Whose Son Is the Messiah?

[41]Then, surrounded by the Pharisees, Jesus asked them a question: [42]"What do you think about the Messiah? Whose son is he?"

They replied, "He is the son of David."

[43]Jesus responded, "Then why does David, speaking under the inspiration of the Spirit, call the Messiah 'my Lord'? For David said,

[44] 'The LORD said to my Lord,
   Sit in the place of honor at my
      right hand
   until I humble your enemies beneath
      your feet.'*

[45]Since David called the Messiah 'my Lord,' how can the Messiah be his son?"

[46]No one could answer him. And after that, no one dared to ask him any more questions.

CHAPTER **23**
Jesus Criticizes the Religious Leaders

Then Jesus said to the crowds and to his disciples, [2]"The teachers of religious law and the Pharisees are the official interpreters of the law of Moses.* [3]So practice and obey whatever they tell you, but don't follow their example. For they don't practice what they teach. [4]They crush people with unbearable religious demands and never lift a finger to ease the burden.

[5]"Everything they do is for show. On their arms they wear extra wide prayer boxes with Scripture verses inside, and they wear robes with extra long tassels.* [6]And they love to sit at the head table at banquets and in the seats of honor in the synagogues. [7]They love to receive respectful greetings as they walk in the marketplaces, and to be called 'Rabbi.'*

[8]"Don't let anyone call you 'Rabbi,' for you have only one teacher, and all of you are equal as brothers and sisters.* [9]And don't address anyone here on earth as 'Father,' for only God in heaven is your spiritual Father. [10]And don't let anyone call you 'Teacher,' for you have only one teacher, the Messiah. [11]The greatest among you must be a servant. [12]But those who exalt themselves will be humbled, and those who humble themselves will be exalted.

22:19 Greek a denarius.   22:24 Deut 25:5-6.   22:31 Greek read about this? God said.   22:32 Exod 3:6.   22:37 Deut 6:5.
22:39 Lev 19:18.   22:44 Ps 110:1.   23:2 Greek and the Pharisees sit in the seat of Moses.   23:5 Greek They enlarge their
phylacteries and lengthen their tassels.   23:7 Rabbi, from Aramaic, means "master" or "teacher."   23:8 Greek brothers.

cornerstones

WILL WE RECOGNIZE PEOPLE IN HEAVEN?
Read MATTHEW 22:23-33

A number of people in Jesus' day had some aberrant views of life after death. The particular group of religious leaders mentioned here, the Sadducees, did not believe in life beyond the grave. So when Jesus answered the question they tested him with, he immediately addressed the error of their teaching: "Your mistake is that you don't know the Scriptures, and you don't know the power of God" (verse 29). In refuting the error and arrogance of the Sadducees, Jesus revealed these three insights about life in heaven:

1. We Will Not Be Married. We will not participate in the same activities we do now, such as marriage and family life. It would appear that the majority of our time will be spent worshiping God (see Revelation 19:5, p. 333).

2. We Will Recognize One Another. Jesus said that we will be as the angels. We won't become angels, but we will probably have some of the same capabilities or characteristics. We will actually have a real, resurrected body. While no specific passage of Scripture guarantees that we will recognize one another in heaven, many verses suggest that we will. Jesus' disciples were able to recognize his resurrected body, and in the parable of Lazarus and the rich man (see Luke 16:19-31, pp. 87-88), both men retained their identity. The Bible also says that we will have increased knowledge in heaven: "Now we see things imperfectly as in a cloudy mirror, but then we will see everything with perfect clarity. All that I know now is partial and incomplete, but then I will know everything completely, just as God now knows me completely" (1 Corinthians 13:12). With that kind of knowledge, we will probably recognize more people in heaven than we do here on earth!

3. We Will Have a Distinct Personality. Notice that at the end of the text Jesus refers to the Old Testament passage that says, "I *am* the God of Abraham, the God of Isaac, and the God of Jacob." Not only does this verse give great proof for a bodily resurrection, but it also refers to these men by name. When we read that God writes our names in the Book of Life, it indicates that we are distinct personalities in heaven. God didn't write a number—he wrote your *name*.

Some day, "in the blink of an eye," Christ will call us home to heaven, and our bodies will be transformed into "immortal bodies" (see 1 Corinthians 15:50-53, p. 207).

To live forever in our current bodies would be a curse. But to live forever in new bodies—free from sickness and pain—in the presence of God will be a blessing.

For the next note on "What Is Heaven?" turn to p. 324.

---

[13] "What sorrow awaits you teachers of religious law and you Pharisees. Hypocrites! For you shut the door of the Kingdom of Heaven in people's faces. You won't go in yourselves, and you don't let others enter either.*

[15] "What sorrow awaits you teachers of religious law and you Pharisees. Hypocrites! For you cross land and sea to make one convert, and then you turn that person into twice the child of hell* you yourselves are!

[16] "Blind guides! What sorrow awaits you! For you say that it means nothing to swear 'by God's Temple,' but that it is binding to swear 'by the gold in the Temple.' [17] Blind fools! Which is more important—the gold or the Temple that makes the gold sacred? [18] And you say that to swear 'by the altar' is not binding, but to swear 'by the gifts on the altar' is binding. [19] How blind! For which is more important—the gift on the altar or the altar that makes the gift sacred? [20] When you swear 'by the altar,' you are swearing by it and by everything on it. [21] And when you swear 'by the Temple,' you are swearing by it and by God, who lives in it. [22] And when you swear 'by heaven,' you are swearing by the throne of God and by God, who sits on the throne.

[23] "What sorrow awaits you teachers of religious law and you Pharisees. Hypocrites! For you are careful to tithe even the tiniest income

23:13 Some manuscripts add verse 14, *What sorrow awaits you teachers of religious law and you Pharisees. Hypocrites! You shamelessly cheat widows out of their property and then pretend to be pious by making long prayers in public. Because of this, you will be severely punished.* Compare Mark 12:40 and Luke 20:47.   23:15 Greek *of Gehenna;* also in 23:33.

from your herb gardens,* but you ignore the more important aspects of the law—justice, mercy, and faith. You should tithe, yes, but do not neglect the more important things. ²⁴Blind guides! You strain your water so you won't accidentally swallow a gnat, but you swallow a camel!*

²⁵"What sorrow awaits you teachers of religious law and you Pharisees. Hypocrites! For you are so careful to clean the outside of the cup and the dish, but inside you are filthy—full of greed and self-indulgence! ²⁶You blind Pharisee! First wash the inside of the cup and the dish,* and then the outside will become clean, too.

²⁷"What sorrow awaits you teachers of religious law and you Pharisees. Hypocrites! For you are like whitewashed tombs—beautiful on the outside but filled on the inside with dead people's bones and all sorts of impurity. ²⁸Outwardly you look like righteous people, but inwardly your hearts are filled with hypocrisy and lawlessness.

²⁹"What sorrow awaits you teachers of religious law and you Pharisees. Hypocrites! For you build tombs for the prophets your ancestors killed, and you decorate the monuments of the godly people your ancestors destroyed. ³⁰Then you say, 'If we had lived in the days of our ancestors, we would never have joined them in killing the prophets.'

³¹"But in saying that, you testify against yourselves that you are indeed the descendants of those who murdered the prophets. ³²Go ahead and finish what your ancestors started. ³³Snakes! Sons of vipers! How will you escape the judgment of hell?

³⁴"Therefore, I am sending you prophets and wise men and teachers of religious law. But you will kill some by crucifixion, and you will flog others with whips in your synagogues, chasing them from city to city. ³⁵As a result, you will be held responsible for the murder of all godly people of all time—from the murder of righteous Abel to the murder of Zechariah son of Berekiah, whom you killed in the Temple between the sanctuary and the altar. ³⁶I tell you the truth, this judgment will fall on this very generation.

Jesus Grieves over Jerusalem

³⁷"O Jerusalem, Jerusalem, the city that kills the prophets and stones God's messengers! How often I have wanted to gather your children together as a hen protects her chicks beneath her wings, but you wouldn't let me. ³⁸And now, look, your house is abandoned and desolate.* ³⁹For I tell you this, you will never see me again until you say, 'Blessings on the one who comes in the name of the LORD!'* "

CHAPTER **24**

Jesus Foretells the Future

As Jesus was leaving the Temple grounds, his disciples pointed out to him the various Temple buildings. ²But he responded, "Do you see all these buildings? I tell you the truth, they will be completely demolished. Not one stone will be left on top of another!"

³Later, Jesus sat on the Mount of Olives. His disciples came to him privately and said, "Tell us, when will all this happen? What sign will signal your return and the end of the world?*"

⁴Jesus told them, "Don't let anyone mislead you, ⁵for many will come in my name, claiming, 'I am the Messiah.' They will deceive many. ⁶And you will hear of wars and threats of wars, but don't panic. Yes, these things must take place, but the end won't follow immediately. ⁷Nation will go to war against nation, and kingdom against kingdom. There will be famines and earthquakes in many parts of the world. ⁸But all this is only the first of the birth pains, with more to come.

⁹"Then you will be arrested, persecuted, and killed. You will be hated all over the world because you are my followers.* ¹⁰And many will turn away from me and betray and hate each other. ¹¹And many false prophets will appear and will deceive many people. ¹²Sin will be rampant everywhere, and the love of many will grow cold. ¹³But the one who endures to the end will be saved. ¹⁴And the Good News about the Kingdom will be preached throughout the whole world, so that all nations* will hear it; and then the end will come.

¹⁵"The day is coming when you will see what Daniel the prophet spoke about—the sacrilegious object that causes desecration* standing in the Holy Place." (Reader, pay attention!) ¹⁶"Then those in Judea must flee to the hills. ¹⁷A person out on the deck of a roof must not go down into the house to pack. ¹⁸A person out in the field must not return even to get a coat. ¹⁹How terrible it will be for pregnant women and for nursing mothers in those days. ²⁰And pray that your flight will not be in winter or on the Sabbath. ²¹For there will be greater anguish than at any time since the world began. And it will never be so great again. ²²In fact, unless

---

23:23 Greek *tithe the mint, the dill, and the cumin.*   23:24 See Lev 11:4, 23, where gnats and camels are both forbidden as food.   23:26 Some manuscripts do not include *and the dish.*   23:38 Some manuscripts do not include *and desolate.*
23:39 Ps 118:26.   24:3 Or *the age?*   24:9 Greek *on account of my name.*   24:14 Or *all peoples.*   24:15 Greek *the abomination of desolation.* See Dan 9:27; 11:31; 12:11.

that time of calamity is shortened, not a single person will survive. But it will be shortened for the sake of God's chosen ones.

23 "Then if anyone tells you, 'Look, here is the Messiah,' or 'There he is,' don't believe it. 24 For false messiahs and false prophets will rise up and perform great signs and wonders so as to deceive, if possible, even God's chosen ones. 25 See, I have warned you about this ahead of time.

26 "So if someone tells you, 'Look, the Messiah is out in the desert,' don't bother to go and look. Or, 'Look, he is hiding here,' don't believe it! 27 For as the lightning flashes in the east and shines to the west, so it will be when the Son of Man* comes. 28 Just as the gathering of vultures shows there is a carcass nearby, so these signs indicate that the end is near.*

29 "Immediately after the anguish of those days,

the sun will be darkened,
    the moon will give no light,
the stars will fall from the sky,
    and the powers in the heavens will be
        shaken.*

30 And then at last, the sign that the Son of Man is coming will appear in the heavens, and there will be deep mourning among all the peoples of the earth. And they will see the Son of Man coming on the clouds of heaven with power and great glory.* 31 And he will send out his angels with the mighty blast of a trumpet, and they will gather his chosen ones from all over the world*—from the farthest ends of the earth and heaven.

32 "Now learn a lesson from the fig tree. When its branches bud and its leaves begin to sprout, you know that summer is near. 33 In the same way, when you see all these things, you can know his return is very near, right at the door. 34 I tell you the truth, this generation* will not pass from the scene until all these things take place. 35 Heaven and earth will disappear, but my words will never disappear.

36 "However, no one knows the day or hour when these things will happen, not even the angels in heaven or the Son himself.* Only the Father knows.

37 "When the Son of Man returns, it will be like it was in Noah's day. 38 In those days before the flood, the people were enjoying banquets and parties and weddings right up to the time Noah entered his boat. 39 People didn't realize what was going to happen until the flood came and swept them all away. That is the way it will be when the Son of Man comes.

40 "Two men will be working together in the field; one will be taken, the other left. 41 Two women will be grinding flour at the mill; one will be taken, the other left.

42 "So you, too, must keep watch! For you don't know what day your Lord is coming. 43 Understand this: If a homeowner knew exactly when a burglar was coming, he would keep watch and not permit his house to be broken into. 44 You also must be ready all the time, for the Son of Man will come when least expected.

45 "A faithful, sensible servant is one to whom the master can give the responsibility of managing his other household servants and feeding them. 46 If the master returns and finds that the servant has done a good job, there will be a reward. 47 I tell you the truth, the master will put that servant in charge of all he owns. 48 But what if the servant is evil and thinks, 'My master won't be back for a while,' 49 and he begins beating the other servants, partying, and getting drunk? 50 The master will return unan-

24:27 "Son of Man" is a title Jesus used for himself.   24:28 Greek *Wherever the carcass is, the vultures gather.*   24:29 See Isa 13:10; 34:4; Joel 2:10.   24:30 See Dan 7:13.   24:31 Greek *from the four winds.*   24:34 Or *this age,* or *this nation.* 24:36 Some manuscripts do not include *or the Son himself.*

---

off and running

WE WILL FIND HAPPINESS IN LOVING GOD AND SERVING OTHERS

Read MATTHEW 22:37-40

In two commands Jesus summarized the entire Old Testament law. He shows us what we as his followers are to do: love God wholeheartedly and love our neighbors as ourselves. When we do these two things, we will experience real happiness through our obedience to God.

Ironically, real happiness is not found in fulfilling our own appetites and desires but in loving God and others. This is not by chance. God knew the value of loving others even before he proved his love for us on the cross. He also

nounced and unexpected, [51] and he will cut the servant to pieces and assign him a place with the hypocrites. In that place there will be weeping and gnashing of teeth.

CHAPTER **25**

Parable of the Ten Bridesmaids

"Then the Kingdom of Heaven will be like ten bridesmaids* who took their lamps and went to meet the bridegroom. [2] Five of them were foolish, and five were wise. [3] The five who were foolish didn't take enough olive oil for their lamps, [4] but the other five were wise enough to take along extra oil. [5] When the bridegroom was delayed, they all became drowsy and fell asleep.

[6] "At midnight they were roused by the shout, 'Look, the bridegroom is coming! Come out and meet him!'

[7] "All the bridesmaids got up and prepared their lamps. [8] Then the five foolish ones asked the others, 'Please give us some of your oil because our lamps are going out.'

[9] "But the others replied, 'We don't have enough for all of us. Go to a shop and buy some for yourselves.'

[10] "But while they were gone to buy oil, the bridegroom came. Then those who were ready went in with him to the marriage feast, and the door was locked. [11] Later, when the other five bridesmaids returned, they stood outside, calling, 'Lord! Lord! Open the door for us!'

[12] "But he called back, 'Believe me, I don't know you!'

[13] "So you, too, must keep watch! For you do not know the day or hour of my return.

Parable of the Three Servants

[14] "Again, the Kingdom of Heaven can be illustrated by the story of a man going on a long trip. He called together his servants and entrusted his money to them while he was gone. [15] He gave five bags of silver* to one, two bags of silver to another, and one bag of silver to the last—dividing it in proportion to their abilities. He then left on his trip.

[16] "The servant who received the five bags of silver began to invest the money and earned five more. [17] The servant with two bags of silver also went to work and earned two more. [18] But the servant who received the one bag of silver dug a hole in the ground and hid the master's money.

[19] "After a long time their master returned from his trip and called them to give an account of how they had used his money. [20] The servant to whom he had entrusted the five bags of silver came forward with five more and said, 'Master, you gave me five bags of silver to invest, and I have earned five more.'

[21] "The master was full of praise. 'Well done, my good and faithful servant. You have been faithful in handling this small amount, so now I will give you many more responsibilities. Let's celebrate together!*'

[22] "The servant who had received the two bags of silver came forward and said, 'Master, you gave me two bags of silver to invest, and I have earned two more.'

[23] "The master said, 'Well done, my good and faithful servant. You have been faithful in handling this small amount, so now I will give you many more responsibilities. Let's celebrate together!'

[24] "Then the servant with the one bag of silver came and said, 'Master, I knew you were a harsh man, harvesting crops you didn't plant and gathering crops you didn't cultivate. [25] I was afraid I would lose your money, so I hid it in the earth. Look, here is your money back.'

25:1 Or *virgins;* also in 25:7, 11.   25:15 Greek *talents;* also throughout the story. A talent is equal to 75 pounds or 34 kilograms.   25:21 Greek *Enter into the joy of your master* [or *your Lord*]; also in 25:23.

knew how self-absorbed we are as humans and that we would fill our lives with empty pursuits in search of happiness if he didn't command us to love him and to love others.

As Paul tells us, all of our works will be tested by fire on Judgment Day (see 1 Corinthians 3:13, p. 192). Works that were done out of selfishness will not last, but works done out of love for God and others will. Because this love and the works motivated by it are everlasting, we will find real meaning in doing them. In addition, we will experience real joy in giving of ourselves to God and others out of love. It is in giving that we find purpose in life and experience true happiness.

For the next note on "Attitude toward Self," turn to p. 22.

²⁶"But the master replied, 'You wicked and lazy servant! If you knew I harvested crops I didn't plant and gathered crops I didn't cultivate, ²⁷ why didn't you deposit my money in the bank? At least I could have gotten some interest on it.'

²⁸"Then he ordered, 'Take the money from this servant, and give it to the one with the ten bags of silver. ²⁹ To those who use well what they are given, even more will be given, and they will have an abundance. But from those who do nothing, even what little they have will be taken away. ³⁰ Now throw this useless servant into outer darkness, where there will be weeping and gnashing of teeth.'

The Final Judgment

³¹"But when the Son of Man* comes in his glory, and all the angels with him, then he will sit upon his glorious throne. ³² All the nations* will be gathered in his presence, and he will separate the people as a shepherd separates the sheep from the goats. ³³ He will place the sheep at his right hand and the goats at his left.

³⁴"Then the King will say to those on his right, 'Come, you who are blessed by my Father, inherit the Kingdom prepared for you from the creation of the world. ³⁵ For I was hungry, and you fed me. I was thirsty, and you gave me a drink. I was a stranger, and you invited me into your home. ³⁶ I was naked, and you gave me clothing. I was sick, and you cared for me. I was in prison, and you visited me.'

³⁷"Then these righteous ones will reply, 'Lord, when did we ever see you hungry and feed you? Or thirsty and give you something to drink? ³⁸ Or a stranger and show you hospitality? Or naked and give you clothing? ³⁹ When did we ever see you sick or in prison and visit you?'

⁴⁰"And the King will say, 'I tell you the truth, when you did it to one of the least of these my brothers and sisters,* you were doing it to me!'

⁴¹"Then the King will turn to those on the left and say, 'Away with you, you cursed ones, into the eternal fire prepared for the devil and his demons.* ⁴² For I was hungry, and you didn't feed me. I was thirsty, and you didn't give me a drink. ⁴³ I was a stranger, and you didn't invite me into your home. I was naked, and you didn't give me clothing. I was sick and in prison, and you didn't visit me.'

⁴⁴"Then they will reply, 'Lord, when did we ever see you hungry or thirsty or a stranger or naked or sick or in prison, and not help you?'

⁴⁵"And he will answer, 'I tell you the truth, when you refused to help the least of these my brothers and sisters, you were refusing to help me.'

⁴⁶"And they will go away into eternal punishment, but the righteous will go into eternal life."

CHAPTER **26**

The Plot to Kill Jesus

When Jesus had finished saying all these things, he said to his disciples, ²"As you know, Passover begins in two days, and the Son of Man* will be handed over to be crucified."

³ At that same time the leading priests and elders were meeting at the residence of Caiaphas, the high priest, ⁴ plotting how to capture Jesus secretly and kill him. ⁵ "But not during the Passover celebration," they agreed, "or the people may riot."

Jesus Anointed at Bethany

⁶ Meanwhile, Jesus was in Bethany at the home of Simon, a man who had previously had leprosy. ⁷ While he was eating,* a woman came in with a beautiful alabaster jar of expensive perfume and poured it over his head.

⁸ The disciples were indignant when they saw this. "What a waste!" they said. ⁹ "It could have been sold for a high price and the money given to the poor."

¹⁰ But Jesus, aware of this, replied, "Why criticize this woman for doing such a good thing to me? ¹¹ You will always have the poor among you, but you will not always have me. ¹² She has poured this perfume on me to prepare my body for burial. ¹³ I tell you the truth, wherever the Good News is preached throughout the world, this woman's deed will be remembered and discussed."

Judas Agrees to Betray Jesus

¹⁴ Then Judas Iscariot, one of the twelve disciples, went to the leading priests ¹⁵ and asked, "How much will you pay me to betray Jesus to you?" And they gave him thirty pieces of silver. ¹⁶ From that time on, Judas began looking for an opportunity to betray Jesus.

The Last Supper

¹⁷ On the first day of the Festival of Unleavened Bread, the disciples came to Jesus and asked, "Where do you want us to prepare the Passover meal for you?"

¹⁸ "As you go into the city," he told them, "you will see a certain man. Tell him, 'The Teacher says: My time has come, and I will eat the Passover meal with my disciples at your house.' "

25:31 "Son of Man" is a title Jesus used for himself.   **25:32** Or *peoples*.   **25:40** Greek *my brothers*.   **25:41** Greek *his angels*.
26:2 "Son of Man" is a title Jesus used for himself.   **26:7** Or *reclining*.

¹⁹So the disciples did as Jesus told them and prepared the Passover meal there.

²⁰When it was evening, Jesus sat down at the table* with the twelve disciples.* ²¹While they were eating, he said, "I tell you the truth, one of you will betray me."

²²Greatly distressed, each one asked in turn, "Am I the one, Lord?"

²³He replied, "One of you who has just eaten from this bowl with me will betray me. ²⁴For the Son of Man must die, as the Scriptures declared long ago. But how terrible it will be for the one who betrays him. It would be far better for that man if he had never been born!"

²⁵Judas, the one who would betray him, also asked, "Rabbi, am I the one?"

And Jesus told him, "You have said it."

²⁶As they were eating, Jesus took some bread and blessed it. Then he broke it in pieces and gave it to the disciples, saying, "Take this and eat it, for this is my body."

²⁷And he took a cup of wine and gave thanks to God for it. He gave it to them and said, "Each of you drink from it, ²⁸for this is my blood, which confirms the covenant* between God and his people. It is poured out as a sacrifice to forgive the sins of many. ²⁹Mark my words—I will not drink wine again until the day I drink it new with you in my Father's Kingdom."

³⁰Then they sang a hymn and went out to the Mount of Olives.

Jesus Predicts Peter's Denial

³¹On the way, Jesus told them, "Tonight all of you will desert me. For the Scriptures say,

'God will strike* the Shepherd,
    and the sheep of the flock will be
        scattered.'

³²But after I have been raised from the dead, I will go ahead of you to Galilee and meet you there."

³³Peter declared, "Even if everyone else deserts you, I will never desert you."

³⁴Jesus replied, "I tell you the truth, Peter—this very night, before the rooster crows, you will deny three times that you even know me."

³⁵"No!" Peter insisted. "Even if I have to die with you, I will never deny you!" And all the other disciples vowed the same.

Jesus Prays in Gethsemane

³⁶Then Jesus went with them to the olive grove called Gethsemane, and he said, "Sit here while I go over there to pray." ³⁷He took Peter and Zebedee's two sons, James and John, and he became anguished and distressed. ³⁸He told them, "My soul is crushed with grief to the point of death. Stay here and keep watch with me."

³⁹He went on a little farther and bowed with his face to the ground, praying, "My Father! If it is possible, let this cup of suffering be taken away from me. Yet I want your will to be done, not mine."

⁴⁰Then he returned to the disciples and found them asleep. He said to Peter, "Couldn't you watch with me even one hour? ⁴¹Keep watch and pray, so that you will not give in to temptation. For the spirit is willing, but the body is weak!"

⁴²Then Jesus left them a second time and prayed, "My Father! If this cup cannot be taken away* unless I drink it, your will be done." ⁴³When he returned to them again, he found them sleeping, for they couldn't keep their eyes open.

⁴⁴So he went to pray a third time, saying the same things again. ⁴⁵Then he came to the disciples and said, "Go ahead and sleep. Have your rest. But look—the time has come. The Son of Man is betrayed into the hands of sinners. ⁴⁶Up, let's be going. Look, my betrayer is here!"

Jesus Is Betrayed and Arrested

⁴⁷And even as Jesus said this, Judas, one of the twelve disciples, arrived with a crowd of men armed with swords and clubs. They had been sent by the leading priests and elders of the people. ⁴⁸The traitor, Judas, had given them a prearranged signal: "You will know which one to arrest when I greet him with a kiss." ⁴⁹So Judas came straight to Jesus. "Greetings, Rabbi!" he exclaimed and gave him the kiss.

⁵⁰Jesus said, "My friend, go ahead and do what you have come for."

Then the others grabbed Jesus and arrested him. ⁵¹But one of the men with Jesus pulled out his sword and struck the high priest's slave, slashing off his ear.

⁵²"Put away your sword," Jesus told him. "Those who use the sword will die by the sword. ⁵³Don't you realize that I could ask my Father for thousands* of angels to protect us, and he would send them instantly? ⁵⁴But if I did, how would the Scriptures be fulfilled that describe what must happen now?"

⁵⁵Then Jesus said to the crowd, "Am I some dangerous revolutionary, that you come with swords and clubs to arrest me? Why didn't you arrest me in the Temple? I was there teaching every day. ⁵⁶But this is all happening to fulfill the words of the prophets as recorded in the Scriptures." At that point, all the disciples deserted him and fled.

26:20a Or *Jesus reclined.*   **26:20b** Some manuscripts read *the Twelve.*   **26:28** Some manuscripts read *the new covenant.*
26:31 Greek *I will strike.* Zech 13:7.   **26:42** Greek *If this cannot pass.*   **26:53** Greek *twelve legions.*

Jesus before the Council

[57] Then the people who had arrested Jesus led him to the home of Caiaphas, the high priest, where the teachers of religious law and the elders had gathered. [58] Meanwhile, Peter followed him at a distance and came to the high priest's courtyard. He went in and sat with the guards and waited to see how it would all end.

[59] Inside, the leading priests and the entire high council* were trying to find witnesses who would lie about Jesus, so they could put him to death. [60] But even though they found many who agreed to give false witness, they could not use anyone's testimony. Finally, two men came forward [61] who declared, "This man said, 'I am able to destroy the Temple of God and rebuild it in three days.'"

[62] Then the high priest stood up and said to Jesus, "Well, aren't you going to answer these charges? What do you have to say for yourself?" [63] But Jesus remained silent. Then the high priest said to him, "I demand in the name of the living God—tell us if you are the Messiah, the Son of God."

[64] Jesus replied, "You have said it. And in the future you will see the Son of Man seated in the place of power at God's right hand* and coming on the clouds of heaven."*

[65] Then the high priest tore his clothing to show his horror and said, "Blasphemy! Why do we need other witnesses? You have all heard his blasphemy. [66] What is your verdict?"

"Guilty!" they shouted. "He deserves to die!"

[67] Then they began to spit in Jesus' face and beat him with their fists. And some slapped him, [68] jeering, "Prophesy to us, you Messiah! Who hit you that time?"

Peter Denies Jesus

[69] Meanwhile, Peter was sitting outside in the courtyard. A servant girl came over and said to him, "You were one of those with Jesus the Galilean."

[70] But Peter denied it in front of everyone. "I don't know what you're talking about," he said.

[71] Later, out by the gate, another servant girl noticed him and said to those standing around, "This man was with Jesus of Nazareth.*"

[72] Again Peter denied it, this time with an oath. "I don't even know the man," he said.

[73] A little later some of the other bystanders came over to Peter and said, "You must be one of them; we can tell by your Galilean accent."

[74] Peter swore, "A curse on me if I'm lying—I don't know the man!" And immediately the rooster crowed.

[75] Suddenly, Jesus' words flashed through Peter's mind: "Before the rooster crows, you will deny three times that you even know me." And he went away, weeping bitterly.

CHAPTER 27

Judas Hangs Himself

Very early in the morning the leading priests and the elders of the people met again to lay plans for putting Jesus to death. [2] Then they bound him, led him away, and took him to Pilate, the Roman governor.

[3] When Judas, who had betrayed him, realized that Jesus had been condemned to die, he was filled with remorse. So he took the thirty pieces of silver back to the leading priests and the elders. [4] "I have sinned," he declared, "for I have betrayed an innocent man."

"What do we care?" they retorted. "That's your problem."

[5] Then Judas threw the silver coins down in the Temple and went out and hanged himself.

[6] The leading priests picked up the coins. "It wouldn't be right to put this money in the Temple treasury," they said, "since it was payment for murder."* [7] After some discussion they finally decided to buy the potter's field, and they made it into a cemetery for foreigners. [8] That is why the field is still called the Field of Blood. [9] This fulfilled the prophecy of Jeremiah that says,

"They took* the thirty pieces of silver—
> the price at which he was valued by the
> people of Israel,
[10] and purchased the potter's field,
> as the LORD directed.*"

Jesus' Trial before Pilate

[11] Now Jesus was standing before Pilate, the Roman governor. "Are you the king of the Jews?" the governor asked him.

Jesus replied, "You have said it."

[12] But when the leading priests and the elders made their accusations against him, Jesus remained silent. [13] "Don't you hear all these charges they are bringing against you?" Pilate demanded. [14] But Jesus made no response to any of the charges, much to the governor's surprise.

[15] Now it was the governor's custom each year during the Passover celebration to release one prisoner to the crowd—anyone they wanted. [16] This year there was a notorious prisoner, a man named Barabbas.* [17] As the crowds gathered before Pilate's house that morning, he asked them, "Which one do you want me to release to you—Barabbas, or Jesus who is called

---

26:59 Greek *the Sanhedrin.*   26:64a Greek *seated at the right hand of the power.* See Ps 110:1.   26:64b See Dan 7:13.
26:71 Or *Jesus the Nazarene.*   27:6 Greek *since it is the price for blood.*   27:9 Or *I took.*   27:9-10 Greek *as the LORD directed me.* Zech 11:12-13; Jer 32:6-9.   27:16 Some manuscripts read *Jesus Barabbas;* also in 27:17.

the Messiah?" [18](He knew very well that the religious leaders had arrested Jesus out of envy.)

[19]Just then, as Pilate was sitting on the judgment seat, his wife sent him this message: "Leave that innocent man alone. I suffered through a terrible nightmare about him last night."

[20]Meanwhile, the leading priests and the elders persuaded the crowd to ask for Barabbas to be released and for Jesus to be put to death. [21]So the governor asked again, "Which of these two do you want me to release to you?"

The crowd shouted back, "Barabbas!"

[22]Pilate responded, "Then what should I do with Jesus who is called the Messiah?"

They shouted back, "Crucify him!"

[23]"Why?" Pilate demanded. "What crime has he committed?"

But the mob roared even louder, "Crucify him!"

[24]Pilate saw that he wasn't getting anywhere and that a riot was developing. So he sent for a bowl of water and washed his hands before the crowd, saying, "I am innocent of this man's blood. The responsibility is yours!"

[25]And all the people yelled back, "We will take responsibility for his death—we and our children!"*

[26]So Pilate released Barabbas to them. He ordered Jesus flogged with a lead-tipped whip, then turned him over to the Roman soldiers to be crucified.

The Soldiers Mock Jesus

[27]Some of the governor's soldiers took Jesus into their headquarters* and called out the entire regiment. [28]They stripped him and put a scarlet robe on him. [29]They wove thorn branches into a crown and put it on his head, and they placed a reed stick in his right hand as a scepter. Then they knelt before him in mockery and taunted, "Hail! King of the Jews!" [30]And they spit on him and grabbed the stick and struck him on the head with it. [31]When they were finally tired of mocking him, they took off the robe and put his own clothes on him again. Then they led him away to be crucified.

The Crucifixion

[32]Along the way, they came across a man named Simon, who was from Cyrene,* and the soldiers forced him to carry Jesus' cross. [33]And they went out to a place called Golgotha (which means "Place of the Skull"). [34]The soldiers gave

him wine mixed with bitter gall, but when he had tasted it, he refused to drink it.

[35]After they had nailed him to the cross, the soldiers gambled for his clothes by throwing dice.* [36]Then they sat around and kept guard as he hung there. [37]A sign was fastened above Jesus' head, announcing the charge against him. It read: "This is Jesus, the King of the Jews." [38]Two revolutionaries* were crucified with him, one on his right and one on his left.

[39]The people passing by shouted abuse, shaking their heads in mockery. [40]"Look at you now!" they yelled at him. "You said you were going to destroy the Temple and rebuild it in three days. Well then, if you are the Son of God, save yourself and come down from the cross!"

[41]The leading priests, the teachers of religious law, and the elders also mocked Jesus. [42]"He saved others," they scoffed, "but he can't save himself! So he is the King of Israel, is he? Let him come down from the cross right now, and we will believe in him! [43]He trusted God, so let God rescue him now if he wants him! For he said, 'I am the Son of God.'" [44]Even the revolutionaries who were crucified with him ridiculed him in the same way.

The Death of Jesus

[45]At noon, darkness fell across the whole land until three o'clock. [46]At about three o'clock, Jesus called out with a loud voice, *"Eli, Eli,* lema sabachthani?"* which means "My God, my God, why have you abandoned me?"*

[47]Some of the bystanders misunderstood and thought he was calling for the prophet Elijah. [48]One of them ran and filled a sponge with sour wine, holding it up to him on a reed stick so he could drink. [49]But the rest said, "Wait! Let's see whether Elijah comes to save him."*

[50]Then Jesus shouted out again, and he released his spirit. [51]At that moment the curtain in the sanctuary of the Temple was torn in two, from top to bottom. The earth shook, rocks split apart, [52]and tombs opened. The bodies of many godly men and women who had died were raised from the dead. [53]They left the cemetery after Jesus' resurrection, went into the holy city of Jerusalem, and appeared to many people.

[54]The Roman officer* and the other soldiers at the crucifixion were terrified by the earthquake and all that had happened. They said, "This man truly was the Son of God!"

27:25 Greek *"His blood be on us and on our children."*   27:27 Or *into the Praetorium.*   27:32 *Cyrene* was a city in northern Africa.   27:35 Greek *by casting lots.* A few late manuscripts add *This fulfilled the word of the prophet: "They divided my garments among themselves and cast lots for my robe."* See Ps 22:18.   27:38 Or *criminals;* also in 27:44.   27:46a Some manuscripts read *Eloi, Eloi.*   27:46b Ps 22:1.   27:49 Some manuscripts add *And another took a spear and pierced his side, and out flowed water and blood.* Compare John 19:34.   27:54 Greek *The centurion.*

⁵⁵And many women who had come from Galilee with Jesus to care for him were watching from a distance. ⁵⁶Among them were Mary Magdalene, Mary (the mother of James and Joseph), and the mother of James and John, the sons of Zebedee.

The Burial of Jesus

⁵⁷As evening approached, Joseph, a rich man from Arimathea who had become a follower of Jesus, ⁵⁸went to Pilate and asked for Jesus' body. And Pilate issued an order to release it to him. ⁵⁹Joseph took the body and wrapped it in a long sheet of clean linen cloth. ⁶⁰He placed it in his own new tomb, which had been carved out of the rock. Then he rolled a great stone across the entrance and left. ⁶¹Both Mary Magdalene and the other Mary were sitting across from the tomb and watching.

The Guard at the Tomb

⁶²The next day, on the Sabbath,* the leading priests and Pharisees went to see Pilate. ⁶³They told him, "Sir, we remember what that deceiver once said while he was still alive: 'After three days I will rise from the dead.' ⁶⁴So we request that you seal the tomb until the third day. This will prevent his disciples from coming and stealing his body and then telling everyone he was raised from the dead! If that happens, we'll be worse off than we were at first."

⁶⁵Pilate replied, "Take guards and secure it the best you can." ⁶⁶So they sealed the tomb and posted guards to protect it.

CHAPTER **28**
The Resurrection

Early on Sunday morning,* as the new day was dawning, Mary Magdalene and the other Mary went out to visit the tomb.

²Suddenly there was a great earthquake! For an angel of the Lord came down from heaven, rolled aside the stone, and sat on it. ³His face shone like lightning, and his clothing was as white as snow. ⁴The guards shook with fear when they saw him, and they fell into a dead faint.

⁵Then the angel spoke to the women. "Don't be afraid!" he said. "I know you are looking for Jesus, who was crucified. ⁶He isn't here! He is risen from the dead, just as he said would happen. Come, see where his body was lying. ⁷And now, go quickly and tell his disciples that he has risen from the dead, and he is going ahead of you to Galilee. You will see him there. Remember what I have told you."

⁸The women ran quickly from the tomb. They were very frightened but also filled with great joy, and they rushed to give the disciples the angel's message. ⁹And as they went, Jesus met them and greeted them. And they ran to him, grasped his feet, and worshiped him. ¹⁰Then Jesus said to them, "Don't be afraid! Go tell my brothers to leave for Galilee, and they will see me there."

The Report of the Guard

¹¹As the women were on their way, some of the guards went into the city and told the leading priests what had happened. ¹²A meeting with the elders was called, and they decided to give the soldiers a large bribe. ¹³They told the soldiers, "You must say, 'Jesus' disciples came during the night while we were sleeping, and they stole his body.' ¹⁴If the governor hears about it, we'll stand up for you so you won't get in trouble." ¹⁵So the guards accepted the bribe and said what they were told to say. Their story spread widely among the Jews, and they still tell it today.

The Great Commission

¹⁶Then the eleven disciples left for Galilee, going to the mountain where Jesus had told them to go. ¹⁷When they saw him, they worshiped him—but some of them doubted!

¹⁸Jesus came and told his disciples, "I have been given all authority in heaven and on earth. ¹⁹Therefore, go and make disciples of all the nations,* baptizing them in the name of the Father and the Son and the Holy Spirit. ²⁰Teach these new disciples to obey all the commands I have given you. And be sure of this: I am with you always, even to the end of the age."

27:62 Or *On the next day, which is after the Preparation.*   **28:1** Greek *After the Sabbath, on the first day of the week.*
28:19 Or *all peoples.*

Mark

AUTHOR: JOHN MARK | DATE WRITTEN: A.D. 55–65 | GENRE: GOSPEL

The Gospel of Mark is the account of the life, ministry, miracles, and words of Jesus Christ. In contrast to Matthew, who primarily presented Jesus as the "Messiah," Mark emphasizes the Lord's servanthood.

CHAPTER **1**

John the Baptist Prepares the Way

This is the Good News about Jesus the Messiah, the Son of God.* It began ²just as the prophet Isaiah had written:

"Look, I am sending my messenger ahead
  of you,
  and he will prepare your way.*
³ He is a voice shouting in the wilderness,
  'Prepare the way for the Lᴏʀᴅ's coming!
  Clear the road for him!'*"

⁴This messenger was John the Baptist. He was in the wilderness and preached that people should be baptized to show that they had repented of their sins and turned to God to be forgiven. ⁵All of Judea, including all the people of Jerusalem, went out to see and hear John. And when they confessed their sins, he baptized them in the Jordan River. ⁶His clothes were woven from coarse camel hair, and he wore a leather belt around his waist. For food he ate locusts and wild honey.

⁷John announced: "Someone is coming soon who is greater than I am—so much greater that I'm not even worthy to stoop down like a slave and untie the straps of his sandals. ⁸I baptize you with* water, but he will baptize you with the Holy Spirit!"

The Baptism and Temptation of Jesus

⁹One day Jesus came from Nazareth in Galilee, and John baptized him in the Jordan River. ¹⁰As Jesus came up out of the water, he saw the heavens splitting apart and the Holy Spirit descending on him* like a dove. ¹¹And a voice from heaven said, "You are my dearly loved Son, and you bring me great joy."

¹²The Spirit then compelled Jesus to go into the wilderness, ¹³where he was tempted by Satan for forty days. He was out among the wild animals, and angels took care of him.

¹⁴Later on, after John was arrested, Jesus went into Galilee, where he preached God's Good News.* ¹⁵"The time promised by God has come at last!" he announced. "The Kingdom of God is near! Repent of your sins and believe the Good News!"

The First Disciples

¹⁶One day as Jesus was walking along the shore of the Sea of Galilee, he saw Simon* and his brother Andrew throwing a net into the water, for they fished for a living. ¹⁷Jesus called out to them, "Come, follow me, and I will show you how to fish for people!" ¹⁸And they left their nets at once and followed him.

¹⁹A little farther up the shore Jesus saw Zebedee's sons, James and John, in a boat repairing their nets. ²⁰He called them at once, and they also followed him, leaving their father, Zebedee, in the boat with the hired men.

Jesus Casts Out an Evil Spirit

²¹Jesus and his companions went to the town of Capernaum. When the Sabbath day came, he went into the synagogue and began to teach. ²²The people were amazed at his teaching, for he taught with real authority—quite unlike the teachers of religious law.

²³Suddenly, a man in the synagogue who was possessed by an evil* spirit began shouting, ·

1:1 Some manuscripts do not include *the Son of God.* 1:2 Mal 3:1. 1:3 Isa 40:3 (Greek version). 1:8 Or *in;* also in 1:8b. 1:10 Or *toward him,* or *into him.* 1:14 Some manuscripts read *the Good News of the Kingdom of God.* 1:16 *Simon* is called "Peter" in 3:16 and thereafter. 1:23 Greek *unclean;* also in 1:26, 27.

24"Why are you interfering with us, Jesus of Nazareth? Have you come to destroy us? I know who you are—the Holy One of God!"

25 Jesus cut him short. "Be quiet! Come out of the man," he ordered. 26At that, the evil spirit screamed, threw the man into a convulsion, and then came out of him.

27Amazement gripped the audience, and they began to discuss what had happened. "What sort of new teaching is this?" they asked excitedly. "It has such authority! Even evil spirits obey his orders!" 28The news about Jesus spread quickly throughout the entire region of Galilee.

Jesus Heals Many People

29After Jesus left the synagogue with James and John, they went to Simon and Andrew's home. 30Now Simon's mother-in-law was sick in bed with a high fever. They told Jesus about her right away. 31So he went to her bedside, took her by the hand, and helped her sit up. Then the fever left her, and she prepared a meal for them.

32That evening after sunset, many sick and demon-possessed people were brought to Jesus. 33The whole town gathered at the door to watch. 34So Jesus healed many people who were sick with various diseases, and he cast out many demons. But because the demons knew who he was, he did not allow them to speak.

Jesus Preaches in Galilee

35Before daybreak the next morning, Jesus got up and went out to an isolated place to pray. 36Later Simon and the others went out to find him. 37When they found him, they said, "Everyone is looking for you."

38But Jesus replied, "We must go on to other towns as well, and I will preach to them, too. That is why I came." 39So he traveled throughout the region of Galilee, preaching in the synagogues and casting out demons.

Jesus Heals a Man with Leprosy

40A man with leprosy came and knelt in front of Jesus, begging to be healed. "If you are willing, you can heal me and make me clean," he said.

41Moved with compassion,* Jesus reached out and touched him. "I am willing," he said. "Be healed!" 42Instantly the leprosy disappeared, and the man was healed. 43Then Jesus sent him on his way with a stern warning: 44"Don't tell anyone about this. Instead, go to the priest and let him examine you. Take along the offering required in the law of Moses for those who have been healed of leprosy.* This will be a public testimony that you have been cleansed."

45But the man went and spread the word, proclaiming to everyone what had happened. As a result, large crowds soon surrounded Jesus, and he couldn't publicly enter a town anywhere. He had to stay out in the secluded places, but people from everywhere kept coming to him.

CHAPTER **2**

Jesus Heals a Paralyzed Man

When Jesus returned to Capernaum several days later, the news spread quickly that he was back home. 2Soon the house where he was staying was so packed with visitors that there was no more room, even outside the door. While he was preaching God's word to them, 3four men arrived carrying a paralyzed man on a mat. 4They couldn't bring him to Jesus because of the crowd, so they dug a hole through the roof above his head. Then they lowered the man on his mat, right down in front of Jesus. 5Seeing their faith, Jesus said to the paralyzed man, "My child, your sins are forgiven."

6But some of the teachers of religious law who were sitting there thought to themselves, 7"What is he saying? This is blasphemy! Only God can forgive sins!"

8Jesus knew immediately what they were thinking, so he asked them, "Why do you question this in your hearts? 9Is it easier to say to the paralyzed man 'Your sins are forgiven,' or 'Stand up, pick up your mat, and walk'? 10So I will prove to you that the Son of Man* has the authority on earth to forgive sins." Then Jesus turned to the paralyzed man and said, 11"Stand up, pick up your mat, and go home!"

12And the man jumped up, grabbed his mat, and walked out through the stunned onlookers. They were all amazed and praised God, exclaiming, "We've never seen anything like this before!"

Jesus Calls Levi (Matthew)

13Then Jesus went out to the lakeshore again and taught the crowds that were coming to him. 14As he walked along, he saw Levi son of Alphaeus sitting at his tax collector's booth. "Follow me and be my disciple," Jesus said to him. So Levi got up and followed him.

15Later, Levi invited Jesus and his disciples to his home as dinner guests, along with many tax collectors and other disreputable sinners. (There were many people of this kind among Jesus' followers.) 16But when the teachers of religious law who were Pharisees* saw him eating with tax collectors and other sinners, they asked his disciples, "Why does he eat with such scum?*"

1:41 Some manuscripts read *Moved with anger.*   **1:44** See Lev 14:2-32.   **2:10** "Son of Man" is a title Jesus used for himself.
2:16a Greek *the scribes of the Pharisees.*   **2:16b** Greek *with tax collectors and sinners?*

[17]When Jesus heard this, he told them, "Healthy people don't need a doctor—sick people do. I have come to call not those who think they are righteous, but those who know they are sinners."

A Discussion about Fasting

[18]Once when John's disciples and the Pharisees were fasting, some people came to Jesus and asked, "Why don't your disciples fast like John's disciples and the Pharisees do?"

[19]Jesus replied, "Do wedding guests fast while celebrating with the groom? Of course not. They can't fast while the groom is with them. [20]But someday the groom will be taken away from them, and then they will fast.

[21]"Besides, who would patch old clothing with new cloth? For the new patch would shrink and rip away from the old cloth, leaving an even bigger tear than before.

[22]"And no one puts new wine into old wineskins. For the wine would burst the wineskins, and the wine and the skins would both be lost. New wine calls for new wineskins."

A Discussion about the Sabbath

[23]One Sabbath day as Jesus was walking through some grainfields, his disciples began breaking off heads of grain to eat. [24]But the Pharisees said to Jesus, "Look, why are they breaking the law by harvesting grain on the Sabbath?"

[25]Jesus said to them, "Haven't you ever read in the Scriptures what David did when he and his companions were hungry? [26]He went into the house of God (during the days when Abiathar was high priest) and broke the law by eating the sacred loaves of bread that only the priests are allowed to eat. He also gave some to his companions."

[27]Then Jesus said to them, "The Sabbath was made to meet the needs of people, and not people to meet the requirements of the Sabbath. [28]So the Son of Man is Lord, even over the Sabbath!"

CHAPTER 3

Jesus Heals on the Sabbath

Jesus went into the synagogue again and noticed a man with a deformed hand. [2]Since it was the Sabbath, Jesus' enemies watched him closely. If he healed the man's hand, they planned to accuse him of working on the Sabbath.

[3]Jesus said to the man with the deformed hand, "Come and stand in front of everyone." [4]Then he turned to his critics and asked, "Does the law permit good deeds on the Sabbath, or is it a day for doing evil? Is this a day to save life or to destroy it?" But they wouldn't answer him.

[5]He looked around at them angrily and was deeply saddened by their hard hearts. Then he said to the man, "Hold out your hand." So the man held out his hand, and it was restored! [6]At once the Pharisees went away and met with the supporters of Herod to plot how to kill Jesus.

Crowds Follow Jesus

[7]Jesus went out to the lake with his disciples, and a large crowd followed him. They came from all over Galilee, Judea, [8]Jerusalem, Idumea, from east of the Jordan River, and even from as far north as Tyre and Sidon. The news about his miracles had spread far and wide, and vast numbers of people came to see him. [9]Jesus instructed his disciples to have a boat ready so the crowd would not crush him. [10]He had healed many people that day, so all the sick people eagerly pushed forward to touch him. [11]And whenever those possessed by evil* spirits caught sight of him, the spirits would throw them to the ground in front of him shrieking, "You are the Son of God!" [12]But Jesus sternly commanded the spirits not to reveal who he was.

Jesus Chooses the Twelve Apostles

[13]Afterward Jesus went up on a mountain and called out the ones he wanted to go with him. And they came to him. [14]Then he appointed twelve of them and called them his apostles.* They were to accompany him, and he would send them out to preach, [15]giving them authority to cast out demons. [16]These are the twelve he chose:

Simon (whom he named Peter),
[17] James and John (the sons of Zebedee, but Jesus nicknamed them "Sons of Thunder"*),
[18] Andrew,
Philip,
Bartholomew,
Matthew,
Thomas,
James (son of Alphaeus),
Thaddaeus,
Simon (the zealot*),
[19] Judas Iscariot (who later betrayed him).

Jesus and the Prince of Demons

[20]One time Jesus entered a house, and the crowds began to gather again. Soon he and his disciples couldn't even find time to eat. [21]When his family heard what was happening,

---

3:11 Greek *unclean;* also in 3:30.   3:14 Some manuscripts do not include *and called them his apostles.*   3:17 Greek *whom he named Boanerges, which means Sons of Thunder.*   3:18 Greek *the Cananean,* an Aramaic term for Jewish nationalists.

they tried to take him away. "He's out of his mind," they said.

²²But the teachers of religious law who had arrived from Jerusalem said, "He's possessed by Satan,* the prince of demons. That's where he gets the power to cast out demons."

²³Jesus called them over and responded with an illustration. "How can Satan cast out Satan?" he asked. ²⁴"A kingdom divided by civil war will collapse. ²⁵Similarly, a family splintered by feuding will fall apart. ²⁶And if Satan is divided and fights against himself, how can he stand? He would never survive. ²⁷Let me illustrate this further. Who is powerful enough to enter the house of a strong man like Satan and plunder his goods? Only someone even stronger—someone who could tie him up and then plunder his house.

²⁸"I tell you the truth, all sin and blasphemy can be forgiven, ²⁹but anyone who blasphemes the Holy Spirit will never be forgiven. This is a sin with eternal consequences." ³⁰He told them this because they were saying, "He's possessed by an evil spirit."

The True Family of Jesus

³¹Then Jesus' mother and brothers came to see him. They stood outside and sent word for him to come out and talk with them. ³²There was a crowd sitting around Jesus, and someone said, "Your mother and your brothers* are outside asking for you."

³³Jesus replied, "Who is my mother? Who are my brothers?" ³⁴Then he looked at those around him and said, "Look, these are my mother and brothers. ³⁵Anyone who does God's will is my brother and sister and mother."

CHAPTER 4

Parable of the Farmer Scattering Seed

Once again Jesus began teaching by the lakeshore. A very large crowd soon gathered around him, so he got into a boat. Then he sat in the boat while all the people remained on the shore. ²He taught them by telling many stories in the form of parables, such as this one:

³"Listen! A farmer went out to plant some seed. ⁴As he scattered it across his field, some of the seed fell on a footpath, and the birds came and ate it. ⁵Other seed fell on shallow soil with underlying rock. The seed sprouted quickly because the soil was shallow. ⁶But the plant soon wilted under the hot sun, and since it didn't have deep roots, it died. ⁷Other seed fell among thorns that grew up and choked out the tender plants so they produced no grain. ⁸Still other

seeds fell on fertile soil, and they sprouted, grew, and produced a crop that was thirty, sixty, and even a hundred times as much as had been planted!" ⁹Then he said, "Anyone with ears to hear should listen and understand."

¹⁰Later, when Jesus was alone with the twelve disciples and with the others who were gathered around, they asked him what the parables meant.

¹¹He replied, "You are permitted to understand the secret* of the Kingdom of God. But I use parables for everything I say to outsiders, ¹²so that the Scriptures might be fulfilled:

'When they see what I do,
    they will learn nothing.
When they hear what I say,
    they will not understand.
Otherwise, they will turn to me
    and be forgiven.'* "

¹³Then Jesus said to them, "If you can't understand the meaning of this parable, how will you understand all the other parables? ¹⁴The farmer plants seed by taking God's word to others. ¹⁵The seed that fell on the footpath represents those who hear the message, only to have Satan come at once and take it away. ¹⁶The seed on the rocky soil represents those who hear the message and immediately receive it with joy. ¹⁷But since they don't have deep roots, they don't last long. They fall away as soon as they have problems or are persecuted for believing God's word. ¹⁸The seed that fell among the thorns represents others who hear God's word, ¹⁹but all too quickly the message is crowded out by the worries of this life, the lure of wealth, and the desire for other things, so no fruit is produced. ²⁰And the seed that fell on good soil represents those who hear and accept God's word and produce a harvest of thirty, sixty, or even a hundred times as much as had been planted!"

Parable of the Lamp

²¹Then Jesus asked them, "Would anyone light a lamp and then put it under a basket or under a bed? Of course not! A lamp is placed on a stand, where its light will shine. ²²For everything that is hidden will eventually be brought into the open, and every secret will be brought to light. ²³Anyone with ears to hear should listen and understand."

²⁴Then he added, "Pay close attention to what you hear. The closer you listen, the more understanding you will be given*—and you will receive even more. ²⁵To those who listen to my

---

3:22 Greek *Beelzeboul;* other manuscripts read *Beezeboul;* Latin version reads *Beelzebub.*   3:32 Some manuscripts add *and sisters.*   4:11 Greek *mystery.*   4:12 Isa 6:9-10 (Greek version).   4:24 Or *The measure you give will be the measure you get back.*

teaching, more understanding will be given. But for those who are not listening, even what little understanding they have will be taken away from them."

Parable of the Growing Seed

²⁶Jesus also said, "The Kingdom of God is like a farmer who scatters seed on the ground. ²⁷Night and day, while he's asleep or awake, the seed sprouts and grows, but he does not understand how it happens. ²⁸The earth produces the crops on its own. First a leaf blade pushes through, then the heads of wheat are formed, and finally the grain ripens. ²⁹And as soon as the grain is ready, the farmer comes and harvests it with a sickle, for the harvest time has come."

Parable of the Mustard Seed

³⁰Jesus said, "How can I describe the Kingdom of God? What story should I use to illustrate it? ³¹It is like a mustard seed planted in the ground. It is the smallest of all seeds, ³²but it becomes the largest of all garden plants; it grows long branches, and birds can make nests in its shade."

³³Jesus used many similar stories and illustrations to teach the people as much as they could understand. ³⁴In fact, in his public ministry he never taught without using parables; but afterward, when he was alone with his disciples, he explained everything to them.

Jesus Calms the Storm

³⁵As evening came, Jesus said to his disciples, "Let's cross to the other side of the lake." ³⁶So they took Jesus in the boat and started out, leaving the crowds behind (although other boats followed). ³⁷But soon a fierce storm came up. High waves were breaking into the boat, and it began to fill with water.

³⁸Jesus was sleeping at the back of the boat with his head on a cushion. The disciples woke him up, shouting, "Teacher, don't you care that we're going to drown?"

³⁹When Jesus woke up, he rebuked the wind and said to the waves, "Silence! Be still!" Suddenly the wind stopped, and there was a great calm. ⁴⁰Then he asked them, "Why are you afraid? Do you still have no faith?"

⁴¹The disciples were absolutely terrified. "Who is this man?" they asked each other. "Even the wind and waves obey him!"

CHAPTER 5

Jesus Heals a Demon-Possessed Man

So they arrived at the other side of the lake, in the region of the Gerasenes.* ²When Jesus

5:1 Other manuscripts read *Gadarenes;* still others read *Gergesenes.* See Matt 8:28; Luke 8:26.

first steps

JESUS IS WITH US IN LIFE'S STORMS

Read MARK 4:35-41

This story illustrates how God is in control of even the most desperate of circumstances. Here we find the disciples, several of whom were seasoned fishermen and sailors, frantically worried that they would perish in this storm. Although Jesus was with them, they thought he was oblivious to the severity of their situation. Yet Jesus wanted them to discover three important lessons.

1. Jesus Is Aware of Your Situation. Although Jesus, being human, needed physical sleep for his weary body, he was still fully aware of his surroundings. Though the shrieking of the storm did not wake him, the cry of one of his disciples did, and he responded immediately and powerfully. Psalm 121:3 says, "He will not let you stumble; the one who watches over you will not slumber."

2. Jesus Will Answer Your Call for Help. The Lord will do the same for you in the midst of your trials. Sometimes he just lets us reach the point of desperation so we will recognize that he is our only hope. He wants us to remember that he is on board with us.

3. You Can Make It Through. Every one of us is going to face hardship, but only the child of God has the promise that God's presence is with him or her in the midst of the storm. As Jesus didn't leave his disciples, so God will not leave you stranded in the middle of your problem. Although he didn't promise smooth sailing, he did promise safe passage. Paul reminds us that "I am certain that God, who began the good work within you, will continue his work until it is finally finished on the day when Christ Jesus returns" (Philippians 1:6).

For the next note on "Have Courage in Trials," turn to p. 117.

climbed out of the boat, a man possessed by an evil* spirit came out from a cemetery to meet him. ³This man lived among the burial caves and could no longer be restrained, even with a chain. ⁴Whenever he was put into chains and shackles—as he often was—he snapped the chains from his wrists and smashed the shackles. No one was strong enough to subdue him. ⁵Day and night he wandered among the burial caves and in the hills, howling and cutting himself with sharp stones.

⁶When Jesus was still some distance away, the man saw him, ran to meet him, and bowed low before him. ⁷With a shriek, he screamed, "Why are you interfering with me, Jesus, Son of the Most High God? In the name of God, I beg you, don't torture me!" ⁸For Jesus had already said to the spirit, "Come out of the man, you evil spirit."

⁹Then Jesus demanded, "What is your name?"

And he replied, "My name is Legion, because there are many of us inside this man." ¹⁰Then the evil spirits begged him again and again not to send them to some distant place.

¹¹There happened to be a large herd of pigs feeding on the hillside nearby. ¹²"Send us into those pigs," the spirits begged. "Let us enter them."

¹³So Jesus gave them permission. The evil spirits came out of the man and entered the pigs, and the entire herd of about 2,000 pigs plunged down the steep hillside into the lake and drowned in the water.

¹⁴The herdsmen fled to the nearby town and the surrounding countryside, spreading the news as they ran. People rushed out to see what had happened. ¹⁵A crowd soon gathered around Jesus, and they saw the man who had been possessed by the legion of demons. He was sitting there fully clothed and perfectly sane, and they were all afraid. ¹⁶Then those who had seen what happened told the others about the demon-possessed man and the pigs. ¹⁷And the crowd began pleading with Jesus to go away and leave them alone.

¹⁸As Jesus was getting into the boat, the man who had been demon possessed begged to go with him. ¹⁹But Jesus said, "No, go home to your family, and tell them everything the Lord has done for you and how merciful he has been." ²⁰So the man started off to visit the Ten Towns* of that region and began to proclaim the great things Jesus had done for him; and everyone was amazed at what he told them.

Jesus Heals in Response to Faith

²¹Jesus got into the boat again and went back to the other side of the lake, where a large crowd gathered around him on the shore. ²²Then a leader of the local synagogue, whose name was Jairus, arrived. When he saw Jesus, he fell at his feet, ²³pleading fervently with him. "My little daughter is dying," he said. "Please come and lay your hands on her; heal her so she can live."

²⁴Jesus went with him, and all the people followed, crowding around him. ²⁵A woman in the crowd had suffered for twelve years with constant bleeding. ²⁶She had suffered a great deal from many doctors, and over the years she had spent everything she had to pay them, but she had gotten no better. In fact, she had gotten worse. ²⁷She had heard about Jesus, so she came up behind him through the crowd and touched his robe. ²⁸For she thought to herself, "If I can just touch his robe, I will be healed." ²⁹Immediately the bleeding stopped, and she could feel in her body that she had been healed of her terrible condition.

³⁰Jesus realized at once that healing power had gone out from him, so he turned around in the crowd and asked, "Who touched my robe?"

³¹His disciples said to him, "Look at this crowd pressing around you. How can you ask, 'Who touched me?'"

³²But he kept on looking around to see who had done it. ³³Then the frightened woman, trembling at the realization of what had happened to her, came and fell to her knees in front of him and told him what she had done. ³⁴And he said to her, "Daughter, your faith has made you well. Go in peace. Your suffering is over."

³⁵While he was still speaking to her, messengers arrived from the home of Jairus, the leader of the synagogue. They told him, "Your daughter is dead. There's no use troubling the Teacher now."

³⁶But Jesus overheard* them and said to Jairus, "Don't be afraid. Just have faith."

³⁷Then Jesus stopped the crowd and wouldn't let anyone go with him except Peter, James, and John (the brother of James). ³⁸When they came to the home of the synagogue leader, Jesus saw much commotion and weeping and wailing. ³⁹He went inside and asked, "Why all this commotion and weeping? The child isn't dead; she's only asleep."

⁴⁰The crowd laughed at him. But he made them all leave, and he took the girl's father and mother and his three disciples into the room where the girl was lying. ⁴¹Holding her hand, he said to her, *"Talitha koum,"* which means "Little girl, get up!" ⁴²And the girl, who was twelve years old, immediately stood up and walked around! They were overwhelmed and

5:2 Greek *unclean;* also in 5:8, 13.   5:20 Greek *Decapolis.*   5:36 Or *ignored.*

totally amazed. [43] Jesus gave them strict orders not to tell anyone what had happened, and then he told them to give her something to eat.

CHAPTER 6

Jesus Rejected at Nazareth

Jesus left that part of the country and returned with his disciples to Nazareth, his hometown. [2] The next Sabbath he began teaching in the synagogue, and many who heard him were amazed. They asked, "Where did he get all this wisdom and the power to perform such miracles?" [3] Then they scoffed, "He's just a carpenter, the son of Mary* and the brother of James, Joseph,* Judas, and Simon. And his sisters live right here among us." They were deeply offended and refused to believe in him.

[4] Then Jesus told them, "A prophet is honored everywhere except in his own hometown and among his relatives and his own family." [5] And because of their unbelief, he couldn't do any miracles among them except to place his hands on a few sick people and heal them. [6] And he was amazed at their unbelief.

Jesus Sends Out the Twelve Disciples

Then Jesus went from village to village, teaching the people. [7] And he called his twelve disciples together and began sending them out two by two, giving them authority to cast out evil* spirits. [8] He told them to take nothing for their journey except a walking stick—no food, no traveler's bag, no money.* [9] He allowed them to wear sandals but not to take a change of clothes.

[10] "Wherever you go," he said, "stay in the same house until you leave town. [11] But if any place refuses to welcome you or listen to you, shake its dust from your feet as you leave to show that you have abandoned those people to their fate."

[12] So the disciples went out, telling everyone they met to repent of their sins and turn to God. [13] And they cast out many demons and healed many sick people, anointing them with olive oil.

The Death of John the Baptist

[14] Herod Antipas, the king, soon heard about Jesus, because everyone was talking about him. Some were saying,* "This must be John the Baptist raised from the dead. That is why he can do such miracles." [15] Others said, "He's the prophet Elijah." Still others said, "He's a prophet like the other great prophets of the past."

[16] When Herod heard about Jesus, he said, "John, the man I beheaded, has come back from the dead."

[17] For Herod had sent soldiers to arrest and imprison John as a favor to Herodias. She had been his brother Philip's wife, but Herod had married her. [18] John had been telling Herod, "It is against God's law for you to marry your brother's wife." [19] So Herodias bore a grudge against John and wanted to kill him. But without Herod's approval she was powerless, [20] for Herod respected John; and knowing that he was a good and holy man, he protected him. Herod was greatly disturbed whenever he talked with John, but even so, he liked to listen to him.

[21] Herodias's chance finally came on Herod's birthday. He gave a party for his high government officials, army officers, and the leading citizens of Galilee. [22] Then his daughter, also named Herodias,* came in and performed a dance that greatly pleased Herod and his guests. "Ask me for anything you like," the king said to the girl, "and I will give it to you." [23] He even vowed, "I will give you whatever you ask, up to half my kingdom!"

[24] She went out and asked her mother, "What should I ask for?"

Her mother told her, "Ask for the head of John the Baptist!"

[25] So the girl hurried back to the king and told him, "I want the head of John the Baptist, right now, on a tray!"

[26] Then the king deeply regretted what he had said; but because of the vows he had made in front of his guests, he couldn't refuse her. [27] So he immediately sent an executioner to the prison to cut off John's head and bring it to him. The soldier beheaded John in the prison, [28] brought his head on a tray, and gave it to the girl, who took it to her mother. [29] When John's disciples heard what had happened, they came to get his body and buried it in a tomb.

Jesus Feeds Five Thousand

[30] The apostles returned to Jesus from their ministry tour and told him all they had done and taught. [31] Then Jesus said, "Let's go off by ourselves to a quiet place and rest awhile." He said this because there were so many people coming and going that Jesus and his apostles didn't even have time to eat.

[32] So they left by boat for a quiet place, where they could be alone. [33] But many people recognized them and saw them leaving, and people from many towns ran ahead along the shore

---

6:3a Some manuscripts read *He's just the son of the carpenter and of Mary.*   6:3b Most manuscripts read *Joses;* see Matt 13:55.   6:7 Greek *unclean.*   6:8 Greek *no copper coins in their money belts.*   6:14 Some manuscripts read *He was saying.*
6:22 Some manuscripts read *the daughter of Herodias herself.*

and got there ahead of them. ³⁴Jesus saw the huge crowd as he stepped from the boat, and he had compassion on them because they were like sheep without a shepherd. So he began teaching them many things.

³⁵Late in the afternoon his disciples came to him and said, "This is a remote place, and it's already getting late. ³⁶Send the crowds away so they can go to the nearby farms and villages and buy something to eat."

³⁷But Jesus said, "You feed them."

"With what?" they asked. "We'd have to work for months to earn enough money* to buy food for all these people!"

³⁸"How much bread do you have?" he asked. "Go and find out."

They came back and reported, "We have five loaves of bread and two fish."

³⁹Then Jesus told the disciples to have the people sit down in groups on the green grass. ⁴⁰So they sat down in groups of fifty or a hundred.

⁴¹Jesus took the five loaves and two fish, looked up toward heaven, and blessed them. Then, breaking the loaves into pieces, he kept giving the bread to the disciples so they could distribute it to the people. He also divided the fish for everyone to share. ⁴²They all ate as much as they wanted, ⁴³and afterward, the disciples picked up twelve baskets of leftover bread and fish. ⁴⁴A total of 5,000 men and their families were fed from those loaves!

Jesus Walks on Water

⁴⁵Immediately after this, Jesus insisted that his disciples get back into the boat and head across the lake to Bethsaida, while he sent the people home. ⁴⁶After telling everyone goodbye, he went up into the hills by himself to pray.

⁴⁷Late that night, the disciples were in their boat in the middle of the lake, and Jesus was alone on land. ⁴⁸He saw that they were in serious trouble, rowing hard and struggling against the wind and waves. About three o'clock in the morning* Jesus came toward them, walking on the water. He intended to go past them, ⁴⁹but when they saw him walking on the water, they cried out in terror, thinking he was a ghost. ⁵⁰They were all terrified when they saw him.

But Jesus spoke to them at once. "Don't be afraid," he said. "Take courage! I am here!*" ⁵¹Then he climbed into the boat, and the wind stopped. They were totally amazed, ⁵²for they still didn't understand the significance of the miracle of the loaves. Their hearts were too hard to take it in.

⁵³After they had crossed the lake, they landed at Gennesaret. They brought the boat to shore ⁵⁴and climbed out. The people recognized Jesus at once, ⁵⁵and they ran throughout the whole area, carrying sick people on mats to wherever they heard he was. ⁵⁶Wherever he went—in villages, cities, or the countryside— they brought the sick out to the marketplaces. They begged him to let the sick touch at least the fringe of his robe, and all who touched him were healed.

CHAPTER 7

Jesus Teaches about Inner Purity

One day some Pharisees and teachers of religious law arrived from Jerusalem to see Jesus. ²They noticed that some of his disciples failed to follow the Jewish ritual of hand washing before eating. ³(The Jews, especially the Pharisees, do not eat until they have poured water over their cupped hands,* as required by their ancient traditions. ⁴Similarly, they don't eat anything from the market until they immerse their hands* in water. This is but one of many traditions they have clung to—such as their ceremonial washing of cups, pitchers, and kettles.*)

⁵So the Pharisees and teachers of religious law asked him, "Why don't your disciples follow our age-old tradition? They eat without first performing the hand-washing ceremony."

⁶Jesus replied, "You hypocrites! Isaiah was right when he prophesied about you, for he wrote,

'These people honor me with their lips,
　　but their hearts are far from me.
⁷ Their worship is a farce,
　　for they teach man-made ideas as
　　　　commands from God.'*

⁸For you ignore God's law and substitute your own tradition."

⁹Then he said, "You skillfully sidestep God's law in order to hold on to your own tradition. ¹⁰For instance, Moses gave you this law from God: 'Honor your father and mother,'* and 'Anyone who speaks disrespectfully of father or mother must be put to death.'* ¹¹But you say it is all right for people to say to their parents, 'Sorry, I can't help you. For I have vowed to give to God what I would have given to you.'* ¹²In this way, you let them disregard their needy

---

6:37 Greek *It would take 200 denarii.* A denarius was equivalent to a laborer's full day's wage.　6:48 Greek *About the fourth watch of the night.*　6:50 Or *The 'I AM' is here;* Greek reads *I am.* See Exod 3:14.　7:3 Greek *have washed with the fist.* 7:4a Some manuscripts read *sprinkle themselves.*　7:4b Some manuscripts add *and dining couches.*　7:7 Isa 29:13 (Greek version).　7:10a Exod 20:12; Deut 5:16.　7:10b Exod 21:17 (Greek version); Lev 20:9 (Greek version).　7:11 Greek *'What I would have given to you is Corban' (that is, a gift).*

parents. [13] And so you cancel the word of God in order to hand down your own tradition. And this is only one example among many others."

[14] Then Jesus called to the crowd to come and hear. "All of you listen," he said, "and try to understand. [15] It's not what goes into your body that defiles you; you are defiled by what comes from your heart.*"

[17] Then Jesus went into a house to get away from the crowd, and his disciples asked him what he meant by the parable he had just used. [18] "Don't you understand either?" he asked. "Can't you see that the food you put into your body cannot defile you? [19] Food doesn't go into your heart, but only passes through the stomach and then goes into the sewer." (By saying this, he declared that every kind of food is acceptable in God's eyes.)

[20] And then he added, "It is what comes from inside that defiles you. [21] For from within, out of a person's heart, come evil thoughts, sexual immorality, theft, murder, [22] adultery, greed, wickedness, deceit, lustful desires, envy, slander, pride, and foolishness. [23] All these vile things come from within; they are what defile you."

The Faith of a Gentile Woman

[24] Then Jesus left Galilee and went north to the region of Tyre.* He didn't want anyone to know which house he was staying in, but he couldn't keep it a secret. [25] Right away a woman who had heard about him came and fell at his feet. Her little girl was possessed by an evil* spirit, [26] and she begged him to cast out the demon from her daughter.

Since she was a Gentile, born in Syrian Phoenicia, [27] Jesus told her, "First I should feed the children—my own family, the Jews.* It isn't right to take food from the children and throw it to the dogs."

[28] She replied, "That's true, Lord, but even the dogs under the table are allowed to eat the scraps from the children's plates."

[29] "Good answer!" he said. "Now go home, for the demon has left your daughter." [30] And when she arrived home, she found her little girl lying quietly in bed, and the demon was gone.

Jesus Heals a Deaf Man

[31] Jesus left Tyre and went up to Sidon before going back to the Sea of Galilee and the region of the Ten Towns.* [32] A deaf man with a speech impediment was brought to him, and the people begged Jesus to lay his hands on the man to heal him.

[33] Jesus led him away from the crowd so they could be alone. He put his fingers into the man's ears. Then, spitting on his own fingers, he touched the man's tongue. [34] Looking up to heaven, he sighed and said, "Ephphatha," which means, "Be opened!" [35] Instantly the man could hear perfectly, and his tongue was freed so he could speak plainly!

[36] Jesus told the crowd not to tell anyone, but the more he told them not to, the more they spread the news. [37] They were completely amazed and said again and again, "Everything he does is wonderful. He even makes the deaf to hear and gives speech to those who cannot speak."

CHAPTER 8

Jesus Feeds Four Thousand

About this time another large crowd had gathered, and the people ran out of food again. Jesus called his disciples and told them, [2] "I feel sorry for these people. They have been here with me for three days, and they have nothing left to eat. [3] If I send them home hungry, they will faint along the way. For some of them have come a long distance."

[4] His disciples replied, "How are we supposed to find enough food to feed them out here in the wilderness?"

[5] Jesus asked, "How much bread do you have?"

"Seven loaves," they replied.

[6] So Jesus told all the people to sit down on the ground. Then he took the seven loaves, thanked God for them, and broke them into pieces. He gave them to his disciples, who distributed the bread to the crowd. [7] A few small fish were found, too, so Jesus also blessed these and told the disciples to distribute them.

[8] They ate as much as they wanted. Afterward, the disciples picked up seven large baskets of leftover food. [9] There were about 4,000 people in the crowd that day, and Jesus sent them home after they had eaten. [10] Immediately after this, he got into a boat with his disciples and crossed over to the region of Dalmanutha.

Pharisees Demand a Miraculous Sign

[11] When the Pharisees heard that Jesus had arrived, they came and started to argue with him. Testing him, they demanded that he show them a miraculous sign from heaven to prove his authority.

[12] When he heard this, he sighed deeply in his spirit and said, "Why do these people keep demanding a miraculous sign? I tell you the truth, I will not give this generation any such

---

7:15 Some manuscripts add verse 16, *Anyone with ears to hear should listen and understand.* Compare 4:9, 23.   **7:24** Some manuscripts add *and Sidon.*   **7:25** Greek *unclean.*   **7:27** Greek *Let the children eat first.*   **7:31** Greek *Decapolis.*

sign." [13]So he got back into the boat and left them, and he crossed to the other side of the lake.

Yeast of the Pharisees and Herod

[14]But the disciples had forgotten to bring any food. They had only one loaf of bread with them in the boat. [15]As they were crossing the lake, Jesus warned them, "Watch out! Beware of the yeast of the Pharisees and of Herod."

[16]At this they began to argue with each other because they hadn't brought any bread. [17]Jesus knew what they were saying, so he said, "Why are you arguing about having no bread? Don't you know or understand even yet? Are your hearts too hard to take it in? [18]'You have eyes—can't you see? You have ears—can't you hear?'* Don't you remember anything at all? [19]When I fed the 5,000 with five loaves of bread, how many baskets of leftovers did you pick up afterward?"

"Twelve," they said.

[20]"And when I fed the 4,000 with seven loaves, how many large baskets of leftovers did you pick up?"

"Seven," they said.

[21]"Don't you understand yet?" he asked them.

Jesus Heals a Blind Man

[22]When they arrived at Bethsaida, some people brought a blind man to Jesus, and they begged him to touch the man and heal him. [23]Jesus took the blind man by the hand and led him out of the village. Then, spitting on the man's eyes, he laid his hands on him and asked, "Can you see anything now?"

[24]The man looked around. "Yes," he said, "I see people, but I can't see them very clearly. They look like trees walking around."

[25]Then Jesus placed his hands on the man's eyes again, and his eyes were opened. His sight was completely restored, and he could see everything clearly. [26]Jesus sent him away, saying, "Don't go back into the village on your way home."

Peter's Declaration about Jesus

[27]Jesus and his disciples left Galilee and went up to the villages near Caesarea Philippi. As they were walking along, he asked them, "Who do people say I am?"

[28]"Well," they replied, "some say John the Baptist, some say Elijah, and others say you are one of the other prophets."

[29]Then he asked them, "But who do you say I am?"

Peter replied, "You are the Messiah.*"

[30]But Jesus warned them not to tell anyone about him.

Jesus Predicts His Death

[31]Then Jesus began to tell them that the Son of Man* must suffer many terrible things and be rejected by the elders, the leading priests, and the teachers of religious law. He would be killed, but three days later he would rise from the dead. [32]As he talked about this openly with his disciples, Peter took him aside and began to reprimand him for saying such things.*

[33]Jesus turned around and looked at his disciples, then reprimanded Peter. "Get away from me, Satan!" he said. "You are seeing things merely from a human point of view, not from God's."

[34]Then, calling the crowd to join his disciples, he said, "If any of you wants to be my follower, you must turn from your selfish ways, take up your cross, and follow me. [35]If you try to hang on to your life, you will lose it. But if you give up your life for my sake and for the sake of the Good News, you will save it. [36]And what do you benefit if you gain the whole world but lose your own soul?* [37]Is anything worth more than your soul? [38]If anyone is ashamed of me and my message in these adulterous and sinful days, the Son of Man will be ashamed of that person when he returns in the glory of his Father with the holy angels."

CHAPTER 9

Jesus went on to say, "I tell you the truth, some standing here right now will not die before they see the Kingdom of God arrive in great power!"

The Transfiguration

[2]Six days later Jesus took Peter, James, and John, and led them up a high mountain to be alone. As the men watched, Jesus' appearance was transformed, [3]and his clothes became dazzling white, far whiter than any earthly bleach could ever make them. [4]Then Elijah and Moses appeared and began talking with Jesus.

[5]Peter exclaimed, "Rabbi, it's wonderful for us to be here! Let's make three shelters as memorials*—one for you, one for Moses, and one for Elijah." [6]He said this because he didn't really know what else to say, for they were all terrified.

[7]Then a cloud overshadowed them, and a voice from the cloud said, "This is my dearly loved Son. Listen to him." [8]Suddenly, when they looked around, Moses and Elijah were gone, and they saw only Jesus with them.

8:18 Jer 5:21.   8:29 Or *the Christ. Messiah* (a Hebrew term) and *Christ* (a Greek term) both mean "the anointed one."
8:31 "Son of Man" is a title Jesus used for himself.   8:32 Or *began to correct him.*   8:36 Or *your self?* also in 8:37.
9:5 Greek *three tabernacles.*

[9]As they went back down the mountain, he told them not to tell anyone what they had seen until the Son of Man* had risen from the dead. [10]So they kept it to themselves, but they often asked each other what he meant by "rising from the dead."

[11]Then they asked him, "Why do the teachers of religious law insist that Elijah must return before the Messiah comes?*"

[12]Jesus responded, "Elijah is indeed coming first to get everything ready. Yet why do the Scriptures say that the Son of Man must suffer greatly and be treated with utter contempt? [13]But I tell you, Elijah has already come, and they chose to abuse him, just as the Scriptures predicted."

Jesus Heals a Demon-Possessed Boy

[14]When they returned to the other disciples, they saw a large crowd surrounding them, and some teachers of religious law were arguing with them. [15]When the crowd saw Jesus, they were overwhelmed with awe, and they ran to greet him.

[16]"What is all this arguing about?" Jesus asked.

[17]One of the men in the crowd spoke up and said, "Teacher, I brought my son so you could heal him. He is possessed by an evil spirit that won't let him talk. [18]And whenever this spirit seizes him, it throws him violently to the ground. Then he foams at the mouth and grinds his teeth and becomes rigid.* So I asked your disciples to cast out the evil spirit, but they couldn't do it."

[19]Jesus said to them,* "You faithless people! How long must I be with you? How long must I put up with you? Bring the boy to me."

[20]So they brought the boy. But when the evil spirit saw Jesus, it threw the child into a violent convulsion, and he fell to the ground, writhing and foaming at the mouth.

[21]"How long has this been happening?" Jesus asked the boy's father.

He replied, "Since he was a little boy. [22]The spirit often throws him into the fire or into water, trying to kill him. Have mercy on us and help us, if you can."

[23]"What do you mean, 'If I can'?" Jesus asked. "Anything is possible if a person believes."

[24]The father instantly cried out, "I do believe, but help me overcome my unbelief!"

[25]When Jesus saw that the crowd of onlookers was growing, he rebuked the evil* spirit. "Listen, you spirit that makes this boy unable to hear and speak," he said. "I command you to come out of this child and never enter him again!"

[26]Then the spirit screamed and threw the boy into another violent convulsion and left him. The boy appeared to be dead. A murmur ran through the crowd as people said, "He's dead." [27]But Jesus took him by the hand and helped him to his feet, and he stood up.

[28]Afterward, when Jesus was alone in the house with his disciples, they asked him, "Why couldn't we cast out that evil spirit?"

[29]Jesus replied, "This kind can be cast out only by prayer.*"

Jesus Again Predicts His Death

[30]Leaving that region, they traveled through Galilee. Jesus didn't want anyone to know he was there, [31]for he wanted to spend more time with his disciples and teach them. He said to them, "The Son of Man is going to be betrayed into the hands of his enemies. He will be killed, but three days later he will rise from the dead." [32]They didn't understand what he was saying, however, and they were afraid to ask him what he meant.

The Greatest in the Kingdom

[33]After they arrived at Capernaum and settled in a house, Jesus asked his disciples, "What were you discussing out on the road?" [34]But they didn't answer, because they had been arguing about which of them was the greatest. [35]He sat down, called the twelve disciples over to him, and said, "Whoever wants to be first must take last place and be the servant of everyone else."

[36]Then he put a little child among them. Taking the child in his arms, he said to them, [37]"Anyone who welcomes a little child like this on my behalf* welcomes me, and anyone who welcomes me welcomes not only me but also my Father who sent me."

Using the Name of Jesus

[38]John said to Jesus, "Teacher, we saw someone using your name to cast out demons, but we told him to stop because he wasn't in our group."

[39]"Don't stop him!" Jesus said. "No one who performs a miracle in my name will soon be able to speak evil of me. [40]Anyone who is not against us is for us. [41]If anyone gives you even a cup of water because you belong to the Messiah, I tell you the truth, that person will surely be rewarded.

[42]"But if you cause one of these little ones who trusts in me to fall into sin, it would be better for you to be thrown into the sea with a large millstone hung around your neck. [43]If

---

9:9 "Son of Man" is a title Jesus used for himself.   **9:11** Greek *that Elijah must come first?*   **9:18** Or *becomes weak.*   **9:19** Or *said to his disciples.*   **9:25** Greek *unclean.*   **9:29** Some manuscripts read *by prayer and fasting.*   **9:37** Greek *in my name.*

your hand causes you to sin, cut it off. It's better to enter eternal life with only one hand than to go into the unquenchable fires of hell* with two hands.* ⁴⁵If your foot causes you to sin, cut it off. It's better to enter eternal life with only one foot than to be thrown into hell with two feet.* ⁴⁷And if your eye causes you to sin, gouge it out. It's better to enter the Kingdom of God with only one eye than to have two eyes and be thrown into hell, ⁴⁸'where the maggots never die and the fire never goes out.'*

⁴⁹"For everyone will be tested with fire.* ⁵⁰Salt is good for seasoning. But if it loses its flavor, how do you make it salty again? You must have the qualities of salt among yourselves and live in peace with each other."

CHAPTER 10
Discussion about Divorce and Marriage
Then Jesus left Capernaum and went down to the region of Judea and into the area east of the Jordan River. Once again crowds gathered around him, and as usual he was teaching them.

²Some Pharisees came and tried to trap him with this question: "Should a man be allowed to divorce his wife?"

³Jesus answered them with a question: "What did Moses say in the law about divorce?"

⁴"Well, he permitted it," they replied. "He said a man can give his wife a written notice of divorce and send her away."*

⁵But Jesus responded, "He wrote this commandment only as a concession to your hard hearts. ⁶But 'God made them male and female'* from the beginning of creation. ⁷'This explains why a man leaves his father and mother and is joined to his wife,* ⁸and the two are united into one.'* Since they are no longer two but one, ⁹let no one split apart what God has joined together."

¹⁰Later, when he was alone with his disciples in the house, they brought up the subject again. ¹¹He told them, "Whoever divorces his wife and marries someone else commits adultery against her. ¹²And if a woman divorces her husband and marries someone else, she commits adultery."

Jesus Blesses the Children
¹³One day some parents brought their children to Jesus so he could touch and bless them. But the disciples scolded the parents for bothering him.

¹⁴When Jesus saw what was happening, he was angry with his disciples. He said to them, "Let the children come to me. Don't stop them! For the Kingdom of God belongs to those who are like these children. ¹⁵I tell you the truth, anyone who doesn't receive the Kingdom of God like a child will never enter it." ¹⁶Then he took the children in his arms and placed his hands on their heads and blessed them.

The Rich Man
¹⁷As Jesus was starting out on his way to Jerusalem, a man came running up to him, knelt

9:43a Greek *Gehenna*; also in 9:45, 47. 9:43b Some manuscripts add verse 44, *'where the maggots never die and the fire never goes out.'* See 9:48. 9:45 Some manuscripts add verse 46, *'where the maggots never die and the fire never goes out.'* See 9:48. 9:48 Isa 66:24. 9:49 Greek *salted with fire*; other manuscripts add *and every sacrifice will be salted with salt.* 10:4 See Deut 24:1. 10:6 Gen 1:27; 5:2. 10:7 Some manuscripts do not include *and is joined to his wife.* 10:7-8 Gen 2:24.

off and running
DIVORCE IS NOT PART OF GOD'S PLAN
Read MARK 10:2-12

At the time Jesus was asked about divorce, some people had a liberal attitude toward it. Much like today, one could dissolve a marriage for practically any reason. But Jesus reminded the people of God's original plan for marriage (verses 6-9)—that a man and woman make a lifelong commitment to each other. Divorce should never be a consideration.

Perhaps one of the greatest deterrents for divorce is to see how much God really hates it:

"You cry out, 'Why doesn't the LORD accept my worship?' I'll tell you why! Because the LORD witnessed the vows you and your wife made when you were young. But you have been unfaithful to her, though she remained your faithful partner, the wife of your marriage vows. Didn't the LORD make you one with your wife? In body and spirit you are his. And what does he want? Godly childown, and asked, "Good Teacher, what must I do to inherit eternal life?"

[18]"Why do you call me good?" Jesus asked. "Only God is truly good. [19]But to answer your question, you know the commandments: 'You must not murder. You must not commit adultery. You must not steal. You must not testify falsely. You must not cheat anyone. Honor your father and mother.'* "

[20]"Teacher," the man replied, "I've obeyed all these commandments since I was young."

[21]Looking at the man, Jesus felt genuine love for him. "There is still one thing you haven't done," he told him. "Go and sell all your possessions and give the money to the poor, and you will have treasure in heaven. Then come, follow me."

[22]At this the man's face fell, and he went away sad, for he had many possessions.

[23]Jesus looked around and said to his disciples, "How hard it is for the rich to enter the Kingdom of God!" [24]This amazed them. But Jesus said again, "Dear children, it is very hard* to enter the Kingdom of God. [25]In fact, it is easier for a camel to go through the eye of a needle than for a rich person to enter the Kingdom of God!"

[26]The disciples were astounded. "Then who in the world can be saved?" they asked.

[27]Jesus looked at them intently and said, "Humanly speaking, it is impossible. But not with God. Everything is possible with God."

[28]Then Peter began to speak up. "We've given up everything to follow you," he said.

[29]"Yes," Jesus replied, "and I assure you that everyone who has given up house or brothers or sisters or mother or father or children or property, for my sake and for the Good News, [30]will receive now in return a hundred times as many houses, brothers, sisters, mothers, children, and property—along with persecution. And in the world to come that person will have eternal life. [31]But many who are the greatest now will be least important then, and those who seem least important now will be the greatest then.*"

Jesus Again Predicts His Death

[32]They were now on the way up to Jerusalem, and Jesus was walking ahead of them. The disciples were filled with awe, and the people following behind were overwhelmed with fear. Taking the twelve disciples aside, Jesus once more began to describe everything that was about to happen to him. [33]"Listen," he said, "we're going up to Jerusalem, where the Son of Man* will be betrayed to the leading priests and the teachers of religious law. They will sentence him to die and hand him over to the Romans.* [34]They will mock him, spit on him, flog him with a whip, and kill him, but after three days he will rise again."

Jesus Teaches about Serving Others

[35]Then James and John, the sons of Zebedee, came over and spoke to him. "Teacher," they said, "we want you to do us a favor."

[36]"What is your request?" he asked.

[37]They replied, "When you sit on your glorious throne, we want to sit in places of honor

10:19 Exod 20:12-16; Deut 5:16-20. **10:24** Some manuscripts read *very hard for those who trust in riches.* **10:31** Greek *But many who are first will be last; and the last, first.* **10:33a** "Son of Man" is a title Jesus used for himself. **10:33b** Greek *the Gentiles.*

---

dren from your union. So guard your heart; remain loyal to the wife of your youth. 'For I hate divorce!'" (Malachi 2:14-16). Just as one should count the cost of marriage, one should also count the cost of divorce. Not only does it devastate the companionship God desires between husband and wife, but it will also greatly affect any children they may have. God wants his people to bring up godly children from their union. When a home is broken by divorce, it becomes more difficult to raise children in obedience to the Lord.

Does God ever permit divorce? While the Bible cites two instances (adultery and a non-believing spouse choosing to leave a believing spouse), God's will is that married couples stay together.

Winston Churchill astutely observed, "Victory is not obtained through evacuation." If you are married, ask God today to strengthen your marriage. Remember that God has joined you and your spouse. Stand by your commitment. Don't retreat from your problems, but ask God to help you face and overcome them. Cultivate oneness and friendship in your marriage, and get back to God's original design.

For the next note on "Marriage," turn to p. 198.

next to you, one on your right and the other on your left."

38 But Jesus said to them, "You don't know what you are asking! Are you able to drink from the bitter cup of suffering I am about to drink? Are you able to be baptized with the baptism of suffering I must be baptized with?"

39 "Oh yes," they replied, "we are able!"

Then Jesus told them, "You will indeed drink from my bitter cup and be baptized with my baptism of suffering. 40 But I have no right to say who will sit on my right or my left. God has prepared those places for the ones he has chosen."

41 When the ten other disciples heard what James and John had asked, they were indignant. 42 So Jesus called them together and said, "You know that the rulers in this world lord it over their people, and officials flaunt their authority over those under them. 43 But among you it will be different. Whoever wants to be a leader among you must be your servant, 44 and whoever wants to be first among you must be the slave of everyone else. 45 For even the Son of Man came not to be served but to serve others and to give his life as a ransom for many."

Jesus Heals Blind Bartimaeus

46 Then they reached Jericho, and as Jesus and his disciples left town, a large crowd followed him. A blind beggar named Bartimaeus (son of Timaeus) was sitting beside the road. 47 When Bartimaeus heard that Jesus of Nazareth was nearby, he began to shout, "Jesus, Son of David, have mercy on me!"

48 "Be quiet!" many of the people yelled at him.

But he only shouted louder, "Son of David, have mercy on me!"

49 When Jesus heard him, he stopped and said, "Tell him to come here."

So they called the blind man. "Cheer up," they said. "Come on, he's calling you!" 50 Bartimaeus threw aside his coat, jumped up, and came to Jesus.

51 "What do you want me to do for you?" Jesus asked.

"My rabbi,*" the blind man said, "I want to see!"

52 And Jesus said to him, "Go, for your faith has healed you." Instantly the man could see, and he followed Jesus down the road.*

CHAPTER 11

Jesus' Triumphant Entry

As Jesus and his disciples approached Jerusalem, they came to the towns of Bethphage and Bethany on the Mount of Olives. Jesus sent two

of them on ahead. 2 "Go into that village over there," he told them. "As soon as you enter it, you will see a young donkey tied there that no one has ever ridden. Untie it and bring it here. 3 If anyone asks, 'What are you doing?' just say, 'The Lord needs it and will return it soon.' "

4 The two disciples left and found the colt standing in the street, tied outside the front door. 5 As they were untying it, some bystanders demanded, "What are you doing, untying that colt?" 6 They said what Jesus had told them to say, and they were permitted to take it. 7 Then they brought the colt to Jesus and threw their garments over it, and he sat on it.

8 Many in the crowd spread their garments on the road ahead of him, and others spread leafy branches they had cut in the fields. 9 Jesus was in the center of the procession, and the people all around him were shouting,

"Praise God!*
     Blessings on the one who comes in the
          name of the LORD!
10 Blessings on the coming Kingdom of our
          ancestor David!
     Praise God in highest heaven!"*

11 So Jesus came to Jerusalem and went into the Temple. After looking around carefully at everything, he left because it was late in the afternoon. Then he returned to Bethany with the twelve disciples.

Jesus Curses the Fig Tree

12 The next morning as they were leaving Bethany, Jesus was hungry. 13 He noticed a fig tree in full leaf a little way off, so he went over to see if he could find any figs. But there were only leaves because it was too early in the season for fruit. 14 Then Jesus said to the tree, "May no one ever eat your fruit again!" And the disciples heard him say it.

Jesus Clears the Temple

15 When they arrived back in Jerusalem, Jesus entered the Temple and began to drive out the people buying and selling animals for sacrifices. He knocked over the tables of the money changers and the chairs of those selling doves, 16 and he stopped everyone from using the Temple as a marketplace.* 17 He said to them, "The Scriptures declare, 'My Temple will be called a house of prayer for all nations,' but you have turned it into a den of thieves."*

18 When the leading priests and teachers of religious law heard what Jesus had done, they began planning how to kill him. But they were

---

10:51 Greek uses the Hebrew term *Rabboni*.   10:52 Or *on the way*.   11:9 Greek *Hosanna*, an exclamation of praise that literally means "save now"; also in 11:10.   11:9-10 Pss 118:25-26; 148:1.   11:16 Or *from carrying merchandise through the Temple*.   11:17 Isa 56:7; Jer 7:11.

afraid of him because the people were so amazed at his teaching.

¹⁹That evening Jesus and the disciples left* the city.

²⁰The next morning as they passed by the fig tree he had cursed, the disciples noticed it had withered from the roots up. ²¹Peter remembered what Jesus had said to the tree on the previous day and exclaimed, "Look, Rabbi! The fig tree you cursed has withered and died!"

²²Then Jesus said to the disciples, "Have faith in God. ²³I tell you the truth, you can say to this mountain, 'May you be lifted up and thrown into the sea,' and it will happen. But you must really believe it will happen and have no doubt in your heart. ²⁴I tell you, you can pray for anything, and if you believe that you've received it, it will be yours. ²⁵But when you are praying, first forgive anyone you are holding a grudge against, so that your Father in heaven will forgive your sins, too.*"

The Authority of Jesus Challenged

²⁷Again they entered Jerusalem. As Jesus was walking through the Temple area, the leading priests, the teachers of religious law, and the elders came up to him. ²⁸They demanded, "By what authority are you doing all these things? Who gave you the right to do them?"

²⁹"I'll tell you by what authority I do these things if you answer one question," Jesus replied. ³⁰"Did John's authority to baptize come from heaven, or was it merely human? Answer me!"

³¹They talked it over among themselves. "If we say it was from heaven, he will ask why we didn't believe John. ³²But do we dare say it was merely human?" For they were afraid of what the people would do, because everyone believed that John was a prophet. ³³So they finally replied, "We don't know."

And Jesus responded, "Then I won't tell you by what authority I do these things."

CHAPTER 12
Parable of the Evil Farmers

Then Jesus began teaching them with stories: "A man planted a vineyard. He built a wall around it, dug a pit for pressing out the grape juice, and built a lookout tower. Then he leased the vineyard to tenant farmers and moved to another country. ²At the time of the grape harvest, he sent one of his servants to collect his share of the crop. ³But the farmers grabbed the servant, beat him up, and sent him back empty-handed. ⁴The owner then sent another servant, but they insulted him and beat him over the

head. ⁵The next servant he sent was killed. Others he sent were either beaten or killed, ⁶until there was only one left—his son whom he loved dearly. The owner finally sent him, thinking, 'Surely they will respect my son.'

⁷"But the tenant farmers said to one another, 'Here comes the heir to this estate. Let's kill him and get the estate for ourselves!' ⁸So they grabbed him and murdered him and threw his body out of the vineyard.

⁹"What do you suppose the owner of the vineyard will do?" Jesus asked. "I'll tell you—he will come and kill those farmers and lease the vineyard to others. ¹⁰Didn't you ever read this in the Scriptures?

'The stone that the builders rejected
   has now become the cornerstone.
¹¹ This is the LORD's doing,
   and it is wonderful to see.'* "

¹²The religious leaders* wanted to arrest Jesus because they realized he was telling the story against them—they were the wicked farmers. But they were afraid of the crowd, so they left him and went away.

Taxes for Caesar

¹³Later the leaders sent some Pharisees and supporters of Herod to trap Jesus into saying something for which he could be arrested. ¹⁴"Teacher," they said, "we know how honest you are. You are impartial and don't play favorites. You teach the way of God truthfully. Now tell us—is it right to pay taxes to Caesar or not? ¹⁵Should we pay them, or shouldn't we?"

Jesus saw through their hypocrisy and said, "Why are you trying to trap me? Show me a Roman coin,* and I'll tell you." ¹⁶When they handed it to him, he asked, "Whose picture and title are stamped on it?"

"Caesar's," they replied.

¹⁷"Well, then," Jesus said, "give to Caesar what belongs to Caesar, and give to God what belongs to God."

His reply completely amazed them.

Discussion about Resurrection

¹⁸Then Jesus was approached by some Sadducees—religious leaders who say there is no resurrection from the dead. They posed this question: ¹⁹"Teacher, Moses gave us a law that if a man dies, leaving a wife without children, his brother should marry the widow and have a child who will carry on the brother's name.* ²⁰Well, suppose there were seven brothers. The oldest one married and then died without children. ²¹So

---

11:19 Greek they left; other manuscripts read he left.   11:25 Some manuscripts add verse 26, But if you refuse to forgive, your Father in heaven will not forgive your sins. Compare Matt 6:15.   12:10-11 Ps 118:22-23.   12:12 Greek They.
12:15 Greek a denarius.   12:19 See Deut 25:5-6.

cornerstones

FORGIVENESS FIRST COMES FROM GOD
Read MARK 11:25

Be careful how you approach God in prayer. An attitude of unforgiveness can actually hinder our prayer life. The psalmist wrote, "If I had not confessed the sin in my heart, the LORD would not have listened" (Psalm 66:18).

Jesus is not saying that God's forgiveness is dependent upon your forgiveness of others. God's acceptance and forgiveness is entirely dependent upon what he did for you at the cross. He is simply stressing that if you are truly a forgiven person, you should be willing to forgive others. At the same time, if you aren't willing to forgive others, one would wonder if you know anything of God's forgiveness.

Don't let unforgiveness rob you of your joy. Forgive as Christ forgave you.

For the next note on "Forgiveness," turn to p. 26.

---

the second brother married the widow, but he also died without children. Then the third brother married her. ²²This continued with all seven of them, and still there were no children. Last of all, the woman also died. ²³So tell us, whose wife will she be in the resurrection? For all seven were married to her."

²⁴Jesus replied, "Your mistake is that you don't know the Scriptures, and you don't know the power of God. ²⁵For when the dead rise, they will neither marry nor be given in marriage. In this respect they will be like the angels in heaven.

²⁶"But now, as to whether the dead will be raised—haven't you ever read about this in the writings of Moses, in the story of the burning bush? Long after Abraham, Isaac, and Jacob had died, God said to Moses,* 'I am the God of Abraham, the God of Isaac, and the God of Jacob.'* ²⁷So he is the God of the living, not the dead. You have made a serious error."

The Most Important Commandment
²⁸One of the teachers of religious law was standing there listening to the debate. He realized that Jesus had answered well, so he asked, "Of all the commandments, which is the most important?"

²⁹Jesus replied, "The most important commandment is this: 'Listen, O Israel! The LORD our God is the one and only LORD. ³⁰And you must love the LORD your God with all your heart, all your soul, all your mind, and all your strength.'* ³¹The second is equally important: 'Love your neighbor as yourself.'* No other commandment is greater than these."

³²The teacher of religious law replied, "Well said, Teacher. You have spoken the truth by saying that there is only one God and no other.

³³And I know it is important to love him with all my heart and all my understanding and all my strength, and to love my neighbor as myself. This is more important than to offer all of the burnt offerings and sacrifices required in the law."

³⁴Realizing how much the man understood, Jesus said to him, "You are not far from the Kingdom of God." And after that, no one dared to ask him any more questions.

Whose Son Is the Messiah?
³⁵Later, as Jesus was teaching the people in the Temple, he asked, "Why do the teachers of religious law claim that the Messiah is the son of David? ³⁶For David himself, speaking under the inspiration of the Holy Spirit, said,

'The LORD said to my Lord,
Sit in the place of honor at my right hand
until I humble your enemies beneath
your feet.'*

³⁷Since David himself called the Messiah 'my Lord,' how can the Messiah be his son?" The large crowd listened to him with great delight.

³⁸Jesus also taught: "Beware of these teachers of religious law! For they like to parade around in flowing robes and receive respectful greetings as they walk in the marketplaces. ³⁹And how they love the seats of honor in the synagogues and the head table at banquets. ⁴⁰Yet they shamelessly cheat widows out of their property and then pretend to be pious by making long prayers in public. Because of this, they will be more severely punished."

The Widow's Offering
⁴¹Jesus sat down near the collection box in the Temple and watched as the crowds dropped in their money. Many rich people put in large

---

12:26a Greek *in the story of the bush? God said to him.* **12:26b** Exod 3:6. **12:29-30** Deut 6:4-5. **12:31** Lev 19:18. **12:36** Ps 110:1.

amounts. [42] Then a poor widow came and dropped in two small coins.*

[43] Jesus called his disciples to him and said, "I tell you the truth, this poor widow has given more than all the others who are making contributions. [44] For they gave a tiny part of their surplus, but she, poor as she is, has given everything she had to live on."

CHAPTER 13

Jesus Foretells the Future

As Jesus was leaving the Temple that day, one of his disciples said, "Teacher, look at these magnificent buildings! Look at the impressive stones in the walls."

[2] Jesus replied, "Yes, look at these great buildings. But they will be completely demolished. Not one stone will be left on top of another!"

[3] Later, Jesus sat on the Mount of Olives across the valley from the Temple. Peter, James, John, and Andrew came to him privately and asked him, [4] "Tell us, when will all this happen? What sign will show us that these things are about to be fulfilled?"

[5] Jesus replied, "Don't let anyone mislead you, [6] for many will come in my name, claiming, 'I am the Messiah.'* They will deceive many. [7] And you will hear of wars and threats of wars, but don't panic. Yes, these things must take place, but the end won't follow immediately. [8] Nation will go to war against nation, and kingdom against kingdom. There will be earthquakes in many parts of the world, as well as famines. But this is only the first of the birth pains, with more to come.

[9] "When these things begin to happen, watch out! You will be handed over to the local councils and beaten in the synagogues. You will stand trial before governors and kings because you are my followers. But this will be your opportunity to tell them about me.* [10] For the Good News must first be preached to all nations.* [11] But when you are arrested and stand trial, don't worry in advance about what to say. Just say what God tells you at that time, for it is not you who will be speaking, but the Holy Spirit.

[12] "A brother will betray his brother to death, a father will betray his own child, and children will rebel against their parents and cause them to be killed. [13] And everyone will hate you because you are my followers.* But the one who endures to the end will be saved.

[14] "The day is coming when you will see the sacrilegious object that causes desecration*

first steps

HOW MUCH SHOULD YOU GIVE?

Read MARK 12:41-44

Generosity is not measured by the size of the gift itself, but by the motivation. Jesus valued the small offering of this poor widow over the large sums of money from the wealthy people. Jesus knew that she had given all she had and that her heart was in the right place.

David, psalmist and king of Israel, said he would not give to the Lord that which cost him nothing. We are not to give our leftovers to God. Is it too much to ask us to give our best to him since he gave his best to us when he sent us his own Son to die in our place?

Our attitude toward giving should be like that of the believers in Macedonia, who eagerly came to the aid of the church in Jerusalem during its time of need: "For I can testify that they gave not only what they could afford, but far more. And they did it of their own free will. They begged us again and again for the privilege of sharing in the gift for the believers in Jerusalem" (2 Corinthians 8:3-4).

When you consider how much of your income should be spent on God's work, remember this promise from the book of Proverbs: "The generous will prosper; those who refresh others will themselves be refreshed" (Proverbs 11:25).

For the next note on "Give to God," turn to p. 219.

standing where he* should not be." (Reader, pay attention!) "Then those in Judea must flee to the hills. [15] A person out on the deck of a roof must not go down into the house to pack. [16] A person out in the field must not return even to get a coat. [17] How terrible it will be for pregnant women and for nursing mothers in those days. [18] And pray that your flight will not be in winter. [19] For there will be greater anguish in those days than at any time since God created the world. And it will never be so great again. [20] In fact, unless the Lord shortens that time of calamity, not a single person will survive. But for the sake of his chosen ones he has shortened those days.

12:42 Greek *two lepta, which is a kodrantes* [i.e., a quadrans].   13:6 Greek *claiming, 'I am.'*   13:9 Or *But this will be your testimony against them.*   13:10 Or *all peoples.*   13:13 Greek *on account of my name.*   13:14a Greek *the abomination of desolation.* See Dan 9:27; 11:31; 12:11.   13:14b Or *it.*

²¹"Then if anyone tells you, 'Look, here is the Messiah,' or 'There he is,' don't believe it. ²²For false messiahs and false prophets will rise up and perform signs and wonders so as to deceive, if possible, even God's chosen ones. ²³Watch out! I have warned you about this ahead of time!

²⁴"At that time, after the anguish of those days,

the sun will be darkened,
the moon will give no light,
²⁵ the stars will fall from the sky,
and the powers in the heavens will be shaken.*

²⁶Then everyone will see the Son of Man* coming on the clouds with great power and glory.* ²⁷And he will send out his angels to gather his chosen ones from all over the world*—from the farthest ends of the earth and heaven.

²⁸"Now learn a lesson from the fig tree. When its branches bud and its leaves begin to sprout, you know that summer is near. ²⁹In the same way, when you see all these things taking place, you can know that his return is very near, right at the door. ³⁰I tell you the truth, this generation* will not pass from the scene before all these things take place. ³¹Heaven and earth will disappear, but my words will never disappear.

³²"However, no one knows the day or hour when these things will happen, not even the angels in heaven or the Son himself. Only the Father knows. ³³And since you don't know when that time will come, be on guard! Stay alert*!

³⁴"The coming of the Son of Man can be illustrated by the story of a man going on a long trip. When he left home, he gave each of his slaves instructions about the work they were to do, and he told the gatekeeper to watch for his return. ³⁵You, too, must keep watch! For you don't know when the master of the household will return—in the evening, at midnight, before dawn, or at daybreak. ³⁶Don't let him find you sleeping when he arrives without warning. ³⁷I say to you what I say to everyone: Watch for him!"

CHAPTER 14

Jesus Anointed at Bethany

It was now two days before Passover and the Festival of Unleavened Bread. The leading priests and the teachers of religious law were still looking for an opportunity to capture Jesus secretly and kill him. ²"But not during the Passover celebration," they agreed, "or the people may riot."

³Meanwhile, Jesus was in Bethany at the home of Simon, a man who had previously had leprosy. While he was eating,* a woman came in with a beautiful alabaster jar of expensive perfume made from essence of nard. She broke open the jar and poured the perfume over his head.

⁴Some of those at the table were indignant. "Why waste such expensive perfume?" they asked. ⁵"It could have been sold for a year's wages* and the money given to the poor!" So they scolded her harshly.

⁶But Jesus replied, "Leave her alone. Why criticize her for doing such a good thing to me? ⁷You will always have the poor among you, and you can help them whenever you want to. But you will not always have me. ⁸She has done what she could and has anointed my body for burial ahead of time. ⁹I tell you the truth, wherever the Good News is preached throughout the world, this woman's deed will be remembered and discussed."

Judas Agrees to Betray Jesus

¹⁰Then Judas Iscariot, one of the twelve disciples, went to the leading priests to arrange to betray Jesus to them. ¹¹They were delighted when they heard why he had come, and they promised to give him money. So he began looking for an opportunity to betray Jesus.

The Last Supper

¹²On the first day of the Festival of Unleavened Bread, when the Passover lamb is sacrificed, Jesus' disciples asked him, "Where do you want us to go to prepare the Passover meal for you?"

¹³So Jesus sent two of them into Jerusalem with these instructions: "As you go into the city, a man carrying a pitcher of water will meet you. Follow him. ¹⁴At the house he enters, say to the owner, 'The Teacher asks: Where is the guest room where I can eat the Passover meal with my disciples?' ¹⁵He will take you upstairs to a large room that is already set up. That is where you should prepare our meal." ¹⁶So the two disciples went into the city and found everything just as Jesus had said, and they prepared the Passover meal there.

¹⁷In the evening Jesus arrived with the twelve disciples.* ¹⁸As they were at the table* eating, Jesus said, "I tell you the truth, one of you eating with me here will betray me."

¹⁹Greatly distressed, each one asked in turn, "Am I the one?"

13:24-25 See Isa 13:10; 34:4; Joel 2:10.   13:26a "Son of Man" is a title Jesus used for himself.   13:26b See Dan 7:13.   13:27 Greek *from the four winds.*   13:30 Or *this age,* or *this nation.*   13:33 Some manuscripts add *and pray.*   14:3 Or *reclining.*   14:5 Greek *for 300 denarii.* A denarius was equivalent to a laborer's full day's wage.   14:17 Greek *the Twelve.*   14:18 Or *As they reclined.*

²⁰He replied, "It is one of you twelve who is eating from this bowl with me. ²¹For the Son of Man* must die, as the Scriptures declared long ago. But how terrible it will be for the one who betrays him. It would be far better for that man if he had never been born!"

²²As they were eating, Jesus took some bread and blessed it. Then he broke it in pieces and gave it to the disciples, saying, "Take it, for this is my body."

²³And he took a cup of wine and gave thanks to God for it. He gave it to them, and they all drank from it. ²⁴And he said to them, "This is my blood, which confirms the covenant* between God and his people. It is poured out as a sacrifice for many. ²⁵I tell you the truth, I will not drink wine again until the day I drink it new in the Kingdom of God."

²⁶Then they sang a hymn and went out to the Mount of Olives.

Jesus Predicts Peter's Denial

²⁷On the way, Jesus told them, "All of you will desert me. For the Scriptures say,

'God will strike* the Shepherd,
  and the sheep will be scattered.'

²⁸But after I am raised from the dead, I will go ahead of you to Galilee and meet you there."

²⁹Peter said to him, "Even if everyone else deserts you, I never will."

³⁰Jesus replied, "I tell you the truth, Peter—this very night, before the rooster crows twice, you will deny three times that you even know me."

³¹"No!" Peter declared emphatically. "Even if I have to die with you, I will never deny you!" And all the others vowed the same.

Jesus Prays in Gethsemane

³²They went to the olive grove called Gethsemane, and Jesus said, "Sit here while I go and pray." ³³He took Peter, James, and John with him, and he became deeply troubled and distressed. ³⁴He told them, "My soul is crushed with grief to the point of death. Stay here and keep watch with me."

³⁵He went on a little farther and fell to the ground. He prayed that, if it were possible, the awful hour awaiting him might pass him by. ³⁶"Abba, Father,"* he cried out, "everything is possible for you. Please take this cup of suffering away from me. Yet I want your will to be done, not mine."

³⁷Then he returned and found the disciples asleep. He said to Peter, "Simon, are you asleep? Couldn't you watch with me even one hour?

³⁸Keep watch and pray, so that you will not give in to temptation. For the spirit is willing, but the body is weak."

³⁹Then Jesus left them again and prayed the same prayer as before. ⁴⁰When he returned to them again, he found them sleeping, for they couldn't keep their eyes open. And they didn't know what to say.

⁴¹When he returned to them the third time, he said, "Go ahead and sleep. Have your rest. But no—the time has come. The Son of Man is betrayed into the hands of sinners. ⁴²Up, let's be going. Look, my betrayer is here!"

Jesus Is Betrayed and Arrested

⁴³And immediately, even as Jesus said this, Judas, one of the twelve disciples, arrived with a crowd of men armed with swords and clubs. They had been sent by the leading priests, the teachers of religious law, and the elders. ⁴⁴The traitor, Judas, had given them a prearranged signal: "You will know which one to arrest when I greet him with a kiss. Then you can take him away under guard." ⁴⁵As soon as they arrived, Judas walked up to Jesus. "Rabbi!" he exclaimed, and gave him the kiss.

⁴⁶Then the others grabbed Jesus and arrested him. ⁴⁷But one of the men with Jesus pulled out his sword and struck the high priest's slave, slashing off his ear.

⁴⁸Jesus asked them, "Am I some dangerous revolutionary, that you come with swords and clubs to arrest me? ⁴⁹Why didn't you arrest me in the Temple? I was there among you teaching every day. But these things are happening to fulfill what the Scriptures say about me."

⁵⁰Then all his disciples deserted him and ran away. ⁵¹One young man following behind was clothed only in a long linen shirt. When the mob tried to grab him, ⁵²he slipped out of his shirt and ran away naked.

Jesus before the Council

⁵³They took Jesus to the high priest's home where the leading priests, the elders, and the teachers of religious law had gathered. ⁵⁴Meanwhile, Peter followed him at a distance and went right into the high priest's courtyard. There he sat with the guards, warming himself by the fire.

⁵⁵Inside, the leading priests and the entire high council* were trying to find evidence against Jesus, so they could put him to death. But they couldn't find any. ⁵⁶Many false witnesses spoke against him, but they contradicted each other. ⁵⁷Finally, some men stood up and gave this false testimony: ⁵⁸"We heard

14:21 "Son of Man" is a title Jesus used for himself.   14:24 Some manuscripts read *the new covenant.*   14:27 Greek *I will strike.* Zech 13:7.   14:36 *Abba* is an Aramaic term for "father."   14:55 Greek *the Sanhedrin.*

him say, 'I will destroy this Temple made with human hands, and in three days I will build another, made without human hands.' " [59] But even then they didn't get their stories straight!

[60] Then the high priest stood up before the others and asked Jesus, "Well, aren't you going to answer these charges? What do you have to say for yourself?" [61] But Jesus was silent and made no reply. Then the high priest asked him, "Are you the Messiah, the Son of the Blessed One?"

[62] Jesus said, "I Am.* And you will see the Son of Man seated in the place of power at God's right hand* and coming on the clouds of heaven.*"

[63] Then the high priest tore his clothing to show his horror and said, "Why do we need other witnesses? [64] You have all heard his blasphemy. What is your verdict?"

"Guilty!" they all cried. "He deserves to die!"

[65] Then some of them began to spit at him, and they blindfolded him and beat him with their fists. "Prophesy to us," they jeered. And the guards slapped him as they took him away.

Peter Denies Jesus

[66] Meanwhile, Peter was in the courtyard below. One of the servant girls who worked for the high priest came by [67] and noticed Peter warming himself at the fire. She looked at him closely and said, "You were one of those with Jesus of Nazareth.*"

[68] But Peter denied it. "I don't know what you're talking about," he said, and he went out into the entryway. Just then, a rooster crowed.*

[69] When the servant girl saw him standing there, she began telling the others, "This man is definitely one of them!" [70] But Peter denied it again.

A little later some of the other bystanders confronted Peter and said, "You must be one of them, because you are a Galilean."

[71] Peter swore, "A curse on me if I'm lying—I don't know this man you're talking about!" [72] And immediately the rooster crowed the second time.

Suddenly, Jesus' words flashed through Peter's mind: "Before the rooster crows twice, you will deny three times that you even know me." And he broke down and wept.

CHAPTER 15
Jesus' Trial before Pilate

Very early in the morning the leading priests, the elders, and the teachers of religious law—the entire high council*—met to discuss their next step. They bound Jesus, led him away, and took him to Pilate, the Roman governor.

[2] Pilate asked Jesus, "Are you the king of the Jews?"

Jesus replied, "You have said it."

[3] Then the leading priests kept accusing him of many crimes, [4] and Pilate asked him, "Aren't you going to answer them? What about all these charges they are bringing against you?" [5] But Jesus said nothing, much to Pilate's surprise.

[6] Now it was the governor's custom each year during the Passover celebration to release one prisoner—anyone the people requested. [7] One of the prisoners at that time was Barabbas, a revolutionary who had committed murder in an uprising. [8] The crowd went to Pilate and asked him to release a prisoner as usual.

[9] "Would you like me to release to you this 'King of the Jews'?" Pilate asked. [10] (For he realized by now that the leading priests had arrested Jesus out of envy.) [11] But at this point the leading priests stirred up the crowd to demand the release of Barabbas instead of Jesus. [12] Pilate asked them, "Then what should I do with this man you call the king of the Jews?"

[13] They shouted back, "Crucify him!"

[14] "Why?" Pilate demanded. "What crime has he committed?"

But the mob roared even louder, "Crucify him!"

[15] So to pacify the crowd, Pilate released Barabbas to them. He ordered Jesus flogged with a lead-tipped whip, then turned him over to the Roman soldiers to be crucified.

The Soldiers Mock Jesus

[16] The soldiers took Jesus into the courtyard of the governor's headquarters (called the Praetorium) and called out the entire regiment. [17] They dressed him in a purple robe, and they wove thorn branches into a crown and put it on his head. [18] Then they saluted him and taunted, "Hail! King of the Jews!" [19] And they struck him on the head with a reed stick, spit on him, and dropped to their knees in mock worship. [20] When they were finally tired of mocking him, they took off the purple robe and put his own clothes on him again. Then they led him away to be crucified.

The Crucifixion

[21] A passerby named Simon, who was from Cyrene,* was coming in from the countryside just then, and the soldiers forced him to carry Jesus' cross. (Simon was the father of Alexander and

---

14:62a Or *The 'I AM' is here;* or *I am the LORD.* See Exod 3:14.   14:62b Greek *at the right hand of the power.* See Ps 110:1.
14:62c See Dan 7:13.   14:67 Or *Jesus the Nazarene.*   14:68 Some manuscripts do not include *Just then, a rooster crowed.*
15:1 Greek *the Sanhedrin;* also in 15:43.   15:21 *Cyrene* was a city in northern Africa.

Rufus.) ²²And they brought Jesus to a place called Golgotha (which means "Place of the Skull"). ²³They offered him wine drugged with myrrh, but he refused it.

²⁴Then the soldiers nailed him to the cross. They divided his clothes and threw dice* to decide who would get each piece. ²⁵It was nine o'clock in the morning when they crucified him. ²⁶A sign announced the charge against him. It read, "The King of the Jews." ²⁷Two revolutionaries* were crucified with him, one on his right and one on his left.*

²⁹The people passing by shouted abuse, shaking their heads in mockery. "Ha! Look at you now!" they yelled at him. "You said you were going to destroy the Temple and rebuild it in three days. ³⁰Well then, save yourself and come down from the cross!"

³¹The leading priests and teachers of religious law also mocked Jesus. "He saved others," they scoffed, "but he can't save himself! ³²Let this Messiah, this King of Israel, come down from the cross so we can see it and believe him!" Even the men who were crucified with Jesus ridiculed him.

The Death of Jesus

³³At noon, darkness fell across the whole land until three o'clock. ³⁴Then at three o'clock Jesus called out with a loud voice, *"Eloi, Eloi, lema sabachthani?"* which means "My God, my God, why have you abandoned me?"*

³⁵Some of the bystanders misunderstood and thought he was calling for the prophet Elijah. ³⁶One of them ran and filled a sponge with sour wine, holding it up to him on a reed stick so he could drink. "Wait!" he said. "Let's see whether Elijah comes to take him down!"

³⁷Then Jesus uttered another loud cry and breathed his last. ³⁸And the curtain in the sanctuary of the Temple was torn in two, from top to bottom.

³⁹When the Roman officer* who stood facing him* saw how he had died, he exclaimed, "This man truly was the Son of God!"

⁴⁰Some women were there, watching from a distance, including Mary Magdalene, Mary (the mother of James the younger and of Joseph*), and Salome. ⁴¹They had been followers of Jesus and had cared for him while he was in Galilee. Many other women who had come with him to Jerusalem were also there.

The Burial of Jesus

⁴²This all happened on Friday, the day of preparation,* the day before the Sabbath. As evening approached, ⁴³Joseph of Arimathea took a risk and went to Pilate and asked for Jesus' body. (Joseph was an honored member of the high council, and he was waiting for the Kingdom of God to come.) ⁴⁴Pilate couldn't believe that Jesus was already dead, so he called for the Roman officer and asked if he had died yet. ⁴⁵The officer confirmed that Jesus was dead, so Pilate told Joseph he could have the body. ⁴⁶Joseph bought a long sheet of linen cloth. Then he took Jesus' body down from the cross, wrapped it in the cloth, and laid it in a tomb that had been carved out of the rock. Then he rolled a stone in front of the entrance. ⁴⁷Mary Magdalene and Mary the mother of Joseph saw where Jesus' body was laid.

CHAPTER 16

The Resurrection

Saturday evening, when the Sabbath ended, Mary Magdalene, Mary the mother of James, and Salome went out and purchased burial spices so they could anoint Jesus' body. ²Very early on Sunday morning,* just at sunrise, they went to the tomb. ³On the way they were asking each other, "Who will roll away the stone for us from the entrance to the tomb?" ⁴But as they arrived, they looked up and saw that the stone, which was very large, had already been rolled aside.

⁵When they entered the tomb, they saw a young man clothed in a white robe sitting on the right side. The women were shocked, ⁶but the angel said, "Don't be alarmed. You are looking for Jesus of Nazareth,* who was crucified. He isn't here! He is risen from the dead! Look, this is where they laid his body. ⁷Now go and tell his disciples, including Peter, that Jesus is going ahead of you to Galilee. You will see him there, just as he told you before he died."

⁸The women fled from the tomb, trembling and bewildered, and they said nothing to anyone because they were too frightened.*

[Shorter Ending of Mark]

Then they briefly reported all this to Peter and his companions. Afterward Jesus himself sent them out from east to west with the sacred

15:24 Greek *cast lots.* See Ps 22:18.   15:27a Or *Two criminals.*   15:27b Some manuscripts add verse 28, *And the Scripture was fulfilled that said, "He was counted among those who were rebels."* See Isa 53:12; also compare Luke 22:37.   15:34 Ps 22:1.   15:39a Greek *the centurion;* similarly in 15:44, 45.   15:39b Some manuscripts add *heard his cry and.*   15:40 Greek *Joses;* also in 15:47. See Matt 27:56.   15:42 Greek *It was the day of preparation.*   16:2 Greek *on the first day of the week;* also in 16:9.   16:6 Or *Jesus the Nazarene.*   16:8 The most reliable early manuscripts of the Gospel of Mark end at verse 8. Other manuscripts include various endings to the Gospel. A few include both the "shorter ending" and the "longer ending." The majority of manuscripts include the "longer ending" immediately after verse 8.

and unfailing message of salvation that gives eternal life. Amen.

[Longer Ending of Mark]

[9] After Jesus rose from the dead early on Sunday morning, the first person who saw him was Mary Magdalene, the woman from whom he had cast out seven demons. [10] She went to the disciples, who were grieving and weeping, and told them what had happened. [11] But when she told them that Jesus was alive and she had seen him, they didn't believe her.

[12] Afterward he appeared in a different form to two of his followers who were walking from Jerusalem into the country. [13] They rushed back to tell the others, but no one believed them.

[14] Still later he appeared to the eleven disciples as they were eating together. He rebuked them for their stubborn unbelief because they refused to believe those who had seen him after he had been raised from the dead.*

[15] And then he told them, "Go into all the world and preach the Good News to everyone. [16] Anyone who believes and is baptized will be saved. But anyone who refuses to believe will be condemned. [17] These miraculous signs will accompany those who believe: They will cast out demons in my name, and they will speak in new languages.* [18] They will be able to handle snakes with safety, and if they drink anything poisonous, it won't hurt them. They will be able to place their hands on the sick, and they will be healed."

[19] When the Lord Jesus had finished talking with them, he was taken up into heaven and sat down in the place of honor at God's right hand. [20] And the disciples went everywhere and preached, and the Lord worked through them, confirming what they said by many miraculous signs.

16:14 Some early manuscripts add: *And they excused themselves, saying, "This age of lawlessness and unbelief is under Satan, who does not permit God's truth and power to conquer the evil [unclean] spirits. Therefore, reveal your justice now." This is what they said to Christ. And Christ replied to them, "The period of years of Satan's power has been fulfilled, but other dreadful things will happen soon. And I was handed over to death for those who have sinned, so that they may return to the truth and sin no more, and so they may inherit the spiritual, incorruptible, and righteous glory in heaven."* **16:17** Or *new tongues;* some manuscripts do not include *new.*

Luke

AUTHOR: **LUKE** | DATE WRITTEN: **A.D. 60** | GENRE: **GOSPEL**

Luke was a Gentile who put his faith in Jesus Christ. *His purpose for writing an account of Jesus Christ's life, death, and resurrection was to make the message of salvation understandable to those outside the Jewish faith and culture.*

CHAPTER 1

Introduction

Many people have set out to write accounts about the events that have been fulfilled among us. ²They used the eyewitness reports circulating among us from the early disciples.* ³Having carefully investigated everything from the beginning, I also have decided to write a careful account for you, most honorable Theophilus, ⁴so you can be certain of the truth of everything you were taught.

The Birth of John the Baptist Foretold

⁵When Herod was king of Judea, there was a Jewish priest named Zechariah. He was a member of the priestly order of Abijah, and his wife, Elizabeth, was also from the priestly line of Aaron. ⁶Zechariah and Elizabeth were righteous in God's eyes, careful to obey all of the Lord's commandments and regulations. ⁷They had no children because Elizabeth was unable to conceive, and they were both very old.

⁸One day Zechariah was serving God in the Temple, for his order was on duty that week. ⁹As was the custom of the priests, he was chosen by lot to enter the sanctuary of the Lord and burn incense. ¹⁰While the incense was being burned, a great crowd stood outside, praying.

¹¹While Zechariah was in the sanctuary, an angel of the Lord appeared to him, standing to the right of the incense altar. ¹²Zechariah was shaken and overwhelmed with fear when he saw him. ¹³But the angel said, "Don't be afraid, Zechariah! God has heard your prayer. Your wife, Elizabeth, will give you a son, and you are to name him John. ¹⁴You will have great joy and gladness, and many will rejoice at his birth,

¹⁵for he will be great in the eyes of the Lord. He must never touch wine or other alcoholic drinks. He will be filled with the Holy Spirit, even before his birth.* ¹⁶And he will turn many Israelites to the Lord their God. ¹⁷He will be a man with the spirit and power of Elijah. He will prepare the people for the coming of the Lord. He will turn the hearts of the fathers to their children,* and he will cause those who are rebellious to accept the wisdom of the godly."

¹⁸Zechariah said to the angel, "How can I be sure this will happen? I'm an old man now, and my wife is also well along in years."

¹⁹Then the angel said, "I am Gabriel! I stand in the very presence of God. It was he who sent me to bring you this good news! ²⁰But now, since you didn't believe what I said, you will be silent and unable to speak until the child is born. For my words will certainly be fulfilled at the proper time."

²¹Meanwhile, the people were waiting for Zechariah to come out of the sanctuary, wondering why he was taking so long. ²²When he finally did come out, he couldn't speak to them. Then they realized from his gestures and his silence that he must have seen a vision in the sanctuary.

²³When Zechariah's week of service in the Temple was over, he returned home. ²⁴Soon afterward his wife, Elizabeth, became pregnant and went into seclusion for five months. ²⁵"How kind the Lord is!" she exclaimed. "He has taken away my disgrace of having no children."

The Birth of Jesus Foretold

²⁶In the sixth month of Elizabeth's pregnancy, God sent the angel Gabriel to Nazareth, a village in Galilee, ²⁷to a virgin named Mary. She

---

1:2 Greek *from those who from the beginning were servants of the word.* **1:15** Or *even from birth.* **1:17** See Mal 4:5-6.

was engaged to be married to a man named Joseph, a descendant of King David. 28 Gabriel appeared to her and said, "Greetings, favored woman! The Lord is with you!*"

29 Confused and disturbed, Mary tried to think what the angel could mean. 30 "Don't be afraid, Mary," the angel told her, "for you have found favor with God! 31 You will conceive and give birth to a son, and you will name him Jesus. 32 He will be very great and will be called the Son of the Most High. The Lord God will give him the throne of his ancestor David. 33 And he will reign over Israel* forever; his Kingdom will never end!"

34 Mary asked the angel, "But how can this happen? I am a virgin."

35 The angel replied, "The Holy Spirit will come upon you, and the power of the Most High will overshadow you. So the baby to be born will be holy, and he will be called the Son of God. 36 What's more, your relative Elizabeth has become pregnant in her old age! People used to say she was barren, but she has conceived a son and is now in her sixth month. 37 For nothing is impossible with God.*"

38 Mary responded, "I am the Lord's servant. May everything you have said about me come true." And then the angel left her.

Mary Visits Elizabeth

39 A few days later Mary hurried to the hill country of Judea, to the town 40 where Zechariah lived. She entered the house and greeted Elizabeth. 41 At the sound of Mary's greeting, Elizabeth's child leaped within her, and Elizabeth was filled with the Holy Spirit.

42 Elizabeth gave a glad cry and exclaimed to Mary, "God has blessed you above all women, and your child is blessed. 43 Why am I so honored, that the mother of my Lord should visit me? 44 When I heard your greeting, the baby in my womb jumped for joy. 45 You are blessed because you believed that the Lord would do what he said."

The Magnificat: Mary's Song of Praise

46 Mary responded,

"Oh, how my soul praises the Lord.
47   How my spirit rejoices in God my Savior!
48 For he took notice of his lowly servant girl,
      and from now on all generations
         will call me blessed.
49 For the Mighty One is holy,
      and he has done great things for me.
50 He shows mercy from generation to
         generation
      to all who fear him.

51 His mighty arm has done tremendous
         things!
      He has scattered the proud and haughty
         ones.
52 He has brought down princes from their
         thrones
      and exalted the humble.
53 He has filled the hungry with good things
      and sent the rich away with empty hands.
54 He has helped his servant Israel
      and remembered to be merciful.
55 For he made this promise to our ancestors,
      to Abraham and his children forever."

56 Mary stayed with Elizabeth about three months and then went back to her own home.

The Birth of John the Baptist

57 When it was time for Elizabeth's baby to be born, she gave birth to a son. 58 And when her neighbors and relatives heard that the Lord had been very merciful to her, everyone rejoiced with her.

59 When the baby was eight days old, they all came for the circumcision ceremony. They wanted to name him Zechariah, after his father. 60 But Elizabeth said, "No! His name is John!"

61 "What?" they exclaimed. "There is no one in all your family by that name." 62 So they used gestures to ask the baby's father what he wanted to name him. 63 He motioned for a writing tablet, and to everyone's surprise he wrote, "His name is John." 64 Instantly Zechariah could speak again, and he began praising God.

65 Awe fell upon the whole neighborhood, and the news of what had happened spread throughout the Judean hills. 66 Everyone who heard about it reflected on these events and asked, "What will this child turn out to be?" For the hand of the Lord was surely upon him in a special way.

Zechariah's Prophecy

67 Then his father, Zechariah, was filled with the Holy Spirit and gave this prophecy:

68 "Praise the Lord, the God of Israel,
      because he has visited and redeemed his
         people.
69 He has sent us a mighty Savior*
      from the royal line of his servant David,
70 just as he promised
      through his holy prophets long ago.
71 Now we will be saved from our enemies
      and from all who hate us.
72 He has been merciful to our ancestors
      by remembering his sacred
         covenant—

1:28 Some manuscripts add *Blessed are you among women.* **1:33** Greek *over the house of Jacob.* **1:37** Some manuscripts read *For the word of God will never fail.* **1:69** Greek *has raised up a horn of salvation for us.*

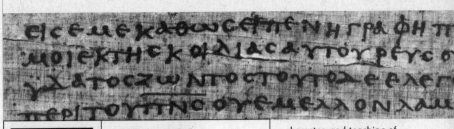

Is the Bible Believable?

Read LUKE 1:1-4

In writing this Gospel, Luke took painstaking efforts to confirm the accuracy of his work. He made it clear that he meticulously put this book together, going so far as to recheck the disciples' accounts "from the beginning."

Although Luke and other writers of the books of the Bible have taken great pains to accurately record the events within, some people have tried to point out contradictions or inconsistencies in the Bible. These same people argue that the Bible is not credible based on what they believe to be contradictions. But here are three reasons why the Bible is believable:

1. God Is the Author. Despite the fact that the Bible was written by more than forty authors, we must recognize one important fact: The people who put the pen to the paper were but instruments in the hand of God. The real

author of the Bible is God. As the apostle Paul wrote, "All Scripture is inspired by God" (2 Timothy 3:16). God chose to speak through these different people much like an artist uses different brushes to paint on a canvas. Each one had his own unique style, but the truth was the same.

2. The Main Story of the Bible Is Too Complex to Be a Hoax. The renowned historian Will Durant, who devoted his life to the study of records of antiquity, made this observation concerning the accounts of Jesus and the early church in Scripture: "That a few simple men should in one generation have invented so powerful and appealing a personality, so lofty an ethic, and so inspiring a vision of human brotherhood, would be a miracle far more incredible than any recorded in the Gospels. After two centuries of Higher Criticism the outlines of life,

character, and teaching of Christ remain reasonably clear, and constitute the most fascinating feature in the history of Western man" [*Caesar and Christ,* in The Story of Civilization, vol. 3 (New York: Simon & Schuster, 1944), p. 557].

3. Scientific Evidence Supports the Bible's Accuracy. Archaeological findings have supported many of the complex historical passages found in the Bible. In addition, the Bible has greater documented accuracy than any other ancient literary work [see Norman L. Geisler & William E. Nix, *A General Introduction to the Bible* (Chicago: Moody Press, Moody Bible Institute, 1986)].

In spite of the evidence, God's Word must be accepted by faith. You, as an individual, must come to recognize that the words of the Lord are perfect, trustworthy, and right (Psalm 19:7-11). Your belief in and practice of the truths found in this book—God's message to us—will make the most profound impact on your life for time and eternity.

For the next "Big Question" note, turn to p. 97.

---

⁷³ the covenant he swore with an oath
    to our ancestor Abraham.
⁷⁴ We have been rescued from our enemies
    so we can serve God without fear,
⁷⁵ in holiness and righteousness
    for as long as we live.
⁷⁶ "And you, my little son,
    will be called the prophet of the
      Most High,

because you will prepare the way
    for the Lord.
⁷⁷ You will tell his people how to
    find salvation
through forgiveness of
    their sins.
⁷⁸ Because of God's tender mercy,
    the morning light from heaven
    is about to break upon us,*

1:78 Or *the Morning Light from Heaven is about to visit us.*

[79] to give light to those who sit in darkness
and in the shadow of death,
and to guide us to the path of peace."

[80] John grew up and became strong in spirit. And he lived in the wilderness until he began his public ministry to Israel.

CHAPTER 2
The Birth of Jesus

At that time the Roman emperor, Augustus, decreed that a census should be taken throughout the Roman Empire. [2] (This was the first census taken when Quirinius was governor of Syria.) [3] All returned to their own ancestral towns to register for this census. [4] And because Joseph was a descendant of King David, he had to go to Bethlehem in Judea, David's ancient home. He traveled there from the village of Nazareth in Galilee. [5] He took with him Mary, his fiancée, who was now obviously pregnant.

[6] And while they were there, the time came for her baby to be born. [7] She gave birth to her first child, a son. She wrapped him snugly in strips of cloth and laid him in a manger, because there was no lodging available for them.

The Shepherds and Angels

[8] That night there were shepherds staying in the fields nearby, guarding their flocks of sheep. [9] Suddenly, an angel of the Lord appeared among them, and the radiance of the Lord's glory surrounded them. They were terrified, [10] but the angel reassured them. "Don't be afraid!" he said. "I bring you good news that will bring great joy to all people. [11] The Savior—yes, the Messiah, the Lord—has been born today in Bethlehem, the city of David! [12] And you will recognize him by this sign: You will find a baby wrapped snugly in strips of cloth, lying in a manger."

[13] Suddenly, the angel was joined by a vast host of others—the armies of heaven—praising God and saying,

[14] "Glory to God in highest heaven,
and peace on earth to those with whom
God is pleased."

[15] When the angels had returned to heaven, the shepherds said to each other, "Let's go to Bethlehem! Let's see this thing that has happened, which the Lord has told us about."

[16] They hurried to the village and found Mary and Joseph. And there was the baby, lying in the manger. [17] After seeing him, the shepherds told everyone what had happened and what the angel had said to them about this child. [18] All who heard the shepherds' story was astonished,

[19] but Mary kept all these things in her heart and thought about them often. [20] The shepherds went back to their flocks, glorifying and praising God for all they had heard and seen. It was just as the angel had told them.

Jesus Is Presented in the Temple

[21] Eight days later, when the baby was circumcised, he was named Jesus, the name given him by the angel even before he was conceived.

[22] Then it was time for their purification offering, as required by the law of Moses after the birth of a child; so his parents took him to Jerusalem to present him to the Lord. [23] The law of the Lord says, "If a woman's first child is a boy, he must be dedicated to the LORD."* [24] So they offered the sacrifice required in the law of the Lord—"either a pair of turtledoves or two young pigeons."*

The Prophecy of Simeon

[25] At that time there was a man in Jerusalem named Simeon. He was righteous and devout and was eagerly waiting for the Messiah to come and rescue Israel. The Holy Spirit was upon him [26] and had revealed to him that he would not die until he had seen the Lord's Messiah. [27] That day the Spirit led him to the Temple. So when Mary and Joseph came to present the baby Jesus to the Lord as the law required, [28] Simeon was there. He took the child in his arms and praised God, saying,

[29] "Sovereign Lord, now let your servant die in peace,
as you have promised.
[30] I have seen your salvation,
[31]   which you have prepared for all people.
[32] He is a light to reveal God to the nations,
and he is the glory of your people Israel!"

[33] Jesus' parents were amazed at what was being said about him. [34] Then Simeon blessed them, and he said to Mary, the baby's mother, "This child is destined to cause many in Israel to fall, but he will be a joy to many others. He has been sent as a sign from God, but many will oppose him. [35] As a result, the deepest thoughts of many hearts will be revealed. And a sword will pierce your very soul."

The Prophecy of Anna

[36] Anna, a prophet, was also there in the Temple. She was the daughter of Phanuel from the tribe of Asher, and she was very old. Her husband died when they had been married only seven years. [37] Then she lived as a widow to the age of eighty-four.* She never left the Temple

---

2:23 Exod 13:2.   2:24 Lev 12:8.   2:37 Or She had been a widow for eighty-four years.

but stayed there day and night, worshiping God with fasting and prayer. ³⁸She came along just as Simeon was talking with Mary and Joseph, and she began praising God. She talked about the child to everyone who had been waiting expectantly for God to rescue Jerusalem.

³⁹When Jesus' parents had fulfilled all the requirements of the law of the Lord, they returned home to Nazareth in Galilee. ⁴⁰There the child grew up healthy and strong. He was filled with wisdom, and God's favor was on him.

Jesus Speaks with the Teachers

⁴¹Every year Jesus' parents went to Jerusalem for the Passover festival. ⁴²When Jesus was twelve years old, they attended the festival as usual. ⁴³After the celebration was over, they started home to Nazareth, but Jesus stayed behind in Jerusalem. His parents didn't miss him at first, ⁴⁴because they assumed he was among the other travelers. But when he didn't show up that evening, they started looking for him among their relatives and friends.

⁴⁵When they couldn't find him, they went back to Jerusalem to search for him there. ⁴⁶Three days later they finally discovered him in the Temple, sitting among the religious teachers, listening to them and asking questions. ⁴⁷All who heard him were amazed at his understanding and his answers.

⁴⁸His parents didn't know what to think. "Son," his mother said to him, "why have you done this to us? Your father and I have been frantic, searching for you everywhere."

⁴⁹"But why did you need to search?" he asked. "Didn't you know that I must be in my Father's house?"* ⁵⁰But they didn't understand what he meant.

⁵¹Then he returned to Nazareth with them and was obedient to them. And his mother stored all these things in her heart.

⁵²Jesus grew in wisdom and in stature and in favor with God and all the people.

CHAPTER 3

John the Baptist Prepares the Way

It was now the fifteenth year of the reign of Tiberius, the Roman emperor. Pontius Pilate was governor over Judea; Herod Antipas was ruler* over Galilee; his brother Philip was ruler* over Iturea and Traconitis; Lysanias was ruler over Abilene. ²Annas and Caiaphas were the high priests. At this time a message from God came to John son of Zechariah, who was living in the wilderness. ³Then John went from place to place on both sides of the Jordan River, preaching that people should be baptized to show that they had repented of their sins and turned to God to be forgiven. ⁴Isaiah had spoken of John when he said,

"He is a voice shouting in the wilderness,
'Prepare the way for the Lord's coming!
    Clear the road for him!
⁵ The valleys will be filled,
    and the mountains and hills made level.
The curves will be straightened,
    and the rough places made smooth.
⁶ And then all people will see
    the salvation sent from God.'"*

⁷When the crowds came to John for baptism, he said, "You brood of snakes! Who warned you to flee God's coming wrath? ⁸Prove by the way you live that you have repented of your sins and turned to God. Don't just say to each other, 'We're safe, for we are descendants of Abraham.' That means nothing, for I tell you, God can create children of Abraham from these very stones. ⁹Even now the ax of God's judgment is poised, ready to sever the roots of the trees. Yes, every tree that does not produce good fruit will be chopped down and thrown into the fire."

¹⁰The crowds asked, "What should we do?"

¹¹John replied, "If you have two shirts, give one to the poor. If you have food, share it with those who are hungry."

¹²Even corrupt tax collectors came to be baptized and asked, "Teacher, what should we do?"

¹³He replied, "Collect no more taxes than the government requires."

¹⁴"What should we do?" asked some soldiers.

John replied, "Don't extort money or make false accusations. And be content with your pay."

¹⁵Everyone was expecting the Messiah to come soon, and they were eager to know whether John might be the Messiah. ¹⁶John answered their questions by saying, "I baptize you with* water; but someone is coming soon who is greater than I am—so much greater that I'm not even worthy to be his slave and untie the straps of his sandals. He will baptize you with the Holy Spirit and with fire.* ¹⁷He is ready to separate the chaff from the wheat with his winnowing fork. Then he will clean up the threshing area, gathering the wheat into his barn but burning the chaff with never-ending fire." ¹⁸John used many such warnings as he announced the Good News to the people.

2:49 Or "Didn't you realize that I should be involved with my Father's affairs?" 3:1a Greek Herod was tetrarch. Herod Antipas was a son of King Herod. 3:1b Greek tetrarch; also in 3:1c. 3:4-6 Isa 40:3-5 (Greek version). 3:16a Or in.
3:16b Or in the Holy Spirit and in fire.

[19]John also publicly criticized Herod Antipas, the ruler of Galilee,* for marrying Herodias, his brother's wife, and for many other wrongs he had done. [20]So Herod put John in prison, adding this sin to his many others.

The Baptism of Jesus

[21]One day when the crowds were being baptized, Jesus himself was baptized. As he was praying, the heavens opened, [22]and the Holy Spirit, in bodily form, descended on him like a dove. And a voice from heaven said, "You are my dearly loved Son, and you bring me great joy.*"

The Ancestors of Jesus

[23]Jesus was about thirty years old when he began his public ministry.

Jesus was known as the son of Joseph.
Joseph was the son of Heli.
[24]Heli was the son of Matthat.
Matthat was the son of Levi.
Levi was the son of Melki.
Melki was the son of Jannai.
Jannai was the son of Joseph.
[25]Joseph was the son of Mattathias.
Mattathias was the son of Amos.
Amos was the son of Nahum.
Nahum was the son of Esli.
Esli was the son of Naggai.
[26]Naggai was the son of Maath.
Maath was the son of Mattathias.
Mattathias was the son of Semein.
Semein was the son of Josech.
Josech was the son of Joda.
[27]Joda was the son of Joanan.
Joanan was the son of Rhesa.
Rhesa was the son of Zerubbabel.
Zerubbabel was the son of Shealtiel.
Shealtiel was the son of Neri.
[28]Neri was the son of Melki.
Melki was the son of Addi.
Addi was the son of Cosam.
Cosam was the son of Elmadam.
Elmadam was the son of Er.
[29]Er was the son of Joshua.
Joshua was the son of Eliezer.
Eliezer was the son of Jorim.
Jorim was the son of Matthat.
Matthat was the son of Levi.
[30]Levi was the son of Simeon.
Simeon was the son of Judah.
Judah was the son of Joseph.
Joseph was the son of Jonam.
Jonam was the son of Eliakim.
[31]Eliakim was the son of Melea.

Melea was the son of Menna.
Menna was the son of Mattatha.
Mattatha was the son of Nathan.
Nathan was the son of David.
[32]David was the son of Jesse.
Jesse was the son of Obed.
Obed was the son of Boaz.
Boaz was the son of Salmon.*
Salmon was the son of Nahshon.
[33]Nahshon was the son of Amminadab.
Amminadab was the son of Admin.
Admin was the son of Arni.*
Arni was the son of Hezron.
Hezron was the son of Perez.
Perez was the son of Judah.
[34]Judah was the son of Jacob.
Jacob was the son of Isaac.
Isaac was the son of Abraham.
Abraham was the son of Terah.
Terah was the son of Nahor.
[35]Nahor was the son of Serug.
Serug was the son of Reu.
Reu was the son of Peleg.
Peleg was the son of Eber.
Eber was the son of Shelah.
[36]Shelah was the son of Cainan.
Cainan was the son of Arphaxad.
Arphaxad was the son of Shem.
Shem was the son of Noah.
Noah was the son of Lamech.
[37]Lamech was the son of Methuselah.
Methuselah was the son of Enoch.
Enoch was the son of Jared.
Jared was the son of Mahalalel.
Mahalalel was the son of Kenan.
[38]Kenan was the son of Enosh.*
Enosh was the son of Seth.
Seth was the son of Adam.
Adam was the son of God.

CHAPTER **4**

The Temptation of Jesus

Then Jesus, full of the Holy Spirit, returned from the Jordan River. He was led by the Spirit in the wilderness,* [2]where he was tempted by the devil for forty days. Jesus ate nothing all that time and became very hungry.

[3]Then the devil said to him, "If you are the Son of God, tell this stone to become a loaf of bread."

[4]But Jesus told him, "No! The Scriptures say, 'People do not live by bread alone.'*"

[5]Then the devil took him up and revealed to him all the kingdoms of the world in a moment of time. [6]"I will give you the glory of these kingdoms and authority over them," the devil said,

3:19 Greek Herod the tetrarch.   3:22 Some manuscripts read my Son, and today I have become your Father.   3:32 Greek Sala, a variant spelling of Salmon; also in 3:32b. See Ruth 4:20.   3:33 Some manuscripts read Amminadab was the son of Aram. Arni and Aram are alternate spellings of Ram. See 1 Chr 2:9-10.   3:38 Greek Enos, a variant spelling of Enosh; also in 3:38b. See Gen 5:6.   4:1 Some manuscripts read into the wilderness.   4:4 Deut 8:3.

"because they are mine to give to anyone I please. [7] I will give it all to you if you will worship me."

[8] Jesus replied, "The Scriptures say,

'You must worship the Lord your God
and serve only him.'* "

[9] Then the devil took him to Jerusalem, to the highest point of the Temple, and said, "If you are the Son of God, jump off! [10] For the Scriptures say,

'He will order his angels to protect and
guard you.
[11] And they will hold you up with their hands
so you won't even hurt your foot on a
stone.'*"

[12] Jesus responded, "The Scriptures also say, 'You must not test the Lord your God.'* "

[13] When the devil had finished tempting Jesus, he left him until the next opportunity came.

Jesus Rejected at Nazareth

[14] Then Jesus returned to Galilee, filled with the Holy Spirit's power. Reports about him spread quickly through the whole region. [15] He taught regularly in their synagogues and was praised by everyone.

[16] When he came to the village of Nazareth, his boyhood home, he went as usual to the synagogue on the Sabbath and stood up to read the Scriptures. [17] The scroll of Isaiah the prophet was handed to him. He unrolled the scroll and found the place where this was written:

[18] "The Spirit of the Lord is upon me,
for he has anointed me to bring
Good News to the poor.
He has sent me to proclaim that
captives will be released,
that the blind will see,
that the oppressed will be set free,
[19] and that the time of the Lord's
favor has come.*"

[20] He rolled up the scroll, handed it back to the attendant, and sat down. All eyes in the synagogue looked at him intently. [21] Then he began to speak to them. "The Scripture you've just heard has been fulfilled this very day!"

[22] Everyone spoke well of him and was amazed by the gracious words that came from his lips. "How can this be?" they asked. "Isn't this Joseph's son?"

[23] Then he said, "You will undoubtedly quote me this proverb: 'Physician, heal yourself'—meaning, 'Do miracles here in your hometown like those you did in Capernaum.' [24] But I tell you the truth, no prophet is accepted in his own hometown.

[25] "Certainly there were many needy widows in Israel in Elijah's time, when the heavens were closed for three and a half years, and a severe famine devastated the land. [26] Yet Elijah was not sent to any of them. He was sent instead to a foreigner—a widow of Zarephath in the land of Sidon. [27] And there were many lepers in Israel in the time of the prophet Elisha, but the only one healed was Naaman, a Syrian."

[28] When they heard this, the people in the synagogue were furious. [29] Jumping up, they mobbed him and forced him to the edge of the hill on which the town was built. They intended to push him over the cliff, [30] but he passed right through the crowd and went on his way.

Jesus Casts Out a Demon

[31] Then Jesus went to Capernaum, a town in Galilee, and taught there in the synagogue every Sabbath day. [32] There, too, the people were amazed at his teaching, for he spoke with authority.

[33] Once when he was in the synagogue, a man possessed by a demon—an evil* spirit—began shouting at Jesus, [34] "Go away! Why are you interfering with us, Jesus of Nazareth? Have you come to destroy us? I know who you are—the Holy One of God!"

[35] Jesus cut him short. "Be quiet! Come out of the man," he ordered. At that, the demon threw the man to the floor as the crowd watched; then it came out of him without hurting him further.

[36] Amazed, the people exclaimed, "What authority and power this man's words possess! Even evil spirits obey him, and they flee at his command!" [37] The news about Jesus spread through every village in the entire region.

Jesus Heals Many People

[38] After leaving the synagogue that day, Jesus went to Simon's home, where he found Simon's mother-in-law very sick with a high fever. "Please heal her," everyone begged. [39] Standing at her bedside, he rebuked the fever, and it left her. And she got up at once and prepared a meal for them.

[40] As the sun went down that evening, people throughout the village brought sick family members to Jesus. No matter what their diseases were, the touch of his hand healed every one. [41] Many were possessed by demons; and the demons came out at his command, shouting,

---

4:8 Deut 6:13.   **4:10-11** Ps 91:11-12.   **4:12** Deut 6:16.   **4:18-19** Or and to proclaim the acceptable year of the Lord. Isa 61:1-2 (Greek version); 58:6.   **4:33** Greek unclean; also in 4:36.

cornerstones

JESUS HAD A SPECIFIC MISSION TO ACCOMPLISH
Read LUKE 4:16-21

When Jesus returned to his hometown of Nazareth, he quoted Isaiah 61:1-2 to describe the purpose of his ministry. There are five goals of Jesus' personal ministry on earth that can be gleaned from this passage:

1. Preach the Good News to the Poor. Jesus ministered to people from all walks of life—from the wealthy tax collectors, to the blue collar fishermen, to the beggars on the street. People's financial status didn't concern him. Rather, he looked beyond people's outward need to their inward need—the poverty of their soul. And to those who will listen, Jesus offers the good news of the gospel.

2. Heal the Brokenhearted. When your heart is broken, you may feel as though no one understands or cares. But Jesus understands. He knows what it is like to be abandoned by friends and has experienced being let down. He understands the sting of death. For that reason, he wants to heal your broken heart.

3. Bring Deliverance to the Captives. The Bible teaches that before we give our lives to God, we are held captive by sin. Jesus wants to release you from the spiritual bondage of our vices and sins. Just admit your sinful condition and turn from it, and ask God to give you a new heart. Then yield yourself to the help and power of the Holy Spirit, and you will know true freedom.

4. Give Sight to the Blind. The Bible also teaches that before we give our lives to Jesus Christ, we are spiritually blind: "Satan, who is the god of this world, has blinded the minds of those who don't believe. They are unable to see the glorious light of the Good News. They don't understand this message about the glory of Christ, who is the exact likeness of God" (2 Corinthians 4:4). Jesus wants to open our eyes so that we can understand and respond to the gospel message.

5. Bring Liberty to the Oppressed. The word *downtrodden* can also be translated "those who are crushed with life." Jesus understands your worries and hurts, and he wants to lift those burdens from your shoulders.

For the next note on "Who Is Jesus?" turn to p. 134.

"You are the Son of God!" But because they knew he was the Messiah, he rebuked them and refused to let them speak.

Jesus Continues to Preach
[42] Early the next morning Jesus went out to an isolated place. The crowds searched everywhere for him, and when they finally found him, they begged him not to leave them. [43] But he replied, "I must preach the Good News of the Kingdom of God in other towns, too, because that is why I was sent." [44] So he continued to travel around, preaching in synagogues throughout Judea.*

CHAPTER **5**
The First Disciples
One day as Jesus was preaching on the shore of the Sea of Galilee,* great crowds pressed in on him to listen to the word of God. [2] He noticed two empty boats at the water's edge, for the fishermen had left them and were washing their nets. [3] Stepping into one of the boats, Jesus asked Simon,* its owner, to push it out into the water. So he sat in the boat and taught the crowds from there.

[4] When he had finished speaking, he said to Simon, "Now go out where it is deeper, and let down your nets to catch some fish."

[5] "Master," Simon replied, "we worked hard all last night and didn't catch a thing. But if you say so, I'll let the nets down again." [6] And this time their nets were so full of fish they began to tear! [7] A shout for help brought their partners in the other boat, and soon both boats were filled with fish and on the verge of sinking.

[8] When Simon Peter realized what had happened, he fell to his knees before Jesus and

4:44 Some manuscripts read *Galilee.*   **5:1** Greek *Lake Gennesaret,* another name for the Sea of Galilee.   **5:3** *Simon* is called "Peter" in 6:14 and thereafter.

said, "Oh, Lord, please leave me—I'm too much of a sinner to be around you." [9]For he was awe-struck by the number of fish they had caught, as were the others with him. [10]His partners, James and John, the sons of Zebedee, were also amazed.

Jesus replied to Simon, "Don't be afraid! From now on you'll be fishing for people!" [11]And as soon as they landed, they left every-thing and followed Jesus.

Jesus Heals a Man with Leprosy

[12]In one of the villages, Jesus met a man with an advanced case of leprosy. When the man saw Jesus, he bowed with his face to the ground, begging to be healed. "Lord," he said, "if you are willing, you can heal me and make me clean."

[13]Jesus reached out and touched him. "I am willing," he said. "Be healed!" And instantly the leprosy disappeared. [14]Then Jesus instructed him not to tell anyone what had happened. He said, "Go to the priest and let him examine you. Take along the offering required in the law of Moses for those who have been healed of lep-rosy.* This will be a public testimony that you have been cleansed."

[15]But despite Jesus' instructions, the report of his power spread even faster, and vast crowds came to hear him preach and to be healed of their diseases. [16]But Jesus often with-drew to the wilderness for prayer.

Jesus Heals a Paralyzed Man

[17]One day while Jesus was teaching, some Pharisees and teachers of religious law were sitting nearby. (It seemed that these men showed up from every village in all Galilee and Judea, as well as from Jerusalem.) And the Lord's healing power was strongly with Jesus.

[18]Some men came carrying a paralyzed man on a sleeping mat. They tried to take him inside to Jesus, [19]but they couldn't reach him because of the crowd. So they went up to the roof and took off some tiles. Then they lowered the sick man on his mat down into the crowd, right in front of Jesus. [20]Seeing their faith, Jesus said to the man, "Young man, your sins are forgiven."

[21]But the Pharisees and teachers of religious law said to themselves, "Who does he think he is? That's blasphemy! Only God can forgive sins!"

[22]Jesus knew what they were thinking, so he asked them, "Why do you question this in your hearts? [23]Is it easier to say 'Your sins are for-given,' or 'Stand up and walk'? [24]So I will prove to you that the Son of Man* has the authority on earth to forgive sins." Then Jesus turned to the paralyzed man and said, "Stand up, pick up your mat, and go home!"

[25]And immediately, as everyone watched, the man jumped up, picked up his mat, and went home praising God. [26]Everyone was gripped with great wonder and awe, and they praised God, exclaiming, "We have seen amaz-ing things today!"

Jesus Calls Levi (Matthew)

[27]Later, as Jesus left the town, he saw a tax col-lector named Levi sitting at his tax collector's booth. "Follow me and be my disciple," Jesus said to him. [28]So Levi got up, left everything, and followed him.

[29]Later, Levi held a banquet in his home with Jesus as the guest of honor. Many of Levi's fel-low tax collectors and other guests also ate with them. [30]But the Pharisees and their teach-ers of religious law complained bitterly to Jesus' disciples, "Why do you eat and drink with such scum?*"

[31]Jesus answered them, "Healthy people don't need a doctor—sick people do. [32]I have come to call not those who think they are righ-teous, but those who know they are sinners and need to repent."

A Discussion about Fasting

[33]One day some people said to Jesus, "John the Baptist's disciples fast and pray regularly, and so do the disciples of the Pharisees. Why are your disciples always eating and drinking?"

[34]Jesus responded, "Do wedding guests fast while celebrating with the groom? Of course not. [35]But someday the groom will be taken away from them, and then they will fast."

[36]Then Jesus gave them this illustration: "No one tears a piece of cloth from a new garment and uses it to patch an old garment. For then the new garment would be ruined, and the new patch wouldn't even match the old garment.

[37]"And no one puts new wine into old wine-skins. For the new wine would burst the wine-skins, spilling the wine and ruining the skins. [38]New wine must be stored in new wineskins. [39]But no one who drinks the old wine seems to want the new wine. 'The old is just fine,' they say."

CHAPTER 6

A Discussion about the Sabbath

One Sabbath day as Jesus was walking through some grainfields, his disciples broke off heads of grain, rubbed off the husks in their hands, and ate the grain. [2]But some Pharisees said, "Why are you breaking the law by harvesting grain on the Sabbath?"

5:14 See Lev 14:2-32.   **5:24** "Son of Man" is a title Jesus used for himself.   **5:30** Greek *with tax collectors and sinners?*

³Jesus replied, "Haven't you read in the Scriptures what David did when he and his companions were hungry? ⁴He went into the house of God and broke the law by eating the sacred loaves of bread that only the priests can eat. He also gave some to his companions." ⁵And Jesus added, "The Son of Man* is Lord, even over the Sabbath."

Jesus Heals on the Sabbath

⁶On another Sabbath day, a man with a deformed right hand was in the synagogue while Jesus was teaching. ⁷The teachers of religious law and the Pharisees watched Jesus closely. If he healed the man's hand, they planned to accuse him of working on the Sabbath.

⁸But Jesus knew their thoughts. He said to the man with the deformed hand, "Come and stand in front of everyone." So the man came forward. ⁹Then Jesus said to his critics, "I have a question for you. Does the law permit good deeds on the Sabbath, or is it a day for doing evil? Is this a day to save life or to destroy it?"

¹⁰He looked around at them one by one and then said to the man, "Hold out your hand." So the man held out his hand, and it was restored! ¹¹At this, the enemies of Jesus were wild with rage and began to discuss what to do with him.

Jesus Chooses the Twelve Apostles

¹²One day soon afterward Jesus went up on a mountain to pray, and he prayed to God all night. ¹³At daybreak he called together all of his disciples and chose twelve of them to be apostles. Here are their names:

¹⁴ Simon (whom he named Peter),
   Andrew (Peter's brother),
   James,
   John,
   Philip,
   Bartholomew,
¹⁵ Matthew,
   Thomas,
   James (son of Alphaeus),
   Simon (who was called the zealot),
¹⁶ Judas (son of James),
   Judas Iscariot (who later betrayed him).

Crowds Follow Jesus

¹⁷When they came down from the mountain, the disciples stood with Jesus on a large, level area, surrounded by many of his followers and by the crowds. There were people from all over Judea and from Jerusalem and from as far north as the seacoasts of Tyre and Sidon. ¹⁸They had come to hear him and to be healed of their diseases; and those troubled by evil*

spirits were healed. ¹⁹Everyone tried to touch him, because healing power went out from him, and he healed everyone.

The Beatitudes

²⁰Then Jesus turned to his disciples and said,

"God blesses you who are poor,
   for the Kingdom of God is yours.
²¹ God blesses you who are hungry now,
   for you will be satisfied.
God blesses you who weep now,
   for in due time you will laugh.

²²What blessings await you when people hate you and exclude you and mock you and curse you as evil because you follow the Son of Man. ²³When that happens, be happy! Yes, leap for joy! For a great reward awaits you in heaven. And remember, their ancestors treated the ancient prophets that same way.

Sorrows Foretold

²⁴ "What sorrow awaits you who are rich,
   for you have your only happiness now.
²⁵ What sorrow awaits you who are fat and
      prosperous now,
   for a time of awful hunger awaits you.
What sorrow awaits you who laugh now,
   for your laughing will turn to mourning
      and sorrow.
²⁶ What sorrow awaits you who are praised by
      the crowds,
   for their ancestors also praised false
      prophets.

Love for Enemies

²⁷"But to you who are willing to listen, I say, love your enemies! Do good to those who hate you. ²⁸Bless those who curse you. Pray for those who hurt you. ²⁹If someone slaps you on one cheek, offer the other cheek also. If someone demands your coat, offer your shirt also. ³⁰Give to anyone who asks; and when things are taken away from you, don't try to get them back. ³¹Do to others as you would like them to do to you.

³²"If you love only those who love you, why should you get credit for that? Even sinners love those who love them! ³³And if you do good only to those who do good to you, why should you get credit? Even sinners do that much! ³⁴And if you lend money only to those who can repay you, why should you get credit? Even sinners will lend to other sinners for a full return.

³⁵"Love your enemies! Do good to them. Lend to them without expecting to be repaid. Then your reward from heaven will be very great, and you will truly be acting as children of the Most High, for he is kind to those who are unthankful

and wicked. [36] You must be compassionate, just as your Father is compassionate.

Do Not Judge Others

[37] "Do not judge others, and you will not be judged. Do not condemn others, or it will all come back against you. Forgive others, and you will be forgiven. [38] Give, and you will receive. Your gift will return to you in full—pressed down, shaken together to make room for more, running over, and poured into your lap. The amount you give will determine the amount you get back.*"

[39] Then Jesus gave the following illustration: "Can one blind person lead another? Won't they both fall into a ditch? [40] Students* are not greater than their teacher. But the student who is fully trained will become like the teacher.

[41] "And why worry about a speck in your friend's eye* when you have a log in your own? [42] How can you think of saying, 'Friend,* let me help you get rid of that speck in your eye,' when you can't see past the log in your own eye? Hypocrite! First get rid of the log in your own eye; then you will see well enough to deal with the speck in your friend's eye.

The Tree and Its Fruit

[43] "A good tree can't produce bad fruit, and a bad tree can't produce good fruit. [44] A tree is identified by its fruit. Figs are never gathered from thornbushes, and grapes are not picked from bramble bushes. [45] A good person produces good things from the treasury of a good heart, and an evil person produces evil things from the treasury of an evil heart. What you say flows from what is in your heart.

Building on a Solid Foundation

[46] "So why do you keep calling me 'Lord, Lord!' when you don't do what I say? [47] I will show you what it's like when someone comes to me, listens to my teaching, and then follows it. [48] It is like a person building a house who digs deep and lays the foundation on solid rock. When the floodwaters rise and break against that house, it stands firm because it is well built. [49] But anyone who hears and doesn't obey is like a person who builds a house without a foundation. When the floods sweep down against that house, it will collapse into a heap of ruins."

CHAPTER 7

The Faith of a Roman Officer

When Jesus had finished saying all this to the people, he returned to Capernaum. [2] At that time the highly valued slave of a Roman officer* was sick and near death. [3] When the officer heard about Jesus, he sent some respected Jewish elders to ask him to come and heal his slave. [4] So they earnestly begged Jesus to help the man. "If anyone deserves your help, he does," they said, [5] "for he loves the Jewish people and even built a synagogue for us."

[6] So Jesus went with them. But just before they arrived at the house, the officer sent some friends to say, "Lord, don't trouble yourself by coming to my home, for I am not worthy of such an honor. [7] I am not even worthy to come and meet you. Just say the word from where you are, and my servant will be healed. [8] I know this because I am under the authority of my superior officers, and I have authority over my soldiers. I only need to say, 'Go,' and they go, or 'Come,' and they come. And if I say to my slaves, 'Do this,' they do it."

[9] When Jesus heard this, he was amazed. Turning to the crowd that was following him, he said, "I tell you, I haven't seen faith like this in all Israel!" [10] And when the officer's friends returned to his house, they found the slave completely healed.

Jesus Raises a Widow's Son

[11] Soon afterward Jesus went with his disciples to the village of Nain, and a large crowd followed him. [12] A funeral procession was coming out as he approached the village gate. The young man who had died was a widow's only son, and a large crowd from the village was with her. [13] When the Lord saw her, his heart overflowed with compassion. "Don't cry!" he said. [14] Then he walked over to the coffin and touched it, and the bearers stopped. "Young man," he said, "I tell you, get up." [15] Then the dead boy sat up and began to talk! And Jesus gave him back to his mother.

[16] Great fear swept the crowd, and they praised God, saying, "A mighty prophet has risen among us," and "God has visited his people today." [17] And the news about Jesus spread throughout Judea and the surrounding countryside.

Jesus and John the Baptist

[18] The disciples of John the Baptist told John about everything Jesus was doing. So John called for two of his disciples, [19] and he sent them to the Lord to ask him, "Are you the Messiah we've been expecting,* or should we keep looking for someone else?"

[20] John's two disciples found Jesus and said

6:38 Or *The measure you give will be the measure you get back.*   **6:40** Or *Disciples.*   **6:41** Greek *your brother's eye;* also in 6:42.   **6:42** Greek *Brother.*   **7:2** Greek *a centurion;* similarly in 7:6.   **7:19** Greek *Are you the one who is coming?* Also in 7:20.

to him, "John the Baptist sent us to ask, 'Are you the Messiah we've been expecting, or should we keep looking for someone else?'"

²¹At that very time, Jesus cured many people of their diseases, illnesses, and evil spirits, and he restored sight to many who were blind. ²²Then he told John's disciples, "Go back to John and tell him what you have seen and heard—the blind see, the lame walk, the lepers are cured, the deaf hear, the dead are raised to life, and the Good News is being preached to the poor. ²³And tell him, 'God blesses those who do not turn away because of me.*'"

²⁴After John's disciples left, Jesus began talking about him to the crowds. "What kind of man did you go into the wilderness to see? Was he a weak reed, swayed by every breath of wind? ²⁵Or were you expecting to see a man dressed in expensive clothes? No, people who wear beautiful clothes and live in luxury are found in palaces. ²⁶Were you looking for a prophet? Yes, and he is more than a prophet. ²⁷John is the man to whom the Scriptures refer when they say,

'Look, I am sending my messenger
    ahead of you,
and he will prepare your way
    before you.'*

²⁸I tell you, of all who have ever lived, none is greater than John. Yet even the least person in the Kingdom of God is greater than he is!"

²⁹When they heard this, all the people—even the tax collectors—agreed that God's way was right,* for they had been baptized by John. ³⁰But the Pharisees and experts in religious law rejected God's plan for them, for they had refused John's baptism.

³¹"To what can I compare the people of this generation?" Jesus asked. "How can I describe them? ³²They are like children playing a game in the public square. They complain to their friends,

'We played wedding songs,
    and you didn't dance,
so we played funeral songs,
    and you didn't weep.'

³³For John the Baptist didn't spend his time eating bread or drinking wine, and you say, 'He's possessed by a demon.' ³⁴The Son of Man,* on the other hand, feasts and drinks, and you say, 'He's a glutton and a drunkard, and a friend of tax collectors and other sinners!' ³⁵But wisdom is shown to be right by the lives of those who follow it.*"

Jesus Anointed by a Sinful Woman

³⁶One of the Pharisees asked Jesus to have dinner with him, so Jesus went to his home and sat down to eat.* ³⁷When a certain immoral woman from that city heard he was eating there, she brought a beautiful alabaster jar filled with expensive perfume. ³⁸Then she knelt behind him at his feet, weeping. Her tears fell on his feet, and she wiped them off with her hair. Then she kept kissing his feet and putting perfume on them.

³⁹When the Pharisee who had invited him saw this, he said to himself, "If this man were a prophet, he would know what kind of woman is touching him. She's a sinner!"

⁴⁰Then Jesus answered his thoughts. "Simon," he said to the Pharisee, "I have something to say to you."

"Go ahead, Teacher," Simon replied.

⁴¹Then Jesus told him this story: "A man loaned money to two people—500 pieces of silver* to one and 50 pieces to the other. ⁴²But neither of them could repay him, so he kindly forgave them both, canceling their debts. Who do you suppose loved him more after that?"

⁴³Simon answered, "I suppose the one for whom he canceled the larger debt."

"That's right," Jesus said. ⁴⁴Then he turned to the woman and said to Simon, "Look at this woman kneeling here. When I entered your home, you didn't offer me water to wash the dust from my feet, but she has washed them with her tears and wiped them with her hair. ⁴⁵You didn't greet me with a kiss, but from the time I first came in, she has not stopped kissing my feet. ⁴⁶You neglected the courtesy of olive oil to anoint my head, but she has anointed my feet with rare perfume.

⁴⁷"I tell you, her sins—and they are many—have been forgiven, so she has shown me much love. But a person who is forgiven little shows only little love." ⁴⁸Then Jesus said to the woman, "Your sins are forgiven."

⁴⁹The men at the table said among themselves, "Who is this man, that he goes around forgiving sins?"

⁵⁰And Jesus said to the woman, "Your faith has saved you; go in peace."

CHAPTER 8

Women Who Followed Jesus

Soon afterward Jesus began a tour of the nearby towns and villages, preaching and announcing the Good News about the Kingdom of God. He took his twelve disciples with him, ²along with some women who had been cured

---

7:23 Or who are not offended by me.　7:27 Mal 3:1.　7:29 Or praised God for his justice.　7:34 "Son of Man" is a title Jesus used for himself.　7:35 Or But wisdom is justified by all her children.　7:36 Or and reclined.　7:41 Greek 500 denarii. A denarius was equivalent to a laborer's full day's wage.

of evil spirits and diseases. Among them were Mary Magdalene, from whom he had cast out seven demons; [3] Joanna, the wife of Chuza, Herod's business manager; Susanna; and many others who were contributing from their own resources to support Jesus and his disciples.

Parable of the Farmer Scattering Seed

[4] One day Jesus told a story in the form of a parable to a large crowd that had gathered from many towns to hear him: [5] "A farmer went out to plant his seed. As he scattered it across his field, some seed fell on a footpath, where it was stepped on, and the birds ate it. [6] Other seed fell among rocks. It began to grow, but the plant soon wilted and died for lack of moisture. [7] Other seed fell among thorns that grew up with it and choked out the tender plants. [8] Still other seed fell on fertile soil. This seed grew and produced a crop that was a hundred times as much as had been planted!" When he had said this, he called out, "Anyone with ears to hear should listen and understand."

[9] His disciples asked him what this parable meant. [10] He replied, "You are permitted to understand the secrets* of the Kingdom of God. But I use parables to teach the others so that the Scriptures might be fulfilled:

'When they look, they won't really see.
    When they hear, they won't
        understand.'*

[11] "This is the meaning of the parable: The seed is God's word. [12] The seeds that fell on the footpath represent those who hear the message, only to have the devil come and take it away from their hearts and prevent them from believing and being saved. [13] The seeds on the rocky soil represent those who hear the message and receive it with joy. But since they don't have deep roots, they believe for a while, then they fall away when they face temptation. [14] The seeds that fell among the thorns represent those who hear the message, but all too quickly the message is crowded out by the cares and riches and pleasures of this life. And so they never grow into maturity. [15] And the seeds that fell on the good soil represent honest, good-hearted people who hear God's word, cling to it, and patiently produce a huge harvest.

Parable of the Lamp

[16] "No one lights a lamp and then covers it with a bowl or hides it under a bed. A lamp is placed on a stand, where its light can be seen by all who enter the house. [17] For all that is secret will eventually be brought into the open, and every-

---

first steps

TRIALS TEST OUR FOUNDATION
Read LUKE 6:47-49

From all outward appearances, these homes probably looked alike. They may have even had similar floor plans. The only thing that set them apart was their foundation, which became apparent when the storm hit. In the same way, when the storms of life hit us, the true foundation of our lives will be revealed. Upon which foundation have you built your life?

The Faulty (or Nonexistent) Foundation. The person who builds upon this foundation is known as a "hearer." This individual may be quick to read, listen, or talk about what Jesus has to say in his Word but will fail to apply those teachings to his or her own life. When the storms of life come, this person will be spiritually weakened and will likely give up on his or her faith because he or she does not have a good foothold.

The Rock-Solid Foundation. The person who builds upon this foundation is known as a "doer." This individual not only listens to Jesus' teachings, but follows them in his or her day-to-day life. This person will be able to withstand even the most devastating tempest, because he or she is grounded in the teachings of the Lord.

If you find yourself on the faulty foundation, you still have time to remodel. But you are the only architect who can make that change.

For the next note on "Have Courage in Trials," turn to p. 43.

---

thing that is concealed will be brought to light and made known to all.

[18] "So pay attention to how you hear. To those who listen to my teaching, more understanding will be given. But for those who are not listening, even what they think they understand will be taken away from them."

The True Family of Jesus

[19] Then Jesus' mother and brothers came to see him, but they couldn't get to him because of the crowd. [20] Someone told Jesus, "Your mother

cornerstones
PERSEVERANCE PRODUCES RESULTS
Read LUKE 8:15

In Luke 8:4-8, Jesus tells a large crowd the well-known parable of the sower to illustrate four different reactions to his message.

The seed that falls on the footpath represents those who hear the gospel, but who do not allow it to penetrate their hearts and minds (verse 12). The seed that lands on the rocky soil represents those who hear God's Word and receive it with joy, but over time their commitment is shown to be shallow and superficial (verse 13). The seed that lands among the thorns represents those who appear to believe, but who let the cares of this life slowly choke out any growth (verse 14). The seed that falls on the fertile soil is the seed that actually takes root to produce spiritual fruit.

What is the difference between this group of individuals and the rest? The key to their success can be broken down into three steps: (1) They *listen* to God's Word; (2) they *obey* God's Word; and (3) they *persevere* to "produce a huge harvest."

Describing their perseverance in the faith, Jesus uses the Greek word *hupomone*, which means "a patient enduring." It is this perseverance that produces spiritual fruit—new believers.

By letting God's Word take root in your heart and life, you will not only grow stronger and be able to withstand the storms of life, but your life will help to draw many others to the Lord Jesus Christ.

For the next note on "Perseverance," turn to p. 290.

and your brothers are outside, and they want to see you."

²¹ Jesus replied, "My mother and my brothers are all those who hear God's word and obey it."

Jesus Calms the Storm

²² One day Jesus said to his disciples, "Let's cross to the other side of the lake." So they got into a boat and started out. ²³ As they sailed across, Jesus settled down for a nap. But soon a fierce storm came down on the lake. The boat was filling with water, and they were in real danger.

²⁴ The disciples went and woke him up, shouting, "Master, Master, we're going to drown!"

When Jesus woke up, he rebuked the wind and the raging waves. Suddenly the storm stopped and all was calm. ²⁵ Then he asked them, "Where is your faith?"

The disciples were terrified and amazed. "Who is this man?" they asked each other. "When he gives a command, even the wind and waves obey him!"

Jesus Heals a Demon-Possessed Man

²⁶ So they arrived in the region of the Gerasenes,* across the lake from Galilee. ²⁷ As Jesus was climbing out of the boat, a man who was possessed by demons came out to meet him. For a long time he had been homeless and naked, living in a cemetery outside the town.

²⁸ As soon as he saw Jesus, he shrieked and fell down in front of him. Then he screamed, "Why are you interfering with me, Jesus, Son of the Most High God? Please, I beg you, don't torture me!" ²⁹ For Jesus had already commanded the evil* spirit to come out of him. This spirit had often taken control of the man. Even when he was placed under guard and put in chains and shackles, he simply broke them and rushed out into the wilderness, completely under the demon's power.

³⁰ Jesus demanded, "What is your name?"

"Legion," he replied, for he was filled with many demons. ³¹ The demons kept begging Jesus not to send them into the bottomless pit.*

³² There happened to be a large herd of pigs feeding on the hillside nearby, and the demons begged him to let them enter into the pigs. So Jesus gave them permission. ³³ Then the demons came out of the man and entered the pigs, and the entire herd plunged down the steep hillside into the lake and drowned.

³⁴ When the herdsmen saw it, they fled to the nearby town and the surrounding countryside,

8:26 Other manuscripts read *Gadarenes;* still others read *Gergesenes;* also in 8:37. See Matt 8:28; Mark 5:1.   **8:29** Greek *unclean.*   **8:31** Or *the abyss,* or *the underworld.*

spreading the news as they ran. [35] People rushed out to see what had happened. A crowd soon gathered around Jesus, and they saw the man who had been freed from the demons. He was sitting at Jesus' feet, fully clothed and perfectly sane, and they were all afraid. [36] Then those who had seen what happened told the others how the demon-possessed man had been healed. [37] And all the people in the region of the Gerasenes begged Jesus to go away and leave them alone, for a great wave of fear swept over them.

So Jesus returned to the boat and left, crossing back to the other side of the lake. [38] The man who had been freed from the demons begged to go with him. But Jesus sent him home, saying, [39] "No, go back to your family, and tell them everything God has done for you." So he went all through the town proclaiming the great things Jesus had done for him.

Jesus Heals in Response to Faith

[40] On the other side of the lake the crowds welcomed Jesus, because they had been waiting for him. [41] Then a man named Jairus, a leader of the local synagogue, came and fell at Jesus' feet, pleading with him to come home with him. [42] His only daughter,* who was about twelve years old, was dying.

As Jesus went with him, he was surrounded by the crowds. [43] A woman in the crowd had suffered for twelve years with constant bleeding,* and she could find no cure. [44] Coming up behind Jesus, she touched the fringe of his robe. Immediately, the bleeding stopped.

[45] "Who touched me?" Jesus asked.

Everyone denied it, and Peter said, "Master, this whole crowd is pressing up against you."

[46] But Jesus said, "Someone deliberately touched me, for I felt healing power go out from me." [47] When the woman realized that she could not stay hidden, she began to tremble and fell to her knees in front of him. The whole crowd heard her explain why she had touched him and that she had been immediately healed. [48] "Daughter," he said to her, "your faith has made you well. Go in peace."

[49] While he was still speaking to her, a messenger arrived from the home of Jairus, the leader of the synagogue. He told him, "Your daughter is dead. There's no use troubling the Teacher now."

[50] But when Jesus heard what had happened, he said to Jairus, "Don't be afraid. Just have faith, and she will be healed."

[51] When they arrived at the house, Jesus wouldn't let anyone go in with him except Peter, John, James, and the little girl's father and mother. [52] The house was filled with people weeping and wailing, but he said, "Stop the weeping! She isn't dead; she's only asleep."

[53] But the crowd laughed at him because they all knew she had died. [54] Then Jesus took her by the hand and said in a loud voice, "My child, get up!" [55] And at that moment her life* returned, and she immediately stood up! Then Jesus told them to give her something to eat. [56] Her parents were overwhelmed, but Jesus insisted that they not tell anyone what had happened.

CHAPTER 9

Jesus Sends Out the Twelve Disciples

One day Jesus called together his twelve disciples* and gave them power and authority to cast out all demons and to heal all diseases. [2] Then he sent them out to tell everyone about the Kingdom of God and to heal the sick. [3] "Take nothing for your journey," he instructed them. "Don't take a walking stick, a traveler's bag, food, money,* or even a change of clothes. [4] Wherever you go, stay in the same house until you leave town. [5] And if a town refuses to welcome you, shake its dust from your feet as you leave to show that you have abandoned those people to their fate."

[6] So they began their circuit of the villages, preaching the Good News and healing the sick.

Herod's Confusion

[7] When Herod Antipas, the ruler of Galilee,* heard about everything Jesus was doing, he was puzzled. Some were saying that John the Baptist had been raised from the dead. [8] Others thought Jesus was Elijah or one of the other prophets risen from the dead.

[9] "I beheaded John," Herod said, "so who is this man about whom I hear such stories?" And he kept trying to see him.

Jesus Feeds Five Thousand

[10] When the apostles returned, they told Jesus everything they had done. Then he slipped quietly away with them toward the town of Bethsaida. [11] But the crowds found out where he was going, and they followed him. He welcomed them and taught them about the Kingdom of God, and he healed those who were sick.

[12] Late in the afternoon the twelve disciples came to him and said, "Send the crowds away to the nearby villages and farms, so they can find food and lodging for the night. There is nothing to eat here in this remote place."

8:42 Or *His only child, a daughter.*   8:43 Some manuscripts add *having spent everything she had on doctors.*   8:55 Or *her spirit.*   9:1 Greek *the Twelve;* other manuscripts read *the twelve apostles.*   9:3 Or *silver coins.*   9:7 Greek *Herod the tetrarch.* Herod Antipas was a son of King Herod and was ruler over Galilee.

[13]But Jesus said, "You feed them."

"But we have only five loaves of bread and two fish," they answered. "Or are you expecting us to go and buy enough food for this whole crowd?" [14]For there were about 5,000 men there.

Jesus replied, "Tell them to sit down in groups of about fifty each." [15]So the people all sat down. [16]Jesus took the five loaves and two fish, looked up toward heaven, and blessed them. Then, breaking the loaves into pieces, he kept giving the bread and fish to the disciples so they could distribute it to the people. [17]They all ate as much as they wanted, and afterward, the disciples picked up twelve baskets of leftovers!

Peter's Declaration about Jesus

[18]One day Jesus left the crowds to pray alone. Only his disciples were with him, and he asked them, "Who do people say I am?"

[19]"Well," they replied, "some say John the Baptist, some say Elijah, and others say you are one of the other ancient prophets risen from the dead."

[20]Then he asked them, "But who do you say I am?"

Peter replied, "You are the Messiah* sent from God!"

Jesus Predicts His Death

[21]Jesus warned his disciples not to tell anyone who he was. [22]"The Son of Man* must suffer many terrible things," he said. "He will be rejected by the elders, the leading priests, and the teachers of religious law. He will be killed, but on the third day he will be raised from the dead."

[23]Then he said to the crowd, "If any of you wants to be my follower, you must turn from your selfish ways, take up your cross daily, and follow me. [24]If you try to hang on to your life, you will lose it. But if you give up your life for my sake, you will save it. [25]And what do you benefit if you gain the whole world but are yourself lost or destroyed? [26]If anyone is ashamed of me and my message, the Son of Man will be ashamed of that person when he returns in his glory and in the glory of the Father and the holy angels. [27]I tell you the truth, some standing here right now will not die before they see the Kingdom of God."

The Transfiguration

[28]About eight days later Jesus took Peter, John, and James up on a mountain to pray. [29]And as he was praying, the appearance of his face was transformed, and his clothes became dazzling white. [30]Suddenly, two men, Moses and Elijah, appeared and began talking with Jesus. [31]They were glorious to see. And they were speaking about his exodus from this world, which was about to be fulfilled in Jerusalem.

[32]Peter and the others had fallen asleep. When they woke up, they saw Jesus' glory and the two men standing with him. [33]As Moses and Elijah were starting to leave, Peter, not even knowing what he was saying, blurted out, "Master, it's wonderful for us to be here! Let's make three shelters as memorials*—one for you, one for Moses, and one for Elijah." [34]But even as he was saying this, a cloud overshadowed them, and terror gripped them as the cloud covered them.

[35]Then a voice from the cloud said, "This is my Son, my Chosen One.* Listen to him." [36]When the voice finished, Jesus was there alone. They didn't tell anyone at that time what they had seen.

Jesus Heals a Demon-Possessed Boy

[37]The next day, after they had come down the mountain, a large crowd met Jesus. [38]A man in the crowd called out to him, "Teacher, I beg you to look at my son, my only child. [39]An evil spirit keeps seizing him, making him scream. It throws him into convulsions so that he foams at the mouth. It batters him and hardly ever leaves him alone. [40]I begged your disciples to cast out the spirit, but they couldn't do it."

[41]Jesus said, "You faithless and corrupt people! How long must I be with you and put up with you?" Then he said to the man, "Bring your son here."

[42]As the boy came forward, the demon knocked him to the ground and threw him into a violent convulsion. But Jesus rebuked the evil* spirit and healed the boy. Then he gave him back to his father. [43]Awe gripped the people as they saw this majestic display of God's power.

Jesus Again Predicts His Death

While everyone was marveling at everything he was doing, Jesus said to his disciples, [44]"Listen to me and remember what I say. The Son of Man is going to be betrayed into the hands of his enemies." [45]But they didn't know what he meant. Its significance was hidden from them, so they couldn't understand it, and they were afraid to ask him about it.

The Greatest in the Kingdom

[46]Then his disciples began arguing about which of them was the greatest. [47]But Jesus

9:20 Or the Christ. Messiah (a Hebrew term) and Christ (a Greek term) both mean "the anointed one."   9:22 "Son of Man" is a title Jesus used for himself.   9:33 Greek three tabernacles.   9:35 Some manuscripts read This is my dearly loved Son.   9:42 Greek unclean.

knew their thoughts, so he brought a little child to his side. [48]Then he said to them, "Anyone who welcomes a little child like this on my behalf* welcomes me, and anyone who welcomes me also welcomes my Father who sent me. Whoever is the least among you is the greatest."

Using the Name of Jesus

[49]John said to Jesus, "Master, we saw someone using your name to cast out demons, but we told him to stop because he isn't in our group."

[50]But Jesus said, "Don't stop him! Anyone who is not against you is for you."

Opposition from Samaritans

[51]As the time drew near for him to ascend to heaven, Jesus resolutely set out for Jerusalem. [52]He sent messengers ahead to a Samaritan village to prepare for his arrival. [53]But the people of the village did not welcome Jesus because he was on his way to Jerusalem. [54]When James and John saw this, they said to Jesus, "Lord, should we call down fire from heaven to burn them up*?" [55]But Jesus turned and rebuked them.* [56]So they went on to another village.

The Cost of Following Jesus

[57]As they were walking along, someone said to Jesus, "I will follow you wherever you go."

[58]But Jesus replied, "Foxes have dens to live in, and birds have nests, but the Son of Man has no place even to lay his head."

[59]He said to another person, "Come, follow me."

The man agreed, but he said, "Lord, first let me return home and bury my father."

[60]But Jesus told him, "Let the spiritually dead bury their own dead!* Your duty is to go and preach about the Kingdom of God."

[61]Another said, "Yes, Lord, I will follow you, but first let me say good-bye to my family."

[62]But Jesus told him, "Anyone who puts a hand to the plow and then looks back is not fit for the Kingdom of God."

CHAPTER 10

Jesus Sends Out His Disciples

The Lord now chose seventy-two* other disciples and sent them ahead in pairs to all the towns and places he planned to visit. [2]These were his instructions to them: "The harvest is great, but the workers are few. So pray to the

9:48 Greek *in my name.* 9:54 Some manuscripts add *as Elijah did.* 9:55 Some manuscripts add an expanded conclusion to verse 55 and an additional sentence in verse 56: *And he said, "You don't realize what your hearts are like. [56]For the Son of Man has not come to destroy people's lives, but to save them."* 9:60 Greek *Let the dead bury their own dead.* 10:1 Some manuscripts read *seventy;* also in 10:17.

first steps

A DISCIPLE TAKES UP HIS OR HER CROSS AND FOLLOWS CHRIST

Read LUKE 9:23-25

Choosing to be a disciple of Jesus Christ takes more than just verbal affirmation. It takes daily sacrifice and commitment. When you follow Christ's guidelines for discipleship, you will find that the end result is far better than you could ever have imagined. Here are three things a true disciple of Christ should do:

1. Your Desires Must Take a Backseat to His Desires for Your Life. Being a disciple means recognizing that God's plans for your life are ultimately better than your own. That may mean making some sacrifices in your life, such as spending more of your time in God's Word, volunteering to teach children's Sunday school, or putting off that vacation to work on a ministry project. Yet, in relinquishing your own plans, you will find yourself drawn closer to the Lord.

2. You Must Take Up Your Cross Daily. Jesus is not simply referring to a religious symbol. At this time in history, anyone seen carrying a cross was headed for a horrible death—by far the cruelest of all deaths. Some have misunderstood this statement by Jesus to mean that your cross is your personal inconvenience or problem. In this passage, however, Jesus is talking about the act of dying to yourself. In essence, he wants you to lay yourself at his feet and say, "I want your will more than my own." Once you have taken up that cross, you will experience the abundant life that Jesus promises to those who follow him.

3. You Must Lose Yourself to Save Yourself. Verse 24 may sound like a contradiction when you first read it. Yet, if you truly want to find happiness and fulfillment, you must relinquish full control of your life to Jesus Christ. Paul wrote, "It is no longer I who live, but Christ lives in me" (Galatians 2:20). Taking up the cross is no more a burden to the disciple than wings are to a bird. A surrendered life holds the key to a fulfilling walk.

It is true that it costs to be a disciple, but it is also true that it costs a lot more not to be!

For the next note on "Live as a Disciple," turn to p. 87.

cornerstones
WHAT MAKES DEMONS POWERLESS?
Read LUKE 10:1-20

Some Christians cower in fear of Satan and his army of demons. Yet every person who has put his or her faith and trust in Jesus Christ comes under God's protection. Scripture says that God has placed a wall of protection around us (Job 1:10). Demons have real powers, but we do not have to fear them. But we do need to recognize the power Christ has given us in the face of our enemy.

As Jesus' disciples found out, demons are drastically limited in their power before the true follower of Christ (verse 17). The power they had came from God. Jesus was quick to warn them not to rejoice in the power they had been given over demons. Rather, Jesus told them to rejoice that their names were "registered in heaven" (verse 20).

Today you may find people who say they have conversations with demons who remind them how powerless they are. Yet even Michael the archangel simply said, "The Lord rebuke you" (see Jude 1:9, p. 317). Our focus should not be upon the power we have been given but on the Giver of that power.

To begin the next topic, turn to p. A27.

Lord who is in charge of the harvest; ask him to send more workers into his fields. ³Now go, and remember that I am sending you out as lambs among wolves. ⁴Don't take any money with you, nor a traveler's bag, nor an extra pair of sandals. And don't stop to greet anyone on the road.

⁵"Whenever you enter someone's home, first say, 'May God's peace be on this house.' ⁶If those who live there are peaceful, the blessing will stand; if they are not, the blessing will return to you. ⁷Don't move around from home to home. Stay in one place, eating and drinking what they provide. Don't hesitate to accept hospitality, because those who work deserve their pay.

⁸"If you enter a town and it welcomes you, eat whatever is set before you. ⁹Heal the sick, and tell them, 'The Kingdom of God is near you now.' ¹⁰But if a town refuses to welcome you, go out into its streets and say, ¹¹'We wipe even the dust of your town from our feet to show that we have abandoned you to your fate. And know this—the Kingdom of God is near!' ¹²I assure you, even wicked Sodom will be better off than such a town on judgment day.

¹³"What sorrow awaits you, Korazin and Bethsaida! For if the miracles I did in you had been done in wicked Tyre and Sidon, their people would have repented of their sins long ago, clothing themselves in burlap and throwing ashes on their heads to show their remorse. ¹⁴Yes, Tyre and Sidon will be better off on judgment day than you. ¹⁵And you people of Capernaum, will you be honored in heaven? No, you will go down to the place of the dead.*"

10:15 Greek *to Hades.*

¹⁶Then he said to the disciples, "Anyone who accepts your message is also accepting me. And anyone who rejects you is rejecting me. And anyone who rejects me is rejecting God, who sent me."

¹⁷When the seventy-two disciples returned, they joyfully reported to him, "Lord, even the demons obey us when we use your name!"

¹⁸"Yes," he told them, "I saw Satan fall from heaven like lightning! ¹⁹Look, I have given you authority over all the power of the enemy, and you can walk among snakes and scorpions and crush them. Nothing will injure you. ²⁰But don't rejoice because evil spirits obey you; rejoice because your names are registered in heaven."

Jesus' Prayer of Thanksgiving
²¹At that same time Jesus was filled with the joy of the Holy Spirit, and he said, "O Father, Lord of heaven and earth, thank you for hiding these things from those who think themselves wise and clever, and for revealing them to the childlike. Yes, Father, it pleased you to do it this way.

²²"My Father has entrusted everything to me. No one truly knows the Son except the Father, and no one truly knows the Father except the Son and those to whom the Son chooses to reveal him."

²³Then when they were alone, he turned to the disciples and said, "Blessed are the eyes that see what you have seen. ²⁴I tell you, many prophets and kings longed to see what you see, but they didn't see it. And they longed to hear what you hear, but they didn't hear it."

The Most Important Commandment

25 One day an expert in religious law stood up to test Jesus by asking him this question: "Teacher, what should I do to inherit eternal life?"

26 Jesus replied, "What does the law of Moses say? How do you read it?"

27 The man answered, " 'You must love the LORD your God with all your heart, all your soul, all your strength, and all your mind.' And, 'Love your neighbor as yourself.' "*

28 "Right!" Jesus told him. "Do this and you will live!"

29 The man wanted to justify his actions, so he asked Jesus, "And who is my neighbor?"

Parable of the Good Samaritan

30 Jesus replied with a story: "A Jewish man was traveling from Jerusalem down to Jericho, and he was attacked by bandits. They stripped him of his clothes, beat him up, and left him half dead beside the road.

31 "By chance a priest came along. But when he saw the man lying there, he crossed to the other side of the road and passed him by. 32 A Temple assistant* walked over and looked at him lying there, but he also passed by on the other side.

33 "Then a despised Samaritan came along, and when he saw the man, he felt compassion for him. 34 Going over to him, the Samaritan soothed his wounds with olive oil and wine and bandaged them. Then he put the man on his own donkey and took him to an inn, where he took care of him. 35 The next day he handed the innkeeper two silver coins,* telling him, 'Take care of this man. If his bill runs higher than this, I'll pay you the next time I'm here.'

36 "Now which of these three would you say was a neighbor to the man who was attacked by bandits?" Jesus asked.

37 The man replied, "The one who showed him mercy."

Then Jesus said, "Yes, now go and do the same."

Jesus Visits Martha and Mary

38 As Jesus and the disciples continued on their way to Jerusalem, they came to a certain village where a woman named Martha welcomed him into her home. 39 Her sister, Mary, sat at the Lord's feet, listening to what he taught. 40 But Martha was distracted by the big dinner she was preparing. She came to Jesus and said,

"Lord, doesn't it seem unfair to you that my sister just sits here while I do all the work? Tell her to come and help me."

41 But the Lord said to her, "My dear Martha, you are worried and upset over all these details! 42 There is only one thing worth being concerned about. Mary has discovered it, and it will not be taken away from her."

CHAPTER 11

Teaching about Prayer

Once Jesus was in a certain place praying. As he finished, one of his disciples came to him and said, "Lord, teach us to pray, just as John taught his disciples."

2 Jesus said, "This is how you should pray:*

"Father, may your name be kept holy.
　　May your Kingdom come soon.
3 Give us each day the food we need,*
4 and forgive us our sins,
　　as we forgive those who sin against us.
　　And don't let us yield to temptation.*"

5 Then, teaching them more about prayer, he used this story: "Suppose you went to a friend's house at midnight, wanting to borrow three loaves of bread. You say to him, 6 'A friend of mine has just arrived for a visit, and I have nothing for him to eat.' 7 And suppose he calls out from his bedroom, 'Don't bother me. The door is locked for the night, and my family and I are all in bed. I can't help you.' 8 But I tell you this—though he won't do it for friendship's sake, if you keep knocking long enough, he will get up and give you whatever you need because of your shameless persistence.*

9 "And so I tell you, keep on asking, and you will receive what you ask for. Keep on seeking, and you will find. Keep on knocking, and the door will be opened to you. 10 For everyone who asks, receives. Everyone who seeks, finds. And to everyone who knocks, the door will be opened.

11 "You fathers—if your children ask* for a fish, do you give them a snake instead? 12 Or if they ask for an egg, do you give them a scorpion? Of course not! 13 So if you sinful people know how to give good gifts to your children, how much more will your heavenly Father give the Holy Spirit to those who ask him."

Jesus and the Prince of Demons

14 One day Jesus cast out a demon from a man who couldn't speak, and when the demon was gone, the man began to speak. The crowds

---

10:27 Deut 6:5; Lev 19:18.　10:32 Greek *A Levite*.　10:35 Greek *two denarii*. A denarius was equivalent to a laborer's full day's wage.　11:2 Some manuscripts add additional phrases from the Lord's Prayer as it reads in Matt 6:9-13.　11:3 Or *Give us each day our food for the day;* or *Give us each day our food for tomorrow.*　11:4 Or *And keep us from being tested.*　11:8 Or *in order to avoid shame,* or *so his reputation won't be damaged.*　11:11 Some manuscripts add *for bread, do you give them a stone? Or [if they ask].*

were amazed, [15]but some of them said, "No wonder he can cast out demons. He gets his power from Satan,* the prince of demons." [16]Others, trying to test Jesus, demanded that he show them a miraculous sign from heaven to prove his authority.

[17]He knew their thoughts, so he said, "Any kingdom divided by civil war is doomed. A family splintered by feuding will fall apart. [18]You say I am empowered by Satan. But if Satan is divided and fighting against himself, how can his kingdom survive? [19]And if I am empowered by Satan, what about your own exorcists? They cast out demons, too, so they will condemn you for what you have said. [20]But if I am casting out demons by the power of God,* then the Kingdom of God has arrived among you. [21]For when a strong man like Satan is fully armed and guards his palace, his possessions are safe—[22]until someone even stronger attacks and overpowers him, strips him of his weapons, and carries off his belongings.

[23]"Anyone who isn't with me opposes me, and anyone who isn't working with me is actually working against me.

[24]"When an evil* spirit leaves a person, it goes into the desert, searching for rest. But when it finds none, it says, 'I will return to the person I came from.' [25]So it returns and finds that its former home is all swept and in order. [26]Then the spirit finds seven other spirits more evil than itself, and they all enter the person and live there. And so that person is worse off than before."

[27]As he was speaking, a woman in the crowd called out, "God bless your mother—the womb from which you came, and the breasts that nursed you!"

[28]Jesus replied, "But even more blessed are all who hear the word of God and put it into practice."

The Sign of Jonah

[29]As the crowd pressed in on Jesus, he said, "This evil generation keeps asking me to show them a miraculous sign. But the only sign I will give them is the sign of Jonah. [30]What happened to him was a sign to the people of Nineveh that God had sent him. What happens to the Son of Man* will be a sign to these people that he was sent by God.

[31]"The queen of Sheba* will stand up against this generation on judgment day and condemn it, for she came from a distant land to hear the wisdom of Solomon. Now someone greater than Solomon is here—but you refuse to listen. [32]The people of Nineveh will also stand up against this generation on judgment day and condemn it, for they repented of their sins at the preaching of Jonah. Now someone greater than Jonah is here—but you refuse to repent.

Receiving the Light

[33]"No one lights a lamp and then hides it or puts it under a basket.* Instead, a lamp is placed on a stand, where its light can be seen by all who enter the house.

[34]"Your eye is a lamp that provides light for

11:15 Greek *Beelzeboul;* also in 11:18, 19. Other manuscripts read *Beezeboul;* Latin version reads *Beelzebub.* 11:20 Greek *by the finger of God.* 11:24 Greek *unclean.* 11:30 "Son of Man" is a title Jesus used for himself. 11:31 Greek *The queen of the south.* 11:33 Some manuscripts do not include *or puts it under a basket.*

---

off and running

BALANCE CHRISTIAN SERVICE WITH WORSHIP

Read LUKE 10:38-42

It is easy to lose sight of Jesus in the midst of all our activity for him. This story shows the necessity of balancing our work with our worship. Here we see two personalities, represented by Martha and Mary.

Martha: the Doer. Martha was a practical type of person. Deep down, she probably wanted to please the Lord, but she made the common mistake of offering work for worship. She received Jesus into her house, but then neglected him. Jesus wanted her attention, and she offered him a flurry of activity. As a result, she felt tired and overworked. Like Martha, we can become weary in our work for the Lord when we fail to take time to sit at his feet and draw from the spiritual resources available to us.

Mary: the Worshiper. Mary had a balanced life. She recognized that there

your body. When your eye is good, your whole body is filled with light. But when it is bad, your body is filled with darkness. ³⁵ Make sure that the light you think you have is not actually darkness. ³⁶ If you are filled with light, with no dark corners, then your whole life will be radiant, as though a floodlight were filling you with light."

Jesus Criticizes the Religious Leaders

³⁷ As Jesus was speaking, one of the Pharisees invited him home for a meal. So he went in and took his place at the table.* ³⁸ His host was amazed to see that he sat down to eat without first performing the hand-washing ceremony required by Jewish custom. ³⁹ Then the Lord said to him, "You Pharisees are so careful to clean the outside of the cup and the dish, but inside you are filthy—full of greed and wickedness! ⁴⁰ Fools! Didn't God make the inside as well as the outside? ⁴¹ So clean the inside by giving gifts to the poor, and you will be clean all over.

⁴² "What sorrow awaits you Pharisees! For you are careful to tithe even the tiniest income from your herb gardens,* but you ignore justice and the love of God. You should tithe, yes, but do not neglect the more important things.

⁴³ "What sorrow awaits you Pharisees! For you love to sit in the seats of honor in the synagogues and receive respectful greetings as you walk in the marketplaces. ⁴⁴ Yes, what sorrow awaits you! For you are like hidden graves in a field. People walk over them without knowing the corruption they are stepping on."

⁴⁵ "Teacher," said an expert in religious law, "you have insulted us, too, in what you just said."

⁴⁶ "Yes," said Jesus, "what sorrow also awaits you experts in religious law! For you crush people with unbearable religious demands, and you never lift a finger to ease the burden. ⁴⁷ What sorrow awaits you! For you build monuments for the prophets your own ancestors killed long ago. ⁴⁸ But in fact, you stand as witnesses who agree with what your ancestors did. They killed the prophets, and you join in their crime by building the monuments! ⁴⁹ This is what God in his wisdom said about you:* 'I will send prophets and apostles to them, but they will kill some and persecute the others.'

⁵⁰ "As a result, this generation will be held responsible for the murder of all God's prophets from the creation of the world—⁵¹ from the murder of Abel to the murder of Zechariah, who was killed between the altar and the sanctuary. Yes, it will certainly be charged against this generation.

⁵² "What sorrow awaits you experts in religious law! For you remove the key to knowledge from the people. You don't enter the Kingdom yourselves, and you prevent others from entering."

⁵³ As Jesus was leaving, the teachers of religious law and the Pharisees became hostile and tried to provoke him with many questions. ⁵⁴ They wanted to trap him into saying something they could use against him.

CHAPTER **12**

A Warning against Hypocrisy

Meanwhile, the crowds grew until thousands were milling about and stepping on each other. Jesus turned first to his disciples and warned

---

11:37 Or *and reclined.*   11:42 Greek *tithe the mint, the rue, and every herb.*   11:49 Greek *Therefore, the wisdom of God said.*

---

was a time to work and a time to worship. She knew when it was time to take off the apron and converse with this most honored guest. While Martha wanted to get the housework done, Mary wanted to seize this wonderful moment to sit at the feet of the Creator.

Few things are as damaging to the Christian life as trying to work for Christ without taking time to commune with him. In his letter to young Timothy, the apostle Paul writes, "Hardworking farmers should be the first to enjoy the fruit of their labor" (2 Timothy 2:6). In other words, you can't effectively feed others until you yourself have been fed.

What we do *with* Christ is far more important than what we do *for* Christ. Those who strike a balance between work and worship will keep themselves from spiritual burnout and will become more effective in their service to the Lord.

For the next note on "Priorities," turn to p. 178.

them, "Beware of the yeast of the Pharisees—their hypocrisy. [2] The time is coming when everything that is covered up will be revealed, and all that is secret will be made known to all. [3] Whatever you have said in the dark will be heard in the light, and what you have whispered behind closed doors will be shouted from the housetops for all to hear!

[4] "Dear friends, don't be afraid of those who want to kill your body; they cannot do any more to you after that. [5] But I'll tell you whom to fear. Fear God, who has the power to kill you and then throw you into hell.* Yes, he's the one to fear.

[6] "What is the price of five sparrows—two copper coins*? Yet God does not forget a single one of them. [7] And the very hairs on your head are all numbered. So don't be afraid; you are more valuable to God than a whole flock of sparrows.

[8] "I tell you the truth, everyone who acknowledges me publicly here on earth, the Son of Man* will also acknowledge in the presence of God's angels. [9] But anyone who denies me here on earth will be denied before God's angels. [10] Anyone who speaks against the Son of Man can be forgiven, but anyone who blasphemes the Holy Spirit will not be forgiven.

[11] "And when you are brought to trial in the synagogues and before rulers and authorities, don't worry about how to defend yourself or what to say, [12] for the Holy Spirit will teach you at that time what needs to be said."

Parable of the Rich Fool

[13] Then someone called from the crowd, "Teacher, please tell my brother to divide our father's estate with me."

[14] Jesus replied, "Friend, who made me a judge over you to decide such things as that?" [15] Then he said, "Beware! Guard against every kind of greed. Life is not measured by how much you own."

[16] Then he told them a story: "A rich man had a fertile farm that produced fine crops. [17] He said to himself, 'What should I do? I don't have room for all my crops.' [18] Then he said, 'I know! I'll tear down my barns and build bigger ones. Then I'll have room enough to store all my wheat and other goods. [19] And I'll sit back and say to myself, "My friend, you have enough stored away for years to come. Now take it easy! Eat, drink, and be merry!"'

[20] "But God said to him, 'You fool! You will die this very night. Then who will get everything you worked for?'

[21] "Yes, a person is a fool to store up earthly wealth but not have a rich relationship with God."

Teaching about Money and Possessions

[22] Then, turning to his disciples, Jesus said, "That is why I tell you not to worry about everyday life—whether you have enough food to eat or enough clothes to wear. [23] For life is more than food, and your body more than clothing. [24] Look at the ravens. They don't plant or harvest or store food in barns, for God feeds them. And you are far more valuable to him than any birds! [25] Can all your worries add a single moment to your life? [26] And if worry can't accomplish a little thing like that, what's the use of worrying over bigger things?

[27] "Look at the lilies and how they grow. They don't work or make their clothing, yet Solomon in all his glory was not dressed as beautifully as they are. [28] And if God cares so wonderfully for

12:5 Greek *Gehenna*.   12:6 Greek *two assaria* [Roman coins equal to ¹⁄₁₆ of a denarius].   12:8 "Son of Man" is a title Jesus used for himself.

---

off and running

DON'T NEGLECT YOUR SPIRITUAL HEALTH

Read LUKE 12:15-21

As this parable illustrates, it is easy to allow other pursuits to cloud our spiritual vision. We have to make enough money to get that new car, buy that house, or take that dream vacation. But we get so caught up in chasing after money and success that we leave God out of the equation altogether.

God's answer to this dilemma is for us to seek first his will in our lives. Then everything else will come into balance. The more you channel your energy, ambition, and life into this one, holy pursuit, the less obsessed you will be with the cares and concerns of this world. Seek God's kingdom in all that you do. Failure to do so will only guarantee confusion, failure, and emptiness.

To begin the next topic, turn to p. A51.

flowers that are here today and thrown into the fire tomorrow, he will certainly care for you. Why do you have so little faith?

29"And don't be concerned about what to eat and what to drink. Don't worry about such things. 30These things dominate the thoughts of unbelievers all over the world, but your Father already knows your needs. 31Seek the Kingdom of God above all else, and he will give you everything you need.

32"So don't be afraid, little flock. For it gives your Father great happiness to give you the Kingdom.

33"Sell your possessions and give to those in need. This will store up treasure for you in heaven! And the purses of heaven never get old or develop holes. Your treasure will be safe; no thief can steal it and no moth can destroy it. 34Wherever your treasure is, there the desires of your heart will also be.

Be Ready for the Lord's Coming

35"Be dressed for service and keep your lamps burning, 36as though you were waiting for your master to return from the wedding feast. Then you will be ready to open the door and let him in the moment he arrives and knocks. 37The servants who are ready and waiting for his return will be rewarded. I tell you the truth, he himself will seat them, put on an apron, and serve them as they sit and eat! 38He may come in the middle of the night or just before dawn.* But whenever he comes, he will reward the servants who are ready.

39"Understand this: If a homeowner knew exactly when a burglar was coming, he would not permit his house to be broken into. 40You also must be ready all the time, for the Son of Man will come when least expected."

41Peter asked, "Lord, is that illustration just for us or for everyone?"

42And the Lord replied, "A faithful, sensible servant is one to whom the master can give the responsibility of managing his other household servants and feeding them. 43If the master returns and finds that the servant has done a good job, there will be a reward. 44I tell you the truth, the master will put that servant in charge of all he owns. 45But what if the servant thinks, 'My master won't be back for a while,' and he begins beating the other servants, partying, and getting drunk? 46The master will return unannounced and unexpected, and he will cut the servant in pieces and banish him with the unfaithful.

47"And a servant who knows what the master wants, but isn't prepared and doesn't carry out those instructions, will be severely punished. 48But someone who does not know, and then does something wrong, will be punished only lightly. When someone has been given much, much will be required in return; and when someone has been entrusted with much, even more will be required.

Jesus Causes Division

49"I have come to set the world on fire, and I wish it were already burning! 50I have a terrible baptism of suffering ahead of me, and I am under a heavy burden until it is accomplished. 51Do you think I have come to bring peace to the earth? No, I have come to divide people against each other! 52From now on families will be split apart, three in favor of me, and two against—or two in favor and three against.

53 'Father will be divided against son
    and son against father;
  mother against daughter
    and daughter against mother;
  and mother-in-law against
      daughter-in-law
    and daughter-in-law against
      mother-in-law.'* "

54Then Jesus turned to the crowd and said, "When you see clouds beginning to form in the west, you say, 'Here comes a shower.' And you are right. 55When the south wind blows, you say, 'Today will be a scorcher.' And it is. 56You fools! You know how to interpret the weather signs of the earth and sky, but you don't know how to interpret the present times.

57"Why can't you decide for yourselves what is right? 58When you are on the way to court with your accuser, try to settle the matter before you get there. Otherwise, your accuser may drag you before the judge, who will hand you over to an officer, who will throw you into prison. 59And if that happens, you won't be free again until you have paid the very last penny.*"

CHAPTER 13

A Call to Repentance

About this time Jesus was informed that Pilate had murdered some people from Galilee as they were offering sacrifices at the Temple. 2"Do you think those Galileans were worse sinners than all the other people from Galilee?" Jesus asked. "Is that why they suffered? 3Not at all! And you will perish, too, unless you repent of your sins and turn to God. 4And what about the eighteen people who died when the tower in Siloam fell on them? Were they the worst sinners in Jerusalem? 5No, and I tell you again that unless you repent, you will perish, too."

12:38 Greek *in the second or third watch.*   12:53 Mic 7:6.   12:59 Greek *last lepton* [the smallest Jewish coin].

cornerstones

THE MORE WE KNOW, THE GREATER OUR RESPONSIBILITY WILL BE
Read LUKE 12:48

According to this verse, you will be held accountable for what you know, from your personal behavior to the work you do for God's Kingdom. For instance, you now know that you should not lie, cheat, steal, or live an immoral lifestyle. If you disregard God's commands, you know that you will reap the consequences. On the other hand, you must also share your spiritual knowledge with others—especially non-Christians. Our attitude should be as Paul's, who wrote, "For we speak as messengers approved by God to be entrusted with the Good News. Our purpose is to please God, not people. He alone examines the motives of our hearts" (1 Thessalonians 2:4).

Are you using the spiritual knowledge and insight God has given you to his glory?

For the next note on "Accountability," turn to p. 92.

Parable of the Barren Fig Tree

⁶Then Jesus told this story: "A man planted a fig tree in his garden and came again and again to see if there was any fruit on it, but he was always disappointed. ⁷Finally, he said to his gardener, 'I've waited three years, and there hasn't been a single fig! Cut it down. It's just taking up space in the garden.'

⁸"The gardener answered, 'Sir, give it one more chance. Leave it another year, and I'll give it special attention and plenty of fertilizer. ⁹If we get figs next year, fine. If not, then you can cut it down.'"

Jesus Heals on the Sabbath

¹⁰One Sabbath day as Jesus was teaching in a synagogue, ¹¹he saw a woman who had been crippled by an evil spirit. She had been bent double for eighteen years and was unable to stand up straight. ¹²When Jesus saw her, he called her over and said, "Dear woman, you are healed of your sickness!" ¹³Then he touched her, and instantly she could stand straight. How she praised God!

¹⁴But the leader in charge of the synagogue was indignant that Jesus had healed her on the Sabbath day. "There are six days of the week for working," he said to the crowd. "Come on those days to be healed, not on the Sabbath."

¹⁵But the Lord replied, "You hypocrites! Each of you works on the Sabbath day! Don't you untie your ox or your donkey from its stall on the Sabbath and lead it out for water? ¹⁶This dear woman, a daughter of Abraham, has been held in bondage by Satan for eighteen years. Isn't it right that she be released, even on the Sabbath?"

¹⁷This shamed his enemies, but all the people rejoiced at the wonderful things he did.

Parable of the Mustard Seed

¹⁸Then Jesus said, "What is the Kingdom of God like? How can I illustrate it? ¹⁹It is like a tiny mustard seed that a man planted in a garden; it grows and becomes a tree, and the birds make nests in its branches."

Parable of the Yeast

²⁰He also asked, "What else is the Kingdom of God like? ²¹It is like the yeast a woman used in making bread. Even though she put only a little yeast in three measures of flour, it permeated every part of the dough."

The Narrow Door

²²Jesus went through the towns and villages, teaching as he went, always pressing on toward Jerusalem. ²³Someone asked him, "Lord, will only a few be saved?"

He replied, ²⁴"Work hard to enter the narrow door to God's Kingdom, for many will try to enter but will fail. ²⁵When the master of the house has locked the door, it will be too late. You will stand outside knocking and pleading, 'Lord, open the door for us!' But he will reply, 'I don't know you or where you come from.' ²⁶Then you will say, 'But we ate and drank with you, and you taught in our streets.' ²⁷And he will reply, 'I tell you, I don't know you or where you come from. Get away from me, all you who do evil.'

²⁸"There will be weeping and gnashing of teeth, for you will see Abraham, Isaac, Jacob, and all the prophets in the Kingdom of God, but you will be thrown out. ²⁹And people will come from all over the world—from east and west, north and south—to take their places in the Kingdom of God. ³⁰And note this: Some who seem least important now will be the

greatest then, and some who are the greatest now will be least important then.*"

Jesus Grieves over Jerusalem

31At that time some Pharisees said to him, "Get away from here if you want to live! Herod Antipas wants to kill you!"

32Jesus replied, "Go tell that fox that I will keep on casting out demons and healing people today and tomorrow; and the third day I will accomplish my purpose. 33Yes, today, tomorrow, and the next day I must proceed on my way. For it wouldn't do for a prophet of God to be killed except in Jerusalem!

34"O Jerusalem, Jerusalem, the city that kills the prophets and stones God's messengers! How often I have wanted to gather your children together as a hen protects her chicks beneath her wings, but you wouldn't let me. 35And now, look, your house is abandoned. And you will never see me again until you say, 'Blessings on the one who comes in the name of the Lord!'* "

CHAPTER 14

Jesus Heals on the Sabbath

One Sabbath day Jesus went to eat dinner in the home of a leader of the Pharisees, and the people were watching him closely. 2There was a man there whose arms and legs were swollen.* 3Jesus asked the Pharisees and experts in religious law, "Is it permitted in the law to heal people on the Sabbath day, or not?" 4When they refused to answer, Jesus touched the sick man and healed him and sent him away. 5Then he turned to them and said, "Which of you doesn't work on the Sabbath? If your son* or your cow falls into a pit, don't you rush to get him out?" 6Again they could not answer.

Jesus Teaches about Humility

7When Jesus noticed that all who had come to the dinner were trying to sit in the seats of honor near the head of the table, he gave them this advice: 8"When you are invited to a wedding feast, don't sit in the seat of honor. What if someone who is more distinguished than you has also been invited? 9The host will come and say, 'Give this person your seat.' Then you will be embarrassed, and you will have to take whatever seat is left at the foot of the table!

10"Instead, take the lowest place at the foot of the table. Then when your host sees you, he will come and say, 'Friend, we have a better place for you!' Then you will be honored in front of all the other guests. 11For those who exalt themselves will be humbled, and those who humble themselves will be exalted."

12Then he turned to his host. "When you put on a luncheon or a banquet," he said, "don't invite your friends, brothers, relatives, and rich neighbors. For they will invite you back, and that will be your only reward. 13Instead, invite the poor, the crippled, the lame, and the blind. 14Then at the resurrection of the righteous, God will reward you for inviting those who could not repay you."

Parable of the Great Feast

15Hearing this, a man sitting at the table with Jesus exclaimed, "What a blessing it will be to attend a banquet* in the Kingdom of God!"

16Jesus replied with this story: "A man prepared a great feast and sent out many invitations. 17When the banquet was ready, he sent his servant to tell the guests, 'Come, the banquet is ready.' 18But they all began making excuses. One said, 'I have just bought a field and must inspect it. Please excuse me.' 19Another said, 'I have just bought five pairs of oxen, and I want to try them out. Please excuse me.' 20Another said, 'I now have a wife, so I can't come.'

21"The servant returned and told his master what they had said. His master was furious and said, 'Go quickly into the streets and alleys of the town and invite the poor, the crippled, the blind, and the lame.' 22After the servant had done this, he reported, 'There is still room for more.' 23So his master said, 'Go out into the country lanes and behind the hedges and urge anyone you find to come, so that the house will be full. 24For none of those I first invited will get even the smallest taste of my banquet.' "

The Cost of Being a Disciple

25A large crowd was following Jesus. He turned around and said to them, 26"If you want to be my disciple, you must hate everyone else by comparison—your father and mother, wife and children, brothers and sisters—yes, even your own life. Otherwise, you cannot be my disciple. 27And if you do not carry your own cross and follow me, you cannot be my disciple.

28"But don't begin until you count the cost. For who would begin construction of a building without first calculating the cost to see if there is enough money to finish it? 29Otherwise, you might complete only the foundation before running out of money, and then everyone would laugh at you. 30They would say, 'There's the person who started that building and couldn't afford to finish it!'

31"Or what king would go to war against

13:30 Greek Some are last who will be first, and some are first who will be last.   13:35 Ps 118:26.   14:2 Or who had dropsy.   14:5 Some manuscripts read donkey.   14:15 Greek to eat bread.

another king without first sitting down with his counselors to discuss whether his army of 10,000 could defeat the 20,000 soldiers marching against him? [32] And if he can't, he will send a delegation to discuss terms of peace while the enemy is still far away. [33] So you cannot become my disciple without giving up everything you own.

[34] "Salt is good for seasoning. But if it loses its flavor, how do you make it salty again? [35] Flavorless salt is good neither for the soil nor for the manure pile. It is thrown away. Anyone with ears to hear should listen and understand!"

CHAPTER **15**

Parable of the Lost Sheep

Tax collectors and other notorious sinners often came to listen to Jesus teach. [2] This made the Pharisees and teachers of religious law complain that he was associating with such sinful people—even eating with them!

[3] So Jesus told them this story: [4] "If a man has a hundred sheep and one of them gets lost, what will he do? Won't he leave the ninety-nine others in the wilderness and go to search for the one that is lost until he finds it? [5] And when he has found it, he will joyfully carry it home on his shoulders. [6] When he arrives, he will call together his friends and neighbors, saying, 'Rejoice with me because I have found my lost sheep.' [7] In the same way, there is more joy in heaven over one lost sinner who repents and returns to God than over ninety-nine others who are righteous and haven't strayed away!

Parable of the Lost Coin

[8] "Or suppose a woman has ten silver coins* and loses one. Won't she light a lamp and sweep the entire house and search carefully until she finds it? [9] And when she finds it, she will call in her friends and neighbors and say, 'Rejoice with me because I have found my lost coin.' [10] In the same way, there is joy in the presence of God's angels when even one sinner repents."

Parable of the Lost Son

[11] To illustrate the point further, Jesus told them this story: "A man had two sons. [12] The younger son told his father, 'I want my share of your estate now before you die.' So his father agreed to divide his wealth between his sons.

[13] "A few days later this younger son packed all his belongings and moved to a distant land, and there he wasted all his money in wild living. [14] About the time his money ran out, a great famine swept over the land, and he began to starve. [15] He persuaded a local farmer to hire

him, and the man sent him into his fields to feed the pigs. [16] The young man became so hungry that even the pods he was feeding the pigs looked good to him. But no one gave him anything.

[17] "When he finally came to his senses, he said to himself, 'At home even the hired servants have food enough to spare, and here I am dying of hunger! [18] I will go home to my father and say, "Father, I have sinned against both heaven and you, [19] and I am no longer worthy of being called your son. Please take me on as a hired servant." '

[20] "So he returned home to his father. And while he was still a long way off, his father saw him coming. Filled with love and compassion, he ran to his son, embraced him, and kissed him. [21] His son said to him, 'Father, I have sinned against both heaven and you, and I am no longer worthy of being called your son.*'

[22] "But his father said to the servants, 'Quick! Bring the finest robe in the house and put it on him. Get a ring for his finger and sandals for his feet. [23] And kill the calf we have been fattening. We must celebrate with a feast, [24] for this son of mine was dead and has now returned to life. He was lost, but now he is found.' So the party began.

[25] "Meanwhile, the older son was in the fields working. When he returned home, he heard music and dancing in the house, [26] and he asked one of the servants what was going on. [27] 'Your brother is back,' he was told, 'and your father has killed the fattened calf. We are celebrating because of his safe return.'

[28] "The older brother was angry and wouldn't go in. His father came out and begged him, [29] but he replied, 'All these years I've slaved for you and never once refused to do a single thing you told me to. And in all that time you never gave me even one young goat for a feast with my friends. [30] Yet when this son of yours comes back after squandering your money on prostitutes, you celebrate by killing the fattened calf!'

[31] "His father said to him, 'Look, dear son, you have always stayed by me, and everything I have is yours. [32] We had to celebrate this happy day. For your brother was dead and has come back to life! He was lost, but now he is found!' "

CHAPTER **16**

Parable of the Shrewd Manager

Jesus told this story to his disciples: "There was a certain rich man who had a manager handling his affairs. One day a report came that the manager was wasting his employer's money. [2] So the employer called him in and said,

---

15:8 Greek *ten drachmas.* A drachma was the equivalent of a full day's wage.   **15:21** Some manuscripts add *Please take me on as a hired servant.*

'What's this I hear about you? Get your report in order, because you are going to be fired.'

[3] "The manager thought to himself, 'Now what? My boss has fired me. I don't have the strength to dig ditches, and I'm too proud to beg. [4] Ah, I know how to ensure that I'll have plenty of friends who will give me a home when I am fired.'

[5] "So he invited each person who owed money to his employer to come and discuss the situation. He asked the first one, 'How much do you owe him?' [6] The man replied, 'I owe him 800 gallons of olive oil.' So the manager told him, 'Take the bill and quickly change it to 400 gallons.*'

[7] "'And how much do you owe my employer?' he asked the next man. 'I owe him 1,000 bushels of wheat,' was the reply. 'Here,' the manager said, 'take the bill and change it to 800 bushels.*'

[8] "The rich man had to admire the dishonest rascal for being so shrewd. And it is true that the children of this world are more shrewd in dealing with the world around them than are the children of the light. [9] Here's the lesson: Use your worldly resources to benefit others and make friends. Then, when your earthly possessions are gone, they will welcome you to an eternal home.*

[10] "If you are faithful in little things, you will be faithful in large ones. But if you are dishonest in little things, you won't be honest with greater responsibilities. [11] And if you are untrustworthy about worldly wealth, who will trust you with the true riches of heaven? [12] And if you are not faithful with other people's things, why should you be trusted with things of your own?

[13] "No one can serve two masters. For you will hate one and love the other; you will be devoted to one and despise the other. You cannot serve both God and money."

[14] The Pharisees, who dearly loved their money, heard all this and scoffed at him. [15] Then he said to them, "You like to appear righteous in public, but God knows your hearts. What this world honors is detestable in the sight of God.

[16] "Until John the Baptist, the law of Moses and the messages of the prophets were your guides. But now the Good News of the Kingdom of God is preached, and everyone is eager to get in.* [17] But that doesn't mean that the law has lost its force. It is easier for heaven and earth to disappear than for the smallest point of God's law to be overturned.

[18] "For example, a man who divorces his wife and marries someone else commits adultery.

first steps

A DISCIPLE COUNTS THE COST
Read LUKE 14:25-33

At the time Jesus said these words, he had become quite a popular figure. Crowds flocked around him wherever he went, but not always for the right reasons. Consequently, Jesus directed his solemn and searching words to those people who followed him for selfish purposes or because it was the thing to do.

Likewise, Jesus doesn't want you to follow him only when it is convenient or socially acceptable. He wants you to be his disciple for the long haul—regardless of how easy or difficult it might be. That is why you must count the cost of being a true disciple of Jesus Christ. What does it mean to count the cost? The following four questions will give you a concrete idea:

- Do you love Jesus more than anyone or anything else in your life?
- Do you love Jesus and desire his will for your life over your own?
- Are you willing to accept ridicule and sacrifice for the cause of Christ?
- Will you commit to following Jesus, even if it isn't popular or expedient?

If you have carefully examined your heart, counted the cost, and can truthfully answer yes to these questions, then you are on the road to lifelong discipleship and friendship with Christ. Jesus is not looking for half-hearted followers. He wants wholehearted commitment.

For the next note on "Live as a Disciple," *turn to p. 119.*

And anyone who marries a woman divorced from her husband commits adultery."

Parable of the Rich Man and Lazarus
[19] Jesus said, "There was a certain rich man who was splendidly clothed in purple and fine linen and who lived each day in luxury. [20] At his gate lay a poor man named Lazarus who was covered with sores. [21] As Lazarus lay there longing for scraps from the rich man's table, the dogs would come and lick his open sores.

16:6 Greek *100 baths . . . 50 [baths].*   16:7 Greek *100 korous . . . 80 [korous].*   16:9 Or *you will be welcomed into eternal homes.*   16:16 Or *everyone is urged to enter in.*

cornerstones

WHAT IS HELL LIKE?
Read LUKE 16:19-31

Jesus reveals some information about hell in this parable.

People's Lifestyles on Earth Will Not Be the Same in Eternity. Things dramatically changed for the rich man when he passed into eternity. Because he did not know God, he immediately entered into the dark torment of hell, penniless and in agony. Those whose hearts are not right with God face the same future as the rich man in this story. After death, it is possible that they will be held in hell until they are brought before God at what is called the Great White Throne Judgment, though no one knows for sure (see "Why Would a Good God Send Anyone to Hell?" p. 277).

Hell Is a Place of Flames and Torment. The rich man in this parable experienced unrelenting heat and an unquenchable thirst. He was in so much agony that he called out to Abraham to have Lazarus come and dip his finger in water to cool his (the rich man's) tongue. If you have ever been badly burned, then you have an idea of the torment an eternity in hell will bring. Add to that darkness and isolation, and you have an incredibly bleak scenario.

People Do Not "Have a Good Time" in Hell. Some people say, "I want to go to hell. All of my friends will be there." That may be true, but there's no party. As this parable states, the rich man is so alarmed by his situation that he wants Lazarus to go and warn his brothers, so that they will *not* join him in torment.

If you want to know about the reality of hell, you don't need tabloid accounts of near-death experiences. Study the words of the living God, who died and rose again, and who can tell you exactly what to expect in eternity. Our acceptance or rejection of his words determines where we will spend the rest of our lives.

For the next note on "What Is Hell?" turn to p. 334.

---

22 "Finally, the poor man died and was carried by the angels to be with Abraham.* The rich man also died and was buried, 23 and his soul went to the place of the dead.* There, in torment, he saw Abraham in the far distance with Lazarus at his side.

24 "The rich man shouted, 'Father Abraham, have some pity! Send Lazarus over here to dip the tip of his finger in water and cool my tongue. I am in anguish in these flames.'

25 "But Abraham said to him, 'Son, remember that during your lifetime you had everything you wanted, and Lazarus had nothing. So now he is here being comforted, and you are in anguish. 26 And besides, there is a great chasm separating us. No one can cross over to you from here, and no one can cross over to us from there.'

27 "Then the rich man said, 'Please, Father Abraham, at least send him to my father's home. 28 For I have five brothers, and I want him to warn them so they don't end up in this place of torment.'

29 "But Abraham said, 'Moses and the prophets have warned them. Your brothers can read what they wrote.'

30 "The rich man replied, 'No, Father Abraham! But if someone is sent to them from the dead, then they will repent of their sins and turn to God.'

31 "But Abraham said, 'If they won't listen to Moses and the prophets, they won't listen even if someone rises from the dead.' "

CHAPTER 17
Teachings about Forgiveness and Faith

One day Jesus said to his disciples, "There will always be temptations to sin, but what sorrow awaits the person who does the tempting! 2 It would be better to be thrown into the sea with a millstone hung around your neck than to cause one of these little ones to fall into sin. 3 So watch yourselves!

"If another believer* sins, rebuke that person; then if there is repentance, forgive. 4 Even if that person wrongs you seven times a day and each time turns again and asks forgiveness, you must forgive."

5 The apostles said to the Lord, "Show us how to increase our faith."

6 The Lord answered, "If you had faith even

16:22 Greek *into Abraham's bosom.*   **16:23** Greek *to Hades.*   **17:3** Greek *If your brother.*

as small as a mustard seed, you could say to this mulberry tree, 'May you be uprooted and thrown into the sea,' and it would obey you!

7 "When a servant comes in from plowing or taking care of sheep, does his master say, 'Come in and eat with me'? 8 No, he says, 'Prepare my meal, put on your apron, and serve me while I eat. Then you can eat later.' 9 And does the master thank the servant for doing what he was told to do? Of course not. 10 In the same way, when you obey me you should say, 'We are unworthy servants who have simply done our duty.' "

Ten Healed of Leprosy

11 As Jesus continued on toward Jerusalem, he reached the border between Galilee and Samaria. 12 As he entered a village there, ten lepers stood at a distance, 13 crying out, "Jesus, Master, have mercy on us!"

14 He looked at them and said, "Go show yourselves to the priests."* And as they went, they were cleansed of their leprosy.

15 One of them, when he saw that he was healed, came back to Jesus, shouting, "Praise God!" 16 He fell to the ground at Jesus' feet, thanking him for what he had done. This man was a Samaritan.

17 Jesus asked, "Didn't I heal ten men? Where are the other nine? 18 Has no one returned to give glory to God except this foreigner?" 19 And Jesus said to the man, "Stand up and go. Your faith has healed you.*"

The Coming of the Kingdom

20 One day the Pharisees asked Jesus, "When will the Kingdom of God come?"

Jesus replied, "The Kingdom of God can't be detected by visible signs.* 21 You won't be able to say, 'Here it is!' or 'It's over there!' For the Kingdom of God is already among you.*"

22 Then he said to his disciples, "The time is coming when you will long to see the day when the Son of Man returns,* but you won't see it. 23 People will tell you, 'Look, there is the Son of Man,' or 'Here he is,' but don't go out and follow them. 24 For as the lightning flashes and lights up the sky from one end to the other, so it will be on the day when the Son of Man comes. 25 But first the Son of Man must suffer terribly* and be rejected by this generation.

26 "When the Son of Man returns, it will be like it was in Noah's day. 27 In those days, the people enjoyed banquets and parties and weddings right up to the time Noah entered his boat and the flood came and destroyed them all.

28 "And the world will be as it was in the days of Lot. People went about their daily business—eating and drinking, buying and selling, farming and building—29 until the morning Lot left Sodom. Then fire and burning sulfur rained down from heaven and destroyed them all. 30 Yes, it will be 'business as usual' right up to the day when the Son of Man is revealed. 31 On that day a person out on the deck of a roof must not go down into the house to pack. A person out in the field must not return home. 32 Remember what happened to Lot's wife! 33 If you cling to your life, you will lose it, and if you let your life go, you will save it. 34 That night two people will be asleep in one bed; one will be taken, the other left. 35 Two women will be grinding flour together at the mill; one will be taken, the other left.*"

37 "Where will this happen, Lord?"* the disciples asked.

Jesus replied, "Just as the gathering of vultures shows there is a carcass nearby, so these signs indicate that the end is near."*

CHAPTER **18**

Parable of the Persistent Widow

One day Jesus told his disciples a story to show that they should always pray and never give up. 2 "There was a judge in a certain city," he said, "who neither feared God nor cared about people. 3 A widow of that city came to him repeatedly, saying, 'Give me justice in this dispute with my enemy.' 4 The judge ignored her for a while, but finally he said to himself, 'I don't fear God or care about people, 5 but this woman is driving me crazy. I'm going to see that she gets justice, because she is wearing me out with her constant requests!' "

6 Then the Lord said, "Learn a lesson from this unjust judge. 7 Even he rendered a just decision in the end. So don't you think God will surely give justice to his chosen people who cry out to him day and night? Will he keep putting them off? 8 I tell you, he will grant justice to them quickly! But when the Son of Man* returns, how many will he find on the earth who have faith?"

Parable of the Pharisee and Tax Collector

9 Then Jesus told this story to some who had great confidence in their own righteousness and scorned everyone else: 10 "Two men went to the Temple to pray. One was a Pharisee, and the other was a despised tax collector. 11 The Pharisee stood by himself and prayed this

17:14 See Lev 14:2-32.   17:19 Or *Your faith has saved you.*   17:20 Or *by your speculations.*   17:21 Or *is within you,* or *is in your grasp.*   17:22 Or *long for even one day with the Son of Man.* "Son of Man" is a title Jesus used for himself.   17:25 Or *suffer many things.*   17:35 Some manuscripts add verse 36, *Two men will be working in the field; one will be taken, the other left.* Compare Matt 24:40.   17:37a Greek *"Where, Lord?"*   17:37b Greek *"Wherever the carcass is, the vultures gather."*   18:8 "Son of Man" is a title Jesus used for himself.

prayer*: 'I thank you, God, that I am not a sinner like everyone else. For I don't cheat, I don't sin, and I don't commit adultery. I'm certainly not like that tax collector! [12] I fast twice a week, and I give you a tenth of my income.'

[13] "But the tax collector stood at a distance and dared not even lift his eyes to heaven as he prayed. Instead, he beat his chest in sorrow, saying, 'O God, be merciful to me, for I am a sinner.' [14] I tell you, this sinner, not the Pharisee, returned home justified before God. For those who exalt themselves will be humbled, and those who humble themselves will be exalted."

Jesus Blesses the Children

[15] One day some parents brought their little children to Jesus so he could touch and bless them. But when the disciples saw this, they scolded the parents for bothering him.

[16] Then Jesus called for the children and said to the disciples, "Let the children come to me. Don't stop them! For the Kingdom of God belongs to those who are like these children. [17] I tell you the truth, anyone who doesn't receive the Kingdom of God like a child will never enter it."

The Rich Man

[18] Once a religious leader asked Jesus this question: "Good Teacher, what should I do to inherit eternal life?"

[19] "Why do you call me good?" Jesus asked him. "Only God is truly good. [20] But to answer your question, you know the commandments: 'You must not commit adultery. You must not murder. You must not steal. You must not testify falsely. Honor your father and mother.'* "

[21] The man replied, "I've obeyed all these commandments since I was young."

[22] When Jesus heard his answer, he said, "There is still one thing you haven't done. Sell all your possessions and give the money to the poor, and you will have treasure in heaven. Then come, follow me."

[23] But when the man heard this he became very sad, for he was very rich.

[24] When Jesus saw this,* he said, "How hard it is for the rich to enter the Kingdom of God! [25] In fact, it is easier for a camel to go through the eye of a needle than for a rich person to enter the Kingdom of God!"

[26] Those who heard this said, "Then who in the world can be saved?"

[27] He replied, "What is impossible for people is possible with God."

[28] Peter said, "We've left our homes to follow you."

[29] "Yes," Jesus replied, "and I assure you that everyone who has given up house or wife or brothers or parents or children, for the sake of the Kingdom of God, [30] will be repaid many times over in this life, and will have eternal life in the world to come."

Jesus Again Predicts His Death

[31] Taking the twelve disciples aside, Jesus said, "Listen, we're going up to Jerusalem, where all the predictions of the prophets concerning the Son of Man will come true. [32] He will be handed over to the Romans,* and he will be mocked, treated shamefully, and spit upon. [33] They will flog him with a whip and kill him, but on the third day he will rise again."

[34] But they didn't understand any of this. The significance of his words was hidden from them, and they failed to grasp what he was talking about.

Jesus Heals a Blind Beggar

[35] As Jesus approached Jericho, a blind beggar was sitting beside the road. [36] When he heard

18:11 Some manuscripts read *stood and prayed this prayer to himself.*　**18:20** Exod 20:12-16; Deut 5:16-20.　**18:24** Some manuscripts read *When Jesus saw how sad the man was.*　**18:32** Greek *the Gentiles.*

---

off and running

PRAY PERSISTENTLY
Read LUKE 18:1-8

This parable illustrates the need for persistence in prayer. Jesus chose two unlikely characters for this parable: a poor widow and a corrupt judge. These characters hardly seem like the proper comparison for describing our relationship with God, but Jesus wants us to focus on several important contrasts in this story:

- The widow had to go to a corrupt judge. . . . We can go to our heavenly Father (see Ephesians 3:14, p. 229).
- The widow was a stranger. . . . We are God's children (see John 1:12, p. 101).

the noise of a crowd going past, he asked what was happening. [37] They told him that Jesus the Nazarene* was going by. [38] So he began shouting, "Jesus, Son of David, have mercy on me!"

[39] "Be quiet!" the people in front yelled at him.

But he only shouted louder, "Son of David, have mercy on me!"

[40] When Jesus heard him, he stopped and ordered that the man be brought to him. As the man came near, Jesus asked him, [41] "What do you want me to do for you?"

"Lord," he said, "I want to see!"

[42] And Jesus said, "All right, receive your sight! Your faith has healed you." [43] Instantly the man could see, and he followed Jesus, praising God. And all who saw it praised God, too.

CHAPTER 19

Jesus and Zacchaeus

Jesus entered Jericho and made his way through the town. [2] There was a man there named Zacchaeus. He was the chief tax collector in the region, and he had become very rich. [3] He tried to get a look at Jesus, but he was too short to see over the crowd. [4] So he ran ahead and climbed a sycamore-fig tree beside the road, for Jesus was going to pass that way.

[5] When Jesus came by, he looked up at Zacchaeus and called him by name. "Zacchaeus!" he said. "Quick, come down! I must be a guest in your home today."

[6] Zacchaeus quickly climbed down and took Jesus to his house in great excitement and joy. [7] But the people were displeased. "He has gone to be the guest of a notorious sinner," they grumbled.

[8] Meanwhile, Zacchaeus stood before the Lord and said, "I will give half my wealth to the poor, Lord, and if I have cheated people on their taxes, I will give them back four times as much!"

[9] Jesus responded, "Salvation has come to this home today, for this man has shown himself to be a true son of Abraham. [10] For the Son of Man* came to seek and save those who are lost."

Parable of the Ten Servants

[11] The crowd was listening to everything Jesus said. And because he was nearing Jerusalem, he told them a story to correct the impression that the Kingdom of God would begin right away. [12] He said, "A nobleman was called away to a distant empire to be crowned king and then return. [13] Before he left, he called together ten of his servants and divided among them ten pounds of silver,* saying, 'Invest this for me while I am gone.' [14] But his people hated him and sent a delegation after him to say, 'We do not want him to be our king.'

[15] "After he was crowned king, he returned and called in the servants to whom he had given the money. He wanted to find out what their profits were. [16] The first servant reported, 'Master, I invested your money and made ten times the original amount!'

[17] "'Well done!' the king exclaimed. 'You are a good servant. You have been faithful with the little I entrusted to you, so you will be governor of ten cities as your reward.'

[18] "The next servant reported, 'Master, I invested your money and made five times the original amount.'

[19] "'Well done!' the king said. 'You will be governor over five cities.'

[20] "But the third servant brought back only the original amount of money and said, 'Master, I hid your money and kept it safe. [21] I was afraid because you are a hard man to deal with, taking what isn't yours and harvesting crops you didn't plant.'

[22] "'You wicked servant!' the king roared.

18:37 Or *Jesus of Nazareth.*   19:10 "Son of Man" is a title Jesus used for himself.   19:13 Greek *ten minas;* one mina was worth about three months' wages.

- The widow had no access to the judge. . . . We have constant access to God (see Hebrews 10:19, p. 283).
- The widow came to the court of law. . . . We come to the throne of grace (see Hebrews 4:16, pp. 278-279).
- The widow had no lawyer. . . . We have Jesus as our advocate (see 1 John 2:1, p. 305).
- The widow had to wear down the judge before he really listened. . . . We already know that God hears our requests (Psalm 4:3).

If this poor woman received what she deserved from a corrupt judge, how much more will we receive from our loving heavenly Father? As Jesus illustrated, persistence pays off. Keep on praying!

To begin the next topic, turn to p. A48.

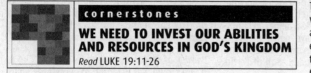

cornerstones

WE NEED TO INVEST OUR ABILITIES AND RESOURCES IN GOD'S KINGDOM
Read LUKE 19:11-26

This parable explains what Jesus expects of us as we await his return to earth. The nobleman in this story represents Christ. The servants refer to his followers. In essence, he is saying that we are to work diligently on his behalf until he returns.

Like the men who were given ten pounds of silver, every believer has an equal opportunity and responsibility to invest his or her life in God's Kingdom. It is the simple commission to proclaim the gospel to the world and make disciples. Here we see three levels of investment.

1. The Servant with Tremendous Gain. This ambitious servant gave the king back ten times more than he had been given. This type of person is truly a disciple. He or she actively shares his or her faith with every person, then takes these individuals under his or her wing to help them mature in their faith.

2. The Servant with Splendid Gain. The second servant was a little less ambitious than the first, but he did make some gain. This type of person seems somewhat satisfied with the status quo. He or she gets the gospel out slowly but surely, but he or she doesn't see the same results as the first person. This person fails to recognize and use all of the resources God has given him or her, and usually falls a little short of his or her full potential.

3. The Servant with No Gain. The third servant wanted to play it safe, so he buried his money. He had a false perception of his master. He claimed that his master was hard and unfair. This person is often motivated out of fear of God rather than love for God. He or she sees witnessing as a duty rather than a privilege. That is why Paul tells us that Christ's love needs to be the motivating force in all that we do (see 2 Corinthians 5:14, p. 212). We can only give out what we ourselves have taken in. And this person knows little of the Savior he or she serves.

In the Kingdom of God, God expects investment as well as results. Don't take this sacred trust he has given to you and bury it in the ground. Use it. Multiply it. Remember, God isn't asking you to work *for* him. He is asking to work *through* you. Yield to the power of the Holy Spirit and ask God for directions as to how you can be used by him. Then you will see results.

For the next note on "Accountability," turn to p. 192.

'Your own words condemn you. If you knew that I'm a hard man who takes what isn't mine and harvests crops I didn't plant, [23] why didn't you deposit my money in the bank? At least I could have gotten some interest on it.'

[24] "Then, turning to the others standing nearby, the king ordered, 'Take the money from this servant, and give it to the one who has ten pounds.'

[25] "But, master,' they said, 'he already has ten pounds!'

[26] "'Yes,' the king replied, 'and to those who use well what they are given, even more will be given. But from those who do nothing, even what little they have will be taken away. [27] And as for these enemies of mine who didn't want me to be their king—bring them in and execute them right here in front of me.'"

Jesus' Triumphant Entry

[28] After telling this story, Jesus went on toward Jerusalem, walking ahead of his disciples. [29] As he came to the towns of Bethphage and Bethany on the Mount of Olives, he sent two disciples ahead. [30] "Go into that village over there," he told them. "As you enter it, you will see a young donkey tied there that no one has ever ridden. Untie it and bring it here. [31] If anyone asks, 'Why are you untying that colt?' just say, 'The Lord needs it.'"

[32] So they went and found the colt, just as Jesus had said. [33] And sure enough, as they were untying it, the owners asked them, "Why are you untying that colt?"

[34] And the disciples simply replied, "The Lord needs it." [35] So they brought the colt to Jesus and threw their garments over it for him to ride on.

[36]As he rode along, the crowds spread out their garments on the road ahead of him. [37]When he reached the place where the road started down the Mount of Olives, all of his followers began to shout and sing as they walked along, praising God for all the wonderful miracles they had seen.

[38] "Blessings on the King who comes in the
        name of the LORD!
    Peace in heaven, and glory in highest
        heaven!"*

[39]But some of the Pharisees among the crowd said, "Teacher, rebuke your followers for saying things like that!"

[40]He replied, "If they kept quiet, the stones along the road would burst into cheers!"

Jesus Weeps over Jerusalem

[41]But as he came closer to Jerusalem and saw the city ahead, he began to weep. [42]"How I wish today that you of all people would understand the way to peace. But now it is too late, and peace is hidden from your eyes. [43]Before long your enemies will build ramparts against your walls and encircle you and close in on you from every side. [44]They will crush you into the ground, and your children with you. Your enemies will not leave a single stone in place, because you did not accept your opportunity for salvation."

Jesus Clears the Temple

[45]Then Jesus entered the Temple and began to drive out the people selling animals for sacrifices. [46]He said to them, "The Scriptures declare, 'My Temple will be a house of prayer,' but you have turned it into a den of thieves."*

[47]After that, he taught daily in the Temple, but the leading priests, the teachers of religious law, and the other leaders of the people began planning how to kill him. [48]But they could think of nothing, because all the people hung on every word he said.

CHAPTER 20

The Authority of Jesus Challenged

One day as Jesus was teaching the people and preaching the Good News in the Temple, the leading priests, the teachers of religious law, and the elders came up to him. [2]They demanded, "By what authority are you doing all these things? Who gave you the right?"

[3]"Let me ask you a question first," he replied. [4]"Did John's authority to baptize come from heaven, or was it merely human?"

[5]They talked it over among themselves. "If we say it was from heaven, he will ask why we didn't believe John. [6]But if we say it was merely human, the people will stone us because they are convinced John was a prophet." [7]So they finally replied that they didn't know.

[8]And Jesus responded, "Then I won't tell you by what authority I do these things."

Parable of the Evil Farmers

[9]Now Jesus turned to the people again and told them this story: "A man planted a vineyard, leased it to tenant farmers, and moved to another country to live for several years. [10]At the time of the grape harvest, he sent one of his servants to collect his share of the crop. But the farmers attacked the servant, beat him up, and sent him back empty-handed. [11]So the owner sent another servant, but they also insulted him, beat him up, and sent him away empty-handed. [12]A third man was sent, and they wounded him and chased him away.

[13]"'What will I do?' the owner asked himself. 'I know! I'll send my cherished son. Surely they will respect him.'

[14]"But when the tenant farmers saw his son, they said to each other, 'Here comes the heir to this estate. Let's kill him and get the estate for ourselves!' [15]So they dragged him out of the vineyard and murdered him.

"What do you suppose the owner of the vineyard will do to them?" Jesus asked. [16]"I'll tell you—he will come and kill those farmers and lease the vineyard to others."

"How terrible that such a thing should ever happen," his listeners protested.

[17]Jesus looked at them and said, "Then what does this Scripture mean?

'The stone that the builders rejected
    has now become the cornerstone.'*

[18]Everyone who stumbles over that stone will be broken to pieces, and it will crush anyone it falls on."

[19]The teachers of religious law and the leading priests wanted to arrest Jesus immediately because they realized he was telling the story against them—they were the wicked farmers. But they were afraid of the people's reaction.

Taxes for Caesar

[20]Watching for their opportunity, the leaders sent spies pretending to be honest men. They tried to get Jesus to say something that could be reported to the Roman governor so he would arrest Jesus. [21]"Teacher," they said, "we know that you speak and teach what is right and are not influenced by what others think. You teach the way of God truthfully. [22]Now tell us—is it right for us to pay taxes to Caesar or not?"

19:38 Pss 118:26; 148:1.   19:46 Isa 56:7; Jer 7:11.   20:17 Ps 118:22.

²³He saw through their trickery and said, ²⁴"Show me a Roman coin.* Whose picture and title are stamped on it?"

"Caesar's," they replied.

²⁵"Well then," he said, "give to Caesar what belongs to Caesar, and give to God what belongs to God."

²⁶So they failed to trap him by what he said in front of the people. Instead, they were amazed by his answer, and they became silent.

Discussion about Resurrection

²⁷Then Jesus was approached by some Sadducees—religious leaders who say there is no resurrection from the dead. ²⁸They posed this question: "Teacher, Moses gave us a law that if a man dies, leaving a wife but no children, his brother should marry the widow and have a child who will carry on the brother's name.* ²⁹Well, suppose there were seven brothers. The oldest one married and then died without children. ³⁰So the second brother married the widow, but he also died. ³¹Then the third brother married her. This continued with all seven of them, who died without children. ³²Finally, the woman also died. ³³So tell us, whose wife will she be in the resurrection? For all seven were married to her!"

³⁴Jesus replied, "Marriage is for people here on earth. ³⁵But in the age to come, those worthy of being raised from the dead will neither marry nor be given in marriage. ³⁶And they will never die again. In this respect they will be like angels. They are children of God and children of the resurrection.

³⁷"But now, as to whether the dead will be raised—even Moses proved this when he wrote about the burning bush. Long after Abraham, Isaac, and Jacob had died, he referred to the Lord* as 'the God of Abraham, the God of Isaac, and the God of Jacob.'* ³⁸So he is the God of the living, not the dead, for they are all alive to him."

³⁹"Well said, Teacher!" remarked some of the teachers of religious law who were standing there. ⁴⁰And then no one dared to ask him any more questions.

Whose Son Is the Messiah?

⁴¹Then Jesus presented them with a question. "Why is it," he asked, "that the Messiah is said to be the son of David? ⁴²For David himself wrote in the book of Psalms:

'The LORD said to my Lord,
Sit in the place of honor
at my right hand

⁴³until I humble your enemies,
making them a footstool under your
feet.'*

⁴⁴Since David called the Messiah 'Lord,' how can the Messiah be his son?"

⁴⁵Then, with the crowds listening, he turned to his disciples and said, ⁴⁶"Beware of these teachers of religious law! For they like to parade around in flowing robes and love to receive respectful greetings as they walk in the marketplaces. And how they love the seats of honor in the synagogues and the head table at banquets. ⁴⁷Yet they shamelessly cheat widows out of their property and then pretend to be pious by making long prayers in public. Because of this, they will be severely punished."

CHAPTER 21
The Widow's Offering

While Jesus was in the Temple, he watched the rich people dropping their gifts in the collection box. ²Then a poor widow came by and dropped in two small coins.*

³"I tell you the truth," Jesus said, "this poor widow has given more than all the rest of them. ⁴For they have given a tiny part of their surplus, but she, poor as she is, has given everything she has."

Jesus Foretells the Future

⁵Some of his disciples began talking about the majestic stonework of the Temple and the memorial decorations on the walls. But Jesus said, ⁶"The time is coming when all these things will be completely demolished. Not one stone will be left on top of another!"

⁷"Teacher," they asked, "when will all this happen? What sign will show us that these things are about to take place?"

⁸He replied, "Don't let anyone mislead you, for many will come in my name, claiming, 'I am the Messiah,'* and saying, 'The time has come!' But don't believe them. ⁹And when you hear of wars and insurrections, don't panic. Yes, these things must take place first, but the end won't follow immediately." ¹⁰Then he added, "Nation will go to war against nation, and kingdom against kingdom. ¹¹There will be great earthquakes, and there will be famines and plagues in many lands, and there will be terrifying things and great miraculous signs from heaven.

¹²"But before all this occurs, there will be a time of great persecution. You will be dragged into synagogues and prisons, and you will stand trial before kings and governors because

---

20:24 Greek *a denarius.*   20:28 See Deut 25:5-6.   20:37a Greek *when he wrote about the bush. He referred to the Lord.*
20:37b Exod 3:6.   20:42-43 Ps 110:1.   21:2 Greek *two lepta* [the smallest of Jewish coins].   21:8 Greek *claiming, 'I am.'*

you are my followers. [13] But this will be your opportunity to tell them about me.* [14] So don't worry in advance about how to answer the charges against you, [15] for I will give you the right words and such wisdom that none of your opponents will be able to reply or refute you! [16] Even those closest to you—your parents, brothers, relatives, and friends—will betray you. They will even kill some of you. [17] And everyone will hate you because you are my followers.* [18] But not a hair of your head will perish! [19] By standing firm, you will win your souls.

[20] "And when you see Jerusalem surrounded by armies, then you will know that the time of its destruction has arrived. [21] Then those in Judea must flee to the hills. Those in Jerusalem must get out, and those out in the country should not return to the city. [22] For those will be days of God's vengeance, and the prophetic words of the Scriptures will be fulfilled. [23] How terrible it will be for pregnant women and for nursing mothers in those days. For there will be disaster in the land and great anger against this people. [24] They will be killed by the sword or sent away as captives to all the nations of the world. And Jerusalem will be trampled down by the Gentiles until the period of the Gentiles comes to an end.

[25] "And there will be strange signs in the sun, moon, and stars. And here on earth the nations will be in turmoil, perplexed by the roaring seas and strange tides. [26] People will be terrified at what they see coming upon the earth, for the powers in the heavens will be shaken. [27] Then everyone will see the Son of Man* coming on a cloud with power and great glory.* [28] So when all these things begin to happen, stand and look up, for your salvation is near!"

[29] Then he gave them this illustration: "Notice the fig tree, or any other tree. [30] When the leaves come out, you know without being told that summer is near. [31] In the same way, when you see all these things taking place, you can know that the Kingdom of God is near. [32] I tell you the truth, this generation will not pass from the scene until all these things have taken place. [33] Heaven and earth will disappear, but my words will never disappear.

[34] "Watch out! Don't let your hearts be dulled by carousing and drunkenness, and by the worries of this life. Don't let that day catch you unaware, [35] like a trap. For that day will come upon everyone living on the earth. [36] Keep alert at all times. And pray that you might be strong enough to escape these coming horrors and stand before the Son of Man."

[37] Every day Jesus went to the Temple to teach, and each evening he returned to spend the night on the Mount of Olives. [38] The crowds gathered at the Temple early each morning to hear him.

CHAPTER 22

Judas Agrees to Betray Jesus

The Festival of Unleavened Bread, which is also called Passover, was approaching. [2] The leading priests and teachers of religious law were plotting how to kill Jesus, but they were afraid of the people's reaction.

[3] Then Satan entered into Judas Iscariot, who was one of the twelve disciples, [4] and he went to the leading priests and captains of the Temple guard to discuss the best way to betray Jesus to them. [5] They were delighted, and they promised to give him money. [6] So he agreed and began looking for an opportunity to betray Jesus so they could arrest him when the crowds weren't around.

The Last Supper

[7] Now the Festival of Unleavened Bread arrived, when the Passover lamb is sacrificed. [8] Jesus sent Peter and John ahead and said, "Go and prepare the Passover meal, so we can eat it together."

[9] "Where do you want us to prepare it?" they asked him.

[10] He replied, "As soon as you enter Jerusalem, a man carrying a pitcher of water will meet you. Follow him. At the house he enters, [11] say to the owner, 'The Teacher asks: Where is the guest room where I can eat the Passover meal with my disciples?' [12] He will take you upstairs to a large room that is already set up. That is where you should prepare our meal." [13] They went off to the city and found everything just as Jesus had said, and they prepared the Passover meal there.

[14] When the time came, Jesus and the apostles sat down together at the table.* [15] Jesus said, "I have been very eager to eat this Passover meal with you before my suffering begins. [16] For I tell you now that I won't eat this meal again until its meaning is fulfilled in the Kingdom of God."

[17] Then he took a cup of wine and gave thanks to God for it. Then he said, "Take this and share it among yourselves. [18] For I will not drink wine again until the Kingdom of God has come."

[19] He took some bread and gave thanks to God for it. Then he broke it in pieces and gave it to the disciples, saying, "This is my body, which is given for you. Do this to remember me."

[20] After supper he took another cup of wine

and said, "This cup is the new covenant between God and his people—an agreement confirmed with my blood, which is poured out as a sacrifice for you.*

21"But here at this table, sitting among us as a friend, is the man who will betray me. 22For it has been determined that the Son of Man* must die. But what sorrow awaits the one who betrays him." 23The disciples began to ask each other which of them would ever do such a thing.

24Then they began to argue among themselves about who would be the greatest among them. 25Jesus told them, "In this world the kings and great men lord it over their people, yet they are called 'friends of the people.' 26But among you it will be different. Those who are the greatest among you should take the lowest rank, and the leader should be like a servant. 27Who is more important, the one who sits at the table or the one who serves? The one who sits at the table, of course. But not here! For I am among you as one who serves.

28"You have stayed with me in my time of trial. 29And just as my Father has granted me a Kingdom, I now grant you the right 30to eat and drink at my table in my Kingdom. And you will sit on thrones, judging the twelve tribes of Israel.

Jesus Predicts Peter's Denial

31"Simon, Simon, Satan has asked to sift each of you like wheat. 32But I have pleaded in prayer for you, Simon, that your faith should not fail. So when you have repented and turned to me again, strengthen your brothers."

33Peter said, "Lord, I am ready to go to prison with you, and even to die with you."

34But Jesus said, "Peter, let me tell you something. Before the rooster crows tomorrow morning, you will deny three times that you even know me."

35Then Jesus asked them, "When I sent you out to preach the Good News and you did not have money, a traveler's bag, or an extra pair of sandals, did you need anything?"

"No," they replied.

36"But now," he said, "take your money and a traveler's bag. And if you don't have a sword, sell your cloak and buy one! 37For the time has come for this prophecy about me to be fulfilled: 'He was counted among the rebels.'* Yes, everything written about me by the prophets will come true."

38"Look, Lord," they replied, "we have two swords among us."

"That's enough," he said.

Jesus Prays on the Mount of Olives

39Then, accompanied by the disciples, Jesus left the upstairs room and went as usual to the Mount of Olives. 40There he told them, "Pray that you will not give in to temptation."

41He walked away, about a stone's throw, and knelt down and prayed, 42"Father, if you are willing, please take this cup of suffering away from me. Yet I want your will to be done, not mine." 43Then an angel from heaven appeared and strengthened him. 44He prayed more fervently, and he was in such agony of spirit that his sweat fell to the ground like great drops of blood.*

45At last he stood up again and returned to the disciples, only to find them asleep, exhausted from grief. 46"Why are you sleeping?" he asked them. "Get up and pray, so that you will not give in to temptation."

Jesus Is Betrayed and Arrested

47But even as Jesus said this, a crowd approached, led by Judas, one of the twelve disciples. Judas walked over to Jesus to greet him with a kiss. 48But Jesus said, "Judas, would you betray the Son of Man with a kiss?"

49When the other disciples saw what was about to happen, they exclaimed, "Lord, should we fight? We brought the swords!" 50And one of them struck at the high priest's slave, slashing off his right ear.

51But Jesus said, "No more of this." And he touched the man's ear and healed him.

52Then Jesus spoke to the leading priests, the captains of the Temple guard, and the elders who had come for him. "Am I some dangerous revolutionary," he asked, "that you come with swords and clubs to arrest me? 53Why didn't you arrest me in the Temple? I was there every day. But this is your moment, the time when the power of darkness reigns."

Peter Denies Jesus

54So they arrested him and led him to the high priest's home. And Peter followed at a distance. 55The guards lit a fire in the middle of the courtyard and sat around it, and Peter joined them there. 56A servant girl noticed him in the firelight and began staring at him. Finally she said, "This man was one of Jesus' followers!"

57But Peter denied it. "Woman," he said, "I don't even know him!"

58After a while someone else looked at him and said, "You must be one of them!"

"No, man, I'm not!" Peter retorted.

59About an hour later someone else insisted,

22:19-20 Some manuscripts do not include 22:19b-20, *which is given for you . . . which is poured out as a sacrifice for you.*
22:22 "Son of Man" is a title Jesus used for himself.   22:37 Isa 53:12.   22:43-44 Verses 43 and 44 are not included in many ancient manuscripts.

BIG QUESTIONS

What Is Backsliding?

Read LUKE 22:31-62

As believers we have been given a "new nature"—a part of us that hungers after God, a supernatural inclination to do what is right. Unfortunately, being human, we also have an "old nature"—a natural inclination to do wrong. Sometimes Christians begin to fall back spiritually or "backslide." God speaks of this in Jeremiah 3:22, where he says, "Come back to me, and I will heal your wayward hearts."

Perhaps the best way to understand the dangers of backsliding is to examine the biblical account of how one believer fell into this trap. He was Simon Peter, one of Jesus' closest disciples. In Luke 22 we are given the account of his spiritual regression. His story serves as a warning that even the most mature believers have the potential to fall if they let their guard down.

Self-Confidence and False Security. Peter not only revealed his unfounded confidence in himself (that he would die with Jesus), but he also directly contradicted the Lord's prediction that he would fall (verse 34). He denied his own weakness to sin. The Bible warns, "If you think you are standing strong, be careful not to fall" (1 Corinthians 10:12).

Prayerlessness. Even after Jesus specifically instructed Peter to pray, he decided to sleep instead. In Matthew's account of this incident, Jesus had even warned them, "The spirit is willing, but the body is weak!" (Matthew 26:41). Yet he felt no weakness and saw no need to be prayerful and watchful. Prayerlessness is as much a sin as directly breaking a commandment, for throughout Scripture God has specifically instructed us to pray.

Following God at a Distance. A lack of closeness and fellowship with the Lord will always be at the foundation of all spiritual regression. Although Peter was still following Jesus, he wasn't following as closely as he could have been. There are some Christians who try to live in both worlds. They want to be believers, but they don't want to be too committed. You endanger yourself when you live this way.

Warming Up at the Enemies' Fire. Following in the distance, Peter became cold and was attracted to the fire. Peter hoped to go unnoticed in the larger crowd, so he settled in with the very people who were responsible for arresting his Lord. The Bible tells us, "Oh, the joys of those who do not follow the advice of the wicked, or stand around with sinners, or join in with mockers" (Psalm 1:1). Tragically, Peter was doing exactly the opposite. When that spiritual passion in our heart begins to die, that fire for Jesus Christ will grow cold, and we will look elsewhere for warmth.

Denial and Disassociations. Peter reached this final step of spiritual regression when he denied knowing or being with Jesus. Matthew tells us that he began to curse and swear, which means he took an oath, saying, "A curse on me if I'm lying—I don't know the man!" (Matthew 26:74). Peter had lost all sense of reality and, seemingly, all awareness of God.

Despite Peter's fall, he was restored. In Luke 22:61, his eyes met those of Jesus, and Peter cried bitterly. As Peter grieved over his sin, Jesus saw his heart. The Bible says, "For the kind of sorrow God wants us to experience leads us away from sin and results in salvation" (2 Corinthians 7:10). Interestingly enough, three days later, after Jesus' resurrection, the angel at the tomb specifically told Mary, "Now go and tell his disciples, *including Peter,* that Jesus is going ahead of you to Galilee. You will see him there, just as he told you before he died" (Mark 16:7, emphasis added). Jesus wanted Peter to know that he still loved him.

As Christians we will sin. Scripture says, "If we claim we have no sin, we are only fooling ourselves and not living in the truth" (1 John 1:8). But the Holy Spirit will lovingly convict us of that sin and lead us back to the cross, where we can confess it and turn from it. Remember, when we sin we should run to—not away from—the Lord.

For the next "Big Question" note, turn to p. 135.

"This must be one of them, because he is a Galilean, too."

[60] But Peter said, "Man, I don't know what you are talking about." And immediately, while he was still speaking, the rooster crowed.

[61] At that moment the Lord turned and looked at Peter. Suddenly, the Lord's words flashed through Peter's mind: "Before the rooster crows tomorrow morning, you will deny three times that you even know me." [62] And Peter left the courtyard, weeping bitterly.

[63] The guards in charge of Jesus began mocking and beating him. [64] They blindfolded him and said, "Prophesy to us! Who hit you that time?" [65] And they hurled all sorts of terrible insults at him.

Jesus before the Council

[66] At daybreak all the elders of the people assembled, including the leading priests and the teachers of religious law. Jesus was led before this high council,* [67] and they said, "Tell us, are you the Messiah?"

But he replied, "If I tell you, you won't believe me. [68] And if I ask you a question, you won't answer. [69] But from now on the Son of Man will be seated in the place of power at God's right hand.*"

[70] They all shouted, "So, are you claiming to be the Son of God?"

And he replied, "You say that I am."

[71] "Why do we need other witnesses?" they said. "We ourselves heard him say it."

CHAPTER 23

Jesus' Trial before Pilate

Then the entire council took Jesus to Pilate, the Roman governor. [2] They began to state their case: "This man has been leading our people astray by telling them not to pay their taxes to the Roman government and by claiming he is the Messiah, a king."

[3] So Pilate asked him, "Are you the king of the Jews?"

Jesus replied, "You have said it."

[4] Pilate turned to the leading priests and to the crowd and said, "I find nothing wrong with this man!"

[5] Then they became insistent. "But he is causing riots by his teaching wherever he goes—all over Judea, from Galilee to Jerusalem!"

[6] "Oh, is he a Galilean?" Pilate asked. [7] When they said that he was, Pilate sent him to Herod Antipas, because Galilee was under Herod's jurisdiction, and Herod happened to be in Jerusalem at the time.

[8] Herod was delighted at the opportunity to see Jesus, because he had heard about him and had been hoping for a long time to see him perform a miracle. [9] He asked Jesus question after question, but Jesus refused to answer. [10] Meanwhile, the leading priests and the teachers of religious law stood there shouting their accusations. [11] Then Herod and his soldiers began mocking and ridiculing Jesus. Finally, they put a royal robe on him and sent him back to Pilate. [12] (Herod and Pilate, who had been enemies before, became friends that day.)

[13] Then Pilate called together the leading priests and other religious leaders, along with the people, [14] and he announced his verdict. "You brought this man to me, accusing him of leading a revolt. I have examined him thoroughly on this point in your presence and find him innocent. [15] Herod came to the same conclusion and sent him back to us. Nothing this man has done calls for the death penalty. [16] So I will have him flogged, and then I will release him."*

[18] Then a mighty roar rose from the crowd, and with one voice they shouted, "Kill him, and release Barabbas to us!" [19] (Barabbas was in prison for taking part in an insurrection in Jerusalem against the government, and for murder.) [20] Pilate argued with them, because he wanted to release Jesus. [21] But they kept shouting, "Crucify him! Crucify him!"

[22] For the third time he demanded, "Why? What crime has he committed? I have found no reason to sentence him to death. So I will have him flogged, and then I will release him."

[23] But the mob shouted louder and louder, demanding that Jesus be crucified, and their voices prevailed. [24] So Pilate sentenced Jesus to die as they demanded. [25] As they had requested, he released Barabbas, the man in prison for insurrection and murder. But he turned Jesus over to them to do as they wished.

The Crucifixion

[26] As they led Jesus away, a man named Simon, who was from Cyrene,* happened to be coming in from the countryside. The soldiers seized him and put the cross on him and made him carry it behind Jesus. [27] A large crowd trailed behind, including many grief-stricken women. [28] But Jesus turned and said to them, "Daughters of Jerusalem, don't weep for me, but weep for yourselves and for your children. [29] For the

---

22:66 Greek *before their Sanhedrin.*   22:69 See Ps 110:1.   23:16 Some manuscripts add verse 17, *Now it was necessary for him to release one prisoner to them during the Passover celebration.* Compare Matt 27:15; Mark 15:6; John 18:39.
23:26 *Cyrene* was a city in northern Africa.

days are coming when they will say, 'Fortunate indeed are the women who are childless, the wombs that have not borne a child and the breasts that have never nursed.' ³⁰People will beg the mountains, 'Fall on us,' and plead with the hills, 'Bury us.'* ³¹For if these things are done when the tree is green, what will happen when it is dry?*"

³²Two others, both criminals, were led out to be executed with him. ³³When they came to a place called The Skull,* they nailed him to the cross. And the criminals were also crucified—one on his right and one on his left.

³⁴Jesus said, "Father, forgive them, for they don't know what they are doing."* And the soldiers gambled for his clothes by throwing dice.*

³⁵The crowd watched and the leaders scoffed. "He saved others," they said, "let him save himself if he is really God's Messiah, the Chosen One." ³⁶The soldiers mocked him, too, by offering him a drink of sour wine. ³⁷They called out to him, "If you are the King of the Jews, save yourself!" ³⁸A sign was fastened above him with these words: "This is the King of the Jews."

³⁹One of the criminals hanging beside him scoffed, "So you're the Messiah, are you? Prove it by saving yourself—and us, too, while you're at it!"

⁴⁰But the other criminal protested, "Don't you fear God even when you have been sentenced to die? ⁴¹We deserve to die for our crimes, but this man hasn't done anything wrong." ⁴²Then he said, "Jesus, remember me when you come into your Kingdom."

⁴³And Jesus replied, "I assure you, today you will be with me in paradise."

The Death of Jesus

⁴⁴By this time it was about noon, and darkness fell across the whole land until three o'clock. ⁴⁵The light from the sun was gone. And suddenly, the curtain in the sanctuary of the Temple was torn down the middle. ⁴⁶Then Jesus shouted, "Father, I entrust my spirit into your hands!"* And with those words he breathed his last.

⁴⁷When the Roman officer* overseeing the execution saw what had happened, he worshiped God and said, "Surely this man was innocent.*" ⁴⁸And when all the crowd that came to see the crucifixion saw what had happened, they went home in deep sorrow.* ⁴⁹But Jesus' friends, including the women who had followed him from Galilee, stood at a distance watching.

The Burial of Jesus

⁵⁰Now there was a good and righteous man named Joseph. He was a member of the Jewish high council, ⁵¹but he had not agreed with the decision and actions of the other religious leaders. He was from the town of Arimathea in Judea, and he was waiting for the Kingdom of God to come. ⁵²He went to Pilate and asked for Jesus' body. ⁵³Then he took the body down from the cross and wrapped it in a long sheet of linen cloth and laid it in a new tomb that had been carved out of rock. ⁵⁴This was done late on Friday afternoon, the day of preparation,* as the Sabbath was about to begin.

⁵⁵As his body was taken away, the women from Galilee followed and saw the tomb where his body was placed. ⁵⁶Then they went home and prepared spices and ointments to anoint his body. But by the time they were finished the Sabbath had begun, so they rested as required by the law.

CHAPTER 24

The Resurrection

But very early on Sunday morning* the women went to the tomb, taking the spices they had prepared. ²They found that the stone had been rolled away from the entrance. ³So they went in, but they didn't find the body of the Lord Jesus. ⁴As they stood there puzzled, two men suddenly appeared to them, clothed in dazzling robes.

⁵The women were terrified and bowed with their faces to the ground. Then the men asked, "Why are you looking among the dead for someone who is alive? ⁶He isn't here! He is risen from the dead! Remember what he told you back in Galilee, ⁷that the Son of Man* must be betrayed into the hands of sinful men and be crucified, and that he would rise again on the third day."

⁸Then they remembered that he had said this. ⁹So they rushed back from the tomb to tell his eleven disciples—and everyone else—what had happened. ¹⁰It was Mary Magdalene, Joanna, Mary the mother of James, and several other women who told the apostles what had happened. ¹¹But the story sounded like nonsense to the men, so they didn't believe it. ¹²However, Peter jumped up and ran to the tomb to look. Stooping, he peered in and saw

---

23:30 Hos 10:8.   23:31 Or *If these things are done to me, the living tree, what will happen to you, the dry tree?*   23:33 Sometimes rendered *Calvary*, which comes from the Latin word for "skull."   23:34a This sentence is not included in many ancient manuscripts.   23:34b Greek *by casting lots.* See Ps 22:18.   23:46 Ps 31:5.   23:47a Greek *the centurion.*   23:47b Or *righteous.*   23:48 Greek *went home beating their breasts.*   23:54 Greek *It was the day of preparation.*   24:1 Greek *But on the first day of the week, very early in the morning.*   24:7 "Son of Man" is a title Jesus used for himself.

the empty linen wrappings; then he went home again, wondering what had happened.

The Walk to Emmaus

[13]That same day two of Jesus' followers were walking to the village of Emmaus, seven miles* from Jerusalem. [14]As they walked along they were talking about everything that had happened. [15]As they talked and discussed these things, Jesus himself suddenly came and began walking with them. [16]But God kept them from recognizing him.

[17]He asked them, "What are you discussing so intently as you walk along?"

They stopped short, sadness written across their faces. [18]Then one of them, Cleopas, replied, "You must be the only person in Jerusalem who hasn't heard about all the things that have happened there the last few days."

[19]"What things?" Jesus asked.

"The things that happened to Jesus, the man from Nazareth," they said. "He was a prophet who did powerful miracles, and he was a mighty teacher in the eyes of God and all the people. [20]But our leading priests and other religious leaders handed him over to be condemned to death, and they crucified him. [21]We had hoped he was the Messiah who had come to rescue Israel. This all happened three days ago.

[22]"Then some women from our group of his followers were at his tomb early this morning, and they came back with an amazing report. [23]They said his body was missing, and they had seen angels who told them Jesus is alive! [24]Some of our men ran out to see, and sure enough, his body was gone, just as the women had said."

[25]Then Jesus said to them, "You foolish people! You find it so hard to believe all that the prophets wrote in the Scriptures. [26]Wasn't it clearly predicted that the Messiah would have to suffer all these things before entering his glory?" [27]Then Jesus took them through the writings of Moses and all the prophets, explaining from all the Scriptures the things concerning himself.

[28]By this time they were nearing Emmaus and the end of their journey. Jesus acted as if he were going on, [29]but they begged him, "Stay the night with us, since it is getting late." So he went home with them. [30]As they sat down to eat,* he took the bread and blessed it. Then he broke it and gave it to them. [31]Suddenly, their eyes were opened, and they recognized him. And at that moment he disappeared!

[32]They said to each other, "Didn't our hearts burn within us as he talked with us on the road and explained the Scriptures to us?" [33]And within the hour they were on their way back to Jerusalem. There they found the eleven disciples and the others who had gathered with them, [34]who said, "The Lord has really risen! He appeared to Peter.*"

Jesus Appears to the Disciples

[35]Then the two from Emmaus told their story of how Jesus had appeared to them as they were walking along the road, and how they had recognized him as he was breaking the bread. [36]And just as they were telling about it, Jesus himself was suddenly standing there among them. "Peace be with you," he said. [37]But the whole group was startled and frightened, thinking they were seeing a ghost!

[38]"Why are you frightened?" he asked. "Why are your hearts filled with doubt? [39]Look at my hands. Look at my feet. You can see that it's really me. Touch me and make sure that I am not a ghost, because ghosts don't have bodies, as you see that I do." [40]As he spoke, he showed them his hands and his feet.

[41]Still they stood there in disbelief, filled with joy and wonder. Then he asked them, "Do you have anything here to eat?" [42]They gave him a piece of broiled fish, [43]and he ate it as they watched.

[44]Then he said, "When I was with you before, I told you that everything written about me in the law of Moses and the prophets and in the Psalms must be fulfilled." [45]Then he opened their minds to understand the Scriptures. [46]And he said, "Yes, it was written long ago that the Messiah would suffer and die and rise from the dead on the third day. [47]It was also written that this message would be proclaimed in the authority of his name to all the nations,* beginning in Jerusalem: 'There is forgiveness of sins for all who repent.' [48]You are witnesses of all these things.

[49]"And now I will send the Holy Spirit, just as my Father promised. But stay here in the city until the Holy Spirit comes and fills you with power from heaven."

The Ascension

[50]Then Jesus led them to Bethany, and lifting his hands to heaven, he blessed them. [51]While he was blessing them, he left them and was taken up to heaven. [52]So they worshiped him and then returned to Jerusalem filled with great joy. [53]And they spent all of their time in the Temple, praising God.

24:13 Greek *60 stadia* [11.1 kilometers].   24:30 Or *As they reclined.*   24:34 Greek *Simon.*   24:47 Or *all peoples.*

John

AUTHOR: JOHN | DATE WRITTEN: A.D. 85–90 | GENRE: GOSPEL

While the emphasis in the other three Gospels centers around the description of events in Jesus' life, John focuses on the meaning of those events. For instance, while all four Gospels record the miracle of Jesus' feeding the five thousand, only John gives us Jesus' message on the "bread of life" that followed the miracle.

CHAPTER 1

Prologue: Christ, the Eternal Word

¹ In the beginning the Word already existed.
   The Word was with God,
      and the Word was God.
² He existed in the beginning with God.
³ God created everything through him,
   and nothing was created except through
      him.
⁴ The Word gave life to everything that was
   created,*
   and his life brought light to everyone.
⁵ The light shines in the darkness,
   and the darkness can never extinguish it.*

⁶ God sent a man, John the Baptist,* ⁷ to tell about the light so that everyone might believe because of his testimony. ⁸ John himself was not the light; he was simply a witness to tell about the light. ⁹ The one who is the true light, who gives light to everyone, was coming into the world.

¹⁰ He came into the very world he created, but the world didn't recognize him. ¹¹ He came to his own people, and even they rejected him. ¹² But to all who believed him and accepted him, he gave the right to become children of God. ¹³ They are reborn—not with a physical birth resulting from human passion or plan, but a birth that comes from God.

¹⁴ So the Word became human* and made his home among us. He was full of unfailing love and faithfulness.* And we have seen his glory, the glory of the Father's one and only Son. ¹⁵ John testified about him when he shouted to the crowds, "This is the one I was talking about when I said, 'Someone is coming after me who is far greater than I am, for he existed long before me.'"

¹⁶ From his abundance we have all received one gracious blessing after another.* ¹⁷ For the law was given through Moses, but God's unfailing love and faithfulness came through Jesus Christ. ¹⁸ No one has ever seen God. But the unique One, who is himself God,* is near to the Father's heart. He has revealed God to us.

The Testimony of John the Baptist

¹⁹ This was John's testimony when the Jewish leaders sent priests and Temple assistants* from Jerusalem to ask John, "Who are you?" ²⁰ He came right out and said, "I am not the Messiah."

²¹ "Well then, who are you?" they asked. "Are you Elijah?"

"No," he replied.

"Are you the Prophet we are expecting?"*

"No."

²² "Then who are you? We need an answer for those who sent us. What do you have to say about yourself?"

²³ John replied in the words of the prophet Isaiah:

"I am a voice shouting in the wilderness,
   'Clear the way for the LORD's coming!'"*

²⁴ Then the Pharisees who had been sent ²⁵ asked him, "If you aren't the Messiah or Elijah or the Prophet, what right do you have to baptize?"

²⁶ John told them, "I baptize with* water, but

1:3-4 Or *and nothing that was created was created except through him. The Word gave life to everything.* 1:5 Or *and the darkness has not understood it.* 1:6 Greek *a man named John.* 1:14a Greek *became flesh.* 1:14b Or *grace and truth;* also in 1:17. 1:16 Or *received the grace of Christ rather than the grace of the law;* Greek reads *received grace upon grace.* 1:18 Some manuscripts read *But the one and only Son.* 1:19 Greek *and Levites.* 1:21 Greek *Are you the Prophet?* See Deut 18:15, 18; Mal 4:5-6. 1:23 Isa 40:3. 1:26 Or *in;* also in 1:31, 33.

right here in the crowd is someone you do not recognize. [27] Though his ministry follows mine, I'm not even worthy to be his slave and untie the straps of his sandal."

[28] This encounter took place in Bethany, an area east of the Jordan River, where John was baptizing.

Jesus, the Lamb of God

[29] The next day John saw Jesus coming toward him and said, "Look! The Lamb of God who takes away the sin of the world! [30] He is the one I was talking about when I said, 'A man is coming after me who is far greater than I am, for he existed long before me.' [31] I did not recognize him as the Messiah, but I have been baptizing with water so that he might be revealed to Israel."

[32] Then John testified, "I saw the Holy Spirit descending like a dove from heaven and resting upon him. [33] I didn't know he was the one, but when God sent me to baptize with water, he told me, 'The one on whom you see the Spirit descend and rest is the one who will baptize with the Holy Spirit.' [34] I saw this happen to Jesus, so I testify that he is the Chosen One of God.*"

The First Disciples

[35] The following day John was again standing with two of his disciples. [36] As Jesus walked by, John looked at him and declared, "Look! There is the Lamb of God!" [37] When John's two disciples heard this, they followed Jesus.

[38] Jesus looked around and saw them following. "What do you want?" he asked them.

They replied, "Rabbi" (which means "Teacher"), "where are you staying?"

[39] "Come and see," he said. It was about four o'clock in the afternoon when they went with him to the place where he was staying, and they remained with him the rest of the day.

[40] Andrew, Simon Peter's brother, was one of these men who heard what John said and then followed Jesus. [41] Andrew went to find his brother, Simon, and told him, "We have found the Messiah" (which means "Christ"*).

[42] Then Andrew brought Simon to meet Jesus. Looking intently at Simon, Jesus said, "Your name is Simon, son of John—but you will be called Cephas" (which means "Peter"*).

[43] The next day Jesus decided to go to Galilee. He found Philip and said to him, "Come, follow me." [44] Philip was from Bethsaida, Andrew and Peter's hometown.

[45] Philip went to look for Nathanael and told him, "We have found the very person Moses*

and the prophets wrote about! His name is Jesus, the son of Joseph from Nazareth."

[46] "Nazareth!" exclaimed Nathanael. "Can anything good come from Nazareth?"

"Come and see for yourself," Philip replied.

[47] As they approached, Jesus said, "Now here is a genuine son of Israel—a man of complete integrity."

[48] "How do you know about me?" Nathanael asked.

Jesus replied, "I could see you under the fig tree before Philip found you."

[49] Then Nathanael exclaimed, "Rabbi, you are the Son of God—the King of Israel!"

[50] Jesus asked him, "Do you believe this just because I told you I had seen you under the fig tree? You will see greater things than this." [51] Then he said, "I tell you the truth, you will all see heaven open and the angels of God going up and down on the Son of Man, the one who is the stairway between heaven and earth.*"

CHAPTER 2

The Wedding at Cana

The next day* there was a wedding celebration in the village of Cana in Galilee. Jesus' mother was there, [2] and Jesus and his disciples were also invited to the celebration. [3] The wine supply ran out during the festivities, so Jesus' mother told him, "They have no more wine."

[4] "Dear woman, that's not our problem," Jesus replied. "My time has not yet come."

[5] But his mother told the servants, "Do whatever he tells you."

[6] Standing nearby were six stone water jars, used for Jewish ceremonial washing. Each could hold twenty to thirty gallons.* [7] Jesus told the servants, "Fill the jars with water." When the jars had been filled, [8] he said, "Now dip some out, and take it to the master of ceremonies." So the servants followed his instructions.

[9] When the master of ceremonies tasted the water that was now wine, not knowing where it had come from (though, of course, the servants knew), he called the bridegroom over. [10] "A host always serves the best wine first," he said. "Then, when everyone has had a lot to drink, he brings out the less expensive wine. But you have kept the best until now!"

[11] This miraculous sign at Cana in Galilee was the first time Jesus revealed his glory. And his disciples believed in him.

[12] After the wedding he went to Capernaum for a few days with his mother, his brothers, and his disciples.

1:34 Some manuscripts read *the Son of God.*   1:41 *Messiah* (a Hebrew term) and *Christ* (a Greek term) both mean "the anointed one."   1:42 The names *Cephas* (from Aramaic) and *Peter* (from Greek) both mean "rock."   1:45 Greek *Moses in the law.*   1:51 Greek *going up and down on the Son of Man;* see Gen 28:10-17. "Son of Man" is a title Jesus used for himself.   2:1 Greek *On the third day;* see 1:35, 43.   2:6 Greek *2 or 3 measures* [75 to 113 liters].

Jesus Clears the Temple

¹³It was nearly time for the Jewish Passover celebration, so Jesus went to Jerusalem. ¹⁴In the Temple area he saw merchants selling cattle, sheep, and doves for sacrifices; he also saw dealers at tables exchanging foreign money. ¹⁵Jesus made a whip from some ropes and chased them all out of the Temple. He drove out the sheep and cattle, scattered the money changers' coins over the floor, and turned over their tables. ¹⁶Then, going over to the people who sold doves, he told them, "Get these things out of here. Stop turning my Father's house into a marketplace!"

¹⁷Then his disciples remembered this prophecy from the Scriptures: "Passion for God's house will consume me."*

¹⁸But the Jewish leaders demanded, "What are you doing? If God gave you authority to do this, show us a miraculous sign to prove it."

¹⁹"All right," Jesus replied. "Destroy this temple, and in three days I will raise it up."

²⁰"What!" they exclaimed. "It has taken forty-six years to build this Temple, and you can rebuild it in three days?" ²¹But when Jesus said "this temple," he meant his own body. ²²After he was raised from the dead, his disciples remembered he had said this, and they believed both the Scriptures and what Jesus had said.

Jesus and Nicodemus

²³Because of the miraculous signs Jesus did in Jerusalem at the Passover celebration, many began to trust in him. ²⁴But Jesus didn't trust them, because he knew human nature. ²⁵No one needed to tell him what mankind is really like.

CHAPTER **3**
There was a man named Nicodemus, a Jewish religious leader who was a Pharisee. ²After dark one evening, he came to speak with Jesus. "Rabbi," he said, "we all know that God has sent you to teach us. Your miraculous signs are evidence that God is with you."

³Jesus replied, "I tell you the truth, unless you are born again,* you cannot see the Kingdom of God."

⁴"What do you mean?" exclaimed Nicodemus. "How can an old man go back into his mother's womb and be born again?"

⁵Jesus replied, "I assure you, no one can enter the Kingdom of God without being born of water and the Spirit.* ⁶Humans can reproduce only human life, but the Holy Spirit gives birth

to spiritual life.* ⁷So don't be surprised when I say, 'You* must be born again.' ⁸The wind blows wherever it wants. Just as you can hear the wind but can't tell where it comes from or where it is going, so you can't explain how people are born of the Spirit."

⁹"How are these things possible?" Nicodemus asked.

¹⁰Jesus replied, "You are a respected Jewish teacher, and yet you don't understand these things? ¹¹I assure you, we tell you what we know and have seen, and yet you won't believe our testimony. ¹²But if you don't believe me when I tell you about earthly things, how can you possibly believe if I tell you about heavenly things? ¹³No one has ever gone to heaven and returned. But the Son of Man* has come down from heaven. ¹⁴And as Moses lifted up the bronze snake on a pole in the wilderness, so the Son of Man must be lifted up, ¹⁵so that everyone who believes in him will have eternal life.*

¹⁶"For God loved the world so much that he gave his one and only Son, so that everyone who believes in him will not perish but have eternal life. ¹⁷God sent his Son into the world not to judge the world, but to save the world through him.

¹⁸"There is no judgment against anyone who believes in him. But anyone who does not believe in him has already been judged for not believing in God's one and only Son. ¹⁹And the judgment is based on this fact: God's light came into the world, but people loved the darkness more than the light, for their actions were evil. ²⁰All who do evil hate the light and refuse to go near it for fear their sins will be exposed. ²¹But those who do what is right come to the light so others can see that they are doing what God wants.*"

John the Baptist Exalts Jesus

²²Then Jesus and his disciples left Jerusalem and went into the Judean countryside. Jesus spent some time with them there, baptizing people.

²³At this time John the Baptist was baptizing at Aenon, near Salim, because there was plenty of water there; and people kept coming to him for baptism. ²⁴(This was before John was thrown into prison.) ²⁵A debate broke out between John's disciples and a certain Jew* over ceremonial cleansing. ²⁶So John's disciples came to him and said, "Rabbi, the man you met on the other side of the Jordan River, the one

---

2:17 Or *"Concern for God's house will be my undoing."* Ps 69:9. **3:3** Or *born from above;* also in 3:7. **3:5** Or *and spirit.* The Greek word for *Spirit* can also be translated *wind;* see 3:8. **3:6** Greek *what is born of the Spirit is spirit.* **3:7** The Greek word for *you* is plural; also in 3:12. **3:13** Some manuscripts add *who lives in heaven.* "Son of Man" is a title Jesus used for himself. **3:15** Or *everyone who believes will have eternal life in him.* **3:21** Or *can see God at work in what he is doing.* **3:25** Some manuscripts read *some Jews.*

you identified as the Messiah, is also baptizing people. And everybody is going to him instead of coming to us."

[27] John replied, "No one can receive anything unless God gives it from heaven. [28] You yourselves know how plainly I told you, 'I am not the Messiah. I am only here to prepare the way for him.' [29] It is the bridegroom who marries the bride, and the best man is simply glad to stand with him and hear his vows. Therefore, I am filled with joy at his success. [30] He must become greater and greater, and I must become less and less.

[31] "He has come from above and is greater than anyone else. We are of the earth, and we speak of earthly things, but he has come from heaven and is greater than anyone else.* [32] He testifies about what he has seen and heard, but how few believe what he tells them! [33] Anyone who accepts his testimony can affirm that God is true. [34] For he is sent by God. He speaks God's words, for God gives him the Spirit without limit. [35] The Father loves his Son and has put everything into his hands. [36] And anyone who believes in God's Son has eternal life. Anyone who doesn't obey the Son will never experience eternal life but remains under God's angry judgment."

CHAPTER **4**

Jesus and the Samaritan Woman

Jesus* knew the Pharisees had heard that he was baptizing and making more disciples than John [2] (though Jesus himself didn't baptize them—his disciples did). [3] So he left Judea and returned to Galilee.

[4] He had to go through Samaria on the way. [5] Eventually he came to the Samaritan village of Sychar, near the field that Jacob gave to his son Joseph. [6] Jacob's well was there; and Jesus, tired from the long walk, sat wearily beside the well about noontime. [7] Soon a Samaritan woman came to draw water, and Jesus said to her, "Please give me a drink." [8] He was alone at the time because his disciples had gone into the village to buy some food.

[9] The woman was surprised, for Jews refuse to have anything to do with Samaritans.* She said to Jesus, "You are a Jew, and I am a Samaritan woman. Why are you asking me for a drink?"

[10] Jesus replied, "If you only knew the gift God has for you and who you are speaking to, you would ask me, and I would give you living water."

[11] "But sir, you don't have a rope or a bucket," she said, "and this well is very deep. Where would you get this living water? [12] And besides, do you think you're greater than our ancestor Jacob, who gave us this well? How can you offer better water than he and his sons and his animals enjoyed?"

[13] Jesus replied, "Anyone who drinks this water will soon become thirsty again. [14] But those who drink the water I give will never be thirsty again. It becomes a fresh, bubbling spring within them, giving them eternal life."

[15] "Please, sir," the woman said, "give me this water! Then I'll never be thirsty again, and I won't have to come here to get water."

[16] "Go and get your husband," Jesus told her.

[17] "I don't have a husband," the woman replied.

Jesus said, "You're right! You don't have a husband—[18] for you have had five husbands, and you aren't even married to the man you're living with now. You certainly spoke the truth!"

[19] "Sir," the woman said, "you must be a prophet. [20] So tell me, why is it that you Jews insist that Jerusalem is the only place of worship, while we Samaritans claim it is here at Mount Gerizim,* where our ancestors worshiped?"

[21] Jesus replied, "Believe me, dear woman, the time is coming when it will no longer matter whether you worship the Father on this mountain or in Jerusalem. [22] You Samaritans know very little about the one you worship, while we Jews know all about him, for salvation comes through the Jews. [23] But the time is coming—indeed it's here now—when true worshipers will worship the Father in spirit and in truth. The Father is looking for those who will worship him that way. [24] For God is Spirit, so those who worship him must worship in spirit and in truth."

[25] The woman said, "I know the Messiah is coming—the one who is called Christ. When he comes, he will explain everything to us."

[26] Then Jesus told her, "I Am the Messiah!"*

[27] Just then his disciples came back. They were shocked to find him talking to a woman, but none of them had the nerve to ask, "What do you want with her?" or "Why are you talking to her?" [28] The woman left her water jar beside the well and ran back to the village, telling everyone, [29] "Come and see a man who told me everything I ever did! Could he possibly be the Messiah?" [30] So the people came streaming from the village to see him.

[31] Meanwhile, the disciples were urging Jesus, "Rabbi, eat something." [32] But Jesus replied, "I have a kind of food you know nothing about."

3:31 Some manuscripts do not include *and is greater than anyone else.*   4:1 Some manuscripts read *The Lord.*   4:9 Some manuscripts do not include this sentence.   4:20 Greek *on this mountain.*   4:26 Or *"The 'I Am' is here"*; or *"I am the Lord"*; Greek reads *"I am, the one speaking to you."* See Exod 3:14.

33 "Did someone bring him food while we were gone?" the disciples asked each other.

34 Then Jesus explained: "My nourishment comes from doing the will of God, who sent me, and from finishing his work. 35 You know the saying, 'Four months between planting and harvest.' But I say, wake up and look around. The fields are already ripe* for harvest. 36 The harvesters are paid good wages, and the fruit they harvest is people brought to eternal life. What joy awaits both the planter and the harvester alike! 37 You know the saying, 'One plants and another harvests.' And it's true. 38 I sent you to harvest where you didn't plant; others had already done the work, and now you will get to gather the harvest."

Many Samaritans Believe

39 Many Samaritans from the village believed in Jesus because the woman had said, "He told me everything I ever did!" 40 When they came out to see him, they begged him to stay in their village. So he stayed for two days, 41 long enough for many more to hear his message and believe. 42 Then they said to the woman, "Now we believe, not just because of what you told us, but because we have heard him ourselves. Now we know that he is indeed the Savior of the world."

Jesus Heals an Official's Son

43 At the end of the two days, Jesus went on to Galilee. 44 He himself had said that a prophet is not honored in his own hometown. 45 Yet the Galileans welcomed him, for they had been in Jerusalem at the Passover celebration and had seen everything he did there.

46 As he traveled through Galilee, he came to Cana, where he had turned the water into wine. There was a government official in nearby Capernaum whose son was very sick. 47 When he heard that Jesus had come from Judea to Galilee, he went and begged Jesus to come to Capernaum to heal his son, who was about to die.

48 Jesus asked, "Will you never believe in me unless you see miraculous signs and wonders?"

49 The official pleaded, "Lord, please come now before my little boy dies."

50 Then Jesus told him, "Go back home. Your son will live!" And the man believed what Jesus said and started home.

51 While the man was on his way, some of his servants met him with the news that his son was alive and well. 52 He asked them when the boy had begun to get better, and they replied, "Yesterday afternoon at one o'clock his fever

suddenly disappeared!" 53 Then the father realized that that was the very time Jesus had told him, "Your son will live." And he and his entire household believed in Jesus. 54 This was the second miraculous sign Jesus did in Galilee after coming from Judea.

CHAPTER **5**
Jesus Heals a Lame Man

Afterward Jesus returned to Jerusalem for one of the Jewish holy days. 2 Inside the city, near the Sheep Gate, was the pool of Bethesda,* with five covered porches. 3 Crowds of sick people—blind, lame, or paralyzed—lay on the porches.* 5 One of the men lying there had been sick for thirty-eight years. 6 When Jesus saw him and knew he had been ill for a long time, he asked him, "Would you like to get well?"

7 "I can't, sir," the sick man said, "for I have no one to put me into the pool when the water bubbles up. Someone else always gets there ahead of me."

8 Jesus told him, "Stand up, pick up your mat, and walk!"

9 Instantly, the man was healed! He rolled up his sleeping mat and began walking! But this miracle happened on the Sabbath, 10 so the Jewish leaders objected. They said to the man who was cured, "You can't work on the Sabbath! The law doesn't allow you to carry that sleeping mat!"

11 But he replied, "The man who healed me told me, 'Pick up your mat and walk.'"

12 "Who said such a thing as that?" they demanded.

13 The man didn't know, for Jesus had disappeared into the crowd. 14 But afterward Jesus found him in the Temple and told him, "Now you are well; so stop sinning, or something even worse may happen to you." 15 Then the man went and told the Jewish leaders that it was Jesus who had healed him.

Jesus Claims to Be the Son of God

16 So the Jewish leaders began harassing* Jesus for breaking the Sabbath rules. 17 But Jesus replied, "My Father is always working, and so am I." 18 So the Jewish leaders tried all the harder to find a way to kill him. For he not only broke the Sabbath, he called God his Father, thereby making himself equal with God.

19 So Jesus explained, "I tell you the truth, the Son can do nothing by himself. He does only what he sees the Father doing. Whatever the Father does, the Son also does. 20 For the Father

4:35 Greek *white.*   5:2 Other manuscripts read *Beth-zatha;* still others read *Bethsaida.*   5:3 Some manuscripts add an expanded conclusion to verse 3 and all of verse 4: *waiting for a certain movement of the water,* 4 *for an angel of the Lord came from time to time and stirred up the water. And the first person to step in after the water was stirred was healed of whatever disease he had.*   5:16 Or *persecuting.*

loves the Son and shows him everything he is doing. In fact, the Father will show him how to do even greater works than healing this man. Then you will truly be astonished. ²¹For just as the Father gives life to those he raises from the dead, so the Son gives life to anyone he wants. ²²In addition, the Father judges no one. Instead, he has given the Son absolute authority to judge, ²³so that everyone will honor the Son, just as they honor the Father. Anyone who does not honor the Son is certainly not honoring the Father who sent him.

²⁴"I tell you the truth, those who listen to my message and believe in God who sent me have eternal life. They will never be condemned for their sins, but they have already passed from death into life.

²⁵"And I assure you that the time is coming, indeed it's here now, when the dead will hear my voice—the voice of the Son of God. And those who listen will live. ²⁶The Father has life in himself, and he has granted that same life-giving power to his Son. ²⁷And he has given him authority to judge everyone because he is the Son of Man.* ²⁸Don't be so surprised! Indeed, the time is coming when all the dead in their graves will hear the voice of God's Son, ²⁹and they will rise again. Those who have done good will rise to experience eternal life, and those who have continued in evil will rise to experience judgment. ³⁰I can do nothing on my own. I judge as God tells me. Therefore, my judgment is just, because I carry out the will of the one who sent me, not my own will.

Witnesses to Jesus

³¹"If I were to testify on my own behalf, my testimony would not be valid. ³²But someone else is also testifying about me, and I assure you that everything he says about me is true. ³³In fact, you sent investigators to listen to John the Baptist, and his testimony about me was true. ³⁴Of course, I have no need of human witnesses, but I say these things so you might be saved. ³⁵John was like a burning and shining lamp, and you were excited for a while about his message. ³⁶But I have a greater witness than John—my teachings and my miracles. The Father gave me these works to accomplish, and they prove that he sent me. ³⁷And the Father who sent me has testified about me himself. You have never heard his voice or seen him face to face, ³⁸and you do not have his message in your hearts, because you do not believe me—the one he sent to you.

³⁹"You search the Scriptures because you

think they give you eternal life. But the Scriptures point to me! ⁴⁰Yet you refuse to come to me to receive this life.

⁴¹"Your approval means nothing to me, ⁴²because I know you don't have God's love within you. ⁴³For I have come to you in my Father's name, and you have rejected me. Yet if others come in their own name, you gladly welcome them. ⁴⁴No wonder you can't believe! For you gladly honor each other, but you don't care about the honor that comes from the one who alone is God.*

⁴⁵"Yet it isn't I who will accuse you before the Father. Moses will accuse you! Yes, Moses, in whom you put your hopes. ⁴⁶If you really believed Moses, you would believe me, because he wrote about me. ⁴⁷But since you don't believe what he wrote, how will you believe what I say?"

CHAPTER 6

Jesus Feeds Five Thousand

After this, Jesus crossed over to the far side of the Sea of Galilee, also known as the Sea of Tiberias. ²A huge crowd kept following him wherever he went, because they saw his miraculous signs as he healed the sick. ³Then Jesus climbed a hill and sat down with his disciples around him. ⁴(It was nearly time for the Jewish Passover celebration.) ⁵Jesus soon saw a huge crowd of people coming to look for him. Turning to Philip, he asked, "Where can we buy bread to feed all these people?" ⁶He was testing Philip, for he already knew what he was going to do.

⁷Philip replied, "Even if we worked for months, we wouldn't have enough money* to feed them!"

⁸Then Andrew, Simon Peter's brother, spoke up. ⁹"There's a young boy here with five barley loaves and two fish. But what good is that with this huge crowd?"

¹⁰"Tell everyone to sit down," Jesus said. So they all sat down on the grassy slopes. (The men alone numbered about 5,000.) ¹¹Then Jesus took the loaves, gave thanks to God, and distributed them to the people. Afterward he did the same with the fish. And they all ate as much as they wanted. ¹²After everyone was full, Jesus told his disciples, "Now gather the leftovers, so that nothing is wasted." ¹³So they picked up the pieces and filled twelve baskets with scraps left by the people who had eaten from the five barley loaves.

¹⁴When the people saw him* do this miraculous sign, they exclaimed, "Surely, he is the Prophet we have been expecting!"* ¹⁵When

---

5:27 "Son of Man" is a title Jesus used for himself.   **5:44** Some manuscripts read *from the only One.*   **6:7** Greek *Two hundred denarii would not be enough.* A denarius was equivalent to a laborer's full day's wage.   **6:14a** Some manuscripts read *Jesus.*   **6:14b** See Deut 18:15, 18; Mal 4:5-6.

Jesus saw that they were ready to force him to be their king, he slipped away into the hills by himself.

Jesus Walks on Water

¹⁶That evening Jesus' disciples went down to the shore to wait for him. ¹⁷But as darkness fell and Jesus still hadn't come back, they got into the boat and headed across the lake toward Capernaum. ¹⁸Soon a gale swept down upon them, and the sea grew very rough. ¹⁹They had rowed three or four miles* when suddenly they saw Jesus walking on the water toward the boat. They were terrified, ²⁰but he called out to them, "Don't be afraid. I am here!*" ²¹Then they were eager to let him in the boat, and immediately they arrived at their destination!

Jesus, the Bread of Life

²²The next day the crowd that had stayed on the far shore saw that the disciples had taken the only boat, and they realized Jesus had not gone with them. ²³Several boats from Tiberias landed near the place where the Lord had blessed the bread and the people had eaten. ²⁴So when the crowd saw that neither Jesus nor his disciples were there, they got into the boats and went across to Capernaum to look for him. ²⁵They found him on the other side of the lake and asked, "Rabbi, when did you get here?"

²⁶Jesus replied, "I tell you the truth, you want to be with me because I fed you, not because you understood the miraculous signs. ²⁷But don't be so concerned about perishable things like food. Spend your energy seeking the eternal life that the Son of Man* can give you. For God the Father has given me the seal of his approval."

²⁸They replied, "We want to perform God's works, too. What should we do?"

²⁹Jesus told them, "This is the only work God wants from you: Believe in the one he has sent."

³⁰They answered, "Show us a miraculous sign if you want us to believe in you. What can you do? ³¹After all, our ancestors ate manna while they journeyed through the wilderness! The Scriptures say, 'Moses gave them bread from heaven to eat.'*"

³²Jesus said, "I tell you the truth, Moses didn't give you bread from heaven. My Father did. And now he offers you the true bread from heaven. ³³The true bread of God is the one who comes down from heaven and gives life to the world."

³⁴"Sir," they said, "give us that bread every day."

³⁵Jesus replied, "I am the bread of life. Whoever comes to me will never be hungry again. Whoever believes in me will never be thirsty. ³⁶But you haven't believed in me even though you have seen me. ³⁷However, those the Father has given me will come to me, and I will never reject them. ³⁸For I have come down from heaven to do the will of God who sent me, not to do my own will. ³⁹And this is the will of God, that I should not lose even one of all those he has given me, but that I should raise them up at the last day. ⁴⁰For it is my Father's will that all who see his Son and believe in him should have eternal life. I will raise them up at the last day."

⁴¹Then the people* began to murmur in disagreement because he had said, "I am the bread that came down from heaven." ⁴²They said, "Isn't this Jesus, the son of Joseph? We know his father and mother. How can he say, 'I came down from heaven'?"

⁴³But Jesus replied, "Stop complaining about what I said. ⁴⁴For no one can come to me unless the Father who sent me draws them to me, and at the last day I will raise them up. ⁴⁵As it is written in the Scriptures,* 'They will all be taught by God.' Everyone who listens to the Father and learns from him comes to me. ⁴⁶(Not that anyone has ever seen the Father; only I, who was sent from God, have seen him.)

⁴⁷"I tell you the truth, anyone who believes has eternal life. ⁴⁸Yes, I am the bread of life! ⁴⁹Your ancestors ate manna in the wilderness, but they all died. ⁵⁰Anyone who eats the bread from heaven, however, will never die. ⁵¹I am the living bread that came down from heaven. Anyone who eats this bread will live forever; and this bread, which I will offer so the world may live, is my flesh."

⁵²Then the people began arguing with each other about what he meant. "How can this man give us his flesh to eat?" they asked.

⁵³So Jesus said again, "I tell you the truth, unless you eat the flesh of the Son of Man and drink his blood, you cannot have eternal life within you. ⁵⁴But anyone who eats my flesh and drinks my blood has eternal life, and I will raise that person at the last day. ⁵⁵For my flesh is true food, and my blood is true drink. ⁵⁶Anyone who eats my flesh and drinks my blood remains in me, and I in him. ⁵⁷I live because of the living Father who sent me; in the same way, anyone who feeds on me will live because of me. ⁵⁸I am the true bread that came down from heaven. Anyone who eats this bread will not die as your ancestors did (even though they ate the manna) but will live forever."

6:19 Greek *25 or 30 stadia* [4.6 or 5.5 kilometers]. **6:20** Or *The 'I AM' is here;* Greek reads *I am.* See Exod 3:14. **6:27** "Son of Man" is a title Jesus used for himself. **6:31** Exod 16:4; Ps 78:24. **6:41** Greek *Jewish people;* also in 6:52. **6:45** Greek *in the prophets.* Isa 54:13.

⁵⁹He said these things while he was teaching in the synagogue in Capernaum.

Many Disciples Desert Jesus

⁶⁰Many of his disciples said, "This is very hard to understand. How can anyone accept it?"

⁶¹Jesus was aware that his disciples were complaining, so he said to them, "Does this offend you? ⁶²Then what will you think if you see the Son of Man ascend to heaven again? ⁶³The Spirit alone gives eternal life. Human effort accomplishes nothing. And the very words I have spoken to you are spirit and life. ⁶⁴But some of you do not believe me." (For Jesus knew from the beginning which ones didn't believe, and he knew who would betray him.) ⁶⁵Then he said, "That is why I said that people can't come to me unless the Father gives them to me."

⁶⁶At this point many of his disciples turned away and deserted him. ⁶⁷Then Jesus turned to the Twelve and asked, "Are you also going to leave?"

⁶⁸Simon Peter replied, "Lord, to whom would we go? You have the words that give eternal life. ⁶⁹We believe, and we know you are the Holy One of God.*"

⁷⁰Then Jesus said, "I chose the twelve of you, but one is a devil." ⁷¹He was speaking of Judas, son of Simon Iscariot, one of the Twelve, who would later betray him.

CHAPTER 7

Jesus and His Brothers

After this, Jesus traveled around Galilee. He wanted to stay out of Judea, where the Jewish leaders were plotting his death. ²But soon it was time for the Jewish Festival of Shelters, ³and Jesus' brothers said to him, "Leave here and go to Judea, where your followers can see your miracles! ⁴You can't become famous if you hide like this! If you can do such wonderful things, show yourself to the world!" ⁵For even his brothers didn't believe in him.

⁶Jesus replied, "Now is not the right time for me to go, but you can go anytime. ⁷The world can't hate you, but it does hate me because I accuse it of doing evil. ⁸You go on. I'm not going* to this festival, because my time has not yet come." ⁹After saying these things, Jesus remained in Galilee.

Jesus Teaches Openly at the Temple

¹⁰But after his brothers left for the festival, Jesus also went, though secretly, staying out of public view. ¹¹The Jewish leaders tried to find him at the festival and kept asking if anyone had seen him. ¹²There was a lot of grumbling about him among the crowds. Some argued, "He's a good man," but others said, "He's nothing but a fraud who deceives the people." ¹³But no one had the courage to speak favorably about him in public, for they were afraid of getting in trouble with the Jewish leaders.

¹⁴Then, midway through the festival, Jesus went up to the Temple and began to teach. ¹⁵The people* were surprised when they heard him. "How does he know so much when he hasn't been trained?" they asked.

¹⁶So Jesus told them, "My message is not my own; it comes from God who sent me. ¹⁷Anyone who wants to do the will of God will know whether my teaching is from God or is merely my own. ¹⁸Those who speak for themselves want glory only for themselves, but a person who seeks to honor the one who sent him speaks truth, not lies. ¹⁹Moses gave you the law, but none of you obeys it! In fact, you are trying to kill me."

²⁰The crowd replied, "You're demon possessed! Who's trying to kill you?"

²¹Jesus replied, "I did one miracle on the Sabbath, and you were amazed. ²²But you work on the Sabbath, too, when you obey Moses' law of circumcision. (Actually, this tradition of circumcision began with the patriarchs, long before the law of Moses.) ²³For if the correct time for circumcising your son falls on the Sabbath, you go ahead and do it so as not to break the law of Moses. So why should you be angry with me for healing a man on the Sabbath? ²⁴Look beneath the surface so you can judge correctly."

Is Jesus the Messiah?

²⁵Some of the people who lived in Jerusalem started to ask each other, "Isn't this the man they are trying to kill? ²⁶But here he is, speaking in public, and they say nothing to him. Could our leaders possibly believe that he is the Messiah? ²⁷But how could he be? For we know where this man comes from. When the Messiah comes, he will simply appear; no one will know where he comes from."

²⁸While Jesus was teaching in the Temple, he called out, "Yes, you know me, and you know where I come from. But I'm not here on my own. The one who sent me is true, and you don't know him. ²⁹But I know him because I come from him, and he sent me to you." ³⁰Then the leaders tried to arrest him; but no one laid a hand on him, because his time* had not yet come.

6:69 Other manuscripts read *you are the Christ, the Holy One of God;* still others read *you are the Christ, the Son of God;* and still others read *you are the Christ, the Son of the living God.*   7:8 Some manuscripts read *not yet going.*   7:15 Greek *Jewish people.*   7:30 Greek *his hour.*

[31] Many among the crowds at the Temple believed in him. "After all," they said, "would you expect the Messiah to do more miraculous signs than this man has done?"

[32] When the Pharisees heard that the crowds were whispering such things, they and the leading priests sent Temple guards to arrest Jesus. [33] But Jesus told them, "I will be with you only a little longer. Then I will return to the one who sent me. [34] You will search for me but not find me. And you cannot go where I am going."

[35] The Jewish leaders were puzzled by this statement. "Where is he planning to go?" they asked. "Is he thinking of leaving the country and going to the Jews in other lands?* Maybe he will even teach the Greeks! [36] What does he mean when he says, 'You will search for me but not find me,' and 'You cannot go where I am going'?"

Jesus Promises Living Water

[37] On the last day, the climax of the festival, Jesus stood and shouted to the crowds, "Anyone who is thirsty may come to me! [38] Anyone who believes in me may come and drink! For the Scriptures declare, 'Rivers of living water will flow from his heart.' "* [39] (When he said "living water," he was speaking of the Spirit, who would be given to everyone believing in him. But the Spirit had not yet been given,* because Jesus had not yet entered into his glory.)

Division and Unbelief

[40] When the crowds heard him say this, some of them declared, "Surely this man is the Prophet we've been expecting."* [41] Others said, "He is the Messiah." Still others said, "But he can't be! Will the Messiah come from Galilee? [42] For the Scriptures clearly state that the Messiah will be born of the royal line of David, in Bethlehem, the village where King David was born."* [43] So the crowd was divided about him. [44] Some even wanted him arrested, but no one laid a hand on him.

[45] When the Temple guards returned without having arrested Jesus, the leading priests and Pharisees demanded, "Why didn't you bring him in?"

[46] "We have never heard anyone speak like this!" the guards responded.

[47] "Have you been led astray, too?" the Pharisees mocked. [48] "Is there a single one of us rulers or Pharisees who believes in him? [49] This foolish crowd follows him, but they are ignorant of the law. God's curse is on them!"

[50] Then Nicodemus, the leader who had met with Jesus earlier, spoke up. [51] "Is it legal to convict a man before he is given a hearing?" he asked.

[52] They replied, "Are you from Galilee, too? Search the Scriptures and see for yourself—no prophet ever comes* from Galilee!"

[The most ancient Greek manuscripts do not include John 7:53–8:11.]

[53] Then the meeting broke up, and everybody went home.

CHAPTER 8

A Woman Caught in Adultery

Jesus returned to the Mount of Olives, [2] but early the next morning he was back again at the Temple. A crowd soon gathered, and he sat down and taught them. [3] As he was speaking, the teachers of religious law and the Pharisees brought a woman who had been caught in the act of adultery. They put her in front of the crowd.

[4] "Teacher," they said to Jesus, "this woman was caught in the act of adultery. [5] The law of Moses says to stone her. What do you say?"

[6] They were trying to trap him into saying something they could use against him, but Jesus stooped down and wrote in the dust with his finger. [7] They kept demanding an answer, so he stood up again and said, "All right, but let the one who has never sinned throw the first stone!" [8] Then he stooped down again and wrote in the dust.

[9] When the accusers heard this, they slipped away one by one, beginning with the oldest, until only Jesus was left in the middle of the crowd with the woman. [10] Then Jesus stood up again and said to the woman, "Where are your accusers? Didn't even one of them condemn you?"

[11] "No, Lord," she said.

And Jesus said, "Neither do I. Go and sin no more."

Jesus, the Light of the World

[12] Jesus spoke to the people once more and said, "I am the light of the world. If you follow me, you won't have to walk in darkness, because you will have the light that leads to life."

[13] The Pharisees replied, "You are making those claims about yourself! Such testimony is not valid."

[14] Jesus told them, "These claims are valid even though I make them about myself. For I

7:35 Or *the Jews who live among the Greeks?*   7:37-38 Or *"Let anyone who is thirsty come to me and drink.* [38]*For the Scriptures declare, 'Rivers of living water will flow from the heart of anyone who believes in me.'"*   7:39 Some manuscripts read *But as yet there was no Spirit.* Still others read *But as yet there was no Holy Spirit.*   7:40 See Deut 18:15, 18; Mal 4:5-6. 7:42 See Mic 5:2.   7:52 Some manuscripts read *the prophet does not come.*

know where I came from and where I am going, but you don't know this about me. [15] You judge me by human standards, but I do not judge anyone. [16] And if I did, my judgment would be correct in every respect because I am not alone. The Father* who sent me is with me. [17] Your own law says that if two people agree about something, their witness is accepted as fact.* [18] I am one witness, and my Father who sent me is the other."

[19] "Where is your father?" they asked.

Jesus answered, "Since you don't know who I am, you don't know who my Father is. If you knew me, you would also know my Father." [20] Jesus made these statements while he was teaching in the section of the Temple known as the Treasury. But he was not arrested, because his time* had not yet come.

The Unbelieving People Warned

[21] Later Jesus said to them again, "I am going away. You will search for me but will die in your sin. You cannot come where I am going."

[22] The people* asked, "Is he planning to commit suicide? What does he mean, 'You cannot come where I am going'?"

[23] Jesus continued, "You are from below; I am from above. You belong to this world; I do not. [24] That is why I said that you will die in your sins; for unless you believe that I AM who I claim to be,* you will die in your sins."

[25] "Who are you?" they demanded.

Jesus replied, "The one I have always claimed to be.* [26] I have much to say about you and much to condemn, but I won't. For I say only what I have heard from the one who sent me, and he is completely truthful." [27] But they still didn't understand that he was talking about his Father.

[28] So Jesus said, "When you have lifted up the Son of Man on the cross, then you will understand that I AM he.* I do nothing on my own but say only what the Father taught me. [29] And the one who sent me is with me—he has not deserted me. For I always do what pleases him." [30] Then many who heard him say these things believed in him.

Jesus and Abraham

[31] Jesus said to the people who believed in him, "You are truly my disciples if you remain faithful to my teachings. [32] And you will know the truth, and the truth will set you free."

[33] "But we are descendants of Abraham," they said. "We have never been slaves to anyone. What do you mean, 'You will be set free'?"

[34] Jesus replied, "I tell you the truth, everyone who sins is a slave of sin. [35] A slave is not a permanent member of the family, but a son is part of the family forever. [36] So if the Son sets you free, you are truly free. [37] Yes, I realize that you are descendants of Abraham. And yet some of you are trying to kill me because there's no room in your hearts for my message. [38] I am telling you what I saw when I was with my Father. But you are following the advice of your father."

[39] "Our father is Abraham!" they declared.

"No," Jesus replied, "for if you were really the children of Abraham, you would follow his example.* [40] Instead, you are trying to kill me because I told you the truth, which I heard from God. Abraham never did such a thing. [41] No, you are imitating your real father."

They replied, "We aren't illegitimate children! God himself is our true Father."

[42] Jesus told them, "If God were your Father, you would love me, because I have come to you from God. I am not here on my own, but he sent me. [43] Why can't you understand what I am saying? It's because you can't even hear me! [44] For you are the children of your father the devil, and you love to do the evil things he does. He was a murderer from the beginning. He has always hated the truth, because there is no truth in him. When he lies, it is consistent with his character; for he is a liar and the father of lies. [45] So when I tell the truth, you just naturally don't believe me! [46] Which of you can truthfully accuse me of sin? And since I am telling you the truth, why don't you believe me? [47] Anyone who belongs to God listens gladly to the words of God. But you don't listen because you don't belong to God."

[48] The people retorted, "You Samaritan devil! Didn't we say all along that you were possessed by a demon?"

[49] "No," Jesus said, "I have no demon in me. For I honor my Father—and you dishonor me. [50] And though I have no wish to glorify myself, God is going to glorify me. He is the true judge. [51] I tell you the truth, anyone who obeys my teaching will never die!"

[52] The people said, "Now we know you are possessed by a demon. Even Abraham and the prophets died, but you say, 'Anyone who obeys my teaching will never die!' [53] Are you greater than our father Abraham? He died, and so did the prophets. Who do you think you are?"

8:16 Some manuscripts read *The One.* **8:17** See Deut 19:15. **8:20** Greek *his hour.* **8:22** Greek *Jewish people;* also in 8:31, 48, 52, 57. **8:24** Greek *unless you believe that I am.* See Exod 3:14. **8:25** Or *Why do I speak to you at all?* **8:28** Greek *When you have lifted up the Son of Man, then you will know that I am.* "Son of Man" is a title Jesus used for himself. **8:39** Some manuscripts read *if you are really the children of Abraham, follow his example.*

[54] Jesus answered, "If I want glory for myself, it doesn't count. But it is my Father who will glorify me. You say, 'He is our God,'*' [55] but you don't even know him. I know him. If I said otherwise, I would be as great a liar as you! But I do know him and obey him. [56] Your father Abraham rejoiced as he looked forward to my coming. He saw it and was glad."

[57] The people said, "You aren't even fifty years old. How can you say you have seen Abraham?*"

[58] Jesus answered, "I tell you the truth, before Abraham was even born, I Am!*" [59] At that point they picked up stones to throw at him. But Jesus was hidden from them and left the Temple.

CHAPTER **9**

Jesus Heals a Man Born Blind

As Jesus was walking along, he saw a man who had been blind from birth. [2] "Rabbi," his disciples asked him, "why was this man born blind? Was it because of his own sins or his parents' sins?"

[3] "It was not because of his sins or his parents' sins," Jesus answered. "This happened so the power of God could be seen in him. [4] We must quickly carry out the tasks assigned us by the one who sent us.* The night is coming, and then no one can work. [5] But while I am here in the world, I am the light of the world."

[6] Then he spit on the ground, made mud with the saliva, and spread the mud over the blind man's eyes. [7] He told him, "Go wash yourself in the pool of Siloam" (Siloam means "sent"). So the man went and washed and came back seeing!

[8] His neighbors and others who knew him as a blind beggar asked each other, "Isn't this the man who used to sit and beg?" [9] Some said he was, and others said, "No, he just looks like him!"

But the beggar kept saying, "Yes, I am the same one!"

[10] They asked, "Who healed you? What happened?"

[11] He told them, "The man they call Jesus made mud and spread it over my eyes and told me, 'Go to the pool of Siloam and wash yourself.' So I went and washed, and now I can see!"

[12] "Where is he now?" they asked.

"I don't know," he replied.

[13] Then they took the man who had been blind to the Pharisees, [14] because it was on the Sabbath that Jesus had made the mud and healed him. [15] The Pharisees asked the man all about it. So he told them, "He put the mud over my eyes, and when I washed it away, I could see!"

[16] Some of the Pharisees said, "This man Jesus is not from God, for he is working on the Sabbath." Others said, "But how could an ordinary sinner do such miraculous signs?" So there was a deep division of opinion among them.

[17] Then the Pharisees again questioned the man who had been blind and demanded, "What's your opinion about this man who healed you?"

The man replied, "I think he must be a prophet."

[18] The Jewish leaders still refused to believe the man had been blind and could now see, so they called in his parents. [19] They asked them, "Is this your son? Was he born blind? If so, how can he now see?"

[20] His parents replied, "We know this is our son and that he was born blind, [21] but we don't know how he can see or who healed him. Ask him. He is old enough to speak for himself." [22] His parents said this because they were afraid of the Jewish leaders, who had announced that anyone saying Jesus was the Messiah would be expelled from the synagogue. [23] That's why they said, "He is old enough. Ask him."

[24] So for the second time they called in the man who had been blind and told him, "God should get the glory for this,* because we know this man Jesus is a sinner."

[25] "I don't know whether he is a sinner," the man replied. "But I know this: I was blind, and now I can see!"

[26] "But what did he do?" they asked. "How did he heal you?"

[27] "Look!" the man exclaimed. "I told you once. Didn't you listen? Why do you want to hear it again? Do you want to become his disciples, too?"

[28] Then they cursed him and said, "You are his disciple, but we are disciples of Moses! [29] We know God spoke to Moses, but we don't even know where this man comes from."

[30] "Why, that's very strange!" the man replied. "He healed my eyes, and yet you don't know where he comes from? [31] We know that God doesn't listen to sinners, but he is ready to hear those who worship him and do his will. [32] Ever since the world began, no one has been able to open the eyes of someone born blind. [33] If this man were not from God, he couldn't have done it."

[34] "You were born a total sinner!" they answered. "Are you trying to teach us?" And they threw him out of the synagogue.

8:54 Some manuscripts read *your God.*   8:57 Some manuscripts read *How can you say Abraham has seen you?*   8:58 Or *before Abraham was even born, I have always been alive;* Greek reads *before Abraham was, I am.* See Exod 3:14.   9:4 Other manuscripts read *I must quickly carry out the tasks assigned me by the one who sent me;* still others read *We must quickly carry out the tasks assigned us by the one who sent me.*   9:24 Or *Give glory to God, not to Jesus;* Greek reads *Give glory to God.*

Spiritual Blindness

³⁵ When Jesus heard what had happened, he found the man and asked, "Do you believe in the Son of Man?*"

³⁶ The man answered, "Who is he, sir? I want to believe in him."

³⁷ "You have seen him," Jesus said, "and he is speaking to you!"

³⁸ "Yes, Lord, I believe!" the man said. And he worshiped Jesus.

³⁹ Then Jesus told him,* "I entered this world to render judgment—to give sight to the blind and to show those who think they see* that they are blind."

⁴⁰ Some Pharisees who were standing nearby heard him and asked, "Are you saying we're blind?"

⁴¹ "If you were blind, you wouldn't be guilty," Jesus replied. "But you remain guilty because you claim you can see.

CHAPTER 10

The Good Shepherd and His Sheep

"I tell you the truth, anyone who sneaks over the wall of a sheepfold, rather than going through the gate, must surely be a thief and a robber! ² But the one who enters through the gate is the shepherd of the sheep. ³ The gate-keeper opens the gate for him, and the sheep recognize his voice and come to him. He calls his own sheep by name and leads them out. ⁴ After he has gathered his own flock, he walks ahead of them, and they follow him because they know his voice. ⁵ They won't follow a stranger; they will run from him because they don't know his voice."

⁶ Those who heard Jesus use this illustration didn't understand what he meant, ⁷ so he explained it to them: "I tell you the truth, I am the gate for the sheep. ⁸ All who came before me* were thieves and robbers. But the true sheep did not listen to them. ⁹ Yes, I am the gate. Those who come in through me will be saved.* They will come and go freely and will find good pastures. ¹⁰ The thief's purpose is to steal and kill and destroy. My purpose is to give them a rich and satisfying life.

¹¹ "I am the good shepherd. The good shepherd sacrifices his life for the sheep. ¹² A hired hand will run when he sees a wolf coming. He will abandon the sheep because they don't belong to him and he isn't their shepherd. And so the wolf attacks them and scatters the flock. ¹³ The hired hand runs away because he's work-ing only for the money and doesn't really care about the sheep.

¹⁴ "I am the good shepherd; I know my own sheep, and they know me, ¹⁵ just as my Father knows me and I know the Father. So I sacrifice my life for the sheep. ¹⁶ I have other sheep, too, that are not in this sheepfold. I must bring them also. They will listen to my voice, and there will be one flock with one shepherd.

¹⁷ "The Father loves me because I sacrifice my life so I may take it back again. ¹⁸ No one can take my life from me. I sacrifice it voluntarily. For I have the authority to lay it down when I want to and also to take it up again. For this is what my Father has commanded."

¹⁹ When he said these things, the people* were again divided in their opinions about him. ²⁰ Some said, "He's demon possessed and out of his mind. Why listen to a man like that?" ²¹ Others said, "This doesn't sound like a man possessed by a demon! Can a demon open the eyes of the blind?"

Jesus Claims to Be the Son of God

²² It was now winter, and Jesus was in Jerusalem at the time of Hanukkah, the Festival of Dedication. ²³ He was in the Temple, walking through the section known as Solomon's Colonnade. ²⁴ The people surrounded him and asked, "How long are you going to keep us in suspense? If you are the Messiah, tell us plainly."

²⁵ Jesus replied, "I have already told you, and you don't believe me. The proof is the work I do in my Father's name. ²⁶ But you don't believe me because you are not my sheep. ²⁷ My sheep listen to my voice; I know them, and they follow me. ²⁸ I give them eternal life, and they will never perish. No one can snatch them away from me, ²⁹ for my Father has given them to me, and he is more powerful than anyone else.* No one can snatch them from the Father's hand. ³⁰ The Father and I are one."

³¹ Once again the people picked up stones to kill him. ³² Jesus said, "At my Father's direction I have done many good works. For which one are you going to stone me?"

³³ They replied, "We're stoning you not for any good work, but for blasphemy! You, a mere man, claim to be God."

³⁴ Jesus replied, "It is written in your own Scriptures* that God said to certain leaders of the people, 'I say, you are gods!'* ³⁵ And you know that the Scriptures cannot be altered. So if those people who received God's message

---

9:35 Some manuscripts read the Son of God? "Son of Man" is a title Jesus used for himself.   9:38-39a Some manuscripts do not include "Yes, Lord, I believe!" the man said. And he worshiped Jesus. Then Jesus told him.   9:39b Greek those who see.   10:8 Some manuscripts do not include before me.   10:9 Or will find safety.   10:19 Greek Jewish people; also in 10:24, 31.   10:29 Other manuscripts read for what my Father has given me is more powerful than anything; still others read for regarding that which my Father has given me, he is greater than all.   10:34a Greek your own law.   10:34b Ps 82:6.

were called 'gods,' ³⁶why do you call it blasphemy when I say, 'I am the Son of God'? After all, the Father set me apart and sent me into the world. ³⁷Don't believe me unless I carry out my Father's work. ³⁸But if I do his work, believe in the evidence of the miraculous works I have done, even if you don't believe me. Then you will know and understand that the Father is in me, and I am in the Father."

³⁹Once again they tried to arrest him, but he got away and left them. ⁴⁰He went beyond the Jordan River near the place where John was first baptizing and stayed there awhile. ⁴¹And many followed him. "John didn't perform miraculous signs," they remarked to one another, "but everything he said about this man has come true." ⁴²And many who were there believed in Jesus.

CHAPTER 11
The Raising of Lazarus

A man named Lazarus was sick. He lived in Bethany with his sisters, Mary and Martha. ²This is the Mary who later poured the expensive perfume on the Lord's feet and wiped them with her hair.* Her brother, Lazarus, was sick. ³So the two sisters sent a message to Jesus telling him, "Lord, your dear friend is very sick."

⁴But when Jesus heard about it he said, "Lazarus's sickness will not end in death. No, it happened for the glory of God so that the Son of God will receive glory from this." ⁵So although Jesus loved Martha, Mary, and Lazarus, ⁶he stayed where he was for the next two days. ⁷Finally, he said to his disciples, "Let's go back to Judea."

⁸But his disciples objected. "Rabbi," they said, "only a few days ago the people* in Judea were trying to stone you. Are you going there again?"

⁹Jesus replied, "There are twelve hours of daylight every day. During the day people can walk safely. They can see because they have the light of this world. ¹⁰But at night there is danger of stumbling because they have no light." ¹¹Then he said, "Our friend Lazarus has fallen asleep, but now I will go and wake him up."

¹²The disciples said, "Lord, if he is sleeping, he will soon get better!" ¹³They thought Jesus meant Lazarus was simply sleeping, but Jesus meant Lazarus had died.

¹⁴So he told them plainly, "Lazarus is dead. ¹⁵And for your sakes, I'm glad I wasn't there, for now you will really believe. Come, let's go see him."

¹⁶Thomas, nicknamed the Twin,* said to his

first steps

YOU DON'T NEED ANY TRAINING TO SHARE
Read JOHN 9:1-41

Perhaps one of the biggest reasons many Christians haven't shared their faith is that they feel inadequate. You might say, "I am not qualified to speak for God! He could never use me." In reality, once you invite Jesus Christ into your life as Savior and Lord, you can begin to tell others about your newfound faith.

This passage tells the story of a blind man whose sight was restored when Jesus touched his eyes. After Jesus healed this man, certain religious rulers known as Pharisees challenged him, asking him some rather complex questions about Jesus. The man's response was classic. He said, "I know this: I was blind, and now I can see!"

In many ways, we as believers are like this formerly blind man. We, too, were once blinded by the power and deception of sin. Scripture tells us that "Satan, who is the god of this world, has blinded the minds of those who don't believe" and made them "unable to see the glorious light of the Good News" (2 Corinthians 4:4). But one day God lovingly "opened our eyes" to see our real spiritual need, and we responded to the message of the gospel.

We may not yet be great scholars of Scripture, but we still know more about the gospel than many, and we can start with that. Like that blind man, we can say to others, "Once I was blind, but now I can see. . . ." As we study the Bible on a regular basis, we will be able to answer many of the questions people have about our faith.

For the next note on "Share Your Faith," turn to p. 143.

11:2 This incident is recorded in chapter 12.   11:8 Greek *Jewish people;* also in 11:19, 31, 33, 36, 45, 54.
11:16 Greek *Thomas, who was called Didymus.*

fellow disciples, "Let's go, too—and die with Jesus."

[17] When Jesus arrived at Bethany, he was told that Lazarus had already been in his grave for four days. [18] Bethany was only a few miles* down the road from Jerusalem, [19] and many of the people had come to console Martha and Mary in their loss. [20] When Martha got word that Jesus was coming, she went to meet him. But Mary stayed in the house. [21] Martha said to Jesus, "Lord, if only you had been here, my brother would not have died. [22] But even now I know that God will give you whatever you ask."

[23] Jesus told her, "Your brother will rise again."

[24] "Yes," Martha said, "he will rise when everyone else rises, at the last day."

[25] Jesus told her, "I am the resurrection and the life.* Anyone who believes in me will live, even after dying. [26] Everyone who lives in me and believes in me will never ever die. Do you believe this, Martha?"

[27] "Yes, Lord," she told him. "I have always believed you are the Messiah, the Son of God, the one who has come into the world from God." [28] Then she returned to Mary. She called Mary aside from the mourners and told her, "The Teacher is here and wants to see you." [29] So Mary immediately went to him.

[30] Jesus had stayed outside the village, at the place where Martha met him. [31] When the people who were at the house consoling Mary saw her leave so hastily, they assumed she was going to Lazarus's grave to weep. So they followed her there. [32] When Mary arrived and saw Jesus, she fell at his feet and said, "Lord, if only you had been here, my brother would not have died."

[33] When Jesus saw her weeping and saw the other people wailing with her, a deep anger welled up within him,* and he was deeply troubled. [34] "Where have you put him?" he asked them.

They told him, "Lord, come and see." [35] Then Jesus wept. [36] The people who were standing nearby said, "See how much he loved him!" [37] But some said, "This man healed a blind man. Couldn't he have kept Lazarus from dying?"

[38] Jesus was still angry as he arrived at the tomb, a cave with a stone rolled across its entrance. [39] "Roll the stone aside," Jesus told them.

But Martha, the dead man's sister, protested, "Lord, he has been dead for four days. The smell will be terrible."

[40] Jesus responded, "Didn't I tell you that you would see God's glory if you believe?" [41] So they rolled the stone aside. Then Jesus looked up to heaven and said, "Father, thank you for hearing me. [42] You always hear me, but I said it out loud for the sake of all these people standing here, so that they will believe you sent me." [43] Then Jesus shouted, "Lazarus, come out!" [44] And the dead man came out, his hands and feet bound in graveclothes, his face wrapped in a headcloth. Jesus told them, "Unwrap him and let him go!"

The Plot to Kill Jesus

[45] Many of the people who were with Mary believed in Jesus when they saw this happen. [46] But some went to the Pharisees and told them what Jesus had done. [47] Then the leading priests and Pharisees called the high council* together. "What are we going to do?" they asked each other. "This man certainly performs many miraculous signs. [48] If we allow him to go on like this, soon everyone will believe in him. Then the Roman army will come and destroy both our Temple* and our nation."

[49] Caiaphas, who was high priest at that time,* said, "You don't know what you're talking about! [50] You don't realize that it's better for you that one man should die for the people than for the whole nation to be destroyed."

[51] He did not say this on his own; as high priest at that time he was led to prophesy that Jesus would die for the entire nation. [52] And not only for that nation, but to bring together and unite all the children of God scattered around the world.

[53] So from that time on, the Jewish leaders began to plot Jesus' death. [54] As a result, Jesus stopped his public ministry among the people and left Jerusalem. He went to a place near the wilderness, to the village of Ephraim, and stayed there with his disciples.

[55] It was now almost time for the Jewish Passover celebration, and many people from all over the country arrived in Jerusalem several days early so they could go through the purification ceremony before Passover began. [56] They kept looking for Jesus, but as they stood around in the Temple, they said to each other, "What do you think? He won't come for Passover, will he?" [57] Meanwhile, the leading priests and Pharisees had publicly ordered that anyone seeing Jesus must report it immediately so they could arrest him.

CHAPTER **12**

Jesus Anointed at Bethany

Six days before the Passover celebration began, Jesus arrived in Bethany, the home of Lazarus—

11:18 Greek *was about 15 stadia* [about 2.8 kilometers]. **11:25** Some manuscripts do not include *and the life.* **11:33** Or *he was angry in his spirit.* **11:47** Greek *the Sanhedrin.* **11:48** Or *our position;* Greek reads *our place.* **11:49** Greek *that year;* also in 11:51.

the man he had raised from the dead. [2] A dinner was prepared in Jesus' honor. Martha served, and Lazarus was among those who ate* with him. [3] Then Mary took a twelve-ounce jar* of expensive perfume made from essence of nard, and she anointed Jesus' feet with it, wiping his feet with her hair. The house was filled with the fragrance.

[4] But Judas Iscariot, the disciple who would soon betray him, said, [5] "That perfume was worth a year's wages.* It should have been sold and the money given to the poor." [6] Not that he cared for the poor—he was a thief, and since he was in charge of the disciples' money, he often stole some for himself.

[7] Jesus replied, "Leave her alone. She did this in preparation for my burial. [8] You will always have the poor among you, but you will not always have me."

[9] When all the people* heard of Jesus' arrival, they flocked to see him and also to see Lazarus, the man Jesus had raised from the dead. [10] Then the leading priests decided to kill Lazarus, too, [11] for it was because of him that many of the people had deserted them* and believed in Jesus.

Jesus' Triumphant Entry

[12] The next day, the news that Jesus was on the way to Jerusalem swept through the city. A large crowd of Passover visitors [13] took palm branches and went down the road to meet him. They shouted,

> "Praise God!*
> Blessings on the one who comes in the
> name of the Lord!
> Hail to the King of Israel!"*

[14] Jesus found a young donkey and rode on it, fulfilling the prophecy that said:

> [15] "Don't be afraid, people of Jerusalem.*
> Look, your King is coming,
> riding on a donkey's colt."*

[16] His disciples didn't understand at the time that this was a fulfillment of prophecy. But after Jesus entered into his glory, they remembered what had happened and realized that these things had been written about him.

[17] Many in the crowd had seen Jesus call Lazarus from the tomb, raising him from the dead, and they were telling others* about it. [18] That was the reason so many went out to meet him—because they had heard about this miraculous sign. [19] Then the Pharisees said to each other, "There's nothing we can do. Look, everyone* has gone after him!"

Jesus Predicts His Death

[20] Some Greeks who had come to Jerusalem for the Passover celebration [21] paid a visit to Philip, who was from Bethsaida in Galilee. They said, "Sir, we want to meet Jesus." [22] Philip told Andrew about it, and they went together to ask Jesus.

[23] Jesus replied, "Now the time has come for the Son of Man* to enter into his glory. [24] I tell you the truth, unless a kernel of wheat is planted in the soil and dies, it remains alone. But its death will produce many new kernels—a plentiful harvest of new lives. [25] Those who love their life in this world will lose it. Those who care nothing for their life in this world will keep it for eternity. [26] Anyone who wants to be my disciple must follow me, because my servants must be where I am. And the Father will honor anyone who serves me.

[27] "Now my soul is deeply troubled. Should I pray, 'Father, save me from this hour'? But this is the very reason I came! [28] Father, bring glory to your name."

Then a voice spoke from heaven, saying, "I have already brought glory to my name, and I will do so again." [29] When the crowd heard the voice, some thought it was thunder, while others declared an angel had spoken to him.

[30] Then Jesus told them, "The voice was for your benefit, not mine. [31] The time for judging this world has come, when Satan, the ruler of this world, will be cast out. [32] And when I am lifted up from the earth, I will draw everyone to myself." [33] He said this to indicate how he was going to die.

[34] The crowd responded, "We understood from Scripture* that the Messiah would live forever. How can you say the Son of Man will die? Just who is this Son of Man, anyway?"

[35] Jesus replied, "My light will shine for you just a little longer. Walk in the light while you can, so the darkness will not overtake you. Those who walk in the darkness cannot see where they are going. [36] Put your trust in the light while there is still time; then you will become children of the light."

After saying these things, Jesus went away and was hidden from them.

The Unbelief of the People

[37] But despite all the miraculous signs Jesus had done, most of the people still did not

---

12:2 Or *who reclined.*   12:3 Greek *took 1 litra* [327 grams].   12:5 Greek *worth 300 denarii.* A denarius was equivalent to a laborer's full day's wage.   12:9 Greek *Jewish people;* also in 12:11.   12:11 Or *had deserted their traditions;* Greek reads *had deserted.*   12:13a Greek *Hosanna,* an exclamation of praise adapted from a Hebrew expression that means "save now."   12:13b Ps 118:25-26; Zeph 3:15.   12:15a Greek *daughter of Zion.*   12:15b Zech 9:9.   12:17 Greek *were testifying.*   12:19 Greek *the world.*   12:23 "Son of Man" is a title Jesus used for himself.   12:34 Greek *from the law.*

believe in him. ³⁸This is exactly what Isaiah the prophet had predicted:

"LORD, who has believed our message?
    To whom has the LORD revealed his
        powerful arm?"*

³⁹But the people couldn't believe, for as Isaiah also said,

⁴⁰ "The Lord has blinded their eyes
    and hardened their hearts—
so that their eyes cannot see,
    and their hearts cannot understand,
and they cannot turn to me
    and have me heal them."*

⁴¹Isaiah was referring to Jesus when he said this, because he saw the future and spoke of the Messiah's glory. ⁴²Many people did believe in him, however, including some of the Jewish leaders. But they wouldn't admit it for fear that the Pharisees would expel them from the synagogue. ⁴³For they loved human praise more than the praise of God.

⁴⁴Jesus shouted to the crowds, "If you trust me, you are trusting not only me, but also God who sent me. ⁴⁵For when you see me, you are seeing the one who sent me. ⁴⁶I have come as a light to shine in this dark world, so that all who put their trust in me will no longer remain in the dark. ⁴⁷I will not judge those who hear me but don't obey me, for I have come to save the world and not to judge it. ⁴⁸But all who reject me and my message will be judged on the day of judgment by the truth I have spoken. ⁴⁹I don't speak on my own authority. The Father who sent me has commanded me what to say and how to say it. ⁵⁰And I know his commands lead to eternal life; so I say whatever the Father tells me to say."

CHAPTER 13
Jesus Washes His Disciples' Feet
Before the Passover celebration, Jesus knew that his hour had come to leave this world and return to his Father. He had loved his disciples during his ministry on earth, and now he loved them to the very end.* ²It was time for supper, and the devil had already prompted Judas,* son of Simon Iscariot, to betray Jesus. ³Jesus knew that the Father had given him authority over everything and that he had come from God and would return to God. ⁴So he got up from the table, took off his robe, wrapped a towel around his waist, ⁵and poured water into a basin. Then he began to wash the disciples' feet, drying them with the towel he had around him.

⁶When Jesus came to Simon Peter, Peter said to him, "Lord, are you going to wash my feet?"

⁷Jesus replied, "You don't understand now what I am doing, but someday you will."

⁸"No," Peter protested, "you will never ever wash my feet!"

Jesus replied, "Unless I wash you, you won't belong to me."

⁹Simon Peter exclaimed, "Then wash my hands and head as well, Lord, not just my feet!"

¹⁰Jesus replied, "A person who has bathed all over does not need to wash, except for the feet,* to be entirely clean. And you disciples are clean, but not all of you." ¹¹For Jesus knew who would betray him. That is what he meant when he said, "Not all of you are clean."

¹²After washing their feet, he put on his robe again and sat down and asked, "Do you understand what I was doing? ¹³You call me 'Teacher' and 'Lord,' and you are right, because that's what I am. ¹⁴And since I, your Lord and Teacher, have washed your feet, you ought to wash each other's feet. ¹⁵I have given you an example to follow. Do as I have done to you. ¹⁶I tell you the truth, slaves are not greater than their master. Nor is the messenger more important than the one who sends the message. ¹⁷Now that you know these things, God will bless you for doing them.

Jesus Predicts His Betrayal
¹⁸"I am not saying these things to all of you; I know the ones I have chosen. But this fulfills the Scripture that says, 'The one who eats my food has turned against me.'* ¹⁹I tell you this beforehand, so that when it happens you will believe that I AM the Messiah.* ²⁰I tell you the truth, anyone who welcomes my messenger is welcoming me, and anyone who welcomes me is welcoming the Father who sent me."

²¹Now Jesus was deeply troubled,* and he exclaimed, "I tell you the truth, one of you will betray me!"

²²The disciples looked at each other, wondering whom he could mean. ²³The disciple Jesus loved was sitting next to Jesus at the table.* ²⁴Simon Peter motioned to him to ask, "Who's he talking about?" ²⁵So that disciple leaned over to Jesus and asked, "Lord, who is it?"

²⁶Jesus responded, "It is the one to whom I give the bread I dip in the bowl." And when he had dipped it, he gave it to Judas, son of Simon Iscariot. ²⁷When Judas had eaten the bread, Satan entered into him. Then Jesus told him, "Hurry and do what you're going to do." ²⁸None

---

13:38 Isa 53:1.   12:40 Isa 6:10.   13:1 Or *he showed them the full extent of his love.*   13:2 Or *the devil had already intended for Judas.*   13:10 Some manuscripts do not include *except for the feet.*   13:18 Ps 41:9.   13:19 Or *that the 'I AM' has come;* or *that I am the LORD;* Greek reads *that I am.* See Exod 3:14.   13:21 Greek *was troubled in his spirit.*
13:23 Greek *was reclining on Jesus' bosom.* The "disciple Jesus loved" was probably John.

of the others at the table knew what Jesus meant. ²⁹ Since Judas was their treasurer, some thought Jesus was telling him to go and pay for the food or to give some money to the poor. ³⁰ So Judas left at once, going out into the night.

Jesus Predicts Peter's Denial

³¹ As soon as Judas left the room, Jesus said, "The time has come for the Son of Man* to enter into his glory, and God will be glorified because of him. ³² And since God receives glory because of the Son,* he will soon give glory to the Son. ³³ Dear children, I will be with you only a little longer. And as I told the Jewish leaders, you will search for me, but you can't come where I am going. ³⁴ So now I am giving you a new commandment: Love each other. Just as I have loved you, you should love each other. ³⁵ Your love for one another will prove to the world that you are my disciples."

³⁶ Simon Peter asked, "Lord, where are you going?"

And Jesus replied, "You can't go with me now, but you will follow me later."

³⁷ "But why can't I come now, Lord?" he asked. "I'm ready to die for you."

³⁸ Jesus answered, "Die for me? I tell you the truth, Peter—before the rooster crows tomorrow morning, you will deny three times that you even know me.

CHAPTER **14**
Jesus, the Way to the Father

"Don't let your hearts be troubled. Trust in God, and trust also in me. ² There is more than enough room in my Father's home.* If this were not so, would I have told you that I am going to prepare a place for you?* ³ When everything is ready, I will come and get you, so that you will always be with me where I am. ⁴ And you know the way to where I am going."

⁵ "No, we don't know, Lord," Thomas said. "We have no idea where you are going, so how can we know the way?"

⁶ Jesus told him, "I am the way, the truth, and the life. No one can come to the Father except through me. ⁷ If you had really known me, you would know who my Father is.* From now on, you do know him and have seen him!"

⁸ Philip said, "Lord, show us the Father, and we will be satisfied."

13:31 "Son of Man" is a title Jesus used for himself.
13:32 Some manuscripts do not include *And since God receives glory because of the Son.*   14:2a Or *There are many rooms in my Father's house.*   14:2b Or *If this were not so, I would have told you that I am going to prepare a place for you.* Some manuscripts read *If this were not so, I would have told you. I am going to prepare a place for you.*
14:7 Some manuscripts read *If you have really known me, you will know who my Father is.*

first steps

GOD GIVES HOPE TO OUR TROUBLED HEARTS
Read JOHN 14:1-7

Have you ever felt troubled and uncertain about your future? Have you ever felt God was unaware of your world turning upside down? The disciples may have been experiencing these feelings when Jesus gave them this message. He had just told them that he was going to leave them, and they were extremely concerned. Yet he tells them to not be troubled and gives them three reasons why they should have peace in their hearts:

1. We Can Take God at His Word. When Jesus said, "Trust in God, and trust also in me," he was reminding his disciples to trust in God's Word (verse 1). Scripture had spoken of both Jesus' impending crucifixion *and* his resurrection. Somehow they had missed that. Sometimes we forget to look at the whole picture when our circumstances seem overwhelming. But we must remember that the words found in these pages will "never disappear" (Matthew 24:35).

2. We Are Going to Heaven. The next time you face some kind of difficulty, be it physical, emotional, or spiritual, put it in perspective—remember that you are going to heaven (verse 2). Your trials are only temporary. When in the presence of the Lord, there will be no more fear, death, pain, or sorrow.

3. Jesus Is Coming Back for Us. Notice that Jesus says, "I will come and get you" (verse 3). The Lord is not merely going to send for us. He is going to personally escort us to the Father's house. The Bible tells us to "encourage each other with these words" (1 Thessalonians 4:18). In the midst of your trials, remember that God cares for you so much that he is coming back so that you can be with him forever.

To begin the next reading track, turn to p. A45.

cornerstones
WHO WILL ENTER HEAVEN?
Read JOHN 14:2-6

Hollywood has often depicted the gates of heaven as the place where you plead your case in order to gain entrance. In this passage, Jesus clearly explains that the only ones who will enter heaven will be those who have accepted him as the way, the truth, and the life—not those who have performed the greatest number of good deeds.

Heaven is not a court but a prepared place for prepared people. If you are a Christian, your reservation for heaven was made the moment you received Christ. And when it comes to accommodations, you don't need to worry, because Jesus himself promised to prepare a place for you.

The Bible tells us to prepare to meet our God. Is your reservation in place?

For the next note on "What Is Heaven?" turn to p. 214.

---

⁹Jesus replied, "Have I been with you all this time, Philip, and yet you still don't know who I am? Anyone who has seen me has seen the Father! So why are you asking me to show him to you? ¹⁰Don't you believe that I am in the Father and the Father is in me? The words I speak are not my own, but my Father who lives in me does his work through me. ¹¹Just believe that I am in the Father and the Father is in me. Or at least believe because of the work you have seen me do.

¹²"I tell you the truth, anyone who believes in me will do the same works I have done, and even greater works, because I am going to be with the Father. ¹³You can ask for anything in my name, and I will do it, so that the Son can bring glory to the Father. ¹⁴Yes, ask me for anything in my name, and I will do it!

Jesus Promises the Holy Spirit
¹⁵"If you love me, obey* my commandments. ¹⁶And I will ask the Father, and he will give you another Advocate,* who will never leave you. ¹⁷He is the Holy Spirit, who leads into all truth. The world cannot receive him, because it isn't looking for him and doesn't recognize him. But you know him, because he lives with you now and later will be in you.* ¹⁸No, I will not abandon you as orphans—I will come to you. ¹⁹Soon the world will no longer see me, but you will see me. Since I live, you also will live. ²⁰When I am raised to life again, you will know that I am in my Father, and you are in me, and I am in you. ²¹Those who accept my commandments and obey them are the ones who love me. And because they love me, my Father will love them. And I will love them and reveal myself to each of them."

²²Judas (not Judas Iscariot, but the other dis-

ciple with that name) said to him, "Lord, why are you going to reveal yourself only to us and not to the world at large?"

²³Jesus replied, "All who love me will do what I say. My Father will love them, and we will come and make our home with each of them. ²⁴Anyone who doesn't love me will not obey me. And remember, my words are not my own. What I am telling you is from the Father who sent me. ²⁵I am telling you these things now while I am still with you. ²⁶But when the Father sends the Advocate as my representative—that is, the Holy Spirit—he will teach you everything and will remind you of everything I have told you.

²⁷"I am leaving you with a gift—peace of mind and heart. And the peace I give is a gift the world cannot give. So don't be troubled or afraid. ²⁸Remember what I told you: I am going away, but I will come back to you again. If you really loved me, you would be happy that I am going to the Father, who is greater than I am. ²⁹I have told you these things before they happen so that when they do happen, you will believe.

³⁰"I don't have much more time to talk to you, because the ruler of this world approaches. He has no power over me, ³¹but I will do what the Father requires of me, so that the world will know that I love the Father. Come, let's be going.

CHAPTER 15
Jesus, the True Vine
"I am the true grapevine, and my Father is the gardener. ²He cuts off every branch of mine that doesn't produce fruit, and he prunes the branches that do bear fruit so they will produce even more. ³You have already been pruned and

14:15 Other manuscripts read *you will obey;* still others read *you should obey.*   14:16 Or *Comforter,* or *Encourager,* or *Counselor.* Greek reads *Paraclete;* also in 14:26.   14:17 Some manuscripts read *and is in you.*

purified by the message I have given you. ⁴Remain in me, and I will remain in you. For a branch cannot produce fruit if it is severed from the vine, and you cannot be fruitful unless you remain in me.

⁵"Yes, I am the vine; you are the branches. Those who remain in me, and I in them, will produce much fruit. For apart from me you can do nothing. ⁶Anyone who does not remain in me is thrown away like a useless branch and withers. Such branches are gathered into a pile to be burned. ⁷But if you remain in me and my words remain in you, you may ask for anything you want, and it will be granted! ⁸When you produce much fruit, you are my true disciples. This brings great glory to my Father.

⁹"I have loved you even as the Father has loved me. Remain in my love. ¹⁰When you obey my commandments, you remain in my love, just as I obey my Father's commandments and remain in his love. ¹¹I have told you these things so that you will be filled with my joy. Yes, your joy will overflow! ¹²This is my commandment: Love each other in the same way I have loved you. ¹³There is no greater love than to lay down one's life for one's friends. ¹⁴You are my friends if you do what I command. ¹⁵I no longer call you slaves, because a master doesn't confide in his slaves. Now you are my friends, since I have told you everything the Father told me. ¹⁶You didn't choose me. I chose you. I appointed you to go and produce lasting fruit, so that the Father will give you whatever you ask for, using my name. ¹⁷This is my command: Love each other.

The World's Hatred

¹⁸"If the world hates you, remember that it hated me first. ¹⁹The world would love you as one of its own if you belonged to it, but you are no longer part of the world. I chose you to come out of the world, so it hates you. ²⁰Do you remember what I told you? 'A slave is not greater than the master.' Since they persecuted me, naturally they will persecute you. And if they had listened to me, they would listen to you. ²¹They will do all this to you because of me, for they have rejected the one who sent me. ²²They would not be guilty if I had not come and spoken to them. But now they have no excuse for their sin. ²³Anyone who hates me also hates my Father. ²⁴If I hadn't done such miraculous signs among them that no one else could do, they would not be guilty. But as it is, they have seen everything I did, yet they still hate me and my Father. ²⁵This fulfills what is written in their Scriptures*: 'They hated me without cause.'

15:25 Greek *in their law.* Pss 35:19; 69:4.

first steps

A DISCIPLE ABIDES IN CHRIST
Read JOHN 15:1-17

Jesus knows that his true followers desire to live productive, fulfilling, joy-filled lives. In this passage, he lays out four predominant characteristics of a growing disciple:

1. A Disciple Stays Close to the Master. Jesus encourages us to remain in him (verses 4-5). Another way to translate that is "to abide in him." The word *abide* signifies a permanent position. It means that you let your roots grow deep into your relationship with Jesus, allowing him to fill every part of your life every day. If you maintain this unbroken fellowship with God, your lifestyle will change.

2. A Disciple Is Fruitful. Just as a branch can only be fruitful when attached to the vine, we can only be productive when we draw our strength from Jesus (verses 6, 16). The Bible describes this fruit as love, joy, peace, patience, kindness, goodness, faithfulness, gentleness, and self-control (see Galatians 5:22-23, p. 226).

3. A Disciple Obeys the Master. Another clear sign that you are Christ's disciple is your obedience to the principles and guidelines found in the Bible (verse 10). Only then will you discover what it means to live in God's love.

4. A Disciple Loves Others. Jesus gave us the ultimate example of love by laying down his life for us. He, in essence, is asking us to do nothing less. That may not mean actually dying, but it may mean placing someone else's needs before our own.

In verse 11 we find Jesus' reason for sharing these principles: He wants us to be filled with joy. If you try to find happiness through the pursuit of worldly things, it will elude you. The only way to find happiness is through the pursuit of God. If you prioritize your life as Jesus has laid out in these verses, then "your joy will overflow."

For the next note on "Live as a Disciple," turn to p. 307.

cornerstones

HOW THE HOLY SPIRIT WORKS IN OUR LIVES
Read JOHN 14:15-17

The Bible uses three different Greek prepositions in the New Testament to describe the different ways in which the Holy Spirit works in our lives. This verse shows two of these ways, and a third can be found elsewhere in Scripture:

1. He Works *with* Us as Nonbelievers (*para*). Prior to our conversion to faith in Jesus Christ, the Holy Spirit convicts us of our sin and reveals Christ as the answer (see John 16:8, p. 120). Some might dismiss his prodding as that of one's conscience. Yet it is the Holy Spirit who opens our eyes to our terminally sinful condition, exposing our need to turn our lives over to Jesus Christ.

2. He Comes *into* Our Lives When We Turn to Christ (*en*). Once we accept Jesus Christ as our Savior and invite him into our lives, the Holy Spirit comes and sets up residence, so to speak. First, he starts the process of salvation in our heart. Jesus said, "I assure you, no one can enter the Kingdom of God without being born of . . . the Spirit" (John 3:5). Second, he assures us that we have done the right thing. Scripture says, "For his Spirit joins with our spirit to affirm that we are God's children" (Romans 8:16). Now he can begin changing us from the inside out and develop the new nature within us.

3. He Will Come *upon* Us to Empower Us as Believers (*epi*). Jesus describes the dynamic empowering of the Holy Spirit upon our lives in Luke 24:49, where he said, "And now I will send the Holy Spirit, just as my Father promised." This is what the early Christians experienced in Acts chapter 2, and it dramatically emboldened their witness for Jesus Christ. This power is available to believers today. Scripture says of the giving of his Spirit, "This promise is to you, and to your children, and even to the Gentiles—all who have been called by the Lord our God" (Acts 2:39).

For the next note on "Who Is the Holy Spirit?" turn to p. 138.

---

26 "But I will send you the Advocate*—the Spirit of truth. He will come to you from the Father and will testify all about me. 27 And you must also testify about me because you have been with me from the beginning of my ministry.

CHAPTER 16

"I have told you these things so that you won't abandon your faith. 2 For you will be expelled from the synagogues, and the time is coming when those who kill you will think they are doing a holy service for God. 3 This is because they have never known the Father or me. 4 Yes, I'm telling you these things now, so that when they happen, you will remember my warning. I didn't tell you earlier because I was going to be with you for a while longer.

The Work of the Holy Spirit

5 "But now I am going away to the one who sent me, and not one of you is asking where I am going. 6 Instead, you grieve because of what I've told you. 7 But in fact, it is best for you that I go away, because if I don't, the Advocate* won't come. If I do go away, then I will send him to you. 8 And when he comes, he will convict the world of its sin, and of God's righteousness, and of the coming judgment. 9 The world's sin is that it refuses to believe in me. 10 Righteousness is available because I go to the Father, and you will see me no more. 11 Judgment will come because the ruler of this world has already been judged.

12 "There is so much more I want to tell you, but you can't bear it now. 13 When the Spirit of truth comes, he will guide you into all truth. He will not speak on his own but will tell you what he has heard. He will tell you about the future. 14 He will bring me glory by telling you whatever he receives from me. 15 All that belongs to the Father is mine; this is why I said, 'The Spirit will tell you whatever he receives from me.'

Sadness Will Be Turned to Joy

16 "In a little while you won't see me anymore. But a little while after that, you will see me again."

17 Some of the disciples asked each other, "What does he mean when he says, 'In a little

15:26 Or *Comforter*, or *Encourager*, or *Counselor*. Greek reads *Paraclete*.   16:7 Or *Comforter*, or *Encourager*, or *Counselor*. Greek reads *Paraclete*.

while you won't see me, but then you will see me,' and 'I am going to the Father'? ¹⁸And what does he mean by 'a little while'? We don't understand."

¹⁹Jesus realized they wanted to ask him about it, so he said, "Are you asking yourselves what I meant? I said in a little while you won't see me, but a little while after that you will see me again. ²⁰I tell you the truth, you will weep and mourn over what is going to happen to me, but the world will rejoice. You will grieve, but your grief will suddenly turn to wonderful joy. ²¹It will be like a woman suffering the pains of labor. When her child is born, her anguish gives way to joy because she has brought a new baby into the world. ²²So you have sorrow now, but I will see you again; then you will rejoice, and no one can rob you of that joy. ²³At that time you won't need to ask me for anything. I tell you the truth, you will ask the Father directly, and he will grant your request because you use my name. ²⁴You haven't done this before. Ask, using my name, and you will receive, and you will have abundant joy.

²⁵"I have spoken of these matters in figures of speech, but soon I will stop speaking figuratively and will tell you plainly all about the Father. ²⁶Then you will ask in my name. I'm not saying I will ask the Father on your behalf, ²⁷for the Father himself loves you dearly because you love me and believe that I came from God.* ²⁸Yes, I came from the Father into the world, and now I will leave the world and return to the Father."

²⁹Then his disciples said, "At last you are speaking plainly and not figuratively. ³⁰Now we understand that you know everything, and there's no need to question you. From this we believe that you came from God."

³¹Jesus asked, "Do you finally believe? ³²But the time is coming—indeed it's here now—when you will be scattered, each one going his own way, leaving me alone. Yet I am not alone because the Father is with me. ³³I have told you all this so that you may have peace in me. Here on earth you will have many trials and sorrows. But take heart, because I have overcome the world."

CHAPTER 17
The Prayer of Jesus
After saying all these things, Jesus looked up to heaven and said, "Father, the hour has come. Glorify your Son so he can give glory back to you. ²For you have given him authority over everyone. He gives eternal life to each one you have given him. ³And this is the way to have eternal life—to know you, the only true God,

16:27 Some manuscripts read *from the Father.*

first steps
LIVE IN GOD'S LOVE
Read JOHN 15:9-11

A portion of Jesus' last message to his disciples before his death is recorded here. In preparation for his departure, Jesus emphasized his love for them and how that love should affect their lives. He wanted them to realize that they could experience true and lasting joy in their walk with God—even if he could not personally be with them. For that reason this intimate message and command from Christ applies to us today as well. In this text Jesus gives four simple points that will enable us to live in his love:

1. Realize That You Have the Love of Jesus. Jesus is not simply some authoritative figure who demands our respect. He is a personal being—fully God and fully human—who loved us so much that he died in our place. Knowing that Jesus loves you frees you to love him in return. Because we love Jesus, we will obey his commands, as God requires us to do.

2. Live within God's Love by Obeying His Commands. One of the earmarks of a true follower of Christ is obedience. It is easy to boast of our great love for God or the wonderful affection and devotion we feel toward him. But the way to prove your love for Jesus is to obey his commands. Obeying his commands out of obligation rather than love can produce resentment toward him. That is because there is no joy in mere obligation. But obeying Jesus out of love produces joy.

3. Follow Jesus' Example. Jesus is our perfect model of obedience. Pay careful attention to how Jesus obeyed his heavenly Father throughout the Gospels of Matthew, Mark, Luke, and John.

4. Experience the Reward of Obedience: Overflowing Joy. An obedient Christian is a happy Christian. If you want more joy in your life, make sure that you are following the guidelines God has given you in his Word.

Do you find it hard to obey God and his principles? If so, it is probably time to reexamine your priorities and make sure that getting to know your Creator is right at the top of the list. Then you will discover the joy that comes from living in God's love every day.

For the next note on "Obey God," turn to *p. 183.*

and Jesus Christ, the one you sent to earth. [4]I brought glory to you here on earth by completing the work you gave me to do. [5]Now, Father, bring me into the glory we shared before the world began.

[6]"I have revealed you* to the ones you gave me from this world. They were always yours. You gave them to me, and they have kept your word. [7]Now they know that everything I have is a gift from you, [8]for I have passed on to them the message you gave me. They accepted it and know that I came from you, and they believe you sent me.

[9]"My prayer is not for the world, but for those you have given me, because they belong to you. [10]All who are mine belong to you, and you have given them to me, so they bring me glory. [11]Now I am departing from the world; they are staying in this world, but I am coming to you. Holy Father, you have given me your name;* now protect them by the power of your name so that they will be united just as we are. [12]During my time here, I protected them by the power of the name you gave me.* I guarded them so that not one was lost, except the one headed for destruction, as the Scriptures foretold.

[13]"Now I am coming to you. I told them many things while I was with them in this world so they would be filled with my joy. [14]I have given them your word. And the world hates them because they do not belong to the world, just as I do not belong to the world. [15]I'm not asking you to take them out of the world, but to keep them safe from the evil one. [16]They do not belong to this world any more than I do. [17]Make them holy by your truth; teach them your word, which is truth. [18]Just as you sent me into the world, I am sending them into the world. [19]And I give myself as a holy sacrifice for them so they can be made holy by your truth.

[20]"I am praying not only for these disciples but also for all who will ever believe in me through their message. [21]I pray that they will all be one, just as you and I are one—as you are in me, Father, and I am in you. And may they be in us so that the world will believe you sent me.

[22]"I have given them the glory you gave me, so they may be one as we are one. [23]I am in them and you are in me. May they experience such perfect unity that the world will know that you sent me and that you love them as much as you love me. [24]Father, I want these whom you have given me to be with me where I am. Then they can see all the glory you gave me because you loved me even before the world began!

[25]"O righteous Father, the world doesn't know you, but I do; and these disciples know you sent me. [26]I have revealed you to them, and I will continue to do so. Then your love for me will be in them, and I will be in them."

CHAPTER **18**

Jesus Is Betrayed and Arrested

After saying these things, Jesus crossed the Kidron Valley with his disciples and entered a grove of olive trees. [2]Judas, the betrayer, knew this place, because Jesus had often gone there with his disciples. [3]The leading priests and Pharisees had given Judas a contingent of Roman soldiers and Temple guards to accompany him. Now with blazing torches, lanterns, and weapons, they arrived at the olive grove.

[4]Jesus fully realized all that was going to happen to him, so he stepped forward to meet them. "Who are you looking for?" he asked.

[5]"Jesus the Nazarene,"* they replied.

"I AM he,"* Jesus said. (Judas, who betrayed him, was standing with them.) [6]As Jesus said "I AM he," they all drew back and fell to the ground! [7]Once more he asked them, "Who are you looking for?"

And again they replied, "Jesus the Nazarene."

[8]"I told you that I AM he," Jesus said. "And since I am the one you want, let these others go." [9]He did this to fulfill his own statement: "I did not lose a single one of those you have given me."*

[10]Then Simon Peter drew a sword and slashed off the right ear of Malchus, the high priest's slave. [11]But Jesus said to Peter, "Put your sword back into its sheath. Shall I not drink from the cup of suffering the Father has given me?"

Jesus at the High Priest's House

[12]So the soldiers, their commanding officer, and the Temple guards arrested Jesus and tied him up. [13]First they took him to Annas, the father-in-law of Caiaphas, the high priest at that time.* [14]Caiaphas was the one who had told the other Jewish leaders, "It's better that one man should die for the people."

Peter's First Denial

[15]Simon Peter followed Jesus, as did another of the disciples. That other disciple was acquainted with the high priest, so he was allowed to enter the high priest's courtyard with Jesus. [16]Peter had to stay outside the gate. Then the disciple who knew the high priest spoke to

---

17:6 Greek *have revealed your name;* also in 17:26.   17:11 Some manuscripts read *you have given me these [disciples].*
17:12 Some manuscripts read *I protected those you gave me, by the power of your name.*   18:5a Or *Jesus of Nazareth;* also in 18:7.   18:5b Or *"The 'I AM' is here";* or *"I am the LORD";* Greek reads *I am;* also in 18:6, 8. See Exod 3:14.   18:9 See John 6:39 and 17:12.   18:13 Greek *that year.*

the woman watching at the gate, and she let Peter in. ¹⁷The woman asked Peter, "You're not one of that man's disciples, are you?"

"No," he said, "I am not."

¹⁸Because it was cold, the household servants and the guards had made a charcoal fire. They stood around it, warming themselves, and Peter stood with them, warming himself.

The High Priest Questions Jesus
¹⁹Inside, the high priest began asking Jesus about his followers and what he had been teaching them. ²⁰Jesus replied, "Everyone knows what I teach. I have preached regularly in the synagogues and the Temple, where the people* gather. I have not spoken in secret. ²¹Why are you asking me this question? Ask those who heard me. They know what I said."

²²Then one of the Temple guards standing nearby slapped Jesus across the face. "Is that the way to answer the high priest?" he demanded.

²³Jesus replied, "If I said anything wrong, you must prove it. But if I'm speaking the truth, why are you beating me?"

²⁴Then Annas bound Jesus and sent him to Caiaphas, the high priest.

Peter's Second and Third Denials
²⁵Meanwhile, as Simon Peter was standing by the fire warming himself, they asked him again, "You're not one of his disciples, are you?"

He denied it, saying, "No, I am not."

²⁶But one of the household slaves of the high priest, a relative of the man whose ear Peter had cut off, asked, "Didn't I see you out there in the olive grove with Jesus?" ²⁷Again Peter denied it. And immediately a rooster crowed.

Jesus' Trial before Pilate
²⁸Jesus' trial before Caiaphas ended in the early hours of the morning. Then he was taken to the headquarters of the Roman governor.* His accusers didn't go inside because it would defile them, and they wouldn't be allowed to celebrate the Passover. ²⁹So Pilate, the governor, went out to them and asked, "What is your charge against this man?"

³⁰"We wouldn't have handed him over to you if he weren't a criminal!" they retorted.

³¹"Then take him away and judge him by your own law," Pilate told them.

"Only the Romans are permitted to execute someone," the Jewish leaders replied. ³²(This fulfilled Jesus' prediction about the way he would die.*)

18:20 Greek *Jewish people;* also in 18:38.   18:28 Greek *to the Praetorium;* also in 18:33.   18:32 See John 12:32-33.

first steps
GOD'S SPIRIT WILL GUIDE YOU
Read JOHN 16:13-15

The work of the Holy Spirit in the life of a Christian is multidimensional. We are told that, among other things, the Holy Spirit "joins with our spirit to affirm that we are God's children" (Romans 8:16). In this passage, we see that the Holy Spirit serves as a teacher and a guide.

The Holy Spirit Will Help Us Understand the Bible. Before you became a Christian, understanding the Bible may have been like walking around with blinders on. But those blinders you once had were taken off, so to speak, when the Holy Spirit came into your heart. The Holy Spirit teaches you the truth of the Scripture, helping you grasp hard-to-understand passages.

The Holy Spirit Will Reveal More and More about God and Jesus. The Bible makes it abundantly clear that one of the primary roles of the Holy Spirit is to glorify Christ. The moment you invited Jesus into your heart, God's Spirit began to help you grasp the awesome, praiseworthy attributes of Jesus. Those who do not have a personal relationship with Christ cannot understand the full glory of God, because they do not have the Holy Spirit's assistance.

The Holy Spirit wants to be actively involved in your life, helping you grow in the knowledge of God and his Word so that you can better understand God's will for your life. Every time you open the Bible, pray for the Holy Spirit to show you how the passages you read can apply to your life.

For the next note on "Live in God's Power," turn to p. 131.

33 Then Pilate went back into his headquarters and called for Jesus to be brought to him. "Are you the king of the Jews?" he asked him.

34 Jesus replied, "Is this your own question, or did others tell you about me?"

35 "Am I a Jew?" Pilate retorted. "Your own people and their leading priests brought you to me for trial. Why? What have you done?"

36 Jesus answered, "My Kingdom is not an earthly kingdom. If it were, my followers would fight to keep me from being handed over to the Jewish leaders. But my Kingdom is not of this world."

37 Pilate said, "So you are a king?"

Jesus responded, "You say I am a king. Actually, I was born and came into the world to testify to the truth. All who love the truth recognize that what I say is true."

38 "What is truth?" Pilate asked. Then he went out again to the people and told them, "He is not guilty of any crime. 39 But you have a custom of asking me to release one prisoner each year at Passover. Would you like me to release this 'King of the Jews'?"

40 But they shouted back, "No! Not this man. We want Barabbas!" (Barabbas was a revolutionary.)

CHAPTER **19**

Jesus Sentenced to Death

Then Pilate had Jesus flogged with a lead-tipped whip. 2 The soldiers wove a crown of thorns and put it on his head, and they put a purple robe on him. 3 "Hail! King of the Jews!" they mocked, as they slapped him across the face.

4 Pilate went outside again and said to the people, "I am going to bring him out to you now, but understand clearly that I find him not guilty." 5 Then Jesus came out wearing the crown of thorns and the purple robe. And Pilate said, "Look, here is the man!"

6 When they saw him, the leading priests and Temple guards began shouting, "Crucify him! Crucify him!"

"Take him yourselves and crucify him," Pilate said. "I find him not guilty."

7 The Jewish leaders replied, "By our law he ought to die because he called himself the Son of God."

8 When Pilate heard this, he was more frightened than ever. 9 He took Jesus back into the headquarters* again and asked him, "Where are you from?" But Jesus gave no answer. 10 "Why don't you talk to me?" Pilate demanded. "Don't you realize that I have the power to release you or crucify you?"

11 Then Jesus said, "You would have no power over me at all unless it were given to you from above. So the one who handed me over to you has the greater sin."

12 Then Pilate tried to release him, but the Jewish leaders shouted, "If you release this man, you are no 'friend of Caesar.'* Anyone who declares himself a king is a rebel against Caesar."

13 When they said this, Pilate brought Jesus out to them again. Then Pilate sat down on the judgment seat on the platform that is called the Stone Pavement (in Hebrew, *Gabbatha*). 14 It was now about noon on the day of preparation for the Passover. And Pilate said to the people,* "Look, here is your king!"

15 "Away with him," they yelled. "Away with him! Crucify him!"

"What? Crucify your king?" Pilate asked.

"We have no king but Caesar," the leading priests shouted back.

16 Then Pilate turned Jesus over to them to be crucified.

The Crucifixion

So they took Jesus away. 17 Carrying the cross by himself, he went to the place called Place of the Skull (in Hebrew, *Golgotha*). 18 There they nailed him to the cross. Two others were crucified with him, one on either side, with Jesus between them. 19 And Pilate posted a sign on the cross that read, "Jesus of Nazareth,* the King of the Jews." 20 The place where Jesus was crucified was near the city, and the sign was written in Hebrew, Latin, and Greek, so that many people could read it.

21 Then the leading priests objected and said to Pilate, "Change it from 'The King of the Jews' to 'He said, I am King of the Jews.'"

22 Pilate replied, "No, what I have written, I have written."

23 When the soldiers had crucified Jesus, they divided his clothes among the four of them. They also took his robe, but it was seamless, woven in one piece from top to bottom. 24 So they said, "Rather than tearing it apart, let's throw dice* for it." This fulfilled the Scripture that says, "They divided my garments among themselves and threw dice for my clothing."* So that is what they did.

25 Standing near the cross were Jesus' mother, and his mother's sister, Mary (the wife of Clopas), and Mary Magdalene. 26 When Jesus saw his mother standing there beside the disciple he loved, he said to her, "Dear woman, here is your son." 27 And he said to this disciple, "Here is your mother." And from then on this disciple took her into his home.

19:9 Greek *the Praetorium.*   19:12 "Friend of Caesar" is a technical term that refers to an ally of the emperor.   19:14 Greek *Jewish people;* also in 19:20.   19:19 Or *Jesus the Nazarene.*   19:24a Greek *cast lots.*   19:24b Ps 22:18.

The Death of Jesus

[28] Jesus knew that his mission was now finished, and to fulfill Scripture he said, "I am thirsty."* [29] A jar of sour wine was sitting there, so they soaked a sponge in it, put it on a hyssop branch, and held it up to his lips. [30] When Jesus had tasted it, he said, "It is finished!" Then he bowed his head and released his spirit.

[31] It was the day of preparation, and the Jewish leaders didn't want the bodies hanging there the next day, which was the Sabbath (and a very special Sabbath, because it was the Passover). So they asked Pilate to hasten their deaths by ordering that their legs be broken. Then their bodies could be taken down. [32] So the soldiers came and broke the legs of the two men crucified with Jesus. [33] But when they came to Jesus, they saw that he was already dead, so they didn't break his legs. [34] One of the soldiers, however, pierced his side with a spear, and immediately blood and water flowed out. [35] (This report is from an eyewitness giving an accurate account. He speaks the truth so that you also can believe.*) [36] These things happened in fulfillment of the Scriptures that say, "Not one of his bones will be broken,"* [37] and "They will look on the one they pierced."*

The Burial of Jesus

[38] Afterward Joseph of Arimathea, who had been a secret disciple of Jesus (because he feared the Jewish leaders), asked Pilate for permission to take down Jesus' body. When Pilate gave permission, Joseph came and took the body away. [39] With him came Nicodemus, the man who had come to Jesus at night. He brought about seventy-five pounds* of perfumed ointment made from myrrh and aloes. [40] Following Jewish burial custom, they wrapped Jesus' body with the spices in long sheets of linen cloth. [41] The place of crucifixion was near a garden, where there was a new tomb, never used before. [42] And so, because it was the day of preparation for the Jewish Passover* and since the tomb was close at hand, they laid Jesus there.

CHAPTER 20

The Resurrection

Early on Sunday morning,* while it was still dark, Mary Magdalene came to the tomb and found that the stone had been rolled away from the entrance. [2] She ran and found Simon Peter and the other disciple, the one whom Jesus loved. She said, "They have taken the Lord's body out of the tomb, and we don't know where they have put him!"

[3] Peter and the other disciple started out for the tomb. [4] They were both running, but the other disciple outran Peter and reached the tomb first. [5] He stooped and looked in and saw the linen wrappings lying there, but he didn't go in. [6] Then Simon Peter arrived and went inside. He also noticed the linen wrappings lying there, [7] while the cloth that had covered Jesus' head was folded up and lying apart from the other wrappings. [8] Then the disciple who had reached the tomb first also went in, and he saw and believed— [9] for until then they still hadn't understood the Scriptures that said Jesus must rise from the dead. [10] Then they went home.

Jesus Appears to Mary Magdalene

[11] Mary was standing outside the tomb crying, and as she wept, she stooped and looked in. [12] She saw two white-robed angels, one sitting at the head and the other at the foot of the place where the body of Jesus had been lying. [13] "Dear woman, why are you crying?" the angels asked her.

"Because they have taken away my Lord," she replied, "and I don't know where they have put him."

[14] She turned to leave and saw someone standing there. It was Jesus, but she didn't recognize him. [15] "Dear woman, why are you crying?" Jesus asked her. "Who are you looking for?"

She thought he was the gardener. "Sir," she said, "if you have taken him away, tell me where you have put him, and I will go and get him."

[16] "Mary!" Jesus said.

She turned to him and cried out, "Rabboni!" (which is Hebrew for "Teacher").

[17] "Don't cling to me," Jesus said, "for I haven't yet ascended to the Father. But go find my brothers and tell them, 'I am ascending to my Father and your Father, to my God and your God.'"

[18] Mary Magdalene found the disciples and told them, "I have seen the Lord!" Then she gave them his message.

Jesus Appears to His Disciples

[19] That Sunday evening* the disciples were meeting behind locked doors because they were afraid of the Jewish leaders. Suddenly, Jesus was standing there among them! "Peace be with you," he said. [20] As he spoke, he showed them the wounds in his hands and his side. They were filled with joy when they saw the Lord! [21] Again he said, "Peace be with you. As the Father has sent me, so I am sending you." [22] Then he breathed on them and said, "Receive the Holy Spirit. [23] If you forgive anyone's sins,

19:28 See Pss 22:15; 69:21.   19:35 Some manuscripts read *can continue to believe*.   19:36 Exod 12:46; Num 9:12; Ps 34:20.   19:37 Zech 12:10.   19:39 Greek *100 litras* [32.7 kilograms].   19:42 Greek *because of the Jewish day of preparation*.   20:1 Greek *On the first day of the week*.   20:19 Greek *In the evening of that day, the first day of the week*.

cornerstones

OUR LOVE FOR GOD PREPARES US FOR SERVICE
Read JOHN 21:15-17

Peter knew that he had let Jesus down when he denied him three times prior to the Crucifixion. But Peter also knew that Jesus had forgiven him.

Jesus tested Peter by asking him the searching question, "Do you love me?" three times.

In the original language of this text, Peter's response to Jesus' questions has great significance. When Jesus posed the questions, he had basically asked, "Peter, do you love me with a sacrificial, committed love?" But Peter responded with a different word for "love." Peter essentially said, "Lord, I like you. I love you as a friend."

At least Peter was honest. He told Jesus the truth about his commitment. Interestingly enough, Jesus still enlisted Peter in his service, to care for his sheep. Jesus just wanted Peter to affirm his devotion before giving him directions for ministry. As this story implies, we must love God before we can serve him faithfully. Do you love God?

Here are five ways to tell if you really love God and are growing in that love for him: If you love God,

1. You Will Long for Personal Communion with Him. Can you relate to the words of the psalmist, "As the deer longs for streams of water, so I long for you, O God" (Psalm 42:1)? When you really love God, you will delight in praising and worshiping him because your heart will overflow with love for God. And this love will cause you to look forward to spending time with him and his people.

2. You Will Love the Things He Loves. We know what God loves by what he has declared in his Word, the Bible. So if you love God, you will love his Word. Bible study will not be a drudgery, but a delight.

3. You Will Hate What He Hates. As the Lord's nature becomes your nature, his likes and dislikes become your likes and dislikes. His outlook becomes your outlook. We know from his Word that he hates sin. If we love him, then we should also hate sin.

4. You Will Long for His Return. Jesus described himself as a bridegroom (Mark 2:19). His bride is the church—the body of believers (Ephesians 5:23-29). When Jesus returns, he will be united with his bride. Therefore, if you love the Lord, you will long for his return as a bride longs for her bridegroom.

5. You Will Keep His Commandments. Jesus says, "If you love me, obey my commandments" (John 14:15). Though it is impossible for any of us who loves God to go on an endless course of sin, we will still occasionally fall into individual sins. But if we love God, we will repent of those sins and seek his forgiveness, and our lifestyle will conform to the truths we find in his Word.

Do you love the Lord? Like Peter, you may be tempted to believe that you have no love for Jesus when you sin. Maybe you feel that God could never use you in his service again. Be honest with God; then start rebuilding that relationship. As you reaffirm your love for him, God will open up opportunities for you to serve him and share that love with others. A committed heart leads to committed service.

For the next note on "Love," turn to p. 306.

---

they are forgiven. If you do not forgive them, they are not forgiven."

Jesus Appears to Thomas
24 One of the twelve disciples, Thomas (nicknamed the Twin),* was not with the others

when Jesus came. 25 They told him, "We have seen the Lord!"

But he replied, "I won't believe it unless I see the nail wounds in his hands, put my fingers into them, and place my hand into the wound in his side."

20:24 Greek *Thomas, who was called Didymus.*

26 Eight days later the disciples were together again, and this time Thomas was with them. The doors were locked; but suddenly, as before, Jesus was standing among them. "Peace be with you," he said. 27 Then he said to Thomas, "Put your finger here, and look at my hands. Put your hand into the wound in my side. Don't be faithless any longer. Believe!"

28 "My Lord and my God!" Thomas exclaimed.

29 Then Jesus told him, "You believe because you have seen me. Blessed are those who believe without seeing me."

Purpose of the Book

30 The disciples saw Jesus do many other miraculous signs in addition to the ones recorded in this book. 31 But these are written so that you may continue to believe* that Jesus is the Messiah, the Son of God, and that by believing in him you will have life by the power of his name.

CHAPTER **21**

Epilogue: Jesus Appears to Seven Disciples

Later, Jesus appeared again to the disciples beside the Sea of Galilee.* This is how it happened. 2 Several of the disciples were there— Simon Peter, Thomas (nicknamed the Twin),* Nathanael from Cana in Galilee, the sons of Zebedee, and two other disciples.

3 Simon Peter said, "I'm going fishing."

"We'll come, too," they all said. So they went out in the boat, but they caught nothing all night.

4 At dawn Jesus was standing on the beach, but the disciples couldn't see who he was. 5 He called out, "Fellows,* have you caught any fish?"

"No," they replied.

6 Then he said, "Throw out your net on the right-hand side of the boat, and you'll get some!" So they did, and they couldn't haul in the net because there were so many fish in it.

7 Then the disciple Jesus loved said to Peter, "It's the Lord!" When Simon Peter heard that it was the Lord, he put on his tunic (for he had stripped for work), jumped into the water, and headed to shore. 8 The others stayed with the boat and pulled the loaded net to the shore, for they were only about a hundred yards* from shore. 9 When they got there, they found breakfast waiting for them—fish cooking over a charcoal fire, and some bread.

10 "Bring some of the fish you've just caught," Jesus said. 11 So Simon Peter went aboard and dragged the net to the shore. There were 153 large fish, and yet the net hadn't torn.

12 "Now come and have some breakfast!" Jesus said. None of the disciples dared to ask him, "Who are you?" They knew it was the Lord. 13 Then Jesus served them the bread and the fish. 14 This was the third time Jesus had appeared to his disciples since he had been raised from the dead.

15 After breakfast Jesus asked Simon Peter, "Simon son of John, do you love me more than these?*"

"Yes, Lord," Peter replied, "you know I love you."

"Then feed my lambs," Jesus told him.

16 Jesus repeated the question: "Simon son of John, do you love me?"

"Yes, Lord," Peter said, "you know I love you."

"Then take care of my sheep," Jesus said.

17 A third time he asked him, "Simon son of John, do you love me?"

Peter was hurt that Jesus asked the question a third time. He said, "Lord, you know everything. You know that I love you."

Jesus said, "Then feed my sheep.

18 "I tell you the truth, when you were young, you were able to do as you liked; you dressed yourself and went wherever you wanted to go. But when you are old, you will stretch out your hands, and others* will dress you and take you where you don't want to go." 19 Jesus said this to let him know by what kind of death he would glorify God. Then Jesus told him, "Follow me."

20 Peter turned around and saw behind them the disciple Jesus loved—the one who had leaned over to Jesus during supper and asked, "Lord, who will betray you?" 21 Peter asked Jesus, "What about him, Lord?"

22 Jesus replied, "If I want him to remain alive until I return, what is that to you? As for you, follow me." 23 So the rumor spread among the community of believers* that this disciple wouldn't die. But that isn't what Jesus said at all. He only said, "If I want him to remain alive until I return, what is that to you?"

24 This disciple is the one who testifies to these events and has recorded them here. And we know that his account of these things is accurate.

25 Jesus also did many other things. If they were all written down, I suppose the whole world could not contain the books that would be written.

20:31 Some manuscripts read *that you may believe.*   21:1 Greek *Sea of Tiberias,* another name for the Sea of Galilee.   21:2 Greek *Thomas, who was called Didymus.*   21:5 Greek *Children.*   21:8 Greek *200 cubits* [90 meters].   21:15 Or *more than these others do?*   21:18 Some manuscripts read *and another one.*   21:23 Greek *the brothers.*

Acts

AUTHOR: **LUKE** | DATE WRITTEN: **A.D. 63–70** | GENRE: **HISTORY**

Acts shows the church's early development and rapid growth. It reveals how the dynamic power of the Holy Spirit transformed a diverse group of fishermen, tax collectors, and other ordinary folks into people who turned their world upside-down with the gospel of Jesus Christ.

CHAPTER 1

The Promise of the Holy Spirit

In my first book* I told you, Theophilus, about everything Jesus began to do and teach ²until the day he was taken up to heaven after giving his chosen apostles further instructions through the Holy Spirit. ³During the forty days after his crucifixion, he appeared to the apostles from time to time, and he proved to them in many ways that he was actually alive. And he talked to them about the Kingdom of God.

⁴Once when he was eating with them, he commanded them, "Do not leave Jerusalem until the Father sends you the gift he promised, as I told you before. ⁵John baptized with* water, but in just a few days you will be baptized with the Holy Spirit."

The Ascension of Jesus

⁶So when the apostles were with Jesus, they kept asking him, "Lord, has the time come for you to free Israel and restore our kingdom?"

⁷He replied, "The Father alone has the authority to set those dates and times, and they are not for you to know. ⁸But you will receive power when the Holy Spirit comes upon you. And you will be my witnesses, telling people about me everywhere—in Jerusalem, throughout Judea, in Samaria, and to the ends of the earth."

⁹After saying this, he was taken up into a cloud while they were watching, and they could no longer see him. ¹⁰As they strained to see him rising into heaven, two white-robed men suddenly stood among them. ¹¹"Men of Galilee," they said, "why are you standing here staring into heaven? Jesus has been taken from you into heaven, but someday he will return from heaven in the same way you saw him go!"

Matthias Replaces Judas

¹²Then the apostles returned to Jerusalem from the Mount of Olives, a distance of half a mile.* ¹³When they arrived, they went to the upstairs room of the house where they were staying.

Here are the names of those who were present: Peter, John, James, Andrew, Philip, Thomas, Bartholomew, Matthew, James (son of Alphaeus), Simon (the Zealot), and Judas (son of James). ¹⁴They all met together and were constantly united in prayer, along with Mary the mother of Jesus, several other women, and the brothers of Jesus.

¹⁵During this time, when about 120 believers* were together in one place, Peter stood up and addressed them. ¹⁶"Brothers," he said, "the Scriptures had to be fulfilled concerning Judas, who guided those who arrested Jesus. This was predicted long ago by the Holy Spirit, speaking through King David. ¹⁷Judas was one of us and shared in the ministry with us."

¹⁸(Judas had bought a field with the money he received for his treachery. Falling headfirst there, his body split open, spilling out all his intestines. ¹⁹The news of his death spread to all the people of Jerusalem, and they gave the place the Aramaic name *Akeldama*, which means "Field of Blood.")

²⁰Peter continued, "This was written in the book of Psalms, where it says, 'Let his home become desolate, with no one living in it.' It also says, 'Let someone else take his position.'*

1:1 The reference is to the Gospel of Luke. **1:5** Or *in;* also in 1:5b. **1:12** Greek *a Sabbath day's journey.* **1:15** Greek *brothers.* **1:20** Pss 69:25; 109:8.

²¹"So now we must choose a replacement for Judas from among the men who were with us the entire time we were traveling with the Lord Jesus—²²from the time he was baptized by John until the day he was taken from us. Whoever is chosen will join us as a witness of Jesus' resurrection."

²³So they nominated two men: Joseph called Barsabbas (also known as Justus) and Matthias. ²⁴Then they all prayed, "O Lord, you know every heart. Show us which of these men you have chosen ²⁵as an apostle to replace Judas in this ministry, for he has deserted us and gone where he belongs." ²⁶Then they cast lots, and Matthias was selected to become an apostle with the other eleven.

CHAPTER 2

The Holy Spirit Comes

On the day of Pentecost* all the believers were meeting together in one place. ²Suddenly, there was a sound from heaven like the roaring of a mighty windstorm, and it filled the house where they were sitting. ³Then, what looked like flames or tongues of fire appeared and settled on each of them. ⁴And everyone present was filled with the Holy Spirit and began speaking in other languages,* as the Holy Spirit gave them this ability.

⁵At that time there were devout Jews from every nation living in Jerusalem. ⁶When they heard the loud noise, everyone came running, and they were bewildered to hear their own languages being spoken by the believers.

⁷They were completely amazed. "How can this be?" they exclaimed. "These people are all from Galilee, ⁸and yet we hear them speaking in our own native languages! ⁹Here we are—Parthians, Medes, Elamites, people from Mesopotamia, Judea, Cappadocia, Pontus, the province of Asia, ¹⁰Phrygia, Pamphylia, Egypt, and the areas of Libya around Cyrene, visitors from Rome ¹¹(both Jews and converts to Judaism), Cretans, and Arabs. And we all hear these people speaking in our own languages about the wonderful things God has done!" ¹²They stood there amazed and perplexed. "What can this mean?" they asked each other.

¹³But others in the crowd ridiculed them, saying, "They're just drunk, that's all!"

Peter Preaches to the Crowd

¹⁴Then Peter stepped forward with the eleven other apostles and shouted to the crowd, "Listen carefully, all of you, fellow Jews and residents of Jerusalem! Make no mistake about this. ¹⁵These people are not drunk, as some of

you are assuming. Nine o'clock in the morning is much too early for that. ¹⁶No, what you see was predicted long ago by the prophet Joel:

¹⁷ 'In the last days,' God says,
        'I will pour out my Spirit upon
            all people.
    Your sons and daughters
        will prophesy.
    Your young men will see visions,
        and your old men will dream dreams.
¹⁸ In those days I will pour out my Spirit
        even on my servants—men and women
            alike—
        and they will prophesy.
¹⁹ And I will cause wonders in the heavens
            above
        and signs on the earth below—
        blood and fire and clouds of smoke.
²⁰ The sun will become dark,
        and the moon will turn blood red
        before that great and glorious day
            of the LORD arrives.
²¹ But everyone who calls on the name
            of the LORD
        will be saved.'*

²²"People of Israel, listen! God publicly endorsed Jesus the Nazarene* by doing powerful miracles, wonders, and signs through him, as you well know. ²³But God knew what would happen, and his prearranged plan was carried out when Jesus was betrayed. With the help of lawless Gentiles, you nailed him to a cross and killed him. ²⁴But God released him from the horrors of death and raised him back to life, for death could not keep him in its grip. ²⁵King David said this about him:

    'I see that the LORD is always with me.
        I will not be shaken, for he is right beside
            me.
²⁶ No wonder my heart is glad,
        and my tongue shouts his praises!
        My body rests in hope.
²⁷ For you will not leave my soul among the
            dead*
        or allow your Holy One to rot in the
            grave.
²⁸ You have shown me the way of life,
        and you will fill me with the joy of your
            presence.'*

²⁹"Dear brothers, think about this! You can be sure that the patriarch David wasn't referring to himself, for he died and was buried, and his tomb is still here among us. ³⁰But he was a prophet, and he knew God had promised with an oath that one of David's own descendants

---

2:1 The Festival of Pentecost came 50 days after Passover (when Jesus was crucified).   2:4 Or *in other tongues.*
2:17-21 Joel 2:28-32.   2:22 Or *Jesus of Nazareth.*   2:27 Greek *in Hades;* also in 2:31.   2:25-28 Ps 16:8-11 (Greek version).

would sit on his throne. ³¹David was looking into the future and speaking of the Messiah's resurrection. He was saying that God would not leave him among the dead or allow his body to rot in the grave.

³²"God raised Jesus from the dead, and we are all witnesses of this. ³³Now he is exalted to the place of highest honor in heaven, at God's right hand. And the Father, as he had promised, gave him the Holy Spirit to pour out upon us, just as you see and hear today. ³⁴For David himself never ascended into heaven, yet he said,

'The LORD said to my Lord,
  "Sit in the place of honor at my right
    hand
³⁵ until I humble your enemies,
    making them a footstool under your
      feet."'*

³⁶"So let everyone in Israel know for certain that God has made this Jesus, whom you crucified, to be both Lord and Messiah!"

³⁷Peter's words pierced their hearts, and they said to him and to the other apostles, "Brothers, what should we do?"

³⁸Peter replied, "Each of you must repent of your sins and turn to God, and be baptized in the name of Jesus Christ for the forgiveness of your sins. Then you will receive the gift of the Holy Spirit. ³⁹This promise is to you, and to your children, and even to the Gentiles*—all who have been called by the Lord our God." ⁴⁰Then Peter continued preaching for a long time, strongly urging all his listeners, "Save yourselves from this crooked generation!"

⁴¹Those who believed what Peter said were baptized and added to the church that day—about 3,000 in all.

The Believers Form a Community

⁴²All the believers devoted themselves to the apostles' teaching, and to fellowship, and to sharing in meals (including the Lord's Supper*), and to prayer.

⁴³A deep sense of awe came over them all, and the apostles performed many miraculous signs and wonders. ⁴⁴And all the believers met together in one place and shared everything they had. ⁴⁵They sold their property and possessions and shared the money with those in need. ⁴⁶They worshiped together at the Temple each day, met in homes for the Lord's Supper, and shared their meals with great joy and generosity*—⁴⁷all the while praising God and enjoying the goodwill of all the people. And each day the Lord added to their fellowship those who were being saved.

first steps

GOD'S SPIRIT WILL EMPOWER YOUR WITNESS

Read ACTS 1:8

One of the greatest things the Holy Spirit wants to do in the life of the believer is empower his or her witness. The word for *power* in this verse comes from the Greek word *dunamis,* from which we get the words *dynamite, dynamic,* and *dynamo.* God didn't give us the power of the Holy Spirit to feel something, but to *accomplish* something.

Sometimes the Holy Spirit's power acts like dynamite in our lives, blasting us with zeal, jolting us out of complacency, and motivating us to greater spiritual growth. At other times God's Spirit is like a dynamic, generating power that will help us live from day to day at a level we could not achieve on our own. We need to remember the encouraging words the apostle Paul gave to young Timothy: "For God has not given us a spirit of fear and timidity, but of power, love, and self-discipline" (2 Timothy 1:7).

Are you timid in your witness for Christ? Is it hard for you to speak up for what you believe? Then you need to tap in to that power he has made available to you through his Spirit. God's Holy Spirit will give you an added dimension of boldness, power, and persuasiveness in your witness that you have never experienced before.

For the next note on "Live in God's Power," *turn to p. 173.*

CHAPTER **3**

Peter Heals a Crippled Beggar

Peter and John went to the Temple one afternoon to take part in the three o'clock prayer service. ²As they approached the Temple, a man lame from birth was being carried in. Each day he was put beside the Temple gate, the one called the Beautiful Gate, so he could beg from the people going into the Temple. ³When he saw Peter and John about to enter, he asked them for some money.

⁴Peter and John looked at him intently, and Peter said, "Look at us!" ⁵The lame man looked

2:34-35 Ps 110:1.   2:39 Or *and to people far in the future;* Greek reads *and to those far away.*   2:42 Greek *the breaking of bread;* also in 2:46.   2:46 Or *and sincere hearts.*

Read ACTS 2:1-41

cornerstones
WHO THE HOLY SPIRIT HELPS

The Holy Spirit has been given to all believers to deepen their spiritual walk and to enable them to make an impact upon their world for Jesus Christ. This passage illustrates three aspects of the Holy Spirit's unique work in the lives of believers:

1. The Holy Spirit Fills All Believers. In the Old Testament, the Holy Spirit was given only to a select few to perform specific tasks. This chapter indicates a change in that pattern. The Holy Spirit was poured out on all the believers in the house that day (verse 4), and he was present in each of their lives from that day forward. This outpouring of the Holy Spirit was used by God to establish the church—and to spread the message of the gospel to everyone everywhere (see verse 39).

2. The Holy Spirit Draws Attention to the Savior. Notice that Peter did not focus on the unique happening that had just taken place but turned the crowd's attention to the message of Jesus Christ and their need for repentance. Likewise, the Holy Spirit does not draw attention to himself but to the Savior. And when he fills your life, he will increase your ability to share the gospel with others.

3. The Holy Spirit Inspired Peter's Message. Peter's sermon, inspired by the Holy Spirit, led many in the crowd to a point of decision: "What should we do?" (verse 37). The people were not attracted to Peter but to his message. The Holy Spirit worked powerfully that day, and three thousand people responded to the message.

The Holy Spirit is promised to all who repent and receive Jesus Christ into their lives. Many people fail to understand who the Holy Spirit is and what dimension of power is available to them through him. It may help to examine what took place after the disciples received the filling of the Holy Spirit that Jesus had promised (see Acts 1:8, p. 129).

For the next note on "Who Is the Holy Spirit?" turn to p. 296.

---

at them eagerly, expecting some money. ⁶But Peter said, "I don't have any silver or gold for you. But I'll give you what I have. In the name of Jesus Christ the Nazarene,* get up and* walk!"

⁷Then Peter took the lame man by the right hand and helped him up. And as he did, the man's feet and ankles were instantly healed and strengthened. ⁸He jumped up, stood on his feet, and began to walk! Then, walking, leaping, and praising God, he went into the Temple with them.

⁹All the people saw him walking and heard him praising God. ¹⁰When they realized he was the lame beggar they had seen so often at the Beautiful Gate, they were absolutely astounded! ¹¹They all rushed out in amazement to Solomon's Colonnade, where the man was holding tightly to Peter and John.

Peter Preaches in the Temple

¹²Peter saw his opportunity and addressed the crowd. "People of Israel," he said, "what is so surprising about this? And why stare at us as though we had made this man walk by our own power or godliness? ¹³For it is the God of Abraham, Isaac, and Jacob—the God of all our ancestors—who has brought glory to his servant Jesus by doing this. This is the same Jesus whom you handed over and rejected before Pilate, despite Pilate's decision to release him. ¹⁴You rejected this holy, righteous one and instead demanded the release of a murderer. ¹⁵You killed the author of life, but God raised him from the dead. And we are witnesses of this fact!

¹⁶"Through faith in the name of Jesus, this man was healed—and you know how crippled he was before. Faith in Jesus' name has healed him before your very eyes.

¹⁷"Friends,* I realize that what you and your leaders did to Jesus was done in ignorance. ¹⁸But God was fulfilling what all the prophets had foretold about the Messiah—that he must suffer these things. ¹⁹Now repent of your sins and turn to God, so that your sins may be wiped away. ²⁰Then times of refreshment will come from the presence of the Lord, and he will

3:6a Or *Jesus Christ of Nazareth.*   **3:6b** Some manuscripts do not include *get up and.*   **3:17** Greek *Brothers.*

again send you Jesus, your appointed Messiah. [21]For he must remain in heaven until the time for the final restoration of all things, as God promised long ago through his holy prophets. [22]Moses said, 'The LORD your God will raise up for you a Prophet like me from among your own people. Listen carefully to everything he tells you.'* [23]Then Moses said, 'Anyone who will not listen to that Prophet will be completely cut off from God's people.'*

[24]"Starting with Samuel, every prophet spoke about what is happening today. [25]You are the children of those prophets, and you are included in the covenant God promised to your ancestors. For God said to Abraham, 'Through your descendants* all the families on earth will be blessed.' [26]When God raised up his servant, Jesus, he sent him first to you people of Israel, to bless you by turning each of you back from your sinful ways."

CHAPTER 4
Peter and John before the Council

While Peter and John were speaking to the people, they were confronted by the priests, the captain of the Temple guard, and some of the Sadducees. [2]These leaders were very disturbed that Peter and John were teaching the people that through Jesus there is a resurrection of the dead. [3]They arrested them and, since it was already evening, put them in jail until morning. [4]But many of the people who heard their message believed it, so the number of believers now totaled about 5,000 men, not counting women and children.*

[5]The next day the council of all the rulers and elders and teachers of religious law met in Jerusalem. [6]Annas the high priest was there, along with Caiaphas, John, Alexander, and other relatives of the high priest. [7]They brought in the two disciples and demanded, "By what power, or in whose name, have you done this?"

[8]Then Peter, filled with the Holy Spirit, said to them, "Rulers and elders of our people, [9]are we being questioned today because we've done a good deed for a crippled man? Do you want to know how he was healed? [10]Let me clearly state to all of you and to all the people of Israel that he was healed by the powerful name of Jesus Christ the Nazarene,* the man you crucified but whom God raised from the dead. [11]For Jesus is the one referred to in the Scriptures, where it says,

'The stone that you builders rejected
    has now become the cornerstone.'*

3:22 Deut 18:15.   3:23 Deut 18:19; Lev 23:29.
3:25 Greek *your seed;* see Gen 12:3; 22:18.   4:4 Greek
5,000 adult males.   4:10 Or *Jesus Christ of Nazareth.*
4:11 Ps 118:22.

first steps
WHAT TO LOOK FOR IN A CHURCH
Read ACTS 2:42, 44-47

The first-century church turned the world upside down with its message (see Acts 17:6, p. 152). What made the early church so dynamic was the commitment of its members to follow Christ wholeheartedly. When you look for a church to attend, make sure it has these five characteristics of a healthy church:

1. Look for a Church That Meets Together Regularly. The early believers did not view church as a social club, but as a place for devoted fellowship and valuable instruction. We miss out on a tremendous blessing when we neglect meeting together with God's people. When we are spiritually weak, we should not run from church but to church!

2. Look for a Church That Places a High Priority on Bible Study. The first-century Christians "devoted themselves to the apostles' teaching." The apostles' teachings on the life and ministry of Jesus eventually became the Gospel portion of the New Testament. Studying the Bible is important to every Christian's spiritual growth. Without Bible study, Christians cannot know and understand God's commands and truth.

3. Look for a Church That Is a Place of Corporate Worship and Prayer. The early church recognized the importance of corporate worship and prayer. Corporate worship focused their attention on the praiseworthy character of God and gave them an opportunity to express their thanks to God. Corporate prayer allowed them to express their thanks to God as well, but it was also an opportunity to seek God together and present their requests before him as a body.

4. Look for a Church That Looks after Its Members. The early believers shared food, clothing, and housing with each other. The Bible reminds us to care for fellow believers who are in need (see 2 Corinthians 9:1-15, pp. 216-217).

5. Look for a Church That Is Growing. Church growth is not our responsibility but God's. If we do our part as a church, God will do his. We see proof of this in Acts 2:47.

For the next note on "Look For and Attend the Right Church," turn to p. 283.

cornerstones

JESUS HAS GREAT POWER TO TRANSFORM PEOPLE
Read ACTS 4:1-13

The entire book of Acts is a testimony to the transformation that takes place in the life of a true follower of Jesus Christ. Consider the case of Peter and John. Immediately after Christ's crucifixion, Peter and John went into hiding. In fact, Peter denied knowing Jesus three times before Jesus died! These men were far from bold. But when Jesus came back to life, met with them, and told them to wait for the promised Holy Spirit once he returned to heaven, everything changed.

Why were Peter and John so bold? And how can our lives be so dramatically transformed?

Peter and John Spent Time with Jesus. For three years Peter and John followed Jesus throughout Israel. During this time they saw Jesus perform many miracles. They also listened to his teaching and observed his lifestyle. But they weren't just casual observers. They talked with Jesus and shared their lives with him. They made Jesus a significant part of their lives. Even though we did not walk alongside Jesus during his time on earth, we can invite him into our hearts. In addition, we have his teachings to study and the ability to spend time with him in prayer. We don't have to have lived in Bible times to have a relationship with Jesus.

Peter and John Modeled Their Lives after Jesus' Life and Teachings. Christ's life and resurrection had such an impact on Peter and John that they began to imitate Jesus in their behavior. We can see that impact in the first few chapters of Acts. Here Peter and John proclaim the message boldly in public, heal a crippled beggar, and endure persecution for Jesus. Their actions prove an important point: We need to put into practice what we have learned from spending time with Jesus.

Peter and John Put Their Confidence in Christ, Not in Their Own Abilities. Remember, Peter and John were common fishermen. They had no impressive credentials to flash in front of these people. They simply relied upon Jesus to guide them and help them through any obstacles—and that gave them all the confidence they needed. We should do no less.

If you want to see the power of Jesus Christ in action today, take a look at some of the lives he has turned around. Some of the greatest evidence for Jesus Christ today consists of the countless lives that have been dramatically changed by his touch.

For the next note on "Who Is Jesus?" turn to p. 320.

---

[12] There is salvation in no one else! God has given no other name under heaven by which we must be saved."

[13] The members of the council were amazed when they saw the boldness of Peter and John, for they could see that they were ordinary men with no special training in the Scriptures. They also recognized them as men who had been with Jesus. [14] But since they could see the man who had been healed standing right there among them, there was nothing the council could say. [15] So they ordered Peter and John out of the council chamber* and conferred among themselves.

[16] "What should we do with these men?" they asked each other. "We can't deny that they have performed a miraculous sign, and everybody in Jerusalem knows about it. [17] But to keep them from spreading their propaganda any further,

we must warn them not to speak to anyone in Jesus' name again." [18] So they called the apostles back in and commanded them never again to speak or teach in the name of Jesus.

[19] But Peter and John replied, "Do you think God wants us to obey you rather than him? [20] We cannot stop telling about everything we have seen and heard."

[21] The council then threatened them further, but they finally let them go because they didn't know how to punish them without starting a riot. For everyone was praising God [22] for this miraculous sign—the healing of a man who had been lame for more than forty years.

The Believers Pray for Courage
[23] As soon as they were freed, Peter and John returned to the other believers and told them what the leading priests and elders had said.

4:15 Greek *the Sanhedrin.*

BIG QUESTIONS

Why Is Jesus Christ the Only Way to God?

Read ACTS 4:12

One of the most common criticisms of Christianity is that it is too narrow. Many people just cannot believe that there is only one way to heaven.

Because Christians have championed this truth, they have been criticized for implying that they are better than those who do not believe in Jesus Christ. But it is important to note that the reason Christians believe Jesus Christ is the only way to heaven is because he himself said it. Jesus said, "I am the way, the truth, and the life. No one can come to the Father except through me" (John 14:6).

If humankind could have reached God any other way, Jesus would not have had to die. His voluntary death on the cross clearly illustrates the fact that there is no other way. Those who reject his loving offer of forgiveness—which is extended to all of humankind—do so at their own peril.

For the next "Big Question" note, turn to p. 137.

24 When they heard the report, all the believers lifted their voices together in prayer to God: "O Sovereign Lord, Creator of heaven and earth, the sea, and everything in them—25 you spoke long ago by the Holy Spirit through our ancestor David, your servant, saying,

'Why were the nations so angry?
    Why did they waste their time with futile plans?
26 The kings of the earth prepared for battle;
    the rulers gathered together
against the LORD
    and against his Messiah.'*

27 "In fact, this has happened here in this very city! For Herod Antipas, Pontius Pilate the governor, the Gentiles, and the people of Israel were all united against Jesus, your holy servant, whom you anointed. 28 But everything they did was determined beforehand according to your will. 29 And now, O Lord, hear their threats, and give us, your servants, great boldness in preaching your word. 30 Stretch out your hand with healing power; may miraculous signs and wonders be done through the name of your holy servant Jesus."

31 After this prayer, the meeting place shook, and they were all filled with the Holy Spirit. Then they preached the word of God with boldness.

The Believers Share Their Possessions

32 All the believers were united in heart and mind. And they felt that what they owned was not their own, so they shared everything they had. 33 The apostles testified powerfully to the resurrection of the Lord Jesus, and God's great blessing was upon them all. 34 There were no needy people among them, because those who owned land or houses would sell them 35 and bring the money to the apostles to give to those in need.

36 For instance, there was Joseph, the one the apostles nicknamed Barnabas (which means "Son of Encouragement"). He was from the tribe of Levi and came from the island of Cyprus. 37 He sold a field he owned and brought the money to the apostles.

CHAPTER **5**
Ananias and Sapphira
But there was a certain man named Ananias who, with his wife, Sapphira, sold some property. 2 He brought part of the money to the apostles, claiming it was the full amount. With his wife's consent, he kept the rest.

3 Then Peter said, "Ananias, why have you let Satan fill your heart? You lied to the Holy Spirit, and you kept some of the money for yourself. 4 The property was yours to sell or not sell, as you wished. And after selling it, the money was also

4:25-26 Or *his anointed one;* or *his Christ.* Ps 2:1-2.

yours to give away. How could you do a thing like this? You weren't lying to us but to God!"

[5] As soon as Ananias heard these words, he fell to the floor and died. Everyone who heard about it was terrified. [6] Then some young men got up, wrapped him in a sheet, and took him out and buried him.

[7] About three hours later his wife came in, not knowing what had happened. [8] Peter asked her, "Was this the price you and your husband received for your land?"

"Yes," she replied, "that was the price."

[9] And Peter said, "How could the two of you even think of conspiring to test the Spirit of the Lord like this? The young men who buried your husband are just outside the door, and they will carry you out, too."

[10] Instantly, she fell to the floor and died. When the young men came in and saw that she was dead, they carried her out and buried her beside her husband. [11] Great fear gripped the entire church and everyone else who heard what had happened.

The Apostles Heal Many

[12] The apostles were performing many miraculous signs and wonders among the people. And all the believers were meeting regularly at the Temple in the area known as Solomon's Colonnade. [13] But no one else dared to join them, even though all the people had high regard for them. [14] Yet more and more people believed and were brought to the Lord—crowds of both men and women. [15] As a result of the apostles' work, sick people were brought out into the streets on beds and mats so that Peter's shadow might fall across some of them as he went by. [16] Crowds came from the villages around Jerusalem, bringing their sick and those possessed by evil* spirits, and they were all healed.

The Apostles Meet Opposition

[17] The high priest and his officials, who were Sadducees, were filled with jealousy. [18] They arrested the apostles and put them in the public jail. [19] But an angel of the Lord came at night, opened the gates of the jail, and brought them out. Then he told them, [20] "Go to the Temple and give the people this message of life!"

[21] So at daybreak the apostles entered the Temple, as they were told, and immediately began teaching.

When the high priest and his officials arrived, they convened the high council*—the full assembly of the elders of Israel. Then they sent for the apostles to be brought from the jail for trial. [22] But when the Temple guards went to the jail, the men were gone. So they returned to the council and reported, [23] "The jail was securely locked, with the guards standing outside, but when we opened the gates, no one was there!"

[24] When the captain of the Temple guard and the leading priests heard this, they were perplexed, wondering where it would all end. [25] Then someone arrived with startling news: "The men you put in jail are standing in the Temple, teaching the people!"

[26] The captain went with his Temple guards and arrested the apostles, but without violence, for they were afraid the people would stone them. [27] Then they brought the apostles before the high council, where the high priest confronted them. [28] "Didn't we tell you never again to teach in this man's name?" he demanded. "Instead, you have filled all Jerusalem with your teaching about him, and you want to make us responsible for his death!"

[29] But Peter and the apostles replied, "We must obey God rather than any human authority. [30] The God of our ancestors raised Jesus from the dead after you killed him by hanging him on a cross.* [31] Then God put him in the place of honor at his right hand as Prince and Savior. He did this so the people of Israel would repent of their sins and be forgiven. [32] We are witnesses of these things and so is the Holy Spirit, who is given by God to those who obey him."

[33] When they heard this, the high council was furious and decided to kill them. [34] But one member, a Pharisee named Gamaliel, who was an expert in religious law and respected by all the people, stood up and ordered that the men be sent outside the council chamber for a while. [35] Then he said to his colleagues, "Men of Israel, take care what you are planning to do to these men! [36] Some time ago there was that fellow Theudas, who pretended to be someone great. About 400 others joined him, but he was killed, and all his followers went their various ways. The whole movement came to nothing. [37] After him, at the time of the census, there was Judas of Galilee. He got people to follow him, but he was killed, too, and all his followers were scattered.

[38] "So my advice is, leave these men alone. Let them go. If they are planning and doing these things merely on their own, it will soon be overthrown. [39] But if it is from God, you will not be able to overthrow them. You may even find yourselves fighting against God!"

[40] The others accepted his advice. They called in the apostles and had them flogged. Then they ordered them never again to speak in the name of Jesus, and they let them go.

5:16 Greek *unclean.*   **5:21** Greek *Sanhedrin;* also in 5:27, 41.   **5:30** Greek *on a tree.*

Aren't Other Religions Just As Good As Christianity?

Read ACTS 4:12

Some people say that all religions basically say and teach the same thing, so they must all be "true." To quote another well-used phrase, "If a person is really sincere in what he or she believes, he or she will get to heaven."

In reality, all belief systems cannot be true, because they contradict one another. Many would like to think that all religions blend together beautifully, but they do not. Look at the differences between what the followers of three major world religions believe compared with what Christians believe.

The Existence of a Personal God.
- Buddhists deny the existence of a personal God.
- Hindus believe in two major gods, Vishnu and Siva, as well as in millions of lesser gods.
- Muslims believe in one God named Allah.

- Christians believe that God is a being who created humans in his own image and who loves them and wants to have a personal relationship with them.

The Subject of Salvation.
- Buddhists believe salvation is by self effort only.
- Hindus believe you achieve salvation by devotion, works, and self-control.
- Muslims believe that people earn their own salvation and pay for their own sins.
- Christians believe that Jesus Christ died for their sins. If people turn from their sins and follow Jesus, they can be forgiven and have the hope of being with Jesus in heaven.

The Person of Jesus Christ.
- Buddhists believe that Jesus Christ was a good teacher, though less important than Buddha.
- Hindus believe that Jesus was just one of many incarnations—or sons—of God. Yet they also assert that Christ was not the unique Son of God. He was no more divine than any other man, and he did not die for people's sins.
- Muslims believe that Jesus Christ was the greatest of the prophets below Muhammad. In addition, they do not believe that Christ died for people's sin.
- Christians believe that Jesus is God as well as man, that he was sinless, and that he died and was raised from death to redeem humankind.

As you can see, you cannot believe in all of the major religious beliefs. That is because each religion eventually contradicts the claims of Christianity [Fritz Ridenour, *So What's the Difference?* (Glendale: Gospel Light Publications, 1967)].

For the next "Big Question" note, turn to p. 169.

---

[41] The apostles left the high council rejoicing that God had counted them worthy to suffer disgrace for the name of Jesus.* [42] And every day, in the Temple and from house to house, they continued to teach and preach this message: "Jesus is the Messiah."

5:41 Greek *for the name.* **6:1** Greek *disciples;* also in 6:2, 7.

CHAPTER **6**
Seven Men Chosen to Serve

But as the believers* rapidly multiplied, there were rumblings of discontent. The Greek-speaking believers complained about the Hebrew-speaking believers, saying that their

One way Scripture supports the concept that the Holy Spirit is a person in the Trinity rather than a force is by showing how he can be sinned against.

cornerstones

WHEN THE HOLY SPIRIT CAN BE SINNED AGAINST

Read ACTS 5:1-10

It is important to understand that the Holy Spirit is indeed *God* at work, and to sin against him is to sin against God. In this passage we see one way in which we can sin against the Holy Spirit, but other passages inform us of at least five additional ways in which a person can sin against the Spirit.

1. Lying to the Holy Spirit. Ananias and Sapphira lied to the Holy Spirit by pretending to be thoroughly devoted to God when they really were not. One way people continue to do this today is by "going through the [spiritual] motions" without really meaning it in their hearts.

2. Grieving the Holy Spirit. Only believers can grieve the Holy Spirit (see Ephesians 4:30, pp. 232-233). We grieve him by carrying anger in our heart, slandering others, or doing things that we know go against the new nature that is inside of us.

3. Quenching the Holy Spirit. When the Holy Spirit convicts us of something we need to change in our life and we ignore his promptings, we are extinguishing his power in our life (1 Thessalonians 5:19). He is still in our life, but we are holding back from giving him complete control.

4. Resisting the Holy Spirit. When Stephen, the first recorded Christian martyr, spoke to his persecutors, he shared the message of Jesus Christ but closed with the words: "You stubborn people! . . . Must you forever resist the Holy Spirit?" (Acts 7:51). Committing this sin means that a person may know that the Holy Spirit is trying to bring them to Jesus, but their pride keeps them from acknowledging Christ as Savior and Lord. The danger with this sin is that every time a person resists God's Spirit, it is more difficult later to come to Christ.

5. Insulting the Holy Spirit. To insult the Holy Spirit means to treat "the blood of the covenant, which made us holy, as if it were common and unholy" (Hebrews 10:29). Committing this sin essentially means dismissing the great price that Jesus paid at the cross of Calvary. This person has refused to accept the tremendous gift of salvation that God has offered.

6. Blaspheming the Holy Spirit. Two of the sins listed above, resisting and insulting the Holy Spirit, can lead to what is termed the "unforgivable sin": blasphemy against the Holy Spirit (see Matthew 12:31-32, p. 16). Since the Bible tells us that Christ is the only way of salvation, and the Holy Spirit's initial work in our life as a nonbeliever is to draw us to Christ, to blaspheme the Holy Spirit is to reject Jesus Christ as our Lord and Savior. That is the point of no return. Every time a person resists the Spirit and insults him, he or she comes one step closer to this ultimate sin.

For the next note on "Who Is the Holy Spirit?" turn to p. 222.

widows were being discriminated against in the daily distribution of food.

[2] So the Twelve called a meeting of all the believers. They said, "We apostles should spend our time teaching the word of God, not running a food program. [3] And so, brothers, select seven men who are well respected and are full of the Spirit and wisdom. We will give them this responsibility. [4] Then we apostles can spend our time in prayer and teaching the word."

[5] Everyone liked this idea, and they chose the following: Stephen (a man full of faith and the Holy Spirit), Philip, Procorus, Nicanor, Timon, Parmenas, and Nicolas of Antioch (an earlier convert to the Jewish faith). [6] These seven were presented to the apostles, who prayed for them as they laid their hands on them.

[7] So God's message continued to spread. The number of believers greatly increased in Jerusalem, and many of the Jewish priests were converted, too.

Stephen Is Arrested

[8] Stephen, a man full of God's grace and power, performed amazing miracles and signs among the people. [9] But one day some men from the Synagogue of Freed Slaves, as it was called, started to debate with him. They were Jews

from Cyrene, Alexandria, Cilicia, and the province of Asia. [10]None of them could stand against the wisdom and the Spirit with which Stephen spoke.

[11]So they persuaded some men to lie about Stephen, saying, "We heard him blaspheme Moses, and even God." [12]This roused the people, the elders, and the teachers of religious law. So they arrested Stephen and brought him before the high council.*

[13]The lying witnesses said, "This man is always speaking against the holy Temple and against the law of Moses. [14]We have heard him say that this Jesus of Nazareth* will destroy the Temple and change the customs Moses handed down to us."

[15]At this point everyone in the high council stared at Stephen, because his face became as bright as an angel's.

CHAPTER 7
Stephen Addresses the Council

Then the high priest asked Stephen, "Are these accusations true?"

[2]This was Stephen's reply: "Brothers and fathers, listen to me. Our glorious God appeared to our ancestor Abraham in Mesopotamia before he settled in Haran.* [3]God told him, 'Leave your native land and your relatives, and come into the land that I will show you.'* [4]So Abraham left the land of the Chaldeans and lived in Haran until his father died. Then God brought him here to the land where you now live.

[5]"But God gave him no inheritance here, not even one square foot of land. God did promise, however, that eventually the whole land would belong to Abraham and his descendants—even though he had no children yet. [6]God also told him that his descendants would live in a foreign land, where they would be oppressed as slaves for 400 years. [7]'But I will punish the nation that enslaves them,' God said, 'and in the end they will come out and worship me here in this place.'*

[8]"God also gave Abraham the covenant of circumcision at that time. So when Abraham became the father of Isaac, he circumcised him on the eighth day. And the practice was continued when Isaac became the father of Jacob, and when Jacob became the father of the twelve patriarchs of the Israelite nation.

[9]"These patriarchs were jealous of their brother Joseph, and they sold him to be a slave in Egypt. But God was with him [10]and rescued him from all his troubles. And God gave him favor before Pharaoh, king of Egypt. God also

gave Joseph unusual wisdom, so that Pharaoh appointed him governor over all of Egypt and put him in charge of the palace.

[11]"But a famine came upon Egypt and Canaan. There was great misery, and our ancestors ran out of food. [12]Jacob heard that there was still grain in Egypt, so he sent his sons—our ancestors—to buy some. [13]The second time they went, Joseph revealed his identity to his brothers,* and they were introduced to Pharaoh. [14]Then Joseph sent for his father, Jacob, and all his relatives to come to Egypt, seventy-five persons in all. [15]So Jacob went to Egypt. He died there, as did our ancestors. [16]Their bodies were taken to Shechem and buried in the tomb Abraham had bought for a certain price from Hamor's sons in Shechem.

[17]"As the time drew near when God would fulfill his promise to Abraham, the number of our people in Egypt greatly increased. [18]But then a new king came to the throne of Egypt who knew nothing about Joseph. [19]This king exploited our people and oppressed them, forcing parents to abandon their newborn babies so they would die.

[20]"At that time Moses was born—a beautiful child in God's eyes. His parents cared for him at home for three months. [21]When they had to abandon him, Pharaoh's daughter adopted him and raised him as her own son. [22]Moses was taught all the wisdom of the Egyptians, and he was powerful in both speech and action.

[23]"One day when Moses was forty years old, he decided to visit his relatives, the people of Israel. [24]He saw an Egyptian mistreating an Israelite. So Moses came to the man's defense and avenged him, killing the Egyptian. [25]Moses assumed his fellow Israelites would realize that God had sent him to rescue them, but they didn't.

[26]"The next day he visited them again and saw two men of Israel fighting. He tried to be a peacemaker. 'Men,' he said, 'you are brothers. Why are you fighting each other?'

[27]"But the man in the wrong pushed Moses aside. 'Who made you a ruler and judge over us?' he asked. [28]'Are you going to kill me as you killed that Egyptian yesterday?' [29]When Moses heard that, he fled the country and lived as a foreigner in the land of Midian. There his two sons were born.

[30]"Forty years later, in the desert near Mount Sinai, an angel appeared to Moses in the flame of a burning bush. [31]When Moses saw it, he was amazed at the sight. As he went to take a closer look, the voice of the LORD called out to him, [32]'I am the God of your ancestors—the

---

6:12 Greek *Sanhedrin;* also in 6:15.   **6:14** Or *Jesus the Nazarene.*   **7:2** *Mesopotamia* was the region now called Iraq. *Haran* was a city in what is now called Syria.   **7:3** Gen 12:1.   **7:5-7** Gen 12:7; 15:13-14; Exod 3:12.   **7:13** Other manuscripts read *Joseph was recognized by his brothers.*

God of Abraham, Isaac, and Jacob.' Moses shook with terror and did not dare to look.

³³"Then the Lord said to him, 'Take off your sandals, for you are standing on holy ground. ³⁴I have certainly seen the oppression of my people in Egypt. I have heard their groans and have come down to rescue them. Now go, for I am sending you back to Egypt.'*

³⁵"So God sent back the same man his people had previously rejected when they demanded, 'Who made you a ruler and judge over us?' Through the angel who appeared to him in the burning bush, God sent Moses to be their ruler and savior. ³⁶And by means of many wonders and miraculous signs, he led them out of Egypt, through the Red Sea, and through the wilderness for forty years.

³⁷"Moses himself told the people of Israel, 'God will raise up for you a Prophet like me from among your own people.'* ³⁸Moses was with our ancestors, the assembly of God's people in the wilderness, when the angel spoke to him at Mount Sinai. And there Moses received life-giving words to pass on to us.*

³⁹"But our ancestors refused to listen to Moses. They rejected him and wanted to return to Egypt. ⁴⁰They told Aaron, 'Make us some gods who can lead us, for we don't know what has become of this Moses, who brought us out of Egypt.' ⁴¹So they made an idol shaped like a calf, and they sacrificed to it and celebrated over this thing they had made. ⁴²Then God turned away from them and abandoned them to serve the stars of heaven as their gods! In the book of the prophets it is written,

'Was it to me you were bringing sacrifices
    and offerings
  during those forty years in the
    wilderness, Israel?
⁴³ No, you carried your pagan gods—
    the shrine of Molech,
    the star of your god Rephan,
    and the images you made to worship
      them.
  So I will send you into exile
    as far away as Babylon.'*

⁴⁴"Our ancestors carried the Tabernacle* with them through the wilderness. It was constructed according to the plan God had shown to Moses. ⁴⁵Years later, when Joshua led our ancestors in battle against the nations that God drove out of this land, the Tabernacle was taken with them into their new territory. And it stayed there until the time of King David. ⁴⁶"David found favor with God and asked for

the privilege of building a permanent Temple for the God of Jacob.* ⁴⁷But it was Solomon who actually built it. ⁴⁸However, the Most High doesn't live in temples made by human hands. As the prophet says,

⁴⁹ 'Heaven is my throne,
    and the earth is my footstool.
  Could you build me a temple as good as
      that?'
    asks the Lord.
  'Could you build me such a resting place?
⁵⁰   Didn't my hands make both heaven and
      earth?'*

⁵¹"You stubborn people! You are heathen* at heart and deaf to the truth. Must you forever resist the Holy Spirit? That's what your ancestors did, and so do you! ⁵²Name one prophet your ancestors didn't persecute! They even killed the ones who predicted the coming of the Righteous One—the Messiah whom you betrayed and murdered. ⁵³You deliberately disobeyed God's law, even though you received it from the hands of angels."

⁵⁴The Jewish leaders were infuriated by Stephen's accusation, and they shook their fists at him in rage.* ⁵⁵But Stephen, full of the Holy Spirit, gazed steadily into heaven and saw the glory of God, and he saw Jesus standing in the place of honor at God's right hand. ⁵⁶And he told them, "Look, I see the heavens opened and the Son of Man standing in the place of honor at God's right hand!"

⁵⁷Then they put their hands over their ears and began shouting. They rushed at him ⁵⁸and dragged him out of the city and began to stone him. His accusers took off their coats and laid them at the feet of a young man named Saul.*

⁵⁹As they stoned him, Stephen prayed, "Lord Jesus, receive my spirit." ⁶⁰He fell to his knees, shouting, "Lord, don't charge them with this sin!" And with that, he died.

CHAPTER **8**

Saul was one of the witnesses, and he agreed completely with the killing of Stephen.

Persecution Scatters the Believers

A great wave of persecution began that day, sweeping over the church in Jerusalem; and all the believers except the apostles were scattered through the regions of Judea and Samaria. ²(Some devout men came and buried Stephen with great mourning.) ³But Saul was going everywhere to destroy the church. He went from house to house, dragging out both men and women to throw them into prison.

7:31-34 Exod 3:5-10.   7:37 Deut 18:15.   7:38 Some manuscripts read *to you.*   7:42-43 Amos 5:25-27 (Greek version).
7:44 Greek *the tent of witness.*   7:46 Some manuscripts read *the house of Jacob.*   7:49-50 Isa 66:1-2.   7:51 Greek
uncircumcised.   7:54 Greek *they were grinding their teeth against him.*   7:58 *Saul* is later called Paul; see 13:9.

Philip Preaches in Samaria

[4] But the believers who were scattered preached the Good News about Jesus wherever they went. [5] Philip, for example, went to the city of Samaria and told the people there about the Messiah. [6] Crowds listened intently to Philip because they were eager to hear his message and see the miraculous signs he did. [7] Many evil* spirits were cast out, screaming as they left their victims. And many who had been paralyzed or lame were healed. [8] So there was great joy in that city.

[9] A man named Simon had been a sorcerer there for many years, amazing the people of Samaria and claiming to be someone great. [10] Everyone, from the least to the greatest, often spoke of him as "the Great One—the Power of God." [11] They listened closely to him because for a long time he had astounded them with his magic.

[12] But now the people believed Philip's message of Good News concerning the Kingdom of God and the name of Jesus Christ. As a result, many men and women were baptized. [13] Then Simon himself believed and was baptized. He began following Philip wherever he went, and he was amazed by the signs and great miracles Philip performed.

[14] When the apostles in Jerusalem heard that the people of Samaria had accepted God's message, they sent Peter and John there. [15] As soon as they arrived, they prayed for these new believers to receive the Holy Spirit. [16] The Holy Spirit had not yet come upon any of them, for they had only been baptized in the name of the Lord Jesus. [17] Then Peter and John laid their hands upon these believers, and they received the Holy Spirit.

[18] When Simon saw that the Spirit was given when the apostles laid their hands on people, he offered them money to buy this power. [19] "Let me have this power, too," he exclaimed, "so that when I lay my hands on people, they will receive the Holy Spirit!"

[20] But Peter replied, "May your money be destroyed with you for thinking God's gift can be bought! [21] You can have no part in this, for your heart is not right with God. [22] Repent of your wickedness and pray to the Lord. Perhaps he will forgive your evil thoughts, [23] for I can see that you are full of bitter jealousy and are held captive by sin."

[24] "Pray to the Lord for me," Simon exclaimed, "that these terrible things you've said won't happen to me!"

[25] After testifying and preaching the word of the Lord in Samaria, Peter and John returned to Jerusalem. And they stopped in many Samaritan villages along the way to preach the Good News.

Philip and the Ethiopian Eunuch

[26] As for Philip, an angel of the Lord said to him, "Go south* down the desert road that runs from Jerusalem to Gaza." [27] So he started out, and he met the treasurer of Ethiopia, a eunuch of great authority under the Kandake, the queen of Ethiopia. The eunuch had gone to Jerusalem to worship, [28] and he was now returning. Seated in his carriage, he was reading aloud from the book of the prophet Isaiah.

[29] The Holy Spirit said to Philip, "Go over and walk along beside the carriage."

[30] Philip ran over and heard the man reading from the prophet Isaiah. Philip asked, "Do you understand what you are reading?"

[31] The man replied, "How can I, unless someone instructs me?" And he urged Philip to come up into the carriage and sit with him.

[32] The passage of Scripture he had been reading was this:

> "He was led like a sheep to the slaughter.
>   And as a lamb is silent before the
>   shearers,
>   he did not open his mouth.
> [33] He was humiliated and received no justice.
>   Who can speak of his descendants?
>   For his life was taken from the earth."*

[34] The eunuch asked Philip, "Tell me, was the prophet talking about himself or someone else?" [35] So beginning with this same Scripture, Philip told him the Good News about Jesus.

[36] As they rode along, they came to some water, and the eunuch said, "Look! There's some water! Why can't I be baptized?"* [38] He ordered the carriage to stop, and they went down into the water, and Philip baptized him.

[39] When they came up out of the water, the Spirit of the Lord snatched Philip away. The eunuch never saw him again but went on his way rejoicing. [40] Meanwhile, Philip found himself farther north at the town of Azotus. He preached the Good News there and in every town along the way until he came to Caesarea.

CHAPTER 9

Saul's Conversion

Meanwhile, Saul was uttering threats with every breath and was eager to kill the Lord's followers.* So he went to the high priest. [2] He requested letters addressed to the synagogues in Damascus, asking for their cooperation in

---

8:7 Greek *unclean.*   8:26 Or *Go at noon.*   8:32-33 Isa 53:7-8 (Greek version).   8:36 Some manuscripts add verse 37, *"You can," Philip answered, "if you believe with all your heart." And the eunuch replied, "I believe that Jesus Christ is the Son of God."*   9:1 Greek *disciples.*

the arrest of any followers of the Way he found there. He wanted to bring them—both men and women—back to Jerusalem in chains.

³As he was approaching Damascus on this mission, a light from heaven suddenly shone down around him. ⁴He fell to the ground and heard a voice saying to him, "Saul! Saul! Why are you persecuting me?"

⁵"Who are you, lord?" Saul asked.

And the voice replied, "I am Jesus, the one you are persecuting! ⁶Now get up and go into the city, and you will be told what you must do."

⁷The men with Saul stood speechless, for they heard the sound of someone's voice but saw no one! ⁸Saul picked himself up off the ground, but when he opened his eyes he was blind. So his companions led him by the hand to Damascus. ⁹He remained there blind for three days and did not eat or drink.

¹⁰Now there was a believer* in Damascus named Ananias. The Lord spoke to him in a vision, calling, "Ananias!"

"Yes, Lord!" he replied.

¹¹The Lord said, "Go over to Straight Street, to the house of Judas. When you get there, ask for a man from Tarsus named Saul. He is praying to me right now. ¹²I have shown him a vision of a man named Ananias coming in and laying hands on him so he can see again."

¹³"But Lord," exclaimed Ananias, "I've heard many people talk about the terrible things this man has done to the believers* in Jerusalem! ¹⁴And he is authorized by the leading priests to arrest everyone who calls upon your name."

¹⁵But the Lord said, "Go, for Saul is my chosen instrument to take my message to the Gentiles and to kings, as well as to the people of Israel. ¹⁶And I will show him how much he must suffer for my name's sake."

¹⁷So Ananias went and found Saul. He laid his hands on him and said, "Brother Saul, the Lord Jesus, who appeared to you on the road, has sent me so that you might regain your sight and be filled with the Holy Spirit." ¹⁸Instantly something like scales fell from Saul's eyes, and he regained his sight. Then he got up and was baptized. ¹⁹Afterward he ate some food and regained his strength.

Saul in Damascus and Jerusalem

Saul stayed with the believers* in Damascus for a few days. ²⁰And immediately he began preaching about Jesus in the synagogues, saying, "He is indeed the Son of God!"

²¹All who heard him were amazed. "Isn't this the same man who caused such devastation among Jesus' followers in Jerusalem?" they asked. "And didn't he come here to arrest them and take them in chains to the leading priests?"

²²Saul's preaching became more and more powerful, and the Jews in Damascus couldn't refute his proofs that Jesus was indeed the Messiah. ²³After a while some of the Jews plotted together to kill him. ²⁴They were watching for him day and night at the city gate so they could murder him, but Saul was told about their plot. ²⁵So during the night, some of the other believers* lowered him in a large basket through an opening in the city wall.

²⁶When Saul arrived in Jerusalem, he tried to meet with the believers, but they were all afraid of him. They did not believe he had truly become a believer! ²⁷Then Barnabas brought him to the apostles and told them how Saul had seen the Lord on the way to Damascus and how the Lord had spoken to Saul. He also told them that Saul had preached boldly in the name of Jesus in Damascus.

²⁸So Saul stayed with the apostles and went all around Jerusalem with them, preaching boldly in the name of the Lord. ²⁹He debated with some Greek-speaking Jews, but they tried to murder him. ³⁰When the believers* heard about this, they took him down to Caesarea and sent him away to Tarsus, his hometown.

³¹The church then had peace throughout Judea, Galilee, and Samaria, and it became stronger as the believers lived in the fear of the Lord. And with the encouragement of the Holy Spirit, it also grew in numbers.

Peter Heals Aeneas and Raises Dorcas

³²Meanwhile, Peter traveled from place to place, and he came down to visit the believers in the town of Lydda. ³³There he met a man named Aeneas, who had been paralyzed and bedridden for eight years. ³⁴Peter said to him, "Aeneas, Jesus Christ heals you! Get up, and roll up your sleeping mat!" And he was healed instantly. ³⁵Then the whole population of Lydda and Sharon saw Aeneas walking around, and they turned to the Lord.

³⁶There was a believer in Joppa named Tabitha (which in Greek is Dorcas*). She was always doing kind things for others and helping the poor. ³⁷About this time she became ill and died. Her body was washed for burial and laid in an upstairs room. ³⁸But the believers had heard that Peter was nearby at Lydda, so they sent two men to beg him, "Please come as soon as possible!"

³⁹So Peter returned with them; and as soon

9:10 Greek *disciple;* also in 9:26, 36.   9:13 Greek *God's holy people;* also in 9:32, 41.   9:19 Greek *disciples;* also in 9:26, 38.
9:25 Greek *his disciples.*   9:30 Greek *brothers.*   9:36 The names *Tabitha* in Aramaic and *Dorcas* in Greek both mean "gazelle."

as he arrived, they took him to the upstairs room. The room was filled with widows who were weeping and showing him the coats and other clothes Dorcas had made for them. [40] But Peter asked them all to leave the room; then he knelt and prayed. Turning to the body he said, "Get up, Tabitha." And she opened her eyes! When she saw Peter, she sat up! [41] He gave her his hand and helped her up. Then he called in the widows and all the believers, and he presented her to them alive.

[42] The news spread through the whole town, and many believed in the Lord. [43] And Peter stayed a long time in Joppa, living with Simon, a tanner of hides.

CHAPTER **10**
Cornelius Calls for Peter
In Caesarea there lived a Roman army officer* named Cornelius, who was a captain of the Italian Regiment. [2] He was a devout, God-fearing man, as was everyone in his household. He gave generously to the poor and prayed regularly to God. [3] One afternoon about three o'clock, he had a vision in which he saw an angel of God coming toward him. "Cornelius!" the angel said.

[4] Cornelius stared at him in terror. "What is it, sir?" he asked the angel.

And the angel replied, "Your prayers and gifts to the poor have been received by God as an offering! [5] Now send some men to Joppa, and summon a man named Simon Peter. [6] He is staying with Simon, a tanner who lives near the seashore."

[7] As soon as the angel was gone, Cornelius called two of his household servants and a devout soldier, one of his personal attendants. [8] He told them what had happened and sent them off to Joppa.

Peter Visits Cornelius
[9] The next day as Cornelius's messengers were nearing the town, Peter went up on the flat roof to pray. It was about noon, [10] and he was hungry. But while a meal was being prepared, he fell into a trance. [11] He saw the sky open, and something like a large sheet was let down by its four corners. [12] In the sheet were all sorts of animals, reptiles, and birds. [13] Then a voice said to him, "Get up, Peter; kill and eat them."

[14] "No, Lord," Peter declared. "I have never eaten anything that our Jewish laws have declared impure and unclean.*"

[15] But the voice spoke again: "Do not call something unclean if God has made it clean." [16] The same vision was repeated three times.

10:1 Greek *a centurion;* similarly in 10:22.   **10:14** Greek *anything common and unclean.*

first steps
BE OPEN TO GOD'S LEADING
Read ACTS 8:4-8, 26-38

This text shows two forms of evangelism. In the beginning of this passage, we see Philip engaged in "mass evangelism" (8:4-8). Toward the end of the chapter, we see Philip taking part in personal, "one-on-one evangelism" with the Ethiopian (8:26-38). The text also gives us three principles to follow for effective evangelism:

1. Philip Was Led by God's Spirit. This principle (8:29) can make all the difference in sharing one's faith. This leading will often come in the form of an "impression" or a burden—such as a compelling desire to talk to someone about your faith (see Acts 17:16-31, pp. 152-153). Like Philip, we should simply be open and available to what God would have us to do.

2. Philip Obeyed God's Leading. Philip did exactly what the Lord told him to do without delay (8:27). Jesus said, "My sheep listen to my voice; I know them, and they follow me" (John 10:27). So when God said, "Go," Philip went! Likewise, we need to be on duty at all times, ready to "preach the word of God" (2 Timothy 4:2).

3. Philip Knew Scripture. Philip used the Scripture this man was reading as a starting point. Then he used a number of other passages to tell the Ethiopian about Jesus (8:35). Knowing God's Word is essential for any person who wants to lead others to Jesus Christ. Arguments will not have nearly the impact that God's Word will when we share our faith with others.

The same God who led Philip in his evangelistic work also wants to direct your steps. You might start each day with a prayer like the prophet Isaiah: "Here I am. Send me" (Isaiah 6:8). Remember, God is not looking so much for a person's ability as his or her availability. God is not looking for "strong" people to be his witnesses so much as he is looking for people through whom he can show his strength.

For the next note on "Share Your Faith," *turn to p. 191.*

Then the sheet was suddenly pulled up to heaven.

[17] Peter was very perplexed. What could the vision mean? Just then the men sent by Cornelius found Simon's house. Standing outside the gate, [18] they asked if a man named Simon Peter was staying there.

[19] Meanwhile, as Peter was puzzling over the vision, the Holy Spirit said to him, "Three men have come looking for you. [20] Get up, go downstairs, and go with them without hesitation. Don't worry, for I have sent them."

[21] So Peter went down and said, "I'm the man you are looking for. Why have you come?"

[22] They said, "We were sent by Cornelius, a Roman officer. He is a devout and God-fearing man, well respected by all the Jews. A holy angel instructed him to summon you to his house so that he can hear your message." [23] So Peter invited the men to stay for the night. The next day he went with them, accompanied by some of the brothers from Joppa.

[24] They arrived in Caesarea the following day. Cornelius was waiting for them and had called together his relatives and close friends. [25] As Peter entered his home, Cornelius fell at his feet and worshiped him. [26] But Peter pulled him up and said, "Stand up! I'm a human being just like you!" [27] So they talked together and went inside, where many others were assembled.

[28] Peter told them, "You know it is against our laws for a Jewish man to enter a Gentile home like this or to associate with you. But God has shown me that I should no longer think of anyone as impure or unclean. [29] So I came without objection as soon as I was sent for. Now tell me why you sent for me."

[30] Cornelius replied, "Four days ago I was praying in my house about this same time, three o'clock in the afternoon. Suddenly, a man in dazzling clothes was standing in front of me. [31] He told me, 'Cornelius, your prayer has been heard, and your gifts to the poor have been noticed by God! [32] Now send messengers to Joppa, and summon a man named Simon Peter. He is staying in the home of Simon, a tanner who lives near the seashore.' [33] So I sent for you at once, and it was good of you to come. Now we are all here, waiting before God to hear the message the Lord has given you."

The Gentiles Hear the Good News

[34] Then Peter replied, "I see very clearly that God shows no favoritism. [35] In every nation he accepts those who fear him and do what is right. [36] This is the message of Good News for the people of Israel—that there is peace with God through Jesus Christ, who is Lord of all. [37] You know what happened throughout Judea, beginning in Galilee, after John began preaching his message of baptism. [38] And you know that God anointed Jesus of Nazareth with the Holy Spirit and with power. Then Jesus went around doing good and healing all who were oppressed by the devil, for God was with him.

[39] "And we apostles are witnesses of all he did throughout Judea and in Jerusalem. They put him to death by hanging him on a cross,* [40] but God raised him to life on the third day. Then God allowed him to appear, [41] not to the general public,* but to us whom God had chosen in advance to be his witnesses. We were those who ate and drank with him after he rose from the dead. [42] And he ordered us to preach everywhere and to testify that Jesus is the one appointed by God to be the judge of all—the living and the dead. [43] He is the one all the prophets testified about, saying that everyone who believes in him will have their sins forgiven through his name."

The Gentiles Receive the Holy Spirit

[44] Even as Peter was saying these things, the Holy Spirit fell upon all who were listening to the message. [45] The Jewish believers* who came with Peter were amazed that the gift of the Holy Spirit had been poured out on the Gentiles, too. [46] For they heard them speaking in other tongues* and praising God.

Then Peter asked, [47] "Can anyone object to their being baptized, now that they have received the Holy Spirit just as we did?" [48] So he gave orders for them to be baptized in the name of Jesus Christ. Afterward Cornelius asked him to stay with them for several days.

CHAPTER 11
Peter Explains His Actions

Soon the news reached the apostles and other believers* in Judea that the Gentiles had received the word of God. [2] But when Peter arrived back in Jerusalem, the Jewish believers* criticized him. [3] "You entered the home of Gentiles* and even ate with them!" they said.

[4] Then Peter told them exactly what had happened. [5] "I was in the town of Joppa," he said, "and while I was praying, I went into a trance and saw a vision. Something like a large sheet was let down by its four corners from the sky. And it came right down to me. [6] When I looked inside the sheet, I saw all sorts of tame and wild animals, reptiles, and birds. [7] And I heard a voice say, 'Get up, Peter; kill and eat them.'

10:39 Greek *on a tree.*   **10:41** Greek *the people.*   **10:45** Greek *The faithful ones of the circumcision.*   **10:46** Or *in other languages.*   **11:1** Greek *brothers.*   **11:2** Greek *those of the circumcision.*   **11:3** Greek *of uncircumcised men.*

8 " 'No, Lord,' I replied. 'I have never eaten anything that our Jewish laws have declared impure or unclean.*'

9 "But the voice from heaven spoke again: 'Do not call something unclean if God has made it clean.' 10 This happened three times before the sheet and all it contained was pulled back up to heaven.

11 "Just then three men who had been sent from Caesarea arrived at the house where we were staying. 12 The Holy Spirit told me to go with them and not to worry that they were Gentiles. These six brothers here accompanied me, and we soon entered the home of the man who had sent for us. 13 He told us how an angel had appeared to him in his home and had told him, 'Send messengers to Joppa, and summon a man named Simon Peter. 14 He will tell you how you and everyone in your household can be saved!'

15 "As I began to speak," Peter continued, "the Holy Spirit fell on them, just as he fell on us at the beginning. 16 Then I thought of the Lord's words when he said, 'John baptized with* water, but you will be baptized with the Holy Spirit.' 17 And since God gave these Gentiles the same gift he gave us when we believed in the Lord Jesus Christ, who was I to stand in God's way?"

18 When the others heard this, they stopped objecting and began praising God. They said, "We can see that God has also given the Gentiles the privilege of repenting of their sins and receiving eternal life."

The Church in Antioch of Syria

19 Meanwhile, the believers who had been scattered during the persecution after Stephen's death traveled as far as Phoenicia, Cyprus, and Antioch of Syria. They preached the word of God, but only to Jews. 20 However, some of the believers who went to Antioch from Cyprus and Cyrene began preaching to the Gentiles* about the Lord Jesus. 21 The power of the Lord was with them, and a large number of these Gentiles believed and turned to the Lord.

22 When the church at Jerusalem heard what had happened, they sent Barnabas to Antioch. 23 When he arrived and saw this evidence of God's blessing, he was filled with joy, and he encouraged the believers to stay true to the Lord. 24 Barnabas was a good man, full of the Holy Spirit and strong in faith. And many people were brought to the Lord. 25 Then Barnabas went on to Tarsus to look for Saul. 26 When he found him, he brought him back to Antioch. Both of them stayed there with the church for a full year, teaching large crowds of people. (It was at Antioch that the believers* were first called Christians.)

27 During this time some prophets traveled from Jerusalem to Antioch. 28 One of them named Agabus stood up in one of the meetings and predicted by the Spirit that a great famine was coming upon the entire Roman world. (This was fulfilled during the reign of Claudius.) 29 So the believers in Antioch decided to send relief to the brothers and sisters* in Judea, everyone giving as much as they could. 30 This they did, entrusting their gifts to Barnabas and Saul to take to the elders of the church in Jerusalem.

CHAPTER 12

James Is Killed and Peter Is Imprisoned

About that time King Herod Agrippa* began to persecute some believers in the church. 2 He had the apostle James (John's brother) killed with a sword. 3 When Herod saw how much this pleased the Jewish people, he also arrested Peter. (This took place during the Passover celebration.*) 4 Then he imprisoned him, placing him under the guard of four squads of four soldiers each. Herod intended to bring Peter out for public trial after the Passover. 5 But while Peter was in prison, the church prayed very earnestly for him.

Peter's Miraculous Escape from Prison

6 The night before Peter was to be placed on trial, he was asleep, fastened with two chains between two soldiers. Others stood guard at the prison gate. 7 Suddenly, there was a bright light in the cell, and an angel of the Lord stood before Peter. The angel struck him on the side to awaken him and said, "Quick! Get up!" And the chains fell off his wrists. 8 Then the angel told him, "Get dressed and put on your sandals." And he did. "Now put on your coat and follow me," the angel ordered.

9 So Peter left the cell, following the angel. But all the time he thought it was a vision. He didn't realize it was actually happening. 10 They passed the first and second guard posts and came to the iron gate leading to the city, and this opened for them all by itself. So they passed through and started walking down the street, and then the angel suddenly left him.

11 Peter finally came to his senses. "It's really true!" he said. "The Lord has sent his angel and saved me from Herod and from what the Jewish leaders* had planned to do to me!"

11:8 Greek *anything common or unclean.* 11:16 Or *in;* also in 11:16b. 11:20 Greek *the Hellenists* (i.e., those who speak Greek); other manuscripts read *the Greeks.* 11:26 Greek *disciples;* also in 11:29. 11:29 Greek *the brothers.* 12:1 Greek *Herod the king.* He was the nephew of Herod Antipas and a grandson of Herod the Great. 12:3 Greek *the days of unleavened bread.* 12:11 Or *the Jewish people.*

¹²When he realized this, he went to the home of Mary, the mother of John Mark, where many were gathered for prayer. ¹³He knocked at the door in the gate, and a servant girl named Rhoda came to open it. ¹⁴When she recognized Peter's voice, she was so overjoyed that, instead of opening the door, she ran back inside and told everyone, "Peter is standing at the door!"

¹⁵"You're out of your mind!" they said. When she insisted, they decided, "It must be his angel."

¹⁶Meanwhile, Peter continued knocking. When they finally opened the door and saw him, they were amazed. ¹⁷He motioned for them to quiet down and told them how the Lord had led him out of prison. "Tell James and the other brothers what happened," he said. And then he went to another place.

¹⁸At dawn there was a great commotion among the soldiers about what had happened to Peter. ¹⁹Herod Agrippa ordered a thorough search for him. When he couldn't be found, Herod interrogated the guards and sentenced them to death. Afterward Herod left Judea to stay in Caesarea for a while.

The Death of Herod Agrippa

²⁰Now Herod was very angry with the people of Tyre and Sidon. So they sent a delegation to make peace with him because their cities were dependent upon Herod's country for food. The delegates won the support of Blastus, Herod's personal assistant, ²¹and an appointment with Herod was granted. When the day arrived, Her-

od put on his royal robes, sat on his throne, and made a speech to them. ²²The people gave him a great ovation, shouting, "It's the voice of a god, not of a man!"

²³Instantly, an angel of the Lord struck Herod with a sickness, because he accepted the people's worship instead of giving the glory to God. So he was consumed with worms and died.

²⁴Meanwhile, the word of God continued to spread, and there were many new believers.

²⁵When Barnabas and Saul had finished their mission to Jerusalem, they returned,* taking John Mark with them.

CHAPTER 13

Barnabas and Saul Are Commissioned

Among the prophets and teachers of the church at Antioch of Syria were Barnabas, Simeon (called "the black man"*), Lucius (from Cyrene), Manaen (the childhood companion of King Herod Antipas*), and Saul. ²One day as these men were worshiping the Lord and fasting, the Holy Spirit said, "Dedicate Barnabas and Saul for the special work to which I have called them." ³So after more fasting and prayer, the men laid their hands on them and sent them on their way.

Paul's First Missionary Journey

⁴So Barnabas and Saul were sent out by the Holy Spirit. They went down to the seaport of Seleucia and then sailed for the island of Cyprus. ⁵There, in the town of Salamis, they went to the Jewish

12:25 Or *mission, they returned to Jerusalem.* Other manuscripts read *mission, they returned from Jerusalem;* still others read *mission, they returned from Jerusalem to Antioch.* 13:1a Greek *who was called Niger.* 13:1b Greek *Herod the tetrarch.*

---

off and running
PRAY EFFECTIVELY
Read Acts 12:1-17

This Bible story vividly illustrates how God works in response to the prayers of his people. Though Peter's situation appeared hopeless, the body of believers did all that they could for him—they called on God. What made the prayers of these believers so effective? Their secret is found in Acts 12:5. There we see the three basic steps these Christians took in response to what appeared to be a hopeless situation:

1. They Directed Their Prayer to God. Ironically, many times our prayers often contain little thought of God himself. We fill our mind with thoughts about our own needs instead of our heavenly Father. But Jesus himself encouraged us to respectfully consider whom we are praying to when he gave us the Lord's Prayer (see Matthew 6:9-13, p. 7). This will allow you to take your eyes off of your dilemma and to place them on Jesus, and it will also help to align your will or desire with his.

synagogues and preached the word of God. John Mark went with them as their assistant.

⁶Afterward they traveled from town to town across the entire island until finally they reached Paphos, where they met a Jewish sorcerer, a false prophet named Bar-Jesus. ⁷He had attached himself to the governor, Sergius Paulus, who was an intelligent man. The governor invited Barnabas and Saul to visit him, for he wanted to hear the word of God. ⁸But Elymas, the sorcerer (as his name means in Greek), interfered and urged the governor to pay no attention to what Barnabas and Saul said. He was trying to keep the governor from believing.

⁹Saul, also known as Paul, was filled with the Holy Spirit, and he looked the sorcerer in the eye. ¹⁰Then he said, "You son of the devil, full of every sort of deceit and fraud, and enemy of all that is good! Will you never stop perverting the true ways of the Lord? ¹¹Watch now, for the Lord has laid his hand of punishment upon you, and you will be struck blind. You will not see the sunlight for some time." Instantly mist and darkness came over the man's eyes, and he began groping around begging for someone to take his hand and lead him.

¹²When the governor saw what had happened, he became a believer, for he was astonished at the teaching about the Lord.

Paul Preaches in Antioch of Pisidia

¹³Paul and his companions then left Paphos by ship for Pamphylia, landing at the port town of Perga. There John Mark left them and returned to Jerusalem. ¹⁴But Paul and Barnabas traveled inland to Antioch of Pisidia.*

On the Sabbath they went to the synagogue for the services. ¹⁵After the usual readings from the books of Moses* and the prophets, those in charge of the service sent them this message: "Brothers, if you have any word of encouragement for the people, come and give it."

¹⁶So Paul stood, lifted his hand to quiet them, and started speaking. "Men of Israel," he said, "and you God-fearing Gentiles, listen to me.

¹⁷"The God of this nation of Israel chose our ancestors and made them multiply and grow strong during their stay in Egypt. Then with a powerful arm he led them out of their slavery. ¹⁸He put up with them* through forty years of wandering in the wilderness. ¹⁹Then he destroyed seven nations in Canaan and gave their land to Israel as an inheritance. ²⁰All this took about 450 years.

"After that, God gave them judges to rule until the time of Samuel the prophet. ²¹Then the people begged for a king, and God gave them Saul son of Kish, a man of the tribe of Benjamin, who reigned for forty years. ²²But God removed Saul and replaced him with David, a man about whom God said, 'I have found David son of Jesse, a man after my own heart. He will do everything I want him to do.'*

²³"And it is one of King David's descendants, Jesus, who is God's promised Savior of Israel! ²⁴Before he came, John the Baptist preached that all the people of Israel needed to repent of their sins and turn to God and be baptized. ²⁵As

13:13-14 *Pamphylia* and *Pisidia* were districts in what is now Turkey.   13:15 Greek *from the law.*   13:18 Some manuscripts read *He cared for them;* compare Deut 1:31.   13:22 1 Sam 13:14.

---

2. They Prayed Earnestly. These believers offered constant, fervent prayer on Peter's behalf. Another way to translate this verse is, "They prayed with agony." It is the same phrase used to describe the way Jesus prayed in the garden of Gethsemane. Their prayers had intensity. Many of our prayers have no power because they have little or no heart in them. If we put so little heart into our prayers, we cannot expect God to put much heart into answering them.

3. They Prayed as a Body. There is power in united prayer. Jesus said in Matthew 18:19, "I also tell you this: If two of you agree here on earth concerning anything you ask, my Father in heaven will do it for you." What Jesus meant is that if two or more people who share the same God-given burden are sure of God's will and are in agreement with the Spirit of God and one another as they pray—they will see dynamic results.

Someone once said, "Satan trembles when he sees the weakest saint upon his knees." If you are in a bleak situation today, consider how God worked through the prayers of these early Christians. Don't give up. If you follow these principles, you will see results done God's way and in God's timing.

For the next note on "Prayer Time," turn to p. 90.

John was finishing his ministry he asked, 'Do you think I am the Messiah? No, I am not! But he is coming soon—and I'm not even worthy to be his slave and untie the sandals on his feet.'

26 "Brothers—you sons of Abraham, and also you God-fearing Gentiles—this message of salvation has been sent to us! 27 The people in Jerusalem and their leaders did not recognize Jesus as the one the prophets had spoken about. Instead, they condemned him, and in doing this they fulfilled the prophets' words that are read every Sabbath. 28 They found no legal reason to execute him, but they asked Pilate to have him killed anyway.

29 "When they had done all that the prophecies said about him, they took him down from the cross* and placed him in a tomb. 30 But God raised him from the dead! 31 And over a period of many days he appeared to those who had gone with him from Galilee to Jerusalem. They are now his witnesses to the people of Israel.

32 "And now we are here to bring you this Good News. The promise was made to our ancestors, 33 and God has now fulfilled it for us, their descendants, by raising Jesus. This is what the second psalm says about Jesus:

'You are my Son.
    Today I have become your Father.*'

34 For God had promised to raise him from the dead, not leaving him to rot in the grave. He said, 'I will give you the sacred blessings I promised to David.'* 35 Another psalm explains it more fully: 'You will not allow your Holy One to rot in the grave.'* 36 This is not a reference to David, for after David had done the will of God in his own generation, he died and was buried with his ancestors, and his body decayed. 37 No, it was a reference to someone else—someone whom God raised and whose body did not decay.

38 *"Brothers, listen! We are here to proclaim that through this man Jesus there is forgiveness for your sins. 39 Everyone who believes in him is declared right with God—something the law of Moses could never do. 40 Be careful! Don't let the prophets' words apply to you. For they said,

41 'Look, you mockers,
    be amazed and die!
For I am doing something in your own day,
    something you wouldn't believe
    even if someone told you about it.'*"

42 As Paul and Barnabas left the synagogue that day, the people begged them to speak about these things again the next week.

43 Many Jews and devout converts to Judaism followed Paul and Barnabas, and the two men urged them to continue to rely on the grace of God.

Paul Turns to the Gentiles

44 The following week almost the entire city turned out to hear them preach the word of the Lord. 45 But when some of the Jews saw the crowds, they were jealous; so they slandered Paul and argued against whatever he said.

46 Then Paul and Barnabas spoke out boldly and declared, "It was necessary that we first preach the word of God to you Jews. But since you have rejected it and judged yourselves unworthy of eternal life, we will offer it to the Gentiles. 47 For the Lord gave us this command when he said,

'I have made you a light to the Gentiles,
    to bring salvation to the farthest corners
        of the earth.'*"

48 When the Gentiles heard this, they were very glad and thanked the Lord for his message; and all who were chosen for eternal life became believers. 49 So the Lord's message spread throughout that region.

50 Then the Jews stirred up the influential religious women and the leaders of the city, and they incited a mob against Paul and Barnabas and ran them out of town. 51 So they shook the dust from their feet as a sign of rejection and went to the town of Iconium. 52 And the believers* were filled with joy and with the Holy Spirit.

CHAPTER 14
Paul and Barnabas in Iconium

The same thing happened in Iconium.* Paul and Barnabas went to the Jewish synagogue and preached with such power that a great number of both Jews and Greeks became believers. 2 Some of the Jews, however, spurned God's message and poisoned the minds of the Gentiles against Paul and Barnabas. 3 But the apostles stayed there a long time, preaching boldly about the grace of the Lord. And the Lord proved their message was true by giving them power to do miraculous signs and wonders. 4 But the people of the town were divided in their opinion about them. Some sided with the Jews, and some with the apostles.

5 Then a mob of Gentiles and Jews, along with their leaders, decided to attack and stone them. 6 When the apostles learned of it, they fled to the region of Lycaonia—to the towns of

13:29 Greek from the tree.   13:33 Or Today I reveal you as my Son. Ps 2:7.   13:34 Isa 55:3.   13:35 Ps 16:10.
13:38 English translations divide verses 38 and 39 in various ways.   13:41 Hab 1:5 (Greek version).   13:47 Isa 49:6.
13:52 Greek the disciples.   14:1 Iconium, as well as Lystra and Derbe (14:6), were towns in what is now Turkey.

Lystra and Derbe and the surrounding area. ⁷And there they preached the Good News.

Paul and Barnabas in Lystra and Derbe

⁸While they were at Lystra, Paul and Barnabas came upon a man with crippled feet. He had been that way from birth, so he had never walked. He was sitting ⁹and listening as Paul preached. Looking straight at him, Paul realized he had faith to be healed. ¹⁰So Paul called to him in a loud voice, "Stand up!" And the man jumped to his feet and started walking.

¹¹When the crowd saw what Paul had done, they shouted in their local dialect, "These men are gods in human form!" ¹²They decided that Barnabas was the Greek god Zeus and that Paul was Hermes, since he was the chief speaker. ¹³Now the temple of Zeus was located just outside the town. So the priest of the temple and the crowd brought bulls and wreaths of flowers to the town gates, and they prepared to offer sacrifices to the apostles.

¹⁴But when the apostles Barnabas and Paul heard what was happening, they tore their clothing in dismay and ran out among the people, shouting, ¹⁵"Friends,* why are you doing this? We are merely human beings—just like you! We have come to bring you the Good News that you should turn from these worthless things and turn to the living God, who made heaven and earth, the sea, and everything in them. ¹⁶In the past he permitted all the nations to go their own ways, ¹⁷but he never left them without evidence of himself and his goodness. For instance, he sends you rain and good crops and gives you food and joyful hearts." ¹⁸But even with these words, Paul and Barnabas could scarcely restrain the people from sacrificing to them.

¹⁹Then some Jews arrived from Antioch and Iconium and won the crowds to their side. They stoned Paul and dragged him out of town, thinking he was dead. ²⁰But as the believers* gathered around him, he got up and went back into the town. The next day he left with Barnabas for Derbe.

Paul and Barnabas Return to Antioch of Syria

²¹After preaching the Good News in Derbe and making many disciples, Paul and Barnabas returned to Lystra, Iconium, and Antioch of Pisidia, ²²where they strengthened the believers. They encouraged them to continue in the faith, reminding them that we must suffer many hardships to enter the Kingdom of God. ²³Paul and Barnabas also appointed elders in every church. With prayer and fasting, they turned the elders over to the care of the Lord, in whom

they had put their trust. ²⁴Then they traveled back through Pisidia to Pamphylia. ²⁵They preached the word in Perga, then went down to Attalia.

²⁶Finally, they returned by ship to Antioch of Syria, where their journey had begun. The believers there had entrusted them to the grace of God to do the work they had now completed. ²⁷Upon arriving in Antioch, they called the church together and reported everything God had done through them and how he had opened the door of faith to the Gentiles, too. ²⁸And they stayed there with the believers for a long time.

CHAPTER 15
The Council at Jerusalem

While Paul and Barnabas were at Antioch of Syria, some men from Judea arrived and began to teach the believers*: "Unless you are circumcised as required by the law of Moses, you cannot be saved." ²Paul and Barnabas disagreed with them, arguing vehemently. Finally, the church decided to send Paul and Barnabas to Jerusalem, accompanied by some local believers, to talk to the apostles and elders about this question. ³The church sent the delegates to Jerusalem, and they stopped along the way in Phoenicia and Samaria to visit the believers. They told them—much to everyone's joy—that the Gentiles, too, were being converted.

⁴When they arrived in Jerusalem, Barnabas and Paul were welcomed by the whole church, including the apostles and elders. They reported everything God had done through them. ⁵But then some of the believers who belonged to the sect of the Pharisees stood up and insisted, "The Gentile converts must be circumcised and required to follow the law of Moses."

⁶So the apostles and elders met together to resolve this issue. ⁷At the meeting, after a long discussion, Peter stood and addressed them as follows: "Brothers, you all know that God chose me from among you some time ago to preach to the Gentiles so that they could hear the Good News and believe. ⁸God knows people's hearts, and he confirmed that he accepts Gentiles by giving them the Holy Spirit, just as he did to us. ⁹He made no distinction between us and them, for he cleansed their hearts through faith. ¹⁰So why are you now challenging God by burdening the Gentile believers* with a yoke that neither we nor our ancestors were able to bear? ¹¹We believe that we are all saved the same way, by the undeserved grace of the Lord Jesus."

¹²Everyone listened quietly as Barnabas and Paul told about the miraculous signs and

14:15 Greek Men.   14:20 Greek disciples; also in 14:22, 28.   15:1 Greek brothers; also in 15:3, 23, 32, 33, 36, 40.
15:10 Greek disciples.

wonders God had done through them among the Gentiles.

[13] When they had finished, James stood and said, "Brothers, listen to me. [14] Peter* has told you about the time God first visited the Gentiles to take from them a people for himself. [15] And this conversion of Gentiles is exactly what the prophets predicted. As it is written:

[16] 'Afterward I will return
    and restore the fallen house* of David.
I will rebuild its ruins
    and restore it,
[17] so that the rest of humanity might seek the
        LORD,
    including the Gentiles—
    all those I have called to be mine.
The LORD has spoken—
[18]   he who made these things known so long
        ago.'*

[19] "And so my judgment is that we should not make it difficult for the Gentiles who are turning to God. [20] Instead, we should write and tell them to abstain from eating food offered to idols, from sexual immorality, from eating the meat of strangled animals, and from consuming blood. [21] For these laws of Moses have been preached in Jewish synagogues in every city on every Sabbath for many generations."

The Letter for Gentile Believers

[22] Then the apostles and elders together with the whole church in Jerusalem chose delegates, and they sent them to Antioch of Syria with Paul and Barnabas to report on this decision. The men chosen were two of the church leaders*—Judas (also called Barsabbas) and Silas. [23] This is the letter they took with them:

"This letter is from the apostles and elders, your brothers in Jerusalem. It is written to the Gentile believers in Antioch, Syria, and Cilicia. Greetings!

[24] "We understand that some men from here have troubled you and upset you with their teaching, but we did not send them! [25] So we decided, having come to complete agreement, to send you official representatives, along with our beloved Barnabas and Paul, [26] who have risked their lives for the name of our Lord Jesus Christ. [27] We are sending Judas and Silas to confirm what we have decided concerning your question.

[28] "For it seemed good to the Holy Spirit and to us to lay no greater burden on you than these few requirements: [29] You must abstain from eating food offered to idols, from consuming blood or the meat of strangled animals, and from sexual immorality. If you do this, you will do well. Farewell."

[30] The messengers went at once to Antioch, where they called a general meeting of the believers and delivered the letter. [31] And there was great joy throughout the church that day as they read this encouraging message.

[32] Then Judas and Silas, both being prophets, spoke at length to the believers, encouraging and strengthening their faith. [33] They stayed for a while, and then the believers sent them back to the church in Jerusalem with a blessing of peace.* [35] Paul and Barnabas stayed in Antioch. They and many others taught and preached the word of the Lord there.

Paul and Barnabas Separate

[36] After some time Paul said to Barnabas, "Let's go back and visit each city where we previously preached the word of the Lord, to see how the new believers are doing." [37] Barnabas agreed and wanted to take along John Mark. [38] But Paul disagreed strongly, since John Mark had deserted them in Pamphylia and had not continued with them in their work. [39] Their disagreement was so sharp that they separated. Barnabas took John Mark with him and sailed for Cyprus. [40] Paul chose Silas, and as he left, the believers entrusted him to the Lord's gracious care. [41] Then he traveled throughout Syria and Cilicia, strengthening the churches there.

CHAPTER 16

Paul's Second Missionary Journey

Paul went first to Derbe and then to Lystra, where there was a young disciple named Timothy. His mother was a Jewish believer, but his father was a Greek. [2] Timothy was well thought of by the believers* in Lystra and Iconium, [3] so Paul wanted him to join them on their journey. In deference to the Jews of the area, he arranged for Timothy to be circumcised before they left, for everyone knew that his father was a Greek. [4] Then they went from town to town, instructing the believers to follow the decisions made by the apostles and elders in Jerusalem. [5] So the churches were strengthened in their faith and grew larger every day.

A Call from Macedonia

[6] Next Paul and Silas traveled through the area of Phrygia and Galatia, because the Holy Spirit

---

15:14 Greek *Symeon*.   **15:16** Or *kingdom;* Greek reads *tent*.   **15:16-18** Amos 9:11-12 (Greek version); Isa 45:21.
15:22 Greek *were leaders among the brothers*.   **15:33** Some manuscripts add verse 34, *But Silas decided to stay there*.
16:2 Greek *brothers;* also in 16:40.

had prevented them from preaching the word in the province of Asia at that time. [7] Then coming to the borders of Mysia, they headed north for the province of Bithynia,* but again the Spirit of Jesus did not allow them to go there. [8] So instead, they went on through Mysia to the seaport of Troas.

[9] That night Paul had a vision: A man from Macedonia in northern Greece was standing there, pleading with him, "Come over to Macedonia and help us!" [10] So we* decided to leave for Macedonia at once, having concluded that God was calling us to preach the Good News there.

Lydia of Philippi Believes in Jesus

[11] We boarded a boat at Troas and sailed straight across to the island of Samothrace, and the next day we landed at Neapolis. [12] From there we reached Philippi, a major city of that district of Macedonia and a Roman colony. And we stayed there several days.

[13] On the Sabbath we went a little way outside the city to a riverbank, where we thought people would be meeting for prayer, and we sat down to speak with some women who had gathered there. [14] One of them was Lydia from Thyatira, a merchant of expensive purple cloth, who worshiped God. As she listened to us, the Lord opened her heart, and she accepted what Paul was saying. [15] She was baptized along with other members of her household, and she asked us to be her guests. "If you agree that I am a true believer in the Lord," she said, "come and stay at my home." And she urged us until we agreed.

Paul and Silas in Prison

[16] One day as we were going down to the place of prayer, we met a demon-possessed slave girl. She was a fortune-teller who earned a lot of money for her masters. [17] She followed Paul and the rest of us, shouting, "These men are servants of the Most High God, and they have come to tell you how to be saved."

[18] This went on day after day until Paul got so exasperated that he turned and said to the demon within her, "I command you in the name of Jesus Christ to come out of her." And instantly it left her.

[19] Her masters' hopes of wealth were now shattered, so they grabbed Paul and Silas and dragged them before the authorities at the marketplace. [20] "The whole city is in an uproar because of these Jews!" they shouted to the city officials. [21] "They are teaching customs that are illegal for us Romans to practice."

[22] A mob quickly formed against Paul and Silas, and the city officials ordered them stripped and beaten with wooden rods. [23] They were severely beaten, and then they were thrown into prison. The jailer was ordered to make sure they didn't escape. [24] So the jailer put them into the inner dungeon and clamped their feet in the stocks.

[25] Around midnight Paul and Silas were praying and singing hymns to God, and the other prisoners were listening. [26] Suddenly, there was a massive earthquake, and the prison was shaken to its foundations. All the doors immediately flew open, and the chains of every prisoner fell off! [27] The jailer woke up to see the prison doors wide open. He assumed the prisoners had escaped, so he drew his sword to kill himself. [28] But Paul shouted to him, "Stop! Don't kill yourself! We are all here!"

[29] The jailer called for lights and ran to the dungeon and fell down trembling before Paul and Silas. [30] Then he brought them out and asked, "Sirs, what must I do to be saved?"

[31] They replied, "Believe in the Lord Jesus and you will be saved, along with everyone in your household." [32] And they shared the word of the Lord with him and with all who lived in his household. [33] Even at that hour of the night, the jailer cared for them and washed their wounds. Then he and everyone in his household were immediately baptized. [34] He brought them into his house and set a meal before them, and he and his entire household rejoiced because they all believed in God.

[35] The next morning the city officials sent the police to tell the jailer, "Let those men go!" [36] So the jailer told Paul, "The city officials have said you and Silas are free to leave. Go in peace."

[37] But Paul replied, "They have publicly beaten us without a trial and put us in prison—and we are Roman citizens. So now they want us to leave secretly? Certainly not! Let them come themselves to release us!"

[38] When the police reported this, the city officials were alarmed to learn that Paul and Silas were Roman citizens. [39] So they came to the jail and apologized to them. Then they brought them out and begged them to leave the city. [40] When Paul and Silas left the prison, they returned to the home of Lydia. There they met with the believers and encouraged them once more. Then they left town.

CHAPTER **17**
Paul Preaches in Thessalonica

Paul and Silas then traveled through the towns of Amphipolis and Apollonia and came to Thessalonica, where there was a Jewish

16:6-7 *Phrygia, Galatia, Asia, Mysia,* and *Bithynia* were all districts in what is now Turkey.   **16:10** Luke, the writer of this book, here joined Paul and accompanied him on his journey.

synagogue. [2]As was Paul's custom, he went to the synagogue service, and for three Sabbaths in a row he used the Scriptures to reason with the people. [3]He explained the prophecies and proved that the Messiah must suffer and rise from the dead. He said, "This Jesus I'm telling you about is the Messiah." [4]Some of the Jews who listened were persuaded and joined Paul and Silas, along with many God-fearing Greek men and quite a few prominent women.*

[5]But some of the Jews were jealous, so they gathered some troublemakers from the marketplace to form a mob and start a riot. They attacked the home of Jason, searching for Paul and Silas so they could drag them out to the crowd.* [6]Not finding them there, they dragged out Jason and some of the other believers* instead and took them before the city council. "Paul and Silas have caused trouble all over the world," they shouted, "and now they are here disturbing our city, too. [7]And Jason has welcomed them into his home. They are all guilty of treason against Caesar, for they profess allegiance to another king, named Jesus."

[8]The people of the city, as well as the city council, were thrown into turmoil by these reports. [9]So the officials forced Jason and the other believers to post bond, and then they released them.

Paul and Silas in Berea

[10]That very night the believers sent Paul and Silas to Berea. When they arrived there, they went to the Jewish synagogue. [11]And the people of Berea were more open-minded than those in Thessalonica, and they listened eagerly to Paul's message. They searched the Scriptures day af-ter day to see if Paul and Silas were teaching the truth. [12]As a result, many Jews believed, as did many of the prominent Greek women and men.

[13]But when some Jews in Thessalonica learned that Paul was preaching the word of God in Berea, they went there and stirred up trouble. [14]The believers acted at once, sending Paul on to the coast, while Silas and Timothy remained behind. [15]Those escorting Paul went with him all the way to Athens; then they returned to Berea with instructions for Silas and Timothy to hurry and join him.

Paul Preaches in Athens

[16]While Paul was waiting for them in Athens, he was deeply troubled by all the idols he saw everywhere in the city. [17]He went to the synagogue to reason with the Jews and the God-fearing Gentiles, and he spoke daily in the public square to all who happened to be there.

[18]He also had a debate with some of the Epicurean and Stoic philosophers. When he told them about Jesus and his resurrection, they said, "What's this babbler trying to say with these strange ideas he's picked up?" Others said, "He seems to be preaching about some foreign gods."

[19]Then they took him to the high council of the city.* "Come and tell us about this new teaching," they said. [20]"You are saying some rather strange things, and we want to know what it's all about." [21](It should be explained that all the Athenians as well as the foreigners in Athens seemed to spend all their time discussing the latest ideas.)

[22]So Paul, standing before the council,* addressed them as follows: "Men of Athens, I notice that you are very religious in every way,

17:4 Some manuscripts read *quite a few of the wives of the leading men.*   17:5 Or *the city council.*   17:6 Greek *brothers;* also in 17:10, 14.   17:19 Or *the most learned society of philosophers in the city.* Greek reads *the Areopagus.*
17:22 Traditionally rendered *standing in the middle of Mars Hill;* Greek reads *standing in the middle of the Areopagus.*

off and running

MAKE SURE YOUR CHILDREN HEAR THE GOSPEL MESSAGE
Read ACTS 16:29-34

In this wonderful story, we see how one man looked out for the spiritual welfare of his family. He took the opportunity at hand to expose his family to the message of Christ through the testimony of Paul and Silas.

We, too, need to take advantage of every opportunity to share Christ with our family—and particularly our children. They are never too young (or too old) to be taught about the things of God. Here are four suggestions to help you share the gospel with your family:

1. Set Aside Time for Family Devotions. Study the Bible, pray together, and share how God has been working in your life.

²³for as I was walking along I saw your many shrines. And one of your altars had this inscription on it: 'To an Unknown God.' This God, whom you worship without knowing, is the one I'm telling you about.

²⁴"He is the God who made the world and everything in it. Since he is Lord of heaven and earth, he doesn't live in man-made temples, ²⁵and human hands can't serve his needs—for he has no needs. He himself gives life and breath to everything, and he satisfies every need. ²⁶From one man* he created all the nations throughout the whole earth. He decided beforehand when they should rise and fall, and he determined their boundaries.

²⁷"His purpose was for the nations to seek after God and perhaps feel their way toward him and find him—though he is not far from any one of us. ²⁸For in him we live and move and exist. As some of your* own poets have said, 'We are his offspring.' ²⁹And since this is true, we shouldn't think of God as an idol designed by craftsmen from gold or silver or stone.

³⁰"God overlooked people's ignorance about these things in earlier times, but now he commands everyone everywhere to repent of their sins and turn to him. ³¹For he has set a day for judging the world with justice by the man he has appointed, and he proved to everyone who this is by raising him from the dead."

³²When they heard Paul speak about the resurrection of the dead, some laughed in contempt, but others said, "We want to hear more about this later." ³³That ended Paul's discussion with them, ³⁴but some joined him and became believers. Among them were Dionysius, a member of the council,* a woman named Damaris, and others with them.

CHAPTER **18**

Paul Meets Priscilla and Aquila in Corinth

Then Paul left Athens and went to Corinth.* ²There he became acquainted with a Jew named Aquila, born in Pontus, who had recently arrived from Italy with his wife, Priscilla. They had left Italy when Claudius Caesar deported all Jews from Rome. ³Paul lived and worked with them, for they were tentmakers* just as he was.

⁴Each Sabbath found Paul at the synagogue, trying to convince the Jews and Greeks alike. ⁵And after Silas and Timothy came down from Macedonia, Paul spent all his time preaching the word. He testified to the Jews that Jesus was the Messiah. ⁶But when they opposed and insulted him, Paul shook the dust from his clothes and said, "Your blood is upon your own heads—I am innocent. From now on I will go preach to the Gentiles."

⁷Then he left and went to the home of Titius Justus, a Gentile who worshiped God and lived next door to the synagogue. ⁸Crispus, the leader of the synagogue, and everyone in his household believed in the Lord. Many others in Corinth also heard Paul, became believers, and were baptized.

⁹One night the Lord spoke to Paul in a vision and told him, "Don't be afraid! Speak out! Don't be silent! ¹⁰For I am with you, and no one will attack and harm you, for many people in this city belong to me." ¹¹So Paul stayed there for the next year and a half, teaching the word of God.

¹²But when Gallio became governor of Achaia, some Jews rose up together against Paul and brought him before the governor for judgment. ¹³They accused Paul of "persuading people to worship God in ways that are contrary to our law."

17:26 Greek *From one;* other manuscripts read *From one blood.*   17:28 Some manuscripts read *our.*   17:34 Greek *an Areopagite.*   18:1 *Athens* and *Corinth* were major cities in Achaia, the region in the southern portion of the Greek peninsula. 18:3 Or *leatherworkers.*

2. Invite Other Believers to Your Home. This jailer invited Paul and Silas over for dinner, and we read how the whole household rejoiced because all were now believers. This type of fellowship can be an enriching time for your family.

3. Bring Your Children to Church with You. Your children will probably learn lessons here that they will carry with them the rest of their lives. If they are young, bring them. If they are older, strongly encourage them to join you.

4. Pray for Your Children Daily. As a parent, you cannot "make" your children Christians, but you can pray that their hearts will be sensitive and open to the gospel message.

For the next note on "Children," turn to p. 250.

cornerstones

USE GOD'S WORD TO EVALUATE SOMEONE'S TEACHINGS
Read ACTS 17:11

The group of people in this passage—the Bereans—actually searched the written Word of God to see if Paul's words were true. In the original Greek, the word for "searched" could also be translated "scrutinized." They did this because they knew that they could trust God's Word and use it as the standard against which to evaluate others' teachings.

The same is true for us today. Everything we need to know about God is found in the pages of Scripture. Applying ourselves in the study of his Word helps us determine whether someone's teachings are true or false. If we fail to study the Bible, we may be lured into believing false teachings. But if we consistently study God's Word, it—along with the illumination of the Holy Spirit—will enable us to distinguish truth from error.

Here is a trustworthy saying to keep in mind: If someone says they have a new "word" or "revelation" from the Lord, rest assured that it is not true. If it is true, it is not new. If it is new, it is not true! If it is not in the Word, it is not of the Lord.

To begin the next topic, turn to p. A33.

---

[14] But just as Paul started to make his defense, Gallio turned to Paul's accusers and said, "Listen, you Jews, if this were a case involving some wrongdoing or a serious crime, I would have a reason to accept your case. [15] But since it is merely a question of words and names and your Jewish law, take care of it yourselves. I refuse to judge such matters." [16] And he threw them out of the courtroom.

[17] The crowd* then grabbed Sosthenes, the leader of the synagogue, and beat him right there in the courtroom. But Gallio paid no attention.

Paul Returns to Antioch of Syria
[18] Paul stayed in Corinth for some time after that, then said good-bye to the brothers and sisters* and went to nearby Cenchrea. There he shaved his head according to Jewish custom, marking the end of a vow. Then he set sail for Syria, taking Priscilla and Aquila with him. [19] They stopped first at the port of Ephesus, where Paul left the others behind. While he was there, he went to the synagogue to reason with the Jews. [20] They asked him to stay longer, but he declined. [21] As he left, however, he said, "I will come back later,* God willing." Then he set sail from Ephesus. [22] The next stop was at the port of Caesarea. From there he went up and visited the church at Jerusalem* and then went back to Antioch.

[23] After spending some time in Antioch, Paul went back through Galatia and Phrygia, visiting and strengthening all the believers.*

Apollos Instructed at Ephesus
[24] Meanwhile, a Jew named Apollos, an eloquent speaker who knew the Scriptures well, had arrived in Ephesus from Alexandria in Egypt. [25] He had been taught the way of the Lord, and he taught others about Jesus with an enthusiastic spirit* and with accuracy. However, he knew only about John's baptism. [26] When Priscilla and Aquila heard him preaching boldly in the synagogue, they took him aside and explained the way of God even more accurately.

[27] Apollos had been thinking about going to Achaia, and the brothers and sisters in Ephesus encouraged him to go. They wrote to the believers in Achaia, asking them to welcome him. When he arrived there, he proved to be of great benefit to those who, by God's grace, had believed. [28] He refuted the Jews with powerful arguments in public debate. Using the Scriptures, he explained to them that Jesus was the Messiah.

CHAPTER **19**
Paul's Third Missionary Journey
While Apollos was in Corinth, Paul traveled through the interior regions until he reached Ephesus, on the coast, where he found several believers.* [2] "Did you receive the Holy Spirit when you believed?" he asked them.

18:17 Greek *Everyone;* other manuscripts read *All the Greeks.* **18:18** Greek *brothers;* also in 18:27. **18:21** Some manuscripts read *"I must by all means be at Jerusalem for the upcoming festival, but I will come back later."* **18:22** Greek *the church.* **18:23** Greek *disciples;* also in 18:27. **18:25** Or *with enthusiasm in the Spirit.* **19:1** Greek *disciples;* also in 19:9, 30.

"No," they replied, "we haven't even heard that there is a Holy Spirit."

³"Then what baptism did you experience?" he asked.

And they replied, "The baptism of John."

⁴Paul said, "John's baptism called for repentance from sin. But John himself told the people to believe in the one who would come later, meaning Jesus."

⁵As soon as they heard this, they were baptized in the name of the Lord Jesus. ⁶Then when Paul laid his hands on them, the Holy Spirit came on them, and they spoke in other tongues* and prophesied. ⁷There were about twelve men in all.

Paul Ministers in Ephesus

⁸Then Paul went to the synagogue and preached boldly for the next three months, arguing persuasively about the Kingdom of God. ⁹But some became stubborn, rejecting his message and publicly speaking against the Way. So Paul left the synagogue and took the believers with him. Then he held daily discussions at the lecture hall of Tyrannus. ¹⁰This went on for the next two years, so that people throughout the province of Asia—both Jews and Greeks—heard the word of the Lord.

¹¹God gave Paul the power to perform unusual miracles. ¹²When handkerchiefs or aprons that had merely touched his skin were placed on sick people, they were healed of their diseases, and evil spirits were expelled.

¹³A group of Jews was traveling from town to town casting out evil spirits. They tried to use the name of the Lord Jesus in their incantation, saying, "I command you in the name of Jesus, whom Paul preaches, to come out!" ¹⁴Seven sons of Sceva, a leading priest, were doing this. ¹⁵But one time when they tried it, the evil spirit replied, "I know Jesus, and I know Paul, but who are you?" ¹⁶Then the man with the evil spirit leaped on them, overpowered them, and attacked them with such violence that they fled from the house, naked and battered.

¹⁷The story of what happened spread quickly all through Ephesus, to Jews and Greeks alike. A solemn fear descended on the city, and the name of the Lord Jesus was greatly honored. ¹⁸Many who became believers confessed their sinful practices. ¹⁹A number of them who had been practicing sorcery brought their incantation books and burned them at a public bonfire. The value of the books was several million dollars.* ²⁰So the message about the Lord spread widely and had a powerful effect.

²¹Afterward Paul felt compelled by the Spirit* to go over to Macedonia and Achaia before going to Jerusalem. "And after that," he said, "I must go on to Rome!" ²²He sent his two assistants, Timothy and Erastus, ahead to Macedonia while he stayed awhile longer in the province of Asia.

The Riot in Ephesus

²³About that time, serious trouble developed in Ephesus concerning the Way. ²⁴It began with Demetrius, a silversmith who had a large business manufacturing silver shrines of the Greek goddess Artemis.* He kept many craftsmen busy. ²⁵He called them together, along with others employed in similar trades, and addressed them as follows:

"Gentlemen, you know that our wealth comes from this business. ²⁶But as you have seen and heard, this man Paul has persuaded many people that handmade gods aren't really gods at all. And he's done this not only here in Ephesus but throughout the entire province! ²⁷Of course, I'm not just talking about the loss of public respect for our business. I'm also concerned that the temple of the great goddess Artemis will lose its influence and that Artemis—this magnificent goddess worshiped throughout the province of Asia and all around the world—will be robbed of her great prestige!"

²⁸At this their anger boiled, and they began shouting, "Great is Artemis of the Ephesians!" ²⁹Soon the whole city was filled with confusion. Everyone rushed to the amphitheater, dragging along Gaius and Aristarchus, who were Paul's traveling companions from Macedonia. ³⁰Paul wanted to go in, too, but the believers wouldn't let him. ³¹Some of the officials of the province, friends of Paul, also sent a message to him, begging him not to risk his life by entering the amphitheater.

³²Inside, the people were all shouting, some one thing and some another. Everything was in confusion. In fact, most of them didn't even know why they were there. ³³The Jews in the crowd pushed Alexander forward and told him to explain the situation. He motioned for silence and tried to speak. ³⁴But when the crowd realized he was a Jew, they started shouting again and kept it up for about two hours: "Great is Artemis of the Ephesians! Great is Artemis of the Ephesians!"

³⁵At last the mayor was able to quiet them down enough to speak. "Citizens of Ephesus," he said. "Everyone knows that Ephesus is the official guardian of the temple of the great Artemis, whose image fell down to us from heaven. ³⁶Since this is an undeniable fact, you

19:6 Or *in other languages.*   19:19 Greek *50,000 pieces of silver,* each of which was the equivalent of a day's wage.
19:21 Or *decided in his spirit.*   19:24 *Artemis* is otherwise known as Diana.

cornerstones

GOD IS PERSONAL
Read ACTS 17:22-31

Paul's audience in this passage included people of two different beliefs. The Epicureans were those who did not believe in life after death and lived only for pleasure. The Stoics were those who believed that God existed in every material object and strived to be at peace with the world. In speaking to these two groups, Paul showed them how their philosophies fell short of grasping the true nature of God by bringing out the following truths about who God is:

God Is the All-Powerful Creator

- God made heaven and earth, and every living creature.
- God is too great to be housed in man-made temples or shrines.
- God created all the people of the world from one man.
- God is the architect behind the world stage.

God Is the Personal Supreme Being

- His purpose behind creation was to draw people to himself.
- He is concerned about people's needs.
- He is not far from any of us.
- He makes it easy for us to know him personally (salvation through Jesus Christ).
- He can and will judge every thought and motive on Judgment Day.

The people who listened to Paul speak responded in one of three ways: (1) Some mocked him; (2) some procrastinated and said they would make a decision after listening to him again later; and (3) some believed him and accepted Jesus as their Savior. People today react to the gospel message in much the same way. However, if someone really wants to know the powerful God who created him or her and who is personally interested in his or her life, only the last response will do.

To begin next topic, turn to p. A23.

---

should stay calm and not do anything rash. ³⁷You have brought these men here, but they have stolen nothing from the temple and have not spoken against our goddess.

³⁸"If Demetrius and the craftsmen have a case against them, the courts are in session and the officials can hear the case at once. Let them make formal charges. ³⁹And if there are complaints about other matters, they can be settled in a legal assembly. ⁴⁰I am afraid we are in danger of being charged with rioting by the Roman government, since there is no cause for all this commotion. And if Rome demands an explanation, we won't know what to say." ⁴¹*Then he dismissed them, and they dispersed.

CHAPTER 20
Paul Goes to Macedonia and Greece

When the uproar was over, Paul sent for the believers* and encouraged them. Then he said good-bye and left for Macedonia. ²While there, he encouraged the believers in all the towns he passed through. Then he traveled down to Greece, ³where he stayed for three months. He was preparing to sail back to Syria when he discovered a plot by some Jews against his life, so he decided to return through Macedonia.

⁴Several men were traveling with him. They were Sopater son of Pyrrhus from Berea; Aristarchus and Secundus from Thessalonica; Gaius from Derbe; Timothy; and Tychicus and Trophimus from the province of Asia. ⁵They went on ahead and waited for us at Troas. ⁶After the Passover* ended, we boarded a ship at Philippi in Macedonia and five days later joined them in Troas, where we stayed a week.

Paul's Final Visit to Troas

⁷On the first day of the week, we gathered with the local believers to share in the Lord's Supper.* Paul was preaching to them, and since he was leaving the next day, he kept talking until midnight. ⁸The upstairs room where we met was lighted with many flickering lamps. ⁹As Paul spoke on and on, a young man named Euty-

19:41 Some translations include verse 41 as part of verse 40. **20:1** Greek *disciples.* **20:6** Greek *the days of unleavened bread.* **20:7** Greek *to break bread.*

chus, sitting on the windowsill, became very drowsy. Finally, he fell sound asleep and dropped three stories to his death below. [10] Paul went down, bent over him, and took him into his arms. "Don't worry," he said, "he's alive!" [11] Then they all went back upstairs, shared in the Lord's Supper,* and ate together. Paul continued talking to them until dawn, and then he left. [12] Meanwhile, the young man was taken home unhurt, and everyone was greatly relieved.

Paul Meets the Ephesian Elders

[13] Paul went by land to Assos, where he had arranged for us to join him, while we traveled by ship. [14] He joined us there, and we sailed together to Mitylene. [15] The next day we sailed past the island of Kios. The following day we crossed to the island of Samos, and* a day later we arrived at Miletus.

[16] Paul had decided to sail on past Ephesus, for he didn't want to spend any more time in the province of Asia. He was hurrying to get to Jerusalem, if possible, in time for the Festival of Pentecost. [17] But when we landed at Miletus, he sent a message to the elders of the church at Ephesus, asking them to come and meet him.

[18] When they arrived he declared, "You know that from the day I set foot in the province of Asia until now [19] I have done the Lord's work humbly and with many tears. I have endured the trials that came to me from the plots of the Jews. [20] I never shrank back from telling you what you needed to hear, either publicly or in your homes. [21] I have had one message for Jews and Greeks alike—the necessity of repenting from sin and turning to God, and of having faith in our Lord Jesus.

[22] "And now I am bound by the Spirit* to go to Jerusalem. I don't know what awaits me, [23] except that the Holy Spirit tells me in city after city that jail and suffering lie ahead. [24] But my life is worth nothing to me unless I use it for finishing the work assigned me by the Lord Jesus—the work of telling others the Good News about the wonderful grace of God.

[25] "And now I know that none of you to whom I have preached the Kingdom will ever see me again. [26] I declare today that I have been faithful. If anyone suffers eternal death, it's not my fault,* [27] for I didn't shrink from declaring all that God wants you to know.

[28] "So guard yourselves and God's people. Feed and shepherd God's flock—his church, purchased with his own blood*—over which the Holy Spirit has appointed you as elders.*

[29] I know that false teachers, like vicious wolves, will come in among you after I leave, not sparing the flock. [30] Even some men from your own group will rise up and distort the truth in order to draw a following. [31] Watch out! Remember the three years I was with you—my constant watch and care over you night and day, and my many tears for you.

[32] "And now I entrust you to God and the message of his grace that is able to build you up and give you an inheritance with all those he has set apart for himself.

[33] "I have never coveted anyone's silver or gold or fine clothes. [34] You know that these hands of mine have worked to supply my own needs and even the needs of those who were with me. [35] And I have been a constant example of how you can help those in need by working hard. You should remember the words of the Lord Jesus: 'It is more blessed to give than to receive.'"

[36] When he had finished speaking, he knelt and prayed with them. [37] They all cried as they embraced and kissed him good-bye. [38] They were sad most of all because he had said that they would never see him again. Then they escorted him down to the ship.

CHAPTER 21

Paul's Journey to Jerusalem

After saying farewell to the Ephesian elders, we sailed straight to the island of Cos. The next day we reached Rhodes and then went to Patara. [2] There we boarded a ship sailing for Phoenicia. [3] We sighted the island of Cyprus, passed it on our left, and landed at the harbor of Tyre, in Syria, where the ship was to unload its cargo.

[4] We went ashore, found the local believers,* and stayed with them a week. These believers prophesied through the Holy Spirit that Paul should not go on to Jerusalem. [5] When we returned to the ship at the end of the week, the entire congregation, including women* and children, left the city and came down to the shore with us. There we knelt, prayed, [6] and said our farewells. Then we went aboard, and they returned home.

[7] The next stop after leaving Tyre was Ptolemais, where we greeted the brothers and sisters* and stayed for one day. [8] The next day we went on to Caesarea and stayed at the home of Philip the Evangelist, one of the seven men who had been chosen to distribute food. [9] He had four unmarried daughters who had the gift of prophecy.

20:11 Greek broke the bread.　20:15 Some manuscripts read and having stayed at Trogyllium.　20:22 Or by my spirit, or by an inner compulsion; Greek reads by the spirit.　20:26 Greek I am innocent of the blood of all.　20:28a Or with the blood of his own [Son].　20:28b Greek overseers.　21:4 Greek disciples; also in 21:16.　21:5 Or wives.　21:7 Greek brothers; also in 21:17.

cornerstones

CAN DEMONS PERSONALLY HARM YOU?
Read ACTS 19:13-20

While Christians have the promise of angelic protection over their lives, non-Christians are open targets for the Devil and his demonic forces. As this passage relates, demons will only respond to or avoid the genuine believer. They will not answer to someone who simply uses the name of Jesus without really knowing who Jesus is. Religion will not keep them away, nor will symbols like a crucifix. Certainly the Devil hates what Jesus did on the cross, but wearing a cross will not drive these evil spirits away.

The only thing that will secure you from the Devil's domination— and even possession—of your soul is the presence of Jesus Christ in your life. Once you trust in him, you come under divine protection and become his property. He said that you are his sheep and that no one can take you out of his hand (see John 10:27-29, p. 112). But if you are not a Christian, the Devil can take you at his will.

For the next note on "What Are Demons?" turn to p. 78.

¹⁰Several days later a man named Agabus, who also had the gift of prophecy, arrived from Judea. ¹¹He came over, took Paul's belt, and bound his own feet and hands with it. Then he said, "The Holy Spirit declares, 'So shall the owner of this belt be bound by the Jewish leaders in Jerusalem and turned over to the Gentiles.'" ¹²When we heard this, we and the local believers all begged Paul not to go on to Jerusalem.

¹³But he said, "Why all this weeping? You are breaking my heart! I am ready not only to be jailed at Jerusalem but even to die for the sake of the Lord Jesus." ¹⁴When it was clear that we couldn't persuade him, we gave up and said, "The Lord's will be done."

Paul Arrives at Jerusalem
¹⁵After this we packed our things and left for Jerusalem. ¹⁶Some believers from Caesarea accompanied us, and they took us to the home of Mnason, a man originally from Cyprus and one of the early believers. ¹⁷When we arrived, the brothers and sisters in Jerusalem welcomed us warmly.

¹⁸The next day Paul went with us to meet with James, and all the elders of the Jerusalem church were present. ¹⁹After greeting them, Paul gave a detailed account of the things God had accomplished among the Gentiles through his ministry.

²⁰After hearing this, they praised God. And then they said, "You know, dear brother, how many thousands of Jews have also believed, and they all follow the law of Moses very seriously. ²¹But the Jewish believers here in Jerusalem have been told that you are teaching all the Jews who live among the Gentiles to turn their backs on the laws of Moses. They've heard that you teach them not to circumcise their children or follow other Jewish customs. ²²What should we do? They will certainly hear that you have come.

²³"Here's what we want you to do. We have four men here who have completed their vow. ²⁴Go with them to the Temple and join them in the purification ceremony, paying for them to have their heads ritually shaved. Then everyone will know that the rumors are all false and that you yourself observe the Jewish laws. ²⁵As for the Gentile believers, they should do what we already told them in a letter: They should abstain from eating food offered to idols, from consuming blood or the meat of strangled animals, and from sexual immorality."

Paul Is Arrested
²⁶So Paul went to the Temple the next day with the other men. They had already started the purification ritual, so he publicly announced the date when their vows would end and sacrifices would be offered for each of them.

²⁷The seven days were almost ended when some Jews from the province of Asia saw Paul in the Temple and roused a mob against him. They grabbed him, ²⁸yelling, "Men of Israel, help us! This is the man who preaches against our people everywhere and tells everybody to disobey the Jewish laws. He speaks against the Temple—and even defiles this holy place by bringing in Gentiles.*" ²⁹(For earlier that day they had seen him in the city with Trophimus, a Gentile from Ephesus,* and they assumed Paul had taken him into the Temple.)

³⁰The whole city was rocked by these accu-

21:28 Greek *Greeks.*   21:29 Greek *Trophimus, the Ephesian.*

sations, and a great riot followed. Paul was grabbed and dragged out of the Temple, and immediately the gates were closed behind him. [31]As they were trying to kill him, word reached the commander of the Roman regiment that all Jerusalem was in an uproar. [32]He immediately called out his soldiers and officers* and ran down among the crowd. When the mob saw the commander and the troops coming, they stopped beating Paul.

[33]Then the commander arrested him and ordered him bound with two chains. He asked the crowd who he was and what he had done. [34]Some shouted one thing and some another. Since he couldn't find out the truth in all the uproar and confusion, he ordered that Paul be taken to the fortress. [35]As Paul reached the stairs, the mob grew so violent the soldiers had to lift him to their shoulders to protect him. [36]And the crowd followed behind, shouting, "Kill him, kill him!"

Paul Speaks to the Crowd

[37]As Paul was about to be taken inside, he said to the commander, "May I have a word with you?"

"Do you know Greek?" the commander asked, surprised. [38]"Aren't you the Egyptian who led a rebellion some time ago and took 4,000 members of the Assassins out into the desert?"

[39]"No," Paul replied, "I am a Jew and a citizen of Tarsus in Cilicia, which is an important city. Please, let me talk to these people." [40]The commander agreed, so Paul stood on the stairs and motioned to the people to be quiet. Soon a deep silence enveloped the crowd, and he addressed them in their own language, Aramaic.*

CHAPTER 22

"Brothers and esteemed fathers," Paul said, "listen to me as I offer my defense." [2]When they heard him speaking in their own language,* the silence was even greater.

[3]Then Paul said, "I am a Jew, born in Tarsus, a city in Cilicia, and I was brought up and educated here in Jerusalem under Gamaliel. As his student, I was carefully trained in our Jewish laws and customs. I became very zealous to honor God in everything I did, just like all of you today. [4]And I persecuted the followers of the Way, hounding some to death, arresting both men and women and throwing them in prison. [5]The high priest and the whole council of elders can testify that this is so. For I received letters from them to our Jewish brothers in Damascus, authorizing me to bring the Christians from there to Jerusalem, in chains, to be punished.

[6]"As I was on the road, approaching Damascus about noon, a very bright light from heaven suddenly shone down around me. [7]I fell to the ground and heard a voice saying to me, 'Saul, Saul, why are you persecuting me?'

[8]"'Who are you, lord?' I asked.

"And the voice replied, 'I am Jesus the Nazarene,* the one you are persecuting.' [9]The people with me saw the light but didn't understand the voice speaking to me.

[10]"I asked, 'What should I do, Lord?'

"And the Lord told me, 'Get up and go into Damascus, and there you will be told everything you are to do.'

[11]"I was blinded by the intense light and had to be led by the hand to Damascus by my companions. [12]A man named Ananias lived there. He was a godly man, deeply devoted to the law, and well regarded by all the Jews of Damascus. [13]He came and stood beside me and said, 'Brother Saul, regain your sight.' And that very moment I could see him!

[14]"Then he told me, 'The God of our ancestors has chosen you to know his will and to see the Righteous One and hear him speak. [15]For you are to be his witness, telling everyone what you have seen and heard. [16]What are you waiting for? Get up and be baptized. Have your sins washed away by calling on the name of the Lord.'

[17]"After I returned to Jerusalem, I was praying in the Temple and fell into a trance. [18]I saw a vision of Jesus* saying to me, 'Hurry! Leave Jerusalem, for the people here won't accept your testimony about me.'

[19]"'But Lord,' I argued, 'they certainly know that in every synagogue I imprisoned and beat those who believed in you. [20]And I was in complete agreement when your witness Stephen was killed. I stood by and kept the coats they took off when they stoned him.'

[21]"But the Lord said to me, 'Go, for I will send you far away to the Gentiles!'"

[22]The crowd listened until Paul said that word. Then they all began to shout, "Away with such a fellow! He isn't fit to live!" [23]They yelled, threw off their coats, and tossed handfuls of dust into the air.

Paul Reveals His Roman Citizenship

[24]The commander brought Paul inside and ordered him lashed with whips to make him confess his crime. He wanted to find out why the crowd had become so furious. [25]When they tied Paul down to lash him, Paul said to the officer* standing there, "Is it legal for you to whip a Roman citizen who hasn't even been tried?"

21:32 Greek *centurions*.   21:40 Or *Hebrew*.   22:2 Greek *in Aramaic*, or *in Hebrew*.   22:8 Or *Jesus of Nazareth*.
22:18 Greek *him*.   22:25 Greek *the centurion*; also in 22:26.

26 When the officer heard this, he went to the commander and asked, "What are you doing? This man is a Roman citizen!"

27 So the commander went over and asked Paul, "Tell me, are you a Roman citizen?"

"Yes, I certainly am," Paul replied.

28 "I am, too," the commander muttered, "and it cost me plenty!"

Paul answered, "But I am a citizen by birth!"

29 The soldiers who were about to interrogate Paul quickly withdrew when they heard he was a Roman citizen, and the commander was frightened because he had ordered him bound and whipped.

Paul before the High Council

30 The next day the commander ordered the leading priests into session with the Jewish high council.* He wanted to find out what the trouble was all about, so he released Paul to have him stand before them.

CHAPTER **23**

Gazing intently at the high council,* Paul began: "Brothers, I have always lived before God with a clear conscience!"

2 Instantly Ananias the high priest commanded those close to Paul to slap him on the mouth. 3 But Paul said to him, "God will slap you, you corrupt hypocrite!* What kind of judge are you to break the law yourself by ordering me struck like that?"

4 Those standing near Paul said to him, "Do you dare to insult God's high priest?"

5 "I'm sorry, brothers. I didn't realize he was the high priest," Paul replied, "for the Scriptures say, 'You must not speak evil of any of your rulers.'*"

6 Paul realized that some members of the high council were Sadducees and some were Pharisees, so he shouted, "Brothers, I am a Pharisee, as were my ancestors! And I am on trial because my hope is in the resurrection of the dead!"

7 This divided the council—the Pharisees against the Sadducees—8 for the Sadducees say there is no resurrection or angels or spirits, but the Pharisees believe in all of these. 9 So there was a great uproar. Some of the teachers of religious law who were Pharisees jumped up and began to argue forcefully. "We see nothing wrong with him," they shouted. "Perhaps a spirit or an angel spoke to him." 10 As the conflict grew more violent, the commander was afraid they would tear Paul apart. So he ordered his soldiers to go and rescue him by force and take him back to the fortress.

11 That night the Lord appeared to Paul and said, "Be encouraged, Paul. Just as you have been a witness to me here in Jerusalem, you must preach the Good News in Rome as well."

The Plan to Kill Paul

12 The next morning a group of Jews* got together and bound themselves with an oath not to eat or drink until they had killed Paul. 13 There were more than forty of them in the conspiracy. 14 They went to the leading priests and elders and told them, "We have bound ourselves with an oath to eat nothing until we have killed Paul. 15 So you and the high council should ask the commander to bring Paul back to the council again. Pretend you want to examine his case more fully. We will kill him on the way."

16 But Paul's nephew—his sister's son—heard of their plan and went to the fortress and told Paul. 17 Paul called for one of the Roman officers* and said, "Take this young man to the commander. He has something important to tell him."

18 So the officer did, explaining, "Paul, the prisoner, called me over and asked me to bring this young man to you because he has something to tell you."

19 The commander took his hand, led him aside, and asked, "What is it you want to tell me?"

20 Paul's nephew told him, "Some Jews are going to ask you to bring Paul before the high council tomorrow, pretending they want to get some more information. 21 But don't do it! There are more than forty men hiding along the way ready to ambush him. They have vowed not to eat or drink anything until they have killed him. They are ready now, just waiting for your consent."

22 "Don't let anyone know you told me this," the commander warned the young man.

Paul Is Sent to Caesarea

23 Then the commander called two of his officers and ordered, "Get 200 soldiers ready to leave for Caesarea at nine o'clock tonight. Also take 200 spearmen and 70 mounted troops. 24 Provide horses for Paul to ride, and get him safely to Governor Felix." 25 Then he wrote this letter to the governor:

26 "From Claudius Lysias, to his Excellency, Governor Felix: Greetings!

27 "This man was seized by some Jews, and they were about to kill him when I arrived with the troops. When I learned

22:30 Greek *Sanhedrin.* 23:1 Greek *Sanhedrin;* also in 23:6, 15, 20, 28. 23:3 Greek *you whitewashed wall.* 23:5 Exod 22:28. 23:12 Greek *the Jews.* 23:17 Greek *centurions;* also in 23:23.

that he was a Roman citizen, I removed him to safety. [28] Then I took him to their high council to try to learn the basis of the accusations against him. [29] I soon discovered the charge was something regarding their religious law—certainly nothing worthy of imprisonment or death. [30] But when I was informed of a plot to kill him, I immediately sent him on to you. I have told his accusers to bring their charges before you."

[31] So that night, as ordered, the soldiers took Paul as far as Antipatris. [32] They returned to the fortress the next morning, while the mounted troops took him on to Caesarea. [33] When they arrived in Caesarea, they presented Paul and the letter to Governor Felix. [34] He read it and then asked Paul what province he was from. "Cilicia," Paul answered.

[35] "I will hear your case myself when your accusers arrive," the governor told him. Then the governor ordered him kept in the prison at Herod's headquarters.*

CHAPTER 24
Paul Appears before Felix

Five days later Ananias, the high priest, arrived with some of the Jewish elders and the lawyer* Tertullus, to present their case against Paul to the governor. [2] When Paul was called in, Tertullus presented the charges against Paul in the following address to the governor:

"You have provided a long period of peace for us Jews and with foresight have enacted reforms for us. [3] For all of this, Your Excellency, we are very grateful to you. [4] But I don't want to bore you, so please give me your attention for only a moment. [5] We have found this man to be a troublemaker who is constantly stirring up riots among the Jews all over the world. He is a ringleader of the cult known as the Nazarenes. [6] Furthermore, he was trying to desecrate the Temple when we arrested him.* [8] You can find out the truth of our accusations by examining him yourself." [9] Then the other Jews chimed in, declaring that everything Tertullus said was true.

[10] The governor then motioned for Paul to speak. Paul said, "I know, sir, that you have been a judge of Jewish affairs for many years, so I gladly present my defense before you. [11] You can quickly discover that I arrived in Jerusalem no more than twelve days ago to worship at the Temple. [12] My accusers never found me arguing with anyone in the Temple, nor stirring up a riot in any synagogue or on the streets of the city. [13] These men cannot prove the things they accuse me of doing.

[14] "But I admit that I follow the Way, which they call a cult. I worship the God of our ancestors, and I firmly believe the Jewish law and everything written in the prophets. [15] I have the same hope in God that these men have, that he will raise both the righteous and the unrighteous. [16] Because of this, I always try to maintain a clear conscience before God and all people.

[17] "After several years away, I returned to Jerusalem with money to aid my people and to offer sacrifices to God. [18] My accusers saw me in the Temple as I was completing a purification ceremony. There was no crowd around me and no rioting. [19] But some Jews from the province of Asia were there—and they ought to be here to bring charges if they have anything against me! [20] Ask these men here what crime the Jewish high council* found me guilty of, [21] except for the one time I shouted out, 'I am on trial before you today because I believe in the resurrection of the dead!'"

[22] At that point Felix, who was quite familiar with the Way, adjourned the hearing and said, "Wait until Lysias, the garrison commander, arrives. Then I will decide the case." [23] He ordered an officer* to keep Paul in custody but to give him some freedom and allow his friends to visit him and take care of his needs.

[24] A few days later Felix came back with his wife, Drusilla, who was Jewish. Sending for Paul, they listened as he told them about faith in Christ Jesus. [25] As he reasoned with them about righteousness and self-control and the coming day of judgment, Felix became frightened. "Go away for now," he replied. "When it is more convenient, I'll call for you again." [26] He also hoped that Paul would bribe him, so he sent for him quite often and talked with him.

[27] After two years went by in this way, Felix was succeeded by Porcius Festus. And because Felix wanted to gain favor with the Jewish people, he left Paul in prison.

CHAPTER 25
Paul Appears before Festus

Three days after Festus arrived in Caesarea to take over his new responsibilities, he left for Jerusalem, [2] where the leading priests and other Jewish leaders met with him and made their accusations against Paul. [3] They asked Festus as a favor to transfer Paul to Jerusalem (planning

---

23:35 Greek *Herod's Praetorium.*   24:1 Greek *some elders and an orator.*   24:6 Some manuscripts add an expanded conclusion to verse 6, all of verse 7, and an additional phrase in verse 8: *We would have judged him by our law, [7]but Lysias, the commander of the garrison, came and violently took him away from us, [8]commanding his accusers to come before you.* 24:20 Greek *Sanhedrin.*   24:23 Greek *a centurion.*

to ambush and kill him on the way). ⁴But Festus replied that Paul was at Caesarea and he himself would be returning there soon. ⁵So he said, "Those of you in authority can return with me. If Paul has done anything wrong, you can make your accusations."

⁶About eight or ten days later Festus returned to Caesarea, and on the following day he took his seat in court and ordered that Paul be brought in. ⁷When Paul arrived, the Jewish leaders from Jerusalem gathered around and made many serious accusations they couldn't prove.

⁸Paul denied the charges. "I am not guilty of any crime against the Jewish laws or the Temple or the Roman government," he said.

⁹Then Festus, wanting to please the Jews, asked him, "Are you willing to go to Jerusalem and stand trial before me there?"

¹⁰But Paul replied, "No! This is the official Roman court, so I ought to be tried right here. You know very well I am not guilty of harming the Jews. ¹¹If I have done something worthy of death, I don't refuse to die. But if I am innocent, no one has a right to turn me over to these men to kill me. I appeal to Caesar!"

¹²Festus conferred with his advisers and then replied, "Very well! You have appealed to Caesar, and to Caesar you will go!"

¹³A few days later King Agrippa arrived with his sister, Bernice,* to pay their respects to Festus. ¹⁴During their stay of several days, Festus discussed Paul's case with the king. "There is a prisoner here," he told him, "whose case was left for me by Felix. ¹⁵When I was in Jerusalem, the leading priests and Jewish elders pressed charges against him and asked me to condemn him. ¹⁶I pointed out to them that Roman law does not convict people without a trial. They must be given an opportunity to confront their accusers and defend themselves.

¹⁷"When his accusers came here for the trial, I didn't delay. I called the case the very next day and ordered Paul brought in. ¹⁸But the accusations made against him weren't any of the crimes I expected. ¹⁹Instead, it was something about their religion and a dead man named Jesus, who Paul insists is alive. ²⁰I was at a loss to know how to investigate these things, so I asked him whether he would be willing to stand trial on these charges in Jerusalem. ²¹But Paul appealed to have his case decided by the emperor. So I ordered that he be held in custody until I could arrange to send him to Caesar."

²²"I'd like to hear the man myself," Agrippa said.

And Festus replied, "You will—tomorrow!"

Paul Speaks to Agrippa

²³So the next day Agrippa and Bernice arrived at the auditorium with great pomp, accompanied by military officers and prominent men of the city. Festus ordered that Paul be brought in. ²⁴Then Festus said, "King Agrippa and all who are here, this is the man whose death is demanded by all the Jews, both here and in Jerusalem. ²⁵But in my opinion he has done nothing deserving death. However, since he appealed his case to the emperor, I have decided to send him to Rome. ²⁶But what shall I write the emperor? For there is no clear charge against him. So I have brought him before all of you, and especially you, King Agrippa, so that after we examine him, I might have something to write. ²⁷For it makes no sense to send a prisoner to the emperor without specifying the charges against him!"

CHAPTER **26**

Then Agrippa said to Paul, "You may speak in your defense."

So Paul, gesturing with his hand, started his defense: ²"I am fortunate, King Agrippa, that you are the one hearing my defense today against all these accusations made by the Jewish leaders, ³for I know you are an expert on all Jewish customs and controversies. Now please listen to me patiently!

⁴"As the Jewish leaders are well aware, I was given a thorough Jewish training from my earliest childhood among my own people and in Jerusalem. ⁵If they would admit it, they know that I have been a member of the Pharisees, the strictest sect of our religion. ⁶Now I am on trial because of my hope in the fulfillment of God's promise made to our ancestors. ⁷In fact, that is why the twelve tribes of Israel zealously worship God night and day, and they share the same hope I have. Yet, Your Majesty, they accuse me for having this hope! ⁸Why does it seem incredible to any of you that God can raise the dead?

⁹"I used to believe that I ought to do everything I could to oppose the very name of Jesus the Nazarene.* ¹⁰Indeed, I did just that in Jerusalem. Authorized by the leading priests, I caused many believers* there to be sent to prison. And I cast my vote against them when they were condemned to death. ¹¹Many times I had them punished in the synagogues to get them to curse Jesus.* I was so violently opposed to them that I even chased them down in foreign cities.

¹²"One day I was on such a mission to Damascus, armed with the authority and com-

mission of the leading priests. [13]About noon, Your Majesty, as I was on the road, a light from heaven brighter than the sun shone down on me and my companions. [14]We all fell down, and I heard a voice saying to me in Aramaic,* 'Saul, Saul, why are you persecuting me? It is useless for you to fight against my will.*'

[15]"'Who are you, lord?' I asked.

"And the Lord replied, 'I am Jesus, the one you are persecuting. [16]Now get to your feet! For I have appeared to you to appoint you as my servant and witness. You are to tell the world what you have seen and what I will show you in the future. [17]And I will rescue you from both your own people and the Gentiles. Yes, I am sending you to the Gentiles [18]to open their eyes, so they may turn from darkness to light and from the power of Satan to God. Then they will receive forgiveness for their sins and be given a place among God's people, who are set apart by faith in me.'

[19]"And so, King Agrippa, I obeyed that vision from heaven. [20]I preached first to those in Damascus, then in Jerusalem and throughout all Judea, and also to the Gentiles, that all must repent of their sins and turn to God—and prove they have changed by the good things they do. [21]Some Jews arrested me in the Temple for preaching this, and they tried to kill me. [22]But God has protected me right up to this present time so I can testify to everyone, from the least to the greatest. I teach nothing except what the prophets and Moses said would happen— [23]that the Messiah would suffer and be the first to rise from the dead, and in this way announce God's light to Jews and Gentiles alike."

[24]Suddenly, Festus shouted, "Paul, you are insane. Too much study has made you crazy!"

[25]But Paul replied, "I am not insane, Most Excellent Festus. What I am saying is the sober truth. [26]And King Agrippa knows about these things. I speak boldly, for I am sure these events are all familiar to him, for they were not done in a corner! [27]King Agrippa, do you believe the prophets? I know you do—"

[28]Agrippa interrupted him. "Do you think you can persuade me to become a Christian so quickly?"*

[29]Paul replied, "Whether quickly or not, I pray to God that both you and everyone here in this audience might become the same as I am, except for these chains."

[30]Then the king, the governor, Bernice, and all the others stood and left. [31]As they went out, they talked it over and agreed, "This man hasn't done anything to deserve death or imprisonment."

first steps
SHARE YOUR OWN STORY
Read ACTS 26:1-23

Another useful tool in our "evangelistic toolbox" is the story, or testimony, of how we came to personally know Jesus Christ. Paul used this method effectively when he appeared before King Agrippa. As was often his style, he began his presentation of the gospel by explaining how he had personally come into a relationship with Christ. Then he segued into the proclamation of the gospel message (26:19-23).

Every believer has a testimony. Some may be more dramatic than others. Such was the case with Paul, formerly the notorious Saul of Tarsus, an aggressive persecutor of the church. Regardless of how incredible your testimony may seem, your personal salvation story will help you find common ground with a nonbeliever. You can tell him or her of your former life and attitude before coming to Christ, then explain the changes that came afterward. When a nonbeliever sees that you can relate to his or her own life, he or she may be more open to what you have to say.

Why don't you take a moment to think about the changes that have taken place in your life now that you are a Christian? You may even want to write down your testimony so that you will be ready to share it at the next opportunity.

To begin the next topic, turn to p. A42.

[32]And Agrippa said to Festus, "He could have been set free if he hadn't appealed to Caesar."

CHAPTER 27
Paul Sails for Rome
When the time came, we set sail for Italy. Paul and several other prisoners were placed in the custody of a Roman officer* named Julius, a captain of the Imperial Regiment. [2]Aristarchus, a Macedonian from Thessalonica, was also with us. We left on a ship whose home port was Adramyttium on the northwest coast of the province of Asia;* it was scheduled to make several stops at ports along the coast of the province.

26:14a Or *Hebrew.* **26:14b** Greek *It is hard for you to kick against the oxgoads.* **26:28** Or *"A little more, and your arguments would make me a Christian."* **27:1** Greek *centurion;* similarly in 27:6, 11, 31, 43. **27:2** *Asia* was a Roman province in what is now western Turkey.

³ The next day when we docked at Sidon, Julius was very kind to Paul and let him go ashore to visit with friends so they could provide for his needs. ⁴ Putting out to sea from there, we encountered strong headwinds that made it difficult to keep the ship on course, so we sailed north of Cyprus between the island and the mainland. ⁵ Keeping to the open sea, we passed along the coast of Cilicia and Pamphylia, landing at Myra, in the province of Lycia. ⁶ There the commanding officer found an Egyptian ship from Alexandria that was bound for Italy, and he put us on board.

⁷ We had several days of slow sailing, and after great difficulty we finally neared Cnidus. But the wind was against us, so we sailed across to Crete and along the sheltered coast of the island, past the cape of Salmone. ⁸ We struggled along the coast with great difficulty and finally arrived at Fair Havens, near the town of Lasea. ⁹ We had lost a lot of time. The weather was becoming dangerous for sea travel because it was so late in the fall,* and Paul spoke to the ship's officers about it.

¹⁰ "Men," he said, "I believe there is trouble ahead if we go on—shipwreck, loss of cargo, and danger to our lives as well." ¹¹ But the officer in charge of the prisoners listened more to the ship's captain and the owner than to Paul. ¹² And since Fair Havens was an exposed harbor—a poor place to spend the winter—most of the crew wanted to go on to Phoenix, farther up the coast of Crete, and spend the winter there. Phoenix was a good harbor with only a southwest and northwest exposure.

The Storm at Sea

¹³ When a light wind began blowing from the south, the sailors thought they could make it. So they pulled up anchor and sailed close to the shore of Crete. ¹⁴ But the weather changed abruptly, and a wind of typhoon strength (called a "northeaster") burst across the island and blew us out to sea. ¹⁵ The sailors couldn't turn the ship into the wind, so they gave up and let it run before the gale.

¹⁶ We sailed along the sheltered side of a small island named Cauda,* where with great difficulty we hoisted aboard the lifeboat being towed behind us. ¹⁷ Then the sailors bound ropes around the hull of the ship to strengthen it. They were afraid of being driven across to the sandbars of Syrtis off the African coast, so they lowered the sea anchor to slow the ship and were driven before the wind.

¹⁸ The next day, as gale-force winds continued to batter the ship, the crew began throwing the cargo overboard. ¹⁹ The following day they even took some of the ship's gear and threw it overboard. ²⁰ The terrible storm raged for many days, blotting out the sun and the stars, until at last all hope was gone.

²¹ No one had eaten for a long time. Finally, Paul called the crew together and said, "Men, you should have listened to me in the first place and not left Crete. You would have avoided all this damage and loss. ²² But take courage! None of you will lose your lives, even though the ship will go down. ²³ For last night an angel of the God to whom I belong and whom I serve stood beside me, ²⁴ and he said, 'Don't be afraid, Paul, for you will surely stand trial before Caesar! What's more, God in his goodness has granted safety to everyone sailing with you.' ²⁵ So take courage! For I believe God. It will be just as he said. ²⁶ But we will be shipwrecked on an island."

The Shipwreck

²⁷ About midnight on the fourteenth night of the storm, as we were being driven across the Sea of Adria,* the sailors sensed land was near. ²⁸ They dropped a weighted line and found that the water was 120 feet deep. But a little later they measured again and found it was only 90 feet deep.* ²⁹ At this rate they were afraid we would soon be driven against the rocks along the shore, so they threw out four anchors from the back of the ship and prayed for daylight.

³⁰ Then the sailors tried to abandon the ship; they lowered the lifeboat as though they were going to put out anchors from the front of the ship. ³¹ But Paul said to the commanding officer and the soldiers, "You will all die unless the sailors stay aboard." ³² So the soldiers cut the ropes to the lifeboat and let it drift away.

³³ Just as day was dawning, Paul urged everyone to eat. "You have been so worried that you haven't touched food for two weeks," he said. ³⁴ "Please eat something now for your own good. For not a hair of your heads will perish." ³⁵ Then he took some bread, gave thanks to God before them all, and broke off a piece and ate it. ³⁶ Then everyone was encouraged and began to eat—³⁷ all 276 of us who were on board. ³⁸ After eating, the crew lightened the ship further by throwing the cargo of wheat overboard.

³⁹ When morning dawned, they didn't recognize the coastline, but they saw a bay with a beach and wondered if they could get to shore by running the ship aground. ⁴⁰ So they cut off the anchors and left them in the sea. Then they

---

27:9 Greek *because the fast was now already gone by.* This fast was associated with the Day of Atonement (*Yom Kippur*), which occurred in late September or early October. 27:16 Some manuscripts read *Clauda.* 27:27 The *Sea of Adria* includes the central portion of the Mediterranean. 27:28 Greek *20 fathoms . . . 15 fathoms* [37 meters . . . 27 meters].

lowered the rudders, raised the foresail, and headed toward shore. [41] But they hit a shoal and ran the ship aground too soon. The bow of the ship stuck fast, while the stern was repeatedly smashed by the force of the waves and began to break apart.

[42] The soldiers wanted to kill the prisoners to make sure they didn't swim ashore and escape. [43] But the commanding officer wanted to spare Paul, so he didn't let them carry out their plan. Then he ordered all who could swim to jump overboard first and make for land. [44] The others held on to planks or debris from the broken ship.* So everyone escaped safely to shore.

CHAPTER **28**

Paul on the Island of Malta

Once we were safe on shore, we learned that we were on the island of Malta. [2] The people of the island were very kind to us. It was cold and rainy, so they built a fire on the shore to welcome us.

[3] As Paul gathered an armful of sticks and was laying them on the fire, a poisonous snake, driven out by the heat, bit him on the hand. [4] The people of the island saw it hanging from his hand and said to each other, "A murderer, no doubt! Though he escaped the sea, justice will not permit him to live." [5] But Paul shook off the snake into the fire and was unharmed. [6] The people waited for him to swell up or suddenly drop dead. But when they had waited a long time and saw that he wasn't harmed, they changed their minds and decided he was a god.

[7] Near the shore where we landed was an estate belonging to Publius, the chief official of the island. He welcomed us and treated us kindly for three days. [8] As it happened, Publius's father was ill with fever and dysentery. Paul went in and prayed for him, and laying his hands on him, he healed him. [9] Then all the other sick people on the island came and were healed. [10] As a result we were showered with honors, and when the time came to sail, people supplied us with everything we would need for the trip.

Paul Arrives at Rome

[11] It was three months after the shipwreck that we set sail on another ship that had wintered at the island—an Alexandrian ship with the twin gods* as its figurehead. [12] Our first stop was Syracuse,* where we stayed three days. [13] From there we sailed across to Rhegium.* A day later a south wind began blowing, so the following day we sailed up the coast to Puteoli. [14] There we found some believers,* who invited us to spend a week with them. And so we came to Rome.

[15] The brothers and sisters* in Rome had heard we were coming, and they came to meet us at the Forum* on the Appian Way. Others joined us at The Three Taverns.* When Paul saw them, he was encouraged and thanked God.

[16] When we arrived in Rome, Paul was permitted to have his own private lodging, though he was guarded by a soldier.

Paul Preaches at Rome under Guard

[17] Three days after Paul's arrival, he called together the local Jewish leaders. He said to them, "Brothers, I was arrested in Jerusalem and handed over to the Roman government, even though I had done nothing against our people or the customs of our ancestors. [18] The Romans tried me and wanted to release me, because they found no cause for the death sentence. [19] But when the Jewish leaders protested the decision, I felt it necessary to appeal to Caesar, even though I had no desire to press charges against my own people. [20] I asked you to come here today so we could get acquainted and so I could explain to you that I am bound with this chain because I believe that the hope of Israel—the Messiah—has already come."

[21] They replied, "We have had no letters from Judea or reports against you from anyone who has come here. [22] But we want to hear what you believe, for the only thing we know about this movement is that it is denounced everywhere."

[23] So a time was set, and on that day a large number of people came to Paul's lodging. He explained and testified about the Kingdom of God and tried to persuade them about Jesus from the Scriptures. Using the law of Moses and the books of the prophets, he spoke to them from morning until evening. [24] Some were persuaded by the things he said, but others did not believe. [25] And after they had argued back and forth among themselves, they left with this final word from Paul: "The Holy Spirit was right when he said to your ancestors through Isaiah the prophet,

[26] 'Go and say to this people:
When you hear what I say,
    you will not understand.
When you see what I do,
    you will not comprehend.

27:44 Or *or were helped by members of the ship's crew.*   **28:11** The *twin gods* were the Roman gods Castor and Pollux.
28:12 *Syracuse* was on the island of Sicily.   **28:13** *Rhegium* was on the southern tip of Italy.   **28:14** Greek *brothers.*
28:15a Greek *brothers.*   **28:15b** *The Forum* was about 43 miles (70 kilometers) from Rome.   **28:15c** *The Three Taverns* was about 35 miles (57 kilometers) from Rome.

²⁷ For the hearts of these people are hardened,
    and their ears cannot hear,
    and they have closed their eyes—
so their eyes cannot see,
    and their ears cannot hear,
    and their hearts cannot understand,
and they cannot turn to me
    and let me heal them.'*

²⁸ So I want you to know that this salvation from God has also been offered to the Gentiles, and they will accept it."*

³⁰ For the next two years, Paul lived in Rome at his own expense.* He welcomed all who visited him, ³¹ boldly proclaiming the Kingdom of God and teaching about the Lord Jesus Christ. And no one tried to stop him.

28:26-27 Isa 6:9-10 (Greek version). **28:28** Some manuscripts add verse 29, *And when he had said these words, the Jews departed, greatly disagreeing with each other.* **28:30** Or *in his own rented quarters.*

Romans

AUTHOR: PAUL | DATE WRITTEN: A.D. 58 | GENRE: EPISTLE

This epistle contains some of the prime secrets of the Christian life. It is a hard-hitting diagnosis of the primary source of man's problems: sin. It also shows the futility of thinking that the answers to our problems lie within ourselves.

CHAPTER 1

Greetings from Paul

This letter is from Paul, a slave of Christ Jesus, chosen by God to be an apostle and sent out to preach his Good News. ²God promised this Good News long ago through his prophets in the holy Scriptures. ³The Good News is about his Son. In his earthly life he was born into King David's family line, ⁴and he was shown to be* the Son of God when he was raised from the dead by the power of the Holy Spirit.* He is Jesus Christ our Lord. ⁵Through Christ, God has given us the privilege* and authority as apostles to tell Gentiles everywhere what God has done for them, so that they will believe and obey him, bringing glory to his name.

⁶And you are included among those Gentiles who have been called to belong to Jesus Christ. ⁷I am writing to all of you in Rome who are loved by God and are called to be his own holy people.

May God our Father and the Lord Jesus Christ give you grace and peace.

God's Good News

⁸Let me say first that I thank my God through Jesus Christ for all of you, because your faith in him is being talked about all over the world. ⁹God knows how often I pray for you. Day and night I bring you and your needs in prayer to God, whom I serve with all my heart* by spreading the Good News about his Son. ¹⁰One of the things I always pray for is the opportunity, God willing, to come at last to see you. ¹¹For I long to visit you so I can bring you some spiritual gift that will help you grow strong in the Lord. ¹²When we get together, I want to encourage you in your faith, but I also want to be encouraged by yours.

¹³I want you to know, dear brothers and sisters,* that I planned many times to visit you, but I was prevented until now. I want to work among you and see spiritual fruit, just as I have seen among other Gentiles. ¹⁴For I have a great sense of obligation to people in both the civilized world and the rest of the world,* to the educated and uneducated alike. ¹⁵So I am eager to come to you in Rome, too, to preach the Good News.

¹⁶For I am not ashamed of this Good News about Christ. It is the power of God at work, saving everyone who believes—the Jew first and also the Gentile.* ¹⁷This Good News tells us how God makes us right in his sight. This is accomplished from start to finish by faith. As the Scriptures say, "It is through faith that a righteous person has life."*

God's Anger at Sin

¹⁸But God shows his anger from heaven against all sinful, wicked people who suppress the truth by their wickedness.* ¹⁹They know the truth about God because he has made it obvious to them. ²⁰For ever since the world was created, people have seen the earth and sky. Through everything God made, they can clearly see his invisible qualities—his eternal power and divine nature. So they have no excuse for not knowing God.

²¹Yes, they knew God, but they wouldn't worship him as God or even give him thanks. And they began to think up foolish ideas of what

1:4a Or *and was designated.* 1:4b Or *by the Spirit of holiness;* or *in the new realm of the Spirit.* 1:5 Or *the grace.* 1:9 Or *in my spirit.* 1:13 Greek *brothers.* 1:14 Greek *to Greeks and barbarians.* 1:16 Greek *also the Greek.* 1:17 Or *"The righteous will live by faith"* Hab 2:4. 1:18 Or *who, by their wickedness, prevent the truth from being known.*

God was like. As a result, their minds became dark and confused. [22] Claiming to be wise, they instead became utter fools. [23] And instead of worshiping the glorious, ever-living God, they worshiped idols made to look like mere people and birds and animals and reptiles.

[24] So God abandoned them to do whatever shameful things their hearts desired. As a result, they did vile and degrading things with each other's bodies. [25] They traded the truth about God for a lie. So they worshiped and served the things God created instead of the Creator himself, who is worthy of eternal praise! Amen. [26] That is why God abandoned them to their shameful desires. Even the women turned against the natural way to have sex and instead indulged in sex with each other. [27] And the men, instead of having normal sexual relations with women, burned with lust for each other. Men did shameful things with other men, and as a result of this sin, they suffered within themselves the penalty they deserved.

[28] Since they thought it foolish to acknowledge God, he abandoned them to their foolish thinking and let them do things that should never be done. [29] Their lives became full of every kind of wickedness, sin, greed, hate, envy, murder, quarreling, deception, malicious behavior, and gossip. [30] They are backstabbers, haters of God, insolent, proud, and boastful. They invent new ways of sinning, and they disobey their parents. [31] They refuse to understand, break their promises, are heartless, and have no mercy. [32] They know God's justice requires that those who do these things deserve to die, yet they do them anyway. Worse yet, they encourage others to do them, too.

CHAPTER **2**
God's Judgment of Sin

You may think you can condemn such people, but you are just as bad, and you have no excuse! When you say they are wicked and should be punished, you are condemning yourself, for you who judge others do these very same things. [2] And we know that God, in his justice, will punish anyone who does such things. [3] Since you judge others for doing these things, why do you think you can avoid God's judgment when you do the same things? [4] Don't you see how wonderfully kind, tolerant, and patient God is with you? Does this mean nothing to you? Can't you see that his kindness is intended to turn you from your sin?

[5] But because you are stubborn and refuse to turn from your sin, you are storing up terrible punishment for yourself. For a day of anger is coming, when God's righteous judgment will be revealed. [6] He will judge everyone according to what they have done. [7] He will give eternal life to those who keep on doing good, seeking after the glory and honor and immortality that God offers. [8] But he will pour out his anger and wrath on those who live for themselves, who refuse to obey the truth and instead live lives of wickedness. [9] There will be trouble and calamity for everyone who keeps on doing what is evil—for the Jew first and also for the Gentile.* [10] But there will be glory and honor and peace from God for all who do good—for the Jew first and also for the Gentile. [11] For God does not show favoritism.

[12] When the Gentiles sin, they will be destroyed, even though they never had God's written law. And the Jews, who do have God's law, will be judged by that law when they fail to obey it. [13] For merely listening to the law doesn't make us right with God. It is obeying the law that makes us right in his sight. [14] Even Gentiles, who do not have God's written law, show that they know his law when they instinctively obey it, even without having heard it. [15] They demonstrate that God's law is written in their hearts, for their own conscience and thoughts either accuse them or tell them they are doing right. [16] And this is the message I proclaim—that the day is coming when God, through Christ Jesus, will judge everyone's secret life.

The Jews and the Law

[17] You who call yourselves Jews are relying on God's law, and you boast about your special relationship with him. [18] You know what he wants; you know what is right because you have been taught his law. [19] You are convinced that you are a guide for the blind and a light for people who are lost in darkness. [20] You think you can instruct the ignorant and teach children the ways of God. For you are certain that God's law gives you complete knowledge and truth.

[21] Well then, if you teach others, why don't you teach yourself? You tell others not to steal, but do you steal? [22] You say it is wrong to commit adultery, but do you commit adultery? You condemn idolatry, but do you use items stolen from pagan temples?* [23] You are so proud of knowing the law, but you dishonor God by breaking it. [24] No wonder the Scriptures say, "The Gentiles blaspheme the name of God because of you."*

[25] The Jewish ceremony of circumcision has value only if you obey God's law. But if you don't obey God's law, you are no better off than an

---

2:9 Greek *also for the Greek;* also in 2:10.   **2:22** Greek *do you steal from temples?*   **2:24** Isa 52:5 (Greek version).

What Happens to Those Who Have Never Heard the Gospel?

Read ROMANS 1:18-20

Sometimes the person who asks this question is not so much concerned about those who have never heard the gospel. Rather, this person may be more concerned about trying to put up a smoke screen to keep you—the Christian—from showing his or her need for God. We might remind that person that God is loving and compassionate, and that he will deal fairly and justly with those who have never heard the gospel. But the person who asks you this question needs to recognize that knowledge brings responsibility. Those who know the truth of the gospel will be held accountable.

As we know from the Bible, God will judge us according to what we know of him (see Luke 12:48, p. 83). We will not be held accountable for what we do not know. Still, that does not excuse us from all responsibility. Otherwise we might say, "Ignorance is bliss." But this is not to say that the person who has not heard of Jesus will never know of him.

We, as humans, no matter where we live on God's earth, were born with a soul, an emptiness, a sense that life should have meaning and purpose. In spite of that spiritual longing, we have disregarded God and his Word. But

if we are truly seeking God, he will reveal himself to us. We find proof of this in Acts 10:1-48 (pp. 143-144). There, a man named Cornelius, a religious man who constantly prayed to God, asked the Lord to reveal himself to him. Although Cornelius may have heard of Jesus Christ, he did not know God's plan for salvation. But that did not stop God from answering his prayer by sending the apostle Peter to preach the gospel to him. When Cornelius heard that wonderful message, he believed!

The Bible tells us that God is unchanging (Malachi 3:6; see also James 1:17, p. 289). He is the same yesterday, today, and tomorrow. If he heard Cornelius's prayer, he will also hear the prayers of those who do not know him but desire to.

For the next "Big Question" note, turn to p. 171.

---

uncircumcised Gentile. [26]And if the Gentiles obey God's law, won't God declare them to be his own people? [27]In fact, uncircumcised Gentiles who keep God's law will condemn you Jews who are circumcised and possess God's law but don't obey it.

[28]For you are not a true Jew just because you were born of Jewish parents or because you have gone through the ceremony of circumcision. [29]No, a true Jew is one whose heart is right with God. And true circumcision is not merely obeying the letter of the law; rather, it is a change of heart produced by God's Spirit. And a person with a changed heart seeks praise* from God, not from people.

CHAPTER **3**

God Remains Faithful

Then what's the advantage of being a Jew? Is there any value in the ceremony of circumcision? [2]Yes, there are great benefits! First of all, the Jews were entrusted with the whole revelation of God.*

[3]True, some of them were unfaithful; but just because they were unfaithful, does that mean God will be unfaithful? [4]Of course not! Even if everyone else is a liar, God is true. As the Scriptures say about him,

"You will be proved right in what you say,
and you will win your case in court."*

2:29 Or *receives praise.* **3:2** Greek *the oracles of God.* **3:4** Ps 51:4 (Greek version).

⁵"But," some might say, "our sinfulness serves a good purpose, for it helps people see how righteous God is. Isn't it unfair, then, for him to punish us?" (This is merely a human point of view.) ⁶Of course not! If God were not entirely fair, how would he be qualified to judge the world? ⁷"But," someone might still argue, "how can God condemn me as a sinner if my dishonesty highlights his truthfulness and brings him more glory?" ⁸And some people even slander us by claiming that we say, "The more we sin, the better it is!" Those who say such things deserve to be condemned.

All People Are Sinners

⁹Well then, should we conclude that we Jews are better than others? No, not at all, for we have already shown that all people, whether Jews or Gentiles,* are under the power of sin. ¹⁰As the Scriptures say,

"No one is righteous—
    not even one.
¹¹ No one is truly wise;
    no one is seeking God.
¹² All have turned away;
    all have become useless.
No one does good,
    not a single one."*
¹³ "Their talk is foul, like the stench from an
    open grave.
Their tongues are filled with lies."*
"Snake venom drips from their lips."*
¹⁴   "Their mouths are full of cursing and
    bitterness."*
¹⁵ "They rush to commit murder.
¹⁶   Destruction and misery always follow
    them.
¹⁷ They don't know where to find peace."*
¹⁸   "They have no fear of God at all."*

¹⁹Obviously, the law applies to those to whom it was given, for its purpose is to keep people from having excuses, and to show that the entire world is guilty before God. ²⁰For no one can ever be made right with God by doing what the law commands. The law simply shows us how sinful we are.

Christ Took Our Punishment

²¹But now God has shown us a way to be made right with him without keeping the requirements of the law, as was promised in the writings of Moses* and the prophets long ago. ²²We are made right with God by placing our faith in Jesus Christ. And this is true for everyone who believes, no matter who we are.

²³For everyone has sinned; we all fall short of God's glorious standard. ²⁴Yet God, with undeserved kindness, declares that we are righteous. He did this through Christ Jesus when he freed us from the penalty for our sins. ²⁵For God presented Jesus as the sacrifice for sin. People are made right with God when they believe that Jesus sacrificed his life, shedding his blood. This sacrifice shows that God was being fair when he held back and did not punish those who sinned in times past, ²⁶for he was looking ahead and including them in what he would do in this present time. God did this to demonstrate his righteousness, for he himself is fair and just, and he declares sinners to be right in his sight when they believe in Jesus.

²⁷Can we boast, then, that we have done anything to be accepted by God? No, because our acquittal is not based on obeying the law. It is based on faith. ²⁸So we are made right with God through faith and not by obeying the law.

²⁹After all, is God the God of the Jews only? Isn't he also the God of the Gentiles? Of course he is. ³⁰There is only one God, and he makes people right with himself only by faith, whether they are Jews or Gentiles.* ³¹Well then, if we emphasize faith, does this mean that we can forget about the law? Of course not! In fact, only when we have faith do we truly fulfill the law.

CHAPTER **4**
The Faith of Abraham

Abraham was, humanly speaking, the founder of our Jewish nation. What did he discover about being made right with God? ²If his good deeds had made him acceptable to God, he would have had something to boast about. But that was not God's way. ³For the Scriptures tell us, "Abraham believed God, and God counted him as righteous because of his faith."*

⁴When people work, their wages are not a gift, but something they have earned. ⁵But people are counted as righteous, not because of their work, but because of their faith in God who forgives sinners. ⁶David also spoke of this when he described the happiness of those who are declared righteous without working for it:

⁷ "Oh, what joy for those
    whose disobedience is forgiven,
    whose sins are put out of sight.
⁸ Yes, what joy for those
    whose record the LORD has cleared of
    sin."*

3:9 Greek or Greeks.   **3:10-12** Pss 14:1-3; 53:1-3 (Greek version).   **3:13** Pss 5:9 (Greek version); 140:3.   **3:14** Ps 10:7 (Greek version).   **3:15-17** Isa 59:7-8.   **3:18** Ps 36:1.   **3:21** Greek in the law.   **3:30** Greek whether they are circumcised or uncircumcised.   **4:3** Gen 15:6.   **4:7-8** Ps 32:1-2 (Greek version).

BIG QUESTIONS

If God Is So Good, Why Do Bad Things Happen to His People?

Read ROMANS 5:1-5

Sickness, war, accidents, natural disasters, tragedies—they come to the just and the unjust, the Christian and the non-Christian, the moral and the immoral. Yet, if God is so good and all-powerful, why doesn't he just wipe out evil things in this world? This question often arises after any tragedy, but especially when it affects people who you would think should be "immune" to such things.

In addressing this question, it is important to remember that God originally created the world perfect. But he also gave man the freedom to obey or disobey. When Adam sinned, death and suffering became an inevitable part of life (Romans 5:12). Yet, as Christian thinker C. S. Lewis observed, it is idle for us to speculate about the *origin* of evil. The problem we all face is the *fact* of evil. The only

solution to the fact of evil is God's solution, Jesus Christ [Paul Little, *How to Give Away Your Faith* (Downers Grove, Ill.: InterVarsity Press, 1966), p. 72].

How is Jesus Christ the solution to the fact of evil? The moment you surrendered your life to Jesus Christ, you entered into the master plan that God has for you. Though it is true that you may not know what the future holds, you know who holds the future. And he has promised that all things work together for good to those that love God (see Romans 8:28, p. 177). Not just the good things, but all things. As Scripture says, "Everything serves [God's] plans" (Psalm 119:91).

That is easy to say when things are going smoothly. But when something unexpected comes into the pic-

ture, we may wonder if God is paying attention. That is when we need to realize that God is painting on a large canvas. He is looking at the big picture. We only see what is in front of us at the given moment.

God will allow many events to come into our life—good things, bad things, things that make sense, things that make no sense at all. But every one of these incidents in our lives serves as a part of his plan for us. Tragedy in itself is not good. But God can take tragedy and hardship and use them for his glory. As God's children, we know that everything that happens to us first goes through his screen of protection. And he will never give us more than we can handle (see 1 Corinthians 10:13, p. 200). For that reason we can follow the advice in Romans 5:3 and rejoice. We have the assurance that God is working in our lives to strengthen and develop our character. More important, he will never leave our side (see Hebrews 13:5, p. 287).

For the next "Big Question" note, turn to p. 181.

[9] Now, is this blessing only for the Jews, or is it also for uncircumcised Gentiles?* Well, we have been saying that Abraham was counted as righteous by God because of his faith. [10] But how did this happen? Was he counted as righteous only after he was circumcised, or was it before he was circumcised? Clearly, God accepted Abraham before he was circumcised! [11] Circumcision was a sign that Abraham already had faith and that God had already accepted him and declared him to be righteous—even before he was circumcised. So Abraham is the spiritual father of those who have faith but have not been circumcised. They are counted as righteous because of their faith. [12] And Abraham is also the spiritual father of those who

4:9 Greek *is this blessing only for the circumcised, or is it also for the uncircumcised?*

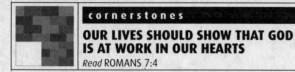

cornerstones

OUR LIVES SHOULD SHOW THAT GOD IS AT WORK IN OUR HEARTS
Read ROMANS 7:4

While we still live on this side of heaven, we will always struggle between the desire to obey God and the desire to follow our sinful instincts. Even the apostle Paul knew what it was like to struggle with sin. In the verses surrounding this text, he describes the six keys to winning this battle and living a life that not only pleases God, but shows that God is working in our heart:

1. Admit the Power of Sin in Your Life (see Romans 7:14, p. 176). Recognize that you have that combustible nature within you, a vulnerability to the enticements of sin. If we fail to see our potential weaknesses, we are even more vulnerable to fall to them. The Bible warns against such an attitude, saying, "If you think you are standing strong, be careful not to fall" (1 Corinthians 10:12).

2. Realize That You Are Powerless to Change on Your Own (see Romans 7:18, p. 176). Your sinful nature is the source of the problem. You will never "master" sin and live a life pleasing to God on your own. Apart from God, you can do nothing.

3. Become "Fed Up" with Your Condition and Cry for Help (see Romans 7:24, p. 176). You cannot control evil in your life by simply determining to do so. You have to come to the end of yourself and ask for God's help in this struggle.

4. Accept Your Freedom (see Romans 7:25, p. 176). Take the hand of help that is offered to you by Jesus.

5. Accept God's Forgiveness and Lack of Condemnation (see Romans 8:1-2, p. 176). Because of your unique union with Christ, God will forgive you—not condemn you—when you acknowledge your failures, struggles, and broken commitments.

6. Cut the Instinctive Actions of Your Sinful Nature (see Romans 8:3-8, p. 176). The only way to stop committing instinctive sinful actions is to stop living by your sinful nature and start living by the power of the Holy Spirit. How do you do this? As Romans 8:6 implies, you must relinquish control of your mind to the Spirit. When you do this, you will be "controlled by the Holy Spirit" and "think about things that please the Spirit" (Romans 8:5).

You will always have the potential to sin. But God has given you the power to overcome sin through his Holy Spirit. The key to drawing on his power is to be obedient to the Holy Spirit.

For the next note on "Faith and Works," turn to p. 292.

---

have been circumcised, but only if they have the same kind of faith Abraham had before he was circumcised.

¹³Clearly, God's promise to give the whole earth to Abraham and his descendants was based not on his obedience to God's law, but on a right relationship with God that comes by faith. ¹⁴If God's promise is only for those who obey the law, then faith is not necessary and the promise is pointless. ¹⁵For the law always brings punishment on those who try to obey it. (The only way to avoid breaking the law is to have no law to break!)

¹⁶So the promise is received by faith. It is given as a free gift. And we are all certain to receive it, whether or not we live according to the law of Moses, if we have faith like Abraham's.

For Abraham is the father of all who believe. ¹⁷That is what the Scriptures mean when God told him, "I have made you the father of many nations."* This happened because Abraham believed in the God who brings the dead back to life and who creates new things out of nothing.

¹⁸Even when there was no reason for hope, Abraham kept hoping—believing that he would become the father of many nations. For God had said to him, "That's how many descendants you will have!"* ¹⁹And Abraham's faith did not weaken, even though, at about 100 years of age, he figured his body was as good as dead—and so was Sarah's womb.

²⁰Abraham never wavered in believing God's promise. In fact, his faith grew stronger, and in this he brought glory to God. ²¹He was fully

4:17 Gen 17:5.   4:18 Gen 15:5.

convinced that God is able to do whatever he promises. ²²And because of Abraham's faith, God counted him as righteous. ²³And when God counted him as righteous, it wasn't just for Abraham's benefit. It was recorded ²⁴for our benefit, too, assuring us that God will also count us as righteous if we believe in him, the one who raised Jesus our Lord from the dead. ²⁵He was handed over to die because of our sins, and he was raised to life to make us right with God.

CHAPTER 5
Faith Brings Joy

Therefore, since we have been made right in God's sight by faith, we have peace with God because of what Jesus Christ our Lord has done for us. ²Because of our faith, Christ has brought us into this place of undeserved privilege where we now stand, and we confidently and joyfully look forward to sharing God's glory.

³We can rejoice, too, when we run into problems and trials, for we know that they help us develop endurance. ⁴And endurance develops strength of character, and character strengthens our confident hope of salvation. ⁵And this hope will not lead to disappointment. For we know how dearly God loves us, because he has given us the Holy Spirit to fill our hearts with his love.

⁶When we were utterly helpless, Christ came at just the right time and died for us sinners. ⁷Now, most people would not be willing to die for an upright person, though someone might perhaps be willing to die for a person who is especially good. ⁸But God showed his great love for us by sending Christ to die for us while we were still sinners. ⁹And since we have been made right in God's sight by the blood of Christ, he will certainly save us from God's condemnation. ¹⁰For since our friendship with God was restored by the death of his Son while we were still his enemies, we will certainly be saved through the life of his Son. ¹¹So now we can rejoice in our wonderful new relationship with God because our Lord Jesus Christ has made us friends of God.

Adam and Christ Contrasted

¹²When Adam sinned, sin entered the world. Adam's sin brought death, so death spread to everyone, for everyone sinned. ¹³Yes, people sinned even before the law was given. But it was not counted as sin because there was not yet any law to break. ¹⁴Still, everyone died—from the time of Adam to the time of Moses—even those who did not disobey an explicit commandment of God, as Adam did. Now Adam is a symbol, a representation of Christ, who was yet to come. ¹⁵But there is a great difference between Adam's sin and God's gracious gift. For the sin of this one man, Adam, brought

first steps

GOD'S SPIRIT WILL HELP YOU OVERCOME SIN
Read ROMANS 8:9-14

This powerful passage of Scripture contains some critical truths we need to know about letting the Holy Spirit lead our lives. Remember, once you became a Christian, God gave you his Holy Spirit to help you live out your faith, guide your steps, empower your witness, and, as this passage attests, overcome sin. Look at four key points the apostle Paul makes here:

1. You Are Controlled by a New Nature. Your old, sinful nature will still try to get a hand on the steering wheel. But now your new nature is in the driver's seat, and your old nature has become like an annoying backseat driver. You can either give in to your old nature's nagging and bad directions, or you can ignore it and let the Holy Spirit direct your path.

2. Even Though You Will Face Physical Death, You Will Not Face Spiritual Death. As a believer, physical death is simply a transition to eternal life in heaven. You have been spared from spiritual death, which leads to everlasting torment and hell (see Revelation 21:8, p. 335). This important fact should reassure you when the devil tries to throw doubts your way.

3. The Same Spirit of God That Raised Jesus from the Dead Resides in *You*. Did you catch that? The Holy Spirit, who had the power to raise Jesus from the dead, now lives in you! If that is indeed true—and God's Word says it is—just think of the supernatural power you now have in your life to resist sin!

4. We Do Not Have to Give In to Our Sinful Nature and Urges. Paul wasn't talking about New Year's resolutions here. If we try to live a morally upright, godly life in our own strength, we will fail—and fail miserably. But, if we rely on the power of the Holy Spirit to help us, we will be overcomers.

To begin the next topic, turn to p. A41.

cornerstones

LIVE TO PLEASE GOD
Read ROMANS 8:5-8

Living to please God may seem like a daunting task. And for some, it is. They struggle to live up to a list of do's and don'ts. They try to obtain God's favor through acts of kindness and compassion. They attempt to "appease" God for their sinful behavior by going to church or making a confession. But this passage—in fact, this entire chapter in Romans—lets you know that it *is* possible to live a life that is pure and pleasing to God.

The beginning verses of this chapter explain that once we enter into a relationship with Jesus Christ, God frees us from the vicious circle of sin and death through the power of his Holy Spirit. This terminology illustrates the basis of our freedom: In essence, the Holy Spirit you received by accepting Jesus Christ into your life has made you a slave of Jesus Christ—not a slave of your sinful nature.

The apostle Paul often identified himself as a slave of Jesus Christ in his writings. He used the word *doulos,* which means "servant by choice." This word was readily understood by those in the Roman culture. A "doulos," or "bondslave," was a slave who had been granted freedom by his master, but who loved his master so deeply that he voluntarily chose to continue on as that master's servant. Likewise, Paul was not a slave to Christ because he had to be; he was a slave to Christ because he *wanted* to be. He had totally surrendered himself to his Master.

The only way to be free from sin is to be "bound" to Jesus. Unless you completely surrender your life to the Lord, all of your efforts to lead a pure life will be futile. That old sinful nature will continue to rear its ugly head and influence your thoughts and actions. But if you are a bondslave of Jesus, following the leading of the Holy Spirit (Romans 8:5), you will not serve God out of fear and duty but out of love and gratitude. Your service will not be motivated by a desire to earn God's approval but will be motivated by a desire to be close to Jesus, recognizing that you already have that approval because of what Jesus did for you. This "blessed" bondage gives you the will, the power, and the motivation to live a life that is pleasing to God.

To begin the next topic, turn to p. A31.

---

death to many. But even greater is God's wonderful grace and his gift of forgiveness to many through this other man, Jesus Christ. [16]And the result of God's gracious gift is very different from the result of that one man's sin. For Adam's sin led to condemnation, but God's free gift leads to our being made right with God, even though we are guilty of many sins. [17]For the sin of this one man, Adam, caused death to rule over many. But even greater is God's wonderful grace and his gift of righteousness, for all who receive it will live in triumph over sin and death through this one man, Jesus Christ.

[18]Yes, Adam's one sin brings condemnation for everyone, but Christ's one act of righteousness brings a right relationship with God and new life for everyone. [19]Because one person disobeyed God, many became sinners. But because one other person obeyed God, many will be made righteous.

[20]God's law was given so that all people could see how sinful they were. But as people sinned more and more, God's wonderful grace became more abundant. [21]So just as sin ruled over all people and brought them to death, now God's wonderful grace rules instead, giving us right standing with God and resulting in eternal life through Jesus Christ our Lord.

CHAPTER **6**
Sin's Power Is Broken
Well then, should we keep on sinning so that God can show us more and more of his wonderful grace? [2]Of course not! Since we have died to sin, how can we continue to live in it? [3]Or have you forgotten that when we were joined with Christ Jesus in baptism, we joined him in his death? [4]For we died and were buried with Christ by baptism. And just as Christ was raised from the dead by the glorious power of the Father, now we also may live new lives.

[5]Since we have been united with him in his death, we will also be raised to life as he was. [6]We know that our old sinful selves were crucified with Christ so that sin might lose its power in our lives. We are no longer slaves to sin. [7]For

when we died with Christ we were set free from the power of sin. ⁸And since we died with Christ, we know we will also live with him. ⁹We are sure of this because Christ was raised from the dead, and he will never die again. Death no longer has any power over him. ¹⁰When he died, he died once to break the power of sin. But now that he lives, he lives for the glory of God. ¹¹So you also should consider yourselves to be dead to the power of sin and alive to God through Christ Jesus.

¹²Do not let sin control the way you live;* do not give in to sinful desires. ¹³Do not let any part of your body become an instrument of evil to serve sin. Instead, give yourselves completely to God, for you were dead, but now you have new life. So use your whole body as an instrument to do what is right for the glory of God. ¹⁴Sin is no longer your master, for you no longer live under the requirements of the law. Instead, you live under the freedom of God's grace.

¹⁵Well then, since God's grace has set us free from the law, does that mean we can go on sinning? Of course not! ¹⁶Don't you realize that you become the slave of whatever you choose to obey? You can be a slave to sin, which leads to death, or you can choose to obey God, which leads to righteous living. ¹⁷Thank God! Once you were slaves of sin, but now you wholeheartedly obey this teaching we have given you. ¹⁸Now you are free from your slavery to sin, and you have become slaves to righteous living.

¹⁹Because of the weakness of your human nature, I am using the illustration of slavery to help you understand all this. Previously, you let yourselves be slaves to impurity and lawlessness, which led ever deeper into sin. Now you must give yourselves to be slaves to righteous living so that you will become holy. ²⁰When you were slaves to sin, you were free from the obligation to do right. ²¹And what was the result? You are now ashamed of the things you used to do, things that end in eternal doom. ²²But now you are free from the power of sin and have become slaves of God. Now you do those things that lead to holiness and result in eternal life. ²³For the wages of sin is death, but the free gift of God is eternal life through Christ Jesus our Lord.

CHAPTER 7
No Longer Bound to the Law
Now, dear brothers and sisters*—you who are familiar with the law—don't you know that the law applies only while a person is living? ²For example, when a woman marries, the law binds her to her husband as long as he is alive. But if he dies,

first steps
PRAYER IS NOT A SOLITARY EXPERIENCE
Read ROMANS 8:26-27

Have you ever wondered what to say to God? Perhaps you have a sick friend that you don't know how to pray for. Or maybe you are unsure of how to pray for your spiritual needs. This portion of Scripture will encourage you. From the moment you asked Jesus to be your personal Lord and Savior, you received a resident guest in your heart: the Holy Spirit.

One of the many things he does is to help you in prayer—especially at those times when you don't know what to pray. As you realize how intimately God is involved in your prayers, you will begin to feel a unique closeness to your Father in heaven. You may even discover a freshness in your prayer life that you never had before.

The next time you don't know what to pray for, ask the Holy Spirit to help you voice your concerns and needs to God.

For the next note on "Pray," turn to p. 291.

the laws of marriage no longer apply to her. ³So while her husband is alive, she would be committing adultery if she married another man. But if her husband dies, she is free from that law and does not commit adultery when she remarries.

⁴So, my dear brothers and sisters, this is the point: You died to the power of the law when you died with Christ. And now you are united with the one who was raised from the dead. As a result, we can produce a harvest of good deeds for God. ⁵When we were controlled by our old nature,* sinful desires were at work within us, and the law aroused these evil desires that produced a harvest of sinful deeds, resulting in death. ⁶But now we have been released from the law, for we died to it and are no longer captive to its power. Now we can serve God, not in the old way of obeying the letter of the law, but in the new way of living in the Spirit.

God's Law Reveals Our Sin
⁷Well then, am I suggesting that the law of God is sinful? Of course not! In fact, it was the law that showed me my sin. I would never have known that coveting is wrong if the law had not

6:12 Or *Do not let sin reign in your body, which is subject to death.*   **7:1** Greek *brothers;* also in 7:4.   **7:5** Greek *When we were in the flesh.*

said, "You must not covet."* [8] But sin used this command to arouse all kinds of covetous desires within me! If there were no law, sin would not have that power. [9] At one time I lived without understanding the law. But when I learned the command not to covet, for instance, the power of sin came to life, [10] and I died. So I discovered that the law's commands, which were supposed to bring life, brought spiritual death instead. [11] Sin took advantage of those commands and deceived me; it used the commands to kill me. [12] But still, the law itself is holy, and its commands are holy and right and good.

[13] But how can that be? Did the law, which is good, cause my death? Of course not! Sin used what was good to bring about my condemnation to death. So we can see how terrible sin really is. It uses God's good commands for its own evil purposes.

Struggling with Sin

[14] So the trouble is not with the law, for it is spiritual and good. The trouble is with me, for I am all too human, a slave to sin. [15] I don't really understand myself, for I want to do what is right, but I don't do it. Instead, I do what I hate. [16] But if I know that what I am doing is wrong, this shows that I agree that the law is good. [17] So I am not the one doing wrong; it is sin living in me that does it.

[18] And I know that nothing good lives in me, that is, in my sinful nature.* I want to do what is right, but I can't. [19] I want to do what is good, but I don't. I don't want to do what is wrong, but I do it anyway. [20] But if I do what I don't want to do, I am not really the one doing wrong; it is sin living in me that does it.

[21] I have discovered this principle of life—that when I want to do what is right, I inevitably do what is wrong. [22] I love God's law with all my heart. [23] But there is another power* within me that is at war with my mind. This power makes me a slave to the sin that is still within me. [24] Oh, what a miserable person I am! Who will free me from this life that is dominated by sin and death? [25] Thank God! The answer is in Jesus Christ our Lord. So you see how it is: In my mind I really want to obey God's law, but because of my sinful nature I am a slave to sin.

CHAPTER **8**

Life in the Spirit

So now there is no condemnation for those who belong to Christ Jesus. [2] And because you belong to him, the power* of the life-giving Spirit has freed you* from the power of sin that leads to death. [3] The law of Moses was unable to save us because of the weakness of our sinful nature.* So God did what the law could not do. He sent his own Son in a body like the bodies we sinners have. And in that body God declared an end to sin's control over us by giving his Son as a sacrifice for our sins. [4] He did this so that the just requirement of the law would be fully satisfied for us, who no longer follow our sinful nature but instead follow the Spirit.

[5] Those who are dominated by the sinful nature think about sinful things, but those who are controlled by the Holy Spirit think about things that please the Spirit. [6] So letting your sinful nature control your mind leads to death. But letting the Spirit control your mind leads to life and peace. [7] For the sinful nature is always hostile to God. It never did obey God's laws, and it never will. [8] That's why those who are still under the control of their sinful nature can never please God.

[9] But you are not controlled by your sinful nature. You are controlled by the Spirit if you have the Spirit of God living in you. (And remember that those who do not have the Spirit of Christ living in them do not belong to him at all.) [10] And Christ lives within you, so even though your body will die because of sin, the Spirit gives you life* because you have been made right with God. [11] The Spirit of God, who raised Jesus from the dead, lives in you. And just as God raised Christ Jesus from the dead, he will give life to your mortal bodies by this same Spirit living within you.

[12] Therefore, dear brothers and sisters,* you have no obligation to do what your sinful nature urges you to do. [13] For if you live by its dictates, you will die. But if through the power of the Spirit you put to death the deeds of your sinful nature,* you will live. [14] For all who are led by the Spirit of God are children* of God.

[15] So you have not received a spirit that makes you fearful slaves. Instead, you received God's Spirit when he adopted you as his own children.* Now we call him, "Abba, Father."* [16] For his Spirit joins with our spirit to affirm that we are God's children. [17] And since we are his children, we are his heirs. In fact, together with Christ we are heirs of God's glory. But if we are to share his glory, we must also share his suffering.

The Future Glory

[18] Yet what we suffer now is nothing compared to the glory he will reveal to us later. [19] For all

---

7:7 Exod 20:17; Deut 5:21.   **7:18** Greek *my flesh;* also in 7:25.   **7:23** Greek *law;* also in 7:23b.   **8:2a** Greek *the law;* also in 8:2b.   **8:2b** Some manuscripts read *me.*   **8:3** Greek *our flesh;* similarly in 8:4, 5, 6, 7, 8, 9, 12.   **8:10** Or *your spirit is alive.* **8:12** Greek *brothers;* also in 8:29.   **8:13** Greek *deeds of the body.*   **8:14** Greek *sons;* also in 8:19.   **8:15a** Greek *you received a spirit of sonship.*   **8:15b** *Abba* is an Aramaic term for "father."

creation is waiting eagerly for that future day when God will reveal who his children really are. [20]Against its will, all creation was subjected to God's curse. But with eager hope, [21]the creation looks forward to the day when it will join God's children in glorious freedom from death and decay. [22]For we know that all creation has been groaning as in the pains of childbirth right up to the present time. [23]And we believers also groan, even though we have the Holy Spirit within us as a foretaste of future glory, for we long for our bodies to be released from sin and suffering. We, too, wait with eager hope for the day when God will give us our full rights as his adopted children,* including the new bodies he has promised us. [24]We were given this hope when we were saved. (If we already have something, we don't need to hope* for it. [25]But if we look forward to something we don't yet have, we must wait patiently and confidently.)

[26]And the Holy Spirit helps us in our weakness. For example, we don't know what God wants us to pray for. But the Holy Spirit prays for us with groanings that cannot be expressed in words. [27]And the Father who knows all hearts knows what the Spirit is saying, for the Spirit pleads for us believers* in harmony with God's own will. [28]And we know that God causes everything to work together* for the good of those who love God and are called according to his purpose for them. [29]For God knew his people in advance, and he chose them to become like his Son, so that his Son would be the firstborn* among many brothers and sisters. [30]And having chosen them, he called them to come to him. And having called them, he gave them right standing with himself. And having given them right standing, he gave them his glory.

Nothing Can Separate Us from God's Love
[31]What shall we say about such wonderful things as these? If God is for us, who can ever be against us? [32]Since he did not spare even his own Son but gave him up for us all, won't he also give us everything else? [33]Who dares accuse us whom God has chosen for his own? No one—for God himself has given us right standing with himself. [34]Who then will condemn us? No one—for Christ Jesus died for us and was raised to life for us, and he is sitting in the place of honor at God's right hand, pleading for us.

[35]Can anything ever separate us from Christ's love? Does it mean he no longer loves us if we

8:23 Greek *wait anxiously for sonship.*   8:24 Some manuscripts read *wait.*   8:27 Greek *for God's holy people.*   8:28 Some manuscripts read *And we know that everything works together.*   8:29 Or *would be supreme.*

first steps

UNCONDITIONALLY SURRENDER YOUR LIFE
Read ROMANS 12:1-2

This passage of Scripture is what we call a conditional promise. The last part of verse 2 contains the promise. Yet if we want to discover God's perfect will for our lives, we must meet the three conditions mentioned at the beginning of these verses.

1. We Must Present Ourselves to God as Living Sacrifices. We need to recognize that we, as Christians, belong to God. The Bible tells us that we no longer own our bodies because Christ paid for them when he died on the cross (see 1 Corinthians 6:19b-20, p. 196). Because our bodies belong to him, we must refrain from sinning. This is what is meant by living sacrifice—putting aside our own will and replacing it with God's.

2. We Must Not Be Conformed to This World. The next step to prepare our hearts to know the will of God is to keep from copying "the behavior and customs of this world" (12:2). When the Bible speaks of the world, it is not referring to the earth. Rather it is speaking of the mentality and thinking of the times—the spiritually bankrupt mind-set that is hostile toward the things of God and primarily focuses on mankind's own selfish desires.

3. We Must Be Transformed by the Renewing of Our Minds. One of the best ways to become "a new person" (12:2) is to literally saturate your mind and heart with those things that spiritually build you up. You can do this by studying God's Word, singing hymns and praises, spending time in prayer, and fellowshiping with other believers. As the apostle Paul tells us, "Fix your thoughts on what is true, and honorable, and right, and pure, and lovely, and admirable. Think about things that are excellent and worthy of praise" (Philippians 4:8).

As we take these preliminary steps, we will be able to more accurately discern the will of God for our lives.

For the next note on "Seek God's Will," turn to p. 251.

have trouble or calamity, or are persecuted, or hungry, or destitute, or in danger, or threatened with death? [36](As the Scriptures say, "For your sake we are killed every day; we are being slaughtered like sheep."*) [37]No, despite all these things, overwhelming victory is ours through Christ, who loved us.

[38]And I am convinced that nothing can ever separate us from God's love. Neither death nor life, neither angels nor demons,* neither our fears for today nor our worries about tomorrow—not even the powers of hell can separate us from God's love. [39]No power in the sky above or in the earth below—indeed, nothing in all creation will ever be able to separate us from the love of God that is revealed in Christ Jesus our Lord.

CHAPTER **9**
God's Selection of Israel
With Christ as my witness, I speak with utter truthfulness. My conscience and the Holy Spirit confirm it. [2]My heart is filled with bitter sorrow and unending grief [3]for my people, my Jewish brothers and sisters.* I would be willing to be forever cursed—cut off from Christ!—if that would save them. [4]They are the people of Israel, chosen to be God's adopted children.* God revealed his glory to them. He made covenants with them and gave them his law. He gave them the privilege of worshiping him and receiving his wonderful promises. [5]Abraham, Isaac, and Jacob are their ancestors, and Christ himself was an Israelite as far as his human nature is concerned. And he is God, the one who rules over everything and is worthy of eternal praise! Amen.*

[6]Well then, has God failed to fulfill his promise to Israel? No, for not all who are born into the nation of Israel are truly members of God's people! [7]Being descendants of Abraham doesn't make them truly Abraham's children. For the Scriptures say, "Isaac is the son through whom your descendants will be counted,"* though Abraham had other children, too. [8]This means that Abraham's physical descendants are not necessarily children of God. Only the children of the promise are considered to be Abraham's children. [9]For God had promised, "I will return about this time next year, and Sarah will have a son."*

[10]This son was our ancestor Isaac. When he married Rebekah, she gave birth to twins.* [11]But before they were born, before they had done anything good or bad, she received a message from God. (This message shows that God chooses people according to his own purposes; [12]he calls people, but not according to their good or bad works.) She was told, "Your older son will serve your younger son."* [13]In the words of the Scriptures, "I loved Jacob, but I rejected Esau."*

[14]Are we saying, then, that God was unfair? Of course not! [15]For God said to Moses,

"I will show mercy to anyone
    I choose,
    and I will show compassion
    to anyone I choose."*

[16]So it is God who decides to show mercy. We can neither choose it nor work for it. [17]For the Scriptures say that God told Pharaoh, "I have appointed you for the very purpose of displaying my power in you and to spread my fame throughout the earth."* [18]So you see, God chooses to show mercy to some,

8:36 Ps 44:22.   **8:38** Greek *nor rulers*.   **9:3** Greek *my brothers*.   **9:4** Greek *chosen for sonship*.   **9:5** Or *May God, the one who rules over everything, be praised forever. Amen.*   **9:7** Gen 21:12.   **9:9** Gen 18:10, 14.   **9:10** Greek *she conceived children through this one man*.   **9:12** Gen 25:23.   **9:13** Mal 1:2-3.   **9:15** Exod 33:19.   **9:17** Exod 9:16 (Greek version).

off and running
KEEP YOUR SPIRITUAL ZEAL ALIVE
Read ROMANS 12:11

This verse not only encourages us to keep our zeal for God alive, it commands us to do so. Another meaning of the phrase "serve the Lord enthusiastically" is to have a burning heart for God. The importance of this is seen in the book of Revelation. There Jesus warned the church in Laodicea that they were in danger of being "spit . . . out of [his] mouth" because they were lukewarm (Revelation 3:15-16). In essence, they had lost the fire of their spiritual zeal and were an offense to Christ. Therefore, Jesus told them to repent or he would reject them.

So what can be done to keep our spiritual zeal alive? We can keep fueling our

and he chooses to harden the hearts of others so they refuse to listen.

¹⁹Well then, you might say, "Why does God blame people for not responding? Haven't they simply done what he makes them do?"

²⁰No, don't say that. Who are you, a mere human being, to argue with God? Should the thing that was created say to the one who created it, "Why have you made me like this?" ²¹When a potter makes jars out of clay, doesn't he have a right to use the same lump of clay to make one jar for decoration and another to throw garbage into? ²²In the same way, even though God has the right to show his anger and his power, he is very patient with those on whom his anger falls, who are destined for destruction. ²³He does this to make the riches of his glory shine even brighter on those to whom he shows mercy, who were prepared in advance for glory. ²⁴And we are among those whom he selected, both from the Jews and from the Gentiles.

²⁵Concerning the Gentiles, God says in the prophecy of Hosea,

"Those who were not my people,
    I will now call my people.
And I will love those
    whom I did not love before."*

²⁶And,

"Then, at the place where they were told,
    'You are not my people,'
there they will be called
    'children of the living God.'"*

²⁷And concerning Israel, Isaiah the prophet cried out,

"Though the people of Israel are as
    numerous as the sand of the seashore,
only a remnant will be saved.

²⁸For the LORD will carry out his sentence
    upon the earth
quickly and with finality."*

²⁹And Isaiah said the same thing in another place:

"If the LORD of Heaven's Armies
    had not spared a few of our children,
we would have been wiped out like Sodom,
    destroyed like Gomorrah."*

Israel's Unbelief

³⁰What does all this mean? Even though the Gentiles were not trying to follow God's standards, they were made right with God. And it was by faith that this took place. ³¹But the people of Israel, who tried so hard to get right with God by keeping the law, never succeeded. ³²Why not? Because they were trying to get right with God by keeping the law* instead of by trusting in him. They stumbled over the great rock in their path. ³³God warned them of this in the Scriptures when he said,

"I am placing a stone in Jerusalem* that
    makes people stumble,
a rock that makes them fall.
But anyone who trusts in him
    will never be disgraced."*

CHAPTER **10**

Dear brothers and sisters,* the longing of my heart and my prayer to God is for the people of Israel to be saved. ²I know what enthusiasm they have for God, but it is misdirected zeal. ³For they don't understand God's way of making people right with himself. Refusing to accept God's way, they cling to their own way of getting right with God by trying to keep the law.

9:25 Hos 2:23.   9:26 Greek *sons of the living God*. Hos 1:10.   9:27-28 Isa 10:22-23 (Greek version).   9:29 Isa 1:9.
9:32 Greek *by works*.   9:33a Greek *in Zion*.   9:33b Isa 8:14; 28:16 (Greek version).   10:1 Greek *Brothers*.

spiritual fire by spending time with God's people in fellowship and prayer. We can also feed the fire with constant input from God's Word. As two discouraged disciples realized, listening to the words of Jesus can rekindle a person's zeal for God: "They said to each other, 'Didn't our hearts burn within us as he talked with us on the road and explained the Scriptures to us?'" (Luke 24:32).

What is your spiritual temperature? Are you passionate about the Lord you serve? Do you make the most of every opportunity to tell others about Jesus? The English evangelist John Wesley once said, "Give me a hundred men who love God with all of their hearts and fear nothing but sin, and I will move the world." If you are aglow with the Spirit, serving the Lord with zeal and enthusiasm, your life *will* make a difference.

To begin the next topic, turn to p. A47.

cornerstones

OUR PEACE CONTINUES AS WE FOLLOW THE HOLY SPIRIT
Read ROMANS 8:5-8

Even if you are a Christian, you still must struggle with your sinful nature. However, if you allow God's Holy Spirit to control your life, that struggle will be much less intense. For, as this passage says, you will want to live to please God.

If you follow your old evil desires, you "can never please God" (Romans 8:8). Your life—whether you realize it or not—will be empty. But if you live the Spirit-controlled life, you will experience "life and peace" (Romans 8:6). To enter into the Spirit-controlled life, follow the advice of the apostle Paul, "Think about the things of heaven, not the things of earth. For you died to this life, and your real life is hidden with Christ in God" (Colossians 3:2-3).

For the next note on "Peace," turn to p. 246).

---

[4] For Christ has already accomplished the purpose for which the law was given.* As a result, all who believe in him are made right with God.

Salvation Is for Everyone
[5] For Moses writes that the law's way of making a person right with God requires obedience to all of its commands.* [6] But faith's way of getting right with God says, "Don't say in your heart, 'Who will go up to heaven?' (to bring Christ down to earth). [7] And don't say, 'Who will go down to the place of the dead?' (to bring Christ back to life again)." [8] In fact, it says,

"The message is very close at hand;
    it is on your lips and in your heart."*

And that message is the very message about faith that we preach: [9] If you confess with your mouth that Jesus is Lord and believe in your heart that God raised him from the dead, you will be saved. [10] For it is by believing in your heart that you are made right with God, and it is by confessing with your mouth that you are saved. [11] As the Scriptures tell us, "Anyone who trusts in him will never be disgraced."* [12] Jew and Gentile* are the same in this respect. They have the same Lord, who gives generously to all who call on him. [13] For "Everyone who calls on the name of the LORD will be saved."*

[14] But how can they call on him to save them unless they believe in him? And how can they believe in him if they have never heard about him? And how can they hear about him unless someone tells them? [15] And how will anyone go and tell them without being sent? That is why the Scriptures say, "How beautiful are the feet of messengers who bring good news!"*

[16] But not everyone welcomes the Good News, for Isaiah the prophet said, "LORD, who

has believed our message?"* [17] So faith comes from hearing, that is, hearing the Good News about Christ. [18] But I ask, have the people of Israel actually heard the message? Yes, they have:

"The message has gone throughout the earth,
    and the words to all the world."*

[19] But I ask, did the people of Israel really understand? Yes, they did, for even in the time of Moses, God said,

"I will rouse your jealousy through people
    who are not even a nation.
I will provoke your anger through the
    foolish Gentiles."*

[20] And later Isaiah spoke boldly for God, saying,

"I was found by people who were not
    looking for me.
I showed myself to those who were not
    asking for me."*

[21] But regarding Israel, God said,

"All day long I opened my arms to them,
    but they were disobedient and
    rebellious."*

CHAPTER 11
God's Mercy on Israel
I ask, then, has God rejected his own people, the nation of Israel? Of course not! I myself am an Israelite, a descendant of Abraham and a member of the tribe of Benjamin.

[2] No, God has not rejected his own people, whom he chose from the very beginning. Do you realize what the Scriptures say about this? Elijah the prophet complained to God about the people of Israel and said, [3] "LORD, they have killed your prophets and torn down your altars.

10:4 Or *For Christ is the end of the law.*   **10:5** See Lev 18:5.   **10:6-8** Deut 30:12-14.   **10:11** Isa 28:16 (Greek version).
10:12 Greek *and Greek.*   **10:13** Joel 2:32.   **10:15** Isa 52:7.   **10:16** Isa 53:1.   **10:18** Ps 19:4.   **10:19** Deut 32:21.
10:20 Isa 65:1 (Greek version).   **10:21** Isa 65:2 (Greek version).

BIG QUESTIONS

How Should I View Authority?

Read ROMANS 13:1-2

When dealing with the subject of authority—particularly how one should act toward those in the government—the Bible gives us some important things to consider.

God Raises Up Rulers. It is true that not every government official has been obedient to God. In fact, far too many have directly violated his Word. Yet God has allowed certain people to rule for his purposes. In the Old Testament God often allowed certain "evil" countries to come to power in order to punish Israel for their wrongdoing and to remind them of their need to return to God. Therefore, we need to respect those in authority, since God has divinely appointed them.

God Uses Those in Government Who Fear Him. While God is ultimately in control of every event that takes place in the world, he still uses his people in strategic positions of power. When Queen Esther, a Jew, faced the prospect of seeing her people put to death,

her Uncle Mordecai challenged her with these words: "If you keep quiet at a time like this, deliverance and relief for the Jews will arise from some other place, but you and your relatives will die. Who knows if perhaps you were made queen for just such a time as this?" (Esther 4:14). Certainly, God does not forbid us to be part of the political process. Sometimes he will even use Christians in government to accomplish his purposes.

We Are to Be a Witness to Those in Authority. Your obedience to the laws of the land serves as a witness to the God you serve. Peter, addressing the early Christians who were suffering persecution under the cruel tyranny of Nero, still challenged believers to be law-abiding citizens (see 1 Peter 2:13-15, p. 297).

Our Allegiance to God Should Always Come First. What about those times when a law or government does something that directly contradicts

God's law? We are accountable to a higher authority. In the Old Testament we read how Daniel defied the king's decree that forbade people to pray to anyone but the king (Daniel 6:1-28). Daniel knew that God had said to worship him alone, so he obeyed God's law instead of man's. As you may recall, he was sent to the lions' den, but God spared his life by shutting the lions' mouths. In the New Testament, Peter told the high priest, when he had been warned not to talk about Jesus, "We must obey God rather than any human authority" (Acts 5:29). In more recent times, Christians in Communist and Muslim countries continue to share Christ and distribute Bibles, despite laws that make such actions illegal.

Perhaps the best approach to those in authority over us is to follow the advice found in 1 Peter 2:17: "Fear God, and respect the king." Here we see a perfect balance, for as we fear God in our daily lives, we will live above reproach and be examples to those in authority. At the same time, we will be able to discern when human laws contradict the divine laws established by God.

For the next "Big Question" note, turn to p. 193.

I am the only one left, and now they are trying to kill me, too."*

⁴And do you remember God's reply? He said, "No, I have 7,000 others who have never bowed down to Baal!"*

⁵It is the same today, for a few of the people of Israel* have remained faithful because of God's grace—his undeserved kindness in choosing them. ⁶And since it is through God's kindness, then it is not by their good works. For in that case, God's grace would not be what it really is—free and undeserved.

11:3 1 Kgs 19:10, 14.   **11:4** 1 Kgs 19:18.   **11:5** Greek *for a remnant.*

⁷So this is the situation: Most of the people of Israel have not found the favor of God they are looking for so earnestly. A few have—the ones God has chosen—but the hearts of the rest were hardened. ⁸As the Scriptures say,

"God has put them into a deep sleep.
To this day he has shut their eyes so they do
    not see,
    and closed their ears so they do not hear."*

⁹Likewise, David said,

"Let their bountiful table become a snare,
    a trap that makes them think all is well.
Let their blessings cause them to stumble,
    and let them get what they deserve.
¹⁰ Let their eyes go blind so they cannot see,
    and let their backs be bent forever."*

¹¹Did God's people stumble and fall beyond recovery? Of course not! They were disobedient, so God made salvation available to the Gentiles. But he wanted his own people to become jealous and claim it for themselves. ¹²Now if the Gentiles were enriched because the people of Israel turned down God's offer of salvation, think how much greater a blessing the world will share when they finally accept it.

¹³I am saying all this especially for you Gentiles. God has appointed me as the apostle to the Gentiles. I stress this, ¹⁴for I want somehow to make the people of Israel jealous of what you Gentiles have, so I might save some of them. ¹⁵For since their rejection meant that God offered salvation to the rest of the world, their acceptance will be even more wonderful. It will be life for those who were dead! ¹⁶And since Abraham and the other patriarchs were holy, their descendants will also be holy—just as the entire batch of dough is holy because the portion given as an offering is holy. For if the roots of the tree are holy, the branches will be, too.

¹⁷But some of these branches from Abraham's tree—some of the people of Israel—have been broken off. And you Gentiles, who were branches from a wild olive tree, have been grafted in. So now you also receive the blessing God has promised Abraham and his children, sharing in the rich nourishment from the root of God's special olive tree. ¹⁸But you must not brag about being grafted in to replace the branches that were broken off. You are just a branch, not the root.

¹⁹"Well," you may say, "those branches were broken off to make room for me." ²⁰Yes, but remember—those branches were broken off because they didn't believe in Christ, and you are there because you do believe. So don't think highly of yourself, but fear what could happen. ²¹For if God did not spare the original branches, he won't* spare you either.

²²Notice how God is both kind and severe. He is severe toward those who disobeyed, but kind to you if you continue to trust in his kindness. But if you stop trusting, you also will be cut off. ²³And if the people of Israel turn from their unbelief, they will be grafted in again, for God has the power to graft them back into the tree. ²⁴You, by nature, were a branch cut from a wild olive tree. So if God was willing to do something contrary to nature by grafting you into his cultivated tree, he will be far more eager to graft the original branches back into the tree where they belong.

God's Mercy Is for Everyone

²⁵I want you to understand this mystery, dear brothers and sisters,* so that you will not feel proud about yourselves. Some of the people of Israel have hard hearts, but this will last only until the full number of Gentiles comes to Christ. ²⁶And so all Israel will be saved. As the Scriptures say,

"The one who rescues will come from
    Jerusalem,*
and he will turn Israel* away from
    ungodliness.
²⁷ And this is my covenant with them,
    that I will take away their sins."*

²⁸Many of the people of Israel are now enemies of the Good News, and this benefits you Gentiles. Yet they are still the people he loves because he chose their ancestors Abraham, Isaac, and Jacob. ²⁹For God's gifts and his call can never be withdrawn. ³⁰Once, you Gentiles were rebels against God, but when the people of Israel rebelled against him, God was merciful to you instead. ³¹Now they are the rebels, and God's mercy has come to you so that they, too, will share* in God's mercy. ³²For God has imprisoned everyone in disobedience so he could have mercy on everyone.

³³Oh, how great are God's riches and wisdom and knowledge! How impossible it is for us to understand his decisions and his ways!

³⁴ For who can know the LORD's thoughts?
    Who knows enough to give him advice?*
³⁵ And who has given him so much
    that he needs to pay it back?*

11:8 Isa 29:10; Deut 29:4.   11:9-10 Ps 69:22-23 (Greek version).   11:21 Some manuscripts read *perhaps he won't*.
11:25 Greek *brothers*.   11:26a Greek *from Zion*.   11:26b Greek *Jacob*.   11:26-27 Isa 59:20-21; 27:9 (Greek version).
11:31 Other manuscripts read *will now share;* still others read *will someday share*.   11:34 Isa 40:13 (Greek version).
11:35 See Job 41:11.

36 For everything comes from him and exists by his power and is intended for his glory. All glory to him forever! Amen.

CHAPTER 12

A Living Sacrifice to God

And so, dear brothers and sisters,* I plead with you to give your bodies to God because of all he has done for you. Let them be a living and holy sacrifice—the kind he will find acceptable. This is truly the way to worship him.* 2 Don't copy the behavior and customs of this world, but let God transform you into a new person by changing the way you think. Then you will learn to know God's will for you, which is good and pleasing and perfect.

3 Because of the privilege and authority* God has given me, I give each of you this warning: Don't think you are better than you really are. Be honest in your evaluation of yourselves, measuring yourselves by the faith God has given us.* 4 Just as our bodies have many parts and each part has a special function, 5 so it is with Christ's body. We are many parts of one body, and we all belong to each other.

6 In his grace, God has given us different gifts for doing certain things well. So if God has given you the ability to prophesy, speak out with as much faith as God has given you. 7 If your gift is serving others, serve them well. If you are a teacher, teach well. 8 If your gift is to encourage others, be encouraging. If it is giving, give generously. If God has given you leadership ability, take the responsibility seriously. And if you have a gift for showing kindness to others, do it gladly.

9 Don't just pretend to love others. Really love them. Hate what is wrong. Hold tightly to what is good. 10 Love each other with genuine affection,* and take delight in honoring each other. 11 Never be lazy, but work hard and serve the Lord enthusiastically.* 12 Rejoice in our confident hope. Be patient in trouble, and keep on praying. 13 When God's people are in need, be ready to help them. Always be eager to practice hospitality.

14 Bless those who persecute you. Don't curse them; pray that God will bless them. 15 Be happy with those who are happy, and weep with those who weep. 16 Live in harmony with each other. Don't be too proud to enjoy the company of ordinary people. And don't think you know it all!

12:1a Greek brothers.   12:1b Or This is your spiritual worship; or This is your reasonable service.   12:3a Or Because of the grace; compare 1:5.   12:3b Or by the faith God has given you; or by the standard of our God-given faith.   12:10 Greek with brotherly love.   12:11 Or but serve the Lord with a zealous spirit; or but let the Spirit excite you as you serve the Lord.

---

first steps

PUT ON GOD'S ARMOR

Read ROMANS 13:11-14

Another way the last verse of this text has been translated is "Be Christ's men from head to foot, and give no chances to the flesh to have its fling." In other words, we need to "clothe ourselves" with Christ. To do this, you need to let him be a part of everything that you do. Let him go with you everywhere you go. Let him act through you in every decision you make. Remember these three simple truths as you strive to obey Christ:

1. Time Is Short. Jesus Christ will return soon, and we need to be the best possible witness for him that we can be.

2. Live in the Light. As Ephesians 5:8 says, "For once you were full of darkness, but now you have light from the Lord. So live as people of light!" The more you live in God's light, the less you will want to be influenced by the darkness of the world around you.

3. Rely upon Christ for Your Strength. You will never be able to stand against the temptations of life on your own. As you follow Christ and his example, you will find it much easier to avoid spiritual pitfalls. As it has been said, "The best defense is a good offense."

Some people want to put God in a little compartment. They will worship God from nine to eleven on Sunday morning, but the rest of the week is theirs. That is not the Christian life. As true followers of Jesus Christ, we need to be identified with our Master twenty-four hours a day, seven days a week, for the rest of our lives.

For the next note on "Obey God," turn to p. 245.

¹⁷Never pay back evil with more evil. Do things in such a way that everyone can see you are honorable. ¹⁸Do all that you can to live in peace with everyone.

¹⁹Dear friends, never take revenge. Leave that to the righteous anger of God. For the Scriptures say,

"I will take revenge;
 I will pay them back,"*
 says the Lord.

²⁰Instead,

"If your enemies are hungry, feed them.
 If they are thirsty, give them something
   to drink.
 In doing this, you will heap
   burning coals of shame on
     their heads."*

²¹Don't let evil conquer you, but conquer evil by doing good.

CHAPTER 13
Respect for Authority

Everyone must submit to governing authorities. For all authority comes from God, and those in positions of authority have been placed there by God. ²So anyone who rebels against authority is rebelling against what God has instituted, and they will be punished. ³For the authorities do not strike fear in people who are doing right, but in those who are doing wrong. Would you like to live without fear of the authorities? Do what is right, and they will honor you. ⁴The authorities are God's servants, sent for your good. But if you are doing wrong, of course you should be afraid, for they have the power to punish you. They are God's servants, sent for the very purpose of punishing those who do what is wrong. ⁵So you must submit to them, not only to avoid punishment, but also to keep a clear conscience.

⁶Pay your taxes, too, for these same reasons. For government workers need to be paid. They are serving God in what they do. ⁷Give to everyone what you owe them: Pay your taxes and government fees to those who collect them, and give respect and honor to those who are in authority.

Love Fulfills God's Requirements

⁸Owe nothing to anyone—except for your obligation to love one another. If you love your neighbor, you will fulfill the requirements of God's law. ⁹For the commandments say, "You must not commit adultery. You must not murder. You must not steal. You must not covet."* These—and other such commandments—are summed up in this one commandment: "Love your neighbor as yourself."* ¹⁰Love does no wrong to others, so love fulfills the requirements of God's law.

¹¹This is all the more urgent, for you know how late it is; time is running out. Wake up, for our salvation is nearer now than when we first believed. ¹²The night is almost gone; the day of salvation will soon be here. So remove your dark deeds like dirty clothes, and put on the shining armor of right living. ¹³Because we belong to the day, we must live decent lives for all to see. Don't participate in the darkness of wild parties and drunkenness, or in sexual promiscuity and immoral living, or in quarreling and jealousy. ¹⁴Instead, clothe yourself with the presence of the Lord Jesus Christ. And don't let yourself think about ways to indulge your evil desires.

CHAPTER 14
The Danger of Criticism

Accept other believers who are weak in faith, and don't argue with them about what they think is right or wrong. ²For instance, one person believes it's all right to eat anything. But another believer with a sensitive conscience will eat only vegetables. ³Those who feel free to eat anything must not look down on those who don't. And those who don't eat certain foods must not con-

12:19 Deut 32:35. **12:20** Prov 25:21-22. **13:9a** Exod 20:13-15, 17. **13:9b** Lev 19:18.

off and running

COULD THIS ACTIVITY CAUSE OTHER CHRISTIANS TO STUMBLE IN THEIR FAITH?
Read ROMANS 14:3-21

Don't do anything that will bring criticism against yourself, even if you know that a certain activity is all right. What we do and become has a direct effect on others—not only

demn those who do, for God has accepted them. [4]Who are you to condemn someone else's servants? Their own master will judge whether they stand or fall. And with the Lord's help, they will stand and receive his approval.

[5]In the same way, some think one day is more holy than another day, while others think every day is alike. You should each be fully convinced that whichever day you choose is acceptable. [6]Those who worship the Lord on a special day do it to honor him. Those who eat any kind of food do so to honor the Lord, since they give thanks to God before eating. And those who refuse to eat certain foods also want to please the Lord and give thanks to God. [7]For we don't live for ourselves or die for ourselves. [8]If we live, it's to honor the Lord. And if we die, it's to honor the Lord. So whether we live or die, we belong to the Lord. [9]Christ died and rose again for this very purpose—to be Lord both of the living and of the dead.

[10]So why do you condemn another believer*? Why do you look down on another believer? Remember, we will all stand before the judgment seat of God. [11]For the Scriptures say,

"'As surely as I live,' says the LORD,
'every knee will bend to me,
    and every tongue will confess and give
        praise to God.*'"

[12]Yes, each of us will give a personal account to God. [13]So let's stop condemning each other. Decide instead to live in such a way that you will not cause another believer to stumble and fall.

[14]I know and am convinced on the authority of the Lord Jesus that no food, in and of itself, is wrong to eat. But if someone believes it is wrong, then for that person it is wrong. [15]And if another believer is distressed by what you eat, you are not acting in love if you eat it. Don't let your eating ruin someone for whom Christ died. [16]Then you will not be criticized for doing something you believe is good. [17]For the Kingdom of God is not a matter of what we eat or drink, but of living a life of goodness and peace and joy in the Holy Spirit. [18]If you serve Christ with this attitude, you will please God, and others will approve of you, too. [19]So then, let us aim for harmony in the church and try to build each other up.

[20]Don't tear apart the work of God over what you eat. Remember, all foods are acceptable, but it is wrong to eat something if it makes another person stumble. [21]It is better not to eat meat or drink wine or do anything else if it might cause another believer to stumble. [22]You may believe there's nothing wrong with what you are doing, but keep it between yourself and God. Blessed are those who don't feel guilty for doing something they have decided is right. [23]But if you have doubts about whether or not you should eat something, you are sinning if you go ahead and do it. For you are not following your convictions. If you do anything you believe is not right, you are sinning.

CHAPTER 15
Living to Please Others

We who are strong must be considerate of those who are sensitive about things like this. We must not just please ourselves. [2]We should help others do what is right and build them up in the Lord. [3]For even Christ didn't live to please himself. As the Scriptures say, "The insults of those who insult you, O God, have fallen on me."* [4]Such things were written in the Scriptures long ago to teach us. And the Scriptures give us hope and encouragement as we wait patiently for God's promises to be fulfilled.

[5]May God, who gives this patience and encouragement, help you live in complete harmony with each other, as is fitting for followers of Christ Jesus. [6]Then all of you can join together with one voice, giving praise and glory to God, the Father of our Lord Jesus Christ.

[7]Therefore, accept each other just as Christ

14:10 Greek *your brother;* also in 14:10b, 13, 15, 21.   **14:11** Or *confess allegiance to God.* Isa 49:18; 45:23 (Greek version).
15:3 Greek *who insult you have fallen on me.* Ps 69:9.

---

for our life here on this earth, but also for eternity. We not only need to live our lives conscious of God's opinion, but we also need to live our lives with consideration for others. We do not want to do anything that has the potential of causing another Christian brother or sister to stumble or fall. Be sensitive to those around you. Don't let your Christian witness be hindered by what you say or do.

To begin the next topic, turn to p. A50.
To begin the next topic, turn to p. A50.

has accepted you so that God will be given glory. [8] Remember that Christ came as a servant to the Jews* to show that God is true to the promises he made to their ancestors. [9] He also came so that the Gentiles might give glory to God for his mercies to them. That is what the psalmist meant when he wrote:

"For this, I will praise you among the
     Gentiles;
  I will sing praises to your name."*

[10] And in another place it is written,

"Rejoice with his people,
  you Gentiles."*

[11] And yet again,

"Praise the LORD, all you Gentiles.
  Praise him, all you people of the earth."*

[12] And in another place Isaiah said,

"The heir to David's throne* will come,
  and he will rule over the Gentiles.
They will place their hope on him."*

[13] I pray that God, the source of hope, will fill you completely with joy and peace because you trust in him. Then you will overflow with confident hope through the power of the Holy Spirit.

Paul's Reason for Writing

[14] I am fully convinced, my dear brothers and sisters,* that you are full of goodness. You know these things so well you can teach each other all about them. [15] Even so, I have been bold enough to write about some of these points, knowing that all you need is this reminder. For by God's grace, [16] I am a special messenger from Christ Jesus to you Gentiles. I bring you the Good News so that I might present you as an acceptable offering to God, made holy by the Holy Spirit. [17] So I have reason to be enthusiastic about all Christ Jesus has done through me in my service to God. [18] Yet I dare not boast about anything except what Christ has done through me, bringing the Gentiles to God by my message and by the way I worked among them. [19] They were convinced by the power of miraculous signs and wonders and by the power of God's Spirit.* In this way, I have fully presented the Good News of Christ from Jerusalem all the way to Illyricum.*

[20] My ambition has always been to preach the Good News where the name of Christ has never been heard, rather than where a church has already been started by someone else. [21] I have been following the plan spoken of in the Scriptures, where it says,

"Those who have never been told about him
     will see,
  and those who have never heard of him
     will understand."*

[22] In fact, my visit to you has been delayed so long because I have been preaching in these places.

Paul's Travel Plans

[23] But now I have finished my work in these regions, and after all these long years of waiting, I am eager to visit you. [24] I am planning to go to Spain, and when I do, I will stop off in Rome. And after I have enjoyed your fellowship for a little while, you can provide for my journey.

[25] But before I come, I must go to Jerusalem to take a gift to the believers* there. [26] For you see, the believers in Macedonia and Achaia* have eagerly taken up an offering for the poor among the believers in Jerusalem. [27] They were glad to do this because they feel they owe a real debt to them. Since the Gentiles received the spiritual blessings of the Good News from the

15:8 Greek *servant of circumcision.*   15:9 Ps 18:49.   15:10 Deut 32:43.   15:11 Ps 117:1.   15:12a Greek *The root of Jesse.* David was the son of Jesse.   15:12b Isa 11:10 (Greek version).   15:14 Greek *brothers;* also in 15:30.   15:19a Other manuscripts read *the Spirit;* still others read *the Holy Spirit.*   15:19b *Illyricum* was a region northeast of Italy.   15:21 Isa 52:15 (Greek version).   15:25 Greek *God's holy people;* also in 15:26, 31.   15:26 *Macedonia* and *Achaia* were the northern and southern regions of Greece.

---

off and running

DO I HAVE AN UNEASY CONSCIENCE ABOUT THIS ACTIVITY?

Read ROMANS 14:23

When it comes to participating in questionable activities, it is easy to rationalize joining in because others are doing it. Yet this verse places the responsibility of your choice squarely on your shoulders. You may protest and say, "Well, so-and-so is doing it!" But you are not that person. You must be obedient to what God tells *you* to do.

believers in Jerusalem, they feel the least they can do in return is to help them financially. [28]As soon as I have delivered this money and completed this good deed of theirs, I will come to see you on my way to Spain. [29]And I am sure that when I come, Christ will richly bless our time together.

[30]Dear brothers and sisters, I urge you in the name of our Lord Jesus Christ to join in my struggle by praying to God for me. Do this because of your love for me, given to you by the Holy Spirit. [31]Pray that I will be rescued from those in Judea who refuse to obey God. Pray also that the believers there will be willing to accept the donation* I am taking to Jerusalem. [32]Then, by the will of God, I will be able to come to you with a joyful heart, and we will be an encouragement to each other.

[33]And now may God, who gives us his peace, be with you all. Amen.*

CHAPTER **16**
Paul Greets His Friends

I commend to you our sister Phoebe, who is a deacon in the church in Cenchrea. [2]Welcome her in the Lord as one who is worthy of honor among God's people. Help her in whatever she needs, for she has been helpful to many, and especially to me.

[3]Give my greetings to Priscilla and Aquila, my co-workers in the ministry of Christ Jesus. [4]In fact, they once risked their lives for me. I am thankful to them, and so are all the Gentile churches. [5]Also give my greetings to the church that meets in their home.

Greet my dear friend Epenetus. He was the first person from the province of Asia to become a follower of Christ. [6]Give my greetings to Mary, who has worked so hard for your benefit. [7]Greet Andronicus and Junia,* my fellow Jews,* who were in prison with me. They are highly respected among the apostles and became followers of Christ before I did. [8]Greet Ampliatus, my dear friend in the Lord. [9]Greet Urbanus, our co-worker in Christ, and my dear friend Stachys.

[10]Greet Apelles, a good man whom Christ approves. And give my greetings to the believers from the household of Aristobulus. [11]Greet Herodion, my fellow Jew.* Greet the Lord's people from the household of Narcissus. [12]Give my greetings to Tryphena and Tryphosa, the Lord's workers, and to dear Persis, who has worked so hard for the Lord. [13]Greet Rufus, whom the Lord picked out to be his very own; and also his dear mother, who has been a mother to me.

[14]Give my greetings to Asyncritus, Phlegon, Hermes, Patrobas, Hermas, and the brothers and sisters* who meet with them. [15]Give my greetings to Philologus, Julia, Nereus and his sister, and to Olympas and all the believers* who meet with them. [16]Greet each other in Christian love.* All the churches of Christ send you their greetings.

Paul's Final Instructions

[17]And now I make one more appeal, my dear brothers and sisters. Watch out for people who cause divisions and upset people's faith by teaching things contrary to what you have been taught. Stay away from them. [18]Such people are not serving Christ our Lord; they are serving their own personal interests. By smooth talk and glowing words they deceive innocent people. [19]But everyone knows that you are obedient to the Lord. This makes me very happy. I want you to be wise in doing right and to stay innocent of any wrong. [20]The God of peace will soon crush Satan under your feet. May the grace of our Lord Jesus* be with you.

[21]Timothy, my fellow worker, sends you his

15:31 Greek *the ministry;* other manuscripts read *the gift.*   **15:33** Some manuscripts do not include *Amen.* One very early manuscript places 16:25-27 here.   **16:7a** *Junia* is a feminine name. Some late manuscripts accent the word so it reads *Junias,* a masculine name; still others read *Julia* (feminine).   **16:7b** Or *compatriots;* also in 16:21.   **16:11** Or *compatriot.*   **16:14** Greek *brothers;* also in 16:17.   **16:15** Greek *all of God's holy people.*   **16:16** Greek *with a sacred kiss.*   **16:20** Some manuscripts read *Lord Jesus Christ.*

How do you know when you should not participate in a certain activity? God's Holy Spirit will often give you an uneasy conscience about something you should not be doing. For example, you may have a sense that you are in the wrong place, with the wrong people, about to do the wrong thing. Or, you may have a lack of peace in your heart about an activity in which you are participating. When this happens, it is up to you to pay attention to your conscience and follow through by being obedient to God.

For the next note on "Responsibility," turn to p. 184.

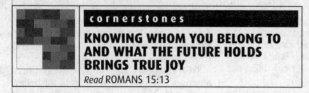

cornerstones

KNOWING WHOM YOU BELONG TO AND WHAT THE FUTURE HOLDS BRINGS TRUE JOY
Read ROMANS 15:13

1. You Have a New Identity. When you accept Jesus Christ into your life, God gives you a new identity. You discover that you are not merely some product of random chance. You are not a speck in the universe. You are a child of God. And as God's child you can rest assured that you will be loved and cared for by your heavenly Father.

2. You Have Power to Face Life. With that new identity and hope in Christ, you also have the promise of the Holy Spirit's presence and power in your life. The Holy Spirit works constantly in your heart, helping you to understand God's Word and to transform your attitudes and behavior (see "Who Is the Holy Spirit?" p. A24). An expanded translation of this verse says that by the power of the Holy Spirit, your whole life and outlook will be "radiant with hope." God has not left you to face life on your own. He has promised to guide and strengthen you with his Spirit.

3. You Have Hope for the Future. As a Christian, you have the hope and knowledge that there is life beyond the grave. Your last breath on earth will be followed by your first breath in heaven. We know this is true, because God has promised it in his Word (see "What Is Heaven?" p. A27). This verse asserts that your belief in Jesus and his promises to us as his followers will fill you with joy and peace.

The world offers many roads to happiness: sex, money, power, personal success. But they are all cheap and worthless substitutes in comparison to knowing that you are God's child and that you have the hope of heaven. This is the only road to lasting—indeed, eternal—joy.

To begin the next topic, turn to p. A35.

greetings, as do Lucius, Jason, and Sosipater, my fellow Jews.

²²I, Tertius, the one writing this letter for Paul, send my greetings, too, as one of the Lord's followers.

²³Gaius says hello to you. He is my host and also serves as host to the whole church. Erastus, the city treasurer, sends you his greetings, and so does our brother Quartus.*

²⁵Now all glory to God, who is able to make you strong, just as my Good News says. This message about Jesus Christ has revealed his plan for you Gentiles, a plan kept secret from the beginning of time. ²⁶But now as the prophets* foretold and as the eternal God has commanded, this message is made known to all Gentiles everywhere, so that they too might believe and obey him. ²⁷All glory to the only wise God, through Jesus Christ, forever. Amen.

16:23 Some manuscripts add verse 24, *May the grace of our Lord Jesus Christ be with you all. Amen.* Still others add this sentence after verse 27. **16:26** Greek *the prophetic writings.*

1 Corinthians

AUTHOR: **PAUL** | DATE WRITTEN: **A.D. 55** | GENRE: **EPISTLE**

Paul wrote this epistle in response to certain situations that arose in the Corinthian church. He straightforwardly dealt with many of the errors that the people of this church believed and practiced. Among the pitfalls were sins of immorality, false teachings, problems regarding marriage, and lawsuits.

CHAPTER 1

Greetings from Paul

This letter is from Paul, chosen by the will of God to be an apostle of Christ Jesus, and from our brother Sosthenes.

²I am writing to God's church in Corinth,* to you who have been called by God to be his own holy people. He made you holy by means of Christ Jesus,* just as he did for all people everywhere who call on the name of our Lord Jesus Christ, their Lord and ours.

³May God our Father and the Lord Jesus Christ give you grace and peace.

Paul Gives Thanks to God

⁴I always thank my God for you and for the gracious gifts he has given you, now that you belong to Christ Jesus. ⁵Through him, God has enriched your church in every way—with all of your eloquent words and all of your knowledge. ⁶This confirms that what I told you about Christ is true. ⁷Now you have every spiritual gift you need as you eagerly wait for the return of our Lord Jesus Christ. ⁸He will keep you strong to the end so that you will be free from all blame on the day when our Lord Jesus Christ returns. ⁹God will do this, for he is faithful to do what he says, and he has invited you into partnership with his Son, Jesus Christ our Lord.

Divisions in the Church

¹⁰I appeal to you, dear brothers and sisters,* by the authority of our Lord Jesus Christ, to live in harmony with each other. Let there be no divisions in the church. Rather, be of one mind, united in thought and purpose. ¹¹For some members of Chloe's household have told me about your quarrels, my dear brothers and sisters. ¹²Some of you are saying, "I am a follower of Paul." Others are saying, "I follow Apollos," or "I follow Peter,*" or "I follow only Christ."

¹³Has Christ been divided into factions? Was I, Paul, crucified for you? Were any of you baptized in the name of Paul? Of course not! ¹⁴I thank God that I did not baptize any of you except Crispus and Gaius, ¹⁵for now no one can say they were baptized in my name. ¹⁶(Oh yes, I also baptized the household of Stephanas, but I don't remember baptizing anyone else.) ¹⁷For Christ didn't send me to baptize, but to preach the Good News—and not with clever speech, for fear that the cross of Christ would lose its power.

The Wisdom of God

¹⁸The message of the cross is foolish to those who are headed for destruction! But we who are being saved know it is the very power of God. ¹⁹As the Scriptures say,

> "I will destroy the wisdom of the wise
> and discard the intelligence of the
> intelligent."*

²⁰So where does this leave the philosophers, the scholars, and the world's brilliant debaters? God has made the wisdom of this world look foolish. ²¹Since God in his wisdom saw to it that the world would never know him through human wisdom, he has used our foolish preaching to save those who believe. ²²It is foolish to the Jews, who ask for signs from heaven. And it is foolish to the Greeks, who seek human wisdom. ²³So when we preach

---

1:2a *Corinth* was the capital city of Achaia, the southern region of the Greek peninsula.   **1:2b** Or *because you belong to Christ Jesus.*   **1:10** Greek *brothers;* also in 1:11, 26.   **1:12** Greek *Cephas.*   **1:19** Isa 29:14.

cornerstones

OVERLOOKING PETTY ISSUES FREES US TO EXPERIENCE JOY
Read 1 CORINTHIANS 1:10-17

In Paul's first letter to the Corinthians, he addressed several problems the church of Corinth was experiencing. One of the church's problems was that the believers were dividing the church by aligning themselves under the teachings of one apostle or another, rather than focusing on the joy of their salvation. Paul, therefore, rebuked the Corinthians for dividing the church over such a petty issue, reminding them that it is Christ they follow and serve, not Apollos, Paul, or Peter.

Like the Corinthians, we can get bogged down in issues that not only divide the church but really don't matter. When we immerse ourselves in petty issues, we rob ourselves of experiencing the joy that Christ has given us. Advocating these issues can become more important to us than salvation itself. It is then that we can become obsessed with others' adherence to our point of view rather than their faith in Christ. However, ignoring petty issues is liberating. It frees us to focus on our own salvation and experience the joy of Christ's forgiveness.

How do we do this? Here are four ways to overlook petty issues and experience joy in Christ:

1. Be Single-Minded in Purpose. The purpose of our life is to serve Christ (see Philippians 1:21, p. 237).

2. Adopt God's Priorities As Your Own. Put God first, others second, and yourself third (see Philippians 2:5-6, p. 238).

3. Keep Moving Forward Spiritually. Acknowledge that you haven't "arrived" spiritually, and keep pressing on to know God more (see Philippians 3:13-14, p. 240).

4. Have a Rejoicing Mind. Don't rejoice in circumstances, but rejoice in God and his faithfulness (see Philippians 4:4-5, p. 240).

Failure to maintain the joy of the Lord in our personal lives leads to spiritual breakdown. Failure to keep the joy of the Lord in our churches cripples the cause of Christ. Let his joy overflow from your life.

For the next note on "Joy," turn to p. 188.

---

that Christ was crucified, the Jews are offended and the Gentiles say it's all nonsense.

²⁴But to those called by God to salvation, both Jews and Gentiles,* Christ is the power of God and the wisdom of God. ²⁵This foolish plan of God is wiser than the wisest of human plans, and God's weakness is stronger than the greatest of human strength.

²⁶Remember, dear brothers and sisters, that few of you were wise in the world's eyes or powerful or wealthy* when God called you. ²⁷Instead, God chose things the world considers foolish in order to shame those who think they are wise. And he chose things that are powerless to shame those who are powerful. ²⁸God chose things despised by the world,* things counted as nothing at all, and used them to bring to nothing what the world considers important. ²⁹As a result, no one can ever boast in the presence of God.

³⁰God has united you with Christ Jesus. For our benefit God made him to be wisdom itself. Christ made us right with God; he made us pure and holy, and he freed us from sin. ³¹Therefore, as the Scriptures say, "If you want to boast, boast only about the LORD."*

CHAPTER **2**
Paul's Message of Wisdom
When I first came to you, dear brothers and sisters,* I didn't use lofty words and impressive wisdom to tell you God's secret plan.* ²For I decided that while I was with you I would forget everything except Jesus Christ, the one who was crucified. ³I came to you in weakness—timid and trembling. ⁴And my message and my preaching were very plain. Rather than using clever and persuasive speeches, I relied only on the power of the Holy Spirit. ⁵I did this so you would trust not in human wisdom but in the power of God.

⁶Yet when I am among mature believers, I

1:24 Greek *and Greeks.* 1:26 Or *high born.* 1:28 Or *God chose those who are low born.* 1:31 Jer 9:24. 2:1a Greek *brothers.* 2:1b Greek *God's mystery;* other manuscripts read *God's testimony.*

do speak with words of wisdom, but not the kind of wisdom that belongs to this world or to the rulers of this world, who are soon forgotten. [7]No, the wisdom we speak of is the mystery of God*—his plan that was previously hidden, even though he made it for our ultimate glory before the world began. [8]But the rulers of this world have not understood it; if they had, they would not have crucified our glorious Lord. [9]That is what the Scriptures mean when they say,

"No eye has seen, no ear has heard,
    and no mind has imagined
what God has prepared
    for those who love him."*

[10]But* it was to us that God revealed these things by his Spirit. For his Spirit searches out everything and shows us God's deep secrets. [11]No one can know a person's thoughts except that person's own spirit, and no one can know God's thoughts except God's own Spirit. [12]And we have received God's Spirit (not the world's spirit), so we can know the wonderful things God has freely given us.

[13]When we tell you these things, we do not use words that come from human wisdom. Instead, we speak words given to us by the Spirit, using the Spirit's words to explain spiritual truths.* [14]But people who aren't spiritual* can't receive these truths from God's Spirit. It all sounds foolish to them and they can't understand it, for only those who are spiritual can understand what the Spirit means. [15]Those who are spiritual can evaluate all things, but they themselves cannot be evaluated by others. [16]For,

"Who can know the Lord's thoughts?
    Who knows enough to teach him?"*

But we understand these things, for we have the mind of Christ.

CHAPTER 3
Paul and Apollos, Servants of Christ

Dear brothers and sisters,* when I was with you I couldn't talk to you as I would to spiritual people.* I had to talk as though you belonged to this world or as though you were infants in the Christian life.* [2]I had to feed you with milk, not with solid food, because you weren't ready for anything stronger. And you still aren't ready,

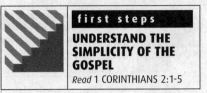

first steps

UNDERSTAND THE SIMPLICITY OF THE GOSPEL
Read 1 CORINTHIANS 2:1-5

Paul reminds us in this text that the heartbeat of the gospel message is the story of the life, death, and resurrection of Jesus Christ. The apostles emphasized this message in their preaching throughout the New Testament—especially in the book of Acts, which chronicles the start of the early church. As you share your faith with others, keep in mind these two points demonstrated in the apostles' own efforts to spread the gospel:

1. Remember the Simplicity of the Gospel. People need to know that they are sinners and that their sin separates them from God, but Jesus came to bring God and humankind together. When he died on the cross, the sins of humankind were placed upon him, and the penalty for those sins was paid in full. Three days after his crucifixion, he rose from the dead, proving that he was the true Son of God, the only one who conquered death and could pay for our sins.

2. Recognize the Power of the Gospel. Although our message is simple, it is incredibly powerful. Paul wrote, "For I am not ashamed of this Good News about Christ. It is the power of God at work, saving everyone who believes" (Romans 1:16). The word Paul uses to describe the power of the gospel is the root for our English words *dynamite* and *dynamic.*

Remember there is power in the simple message of the life, death, and resurrection of Jesus Christ. We should not be ashamed of it but boldly proclaim it.

For the next note on "Share Your Faith," turn to p. 163.

2:7 Greek *But we speak God's wisdom in a mystery.*
2:9 Isa 64:4.   2:10 Some manuscripts read *For.*   2:13 Or *explaining spiritual truths in spiritual language,* or *explaining spiritual truths to spiritual people.*   2:14 Or *who don't have the Spirit;* or *who have only physical life.*
2:16 Isa 40:13 (Greek version).   3:1a Greek *Brothers.*
3:1b Or *to people who have the Spirit.*   3:1c Greek *in Christ.*

cornerstones

THE VALUE OF OUR WORK ON EARTH WILL BE TESTED

Read 1 CORINTHIANS 3:10-15

The British preacher Alan Redpath once said, "It is possible to have a saved soul and a lost life." In other words, it is possible to be saved and forgiven of one's sin but to waste one's life by not serving the Lord.

That is what Paul warned the Corinthians about in this passage. Here Paul describes another judgment—besides the Great White Throne Judgment—specifically for believers. You might call it the Christian's award ceremony. Yet it won't be like any awards ceremony on earth. There the quality of our work for the Lord will be tested, as well as our motives for doing it. Our reward will reflect what we have or haven't done with the talents and abilities God has given us.

One day you are going to stand before Jesus. When you do, you want to be welcomed into the arms of Jesus and hear him say, "Well done, my good and faithful servant" (Matthew 25:21).

Be an "expert builder." Take the gifts and abilities God has given you—however insignificant they may seem to you—and use them for his glory. Then you will have a saved soul *and* an abundant life.

To begin the next reading track, turn to p. A37.

---

³for you are still controlled by your sinful nature. You are jealous of one another and quarrel with each other. Doesn't that prove you are controlled by your sinful nature? Aren't you living like people of the world? ⁴When one of you says, "I am a follower of Paul," and another says, "I follow Apollos," aren't you acting just like people of the world?

⁵After all, who is Apollos? Who is Paul? We are only God's servants through whom you believed the Good News. Each of us did the work the Lord gave us. ⁶I planted the seed in your hearts, and Apollos watered it, but it was God who made it grow. ⁷It's not important who does the planting, or who does the watering. What's important is that God makes the seed grow. ⁸The one who plants and the one who waters work together with the same purpose. And both will be rewarded for their own hard work. ⁹For we are both God's workers. And you are God's field. You are God's building.

¹⁰Because of God's grace to me, I have laid the foundation like an expert builder. Now others are building on it. But whoever is building on this foundation must be very careful. ¹¹For no one can lay any foundation other than the one we already have—Jesus Christ.

¹²Anyone who builds on that foundation may use a variety of materials—gold, silver, jewels, wood, hay, or straw. ¹³But on the judgment day, fire will reveal what kind of work each builder has done. The fire will show if a person's work has any value. ¹⁴If the work survives, that builder will receive a reward. ¹⁵But if the work is burned up, the builder will suffer great loss. The builder will be saved, but like someone barely escaping through a wall of flames.

¹⁶Don't you realize that all of you together are the temple of God and that the Spirit of God lives in* you? ¹⁷God will destroy anyone who destroys this temple. For God's temple is holy, and you are that temple.

¹⁸Stop deceiving yourselves. If you think you are wise by this world's standards, you need to become a fool to be truly wise. ¹⁹For the wisdom of this world is foolishness to God. As the Scriptures say,

"He traps the wise
    in the snare of their own cleverness."*

²⁰And again,

"The LORD knows the thoughts of the wise;
    he knows they are worthless."*

²¹So don't boast about following a particular human leader. For everything belongs to you—²²whether Paul or Apollos or Peter,* or the world, or life and death, or the present and the future. Everything belongs to you, ²³and you belong to Christ, and Christ belongs to God.

CHAPTER 4

Paul's Relationship with the Corinthians

So look at Apollos and me as mere servants of Christ who have been put in charge of explaining God's mysteries. ²Now, a person who is put

3:16 Or *among.*   3:19 Job 5:13.   3:20 Ps 94:11.   3:22 Greek *Cephas.*

Does God Approve of Alternative Lifestyles?

Read 1 CORINTHIANS 6:9-10, 15-20

In this day and age we hear a lot of talk about "alternative lifestyles." But what does God have to say about homosexuality, living together as an unmarried couple, or being promiscuous? While some say that God is accepting of any relationship, the Bible paints a very different picture. Just because these relationships exist does not make them right. In fact, God clearly labels them as sin.

About Homosexuality.

Saying that homosexuality is wrong is not a popular thing to do in our culture today. Yet God is not concerned with what is and what is not popular. He is concerned with people's salvation and their obedience to his Word. Just because homosexuality is viewed as an acceptable lifestyle does not mean that it is not a sin. God declared it to be just that when he gave his law to the Israelites (Leviticus 18:22). Paul reiterated God's command on abstaining from homosexual sex in his letter to the Romans (see Romans 1:26-27, p. 168), as well as in some of his other letters to the early church.

About Living Together before Marriage and Premarital Sex.

Have you ever thought that something was OK to do because "everybody is doing it"? Today, couples living together outside of marriage has become acceptable. In addition, it seems that premarital sex is the norm rather than the exception. But God has not given his approval of these relationships (see Hebrews 13:4, p. 287). Although God created sex, he did not intend us to have it before marriage. That is because he created sex to be a means by which a husband and wife would grow closer in their relationship. He did not create sex to be something cheaply enjoyed outside the bonds of marital commitment, which is what living together and premarital sex are.

About Promiscuity.

Promiscuity is a word that we do not hear as often today as we used to. The problem with promiscuity is that it involves having many sexual partners. We know from God's Word that he intended us to have one sexual partner—our spouse. When a person has more than one partner (with the exception of remarriage after a spouse's death or a divorce on solid biblical grounds), he or she is involved in sexual immorality, if not married, or adultery, if married (see Ephesians 5:3, p. 233; Matthew 5:27-28, p. 5).

Some have questions about whether God's Word on these subjects still applies to us today, or if it was simply meant for the people of that particular time and culture. Yet God has instructed us to obey all of his commands and not to add or subtract from any of them (Deuteronomy 12:32). In addition, we are told that the Word of the Lord stands forever (see 1 Peter 1:25, p. 296). Consequently, these instructions apply just as much to us today as they did to their original audience centuries ago.

God gave us our sexual desires to enjoy within the bounds of marriage (see 1 Corinthians 7:1-5, p. 196). If you go against God's divinely instituted plan and do not repent, you will reap the consequences—not only in this life, but in eternity. You cannot be close to God if you are engaged in any type of immoral behavior. At the same time, you won't be engaged in this type of behavior if you are truly close to God.

For the next "Big Question" note, turn to p. 231.

in charge as a manager must be faithful. [3]As for me, it matters very little how I might be evaluated by you or by any human authority. I don't even trust my own judgment on this point. [4]My conscience is clear, but that doesn't prove I'm right. It is the Lord himself who will examine me and decide.

[5]So don't make judgments about anyone ahead of time—before the Lord returns. For he will bring our darkest secrets to light and will reveal our private motives. Then God will give to each one whatever praise is due.

[6]Dear brothers and sisters,* I have used Apollos and myself to illustrate what I've been saying. If you pay attention to what I have quoted from the Scriptures,* you won't be proud of one of your leaders at the expense of another. [7]For what gives you the right to make such a judgment? What do you have that God hasn't given you? And if everything you have is from God, why boast as though it were not a gift?

[8]You think you already have everything you need. You think you are already rich. You have begun to reign in God's kingdom without us! I wish you really were reigning already, for then we would be reigning with you. [9]Instead, I sometimes think God has put us apostles on display, like prisoners of war at the end of a victor's parade, condemned to die. We have become a spectacle to the entire world—to people and angels alike.

[10]Our dedication to Christ makes us look like fools, but you claim to be so wise in Christ! We are weak, but you are so powerful! You are honored, but we are ridiculed. [11]Even now we go hungry and thirsty, and we don't have enough clothes to keep warm. We are often beaten and have no home. [12]We work wearily with our own hands to earn our living. We bless those who curse us. We are patient with those

who abuse us. [13]We appeal gently when evil things are said about us. Yet we are treated like the world's garbage, like everybody's trash—right up to the present moment.

[14]I am not writing these things to shame you, but to warn you as my beloved children. [15]For even if you had ten thousand others to teach you about Christ, you have only one spiritual father. For I became your father in Christ Jesus when I preached the Good News to you. [16]So I urge you to imitate me.

[17]That's why I have sent Timothy, my beloved and faithful child in the Lord. He will remind you of how I follow Christ Jesus, just as I teach in all the churches wherever I go.

[18]Some of you have become arrogant, thinking I will not visit you again. [19]But I will come—and soon—if the Lord lets me, and then I'll find out whether these arrogant people just give pretentious speeches or whether they really have God's power. [20]For the Kingdom of God is not just a lot of talk; it is living by God's power. [21]Which do you choose? Should I come with a rod to punish you, or should I come with love and a gentle spirit?

CHAPTER 5
Paul Condemns Spiritual Pride

I can hardly believe the report about the sexual immorality going on among you—something that even pagans don't do. I am told that a man in your church is living in sin with his stepmother.* [2]You are so proud of yourselves, but you should be mourning in sorrow and shame. And you should remove this man from your fellowship.

[3]Even though I am not with you in person, I am with you in the Spirit.* And as though I were there, I have already passed judgment on this man [4]in the name of the Lord Jesus. You must call a meeting of the church.* I will be

4:6a Greek *Brothers.*   4:6b Or *If you learn not to go beyond "what is written."*   5:1 Greek *his father's wife.*   5:3 Or *in spirit.*
5:4 Or *In the name of the Lord Jesus, you must call a meeting of the church.*

Some have mistakenly assumed that following Christ means drudgingly obeying a list of "do's and don'ts." In reality, the Christian life, if lived according to Scripture, is one of joy and satisfaction. This verse serves as a case in point. To follow the principle laid out here is not overly restricting but truly liberating!

Some people are controlled by pleasure. For example, they may live for a certain sport and become so fanatical about it that it turns into an obsession. Others

present with you in spirit, and so will the power of our Lord Jesus. ⁵Then you must throw this man out and hand him over to Satan so that his sinful nature will be destroyed* and he himself* will be saved on the day the Lord* returns.

⁶Your boasting about this is terrible. Don't you realize that this sin is like a little yeast that spreads through the whole batch of dough? ⁷Get rid of the old "yeast" by removing this wicked person from among you. Then you will be like a fresh batch of dough made without yeast, which is what you really are. Christ, our Passover Lamb, has been sacrificed for us.* ⁸So let us celebrate the festival, not with the old bread* of wickedness and evil, but with the new bread* of sincerity and truth.

⁹When I wrote to you before, I told you not to associate with people who indulge in sexual sin. ¹⁰But I wasn't talking about unbelievers who indulge in sexual sin, or are greedy, or cheat people, or worship idols. You would have to leave this world to avoid people like that. ¹¹I meant that you are not to associate with anyone who claims to be a believer* yet indulges in sexual sin, or is greedy, or worships idols, or is abusive, or is a drunkard, or cheats people. Don't even eat with such people.

¹²It isn't my responsibility to judge outsiders, but it certainly is your responsibility to judge those inside the church who are sinning. ¹³God will judge those on the outside; but as the Scriptures say, "You must remove the evil person from among you."*

CHAPTER 6
Avoiding Lawsuits with Christians

When one of you has a dispute with another believer, how dare you file a lawsuit and ask a secular court to decide the matter instead of taking it to other believers*! ²Don't you realize that someday we believers will judge the world? And since you are going to judge the world, can't you decide even these little things among yourselves? ³Don't you realize that we will judge angels? So you should surely be able to resolve ordinary disputes in this life. ⁴If you have legal disputes about such matters, why go to outside judges who are not respected by the church? ⁵I am saying this to shame you. Isn't there anyone in all the church who is wise enough to decide these issues? ⁶But instead, one believer* sues another—right in front of unbelievers!

⁷Even to have such lawsuits with one another is a defeat for you. Why not just accept the injustice and leave it at that? Why not let yourselves be cheated? ⁸Instead, you yourselves are the ones who do wrong and cheat even your fellow believers.*

⁹Don't you realize that those who do wrong will not inherit the Kingdom of God? Don't fool yourselves. Those who indulge in sexual sin, or who worship idols, or commit adultery, or are male prostitutes, or practice homosexuality, ¹⁰or are thieves, or greedy people, or drunkards, or are abusive, or cheat people—none of these will inherit the Kingdom of God. ¹¹Some of you were once like that. But you were cleansed; you were made holy; you were made right with God by calling on the name of the Lord Jesus Christ and by the Spirit of our God.

Avoiding Sexual Sin

¹²You say, "I am allowed to do anything"—but not everything is good for you. And even though "I am allowed to do anything," I must

5:5a Or *so that his body will be destroyed;* Greek reads *for the destruction of the flesh.*   5:5b Greek *and the spirit.*   5:5c Other manuscripts read *the Lord Jesus;* still others read *our Lord Jesus Christ.*   5:7 Greek *has been sacrificed.*   5:8a Greek *not with old leaven.*   5:8b Greek *but with unleavened [bread].*   5:11 Greek *a brother.*   5:13 Deut 17:7.   6:1 Greek *God's holy people;* also in 6:2.   6:6 Greek *one brother.*   6:8 Greek *even the brothers.*

---

may be hooked on soap operas, food, or some particular habit that has them under its power. Yet, as a Christian, you should only want to be controlled by and under the power of Jesus Christ.

We need to so treasure our relationship with God—and the ensuing freedom from sin it has brought—that we jealously guard that relationship, wanting nothing or person to get in its way. As the Psalmist prayed, we, too, should pray, "Search me, O God, and know my heart; test me and know my anxious thoughts. Point out anything in me that offends you, and lead me along the path of everlasting life" (Psalm 139:23-24).

For the next note on "Responsibility," turn to p. 186.

not become a slave to anything. [13]You say, "Food was made for the stomach, and the stomach for food." (This is true, though someday God will do away with both of them.) But you can't say that our bodies were made for sexual immorality. They were made for the Lord, and the Lord cares about our bodies. [14]And God will raise us from the dead by his power, just as he raised our Lord from the dead.

[15]Don't you realize that your bodies are actually parts of Christ? Should a man take his body, which is part of Christ, and join it to a prostitute? Never! [16]And don't you realize that if a man joins himself to a prostitute, he becomes one body with her? For the Scriptures say, "The two are united into one."* [17]But the person who is joined to the Lord is one spirit with him.

[18]Run from sexual sin! No other sin so clearly affects the body as this one does. For sexual immorality is a sin against your own body. [19]Don't you realize that your body is the temple of the Holy Spirit, who lives in you and was given to you by God? You do not belong to yourself, [20]for God bought you with a high price. So you must honor God with your body.

CHAPTER **7**

Instruction on Marriage

Now regarding the questions you asked in your letter. Yes, it is good to abstain from sexual relations.* [2]But because there is so much sexual immorality, each man should have his own wife, and each woman should have her own husband.

[3]The husband should fulfill his wife's sexual needs, and the wife should fulfill her husband's needs. [4]The wife gives authority over her body to her husband, and the husband gives authority over his body to his wife.

[5]Do not deprive each other of sexual relations, unless you both agree to refrain from sexual intimacy for a limited time so you can give yourselves more completely to prayer. Afterward, you should come together again so that Satan won't be able to tempt you because of your lack of self-control. [6]I say this as a concession, not as a command. [7]But I wish everyone were single, just as I am. Yet each person has a special gift from God, of one kind or another.

[8]So I say to those who aren't married and to widows—it's better to stay unmarried, just as I am. [9]But if they can't control themselves, they should go ahead and marry. It's better to marry than to burn with lust.

[10]But for those who are married, I have a command that comes not from me, but from the Lord.* A wife must not leave her husband. [11]But if she does leave him, let her remain single or else be reconciled to him. And the husband must not leave his wife.

[12]Now, I will speak to the rest of you, though I do not have a direct command from the Lord. If a Christian man* has a wife who is not a believer and she is willing to continue living with him, he must not leave her. [13]And if a Christian woman has a husband who is not a believer and

6:16 Gen 2:24. 7:1 Or to *live a celibate life*; Greek reads *It is good for a man not to touch a woman.* 7:10 See Matt 5:32; 19:9; Mark 10:11-12; Luke 16:18. 7:12 Greek *a brother.*

MARRIAGE IS NOT FOR EVERYONE

Read 1 CORINTHIANS 7:1-40

Contrary to what popular opinion suggests, God has given some the ability to remain "happily unmarried." Verse 35 of this passage reminds us that, when it comes to marrying, it is vitally important to make sure that your decision "will help you serve the Lord best."

If you are contemplating marriage, here are four important things to consider:

1. Take Time Getting to Know One Another. Don't rush into marriage. If you are really in love with someone, you will want to build your friendship with that person as well. That is the foundation of your marriage. As Benjamin Franklin humorously said, "Keep your eyes wide open before marriage and half shut afterwards"—not the other way around!

2. Test the Depth of Your Love. Love is more than some gooey emotion. It is a commitment. In the Greek language, love was described in three different ways: *eros* (physical attraction), *philia* (love between friends), and *agape* (unconditional love). Marriages that are simply based upon *eros* or *philia* love

he is willing to continue living with her, she must not leave him. [14]For the Christian wife brings holiness to her marriage, and the Christian husband* brings holiness to his marriage. Otherwise, your children would not be holy, but now they are holy. [15](But if the husband or wife who isn't a believer insists on leaving, let them go. In such cases the Christian husband or wife* is no longer bound to the other, for God has called you* to live in peace.) [16]Don't you wives realize that your husbands might be saved because of you? And don't you husbands realize that your wives might be saved because of you?

[17]Each of you should continue to live in whatever situation the Lord has placed you, and remain as you were when God first called you. This is my rule for all the churches. [18]For instance, a man who was circumcised before he became a believer should not try to reverse it. And the man who was uncircumcised when he became a believer should not be circumcised now. [19]For it makes no difference whether or not a man has been circumcised. The important thing is to keep God's commandments.

[20]Yes, each of you should remain as you were when God called you. [21]Are you a slave? Don't let that worry you—but if you get a chance to be free, take it. [22]And remember, if you were a slave when the Lord called you, you are now free in the Lord. And if you were free when the Lord called you, you are now a slave of Christ.

[23]God paid a high price for you, so don't be enslaved by the world.* [24]Each of you, dear brothers and sisters,* should remain as you were when God first called you.

[25]Now regarding your question about the young women who are not yet married. I do not have a command from the Lord for them. But the Lord in his mercy has given me wisdom that can be trusted, and I will share it with you. [26]Because of the present crisis,* I think it is best to remain as you are. [27]If you have a wife, do not seek to end the marriage. If you do not have a wife, do not seek to get married. [28]But if you do get married, it is not a sin. And if a young woman gets married, it is not a sin. However, those who get married at this time will have troubles, and I am trying to spare you those problems.

[29]But let me say this, dear brothers and sisters: The time that remains is very short. So from now on, those with wives should not focus only on their marriage. [30]Those who weep or who rejoice or who buy things should not be absorbed by their weeping or their joy or their possessions. [31]Those who use the things of the world should not become attached to them. For this world as we know it will soon pass away.

[32]I want you to be free from the concerns of this life. An unmarried man can spend his time doing the Lord's work and thinking how to please him. [33]But a married man has to think about his earthly responsibilities and how to

---

7:14 Greek *the brother.*   7:15a Greek *the brother or sister.*   7:15b Some manuscripts read *us.*   7:23 Greek *don't become slaves of people.*   7:24 Greek *brothers;* also in 7:29.   7:26 Or *the pressures of life.*

---

are destined for trouble, but marriages built around the *agape* love that Christ displayed will last. Emotions will come and go, but true love is far more than that. The Bible says, "Many waters cannot quench love, nor can rivers drown it" (Song of Songs 8:7).

3. Make Sure of Your Commitment. Ask yourself the following questions: Are you ready to spend the rest of your life with this person? Can you see yourselves going through parenthood together? Are you willing to make sacrifices in relationships, hobbies, and even your career for the sake of your marriage?

4. Consider Your Witness for Christ. If this other person is not a believer, don't even consider marriage. Scripture gives stern warnings against being teamed with those who are unbelievers (2 Corinthians 6:14, p. 214). You need to also consider the spiritual implications of this relationship. Will the two of you together be a more effective and powerful witness for Christ than the two of you apart?

Whether you marry or remain single, learn to be content in whatever situation the Lord places you. Then you will possess one of the keys to true happiness.

To begin the next topic, turn to p. A46.

please his wife. ³⁴His interests are divided. In the same way, a woman who is no longer married or has never been married can be devoted to the Lord and holy in body and in spirit. But a married woman has to think about her earthly responsibilities and how to please her husband. ³⁵I am saying this for your benefit, not to place restrictions on you. I want you to do whatever will help you serve the Lord best, with as few distractions as possible.

³⁶But if a man thinks that he's treating his fiancée improperly and will inevitably give in to his passion, let him marry her as he wishes. It is not a sin. ³⁷But if he has decided firmly not to marry and there is no urgency and he can control his passion, he does well not to marry. ³⁸So the person who marries his fiancée does well, and the person who doesn't marry does even better.

³⁹A wife is bound to her husband as long as he lives. If her husband dies, she is free to marry anyone she wishes, but only if he loves the Lord.* ⁴⁰But in my opinion it would be better for her to stay single, and I think I am giving you counsel from God's Spirit when I say this.

CHAPTER **8**
Food Sacrificed to Idols
Now regarding your question about food that has been offered to idols. Yes, we know that "we all have knowledge" about this issue. But while knowledge makes us feel important, it is love that strengthens the church. ²Anyone who claims to know all the answers doesn't really know very much. ³But the person who loves God is the one whom God recognizes.*

⁴So, what about eating meat that has been offered to idols? Well, we all know that an idol is not really a god and that there is only one

God. ⁵There may be so-called gods both in heaven and on earth, and some people actually worship many gods and many lords. ⁶But we know that there is only one God, the Father, who created everything, and we live for him. And there is only one Lord, Jesus Christ, through whom God made everything and through whom we have been given life.

⁷However, not all believers know this. Some are accustomed to thinking of idols as being real, so when they eat food that has been offered to idols, they think of it as the worship of real gods, and their weak consciences are violated. ⁸It's true that we can't win God's approval by what we eat. We don't lose anything if we don't eat it, and we don't gain anything if we do.

⁹But you must be careful so that your freedom does not cause others with a weaker conscience to stumble. ¹⁰For if others see you—with your "superior knowledge"—eating in the temple of an idol, won't they be encouraged to violate their conscience by eating food that has been offered to an idol? ¹¹So because of your superior knowledge, a weak believer* for whom Christ died will be destroyed. ¹²And when you sin against other believers* by encouraging them to do something they believe is wrong, you are sinning against Christ. ¹³So if what I eat causes another believer to sin, I will never eat meat again as long as I live—for I don't want to cause another believer to stumble.

CHAPTER **9**
Paul Gives Up His Rights
Am I not as free as anyone else? Am I not an apostle? Haven't I seen Jesus our Lord with my own eyes? Isn't it because of my work that you belong to the Lord? ²Even if others think I am not an apostle, I certainly am to you. You yourselves are proof that I am the Lord's apostle.

7:39 Greek *but only in the Lord.*   **8:3** Some manuscripts read *the person who loves has full knowledge.*   **8:11** Greek *brother;* also in 8:13.   **8:12** Greek *brothers.*

---

off and running
A CHRISTIAN SHOULD NOT LEAVE A NON-CHRISTIAN SPOUSE
Read 1 CORINTHIANS 7:12-16

While it is easy to rationalize leaving an unbelieving spouse who does not support or encourage your faith, it is not biblical. As Paul reiterates here, divorce is not God's intent for married couples. In the case of a Christian and non-Christian spouse, there are two additional reasons to remain married:

1. A Christian Spouse Serves as a Witness to an Unbelieving Spouse. A Christian may play an important role in winning his or her spouse to the Lord. Scripture says that the Christian wife of a nonbelieving husband can have a powerful influence on her spouse through her godly actions and example, which

³This is my answer to those who question my authority.* ⁴Don't we have the right to live in your homes and share your meals? ⁵Don't we have the right to bring a Christian wife with us as the other apostles and the Lord's brothers do, and as Peter* does? ⁶Or is it only Barnabas and I who have to work to support ourselves?

⁷What soldier has to pay his own expenses? What farmer plants a vineyard and doesn't have the right to eat some of its fruit? What shepherd cares for a flock of sheep and isn't allowed to drink some of the milk? ⁸Am I expressing merely a human opinion, or does the law say the same thing? ⁹For the law of Moses says, "You must not muzzle an ox to keep it from eating as it treads out the grain."* Was God thinking only about oxen when he said this? ¹⁰Wasn't he actually speaking to us? Yes, it was written for us, so that the one who plows and the one who threshes the grain might both expect a share of the harvest.

¹¹Since we have planted spiritual seed among you, aren't we entitled to a harvest of physical food and drink? ¹²If you support others who preach to you, shouldn't we have an even greater right to be supported? But we have never used this right. We would rather put up with anything than be an obstacle to the Good News about Christ.

¹³Don't you realize that those who work in the temple get their meals from the offerings brought to the temple? And those who serve at the altar get a share of the sacrificial offerings. ¹⁴In the same way, the Lord ordered that those who preach the Good News should be supported by those who benefit from it. ¹⁵Yet I have never used any of these rights. And I am not writing this to suggest that I want to start now. In fact, I would rather die than lose my right to boast about preaching without charge. ¹⁶Yet preaching the Good News is not something I can boast about. I am compelled by God to do it. How terrible for me if I didn't preach the Good News!

¹⁷If I were doing this on my own initiative, I would deserve payment. But I have no choice, for God has given me this sacred trust. ¹⁸What then is my pay? It is the opportunity to preach the Good News without charging anyone. That's why I never demand my rights when I preach the Good News.

¹⁹Even though I am a free man with no master, I have become a slave to all people to bring many to Christ. ²⁰When I was with the Jews, I lived like a Jew to bring the Jews to Christ. When I was with those who follow the Jewish law, I too lived under that law. Even though I am not subject to the law, I did this so I could bring to Christ those who are under the law. ²¹When I am with the Gentiles who do not follow the Jewish law,* I too live apart from that law so I can bring them to Christ. But I do not ignore the law of God; I obey the law of Christ.

²²When I am with those who are weak, I share their weakness, for I want to bring the weak to Christ. Yes, I try to find common ground with everyone, doing everything I can to save some. ²³I do everything to spread the Good News and share in its blessings.

²⁴Don't you realize that in a race everyone runs, but only one person gets the prize? So run to win! ²⁵All athletes are disciplined in their training. They do it to win a prize that will fade away, but we do it for an eternal prize. ²⁶So I run with purpose in every step. I am not just shadowboxing. ²⁷I discipline my body like an athlete, training it to do what it should. Otherwise, I fear that after preaching to others I myself might be disqualified.

9:3 Greek *those who examine me.*   9:5 Greek *Cephas.*   9:9 Deut 25:4.   9:21 Greek *those without the law.*

---

may encourage him to come to faith in Christ (see 1 Peter 3:1-2, p. 297). The same is true for Christian husbands.

2. A Christian Spouse Can Influence the Couple's Children for Christ. If you separate, as Paul states, there is a good chance your children may not come to faith. It will help them to see your faith in the context of a united family.

If, however, your unbelieving spouse abandons you, and you have done everything you could to keep the marriage together, God will not hold you to that relationship. This is one of the few marriage "release clauses" found in Scripture. God will not force you to stay married to an unbelieving partner who doesn't want to stay married to you.

For the next note on "Marriage," turn to p. 196.

CHAPTER **10**

Lessons from Israel's Idolatry

I don't want you to forget, dear brothers and sisters,* about our ancestors in the wilderness long ago. All of them were guided by a cloud that moved ahead of them, and all of them walked through the sea on dry ground. ²In the cloud and in the sea, all of them were baptized as followers of Moses. ³All of them ate the same spiritual food, ⁴and all of them drank the same spiritual water. For they drank from the spiritual rock that traveled with them, and that rock was Christ. ⁵Yet God was not pleased with most of them, and their bodies were scattered in the wilderness.

⁶These things happened as a warning to us, so that we would not crave evil things as they did, ⁷or worship idols as some of them did. As the Scriptures say, "The people celebrated with feasting and drinking, and then indulged in pagan revelry."* ⁸And we must not engage in sexual immorality as some of them did, causing 23,000 of them to die in one day.

⁹Nor should we put Christ* to the test, as some of them did and then died from snakebites. ¹⁰And don't grumble as some of them did, and then were destroyed by the angel of death. ¹¹These things happened to them as examples for us. They were written down to warn us who live at the end of the age.

¹²If you think you are standing strong, be careful not to fall. ¹³The temptations in your life are no different from what others experience. And God is faithful. He will not allow the temptation to be more than you can stand. When you are tempted, he will show you a way out so that you can endure.

¹⁴So, my dear friends, flee from the worship of idols. ¹⁵You are reasonable people. Decide for yourselves if what I am saying is true. ¹⁶When we bless the cup at the Lord's Table, aren't we sharing in the blood of Christ? And when we break the bread, aren't we sharing in the body of Christ? ¹⁷And though we are many, we all eat from one loaf of bread, showing that we are one body. ¹⁸Think about the people of Israel. Weren't they united by eating the sacrifices at the altar?

¹⁹What am I trying to say? Am I saying that food offered to idols has some significance, or that idols are real gods? ²⁰No, not at all. I am saying that these sacrifices are offered to demons, not to God. And I don't want you to participate with demons. ²¹You cannot drink from the cup of the Lord and from the cup of demons, too. You cannot eat at the Lord's Table and at the table of demons, too. ²²What? Do we dare to rouse the Lord's jealousy? Do you think we are stronger than he is?

²³You say, "I am allowed to do anything"*— but not everything is good for you. You say, "I am allowed to do anything"—but not everything is beneficial. ²⁴Don't be concerned for your own good but for the good of others.

²⁵So you may eat any meat that is sold in the marketplace without raising questions of conscience. ²⁶For "the earth is the LORD's, and everything in it."*

²⁷If someone who isn't a believer asks you home for dinner, accept the invitation if you want to. Eat whatever is offered to you without raising questions of conscience. ²⁸(But suppose someone tells you, "This meat was offered to an idol." Don't eat it, out of consideration for the conscience of the one who told you. ²⁹It might not be a matter of conscience for you, but it is for the other person.) For why should my freedom be limited by what someone else thinks? ³⁰If I can thank God for the food and enjoy it, why should I be condemned for eating it?

³¹So whether you eat or drink, or whatever you do, do it all for the glory of God. ³²Don't give offense to Jews or Gentiles* or the church of God. ³³I, too, try to please everyone in everything I do. I don't just do what is best for me; I do what is best for others so that many may be saved. ¹¹:¹And you should imitate me, just as I imitate Christ.

CHAPTER **11**

Instructions for Public Worship

²I am so glad that you always keep me in your thoughts, and that you are following the teachings I passed on to you. ³But there is one thing I want you to know: The head of every man is Christ, the head of woman is man, and the head of Christ is God.* ⁴A man dishonors his head* if he covers his head while praying or prophesying. ⁵But a woman dishonors her head* if she prays or prophesies without a covering on her head, for this is the same as shaving her head. ⁶Yes, if she refuses to wear a head covering, she should cut off all her hair! But since it is shameful for a woman to have her hair cut or her head shaved, she should wear a covering.*

⁷A man should not wear anything on his head when worshiping, for man is made in

10:1 Greek *brothers.*   **10:7** Exod 32:6.   **10:9** Some manuscripts read *the Lord.*   **10:23** Greek *All things are lawful;* also in 10:23b.   **10:26** Ps 24:1.   **10:32** Greek *or Greeks.*   **11:3** Or *to know: The source of every man is Christ, the source of woman is man, and the source of Christ is God. Or to know: Every man is responsible to Christ, a woman is responsible to her husband, and Christ is responsible to God.*   **11:4** Or *dishonors Christ.*   **11:5** Or *dishonors her husband.*   **11:6** Or *should have long hair.*

God's image and reflects God's glory. And woman reflects man's glory. [8]For the first man didn't come from woman, but the first woman came from man. [9]And man was not made for woman, but woman was made for man. [10]For this reason, and because the angels are watching, a woman should wear a covering on her head to show she is under authority.*

[11]But among the Lord's people, women are not independent of men, and men are not independent of women. [12]For although the first woman came from man, every other man was born from a woman, and everything comes from God.

[13]Judge for yourselves. Is it right for a woman to pray to God in public without covering her head? [14]Isn't it obvious that it's disgraceful for a man to have long hair? [15]And isn't long hair a woman's pride and joy? For it has been given to her as a covering. [16]But if anyone wants to argue about this, I simply say that we have no other custom than this, and neither do God's other churches.

Order at the Lord's Supper

[17]But in the following instructions, I cannot praise you. For it sounds as if more harm than good is done when you meet together. [18]First, I hear that there are divisions among you when you meet as a church, and to some extent I believe it. [19]But, of course, there must be divisions among you so that you who have God's approval will be recognized!

[20]When you meet together, you are not really interested in the Lord's Supper. [21]For some of you hurry to eat your own meal without sharing with others. As a result, some go hungry while others get drunk. [22]What? Don't you have your own homes for eating and drinking? Or do you really want to disgrace God's church and shame the poor? What am I supposed to say? Do you want me to praise you? Well, I certainly will not praise you for this!

[23]For I pass on to you what I received from the Lord himself. On the night when he was betrayed, the Lord Jesus took some bread [24]and gave thanks to God for it. Then he broke it in pieces and said, "This is my body, which is given for you.* Do this to remember me." [25]In the same way, he took the cup of wine after supper, saying, "This cup is the new covenant between God and his people—an agreement confirmed with my blood. Do this to remember me as often as you drink it." [26]For every time you eat this bread and drink this cup, you are announcing the Lord's death until he comes again.

God realizes that we as humans will be tempted by one thing or another in this world. Fortunately for us, God cares so deeply about us that he has taken action to help us through times of temptation. This verse provides two rays of hope for you when you are tempted:

1. Jesus Understands Your Situation. Any temptation you are facing or will face has been faced before. Better yet, Jesus understands what it is like to be tempted, for the Bible teaches that he can sympathize with us, "for he faced all of the same testings we do, yet he did not sin" (Hebrews 4:15).

2. God Will Always Give You the Strength to Get Through the Temptation. When you face temptation, God will always give you the power to resist it or give you a way to escape it. Sometimes the way out of temptation is literal. For instance, if you are at the movie theater and an explicit sexual scene appears on the screen, the way of escape means walking out of the theater. At other times, it may mean relying on God's Holy Spirit to give you the power to resist.

The next time you are tempted or tested, remember this: God will allow hardship in the life of the Christian, but it will always be filtered through the screen of his love. He will never give you more than you can handle.

To begin the next topic, turn to p. A40.

[27]So anyone who eats this bread or drinks this cup of the Lord unworthily is guilty of sinning against* the body and blood of the Lord. [28]That is why you should examine yourself before eating the bread and drinking the cup. [29]For if you eat the bread or drink the cup without honoring the body of Christ,* you are eating and drinking God's judgment upon yourself. [30]That is why many of you are weak and sick and some have even died.

11:10 Greek *should have an authority on her head.*   **11:24** Greek *which is for you;* other manuscripts read *which is broken for you.*   **11:27** Or *is responsible for.*   **11:29** Greek *the body;* other manuscripts read *the Lord's body.*

[31] But if we would examine ourselves, we would not be judged by God in this way. [32] Yet when we are judged by the Lord, we are being disciplined so that we will not be condemned along with the world.

[33] So, my dear brothers and sisters,* when you gather for the Lord's Supper, wait for each other. [34] If you are really hungry, eat at home so you won't bring judgment upon yourselves when you meet together. I'll give you instructions about the other matters after I arrive.

CHAPTER 12
Spiritual Gifts

Now, dear brothers and sisters,* regarding your question about the special abilities the Spirit gives us. I don't want you to misunderstand this. [2] You know that when you were still pagans, you were led astray and swept along in worshiping speechless idols. [3] So I want you to know that no one speaking by the Spirit of God will curse Jesus, and no one can say Jesus is Lord, except by the Holy Spirit.

[4] There are different kinds of spiritual gifts, but the same Spirit is the source of them all. [5] There are different kinds of service, but we serve the same Lord. [6] God works in different ways, but it is the same God who does the work in all of us.

[7] A spiritual gift is given to each of us so we can help each other. [8] To one person the Spirit gives the ability to give wise advice*; to another the same Spirit gives a message of special knowledge.* [9] The same Spirit gives great faith to another, and to someone else the one Spirit gives the gift of healing. [10] He gives one person the power to perform miracles, and another the ability to prophesy. He gives someone else the ability to discern whether a message is from the Spirit of God or from another spirit. Still another person is given the ability to speak in unknown languages,* while another is given the ability to interpret what is being said. [11] It is the one and only Spirit who distributes all these gifts. He alone decides which gift each person should have.

One Body with Many Parts

[12] The human body has many parts, but the many parts make up one whole body. So it is with the body of Christ. [13] Some of us are Jews, some are Gentiles,* some are slaves, and some are free. But we have all been baptized into one body by one Spirit, and we all share the same Spirit.*

[14] Yes, the body has many different parts, not just one part. [15] If the foot says, "I am not a part of the body because I am not a hand," that does not make it any less a part of the body. [16] And if the ear says, "I am not part of the body because I am not an eye," would that make it any less a part of the body? [17] If the whole body were an eye, how would you hear? Or if your whole body were an ear, how would you smell anything?

[18] But our bodies have many parts, and God has put each part just where he wants it. [19] How strange a body would be if it had only one part! [20] Yes, there are many parts, but only one body. [21] The eye can never say to the hand, "I don't need you." The head can't say to the feet, "I don't need you."

[22] In fact, some parts of the body that seem weakest and least important are actually the most necessary. [23] And the parts we regard as less honorable are those we clothe with the greatest care. So we carefully protect those

11:33 Greek *brothers.*   12:1 Greek *brothers.*   12:8a Or *gives a word of wisdom.*   12:8b Or *gives a word of knowledge.*
12:10 Or *in various tongues;* also in 12:28, 30.   12:13a Greek *some are Greeks.*   12:13b Greek *we were all given one Spirit to drink.*

---

off and running

DOES THIS ACTIVITY BUILD ME UP SPIRITUALLY?
Read 1 CORINTHIANS 10:23

This verse tackles the issue of whether certain activities will be spiritually constructive in your life— even if it falls into a so-called "gray" area. A more literal translation of that verse is "All things are permissible, but not all things promote growth in Christian character." The next time you question whether you should be seeing a certain movie, participating in a specific activity, or engaging in a certain habit, ask yourself the following questions:

- Will this activity make the things of this world more appealing than the things of God?

parts that should not be seen, [24] while the more honorable parts do not require this special care. So God has put the body together such that extra honor and care are given to those parts that have less dignity. [25] This makes for harmony among the members, so that all the members care for each other. [26] If one part suffers, all the parts suffer with it, and if one part is honored, all the parts are glad.

[27] All of you together are Christ's body, and each of you is a part of it. [28] Here are some of the parts God has appointed for the church:

first are apostles,
second are prophets,
third are teachers,
then those who do miracles,
those who have the gift of healing,
those who can help others,
those who have the gift of leadership,
those who speak in unknown languages.

[29] Are we all apostles? Are we all prophets? Are we all teachers? Do we all have the power to do miracles? [30] Do we all have the gift of healing? Do we all have the ability to speak in unknown languages? Do we all have the ability to interpret unknown languages? Of course not! [31] So you should earnestly desire the most helpful gifts.

But now let me show you a way of life that is best of all.

CHAPTER **13**
Love Is the Greatest
If I could speak all the languages of earth and of angels, but didn't love others, I would only be a noisy gong or a clanging cymbal. [2] If I had the gift of prophecy, and if I understood all of God's secret plans and possessed all knowledge, and if I had such faith that I could move mountains, but didn't love others, I would be nothing. [3] If I gave everything I have to the poor and even sacrificed my body, I could boast about it;* but if I didn't love others, I would have gained nothing.

[4] Love is patient and kind. Love is not jealous or boastful or proud [5] or rude. It does not demand its own way. It is not irritable, and it keeps no record of being wronged. [6] It does not rejoice about injustice but rejoices whenever the truth wins out. [7] Love never gives up, never loses faith, is always hopeful, and endures through every circumstance.

[8] Prophecy and speaking in unknown languages* and special knowledge will become useless. But love will last forever! [9] Now our knowledge is partial and incomplete, and even the gift of prophecy reveals only part of the whole picture! [10] But when the time of perfection comes, these partial things will become useless.

[11] When I was a child, I spoke and thought and reasoned as a child. But when I grew up, I put away childish things. [12] Now we see things imperfectly, like puzzling reflections in a mirror, but then we will see everything with perfect clarity.* All that I know now is partial and incomplete, but then I will know everything completely, just as God now knows me completely.

[13] Three things will last forever—faith, hope, and love—and the greatest of these is love.

CHAPTER **14**
Tongues and Prophecy
Let love be your highest goal! But you should also desire the special abilities the Spirit gives—especially the ability to prophesy. [2] For if you have the ability to speak in tongues,* you will be talking only to God, since people won't

13:3 Some manuscripts read *sacrificed my body to be burned.*   13:8 Or *in tongues.*   13:12 Greek *see face to face.*
14:2a Or *in unknown languages;* also in 14:4, 5, 13, 14, 18, 22, 26, 27, 28, 39.

- Will it keep me from prayer?
- Will it diminish my hunger for God's Word?
- Will it spiritually tear me down by pulling me away from other Christian believers?

You do not have time for anything that would make this world more attractive, dull your desire for prayer, take away your appetite for Bible study, or keep you from Christian fellowship. Instead, look for things that will benefit and build your Christian character.

For the next note on "Responsibility," turn to p. 194.

be able to understand you. You will be speaking by the power of the Spirit,* but it will all be mysterious. ³But one who prophesies strengthens others, encourages them, and comforts them. ⁴A person who speaks in tongues is strengthened personally, but one who speaks a word of prophecy strengthens the entire church.

⁵I wish you could all speak in tongues, but even more I wish you could all prophesy. For prophecy is greater than speaking in tongues, unless someone interprets what you are saying so that the whole church will be strengthened.

⁶Dear brothers and sisters,* if I should come to you speaking in an unknown language,* how would that help you? But if I bring you a revelation or some special knowledge or prophecy or teaching, that will be helpful. ⁷Even lifeless instruments like the flute or the harp must play the notes clearly, or no one will recognize the melody. ⁸And if the bugler doesn't sound a clear call, how will the soldiers know they are being called to battle?

⁹It's the same for you. If you speak to people in words they don't understand, how will they know what you are saying? You might as well be talking into empty space.

¹⁰There are many different languages in the world, and every language has meaning. ¹¹But if I don't understand a language, I will be a foreigner to someone who speaks it, and the one who speaks it will be a foreigner to me. ¹²And the same is true for you. Since you are so eager to have the special abilities the Spirit gives, seek those that will strengthen the whole church.

¹³So anyone who speaks in tongues should pray also for the ability to interpret what has been said. ¹⁴For if I pray in tongues, my spirit is praying, but I don't understand what I am saying.

¹⁵Well then, what shall I do? I will pray in the spirit,* and I will also pray in words I understand. I will sing in the spirit, and I will also sing in words I understand. ¹⁶For if you praise God only in the spirit, how can those who don't understand you praise God along with you? How can they join you in giving thanks when they don't understand what you are saying? ¹⁷You will be giving thanks very well, but it won't strengthen the people who hear you.

¹⁸I thank God that I speak in tongues more than any of you. ¹⁹But in a church meeting I would rather speak five understandable words to help others than ten thousand words in an unknown language.

²⁰Dear brothers and sisters, don't be childish in your understanding of these things. Be innocent as babies when it comes to evil, but be mature in understanding matters of this kind. ²¹It is written in the Scriptures*:

"I will speak to my own people
    through strange languages
    and through the lips of foreigners.
But even then, they will not listen to me,"*
    says the Lord.

²²So you see that speaking in tongues is a sign, not for believers, but for unbelievers. Prophecy, however, is for the benefit of believers, not unbelievers. ²³Even so, if unbelievers or people who don't understand these things come into your church meeting and hear everyone speaking in an unknown language, they will think you are crazy. ²⁴But if all of you are prophesying, and unbelievers or people who don't understand these things come into your meeting, they will be convicted of sin and judged by what you say. ²⁵As they listen, their secret thoughts will be exposed, and they will fall to their knees and worship God, declaring, "God is truly here among you."

A Call to Orderly Worship

²⁶Well, my brothers and sisters, let's summarize. When you meet together, one will sing, another will teach, another will tell some special revelation God has given, one will speak in tongues, and another will interpret what is said. But everything that is done must strengthen all of you.

²⁷No more than two or three should speak in tongues. They must speak one at a time, and someone must interpret what they say. ²⁸But if no one is present who can interpret, they must be silent in your church meeting and speak in tongues to God privately.

²⁹Let two or three people prophesy, and let the others evaluate what is said. ³⁰But if someone is prophesying and another person receives a revelation from the Lord, the one who is speaking must stop. ³¹In this way, all who prophesy will have a turn to speak, one after the other, so that everyone will learn and be encouraged. ³²Remember that people who prophesy are in control of their spirit and can take turns. ³³For God is not a God of disorder but of peace, as in all the meetings of God's holy people.*

³⁴Women should be silent during the church meetings. It is not proper for them to speak. They should be submissive, just as the law says. ³⁵If they have any questions, they should ask their husbands at home, for it is improper for women to speak in church meetings.*

14:2b Or *speaking in your spirit.*   14:6a Greek *brothers;* also in 14:20, 26, 39.   14:6b Or *in tongues;* also in 14:19, 23. 14:15 Or *in the Spirit;* also in 14:15b, 16.   14:21a Greek *in the law.*   14:21b Isa 28:11-12.   14:33 The phrase *as in all the meetings of God's holy people* could instead be joined to the beginning of 14:34.   14:35 Some manuscripts place verses 34-35 after 14:40.

³⁶ Or do you think God's word originated with you Corinthians? Are you the only ones to whom it was given? ³⁷ If you claim to be a prophet or think you are spiritual, you should recognize that what I am saying is a command from the Lord himself. ³⁸ But if you do not recognize this, you yourself will not be recognized.*

³⁹ So, my dear brothers and sisters, be eager to prophesy, and don't forbid speaking in tongues. ⁴⁰ But be sure that everything is done properly and in order.

CHAPTER 15
The Resurrection of Christ

Let me now remind you, dear brothers and sisters,* of the Good News I preached to you before. You welcomed it then, and you still stand firm in it. ² It is this Good News that saves you if you continue to believe the message I told you—unless, of course, you believed something that was never true in the first place.*

³ I passed on to you what was most important and what had also been passed on to me. Christ died for our sins, just as the Scriptures said. ⁴ He was buried, and he was raised from the dead on the third day, just as the Scriptures said. ⁵ He was seen by Peter* and then by the Twelve. ⁶ After that, he was seen by more than 500 of his followers* at one time, most of whom are still alive, though some have died. ⁷ Then he was seen by James and later by all the apostles. ⁸ Last of all, as though I had been born at the wrong time, I also saw him. ⁹ For I am the least of all the apostles. In fact, I'm not even worthy to be called an apostle after the way I persecuted God's church.

¹⁰ But whatever I am now, it is all because God poured out his special favor on me—and not without results. For I have worked harder than any of the other apostles; yet it was not I but God who was working through me by his grace. ¹¹ So it makes no difference whether I preach or they preach, for we all preach the same message you have already believed.

The Resurrection of the Dead

¹² But tell me this—since we preach that Christ rose from the dead, why are some of you saying there will be no resurrection of the dead? ¹³ For if there is no resurrection of the dead, then Christ has not been raised either. ¹⁴ And if Christ has not been raised, then all our preaching is useless, and your faith is useless. ¹⁵ And we apostles would all be lying about God—for we have said that God raised Christ from the

14:38 Some manuscripts read *If you are ignorant of this, stay in your ignorance.* **15:1** Greek *brothers;* also in 15:31, 50, 58. **15:2** Or *unless you never believed it in the first place.* **15:5** Greek *Cephas.* **15:6** Greek *the brothers.*

first steps

YOU HAVE A PLACE IN THE CHURCH
Read 1 CORINTHIANS 12:12-31

The apostle Paul used this illustration of the physical body to drive home an important point: Every single person has a vital role to play in the body of Christ. That means God has a specific purpose for you to carry out in your local church, and it is up to you to fill that purpose, with God's help. This passage explains why this is so important.

The Church Consists of Different People with Different Roles. When God designed the church, he did not intend for its members to be "Christian clones." Instead, he chose to use the various groups and spiritual gifts found throughout the church to bring attention to the person who unifies us: Jesus Christ (see Ephesians 3:10-11, p. 229). When the church operates as God intended, it serves as a powerful witness to a watching world.

No One Person Is More Valuable than Another. No gift of the Holy Spirit is "better" than another. Therefore, each individual has a special place of significance within the body of Christ. Even though your role may not seem as visible as others—for instance, God may be using you to visit convalescent homes while someone else leads a Bible study—your role is just as vital.

We Need One Another to Function as God Intended. If you fail to use the special gifts and abilities God has given you, you do a disservice to the church. God wants you to realize the importance of working together and building friendships with other committed Christians. One could liken the church to a group of coals burning brightly together. Each coal not only emanates its own heat, but also helps to keep the others hot, benefiting from their warmth as well. If you were to isolate one of those coals from the others, it would only be a matter of time until its heat dissipated. The same holds true for us as believers. We need one another to function as individuals and as the body of Christ.

To begin the next topic, turn to p. A39.

cornerstones

LOVE SURPASSES ALL SPIRITUAL GIFTS

Read 1 CORINTHIANS 13:1-13

This passage gives one of the most complete descriptions of love in the Bible. More importantly, it shows that love needs to be the one thing in life we seek more than anything else. Without it, whatever we do or say really has no lasting value. Compare the love described here with the superficial love found in this world:

- God says love should be directed toward others (verses 1-3). The world says love should be directed toward ourselves.
- God says love is patient and kind (verse 4). The world says love satisfies your immediate needs.
- God says love is never jealous or envious (verse 4). The world says love means that you deserve the "best."
- God says love is never boastful or proud (verse 4). The world says love isn't necessary to make people respect you.
- God says love is never rude (verse 5). The world says love lets you act as you please.
- God says love does not demand its own way (verse 5). The world says love gets in the way of what is in it for me.
- God says love is not irritable or touchy, and it holds no grudges (verse 5). The world says love takes a backseat when it comes to seeking revenge.
- God says love rejoices in justice and truth (verse 6). The world says love understands—even ignores—evil.
- God says love is loyal (verse 7). The world says love should be self-serving.

The kind of love God wants you to give others is impossible to "manufacture" on our own. You might say that it is a "supernatural" love. It is a natural outflow of God's presence in our lives. That is why the Bible says, "[God] has given us the Holy Spirit to fill our hearts with his love" (Romans 5:5).

If you feel your love for others is falling short of God's ideal, ask the Holy Spirit to strengthen you in this area. Your relationships with others will never be the same.

For the next note on "Love," turn to p. 126.

For the next note on "Love," turn to p. 126.

grave. But that can't be true if there is no resurrection of the dead. [16]And if there is no resurrection of the dead, then Christ has not been raised. [17]And if Christ has not been raised, then your faith is useless and you are still guilty of your sins. [18]In that case, all who have died believing in Christ are lost! [19]And if our hope in Christ is only for this life, we are more to be pitied than anyone in the world.

[20]But in fact, Christ has been raised from the dead. He is the first of a great harvest of all who have died.

[21]So you see, just as death came into the world through a man, now the resurrection from the dead has begun through another man. [22]Just as everyone dies because we all belong to Adam, everyone who belongs to Christ will be given new life. [23]But there is an order to this resurrection: Christ was raised as the first of the harvest; then all who belong to Christ will be raised when he comes back.

[24]After that the end will come, when he will turn the Kingdom over to God the Father, having destroyed every ruler and authority and power. [25]For Christ must reign until he humbles all his enemies beneath his feet. [26]And the last enemy to be destroyed is death. [27]For the Scriptures say, "God has put all things under his authority."* (Of course, when it says "all things are under his authority," that does not include God himself, who gave Christ his authority.) [28]Then, when all things are under his authority, the Son will put himself under God's authority, so that God, who gave his Son authority over all things, will be utterly supreme over everything everywhere.

[29]If the dead will not be raised, what point is there in people being baptized for those who

15:27 Ps 8:6.

are dead? Why do it unless the dead will some-day rise again?

³⁰And why should we ourselves risk our lives hour by hour? ³¹For I swear, dear brothers and sisters, that I face death daily. This is as certain as my pride in what Christ Jesus our Lord has done in you. ³²And what value was there in fighting wild beasts—those people of Ephesus*—if there will be no resurrection from the dead? And if there is no resurrection, "Let's feast and drink, for tomorrow we die!"* ³³Don't be fooled by those who say such things, for "bad company corrupts good character." ³⁴Think carefully about what is right, and stop sinning. For to your shame I say that some of you don't know God at all.

The Resurrection Body

³⁵But someone may ask, "How will the dead be raised? What kind of bodies will they have?" ³⁶What a foolish question! When you put a seed into the ground, it doesn't grow into a plant unless it dies first. ³⁷And what you put in the ground is not the plant that will grow, but only a bare seed of wheat or whatever you are planting. ³⁸Then God gives it the new body he wants it to have. A different plant grows from each kind of seed. ³⁹Similarly there are different kinds of flesh—one kind for humans, another for animals, another for birds, and another for fish.

⁴⁰There are also bodies in the heavens and bodies on the earth. The glory of the heavenly bodies is different from the glory of the earthly bodies. ⁴¹The sun has one kind of glory, while the moon and stars each have another kind. And even the stars differ from each other in their glory.

⁴²It is the same way with the resurrection of the dead. Our earthly bodies are planted in the ground when we die, but they will be raised to live forever. ⁴³Our bodies are buried in brokenness, but they will be raised in glory. They are buried in weakness, but they will be raised in strength. ⁴⁴They are buried as natural human bodies, but they will be raised as spiritual bodies. For just as there are natural bodies, there are also spiritual bodies.

⁴⁵The Scriptures tell us, "The first man, Adam, became a living person."* But the last Adam—that is, Christ—is a life-giving Spirit. ⁴⁶What comes first is the natural body, then the spiritual body comes later. ⁴⁷Adam, the first man, was made from the dust of the earth, while Christ, the second man, came from heaven. ⁴⁸Earthly people are like the earthly man, and heavenly people are like the heavenly man. ⁴⁹Just as we are now like the earthly man, we will someday be like* the heavenly man.

⁵⁰What I am saying, dear brothers and sisters, is that our physical bodies cannot inherit the Kingdom of God. These dying bodies cannot inherit what will last forever.

⁵¹But let me reveal to you a wonderful secret. We will not all die, but we will all be transformed! ⁵²It will happen in a moment, in the blink of an eye, when the last trumpet is blown. For when the trumpet sounds, those who have died will be raised to live forever. And we who are living will also be transformed. ⁵³For our dying bodies must be transformed into bodies that will never die; our mortal bodies must be transformed into immortal bodies.

⁵⁴Then, when our dying bodies have been transformed into bodies that will never die,* this Scripture will be fulfilled:

"Death is swallowed up in victory.*
⁵⁵ O death, where is your victory?
　O death, where is your sting?*"

⁵⁶For sin is the sting that results in death, and the law gives sin its power. ⁵⁷But thank God! He gives us victory over sin and death through our Lord Jesus Christ.

⁵⁸So, my dear brothers and sisters, be strong and immovable. Always work enthusiastically for the Lord, for you know that nothing you do for the Lord is ever useless.

CHAPTER 16

The Collection for Jerusalem

Now regarding your question about the money being collected for God's people in Jerusalem. You should follow the same procedure I gave to the churches in Galatia. ²On the first day of each week, you should each put aside a portion of the money you have earned. Don't wait until I get there and then try to collect it all at once. ³When I come, I will write letters of recommendation for the messengers you choose to deliver your gift to Jerusalem. ⁴And if it seems appropriate for me to go along, they can travel with me.

Paul's Final Instructions

⁵I am coming to visit you after I have been to Macedonia,* for I am planning to travel through Macedonia. ⁶Perhaps I will stay awhile with you, possibly all winter, and then you can send me on my way to my next destination. ⁷This time I don't want to make just a short visit and then go right on. I want to come and stay awhile, if the Lord will let me. ⁸In the

---

15:32a Greek *fighting wild beasts in Ephesus.*　15:32b Isa 22:13.　15:45 Gen 2:7.　15:49 Some manuscripts read *let us be like.*　15:54a Some manuscripts add *and our mortal bodies have been transformed into immortal bodies.*　15:54b Isa 25:8.　15:55 Hos 13:14 (Greek version).　16:5 *Macedonia* was in the northern region of Greece.

meantime, I will be staying here at Ephesus until the Festival of Pentecost. [9] There is a wide-open door for a great work here, although many oppose me.

[10] When Timothy comes, don't intimidate him. He is doing the Lord's work, just as I am. [11] Don't let anyone treat him with contempt. Send him on his way with your blessing when he returns to me. I expect him to come with the other believers.*

[12] Now about our brother Apollos—I urged him to visit you with the other believers, but he was not willing to go right now. He will see you later when he has the opportunity.

[13] Be on guard. Stand firm in the faith. Be courageous.* Be strong. [14] And do everything with love.

[15] You know that Stephanas and his household were the first of the harvest of believers in Greece,* and they are spending their lives in service to God's people. I urge you, dear brothers and sisters,* [16] to submit to them and others

like them who serve with such devotion. [17] I am very glad that Stephanas, Fortunatus, and Achaicus have come here. They have been providing the help you weren't here to give me. [18] They have been a wonderful encouragement to me, as they have been to you. You must show your appreciation to all who serve so well.

Paul's Final Greetings

[19] The churches here in the province of Asia* send greetings in the Lord, as do Aquila and Priscilla* and all the others who gather in their home for church meetings. [20] All the brothers and sisters here send greetings to you. Greet each other with Christian love.*

[21] HERE IS MY GREETING IN MY OWN HANDWRITING—PAUL.

[22] If anyone does not love the Lord, that person is cursed. Our Lord, come!*

[23] May the grace of the Lord Jesus be with you.

[24] My love to all of you in Christ Jesus.*

16:11 Greek *with the brothers;* also in 16:12.   16:13 Greek *Be men.*   16:15a Greek *in Achaia,* the southern region of the Greek peninsula.   16:15b Greek *brothers;* also in 16:20.   16:19a *Asia* was a Roman province in what is now western Turkey. 16:19b Greek *Prisca.*   16:20 Greek *with a sacred kiss.*   16:22 From Aramaic, *Marana tha.* Some manuscripts read *Maran atha, "Our Lord has come."*   16:24 Some manuscripts add *Amen.*

2 Corinthians

AUTHOR: **PAUL** | DATE WRITTEN: **A.D. 55–57** | GENRE: **EPISTLE**

Some of the Corinthians who were still living in sin after Paul's first letter denied Paul's authority. Paul wrote this second letter to deal with the problems that persisted within the Corinthian church.

CHAPTER 1

Greetings from Paul

This letter is from Paul, chosen by the will of God to be an apostle of Christ Jesus, and from our brother Timothy.

I am writing to God's church in Corinth and to all of his holy people throughout Greece.*

²May God our Father and the Lord Jesus Christ give you grace and peace.

God Offers Comfort to All

³All praise to God, the Father of our Lord Jesus Christ. God is our merciful Father and the source of all comfort. ⁴He comforts us in all our troubles so that we can comfort others. When they are troubled, we will be able to give them the same comfort God has given us. ⁵For the more we suffer for Christ, the more God will shower us with his comfort through Christ. ⁶Even when we are weighed down with troubles, it is for your comfort and salvation! For when we ourselves are comforted, we will certainly comfort you. Then you can patiently endure the same things we suffer. ⁷We are confident that as you share in our sufferings, you will also share in the comfort God gives us.

⁸We think you ought to know, dear brothers and sisters,* about the trouble we went through in the province of Asia. We were crushed and overwhelmed beyond our ability to endure, and we thought we would never live through it. ⁹In fact, we expected to die. But as a result, we stopped relying on ourselves and learned to rely only on God, who raises the dead. ¹⁰And he did rescue us from mortal danger, and he will rescue us again. We have placed our confidence in him, and he will continue to rescue us. ¹¹And you are helping us by praying for us. Then many people will give thanks because God has graciously answered so many prayers for our safety.

Paul's Change of Plans

¹²We can say with confidence and a clear conscience that we have lived with a God-given holiness* and sincerity in all our dealings. We have depended on God's grace, not on our own human wisdom. That is how we have conducted ourselves before the world, and especially toward you. ¹³Our letters have been straightforward, and there is nothing written between the lines and nothing you can't understand. I hope someday you will fully understand us, ¹⁴even if you don't understand us now. Then on the day when the Lord Jesus* returns, you will be proud of us in the same way we are proud of you.

¹⁵Since I was so sure of your understanding and trust, I wanted to give you a double blessing by visiting you twice—¹⁶first on my way to Macedonia and again when I returned from Macedonia.* Then you could send me on my way to Judea.

¹⁷You may be asking why I changed my plan. Do you think I make my plans carelessly? Do you think I am like people of the world who say "Yes" when they really mean "No"? ¹⁸As surely as God is faithful, our word to you does not waver between "Yes" and "No." ¹⁹For Jesus Christ, the Son of God, does not waver between "Yes" and "No." He is the one whom Silas,* Timothy, and I preached to you, and as God's ultimate "Yes," he always does what he says. ²⁰For all of God's promises have been fulfilled in Christ with a resounding "Yes!" And through Christ,

1:1 Greek *Achaia*, the southern region of the Greek peninsula. 1:8 Greek *brothers*. 1:12 Some manuscripts read *honesty*. 1:14 Some manuscripts read *our Lord Jesus*. 1:16 *Macedonia* was in the northern region of Greece. 1:19 Greek *Silvanus*.

our "Amen" (which means "Yes") ascends to God for his glory.

[21] It is God who enables us, along with you, to stand firm for Christ. He has commissioned us, [22] and he has identified us as his own by placing the Holy Spirit in our hearts as the first installment that guarantees everything he has promised us.

[23] Now I call upon God as my witness that I am telling the truth. The reason I didn't return to Corinth was to spare you from a severe rebuke. [24] But that does not mean we want to dominate you by telling you how to put your faith into practice. We want to work together with you so you will be full of joy, for it is by your own faith that you stand firm.

CHAPTER 2

So I decided that I would not bring you grief with another painful visit. [2] For if I cause you grief, who will make me glad? Certainly not someone I have grieved. [3] That is why I wrote to you as I did, so that when I do come, I won't be grieved by the very ones who ought to give me the greatest joy. Surely you all know that my joy comes from your being joyful. [4] I wrote that letter in great anguish, with a troubled heart and many tears. I didn't want to grieve you, but I wanted to let you know how much love I have for you.

Forgiveness for the Sinner

[5] I am not overstating it when I say that the man who caused all the trouble hurt all of you more than he hurt me. [6] Most of you opposed him, and that was punishment enough. [7] Now, however, it is time to forgive and comfort him. Otherwise he may be overcome by discouragement. [8] So I urge you now to reaffirm your love for him.

[9] I wrote to you as I did to test you and see if you would fully comply with my instructions. [10] When you forgive this man, I forgive him, too. And when I forgive whatever needs to be forgiven, I do so with Christ's authority for your benefit, [11] so that Satan will not outsmart us. For we are familiar with his evil schemes.

[12] When I came to the city of Troas to preach the Good News of Christ, the Lord opened a door of opportunity for me. [13] But I had no peace of mind because my dear brother Titus hadn't yet arrived with a report from you. So I said good-bye and went on to Macedonia to find him.

Ministers of the New Covenant

[14] But thank God! He has made us his captives and continues to lead us along in Christ's tri-

umphal procession. Now he uses us to spread the knowledge of Christ everywhere, like a sweet perfume. [15] Our lives are a Christ-like fragrance rising up to God. But this fragrance is perceived differently by those who are being saved and by those who are perishing. [16] To those who are perishing, we are a dreadful smell of death and doom. But to those who are being saved, we are a life-giving perfume. And who is adequate for such a task as this?

[17] You see, we are not like the many hucksters* who preach for personal profit. We preach the word of God with sincerity and with Christ's authority, knowing that God is watching us.

CHAPTER 3

Are we beginning to praise ourselves again? Are we like others, who need to bring you letters of recommendation, or who ask you to write such letters on their behalf? Surely not! [2] The only letter of recommendation we need is you yourselves. Your lives are a letter written in our* hearts; everyone can read it and recognize our good work among you. [3] Clearly, you are a letter from Christ showing the result of our ministry among you. This "letter" is written not with pen and ink, but with the Spirit of the living God. It is carved not on tablets of stone, but on human hearts.

[4] We are confident of all this because of our great trust in God through Christ. [5] It is not that we think we are qualified to do anything on our own. Our qualification comes from God. [6] He has enabled us to be ministers of his new covenant. This is a covenant not of written laws, but of the Spirit. The old written covenant ends in death; but under the new covenant, the Spirit gives life.

The Glory of the New Covenant

[7] The old way,* with laws etched in stone, led to death, though it began with such glory that the people of Israel could not bear to look at Moses' face. For his face shone with the glory of God, even though the brightness was already fading away. [8] Shouldn't we expect far greater glory under the new way, now that the Holy Spirit is giving life? [9] If the old way, which brings condemnation, was glorious, how much more glorious is the new way, which makes us right with God! [10] In fact, that first glory was not glorious at all compared with the overwhelming glory of the new way. [11] So if the old way, which has been replaced, was glorious, how much more glorious is the new, which remains forever!

[12] Since this new way gives us such confi-

2:17 Some manuscripts read *the rest of the hucksters.*   3:2 Some manuscripts read *your.*   3:7 Or *ministry;* also in 3:8, 9, 10, 11, 12.

dence, we can be very bold. ¹³We are not like Moses, who put a veil over his face so the people of Israel would not see the glory, even though it was destined to fade away. ¹⁴But the people's minds were hardened, and to this day whenever the old covenant is being read, the same veil covers their minds so they cannot understand the truth. And this veil can be removed only by believing in Christ. ¹⁵Yes, even today when they read Moses' writings, their hearts are covered with that veil, and they do not understand.

¹⁶But whenever someone turns to the Lord, the veil is taken away. ¹⁷For the Lord is the Spirit, and wherever the Spirit of the Lord is, there is freedom. ¹⁸So all of us who have had that veil removed can see and reflect the glory of the Lord. And the Lord—who is the Spirit—makes us more and more like him as we are changed into his glorious image.

CHAPTER 4
Treasure in Fragile Clay Jars
Therefore, since God in his mercy has given us this new way,* we never give up. ²We reject all shameful deeds and underhanded methods. We don't try to trick anyone or distort the word of God. We tell the truth before God, and all who are honest know this.

³If the Good News we preach is hidden behind a veil, it is hidden only from people who are perishing. ⁴Satan, who is the god of this world, has blinded the minds of those who don't believe. They are unable to see the glorious light of the Good News. They don't understand this message about the glory of Christ, who is the exact likeness of God.

⁵You see, we don't go around preaching about ourselves. We preach that Jesus Christ is Lord, and we ourselves are your servants for Jesus' sake. ⁶For God, who said, "Let there be light in the darkness," has made this light shine in our hearts so we could know the glory of God that is seen in the face of Jesus Christ.

⁷We now have this light shining in our hearts, but we ourselves are like fragile clay jars containing this great treasure.* This makes it clear that our great power is from God, not from ourselves.

⁸We are pressed on every side by troubles, but we are not crushed. We are perplexed, but not driven to despair. ⁹We are hunted down, but never abandoned by God. We get knocked down, but we are not destroyed. ¹⁰Through suffering, our bodies continue to share in the death of Jesus so that the life of Jesus may also be seen in our bodies.

first steps

TRIALS HELP US COMFORT OTHERS

Read 2 CORINTHIANS 1:3-7

The apostle Paul penned these words from personal experience. He had seen his share of suffering over the years—particularly for the sake of the gospel of Jesus Christ. He was thrown into prison on more than one occasion, but he continued to praise God and share his faith in Christ. He was shipwrecked, abandoned by former friends, pelted by stones, and left for dead. His faith, however, remained firm. Why? Because he learned to draw his comfort from the Lord. This then enabled him to be a greater source of comfort to those around him.

The next time someone ridicules or rejects you because of your commitment to Christ, remember Paul's words. You do not need to fear trials in your life. No matter how great a hardship you face, realize that Jesus *will* comfort and strengthen you. In turn, you will be better equipped to comfort those around you who suffer the same hardships.

For the next note on "Have Courage in Trials," turn to p. 213.

¹¹Yes, we live under constant danger of death because we serve Jesus, so that the life of Jesus will be evident in our dying bodies. ¹²So we live in the face of death, but this has resulted in eternal life for you.

¹³But we continue to preach because we have the same kind of faith the psalmist had when he said, "I believed in God, so I spoke."* ¹⁴We know that God, who raised the Lord Jesus,* will also raise us with Jesus and present us to himself together with you. ¹⁵All of this is for your benefit. And as God's grace reaches more and more people, there will be great thanksgiving, and God will receive more and more glory.

¹⁶That is why we never give up. Though our bodies are dying, our spirits are* being renewed every day. ¹⁷For our present troubles are small and won't last very long. Yet they produce for us a glory that vastly outweighs them and will last forever! ¹⁸So we don't look at the troubles we can see now; rather, we fix our gaze on

---

4:1 Or *ministry.*   **4:7** Greek *We now have this treasure in clay jars.*   **4:13** Ps 116:10.   **4:14** Some manuscripts read *who raised Jesus.*   **4:16** Greek *our inner being is.*

cornerstones

WHAT ARE SATAN'S ABILITIES?

Read 2 CORINTHIANS 4:3-4

Ever since Satan lost his privileges and was cast to this earth, he has been using his abilities to oppose the work that God has been seeking to accomplish. Paul's second letter to the Corinthians reveals at least three of Satan's abilities:

1. He Is the God of This World. This becomes more and more evident as you survey the increasing wickedness around you. While Christ conquered sin and death at the cross, this world is still flawed and evil. But Satan will lose his reign in this world when Christ returns to establish his Kingdom on earth.

2. He Blinds the Minds of Unbelievers. According to this text, Satan wants to keep those who do not have a relationship with God from coming to God. The unbelieving mind has a difficult time understanding the message of the gospel because Satan has darkened or blinded that person's mind. Yet Christ can break through that barrier (see 2 Timothy 2:24-26, p. 266).

3. He Is a Master Counterfeiter. One of Satan's greatest abilities is deception. He is good at making lies look like truth. Paul describes Satan as someone who disguises himself as an angel of light (see 2 Corinthians 11:14, p. 218). That is, he fools people by making them think the lies he offers are truth. His lies take on various forms, such as cults and false doctrines. But we can discern the difference between truth and error when we test them against what is found in God's Word.

For the next note on "Who Is the Devil?" turn to p. 328.

---

things that cannot be seen. For the things we see now will soon be gone, but the things we cannot see will last forever.

CHAPTER 5
New Bodies

For we know that when this earthly tent we live in is taken down (that is, when we die and leave this earthly body), we will have a house in heaven, an eternal body made for us by God himself and not by human hands. ²We grow weary in our present bodies, and we long to put on our heavenly bodies like new clothing. ³For we will put on heavenly bodies; we will not be spirits without bodies.* ⁴While we live in these earthly bodies, we groan and sigh, but it's not that we want to die and get rid of these bodies that clothe us. Rather, we want to put on our new bodies so that these dying bodies will be swallowed up by life. ⁵God himself has prepared us for this, and as a guarantee he has given us his Holy Spirit.

⁶So we are always confident, even though we know that as long as we live in these bodies we are not at home with the Lord. ⁷For we live by believing and not by seeing. ⁸Yes, we are fully confident, and we would rather be away from these earthly bodies, for then we will be at home with the Lord. ⁹So whether we are here in this body or away from this body, our goal is to please him. ¹⁰For we must all stand before Christ to be judged. We will each receive whatever we deserve for the good or evil we have done in this earthly body.

We Are God's Ambassadors

¹¹Because we understand our fearful responsibility to the Lord, we work hard to persuade others. God knows we are sincere, and I hope you know this, too. ¹²Are we commending ourselves to you again? No, we are giving you a reason to be proud of us,* so you can answer those who brag about having a spectacular ministry rather than having a sincere heart. ¹³If it seems we are crazy, it is to bring glory to God. And if we are in our right minds, it is for your benefit. ¹⁴Either way, Christ's love controls us.* Since we believe that Christ died for all, we also believe that we have all died to our old life.* ¹⁵He died for everyone so that those who receive his new life will no longer live for themselves. Instead, they will live for Christ, who died and was raised for them.

¹⁶So we have stopped evaluating others from a human point of view. At one time we thought of Christ merely from a human point of view. How differently we know him now! ¹⁷This means that anyone who belongs to Christ has

5:3 Greek *we will not be naked.*   **5:12** Some manuscripts read *proud of yourselves.*   **5:14a** Or *urges us on.*   **5:14b** Greek *Since one died for all, then all died.*

become a new person. The old life is gone; a new life has begun! [18]And all of this is a gift from God, who brought us back to himself through Christ. And God has given us this task of reconciling people to him. [19]For God was in Christ, reconciling the world to himself, no longer counting people's sins against them. And he gave us this wonderful message of reconciliation. [20]So we are Christ's ambassadors; God is making his appeal through us. We speak for Christ when we plead, "Come back to God!" [21]For God made Christ, who never sinned, to be the offering for our sin,* so that we could be made right with God through Christ.

CHAPTER 6

As God's partners,* we beg you not to accept this marvelous gift of God's kindness and then ignore it. [2]For God says,

"At just the right time, I heard you.
On the day of salvation, I helped you."*

Indeed, the "right time" is now. Today is the day of salvation.

Paul's Hardships

[3]We live in such a way that no one will stumble because of us, and no one will find fault with our ministry. [4]In everything we do, we show that we are true ministers of God. We patiently endure troubles and hardships and calamities of every kind. [5]We have been beaten, been put in prison, faced angry mobs, worked to exhaustion, endured sleepless nights, and gone without food. [6]We prove ourselves by our purity, our understanding, our patience, our kindness, by the Holy Spirit within us,* and by our sincere love. [7]We faithfully preach the truth. God's power is working in us. We use the weapons of righteousness in the right hand for attack and the left hand for defense. [8]We serve God whether people honor us or despise us, whether they slander us or praise us. We are honest, but they call us impostors. [9]We are ignored, even though we are well known. We live close to death, but we are still alive. We have been beaten, but we have not been killed. [10]Our hearts ache, but we always have joy. We are poor, but we give spiritual riches to others. We own nothing, and yet we have everything.

[11]Oh, dear Corinthian friends! We have spoken honestly with you, and our hearts are open to you. [12]There is no lack of love on our part, but you have withheld your love from us. [13]I am

5:21 Or *to become sin itself.* 6:1 Or *As we work together.*
6:2 Isa 49:8 (Greek version). 6:6 Or *by our holiness of spirit.*

---

first steps

TRIALS ARE SURVIVABLE

Read 2 CORINTHIANS 4:7-18

When we face trials in our lives, we can do one of two things. We can either become self-absorbed with our problems and say, "Look at how tough things are!" Or we can keep our eyes on Jesus and say, "This is only temporary." The apostle Paul was able to focus on the temporary nature of his problems because he accepted five important facts:

1. Our Bodies Are Weak and Mortal. Paul wasn't the type to be caught up in his bodily aches and pains. He didn't strive for the perfect body or the perfect image because he knew his body was a "fragile clay jar." The Bible does not teach that we should neglect our bodies, but it does say that spiritual exercise is more important and beneficial (see 1 Timothy 4:8, p. 262).

2. God's Power Is Displayed in Our Weakness. If we become overly obsessed with ourselves, we will never give God the chance to work through our lives. Paul recognized that God's glory shines through our weaknesses.

3. God Does Not Abandon Us. Even though we may be "crushed" and "perplexed," we have the hope that God will protect and strengthen us through these trials.

4. Trials Can Be Witnessing Opportunities. When people see the inner strength we have in Christ, they will take notice. This is well illustrated in the story of Paul and Silas, who were put in prison for preaching the gospel (see Acts 16:16-36, p. 151). Though they had been whipped and had their legs clamped in stocks in a damp, dark dungeon, they began to pray and worship the Lord in song. In an unusual string of events, these men were able to lead their jailer, as well as his entire family, to the Lord. Paul and Silas's godly attitude, which enabled them to rejoice in such a time of trouble, prepared the soil of this man's heart, opening him up to the gospel they preached.

5. We Have the Hope of Heaven. These trials are only a split second in time compared to the eternal joys and blessings of heaven.

For the next note on "Have Courage in Trials," turn to p. 73.

cornerstones
WHEN DOES A CHRISTIAN ENTER HEAVEN?
Read 2 CORINTHIANS 5:6-9

Some people teach that when we die we go into a state of suspended animation. Then later on we are called into the presence of God. But this passage clearly explains that when a believer dies, he or she will go directly to heaven to "be at home with the Lord." This is illustrated in at least two other instances in Scripture:

1. The Thief on the Cross. As Jesus was being crucified, a thief hanging on a cross next to him asked Jesus to remember him when Jesus entered his Kingdom. To this request, Jesus replied, *"Today* you will be with me in paradise" (Luke 23:40-43).

2. The Apostle Paul. The apostle Paul wrote, "I long to go and be with Christ" (Philippians 1:23). He didn't say, "I long to depart and be suspended in a soul sleep for a few thousand years." Paul understood better than most this truth about entering heaven, because he had already had a glimpse of heaven. It is possible that when Paul was stoned, he died and entered the presence of the Lord. But God still had work for Paul to do on earth, so he sent Paul back to carry it out (see 2 Corinthians 12:2-4, pp. 218-219).

The moment you take your last breath on earth, you will take your first breath in heaven. So don't be afraid of death. Instead, enjoy your life in Christ on earth, and spend the rest of your time here introducing others to the one with whom you will spend eternity.

For the next note on "What Is Heaven?" turn to p. 30.

asking you to respond as if you were my own children. Open your hearts to us!

The Temple of the Living God
14 Don't team up with those who are unbelievers. How can righteousness be a partner with wickedness? How can light live with darkness? 15 What harmony can there be between Christ and the devil*? How can a believer be a partner with an unbeliever? 16 And what union can there be between God's temple and idols? For we are the temple of the living God. As God said:

"I will live in them
and walk among them.
I will be their God,
and they will be my people.*
17 Therefore, come out from among
unbelievers,
and separate yourselves from them, says
the LORD.
Don't touch their filthy things,
and I will welcome you.*
18 And I will be your Father,
and you will be my sons and daughters,
says the LORD Almighty.*"

CHAPTER 7
Because we have these promises, dear friends, let us cleanse ourselves from everything that can defile our body or spirit. And let us work toward complete holiness because we fear God.

2 Please open your hearts to us. We have not done wrong to anyone, nor led anyone astray, nor taken advantage of anyone. 3 I'm not saying this to condemn you. I said before that you are in our hearts, and we live or die together with you. 4 I have the highest confidence in you, and I take great pride in you. You have greatly encouraged me and made me happy despite all our troubles.

Paul's Joy at the Church's Repentance
5 When we arrived in Macedonia, there was no rest for us. We faced conflict from every direction, with battles on the outside and fear on the inside. 6 But God, who encourages those who are discouraged, encouraged us by the arrival of Titus. 7 His presence was a joy, but so was the news he brought of the encouragement he received from you. When he told us how much you long to see me, and how sorry you are for what happened, and how loyal you are to me, I was filled with joy!

8 I am not sorry that I sent that severe letter to you, though I was sorry at first, for I know it was painful to you for a little while. 9 Now I am glad I sent it, not because it hurt you, but because the pain caused you to repent and

6:15 Greek *Beliar;* various other manuscripts render this proper name of the devil as *Belian, Beliab,* or *Belial.* **6:16** Lev 26:12; Ezek 37:27 **6:17** Isa 52:11; Ezek 20:34 (Greek version). **6:18** 2 Sam 7:14.

change your ways. It was the kind of sorrow God wants his people to have, so you were not harmed by us in any way. [10] For the kind of sorrow God wants us to experience leads us away from sin and results in salvation. There's no regret for that kind of sorrow. But worldly sorrow, which lacks repentance, results in spiritual death.

[11] Just see what this godly sorrow produced in you! Such earnestness, such concern to clear yourselves, such indignation, such alarm, such longing to see me, such zeal, and such a readiness to punish wrong. You showed that you have done everything necessary to make things right. [12] My purpose, then, was not to write about who did the wrong or who was wronged. I wrote to you so that in the sight of God you could see for yourselves how loyal you are to us. [13] We have been greatly encouraged by this.

In addition to our own encouragement, we were especially delighted to see how happy Titus was about the way all of you welcomed him and set his mind* at ease. [14] I had told him how proud I was of you—and you didn't disappoint me. I have always told you the truth, and now my boasting to Titus has also proved true! [15] Now he cares for you more than ever when he remembers the way all of you obeyed him and welcomed him with such fear and deep respect. [16] I am very happy now because I have complete confidence in you.

CHAPTER **8**

A Call to Generous Giving

Now I want you to know, dear brothers and sisters,* what God in his kindness has done through the churches in Macedonia. [2] They are being tested by many troubles, and they are very poor. But they are also filled with abundant joy, which has overflowed in rich generosity.

[3] For I can testify that they gave not only what they could afford, but far more. And they did it of their own free will. [4] They begged us again and again for the privilege of sharing in the gift for the believers in Jerusalem.* [5] They even did more than we had hoped, for their first action was to give themselves to the Lord and to us, just as God wanted them to do.

[6] So we have urged Titus, who encouraged your giving in the first place, to return to you and encourage you to finish this ministry of giving. [7] Since you excel in so many ways—in your faith, your gifted speakers, your knowledge, your enthusiasm, and your love from us*—I want you to excel also in this gracious act of giving.

7:13 Greek *his spirit.*   **8:1** Greek *brothers.*   **8:4** Greek *for God's holy people.*   **8:7** Some manuscripts read *your love for us.*

first steps

RECOGNIZE THAT YOU ARE A NEW CREATION

Read 2 CORINTHIANS 5:14-17

Although outwardly you may appear to be the same person, when you received Christ you underwent a radical heart transplant. You literally became a "new person" (or "creation") inside. This short passage of Scripture highlights some encouraging points as you endeavor to be obedient to God.

- As "new creations," Christ's love compels us to please God rather than ourselves.
- As "new creations," we can look beyond the "packaging" of a person to what is inside.
- As "new creations," we have become altogether different people.
- As "new creations," we have been given a clean slate, a fresh start, and a new nature.

The new nature you have received is like a tender little flower. It takes time and effort to cultivate. You may find it hard at times to obey God and leave certain old habits behind at first. But as you cultivate that new nature by spending more time with God through activities like prayer and Bible study, you will notice changes as the weeks, months, and years go by.

A man from India was heard to compare our new spiritual nature and our old selfish one to two dogs constantly fighting with each other. He went on to say that he could determine which dog would win. When asked how he determined which dog won, his response was, "The one I feed the most, of course." When you take time to "feed" your new spiritual nature (as you are doing right now), you give it the edge in this ongoing conflict between good and evil.

For the next note on "Obey God," turn to p. 121.

[8] I am not commanding you to do this. But I am testing how genuine your love is by comparing it with the eagerness of the other churches.

[9] You know the generous grace of our Lord Jesus Christ. Though he was rich, yet for your sakes he became poor, so that by his poverty he could make you rich.

[10] Here is my advice: It would be good for you to finish what you started a year ago. Last year you were the first who wanted to give, and you were the first to begin doing it. [11] Now you should finish what you started. Let the eagerness you showed in the beginning be matched now by your giving. Give in proportion to what you have. [12] Whatever you give is acceptable if you give it eagerly. And give according to what you have, not what you don't have. [13] Of course, I don't mean your giving should make life easy for others and hard for yourselves. I only mean that there should be some equality. [14] Right now you have plenty and can help those who are in need. Later, they will have plenty and can share with you when you need it. In this way, things will be equal. [15] As the Scriptures say,

> "Those who gathered a lot had nothing left over,
> and those who gathered only a little had enough."*

Titus and His Companions

[16] But thank God! He has given Titus the same enthusiasm for you that I have. [17] Titus welcomed our request that he visit you again. In fact, he himself was very eager to go and see you. [18] We are also sending another brother with Titus. All the churches praise him as a preacher of the Good News. [19] He was appointed by the churches to accompany us as we take the offering to Jerusalem*—a service that glorifies the Lord and shows our eagerness to help.

[20] We are traveling together to guard against any criticism for the way we are handling this generous gift. [21] We are careful to be honorable before the Lord, but we also want everyone else to see that we are honorable.

[22] We are also sending with them another of our brothers who has proven himself many times and has shown on many occasions how eager he is. He is now even more enthusiastic because of his great confidence in you. [23] If anyone asks about Titus, say that he is my partner who works with me to help you. And the brothers with him have been sent by the churches,* and they bring honor to Christ. [24] So show them your love, and prove to all the churches that our boasting about you is justified.

CHAPTER 9

The Collection for Christians in Jerusalem

I really don't need to write to you about this ministry of giving for the believers in Jerusalem.* [2] For I know how eager you are to help, and I have been boasting to the churches in Macedonia that you in Greece* were ready to send an offering a year ago. In fact, it was your enthusiasm that stirred up many of the Macedonian believers to begin giving.

[3] But I am sending these brothers to be sure you really are ready, as I have been telling them, and that your money is all collected. I don't want to be wrong in my boasting about you. [4] We would be embarrassed—not to mention your own embarrassment—if some Macedonian believers came with me and found that you weren't ready after all I had told them! [5] So I thought I should send these brothers ahead of me to make sure the gift you promised is ready. But I want it to be a willing gift, not one given grudgingly.

[6] Remember this—a farmer who plants only a few seeds will get a small crop. But the one who plants generously will get a generous crop. [7] You must each decide in your heart how much to give. And don't give reluctantly or in response to

8:15 Exod 16:18. 8:19 See 1 Cor 16:3-4. 8:23 Greek *are apostles of the churches.* 9:1 Greek *about the offering for God's holy people.* 9:2 Greek *in Achaia,* the southern region of the Greek peninsula. *Macedonia* was in the northern region of Greece.

---

off and running

AVOID RELATIONSHIPS THAT COULD CAUSE YOU TO SIN

Read 2 CORINTHIANS 6:14–7:1

As a Christian, you should avoid anything that would compromise your relationship with Jesus. That includes entering into a relationship, business deal, or any other association that would tempt you to lower your standards or discredit your integrity. When you team up with someone who does not love

pressure. "For God loves a person who gives cheerfully." [8]And God will generously provide all you need. Then you will always have everything you need and plenty left over to share with others. [9]As the Scriptures say,

"They share freely and give generously to
the poor.
Their good deeds will be remembered
forever."*

[10]For God is the one who provides seed for the farmer and then bread to eat. In the same way, he will provide and increase your resources and then produce a great harvest of generosity* in you.

[11]Yes, you will be enriched in every way so that you can always be generous. And when we take your gifts to those who need them, they will thank God. [12]So two good things will result from this ministry of giving—the needs of the believers in Jerusalem* will be met, and they will joyfully express their thanks to God.

[13]As a result of your ministry, they will give glory to God. For your generosity to them and to all believers will prove that you are obedient to the Good News of Christ. [14]And they will pray for you with deep affection because of the overflowing grace God has given to you. [15]Thank God for this gift* too wonderful for words!

CHAPTER **10**

Paul Defends His Authority

Now I, Paul, appeal to you with the gentleness and kindness of Christ—though I realize you think I am timid in person and bold only when I write from far away. [2]Well, I am begging you now so that when I come I won't have to be bold with those who think we act from human motives.

[3]We are human, but we don't wage war as humans do. [4]*We use God's mighty weapons, not worldly weapons, to knock down the strongholds of human reasoning and to de-

stroy false arguments. [5]We destroy every proud obstacle that keeps people from knowing God. We capture their rebellious thoughts and teach them to obey Christ. [6]And after you have become fully obedient, we will punish everyone who remains disobedient.

[7]Look at the obvious facts.* Those who say they belong to Christ must recognize that we belong to Christ as much as they do. [8]I may seem to be boasting too much about the authority given to us by the Lord. But our authority builds you up; it doesn't tear you down. So I will not be ashamed of using my authority.

[9]I'm not trying to frighten you by my letters. [10]For some say, "Paul's letters are demanding and forceful, but in person he is weak, and his speeches are worthless!" [11]Those people should realize that our actions when we arrive in person will be as forceful as what we say in our letters from far away.

[12]Oh, don't worry; we wouldn't dare say that we are as wonderful as these other men who tell you how important they are! But they are only comparing themselves with each other, using themselves as the standard of measurement. How ignorant!

[13]We will not boast about things done outside our area of authority. We will boast only about what has happened within the boundaries of the work God has given us, which includes our working with you. [14]We are not reaching beyond these boundaries when we claim authority over you, as if we had never visited you. For we were the first to travel all the way to Corinth with the Good News of Christ.

[15]Nor do we boast and claim credit for the work someone else has done. Instead, we hope that your faith will grow so that the boundaries of our work among you will be extended. [16]Then we will be able to go and preach the Good News in other places far beyond you, where no one else is working. Then there will be no question of our boasting about work

9:9 Ps 112:9.   9:10 Greek *righteousness*.   9:12 Greek *of God's holy people*.   9:15 Greek *his gift*.   10:4 English translations divide verses 4 and 5 in various ways.   10:7 Or *You look at things only on the basis of appearance*.

---

and fear the Lord, that relationship can dramatically weaken your spiritual health.

God does not want us to avoid all interaction with nonbelievers. Jesus himself spent time with the "sinners" and social outcasts of his day in order to share the message of salvation. God just wants us to keep from being so closely connected to unbelievers that it ultimately affects our faith and behavior, tempting us to compromise our witness for and obedience to God.

For the next note on "Relationships," turn to p. 306.

done in someone else's territory. [17]As the Scriptures say, "If you want to boast, boast only about the LORD."*

[18]When people commend themselves, it doesn't count for much. The important thing is for the Lord to commend them.

CHAPTER **11**

Paul and the False Apostles

I hope you will put up with a little more of my foolishness. Please bear with me. [2]For I am jealous for you with the jealousy of God himself. I promised you as a pure bride* to one husband—Christ. [3]But I fear that somehow your pure and undivided devotion to Christ will be corrupted, just as Eve was deceived by the cunning ways of the serpent. [4]You happily put up with whatever anyone tells you, even if they preach a different Jesus than the one we preach, or a different kind of Spirit than the one you received, or a different kind of gospel than the one you believed.

[5]But I don't consider myself inferior in any way to these "super apostles" who teach such things. [6]I may be unskilled as a speaker, but I'm not lacking in knowledge. We have made this clear to you in every possible way.

[7]Was I wrong when I humbled myself and honored you by preaching God's Good News to you without expecting anything in return? [8]I "robbed" other churches by accepting their contributions so I could serve you at no cost. [9]And when I was with you and didn't have enough to live on, I did not become a financial burden to anyone. For the brothers who came from Macedonia brought me all that I needed. I have never been a burden to you, and I never will be. [10]As surely as the truth of Christ is in me, no one in all of Greece* will ever stop me from boasting about this. [11]Why? Because I don't love you? God knows that I do.

[12]But I will continue doing what I have always done. This will undercut those who are looking for an opportunity to boast that their work is just like ours. [13]These people are false apostles. They are deceitful workers who disguise themselves as apostles of Christ. [14]But I am not surprised! Even Satan disguises himself as an angel of light. [15]So it is no wonder that his servants also disguise themselves as servants of righteousness. In the end they will get the punishment their wicked deeds deserve.

Paul's Many Trials

[16]Again I say, don't think that I am a fool to talk like this. But even if you do, listen to me, as you would to a foolish person, while I also boast a little. [17]Such boasting is not from the Lord, but I am acting like a fool. [18]And since others boast about their human achievements, I will, too. [19]After all, you think you are so wise, but you enjoy putting up with fools! [20]You put up with it when someone enslaves you, takes everything you have, takes advantage of you, takes control of everything, and slaps you in the face. [21]I'm ashamed to say that we've been too "weak" to do that!

But whatever they dare to boast about—I'm talking like a fool again—I dare to boast about it, too. [22]Are they Hebrews? So am I. Are they Israelites? So am I. Are they descendants of Abraham? So am I. [23]Are they servants of Christ? I know I sound like a madman, but I have served him far more! I have worked harder, been put in prison more often, been whipped times without number, and faced death again and again. [24]Five different times the Jewish leaders gave me thirty-nine lashes. [25]Three times I was beaten with rods. Once I was stoned. Three times I was shipwrecked. Once I spent a whole night and a day adrift at sea. [26]I have traveled on many long journeys. I have faced danger from rivers and from robbers. I have faced danger from my own people, the Jews, as well as from the Gentiles. I have faced danger in the cities, in the deserts, and on the seas. And I have faced danger from men who claim to be believers but are not.* [27]I have worked hard and long, enduring many sleepless nights. I have been hungry and thirsty and have often gone without food. I have shivered in the cold, without enough clothing to keep me warm.

[28]Then, besides all this, I have the daily burden of my concern for all the churches. [29]Who is weak without my feeling that weakness? Who is led astray, and I do not burn with anger?

[30]If I must boast, I would rather boast about the things that show how weak I am. [31]God, the Father of our Lord Jesus, who is worthy of eternal praise, knows I am not lying. [32]When I was in Damascus, the governor under King Aretas kept guards at the city gates to catch me. [33]I had to be lowered in a basket through a window in the city wall to escape from him.

CHAPTER **12**

Paul's Vision and His Thorn in the Flesh

This boasting will do no good, but I must go on. I will reluctantly tell about visions and revelations from the Lord. [2]I* was caught up to the third heaven fourteen years ago. Whether I was in my body or out of my body, I don't know—only God knows. [3]Yes, only God knows whether I was in my body or outside my body. But I do

---

10:17 Jer 9:24.   **11:2** Greek *a virgin*.   **11:10** Greek *Achaia,* the southern region of the Greek peninsula.   **11:26** Greek *from false brothers.*   **12:2** Greek *I know a man in Christ who.*

know [4]that I was caught up* to paradise and heard things so astounding that they cannot be expressed in words, things no human is allowed to tell.

[5]That experience is worth boasting about, but I'm not going to do it. I will boast only about my weaknesses. [6]If I wanted to boast, I would be no fool in doing so, because I would be telling the truth. But I won't do it, because I don't want anyone to give me credit beyond what they can see in my life or hear in my message, [7]even though I have received such wonderful revelations from God. So to keep me from becoming proud, I was given a thorn in my flesh, a messenger from Satan to torment me and keep me from becoming proud.

[8]Three different times I begged the Lord to take it away. [9]Each time he said, "My grace is all you need. My power works best in weakness." So now I am glad to boast about my weaknesses, so that the power of Christ can work through me. [10]That's why I take pleasure in my weaknesses, and in the insults, hardships, persecutions, and troubles that I suffer for Christ. For when I am weak, then I am strong.

Paul's Concern for the Corinthians

[11]You have made me act like a fool—boasting like this.* You ought to be writing commendations for me, for I am not at all inferior to these "super apostles," even though I am nothing at all. [12]When I was with you, I certainly gave you proof that I am an apostle. For I patiently did many signs and wonders and miracles among you. [13]The only thing I failed to do, which I do in the other churches, was to become a financial burden to you. Please forgive me for this wrong!

[14]Now I am coming to you for the third time, and I will not be a burden to you. I don't want what you have—I want you. After all, children don't provide for their parents. Rather, parents provide for their children. [15]I will gladly spend myself and all I have for you, even though it seems that the more I love you, the less you love me.

[16]Some of you admit I was not a burden to you. But others still think I was sneaky and took advantage of you by trickery. [17]But how? Did any of the men I sent to you take advantage of you? [18]When I urged Titus to visit you and sent our other brother with him, did Titus take advantage of you? No! For we have the same spirit and walk in each other's steps, doing things the same way.

[19]Perhaps you think we're saying these things just to defend ourselves. No, we tell you this as Christ's servants, and with God as our

12:3-4 Greek *But I know such a man,* [4]*that he was caught up.*
12:11 Some manuscripts do not include *boasting like this.*

first steps
WHAT HAPPENS WHEN YOU GIVE?
Read 2 CORINTHIANS 9:6-14

One of Paul's goals in his ministry was to mend the division that existed between Jewish and Gentile believers. To do this, he took up a gift offering from the Gentile believers to be given to the needy Jewish believers in Jerusalem. Apparently the believers in Corinth were lagging behind in their giving. So Paul, in this portion of 2 Corinthians, wrote of the benefits of giving to God and the work of his church. Here are three important truths from this passage about our giving as believers:

1. Our Motives Are Important. The passage says that God prizes cheerful givers (2 Corinthians 9:7). The word "cheerfully" could also be translated as "hilariously." We should give hilariously, joyfully—not out of mere duty or guilt. As Jesus said, it is truly "more blessed to give than to receive" (Acts 20:35).

2. As We Give, God Will Give to Us. You can't out-give God (2 Corinthians 9:8, 10). As Jesus said, "Give, and you will receive. Your gift will return to you in full—pressed down, shaken together to make room for more, running over, and poured into your lap. The amount you give will determine the amount you get back" (Luke 6:38). Coming back to our motive for giving, we should not fall into the trap of "giving to get." We should give because God has so graciously and generously given to us.

3. Others Are Helped because of Our Financial Help. We should always be on the lookout to help Christian brothers and sisters who are in need. Paul was not speaking of the tithe you give, but an offering above and beyond your tithe (2 Corinthians 9:11-14). Our tithe goes to the church. Our offerings go to other situations, like helping those in need. When these people receive our gifts, they see that our faith is deeper than mere words.

When you give to the Lord's work, that money, which really had no effect in any spiritual sense before, will be used to touch the lives of others for the glory of God. God is looking for open-handed people—people upon whom he can pour out his blessings, and who, in turn, will give it to others.

For the next note on "Give to God," turn to p. 9.

witness. Everything we do, dear friends, is to strengthen you. [20]For I am afraid that when I come I won't like what I find, and you won't like my response. I am afraid that I will find quarreling, jealousy, anger, selfishness, slander, gossip, arrogance, and disorderly behavior. [21]Yes, I am afraid that when I come again, God will humble me in your presence. And I will be grieved because many of you have not given up your old sins. You have not repented of your impurity, sexual immorality, and eagerness for lustful pleasure.

CHAPTER 13

Paul's Final Advice

This is the third time I am coming to visit you (and as the Scriptures say, "The facts of every case must be established by the testimony of two or three witnesses"*). [2]I have already warned those who had been sinning when I was there on my second visit. Now I again warn them and all others, just as I did before, that next time I will not spare them.

[3]I will give you all the proof you want that Christ speaks through me. Christ is not weak when he deals with you; he is powerful among you. [4]Although he was crucified in weakness, he now lives by the power of God. We, too, are weak, just as Christ was, but when we deal with you we will be alive with him and will have God's power.

[5]Examine yourselves to see if your faith is genuine. Test yourselves. Surely you know that Jesus Christ is among you*; if not, you have failed the test of genuine faith. [6]As you test yourselves, I hope you will recognize that we have not failed the test of apostolic authority.

[7]We pray to God that you will not do what is wrong by refusing our correction. I hope we won't need to demonstrate our authority when we arrive. Do the right thing before we come—even if that makes it look like we have failed to demonstrate our authority. [8]For we cannot oppose the truth, but must always stand for the truth. [9]We are glad to seem weak if it helps show that you are actually strong. We pray that you will become mature.

[10]I am writing this to you before I come, hoping that I won't need to deal severely with you when I do come. For I want to use the authority the Lord has given me to strengthen you, not to tear you down.

Paul's Final Greetings

[11]Dear brothers and sisters,* I close my letter with these last words: Be joyful. Grow to maturity. Encourage each other. Live in harmony and peace. Then the God of love and peace will be with you.

[12]Greet each other with Christian love.* [13]All of God's people here send you their greetings.

[14]*May the grace of the Lord Jesus Christ, the love of God, and the fellowship of the Holy Spirit be with you all.

13:1 Deut 19:15.   **13:5** Or *in you*.   **13:11** Greek *Brothers*.   **13:12** Greek *with a sacred kiss*.   **13:14** Some English translations include verse 13 as part of verse 12, and then verse 14 becomes verse 13.

Galatians

AUTHOR: **PAUL** | DATE WRITTEN: **A.D. 49** | GENRE: **EPISTLE**

Galatians is a foundational study that shows how complete the work of Jesus' death on the cross was for our salvation. Nothing needs to be added to that work, nor does it need to be improved upon, because that work was perfect.

CHAPTER 1

Greetings from Paul

This letter is from Paul, an apostle. I was not appointed by any group of people or any human authority, but by Jesus Christ himself and by God the Father, who raised Jesus from the dead.

2 All the brothers and sisters* here join me in sending this letter to the churches of Galatia.

3 May God our Father and the Lord Jesus Christ* give you grace and peace. 4 Jesus gave his life for our sins, just as God our Father planned, in order to rescue us from this evil world in which we live. 5 All glory to God forever and ever! Amen.

There Is Only One Good News

6 I am shocked that you are turning away so soon from God, who called you to himself through the loving mercy of Christ.* You are following a different way that pretends to be the Good News 7 but is not the Good News at all. You are being fooled by those who deliberately twist the truth concerning Christ.

8 Let God's curse fall on anyone, including us or even an angel from heaven, who preaches a different kind of Good News than the one we preached to you. 9 I say again what we have said before: If anyone preaches any other Good News than the one you welcomed, let that person be cursed.

10 Obviously, I'm not trying to win the approval of people, but of God. If pleasing people were my goal, I would not be Christ's servant.

Paul's Message Comes from Christ

11 Dear brothers and sisters, I want you to understand that the gospel message I preach is not based on mere human reasoning. 12 I received my message from no human source, and no one taught me. Instead, I received it by direct revelation from Jesus Christ.*

13 You know what I was like when I followed the Jewish religion—how I violently persecuted God's church. I did my best to destroy it. 14 I was far ahead of my fellow Jews in my zeal for the traditions of my ancestors.

15 But even before I was born, God chose me and called me by his marvelous grace. Then it pleased him 16 to reveal his Son to me* so that I would proclaim the Good News about Jesus to the Gentiles.

When this happened, I did not rush out to consult with any human being.* 17 Nor did I go up to Jerusalem to consult with those who were apostles before I was. Instead, I went away into Arabia, and later I returned to the city of Damascus.

18 Then three years later I went to Jerusalem to get to know Peter,* and I stayed with him for fifteen days. 19 The only other apostle I met at that time was James, the Lord's brother. 20 I declare before God that what I am writing to you is not a lie.

21 After that visit I went north into the provinces of Syria and Cilicia. 22 And still the Christians in the churches in Judea didn't know me personally. 23 All they knew was that people were saying, "The one who used to persecute us

---

1:2 Greek *brothers;* also in 1:11. 1:3 Some manuscripts read *God the Father and our Lord Jesus Christ.* 1:6 Some manuscripts read *through loving mercy.* 1:12 Or *by the revelation of Jesus Christ.* 1:16a Or *in me.* 1:16b Greek *with flesh and blood.* 1:18 Greek *Cephas.*

cornerstones

WHY CHRISTIANS NEED THE HOLY SPIRIT
Read GALATIANS 5:16-26

This text lays out four important reasons we need to let the Holy Spirit have full control of our lives as believers:

1. The Holy Spirit Helps to Conquer Our Sin Nature. The Holy Spirit will help us make the right decisions if we listen to his advice.

2. The Holy Spirit Makes It Easier to Follow God's Guidelines. The Holy Spirit gives us the power to live by God's guidelines. If we listen to and follow the Holy Spirit's promptings, then we won't have to force ourselves to obey the Lord—we will want to obey him.

3. The Holy Spirit Will Produce Godly Qualities in Our Lives. When we live by the Holy Spirit, he develops godly qualities (known as the fruits of the Spirit) in our lives.

4. The Holy Spirit Encourages Us to Seek God's Approval above Man's. We will seek God's glory above our own when we follow the Holy Spirit's leading.

In essence, the Holy Spirit enables Christians to live lives that are pleasing to God—something that is impossible to do on our own. He makes following Christ a joy rather than a duty.

To begin the next topic, turn to p. A25.

---

is now preaching the very faith he tried to destroy!" ²⁴And they praised God because of me.

CHAPTER **2**

The Apostles Accept Paul

Then fourteen years later I went back to Jerusalem again, this time with Barnabas; and Titus came along, too. ²I went there because God revealed to me that I should go. While I was there I met privately with those considered to be leaders of the church and shared with them the message I had been preaching to the Gentiles. I wanted to make sure that we were in agreement, for fear that all my efforts had been wasted and I was running the race for nothing. ³And they supported me and did not even demand that my companion Titus be circumcised, though he was a Gentile.*

⁴Even that question came up only because of some so-called Christians there—false ones, really*—who were secretly brought in. They sneaked in to spy on us and take away the freedom we have in Christ Jesus. They wanted to enslave us and force us to follow their Jewish regulations. ⁵But we refused to give in to them for a single moment. We wanted to preserve the truth of the gospel message for you.

⁶And the leaders of the church had nothing to add to what I was preaching. (By the way, their reputation as great leaders made no difference to me, for God has no favorites.) ⁷Instead, they saw that God had given me the responsibility of preaching the gospel to the Gentiles, just as he had given Peter the responsibility of preaching to the Jews. ⁸For the same God who worked through Peter as the apostle to the Jews also worked through me as the apostle to the Gentiles.

⁹In fact, James, Peter,* and John, who were known as pillars of the church, recognized the gift God had given me, and they accepted Barnabas and me as their co-workers. They encouraged us to keep preaching to the Gentiles, while they continued their work with the Jews. ¹⁰Their only suggestion was that we keep on helping the poor, which I have always been eager to do.

Paul Confronts Peter

¹¹But when Peter came to Antioch, I had to oppose him to his face, for what he did was very wrong. ¹²When he first arrived, he ate with the Gentile Christians, who were not circumcised. But afterward, when some friends of James came, Peter wouldn't eat with the Gentiles anymore. He was afraid of criticism from these people who insisted on the necessity of circumcision. ¹³As a result, other Jewish Christians followed Peter's hypocrisy, and even Barnabas was led astray by their hypocrisy.

¹⁴When I saw that they were not following the truth of the gospel message, I said to Peter in front of all the others, "Since you, a Jew by birth, have discarded the Jewish laws and are living like a Gentile, why are you now trying to make these Gentiles follow the Jewish traditions?

¹⁵"You and I are Jews by birth, not 'sinners' like the Gentiles. ¹⁶Yet we know that a person is

2:3 Greek *a Greek.*   2:4 Greek *some false brothers.*   2:9 Greek *Cephas;* also in 2:11, 14.

made right with God by faith in Jesus Christ, not by obeying the law. And we have believed in Christ Jesus, so that we might be made right with God because of our faith in Christ, not because we have obeyed the law. For no one will ever be made right with God by obeying the law."*

17 But suppose we seek to be made right with God through faith in Christ and then we are found guilty because we have abandoned the law. Would that mean Christ has led us into sin? Absolutely not! 18 Rather, I am a sinner if I rebuild the old system of law I already tore down. 19 For when I tried to keep the law, it condemned me. So I died to the law—I stopped trying to meet all its requirements—so that I might live for God. 20 My old self has been crucified with Christ.* It is no longer I who live, but Christ lives in me. So I live in this earthly body by trusting in the Son of God, who loved me and gave himself for me. 21 I do not treat the grace of God as meaningless. For if keeping the law could make us right with God, then there was no need for Christ to die.

CHAPTER **3**
The Law and Faith in Christ
Oh, foolish Galatians! Who has cast an evil spell on you? For the meaning of Jesus Christ's death was made as clear to you as if you had seen a picture of his death on the cross. 2 Let me ask you this one question: Did you receive the Holy Spirit by obeying the law of Moses? Of course not! You received the Spirit because you believed the message you heard about Christ. 3 How foolish can you be? After starting your Christian lives in the Spirit, why are you now trying to become perfect by your own human effort? 4 Have you experienced* so much for nothing? Surely it was not in vain, was it?

5 I ask you again, does God give you the Holy Spirit and work miracles among you because you obey the law? Of course not! It is because you believe the message you heard about Christ.

6 In the same way, "Abraham believed God, and God counted him as righteous because of his faith."* 7 The real children of Abraham, then, are those who put their faith in God.

8 What's more, the Scriptures looked forward to this time when God would declare the Gentiles to be righteous because of their faith. God proclaimed this good news to Abraham long ago when he said, "All nations will be blessed through you."* 9 So all who put their

faith in Christ share the same blessing Abraham received because of his faith.

10 But those who depend on the law to make them right with God are under his curse, for the Scriptures say, "Cursed is everyone who does not observe and obey all the commands that are written in God's Book of the Law."* 11 So it is clear that no one can be made right with God by trying to keep the law. For the Scriptures say, "It is through faith that a righteous person has life."* 12 This way of faith is very different from the way of law, which says, "It is through obeying the law that a person has life."*

13 But Christ has rescued us from the curse pronounced by the law. When he was hung on the cross, he took upon himself the curse for our wrongdoing. For it is written in the Scriptures, "Cursed is everyone who is hung on a tree."* 14 Through Christ Jesus, God has blessed the Gentiles with the same blessing he promised to Abraham, so that we who are believers might receive the promised* Holy Spirit through faith.

The Law and God's Promise
15 Dear brothers and sisters,* here's an example from everyday life. Just as no one can set aside or amend an irrevocable agreement, so it is in this case. 16 God gave the promises to Abraham and his child.* And notice that the Scripture doesn't say "to his children,*" as if it meant many descendants. Rather, it says "to his child"—and that, of course, means Christ. 17 This is what I am trying to say: The agreement God made with Abraham could not be canceled 430 years later when God gave the law to Moses. God would be breaking his promise. 18 For if the inheritance could be received by keeping the law, then it would not be the result of accepting God's promise. But God graciously gave it to Abraham as a promise.

19 Why, then, was the law given? It was given alongside the promise to show people their sins. But the law was designed to last only until the coming of the child who was promised. God gave his law through angels to Moses, who was the mediator between God and the people. 20 Now a mediator is helpful if more than one party must reach an agreement. But God, who is one, did not use a mediator when he gave his promise to Abraham.

21 Is there a conflict, then, between God's law and God's promises?* Absolutely not! If the law could give us new life, we could be made right

---

2:16 Some translators hold that the quotation extends through verse 14; others through verse 16; and still others through verse 21. 2:20 Some English translations put this sentence in verse 19. 3:4 Or *Have you suffered.* 3:6 Gen 15:6. 3:8 Gen 12:3; 18:18; 22:18. 3:10 Deut 27:26. 3:11 Hab 2:4. 3:12 Lev 18:5. 3:13 Deut 21:23 (Greek version). 3:14 Some manuscripts read *the blessing of the.* 3:15 Greek *Brothers.* 3:16a Greek *seed;* also in 3:16c, 19. 3:16b Greek *seeds.* 3:21 Some manuscripts read *and the promises?*

with God by obeying it. [22] But the Scriptures declare that we are all prisoners of sin, so we receive God's promise of freedom only by believing in Jesus Christ.

God's Children through Faith

[23] Before the way of faith in Christ was available to us, we were placed under guard by the law. We were kept in protective custody, so to speak, until the way of faith was revealed.

[24] Let me put it another way. The law was our guardian until Christ came; it protected us until we could be made right with God through faith. [25] And now that the way of faith has come, we no longer need the law as our guardian.

[26] For you are all children* of God through faith in Christ Jesus. [27] And all who have been united with Christ in baptism have put on Christ, like putting on new clothes.* [28] There is no longer Jew or Gentile,* slave or free, male and female. For you are all one in Christ Jesus. [29] And now that you belong to Christ, you are the true children* of Abraham. You are his heirs, and God's promise to Abraham belongs to you.

CHAPTER **4**

Think of it this way. If a father dies and leaves an inheritance for his young children, those children are not much better off than slaves until they grow up, even though they actually own everything their father had. [2] They have to obey their guardians until they reach whatever age their father set. [3] And that's the way it was with us before Christ came. We were like children; we were slaves to the basic spiritual principles* of this world.

[4] But when the right time came, God sent his Son, born of a woman, subject to the law. [5] God sent him to buy freedom for us who were slaves to the law, so that he could adopt us as his very own children.* [6] And because we* are his children, God has sent the Spirit of his Son into our hearts, prompting us to call out, "Abba, Father."* [7] Now you are no longer a slave but God's own child.* And since you are his child, God has made you his heir.

Paul's Concern for the Galatians

[8] Before you Gentiles knew God, you were slaves to so-called gods that do not even exist. [9] So now that you know God (or should I say, now that God knows you), why do you want to go back again and become slaves once more to the weak and useless spiritual principles of this world? [10] You are trying to earn favor with God by observing certain days or months or seasons or years. [11] I fear for you. Perhaps all my hard work with you was for nothing. [12] Dear brothers and sisters,* I plead with you to live as I do in freedom from these things, for I have become like you Gentiles—free from those laws.

You did not mistreat me when I first preached to you. [13] Surely you remember that I was sick when I first brought you the Good News. [14] But even though my condition tempted you to reject me, you did not despise me or turn me away. No, you took me in and cared for me as though I were an angel from God or even Christ Jesus himself. [15] Where is that joyful and grateful spirit you felt then? I am sure you would have taken out your own eyes and given them to me if it had been possible. [16] Have I now become your enemy because I am telling you the truth?

[17] Those false teachers are so eager to win your favor, but their intentions are not good. They are trying to shut you off from me so that you will pay attention only to them. [18] If someone is eager to do good things for you, that's all

---

3:26 Greek *sons.*   **3:27** Greek *have put on Christ.*   **3:28** Greek *Jew or Greek.*   **3:29** Greek *seed.*   **4:3** Or *powers;* also in 4:9.
4:5 Greek *sons;* also in 4:6.   **4:6a** Greek *you.*   **4:6b** *Abba* is an Aramaic term for "father."   **4:7** Greek *son;* also in 4:7b.
4:12 Greek *brothers;* also in 4:28, 31.

---

off and running

FIND A CLOSE CHRISTIAN FRIEND
Read GALATIANS 6:1-3

God never intended us to be "solo" Christians. That is why one of the first things you should do after becoming a Christian is find some good, solid Christian friends. Although God wants us to turn to him first in times of trouble, he also knows that we need Christian brothers and sisters here on earth to help us through our difficulties—and they need us, too. Here are three things to look for in a Christian friend:

1. A True Christian Friend Will Let You Know When You Sin. A true friend will care enough about your spiritual condition to tell you the truth. The Bible

right; but let them do it all the time, not just when I'm with you.

[19] Oh, my dear children! I feel as if I'm going through labor pains for you again, and they will continue until Christ is fully developed in your lives. [20] I wish I were with you right now so I could change my tone. But at this distance I don't know how else to help you.

Abraham's Two Children

[21] Tell me, you who want to live under the law, do you know what the law actually says? [22] The Scriptures say that Abraham had two sons, one from his slave wife and one from his freeborn wife.* [23] The son of the slave wife was born in a human attempt to bring about the fulfillment of God's promise. But the son of the freeborn wife was born as God's own fulfillment of his promise.

[24] These two women serve as an illustration of God's two covenants. The first woman, Hagar, represents Mount Sinai where people received the law that enslaved them. [25] And now Jerusalem is just like Mount Sinai in Arabia,* because she and her children live in slavery to the law. [26] But the other woman, Sarah, represents the heavenly Jerusalem. She is the free woman, and she is our mother. [27] As Isaiah said,

"Rejoice, O childless woman,
    you who have never given birth!
Break into a joyful shout,
    you who have never been in labor!
For the desolate woman now has more
        children
    than the woman who lives with her
        husband!"*

[28] And you, dear brothers and sisters, are children of the promise, just like Isaac. [29] But you are now being persecuted by those who want you to keep the law, just as Ishmael, the child born by human effort, persecuted Isaac, the child born by the power of the Spirit.

[30] But what do the Scriptures say about that? "Get rid of the slave and her son, for the son of the slave woman will not share the inheritance with the free woman's son."* [31] So, dear brothers and sisters, we are not children of the slave woman; we are children of the free woman.

CHAPTER 5
Freedom in Christ

So Christ has truly set us free. Now make sure that you stay free, and don't get tied up again in slavery to the law.

[2] Listen! I, Paul, tell you this: If you are counting on circumcision to make you right with God, then Christ will be of no benefit to you. [3] I'll say it again. If you are trying to find favor with God by being circumcised, you must obey every regulation in the whole law of Moses. [4] For if you are trying to make yourselves right with God by keeping the law, you have been cut off from Christ! You have fallen away from God's grace.

[5] But we who live by the Spirit eagerly wait to receive by faith the righteousness God has promised to us. [6] For when we place our faith in Christ Jesus, there is no benefit in being circumcised or being uncircumcised. What is important is faith expressing itself in love.

[7] You were running the race so well. Who has held you back from following the truth? [8] It certainly isn't God, for he is the one who called you to freedom. [9] This false teaching is like a little yeast that spreads through the whole batch of dough! [10] I am trusting the Lord to keep you from believing false teachings. God will judge that person, whoever he is, who has been confusing you.

4:22 See Gen 16:15; 21:2-3.   **4:25** Greek *And Hagar, which is Mount Sinai in Arabia, is now like Jerusalem;* other manuscripts read *And Mount Sinai in Arabia is now like Jerusalem.*   **4:27** Isa 54:1.   **4:30** Gen 21:10.

---

says, "Wounds from a sincere friend are better than many kisses from an enemy" (Proverbs 27:6).

2. A True Christian Friend Is Humble. If you fall spiritually, a friend who is a strong Christian can be counted upon to help restore you without spreading rumors because this friend realizes that he or she is just as susceptible to sin as you are.

3. A True Christian Friend Will Help Carry Your Burdens. He will weep with you when you weep and rejoice with you when you rejoice (see Romans 12:15, p. 183).

Having a friend who is a strong Christian is not just a benefit—it is a necessity! And that is how Jesus wants it to be. Therefore, build your Christian friendships, and in so doing, you will help strengthen yourself and the body of Christ.

For the next note on "Relationships," turn to p. 216.

¹¹Dear brothers and sisters,* if I were still preaching that you must be circumcised—as some say I do—why am I still being persecuted? If I were no longer preaching salvation through the cross of Christ, no one would be offended. ¹²I just wish that those troublemakers who want to mutilate you by circumcision would mutilate themselves.*

¹³For you have been called to live in freedom, my brothers and sisters. But don't use your freedom to satisfy your sinful nature. Instead, use your freedom to serve one another in love. ¹⁴For the whole law can be summed up in this one command: "Love your neighbor as yourself."* ¹⁵But if you are always biting and devouring one another, watch out! Beware of destroying one another.

Living by the Spirit's Power

¹⁶So I say, let the Holy Spirit guide your lives. Then you won't be doing what your sinful nature craves. ¹⁷The sinful nature wants to do evil, which is just the opposite of what the Spirit wants. And the Spirit gives us desires that are the opposite of what the sinful nature desires. These two forces are constantly fighting each other, so you are not free to carry out your good intentions. ¹⁸But when you are directed by the Spirit, you are not under obligation to the law of Moses.

¹⁹When you follow the desires of your sinful nature, the results are very clear: sexual immorality, impurity, lustful pleasures, ²⁰idolatry, sorcery, hostility, quarreling, jealousy, outbursts of anger, selfish ambition, dissension, division, ²¹envy, drunkenness, wild parties, and other sins like these. Let me tell you again, as I have before, that anyone living that sort of life will not inherit the Kingdom of God.

²²But the Holy Spirit produces this kind of fruit in our lives: love, joy, peace, patience, kindness, goodness, faithfulness, ²³gentleness, and self-control. There is no law against these things!

²⁴Those who belong to Christ Jesus have nailed the passions and desires of their sinful nature to his cross and crucified them there. ²⁵Since we are living by the Spirit, let us follow the Spirit's leading in every part of our lives. ²⁶Let us not become conceited, or provoke one another, or be jealous of one another.

CHAPTER 6

We Harvest What We Plant

Dear brothers and sisters, if another believer* is overcome by some sin, you who are godly* should gently and humbly help that person back onto the right path. And be careful not to fall into the same temptation yourself. ²Share each other's burdens, and in this way obey the law of Christ. ³If you think you are too important to help someone, you are only fooling yourself. You are not that important.

⁴Pay careful attention to your own work, for then you will get the satisfaction of a job well done, and you won't need to compare yourself to anyone else. ⁵For we are each responsible for our own conduct.

⁶Those who are taught the word of God should provide for their teachers, sharing all good things with them.

⁷Don't be misled—you cannot mock the justice of God. You will always harvest what you plant. ⁸Those who live only to satisfy their own sinful nature will harvest decay and death from that sinful nature. But those who live to please the Spirit will harvest everlasting life from the Spirit. ⁹So let's not get tired of doing what is good. At just the right time we will reap a harvest of blessing if we don't give up. ¹⁰Therefore, whenever we have the opportunity, we should do good to everyone—especially to those in the family of faith.

Paul's Final Advice

¹¹NOTICE WHAT LARGE LETTERS I USE AS I WRITE THESE CLOSING WORDS IN MY OWN HANDWRITING.

¹²Those who are trying to force you to be circumcised want to look good to others. They don't want to be persecuted for teaching that the cross of Christ alone can save. ¹³And even those who advocate circumcision don't keep the whole law themselves. They only want you to be circumcised so they can boast about it and claim you as their disciples.

¹⁴As for me, may I never boast about anything except the cross of our Lord Jesus Christ. Because of that cross,* my interest in this world has been crucified, and the world's interest in me has also died. ¹⁵It doesn't matter whether we have been circumcised or not. What counts is whether we have been transformed into a new creation. ¹⁶May God's peace and mercy be upon all who live by this principle; they are the new people of God.*

¹⁷From now on, don't let anyone trouble me with these things. For I bear on my body the scars that show I belong to Jesus.

¹⁸Dear brothers and sisters,* may the grace of our Lord Jesus Christ be with your spirit. Amen.

5:11 Greek *Brothers;* similarly in 5:13. **5:12** Or *castrate themselves,* or *cut themselves off from you;* Greek reads *cut themselves off.* **5:14** Lev 19:18. **6:1a** Greek *Brothers, if a man.* **6:1b** Greek *spiritual.* **6:14** Or *Because of him.* **6:16** Greek *this principle, and upon the Israel of God.* **6:18** Greek *Brothers.*

Ephesians

AUTHOR: **PAUL** | DATE WRITTEN: **A.D. 60** | GENRE: **EPISTLE**

The book of Ephesians shows us our rightful position as children of God "in the heavenly realms" with Jesus Christ. It tells us of all that God has done for us, as well as how to fully appreciate and implement it practically in our lives.

CHAPTER 1

Greetings from Paul

This letter is from Paul, chosen by the will of God to be an apostle of Christ Jesus.

I am writing to God's holy people in Ephesus,* who are faithful followers of Christ Jesus.

2 May God our Father and the Lord Jesus Christ give you grace and peace.

Spiritual Blessings

3 All praise to God, the Father of our Lord Jesus Christ, who has blessed us with every spiritual blessing in the heavenly realms because we are united with Christ. 4 Even before he made the world, God loved us and chose us in Christ to be holy and without fault in his eyes. 5 God decided in advance to adopt us into his own family by bringing us to himself through Jesus Christ. This is what he wanted to do, and it gave him great pleasure. 6 So we praise God for the glorious grace he has poured out on us who belong to his dear Son.* 7 He is so rich in kindness and grace that he purchased our freedom with the blood of his Son and forgave our sins. 8 He has showered his kindness on us, along with all wisdom and understanding.

9 God has now revealed to us his mysterious plan regarding Christ, a plan to fulfill his own good pleasure. 10 And this is the plan: At the right time he will bring everything together under the authority of Christ—everything in heaven and on earth. 11 Furthermore, because we are united with Christ, we have received an inheritance from God,* for he chose us in advance, and he makes everything work out according to his plan.

12 God's purpose was that we Jews who were the first to trust in Christ would bring praise and glory to God. 13 And now you Gentiles have also heard the truth, the Good News that God saves you. And when you believed in Christ, he identified you as his own* by giving you the Holy Spirit, whom he promised long ago. 14 The Spirit is God's guarantee that he will give us the inheritance he promised and that he has purchased us to be his own people. He did this so we would praise and glorify him.

Paul's Prayer for Spiritual Wisdom

15 Ever since I first heard of your strong faith in the Lord Jesus and your love for God's people everywhere,* 16 I have not stopped thanking God for you. I pray for you constantly, 17 asking God, the glorious Father of our Lord Jesus Christ, to give you spiritual wisdom* and insight so that you might grow in your knowledge of God. 18 I pray that your hearts will be flooded with light so that you can understand the confident hope he has given to those he called—his holy people who are his rich and glorious inheritance.*

19 I also pray that you will understand the incredible greatness of God's power for us who believe him. This is the same mighty power 20 that raised Christ from the dead and seated him in the place of honor at God's right hand in the heavenly realms. 21 Now he is far above any ruler or authority or power or leader or

1:1 The most ancient manuscripts do not include *in Ephesus.* 1:6 Greek *to us in the beloved.* 1:11 Or *we have become God's inheritance.* 1:13 Or *he put his seal on you.* 1:15 Some manuscripts read *your faithfulness to the Lord Jesus and to God's people everywhere.* 1:17 Or *to give you the Spirit of wisdom.* 1:18 Or *called, and the rich and glorious inheritance he has given to his holy people.*

cornerstones

WHY GOD GIVES US THE HOLY SPIRIT
Read EPHESIANS 1:13-14

You might say that the Holy Spirit is our "identifying mark" as a Christian. In this text we see three specific reasons God gives us his Holy Spirit:

1. The Holy Spirit Is a Promise. Once again, Scripture reminds us that God has promised to send the Holy Spirit to all those who have heard the good news of the gospel and trusted Christ as Savior.

2. The Holy Spirit Is a Seal. The Holy Spirit serves as a mark of ownership, showing that we belong to God.

3. The Holy Spirit Is a Guarantee. The Holy Spirit also represents God's pledge to bring us to our final spiritual inheritance. This word could also be translated as a "first installment" or "deposit," signifying that his sealing in our lives is a foretaste of much more to come!

God gives us the Holy Spirit not only to enable us to live out the Christian life but to prove that we are precious in his sight.

For the next note on "Who Is the Holy Spirit?" *turn to p. 120.*

---

anything else—not only in this world but also in the world to come. ²²God has put all things under the authority of Christ and has made him head over all things for the benefit of the church. ²³And the church is his body; it is made full and complete by Christ, who fills all things everywhere with himself.

CHAPTER **2**
Made Alive with Christ

Once you were dead because of your disobedience and your many sins. ²You used to live in sin, just like the rest of the world, obeying the devil—the commander of the powers in the unseen world.* He is the spirit at work in the hearts of those who refuse to obey God. ³All of us used to live that way, following the passionate desires and inclinations of our sinful nature. By our very nature we were subject to God's anger, just like everyone else.

⁴But God is so rich in mercy, and he loved us so much, ⁵that even though we were dead because of our sins, he gave us life when he raised Christ from the dead. (It is only by God's grace that you have been saved!) ⁶For he raised us from the dead along with Christ and seated us with him in the heavenly realms because we are united with Christ Jesus. ⁷So God can point to us in all future ages as examples of the incredible wealth of his grace and kindness toward us, as shown in all he has done for us who are united with Christ Jesus.

⁸God saved you by his grace when you believed. And you can't take credit for this; it is a gift from God. ⁹Salvation is not a reward for the good things we have done, so none of us can boast about it. ¹⁰For we are God's masterpiece. He has created us anew in Christ Jesus, so we can do the good things he planned for us long ago.

Oneness and Peace in Christ

¹¹Don't forget that you Gentiles used to be outsiders. You were called "uncircumcised heathens" by the Jews, who were proud of their circumcision, even though it affected only their bodies and not their hearts. ¹²In those days you were living apart from Christ. You were excluded from citizenship among the people of Israel, and you did not know the covenant promises God had made to them. You lived in this world without God and without hope. ¹³But now you have been united with Christ Jesus. Once you were far away from God, but now you have been brought near to him through the blood of Christ.

¹⁴For Christ himself has brought peace to us. He united Jews and Gentiles into one people when, in his own body on the cross, he broke down the wall of hostility that separated us. ¹⁵He did this by ending the system of law with its commandments and regulations. He made peace between Jews and Gentiles by creating in himself one new people from the two groups. ¹⁶Together as one body, Christ reconciled both groups to God by means of his death on the cross, and our hostility toward each other was put to death.

¹⁷He brought this Good News of peace to you Gentiles who were far away from him, and

2:2 Greek *obeying the commander of the power of the air.*

peace to the Jews who were near. [18]Now all of us can come to the Father through the same Holy Spirit because of what Christ has done for us.

A Temple for the Lord

[19]So now you Gentiles are no longer strangers and foreigners. You are citizens along with all of God's holy people. You are members of God's family. [20]Together, we are his house, built on the foundation of the apostles and the prophets. And the cornerstone is Christ Jesus himself. [21]We are carefully joined together in him, becoming a holy temple for the Lord. [22]Through him you Gentiles are also being made part of this dwelling where God lives by his Spirit.

CHAPTER **3**

God's Mysterious Plan Revealed

When I think of all this, I, Paul, a prisoner of Christ Jesus for the benefit of you Gentiles* ... [2]assuming, by the way, that you know God gave me the special responsibility of extending his grace to you Gentiles. [3]As I briefly wrote earlier, God himself revealed his mysterious plan to me. [4]As you read what I have written, you will understand my insight into this plan regarding Christ. [5]God did not reveal it to previous generations, but now by his Spirit he has revealed it to his holy apostles and prophets.

[6]And this is God's plan: Both Gentiles and Jews who believe the Good News share equally in the riches inherited by God's children. Both are part of the same body, and both enjoy the promise of blessings because they belong to Christ Jesus.* [7]By God's grace and mighty power, I have been given the privilege of serving him by spreading this Good News.

[8]Though I am the least deserving of all God's people, he graciously gave me the privilege of telling the Gentiles about the endless treasures available to them in Christ. [9]I was chosen to explain to everyone* this mysterious plan that God, the Creator of all things, had kept secret from the beginning.

[10]God's purpose in all this was to use the church to display his wisdom in its rich variety to all the unseen rulers and authorities in the heavenly places. [11]This was his eternal plan, which he carried out through Christ Jesus our Lord.

[12]Because of Christ and our faith in him,* we can now come boldly and confidently into God's presence. [13]So please don't lose heart be-

first steps

WHY THE CHURCH NEEDS YOU

Read EPHESIANS 4:11-16

Not only do you need the church, but the church needs you! As God's child, you are blessed with unique spiritual gifts and talents that can be used to benefit the body of Christ. You can use these gifts in at least two ways to benefit fellow believers:

1. The Gifts God Gives You Promote Spiritual Maturity. God wants you to grow spiritually. In order for this to happen, he has placed gifted people in the church to fulfill different aspects of ministry. If the pastor, teacher, evangelist, and others properly carry out their duties, this not only helps to promote your spiritual growth, but also equips you to do better work for him. For this to take place, however, you must "fit together perfectly," with "each part [doing] its own special work, so that the whole body is healthy and growing and full of love" (Ephesians 4:16).

2. The Gifts God Gives You Bless Others. Although you may not hold a prominent position in your church, you may be able to encourage others, care for the sick or those in need, financially support a ministry outreach, or even clean restrooms. If you fail to regularly fellowship in a church with other believers, you are neglecting a tremendous opportunity to use what God has given you.

For the next note on "Look for and Attend the Right Church," turn to p. 205.

cause of my trials here. I am suffering for you, so you should feel honored.

Paul's Prayer for Spiritual Growth

[14]When I think of all this, I fall to my knees and pray to the Father,* [15]the Creator of everything in heaven and on earth.* [16]I pray that from his glorious, unlimited resources he will empower you with inner strength through his Spirit. [17]Then Christ will make his home in your hearts as you trust in him. Your roots will grow down into God's love and keep you strong.

3:1 Paul resumes this thought in verse 14: "When I think of all this, I fall to my knees and pray to the Father." **3:6** Or *because they are united with Christ Jesus.* **3:9** Some manuscripts do not include *to everyone.* **3:12** Or *Because of Christ's faithfulness.* **3:14** Some manuscripts read *the Father of our Lord Jesus Christ.* **3:15** Or *from whom every family in heaven and on earth takes its name.*

cornerstones

GOD SAVED US FOR A PURPOSE
Read EPHESIANS 2:10

As a nonbeliever, you had nothing to motivate you to live righteously. You may have searched for purpose and meaning in life but found nothing satisfying. As a believer, however, you are "God's masterpiece," which means that his Spirit is working in your life to make you more like Christ and to give you a purpose for living.

This verse describes part of the purpose God has for your life as his child—to do good works by helping others. The amazing and wonderful truth about God's purpose for your life is that he had plans for you to do good works long before you even existed. He has already scheduled the days and events of your life with opportunities to tangibly share his love with others (Psalm 139:16; Jeremiah 29:11).

The next time you see a neighbor in trouble, hear about a friend struggling with a problem, notice a coworker in distress, or see a stranger who genuinely needs a helping hand—take hold of this opportunity God has placed in your path. Let your "good deeds shine" (see Matthew 5:16, p. 5) because you are his child.

navigation cross-referenceFor the next note on "Faith and Works," turn to p. 10.

---

[18]And may you have the power to understand, as all God's people should, how wide, how long, how high, and how deep his love is. [19]May you experience the love of Christ, though it is too great to understand fully. Then you will be made complete with all the fullness of life and power that comes from God.

[20]Now all glory to God, who is able, through his mighty power at work within us, to accomplish infinitely more than we might ask or think. [21]Glory to him in the church and in Christ Jesus through all generations forever and ever! Amen.

CHAPTER **4**
Unity in the Body
Therefore I, a prisoner for serving the Lord, beg you to lead a life worthy of your calling, for you have been called by God. [2]Always be humble and gentle. Be patient with each other, making allowance for each other's faults because of your love. [3]Make every effort to keep yourselves united in the Spirit, binding yourselves together with peace. [4]For there is one body and one Spirit, just as you have been called to one glorious hope for the future. [5]There is one Lord, one faith, one baptism, [6]and one God and Father, who is over all and in all and living through all.

[7]However, he has given each one of us a special gift* through the generosity of Christ. [8]That is why the Scriptures say,

"When he ascended to the heights,
    he led a crowd of captives
    and gave gifts to his people."*

[9]Notice that it says "he ascended." This clearly means that Christ also descended to our lowly world.* [10]And the same one who descended is the one who ascended higher than all the heavens, so that he might fill the entire universe with himself.

[11]Now these are the gifts Christ gave to the church: the apostles, the prophets, the evangelists, and the pastors and teachers. [12]Their responsibility is to equip God's people to do his work and build up the church, the body of Christ. [13]This will continue until we all come to such unity in our faith and knowledge of God's Son that we will be mature in the Lord, measuring up to the full and complete standard of Christ.

[14]Then we will no longer be immature like children. We won't be tossed and blown about by every wind of new teaching. We will not be influenced when people try to trick us with lies so clever they sound like the truth. [15]Instead, we will speak the truth in love, growing in every way more and more like Christ, who is the head of his body, the church. [16]He makes the whole body fit together perfectly. As each part does its own special work, it helps the other parts grow, so that the whole body is healthy and growing and full of love.

Living as Children of Light
[17]With the Lord's authority I say this: Live no longer as the Gentiles do, for they are hopelessly confused. [18]Their minds are full of darkness; they wander far from the life God gives

4:7 Greek *a grace.*   4:8 Ps 68:18.   4:9 Or *to the lowest parts of the earth.*

What Are Spiritual Gifts?

Read EPHESIANS 4:11-16

God has chosen people to do his work. He chose this course of action for reasons only he knows and understands. From a human perspective, we may wonder if this was the best decision. After all, the sky's the limit concerning what God could have done. He could have chosen to use angels to speak to lost humanity. He certainly used them on many significant occasions throughout Scripture. Or God could have created a special category of messengers that would never fail him—a "sin-proof" instrument that would faithfully proclaim his Word. For that matter, God himself could have simply poked his face through the heavens and said, "Hello, world! I'm God, and you're not!" But God has chosen men and women to do his work among humankind.

As we seek to follow and be used by Jesus Christ, we need to utilize all that he has made available to us. One of the great blessings Jesus has given to his church and to us as individuals is the gifts of the Spirit. Why has he given these gifts? The Bible has this to say about the vital role they play in the lives of believers:

Spiritual Gifts Enable Us to Grow in the Knowledge of Christ. Some people get side-tracked with spiritual gifts and become more obsessed with the gifts than with Jesus. Believers begin to follow signs and wonders, instead of signs and wonders following believers. This is a sign of spiritual immaturity. The Christian writer/preacher A. B. Simpson wrote these insightful words:

Once it was the blessing, now it is the Lord.
Once it was the feeling, now it is his Word.
Once his gifts I wanted, now the Giver own.
Once I sought for healing, now himself alone.

Attaining spiritual gifts is not the goal—they are the gateway. They are not a hobby to play with—they are tools to build with, weapons to fight with. We will be more effective as we put them to use for God's glory and not our own.

Spiritual Gifts Are to Be Used. It is possible to let a gift go unused. In doing this, however, you disobey God and cheat the church of a blessing. For this reason, we must use those unique gifts he has given us. In fact, it must be insulting to God for us to demean some gift his Holy Spirit has instilled in our life by saying that it just isn't important enough to use.

Each Spiritual Gift Has a Special Place in the Body of Christ. Every gift that God has placed in the body of Christ, the church, is important. Some gifts such as preaching, teaching, and prophesying may seem more important than others such as hospitality or service. But God has given all of these gifts to build up his church. None of these gifts should be looked down upon or treated lightly.

For the next "Big Question" note, turn to p. 277.

because they have closed their minds and hardened their hearts against him. [19] They have no sense of shame. They live for lustful pleasure and eagerly practice every kind of impurity.

[20] But that isn't what you learned about Christ. [21] Since you have heard about Jesus and have learned the truth that comes from him, [22] throw off your old sinful nature and your former way of life, which is corrupted by lust and deception. [23] Instead, let the Spirit renew your thoughts and attitudes. [24] Put on your new nature, created to be like God—truly righteous and holy.

[25] So stop telling lies. Let us tell our neighbors the truth, for we are all parts of the same

body. ²⁶And "don't sin by letting anger control you."* Don't let the sun go down while you are still angry, ²⁷ for anger gives a foothold to the devil.

²⁸ If you are a thief, quit stealing. Instead, use your hands for good hard work, and then give

4:26 Ps 4:4.

generously to others in need. ²⁹Don't use foul or abusive language. Let everything you say be good and helpful, so that your words will be an encouragement to those who hear them.

³⁰And do not bring sorrow to God's Holy Spirit by the way you live. Remember, he has

---

off and running

HUSBANDS AND WIVES HAVE DISTINCT ROLES IN MARRIAGE
Read EPHESIANS 5:21-33

The reason so many marriages fail is that husbands, wives, or both do not obey the standards God has laid out in Scripture. In this text, we find the specific roles God has given to the husband and the wife.

God's Plan for the Husband

• He is to be the head of his wife as Christ is the head of the church

True authority in the marriage relationship has been given by God to the husband. From the beginning, God designated the man as the leader in the marriage relationship (Ephesians 5:23). Like Christ, a husband should be firm and decisive but also humble and unselfish. Before a husband can expect his wife to submit to him, though, he has to submit to Christ.

• He must love his wife as Christ loved the church

Jesus said, "For even the Son of Man came not to be served but to serve others and to give his life as a ransom for many" (Matthew 20:28). To love as Jesus loved means that a husband focuses primarily on his wife's needs, not his own (Ephesians 5:25). The wife's submission hinges upon the husband's fulfillment of this role. Just as the church loves Jesus because of his incredible display of love for it, so the wife will love and submit to her husband as she sees his demonstration of love toward her. One heart burning with love sets another on fire.

• He must encourage his wife's spiritual growth

One of the husband's first priorities is to make sure his wife has a good relationship with God (Ephesians 5:26). He is to encourage his wife's spiritual growth, recognizing that it affects her personal happiness as a woman, wife, and mother.

• He must love his wife as he loves himself

A husband must recognize that he and his wife are actually "one" (Ephesians 5:31). Therefore, he must do for his wife what he would do for himself. He should give her needs as much attention as he would his own (Ephesians 5:28-29).

God's Plan for the Wife

• She must submit to her husband's leadership Just as a wife submits to God, seeking his will above her own, so she must submit to her husband and his decisions (Ephesians 5:21, 24).

These guidelines for the husband and the wife become much easier to follow if they respect the first code of conduct listed: "Submit to one another out of reverence for Christ" (Ephesians 5:21). The word used for "submit" is a term that means "to arrange or rank under." In other words, we need to put the needs of our spouse before our own—in the fear of God. As we do that, our marriages will flourish as God intended, and you will be a living illustration of Christ's love for the church to an unbelieving world. For marriage is not so much *finding* the right person as it is *being* the right person.

For the next note on "Marriage," turn to p. 286.

identified you as his own,* guaranteeing that you will be saved on the day of redemption.

³¹ Get rid of all bitterness, rage, anger, harsh words, and slander, as well as all types of evil behavior. ³² Instead, be kind to each other, tenderhearted, forgiving one another, just as God through Christ has forgiven you.

CHAPTER 5
Living in the Light
Imitate God, therefore, in everything you do, because you are his dear children. ² Live a life filled with love, following the example of Christ. He loved us* and offered himself as a sacrifice for us, a pleasing aroma to God.

³ Let there be no sexual immorality, impurity, or greed among you. Such sins have no place among God's people. ⁴ Obscene stories, foolish talk, and coarse jokes—these are not for you. Instead, let there be thankfulness to God. ⁵ You can be sure that no immoral, impure, or greedy person will inherit the Kingdom of Christ and of God. For a greedy person is an idolater, worshiping the things of this world.

⁶ Don't be fooled by those who try to excuse these sins, for the anger of God will fall on all who disobey him. ⁷ Don't participate in the things these people do. ⁸ For once you were full of darkness, but now you have light from the Lord. So live as people of light! ⁹ For this light within you produces only what is good and right and true.

¹⁰ Carefully determine what pleases the Lord. ¹¹ Take no part in the worthless deeds of evil and darkness; instead, expose them. ¹² It is shameful even to talk about the things that ungodly people do in secret. ¹³ But their evil intentions will be exposed when the light shines on them, ¹⁴ for the light makes everything visible. This is why it is said,

> "Awake, O sleeper,
> rise up from the dead,
> and Christ will give you light."

Living by the Spirit's Power
¹⁵ So be careful how you live. Don't live like fools, but like those who are wise. ¹⁶ Make the most of every opportunity in these evil days. ¹⁷ Don't act thoughtlessly, but understand what the Lord wants you to do. ¹⁸ Don't be drunk with wine, because that will ruin your life. Instead, be filled with the Holy Spirit, ¹⁹ singing psalms and hymns and spiritual songs among yourselves, and making music to the Lord in your hearts. ²⁰ And give thanks for everything to God the Father in the name of our Lord Jesus Christ.

4:30 Or *has put his seal on you.*   5:2 Some manuscripts read *loved you.*

first steps

REALIZE WHO IS TEMPTING YOU
Read EPHESIANS 6:10-12

In the Bible, the Christian life is not simply compared to a war—it is actually called a war! As in any battle, it helps to know your enemy. In this case, our enemy is the same one who faced off against Christ in the wilderness: Satan. He is incensed that you have surrendered your life to Christ, and he also sees you as a potential threat to his kingdom. But the encouraging news is that Satan is not as powerful as he would like you to think. Here are two things Satan doesn't want you to know:

1. The Devil Was Conquered by Jesus. When Jesus Christ died on the cross, he disarmed the devil and his demon powers. They could no longer control and condemn people for their sin. In addition, they could no longer keep the penalty of death hanging above people's heads (see Colossians 2:13-15, p. 245; Hebrews 2:14, p. 277; 1 John 3:8-9, pp. 309-310). The fact that Jesus defeated Satan does not mean that he has no power today. But it does mean that he does not have the upper hand.

2. The Devil Has Definite Limitations. Satan would love to have us think that he is God's equal, but he has clear and definite limitations as to what he can do (Job 1:1-12). Most important, before he can bring one temptation or hardship our way, Satan has to go through the protective hedge of Jesus Christ.

Temptation will come your way in the Christian life. But if you are wise, you will cling to the Lord that much tighter when the devil comes with his enticements. Then, once you have stood through the temptation, you will be stronger. As Martin Luther once said, "One Christian who has been tempted is worth a thousand who haven't."

For the next note on "Resist Temptation," *turn to p. 293.*

cornerstones

CHRIST'S LOVE SETS THE STANDARD
Read EPHESIANS 5:2

Think back for a moment to when you were a child. What if your parents had never demonstrated how to use a fork and spoon. Then one day they placed you at a table with these utensils and said, "Eat!" You would have had no idea how to use them to get food into your mouth. Consequently, you would have made a mess.

Fortunately, when it comes to loving others, God has given us the greatest example: Jesus Christ. He knew that the best way to teach us how to love was to show us how it is done, and throughout the Gospels, we can see Jesus' love in action. Of course the greatest display of Christ's love for us was when he took the punishment we deserved by dying on the cross. Because of that tremendous sacrifice, we are obligated to love others. Scripture says, "Owe nothing to anyone—except for your obligation to love one another" (Romans 13:8). Because we will never match the depth of love God has for us, we will never be able to fully repay the debt of love we owe him. That is why we have to keep giving out that same kind of love to others.

Perhaps you have grown up in a home where love was seldom expressed, or you have had a distorted view of love, and you feel that you are incapable of truly loving others. Take heart, for as this passage says, you can look to Jesus as your example.

When Christ becomes the standard of your love, you will understand what the apostle Paul meant when he said that Christ's love controls us (see 2 Corinthians 5:14, p. 212).

For the next note on "Love," turn to p. 206.

Spirit-Guided Relationships: Wives and Husbands

²¹And further, submit to one another out of reverence for Christ.

²²For wives, this means submit to your husbands as to the Lord. ²³For a husband is the head of his wife as Christ is the head of the church. He is the Savior of his body, the church. ²⁴As the church submits to Christ, so you wives should submit to your husbands in everything.

²⁵For husbands, this means love your wives, just as Christ loved the church. He gave up his life for her ²⁶to make her holy and clean, washed by the cleansing of God's word.* ²⁷He did this to present her to himself as a glorious church without a spot or wrinkle or any other blemish. Instead, she will be holy and without fault. ²⁸In the same way, husbands ought to love their wives as they love their own bodies. For a man who loves his wife actually shows love for himself. ²⁹No one hates his own body but feeds and cares for it, just as Christ cares for the church. ³⁰And we are members of his body.

³¹As the Scriptures say, "A man leaves his father and mother and is joined to his wife, and the two are united into one."* ³²This is a great mystery, but it is an illustration of the way Christ and the church are one. ³³So again I say, each man must love his wife as he loves himself, and the wife must respect her husband.

CHAPTER 6
Children and Parents

Children, obey your parents because you belong to the Lord,* for this is the right thing to do. ²"Honor your father and mother." This is the first commandment with a promise: ³If you honor your father and mother, "things will go well for you, and you will have a long life on the earth."*

⁴Fathers, do not provoke your children to anger by the way you treat them. Rather, bring them up with the discipline and instruction that comes from the Lord.

Slaves and Masters

⁵Slaves, obey your earthly masters with deep respect and fear. Serve them sincerely as you would serve Christ. ⁶Try to please them all the time, not just when they are watching you. As slaves of Christ, do the will of God with all your heart. ⁷Work with enthusiasm, as though you were working for the Lord rather than for people. ⁸Remember that the Lord will reward each one of us for the good we do, whether we are slaves or free.

5:26 Greek *washed by water with the word.*   **5:31** Gen 2:24.   **6:1** Or *Children, obey your parents who belong to the Lord;* some manuscripts read simply *Children, obey your parents.*   **6:2-3** Exod 20:12; Deut 5:16.

[9] Masters, treat your slaves in the same way. Don't threaten them; remember, you both have the same Master in heaven, and he has no favorites.

The Whole Armor of God

[10] A final word: Be strong in the Lord and in his mighty power. [11] Put on all of God's armor so that you will be able to stand firm against all strategies of the devil. [12] For we* are not fighting against flesh-and-blood enemies, but against evil rulers and authorities of the unseen world, against mighty powers in this dark world, and against evil spirits in the heavenly places.

[13] Therefore, put on every piece of God's armor so you will be able to resist the enemy in the time of evil. Then after the battle you will still be standing firm. [14] Stand your ground, putting on the belt of truth and the body armor of God's righteousness. [15] For shoes, put on the peace that comes from the Good News so that you will be fully prepared.* [16] In addition to all of these, hold up the shield of faith to stop the fiery arrows of the devil.* [17] Put on salvation as your helmet, and take the sword of the Spirit, which is the word of God.

[18] Pray in the Spirit at all times and on every occasion. Stay alert and be persistent in your prayers for all believers everywhere.*

[19] And pray for me, too. Ask God to give me the right words so I can boldly explain God's mysterious plan that the Good News is for Jews and Gentiles alike.* [20] I am in chains now, still preaching this message as God's ambassador. So pray that I will keep on speaking boldly for him, as I should.

Final Greetings

[21] To bring you up to date, Tychicus will give you a full report about what I am doing and how I am getting along. He is a beloved brother and faithful helper in the Lord's work. [22] I have sent him to you for this very purpose—to let you know how we are doing and to encourage you.

[23] Peace be with you, dear brothers and sisters,* and may God the Father and the Lord Jesus Christ give you love with faithfulness. [24] May God's grace be eternally upon all who love our Lord Jesus Christ.

6:12 Some manuscripts read *you*.   **6:15** Or *For shoes, put on the readiness to preach the Good News of peace with God.*
6:16 Greek *the evil one.*   **6:18** Greek *all of God's holy people.*   **6:19** Greek *explain the mystery of the Good News;* some manuscripts read simply *explain the mystery.*   **6:23** Greek *brothers.*

Philippians

AUTHOR: **PAUL** | DATE WRITTEN: **A.D. 61** | GENRE: **EPISTLE**

This book explains the mindset, attitude, and outlook the believer must have if he or she is going to experience the joy of the Lord in a troubled world.

CHAPTER **1**

Greetings from Paul

This letter is from Paul and Timothy, slaves of Christ Jesus.

I am writing to all of God's holy people in Philippi who belong to Christ Jesus, including the elders* and deacons.

2 May God our Father and the Lord Jesus Christ give you grace and peace.

Paul's Thanksgiving and Prayer

3 Every time I think of you, I give thanks to my God. 4 Whenever I pray, I make my requests for all of you with joy, 5 for you have been my partners in spreading the Good News about Christ from the time you first heard it until now. 6 And I am certain that God, who began the good work within you, will continue his work until it is finally finished on the day when Christ Jesus returns.

7 So it is right that I should feel as I do about all of you, for you have a special place in my heart. You share with me the special favor of God, both in my imprisonment and in defending and confirming the truth of the Good News. 8 God knows how much I love you and long for you with the tender compassion of Christ Jesus.

9 I pray that your love will overflow more and more, and that you will keep on growing in knowledge and understanding. 10 For I want you to understand what really matters, so that you may live pure and blameless lives until the day of Christ's return. 11 May you always be filled with the fruit of your salvation—the righteous character produced in your life by Jesus Christ*—for this will bring much glory and praise to God.

Paul's Joy That Christ Is Preached

12 And I want you to know, my dear brothers and sisters,* that everything that has happened to me here has helped to spread the Good News. 13 For everyone here, including the whole palace guard,* knows that I am in chains because of Christ. 14 And because of my imprisonment, most of the believers* here have gained confidence and boldly speak God's message* without fear.

15 It's true that some are preaching out of jealousy and rivalry. But others preach about Christ with pure motives. 16 They preach because they love me, for they know I have been appointed to defend the Good News. 17 Those others do not have pure motives as they preach about Christ. They preach with selfish ambition, not sincerely, intending to make my chains more painful to me. 18 But that doesn't matter. Whether their motives are false or genuine, the message about Christ is being preached either way, so I rejoice. And I will continue to rejoice. 19 For I know that as you pray for me and the Spirit of Jesus Christ helps me, this will lead to my deliverance.

Paul's Life for Christ

20 For I fully expect and hope that I will never be ashamed, but that I will continue to be bold for Christ, as I have been in the past. And I trust that my life will bring honor to Christ, whether I live or die. 21 For to me, living means living for Christ, and dying is even better. 22 But if I live, I

1:1 Or *overseers; or bishops.* 1:11 Greek *with the fruit of righteousness through Jesus Christ.* 1:12 Greek *brothers.* 1:13 Greek *including all the Praetorium.* 1:14a Greek *brothers in the Lord.* 1:14b Some manuscripts read *speak the message.*

cornerstones

JESUS IS HUMAN
Read PHILIPPIANS 2:5-11

This passage of Scripture paints a touching portrait of the Savior while letting us in on some key truths concerning Christ's divinity and humanity. In essence, it shows why we should worship and emulate Jesus in our lives.

Jesus Veiled His Deity without Voiding It. There was never a moment in the life of Jesus when he suddenly *became* God. He was God before he entered this world as a little baby. And he remained God after he became man. When the Scripture says that he "gave up his divine privileges," it does not mean that he ceased being God. He simply veiled his deity. But he never voided it. He always was, always is, and always will be God.

Jesus Experienced Our Experiences. Another way of saying that Jesus "took the humble position of a slave" is to say that "he emptied himself." Again, this does not mean that he emptied himself of his deity, but that he emptied himself of the privileges of deity. For instance, he never performed a miracle for his own benefit. He walked this earth as a man, not a spirit. He experienced human limitations. Jesus—God in human form—experienced hunger. He endured sorrow. He grew tired. He felt the sting of loneliness. He felt the pressure of temptation. For these reasons, we can be assured that our God understands what we are going through (see Hebrews 2:17-18, p. 277).

Jesus' Lordship Will Be Acknowledged by All. Regardless of what anyone thinks of Jesus now, in the end every knee will bow and every tongue will confess that Jesus Christ is Lord. The authority of the Bible backs this claim. Christ's divine nature, which he veiled at times during his time on earth, will then be clearly visible for all to see.

For the next note on "Who Is Jesus?" turn to p. 244.

---

can do more fruitful work for Christ. So I really don't know which is better. ²³I'm torn between two desires: I long to go and be with Christ, which would be far better for me. ²⁴But for your sakes, it is better that I continue to live.

²⁵Knowing this, I am convinced that I will remain alive so I can continue to help all of you grow and experience the joy of your faith. ²⁶And when I come to you again, you will have even more reason to take pride in Christ Jesus because of what he is doing through me.

Live as Citizens of Heaven

²⁷Above all, you must live as citizens of heaven, conducting yourselves in a manner worthy of the Good News about Christ. Then, whether I come and see you again or only hear about you, I will know that you are standing together with one spirit and one purpose, fighting together for the faith, which is the Good News. ²⁸Don't be intimidated in any way by your enemies. This will be a sign to them that they are going to be destroyed, but that you are going to be saved, even by God himself. ²⁹For you have been given not only the privilege of trusting in Christ but also the privilege of suffering for him. ³⁰We are

in this struggle together. You have seen my struggle in the past, and you know that I am still in the midst of it.

CHAPTER 2

Have the Attitude of Christ

Is there any encouragement from belonging to Christ? Any comfort from his love? Any fellowship together in the Spirit? Are your hearts tender and compassionate? ²Then make me truly happy by agreeing wholeheartedly with each other, loving one another, and working together with one mind and purpose.

³Don't be selfish; don't try to impress others. Be humble, thinking of others as better than yourselves. ⁴Don't look out only for your own interests, but take an interest in others, too.

⁵You must have the same attitude that Christ Jesus had.

⁶ Though he was God,*
   he did not think of equality with God
   as something to cling to.
⁷ Instead, he gave up his divine privileges*;
   he took the humble position of a slave*
   and was born as a human being.
   When he appeared in human form,*

2:6 Or *Being in the form of God.*   **2:7a** Greek *he emptied himself.*   **2:7b** Or *the form of a slave.*   **2:7c** Some English translations put this phrase in verse 8.

8 he humbled himself in obedience to God and died a criminal's death on a cross.

9 Therefore, God elevated him to the place of highest honor
and gave him the name above all other names,
10 that at the name of Jesus every knee should bow,
in heaven and on earth and under the earth,
11 and every tongue confess that Jesus Christ is Lord,
to the glory of God the Father.

Shine Brightly for Christ

12 Dear friends, you always followed my instructions when I was with you. And now that I am away, it is even more important. Work hard to show the results of your salvation, obeying God with deep reverence and fear. 13 For God is working in you, giving you the desire and the power to do what pleases him.

14 Do everything without complaining and arguing, 15 so that no one can criticize you. Live clean, innocent lives as children of God, shining like bright lights in a world full of crooked and perverse people. 16 Hold firmly to the word of life; then, on the day of Christ's return, I will be proud that I did not run the race in vain and that my work was not useless. 17 But I will rejoice even if I lose my life, pouring it out like a liquid offering to God,* just like your faithful service is an offering to God. And I want all of you to share that joy. 18 Yes, you should rejoice, and I will share your joy.

Paul Commends Timothy

19 If the Lord Jesus is willing, I hope to send Timothy to you soon for a visit. Then he can cheer me up by telling me how you are getting along. 20 I have no one else like Timothy, who genuinely cares about your welfare. 21 All the others care only for themselves and not for what matters to Jesus Christ. 22 But you know how Timothy has proved himself. Like a son with his father, he has served with me in preaching the Good News. 23 I hope to send him to you just as soon as I find out what is going to happen to me here. 24 And I have confidence from the Lord that I myself will come to see you soon.

Paul Commends Epaphroditus

25 Meanwhile, I thought I should send Epaphroditus back to you. He is a true brother, co-worker, and fellow soldier. And he was your messenger to help me in my need. 26 I am sending him because he has been longing to see you, and he was very distressed that you heard he was ill. 27 And he certainly was ill; in fact, he almost died. But God had mercy on him—and also on me, so that I would not have one sorrow after another.

28 So I am all the more anxious to send him back to you, for I know you will be glad to see him, and then I will not be so worried about you. 29 Welcome him with Christian love* and with great joy, and give him the honor that people like him deserve. 30 For he risked his life for the work of Christ, and he was at the point of death while doing for me what you couldn't do from far away.

CHAPTER **3**

The Priceless Value of Knowing Christ

Whatever happens, my dear brothers and sisters,* rejoice in the Lord. I never get tired of telling you these things, and I do it to safeguard your faith.

2 Watch out for those dogs, those people who do evil, those mutilators who say you must be circumcised to be saved. 3 For we who worship by the Spirit of God* are the ones who are truly circumcised. We rely on what Christ Jesus has done for us. We put no confidence in human effort, 4 though I could have confidence in my own effort if anyone could. Indeed, if others have reason for confidence in their own efforts, I have even more!

5 I was circumcised when I was eight days old. I am a pure-blooded citizen of Israel and a member of the tribe of Benjamin—a real Hebrew if there ever was one! I was a member of the Pharisees, who demand the strictest obedience to the Jewish law. 6 I was so zealous that I harshly persecuted the church. And as for righteousness, I obeyed the law without fault.

7 I once thought these things were valuable, but now I consider them worthless because of what Christ has done. 8 Yes, everything else is worthless when compared with the infinite value of knowing Christ Jesus my Lord. For his sake I have discarded everything else, counting it all as garbage, so that I could gain Christ 9 and become one with him. I no longer count on my own righteousness through obeying the law; rather, I become righteous through faith in Christ.* For God's way of making us right with himself depends on faith. 10 I want to know Christ and experience the mighty power that raised him from the dead. I want to suffer with

---

2:17 Greek *I will rejoice even if I am to be poured out as a liquid offering.*   2:29 Greek *in the Lord.*   3:1 Greek *brothers;* also in 3:13, 17.   3:3 Some manuscripts read *worship God in spirit;* one early manuscript reads *worship in spirit.*   3:9 Or *through the faithfulness of Christ.*

him, sharing in his death, [11]so that one way or another I will experience the resurrection from the dead!

Pressing toward the Goal

[12]I don't mean to say that I have already achieved these things or that I have already reached perfection. But I press on to possess that perfection for which Christ Jesus first possessed me. [13]No, dear brothers and sisters, I have not achieved it,* but I focus on this one thing: Forgetting the past and looking forward to what lies ahead, [14]I press on to reach the end of the race and receive the heavenly prize for which God, through Christ Jesus, is calling us.

[15]Let all who are spiritually mature agree on these things. If you disagree on some point, I believe God will make it plain to you. [16]But we must hold on to the progress we have already made.

[17]Dear brothers and sisters, pattern your lives after mine, and learn from those who follow our example. [18]For I have told you often before, and I say it again with tears in my eyes, that there are many whose conduct shows they are really enemies of the cross of Christ. [19]They are headed for destruction. Their god is their appetite, they brag about shameful things, and they think only about this life here on earth. [20]But we are citizens of heaven, where the Lord Jesus Christ lives. And we are eagerly waiting for him to return as our Savior. [21]He will take our weak mortal bodies and change them into glorious bodies like his own, using the same power with which he will bring everything under his control.

CHAPTER **4**

Therefore, my dear brothers and sisters,* stay true to the Lord. I love you and long to see you, dear friends, for you are my joy and the crown I receive for my work.

Words of Encouragement

[2]Now I appeal to Euodia and Syntyche. Please, because you belong to the Lord, settle your disagreement. [3]And I ask you, my true partner,* to help these two women, for they worked hard with me in telling others the Good News. They worked along with Clement and the rest of my co-workers, whose names are written in the Book of Life.

[4]Always be full of joy in the Lord. I say it again—rejoice! [5]Let everyone see that you are considerate in all you do. Remember, the Lord is coming soon.

[6]Don't worry about anything; instead, pray about everything. Tell God what you need, and thank him for all he has done. [7]Then you will experience God's peace, which exceeds anything we can understand. His peace will guard your hearts and minds as you live in Christ Jesus.

3:13 Some manuscripts read *not yet achieved it.*   4:1 Greek *brothers;* also in 4:8.   4:3 Or *loyal Syzygus.*

---

off and running

PLACE CHRIST BEFORE ALL ELSE

Read PHILIPPIANS 3:4-11

As verses 4-6 attest, the apostle Paul was the epitome of a good Jew. He had been born a member of God's chosen people and had flawlessly kept God's laws. But when Paul met Jesus on the road to Damascus (see Acts 9:1-19, pp. 141-142), Paul realized that everything he was living for was taking him in the wrong direction. For that reason he counted everything else in life—his reputation, his achievements, his pursuits, his possessions—worthless, so that his sole pursuit would be in knowing and serving Jesus.

Do you, like Paul, place Christ above everything else in your life? If you are not sure, ask yourself the following questions: How do you spend your time? What dominates your thoughts? Where are your priorities? What motivates you? If the most important thing in your life is Jesus, then your life will revolve around getting to know him more and more. You will want to spend time learning about his nature, his will, and his purposes for you in his Word. And you will truly be able to say that you have discovered "the infinite value of knowing Christ Jesus."

For the next note on "Priorities," turn to p. 80.

[8] And now, dear brothers and sisters, one final thing. Fix your thoughts on what is true, and honorable, and right, and pure, and lovely, and admirable. Think about things that are excellent and worthy of praise. [9] Keep putting into practice all you learned and received from me—everything you heard from me and saw me doing. Then the God of peace will be with you.

Paul's Thanks for Their Gifts

[10] How I praise the Lord that you are concerned about me again. I know you have always been concerned for me, but you didn't have the chance to help me. [11] Not that I was ever in need, for I have learned how to be content with whatever I have. [12] I know how to live on almost nothing or with everything. I have learned the secret of living in every situation, whether it is with a full stomach or empty, with plenty or little. [13] For I can do everything through Christ,* who gives me strength. [14] Even so, you have done well to share with me in my present difficulty.

[15] As you know, you Philippians were the only ones who gave me financial help when I first brought you the Good News and then traveled on from Macedonia. No other church did this. [16] Even when I was in Thessalonica you sent help more than once. [17] I don't say this because I want a gift from you. Rather, I want you to receive a reward for your kindness.

[18] At the moment I have all I need—and more! I am generously supplied with the gifts you sent me with Epaphroditus. They are a sweet-smelling sacrifice that is acceptable and pleasing to God. [19] And this same God who takes care of me will supply all your needs from his glorious riches, which have been given to us in Christ Jesus.

[20] Now all glory to God our Father forever and ever! Amen.

Paul's Final Greetings

[21] Give my greetings to each of God's holy people—all who belong to Christ Jesus. The brothers who are with me send you their greetings. [22] And all the rest of God's people send you greetings, too, especially those in Caesar's household.

[23] May the grace of the Lord Jesus Christ be with your spirit.

4:13 Greek *through the one.*

PRAYER HELPS US OVERCOME WORRY
Read PHILIPPIANS 4:6-7

Have you ever been gripped by worry or fear? Worry is a completely unproductive emotion. It is the advance interest we pay on troubles that seldom come. But these verses give us the best antidote for worry—prayer. God wants to be the first one we turn to in times of worry or crisis. When we do, he promises a special blessing if we do the following four things:

1. Stop Worrying and Start Praying. Don't ever think that your need is too insignificant for God's attention. He wants us to pray about *everything*.

2. Tell God Your Needs. Even though God is all-knowing and is well aware of your situation, he desires that you verbalize your needs to him and place them in his hands.

3. Present Your Requests with Thanks. Instead of praying with feelings of doubt, we can thank God for his answers in advance because of the promises he has made to us in his Word.

4. Receive God's Peace. Once you do these things, verse 7 says that you will experience God's peace. In the original Greek text, this verse literally means that God's peace will "mount a guard or garrison" around your heart and mind to keep and protect you during those difficult times in your life.

The next time you are tempted to worry about something, channel into prayer all of the energy you would have put into worry. Say something like, "Lord, here is my problem. It looms ever larger in my path, so I am putting it into your hands. I am not going to worry, Lord. Instead, I am going to trust you. I am even going to thank you in advance for what you will do, because you know what you are doing." This may not always be an easy thing to do, but if you want to overcome worry and experience God's peace, it is something you must consciously do.

To begin the next topic, turn to p. A38.

Colossians

AUTHOR: PAUL | DATE WRITTEN: A.D. 60 | GENRE: EPISTLE

Paul wrote this epistle to refute certain false teachings that had found their way into the church. *A common theme of this book is the superiority of Jesus Christ.*

CHAPTER 1

Greetings from Paul

This letter is from Paul, chosen by the will of God to be an apostle of Christ Jesus, and from our brother Timothy.

² We are writing to God's holy people in the city of Colosse, who are faithful brothers and sisters* in Christ.

May God our Father give you grace and peace.

Paul's Thanksgiving and Prayer

³ We always pray for you, and we give thanks to God, the Father of our Lord Jesus Christ. ⁴ For we have heard of your faith in Christ Jesus and your love for all of God's people, ⁵ which come from your confident hope of what God has reserved for you in heaven. You have had this expectation ever since you first heard the truth of the Good News.

⁶ This same Good News that came to you is going out all over the world. It is bearing fruit everywhere by changing lives, just as it changed your lives from the day you first heard and understood the truth about God's wonderful grace.

⁷ You learned about the Good News from Epaphras, our beloved co-worker. He is Christ's faithful servant, and he is helping us on your behalf.* ⁸ He has told us about the love for others that the Holy Spirit has given you.

⁹ So we have not stopped praying for you since we first heard about you. We ask God to give you complete knowledge of his will and to give you spiritual wisdom and understanding. ¹⁰ Then the way you live will always honor and please the Lord, and your lives will produce every kind of good fruit. All the while, you will grow as you learn to know God better and better.

¹¹ We also pray that you will be strengthened with all his glorious power so you will have all the endurance and patience you need. May you be filled with joy,* ¹² always thanking the Father. He has enabled you to share in the inheritance that belongs to his people, who live in the light. ¹³ For he has rescued us from the kingdom of darkness and transferred us into the Kingdom of his dear Son, ¹⁴ who purchased our freedom* and forgave our sins.

Christ Is Supreme

¹⁵ Christ is the visible image of the
     invisible God.
  He existed before anything was created
     and is supreme over all creation,*
¹⁶ for through him God created everything
     in the heavenly realms and on earth.
  He made the things we can see
     and the things we can't see—
  such as thrones, kingdoms, rulers, and
     authorities in the unseen world.
  Everything was created through him
     and for him.
¹⁷ He existed before anything else,
     and he holds all creation together.
¹⁸ Christ is also the head of the church,
     which is his body.
  He is the beginning,
     supreme over all who rise from the dead.*
  So he is first in everything.
¹⁹ For God in all his fullness
     was pleased to live in Christ,

1:2 Greek *faithful brothers.*   1:7 Or *he is ministering on your behalf;* some manuscripts read *he is ministering on our behalf.*
1:11 Or *all the patience and endurance you need with joy.*   1:14 Some manuscripts add *with his blood.*   1:15 Or *He is the firstborn of all creation.*   1:18 Or *the firstborn from the dead.*

cornerstones

JESUS IS DIVINE

Read COLOSSIANS 1:15-20

The most crucial truth of the Christian faith is that Jesus Christ, though he came to earth as a man, was in fact God. This passage lays out six important details about Jesus' divinity and his work in heaven and on earth:

1. Jesus Is Eternal. Being God, Jesus never had a beginning, nor does he have an end (verse 15). The prophet Micah, speaking of the place in which Jesus would be born, said, "But you, O Bethlehem Ephrathah, are only a small village among all the people of Judah. Yet a ruler of Israel will come from you, one whose origins are from the distant past" (Micah 5:2). The phrase "distant past" has also been translated "from everlasting," meaning eternal.

2. Jesus Is the Creator of All Things. This concept makes the whole idea of Jesus' coming as a Savior to this earth so amazing. He understood the way people acted and the hardness of humans' hearts because he created them (verse 16). Yet he loved people so much he was willing to come down to earth and die in order to redeem all humankind.

3. Jesus Holds Everything Together. Jesus has and always will be in control (verses 16-17). Our world is not in some chaotic state but has been created with a purpose in mind—to ultimately bring glory to Christ.

4. Jesus Is the Head of the Church. The church was not established by a group of people but by God himself. Although some leaders in the church may let us down at times, we must remember that Christ, the true head of this body of believers (verse 18), will never fail us.

5. Jesus Is the Leader of All Who Will Rise from the Dead. Christ was the first to actually defeat death and return to life in a resurrected body (verse 18). For that reason, we who follow him have the hope—and the evidence—that we, too, will one day rise again after death to spend eternity with him.

6. Jesus Is the Only Way to Peace with God. God was never surprised that man sinned in the Garden of Eden. The Bible even records that Jesus' sacrifice on the cross was known "before the world was made" (Revelation 17:8). That means that God had already made a provision for our sins long before Adam ate the forbidden fruit (verse 20).

Jesus was much more than a mere prophet, teacher, or messenger. In reality, Jesus was nothing less than God himself come to the earth. To deny this central truth is to deny the basis of the Christian faith. Remember, it was this truth that motivated the Christians of the first century to cause "trouble all over the world" for the sake of the gospel (see Acts 17:6, p. 152).

For the next note on "Who Is Jesus?" turn to p. 68.

---

[20] and through him God reconciled
    everything to himself.
He made peace with everything in heaven
    and on earth
    by means of Christ's blood on the cross.

[21] This includes you who were once far away from God. You were his enemies, separated from him by your evil thoughts and actions. [22] Yet now he has reconciled you to himself through the death of Christ in his physical body. As a result, he has brought you into his own presence, and you are holy and blameless as you stand before him without a single fault. [23] But you must continue to believe this truth and stand firmly in it. Don't drift away from the assurance you received when you heard the Good News. The Good News has been preached all over the world, and I, Paul, have been appointed as God's servant to proclaim it.

Paul's Work for the Church

[24] I am glad when I suffer for you in my body, for I am participating in the sufferings of Christ that continue for his body, the church. [25] God has given me the responsibility of serving his church by proclaiming his entire message to you. [26] This message was kept secret for centuries and generations past, but now it has been revealed to God's people. [27] For God wanted them to know that the riches and glory

of Christ are for you Gentiles, too. And this is the secret: Christ lives in you. This gives you assurance of sharing his glory.

[28]So we tell others about Christ, warning everyone and teaching everyone with all the wisdom God has given us. We want to present them to God, perfect* in their relationship to Christ. [29]That's why I work and struggle so hard, depending on Christ's mighty power that works within me.

CHAPTER 2

I want you to know how much I have agonized for you and for the church at Laodicea, and for many other believers who have never met me personally. [2]I want them to be encouraged and knit together by strong ties of love. I want them to have complete confidence that they understand God's mysterious plan, which is Christ himself. [3]In him lie hidden all the treasures of wisdom and knowledge.

[4]I am telling you this so no one will deceive you with well-crafted arguments. [5]For though I am far away from you, my heart is with you. And I rejoice that you are living as you should and that your faith in Christ is strong.

Freedom from Rules and New Life in Christ

[6]And now, just as you accepted Christ Jesus as your Lord, you must continue to follow him. [7]Let your roots grow down into him, and let your lives be built on him. Then your faith will grow strong in the truth you were taught, and you will overflow with thankfulness.

[8]Don't let anyone capture you with empty philosophies and high-sounding nonsense that come from human thinking and from the spiritual powers* of this world, rather than from Christ. [9]For in Christ lives all the fullness of God in a human body.* [10]So you also are complete through your union with Christ, who is the head over every ruler and authority.

[11]When you came to Christ, you were "circumcised," but not by a physical procedure. Christ performed a spiritual circumcision— the cutting away of your sinful nature.* [12]For you were buried with Christ when you were baptized. And with him you were raised to new life because you trusted the mighty power of God, who raised Christ from the dead.

[13]You were dead because of your sins and because your sinful nature was not yet cut away. Then God made you alive with Christ, for he forgave all our sins. [14]He canceled the record of the charges against us and took it away by nailing it to the cross. [15]In this way, he disarmed* the spiritual rulers and authorities. He

first steps

LET GOD OCCUPY YOUR THOUGHTS

Read COLOSSIANS 3:2-4

A song in the church says, "Turn your eyes upon Jesus, Look full in His wonderful face, And the things of earth will grow strangely dim, In the light of His glory and grace." These are good words to live by, because one of the strongest deterrents against returning to your old way of life is to focus upon your Savior and future. As a believer, you have been promised eternal life, the hope of heaven, and the assurance of spending eternity in the presence of God. When you think about that, the trappings of this world begin to lose their appeal.

The next time you feel inclined to dabble with your old life, or feel weighed down by the worries of this world, or fear that you won't make it as a Christian, remember to do these things:

- Keep your eyes on your final destination.
- Realize that worry should not be a part of your life.
- Picture yourself as dead to this world and alive in Christ.
- Remember that your Redeemer is returning.

If you allow these truths to occupy your thoughts, you will find it much easier to obey God and say no to the alluring, but damaging, enticements of this sinful world.

To begin the next topic, turn to p. A40.

shamed them publicly by his victory over them on the cross.

[16]So don't let anyone condemn you for what you eat or drink, or for not celebrating certain holy days or new moon ceremonies or Sabbaths. [17]For these rules are only shadows of the reality yet to come. And Christ himself is that reality. [18]Don't let anyone condemn you by insisting on pious self-denial or the worship of angels,* saying they have had visions about these things. Their sinful minds have made them proud, [19]and they are not connected to Christ, the head of the body. For he holds the whole body together with its joints and ligaments, and it grows as God nourishes it.

1:28 Or *mature.*   2:8 Or *the spiritual principles;* also in 2:20. 2:9 Or *in him dwells all the completeness of the Godhead*
bodily.   2:11 Greek *the cutting away of the body of the flesh.* 2:15 Or *he stripped off.*   2:18 Or *or worshiping with angels.*

cornerstones

GOD'S PEACE NEEDS TO RULE IN OUR HEARTS
Read COLOSSIANS 3:15

One of the most obvious identifying marks of a Christian is peace. As Paul points out in this verse, the peace a Christian has comes from Christ and rules in a Christian's heart. The Greek verb Paul uses for *rule* suggests that Christ's peace is to act as an "umpire" or a judge in our lives, deciding our outlook and mood in the midst of all circumstances. What characterizes Christ's peace? Here are a few more biblical descriptions:

- It is not anxious about anything but trusts God (see Philippians 4:6-7, p. 240).
- It doesn't doubt that God is in control (see Mark 4:35-41, p. 43).
- It doesn't forget God's blessings and answers to prayer (see Philippians 4:6, p. 240).
- It should be present in our relationships (Psalm 34:14; see also Romans 12:18, p. 184).
- It comes from Christ alone (see John 16:33, p. 121).
- It is produced by the Holy Spirit (see Galatians 5:22, p. 226).
- It promotes peace with others (see James 3:18, pp. 291-292).

Does the peace of Christ rule in your life? If not, you are not living as Jesus really intends you to live. Give God your worries and concerns, and ask him to replace them with his peace. This peace will not only calm your heart, but it will also help encourage harmony between you and your Christian brothers and sisters.

To begin the next topic, turn to p. A34.

---

²⁰You have died with Christ, and he has set you free from the spiritual powers of this world. So why do you keep on following the rules of the world, such as, ²¹"Don't handle! Don't taste! Don't touch!"? ²²Such rules are mere human teachings about things that deteriorate as we use them. ²³These rules may seem wise because they require strong devotion, pious self-denial, and severe bodily discipline. But they provide no help in conquering a person's evil desires.

CHAPTER 3
Living the New Life

Since you have been raised to new life with Christ, set your sights on the realities of heaven, where Christ sits in the place of honor at God's right hand. ²Think about the things of heaven, not the things of earth. ³For you died to this life, and your real life is hidden with Christ in God. ⁴And when Christ, who is your* life, is revealed to the whole world, you will share in all his glory.

⁵So put to death the sinful, earthly things lurking within you. Have nothing to do with sexual immorality, impurity, lust, and evil desires. Don't be greedy, for a greedy person is an idolater, worshiping the things of this world. ⁶Because of these sins, the anger of God is coming.* ⁷You used to do these things when your life was still part of this world. ⁸But now is the time to get rid of anger, rage, malicious behavior, slander, and dirty language. ⁹Don't lie to each other, for you have stripped off your old

3:4 Some manuscripts read *our.*   3:6 Some manuscripts read *is coming on all who disobey him.*

---

off and running

AVOID AGGRAVATING YOUR CHILDREN
Read COLOSSIANS 3:20-21

While discipline is necessary in the lives of children, it is equally necessary that discipline be tempered with love. This means that parents should not scold or nag their children, especially when disciplining them. Other words that have been used for scold and nag are *exasperate* and *aggravate*. The word *aggravate* means to irritate, enrage, harass, tease, and add fuel to the fire.

sinful nature and all its wicked deeds. [10]Put on your new nature, and be renewed as you learn to know your Creator and become like him. [11]In this new life, it doesn't matter if you are a Jew or a Gentile,* circumcised or uncircumcised, barbaric, uncivilized,* slave, or free. Christ is all that matters, and he lives in all of us.

[12]Since God chose you to be the holy people he loves, you must clothe yourselves with tenderhearted mercy, kindness, humility, gentleness, and patience. [13]Make allowance for each other's faults, and forgive anyone who offends you. Remember, the Lord forgave you, so you must forgive others. [14]Above all, clothe yourselves with love, which binds us all together in perfect harmony. [15]And let the peace that comes from Christ rule in your hearts. For as members of one body you are called to live in peace. And always be thankful.

[16]Let the message about Christ, in all its richness, fill your lives. Teach and counsel each other with all the wisdom he gives. Sing psalms and hymns and spiritual songs to God with thankful hearts. [17]And whatever you do or say, do it as a representative of the Lord Jesus, giving thanks through him to God the Father.

Instructions for Christian Households

[18]Wives, submit to your husbands, as is fitting for those who belong to the Lord.

[19]Husbands, love your wives and never treat them harshly.

[20]Children, always obey your parents, for this pleases the Lord. [21]Fathers, do not aggravate your children, or they will become discouraged.

[22]Slaves, obey your earthly masters in everything you do. Try to please them all the time, not just when they are watching you. Serve them sincerely because of your reverent fear of the Lord. [23]Work willingly at whatever you do, as though you were working for the Lord rather than for people. [24]Remember that the Lord will give you an inheritance as your reward, and that the Master you are serving is Christ.* [25]But if you do what is wrong, you will be paid back for the wrong you have done. For God has no favorites.

CHAPTER 4

Masters, be just and fair to your slaves. Remember that you also have a Master—in heaven.

An Encouragement for Prayer

[2]Devote yourselves to prayer with an alert mind and a thankful heart. [3]Pray for us, too, that God will give us many opportunities to speak about his mysterious plan concerning Christ. That is why I am here in chains. [4]Pray that I will proclaim this message as clearly as I should.

[5]Live wisely among those who are not believers, and make the most of every opportunity. [6]Let your conversation be gracious and attractive* so that you will have the right response for everyone.

Paul's Final Instructions and Greetings

[7]Tychicus will give you a full report about how I am getting along. He is a beloved brother and faithful helper who serves with me in the Lord's work. [8]I have sent him to you for this very purpose—to let you know how we are doing and to encourage you. [9]I am also sending Onesimus, a faithful and beloved brother, one of your own people. He and Tychicus will tell you everything that's happening here.

[10]Aristarchus, who is in prison with me, sends you his greetings, and so does Mark, Barnabas's cousin. As you were instructed before, make Mark welcome if he comes your way. [11]Jesus (the one we call Justus) also sends his greetings. These are the only Jewish believers among my co-workers; they are working with me here for the Kingdom of God. And what a comfort they have been!

[12]Epaphras, a member of your own fellowship and a servant of Christ Jesus, sends you his greetings. He always prays earnestly for you, asking God to make you strong and perfect, fully confident that you are following the whole will of God. [13]I can assure you that he

---

3:11a Greek *a Greek.*   **3:11b** Greek *Barbarian, Scythian.*   **3:24** Or *and serve Christ as your Master.*   **4:6** Greek *and seasoned with salt.*

When discipline is administered in an aggravating manner, the consequences can be devastating. Children may not only be angry with their parents and resent them, but children may also disrespect and dishonor their parents. Even worse, they may one day end their relationship with their parents or act out violently against them.

If you really want your children to honor you as a parent, then you must discipline them with love, praise them when they obey, and train them in the instruction of the Lord.

To begin the next topic, turn to p. A47.

off and running

WORK AS IF YOU ARE WORKING FOR THE LORD
Read COLOSSIANS 3:22-24

While the world says to work for the sake of your own welfare, Jesus says to work out of your desire to please him. While the world says to work hard to get ahead, Jesus says to work hard to show the world who you are really working for. When you work as though you are working for the Lord, your whole outlook changes.

Do you want to revolutionize your attitude toward your job? Then take this verse to heart. If you are a mother at home, tackle the dishes, laundry, and cooking as if you are serving the Lord, not just your family. If you work in an office, take care of your tasks and treat your coworkers as you would the Lord himself. Your work may be unappreciated and underpaid in this life, but God promises to give you your full reward in heaven (verse 24).

For the next note on "Job Performance," turn to p. 270.

---

prays hard for you and also for the believers in Laodicea and Hierapolis.

¹⁴Luke, the beloved doctor, sends his greetings, and so does Demas. ¹⁵Please give my greetings to our brothers and sisters* at Laodicea, and to Nympha and the church that meets in her house.

¹⁶After you have read this letter, pass it on to the church at Laodicea so they can read it, too. And you should read the letter I wrote to them.

¹⁷And say to Archippus, "Be sure to carry out the ministry the Lord gave you."

¹⁸HERE IS MY GREETING IN MY OWN HANDWRITING—PAUL.

Remember my chains.

May God's grace be with you.

4:15 Greek *brothers.*

---

off and running

KEEP YOUR CONVERSATION GRACIOUS
Read COLOSSIANS 4:6

Witnessing to others about the Lord can be a bit intimidating at first. We never know what kind of response we will receive. But if you follow the three steps found in these verses, you will become much more effective at sharing your faith:

1. Tell the Good News. Center your conversation on the simple gospel message: (1) Man is separated from God by sin; (2) God sent his Son, Jesus Christ, to die on the cross and pay the price for our sin; and (3) if we will turn from that sin, embrace Christ as Savior and Lord, and follow him, we can be forgiven and have a relationship with God.

2. Be Wise When Sharing Your Faith. Use discernment. Don't push the subject of your faith if you sense the person is not interested. On the other hand, don't end the conversation if you feel the person is sincerely interested. Remember, God softens a person's heart. You simply present the message.

3. Let Your Conversation Be Gracious and Sensible. Don't rely upon sophisticated arguments to prove your point. Let Christ's love shine through you as you speak. Another translation adds that your conversation should also be "seasoned with salt." In other words, give the person a thirst to learn more about Christ.

Jesus communicated his message in a unique way to each individual. We must do the same. The more we share our faith, the easier that will become.

For the next note on "Conversation," turn to p. 298.

1 Thessalonians

AUTHOR: **PAUL** | DATE WRITTEN: **A.D. 51** | GENRE: **EPISTLE**

The theme of this book focuses on living a godly and holy life as we await the return of Jesus Christ. *Paul also offered words of comfort concerning Christian loved ones who died.*

CHAPTER 1
Greetings from Paul

This letter is from Paul, Silas,* and Timothy.

We are writing to the church in Thessalonica, to you who belong to God the Father and the Lord Jesus Christ.

May God give you grace and peace.

The Faith of the Thessalonian Believers

[2] We always thank God for all of you and pray for you constantly. [3] As we pray to our God and Father about you, we think of your faithful work, your loving deeds, and the enduring hope you have because of our Lord Jesus Christ.

[4] We know, dear brothers and sisters,* that God loves you and has chosen you to be his own people. [5] For when we brought you the Good News, it was not only with words but also with power, for the Holy Spirit gave you full assurance* that what we said was true. And you know of our concern for you from the way we lived when we were with you. [6] So you received the message with joy from the Holy Spirit in spite of the severe suffering it brought you. In this way, you imitated both us and the Lord. [7] As a result, you have become an example to all the believers in Greece—throughout both Macedonia and Achaia.*

[8] And now the word of the Lord is ringing out from you to people everywhere, even beyond Macedonia and Achaia, for wherever we go we find people telling us about your faith in God. We don't need to tell them about it, [9] for they keep talking about the wonderful welcome you gave us and how you turned away from idols to serve the living and true God. [10] And they speak of how you are looking forward to the coming of God's Son from heaven—Jesus, whom God raised from the dead. He is the one who has rescued us from the terrors of the coming judgment.

CHAPTER 2
Paul Remembers His Visit

You yourselves know, dear brothers and sisters,* that our visit to you was not a failure. [2] You know how badly we had been treated at Philippi just before we came to you and how much we suffered there. Yet our God gave us the courage to declare his Good News to you boldly, in spite of great opposition. [3] So you can see we were not preaching with any deceit or impure motives or trickery.

[4] For we speak as messengers approved by God to be entrusted with the Good News. Our purpose is to please God, not people. He alone examines the motives of our hearts. [5] Never once did we try to win you with flattery, as you well know. And God is our witness that we were not pretending to be your friends just to get your money! [6] As for human praise, we have never sought it from you or anyone else.

[7] As apostles of Christ we certainly had a right to make some demands of you, but instead we were like children* among you. Or we were like a mother feeding and caring for her own children. [8] We loved you so much that we shared with you not only God's Good News but our own lives, too.

[9] Don't you remember, dear brothers and sisters, how hard we worked among you? Night and day we toiled to earn a living so that we

---

1:1 Greek *Silvanus,* the Greek form of the name.   **1:4** Greek *brothers.*   **1:5** Or *with the power of the Holy Spirit, so you can have full assurance.*   **1:7** *Macedonia* and *Achaia* were the northern and southern regions of Greece.   **2:1** Greek *brothers;* also in 2:9, 14, 17.   **2:7** Some manuscripts read *we were gentle.*

cornerstones
OUR LOVE SHOULD GROW
Read 1 THESSALONIANS 3:12-13

Too many of us think that love is some emotional thing that comes and goes. Yet this passage suggests that our love should not only remain steady but that it should also *grow*. This may seem like an impossible task on our own—and it is. That is why the apostle Paul says, "May the *Lord* make your love for one another and for all people grow and overflow" (1 Thessalonians 3:12, emphasis added). You cannot manufacture sincere love. Christ's love must motivate and compel you (see 2 Corinthians 5:14, p. 212). This love, in turn, will help to strengthen your heart, keep you from sin, and make you holy so that you can be guiltless when Christ returns.

If your love toward God and others seems stagnant, it is likely that you have distanced yourself from the Source of that love. Return to the Lord and ask him to refill and refresh your love for him, then look for ways to share that love with others.

To begin the next topic, turn to p. A30.

---

would not be a burden to any of you as we preached God's Good News to you. [10]You yourselves are our witnesses—and so is God—that we were devout and honest and faultless toward all of you believers. [11]And you know that we treated each of you as a father treats his own children. [12]We pleaded with you, encouraged you, and urged you to live your lives in a way that God would consider worthy. For he called you to share in his Kingdom and glory.

[13]Therefore, we never stop thanking God that when you received his message from us, you didn't think of our words as mere human ideas. You accepted what we said as the very word of God—which, of course, it is. And this word continues to work in you who believe.

[14]And then, dear brothers and sisters, you suffered persecution from your own countrymen. In this way, you imitated the believers in God's churches in Judea who, because of their belief in Christ Jesus, suffered from their own people, the Jews. [15]For some of the Jews killed the prophets,

---

off and running
ENCOURAGE YOUR CHILDREN'S SPIRITUAL GROWTH
Read 1 THESSALONIANS 2:11-12

The apostle Paul compared his relationship with the Thessalonians to that of a father with his children. Although this passage doesn't necessarily deal with the father-child relationship, it does show three ways in which fathers play an important role in developing their children's faith:

1. Fathers Encourage Children in Their Faith. One way in which fathers can do this is to live out their faith before their children. Doing this will show children how one's faith affects the way a person lives.

2. Fathers Comfort Children in Their Faith. Be available for your children when they face challenges to their faith.

3. Fathers Urge Children to Grow in Their Faith. Set rules and boundaries that will help establish the moral foundation children need to live a life pleasing to God.

Fathers may not be able to be with their children twenty-four hours a day, but they can help build conviction in their children's lives so that their children will make the right choices. This is one of the most important investments fathers will ever make.

For the next note on "Children," turn to p. 246.

and some even killed the Lord Jesus. Now they have persecuted us, too. They fail to please God and work against all humanity [16]as they try to keep us from preaching the Good News of salvation to the Gentiles. By doing this, they continue to pile up their sins. But the anger of God has caught up with them at last.

Timothy's Good Report about the Church
[17]Dear brothers and sisters, after we were separated from you for a little while (though our hearts never left you), we tried very hard to come back because of our intense longing to see you again. [18]We wanted very much to come to you, and I, Paul, tried again and again, but Satan prevented us. [19]After all, what gives us hope and joy, and what will be our proud reward and crown as we stand before our Lord Jesus when he returns? It is you! [20]Yes, you are our pride and joy.

CHAPTER **3**
Finally, when we could stand it no longer, we decided to stay alone in Athens, [2]and we sent Timothy to visit you. He is our brother and God's co-worker* in proclaiming the Good News of Christ. We sent him to strengthen you, to encourage you in your faith, [3]and to keep you from being shaken by the troubles you were going through. But you know that we are destined for such troubles. [4]Even while we were with you, we warned you that troubles would soon come—and they did, as you well know. [5]That is why, when I could bear it no longer, I sent Timothy to find out whether your faith was still strong. I was afraid that the tempter had gotten the best of you and that our work had been useless.

[6]But now Timothy has just returned, bringing us good news about your faith and love. He reports that you always remember our visit with joy and that you want to see us as much as we want to see you. [7]So we have been greatly encouraged in the midst of our troubles and suffering, dear brothers and sisters,* because you have remained strong in your faith. [8]It gives us new life to know that you are standing firm in the Lord.

[9]How we thank God for you! Because of you we have great joy as we enter God's presence. [10]Night and day we pray earnestly for you, asking God to let us see you again to fill the gaps in your faith.

[11]May God our Father and our Lord Jesus bring us to you very soon. [12]And may the Lord make your love for one another and for all

3:2 Other manuscripts read *and God's servant*; still others read *and a co-worker*, or *and a servant and co-worker for God*, or *and God's servant and our co-worker*.   3:7 Greek *brothers*.

first steps

ACT UPON WHAT GOD HAS ALREADY REVEALED IN SCRIPTURE
Read 1 THESSALONIANS 4:1-8

We often wonder what God's will may be for us concerning a particular situation. Yet Scripture reveals certain things that are clearly the will of God for every believer—without exception. Here are four things Scripture reveals as God's will:

1. God Wants Us to Live under the Control of the Holy Spirit. God doesn't want us to fill our lives with cheap substitutes, like alcohol, possessions, or worldly pursuits. Instead, he wants us to seek to live under the control of the Holy Spirit (see Ephesians 5:18, p. 233), who produces such attributes as love, joy, peace, patience, kindness, goodness, faithfulness, gentleness, and self-control in our lives. To be controlled by anything or anyone else is outside the will of God.

2. God Wants Us to Live a Pure and Holy Life. It is the clear will of God that we as Christians live sexually pure lives (verses 4-5). The only sexual relationship God will bless is that of a man and woman committed to each other in marriage. Premarital and extramarital sexual relationships are never the will of God for the believer, under any circumstances.

3. God Wants Us to Have an Attitude of Gratitude. No matter what happens, God wants us to be thankful, recognizing that he is in control of all the circumstances that surround our life (see 1 Thessalonians 5:18, p. 254). He has promised to work all things together for good in the life of the Christian. We can rejoice that he has a purpose in mind for whatever we are going through.

4. God Wants Everyone to Come to Repentance. God makes it clear that he desires to see more people come into a relationship with him (see 2 Peter 3:9, p. 303). For that reason, you should take advantage of every opportunity you have to pray for or witness to someone who needs Christ.

To begin the next topic, turn to p. A42.

cornerstones

AVOID ADULTEROUS RELATIONSHIPS
Read 1 THESSALONIANS 4:1-8

This passage gives some strong reasons as to why we should avoid sexual immorality at all costs. Beyond that, there are at least six more damaging consequences the sin of adultery causes:

1. Adultery Inflicts Incredible Pain on the Adulterer's Spouse. A married adulterer violates the oneness with his or her mate by entering into this bond with another person. This sin is so serious that Jesus said it could be grounds for divorce (see Matthew 19:9, p. 25). While a marriage can survive the pain of adultery with God's help, the level of trust will never be the same.

2. Adultery Does Irreparable Damage to the Adulterer. Though God will forgive the person who commits this sin, others will not forgive this person so quickly. This person's reputation will be tarnished, and Satan will undoubtedly riddle him or her with guilt.

3. Adultery Tremendously Hurts the Adulterer's Children. A person who commits this sin may never fully regain his or her children's trust. Worse yet, the adulterer's children may even follow in his or her footsteps and fall into that same sin later in life, as seen in the life of King David.

4. Believers Who Commit Adultery Give the Church a Bad Reputation. Scripture teaches that when one part of the body of Christ suffers, we all suffer (see 1 Corinthians 12:26, p. 203). All Christians are representatives of the church. And when a Christian's sin is exposed, that person has hurt the reputation of the church—especially if that person is in a position of leadership.

5. Adultery Hurts the Cause of Christ. Such behavior hurts a Christian's witness and damages his or her credibility. Those who claim to follow Christ and commit adultery hurt not only their own reputation but also the reputation of Christ.

6. Adultery Is a Sin against the Lord. This should be the primary motive for living a pure life. Remember Joseph's response to Potiphar's wife when faced with this temptation: "How could I do such a wicked thing? It would be a great sin against God" (Genesis 39:9).

As Paul reminds us in this text, God has given us his *Holy* Spirit to live in us. The more his Spirit fills and controls our life, the less likely we will be to give in to the temptation of adultery.

For the next note on "Purity," turn to p. 304.

---

people grow and overflow, just as our love for you overflows. [13] May he, as a result, make your hearts strong, blameless, and holy as you stand before God our Father when our Lord Jesus comes again with all his holy people. Amen.

4:1 Greek *brothers;* also in 4:10, 13.

CHAPTER **4**
Live to Please God
Finally, dear brothers and sisters,* we urge you in the name of the Lord Jesus to live in a way that pleases God, as we have taught you.

---

off and running

STRIVE TO BE RESPONSIBLE
Read 1 THESSALONIANS 4:11-12

As a Christian, you should strive to be the best worker you can be. If you don't, then you disgrace the Lord you serve by doing less than quality work. However, if you work hard and lead a responsible life, you will have many more opportunities to share your faith, because people will respect you.

Consider Joseph of the Old Testament. Although he had been sold into slavery by his own brothers, he worked diligently in every position he held. And his hard

You live this way already, and we encourage you to do so even more. ² For you remember what we taught you by the authority of the Lord Jesus.

³ God's will is for you to be holy, so stay away from all sexual sin. ⁴ Then each of you will control his own body* and live in holiness and honor—⁵ not in lustful passion like the pagans who do not know God and his ways. ⁶ Never harm or cheat a Christian brother in this matter by violating his wife,* for the Lord avenges all such sins, as we have solemnly warned you before. ⁷ God has called us to live holy lives, not impure lives. ⁸ Therefore, anyone who refuses to live by these rules is not disobeying human teaching but is rejecting God, who gives his Holy Spirit to you.

⁹ But we don't need to write to you about the importance of loving each other,* for God himself has taught you to love one another. ¹⁰ Indeed, you already show your love for all the believers* throughout Macedonia. Even so, dear brothers and sisters, we urge you to love them even more.

¹¹ Make it your goal to live a quiet life, minding your own business and working with your hands, just as we instructed you before. ¹² Then people who are not Christians will respect the way you live, and you will not need to depend on others.

The Hope of the Resurrection

¹³ And now, dear brothers and sisters, we want you to know what will happen to the believers who have died* so you will not grieve like people who have no hope. ¹⁴ For since we believe that Jesus died and was raised to life again, we also believe that when Jesus returns, God will bring back with him the believers who have died.

¹⁵ We tell you this directly from the Lord: We who are still living when the Lord returns will not meet him ahead of those who have died.* ¹⁶ For the Lord himself will come down from heaven with a commanding shout, with the voice of the archangel, and with the trumpet call of God. First, the Christians who have died* will rise from their graves. ¹⁷ Then, together with them, we who are still alive and remain on the earth will be caught up in the clouds to meet the Lord in the air. Then we will be with the Lord forever. ¹⁸ So encourage each other with these words.

CHAPTER **5**

Now concerning how and when all this will happen, dear brothers and sisters,* we don't really need to write to you. ² For you know quite well that the day of the Lord's return will come unexpectedly, like a thief in the night. ³ When people are saying, "Everything is peaceful and secure," then disaster will fall on them as suddenly as a pregnant woman's labor pains begin. And there will be no escape.

⁴ But you aren't in the dark about these things, dear brothers and sisters, and you won't be surprised when the day of the Lord comes like a thief.* ⁵ For you are all children of the light and of the day; we don't belong to darkness and night. ⁶ So be on your guard, not asleep like the others. Stay alert and be clearheaded. ⁷ Night is the time when people sleep and drinkers get drunk. ⁸ But let us who live in the light be clearheaded, protected by the armor of faith and love, and wearing as our helmet the confidence of our salvation.

⁹ For God chose to save us through our Lord Jesus Christ, not to pour out his anger on us. ¹⁰ Christ died for us so that, whether we are

---

4:4 Or *will know how to take a wife for himself;* or *will learn to live with his own wife;* Greek reads *will know how to possess his own vessel.*   4:6 Greek *Never harm or cheat a brother in this matter.*   4:9 Greek *about brotherly love.*   4:10 Greek *the brothers.*   4:13 Greek *those who have fallen asleep;* also in 4:14.   4:15 Greek *those who have fallen asleep.*   4:16 Greek *the dead in Christ.*   5:1 Greek *brothers;* also in 5:4, 12, 14, 25, 26, 27.   5:4 Some manuscripts read *comes upon you as if you were thieves.*

---

work made a difference. The Bible records, "The LORD was with Joseph, so he succeeded in everything he did as he served in the home of his Egyptian master. Potiphar noticed this and realized that the LORD was with Joseph, giving him success in everything he did" (Genesis 39:2-3).

You can't expect others to take your message seriously if they don't see that you are serious in what you do. Don't draw attention to yourself by your laziness. Instead, draw attention to the Lord by your diligence. Your faithful, responsible lifestyle will be your greatest sermon.

For the next note on "Job Performance," turn to p. 82.

dead or alive when he returns, we can live with him forever. [11]So encourage each other and build each other up, just as you are already doing.

Paul's Final Advice

[12]Dear brothers and sisters, honor those who are your leaders in the Lord's work. They work hard among you and give you spiritual guidance. [13]Show them great respect and wholehearted love because of their work. And live peacefully with each other.

[14]Brothers and sisters, we urge you to warn those who are lazy. Encourage those who are timid. Take tender care of those who are weak. Be patient with everyone.

[15]See that no one pays back evil for evil, but always try to do good to each other and to all people.

[16]Always be joyful. [17]Never stop praying.

5:26 Greek *with a holy kiss.*

[18]Be thankful in all circumstances, for this is God's will for you who belong to Christ Jesus.

[19]Do not stifle the Holy Spirit. [20]Do not scoff at prophecies, [21]but test everything that is said. Hold on to what is good. [22]Stay away from every kind of evil.

Paul's Final Greetings

[23]Now may the God of peace make you holy in every way, and may your whole spirit and soul and body be kept blameless until our Lord Jesus Christ comes again. [24]God will make this happen, for he who calls you is faithful.

[25]Dear brothers and sisters, pray for us.

[26]Greet all the brothers and sisters with Christian love.*

[27]I command you in the name of the Lord to read this letter to all the brothers and sisters.

[28]May the grace of our Lord Jesus Christ be with you.

---

off and running

THINK OF WAYS TO ENCOURAGE, PRAISE, AND BUILD UP OTHERS

Read 1 THESSALONIANS 5:11

Do the words you use truly benefit and leave a positive impression upon those to whom you speak? In this passage Paul stresses the importance of speaking in a wholesome manner. Below are three insights from this passage that will help you make your conversations more meaningful:

1. Do Not Use Bad Language. As Christians, our speech should be positive and uplifting, not vulgar and crude. Such speech draws attention away from Christ and does nothing to encourage others.

2. Listen before You Speak. Don't just pretend to be interested—*really* listen. You won't know what would be helpful to say to an individual unless you understand his or her needs, questions, and hurts. James instructs us to be quick to listen and slow to speak (see James 1:19, p. 289).

3. Strive to Honor Christ in What You Say. The greatest way we can bless or encourage others with our conversation is to point them to our Savior. This verse has also been translated to say that we should use "words suitable for the occasion, which God can use to help other people." For instance, when someone begins talking about a hurt in his or her life, take that opportunity to somehow bring the hope that Jesus Christ gives you into that discussion.

Unfortunately, with our busy, hectic lives, the quality of our conversations with others often suffers. Our discussions seem to revolve around "surface" issues like the weather, sporting events, the latest headline, or our workday. Yet, as Christians, we should go the extra mile to make our conversations more meaningful so that those who listen to us will be encouraged and refreshed by what we say. Those who follow Paul's advice will not only develop deeper friendships, but will also be effective witnesses for the Lord.

To begin the next topic, turn to p. A49.

2 Thessalonians

AUTHOR: **PAUL** | DATE WRITTEN: **A.D. 51** | GENRE: **EPISTLE**

This letter offered encouragement to the believers who were facing persecution.
It also offered correct teaching on the subject of "the day of the Lord," a confusing matter for some of the Thessalonian believers. In addition, some were not living as they should have been in light of the Lord's return, so Paul addressed that issue as well.

CHAPTER 1

Greetings from Paul

This letter is from Paul, Silas,* and Timothy.

We are writing to the church in Thessalonica, to you who belong to God our Father and the Lord Jesus Christ.

² May God our Father* and the Lord Jesus Christ give you grace and peace.

Encouragement during Persecution

³ Dear brothers and sisters,* we can't help but thank God for you, because your faith is flourishing and your love for one another is growing. ⁴ We proudly tell God's other churches about your endurance and faithfulness in all the persecutions and hardships you are suffering. ⁵ And God will use this persecution to show his justice and to make you worthy of his Kingdom, for which you are suffering. ⁶ In his justice he will pay back those who persecute you.

⁷ And God will provide rest for you who are being persecuted and also for us when the Lord Jesus appears from heaven. He will come with his mighty angels, ⁸ in flaming fire, bringing judgment on those who don't know God and on those who refuse to obey the Good News of our Lord Jesus. ⁹ They will be punished with eternal destruction, forever separated from the Lord and from his glorious power. ¹⁰ When he comes on that day, he will receive glory from his holy people—praise from all who believe. And this includes you, for you believed what we told you about him.

¹¹ So we keep on praying for you, asking our God to enable you to live a life worthy of his call. May he give you the power to accomplish all the good things your faith prompts you to do. ¹² Then the name of our Lord Jesus will be honored because of the way you live, and you will be honored along with him. This is all made possible because of the grace of our God and Lord, Jesus Christ.*

CHAPTER 2

Events prior to the Lord's Second Coming

Now, dear brothers and sisters,* let us clarify some things about the coming of our Lord Jesus Christ and how we will be gathered to meet him. ² Don't be so easily shaken or alarmed by those who say that the day of the Lord has already begun. Don't believe them, even if they claim to have had a spiritual vision, a revelation, or a letter supposedly from us. ³ Don't be fooled by what they say. For that day will not come until there is a great rebellion against God and the man of lawlessness* is revealed—the one who brings destruction.* ⁴ He will exalt himself and defy everything that people call god and every object of worship. He will even sit in the temple of God, claiming that he himself is God.

⁵ Don't you remember that I told you about all this when I was with you? ⁶ And you know what is holding him back, for he can be revealed only when his time comes. ⁷ For this lawlessness is already at work secretly, and it will remain secret until the one who is holding it back steps out of the way. ⁸ Then the man of lawlessness will be revealed, but the Lord Jesus will kill him with the breath of his mouth and destroy him by the splendor of his coming. ⁹ This man will come to do the work of Satan

---

1:1 Greek *Silvanus,* the Greek form of the name.   **1:2** Some manuscripts read *God the Father.*   **1:3** Greek *Brothers.*   **1:12** Or *of our God and our Lord Jesus Christ.*   **2:1** Greek *brothers;* also in 2:13, 15.   **2:3a** Some manuscripts read *the man of sin.* **2:3b** Greek *the son of destruction.*

cornerstones

WHAT IS THE WORST PUNISHMENT OF HELL?

Read 2 THESSALONIANS 1:7-10

As this passage states, the real agony of those who go to hell is that they will be eternally separated from the Lord. To understand how terrible a punishment this is, examine the consequences of being separated from God's presence:

Judgment. When Christ comes back, nonbelievers will face a judgment that believers will not. At this judgment, nonbelievers will have their deeds revealed before everyone and then will be sentenced to spend eternity in the lake of fire (see Revelation 20:11-15, p. 335).

Everlasting Destruction. In hell, nonbelievers will be doomed to exist in unending torment with the Devil and his demons. The torment that they will endure is described by Jesus as an unquenchable, eternal fire (see Matthew 18:8, p. 24; Matthew 25:41, p. 34). Nonbelievers will spend eternity in agony.

Regret. Jesus used many parables to describe the Kingdom of Heaven—who would get into it, and who would not. Those who don't get into the Kingdom are pictured in a place where there will be "weeping and gnashing of teeth" (Matthew 13:42). Their response—weeping and gnashing of teeth—is one of regret when they realize what they will be missing out on for eternity.

Hopelessness. Because their punishment is everlasting, nonbelievers have no hope of their condition ever improving. Their existence is not only one of agony, but of despair.

Those who know Christ have much to gain. Those who do not know Christ have everything to lose.

To begin the next topic, turn to p. A29.

---

with counterfeit power and signs and miracles. [10] He will use every kind of evil deception to fool those on their way to destruction, because they refuse to love and accept the truth that would save them. [11] So God will cause them to be greatly deceived, and they will believe these lies. [12] Then they will be condemned for enjoying evil rather than believing the truth.

Believers Should Stand Firm

[13] As for us, we can't help but thank God for you, dear brothers and sisters loved by the Lord. We are always thankful that God chose you to be among the first* to experience salvation—a salvation that came through the Spirit who makes you holy and through your belief in the truth. [14] He called you to salvation when we told you the Good News; now you can share in the glory of our Lord Jesus Christ.

[15] With all these things in mind, dear brothers and sisters, stand firm and keep a strong grip on the teaching we passed on to you both in person and by letter.

[16] Now may our Lord Jesus Christ himself and God our Father, who loved us and by his grace gave us eternal comfort and a wonderful hope, [17] comfort you and strengthen you in every good thing you do and say.

CHAPTER 3

Paul's Request for Prayer

Finally, dear brothers and sisters,* we ask you to pray for us. Pray that the Lord's message will spread rapidly and be honored wherever it goes, just as when it came to you. [2] Pray, too, that we will be rescued from wicked and evil people, for not everyone is a believer. [3] But the Lord is faithful; he will strengthen you and guard you from the evil one.* [4] And we are confident in the Lord that you are doing and will continue to do the things we commanded you. [5] May the Lord lead your hearts into a full understanding and expression of the love of God and the patient endurance that comes from Christ.

An Exhortation to Proper Living

[6] And now, dear brothers and sisters, we give you this command in the name of our Lord Jesus Christ: Stay away from all believers* who live idle lives and don't follow the tradition they received* from us. [7] For you know that you ought to imitate us. We were not idle when we

2:13 Some manuscripts read *chose you from the very beginning.*   3:1 Greek *brothers;* also in 3:6, 13.   3:3 Or *from evil.*
3:6a Greek *from every brother.*   3:6b Some manuscripts read *you received.*

were with you. [8] We never accepted food from anyone without paying for it. We worked hard day and night so we would not be a burden to any of you. [9] We certainly had the right to ask you to feed us, but we wanted to give you an example to follow. [10] Even while we were with you, we gave you this command: "Those unwilling to work will not get to eat."

[11] Yet we hear that some of you are living idle lives, refusing to work and meddling in other people's business. [12] We command such people and urge them in the name of the Lord Jesus Christ to settle down and work to earn their own living. [13] As for the rest of you, dear brothers and sisters, never get tired of doing good.

3:15 Greek *as a brother.*

[14] Take note of those who refuse to obey what we say in this letter. Stay away from them so they will be ashamed. [15] Don't think of them as enemies, but warn them as you would a brother or sister.*

Paul's Final Greetings

[16] Now may the Lord of peace himself give you his peace at all times and in every situation. The Lord be with you all.

[17] HERE IS MY GREETING IN MY OWN HANDWRITING—PAUL. I DO THIS IN ALL MY LETTERS TO PROVE THEY ARE FROM ME.

[18] May the grace of our Lord Jesus Christ be with you all.

1 Timothy

AUTHOR: **PAUL** | DATE WRITTEN: **A.D. 64** | GENRE: **EPISTLE**

Paul, under the inspiration of the Holy Spirit, laid out what the conduct of the church and its leaders should be. *Though Timothy himself was a pastor, these words apply to all who want to be used by God and have their lives make a difference.*

CHAPTER **1**

Greetings from Paul

This letter is from Paul, an apostle of Christ Jesus, appointed by the command of God our Savior and Christ Jesus, who gives us hope.

²I am writing to Timothy, my true son in the faith.

May God the Father and Christ Jesus our Lord give you grace, mercy, and peace.

Warnings against False Teachings

³When I left for Macedonia, I urged you to stay there in Ephesus and stop those whose teaching is contrary to the truth. ⁴Don't let them waste their time in endless discussion of myths and spiritual pedigrees. These things only lead to meaningless speculations,* which don't help people live a life of faith in God.*

⁵The purpose of my instruction is that all believers would be filled with love that comes from a pure heart, a clear conscience, and genuine faith. ⁶But some people have missed this whole point. They have turned away from these things and spend their time in meaningless discussions. ⁷They want to be known as teachers of the law of Moses, but they don't know what they are talking about, even though they speak so confidently.

⁸We know that the law is good when used correctly. ⁹For the law was not intended for people who do what is right. It is for people who are lawless and rebellious, who are ungodly and sinful, who consider nothing sacred and defile what is holy, who kill their father or mother or commit other murders. ¹⁰The law is for people who are sexually immoral, or who practice homosexuality, or are slave traders,* liars, promise breakers, or who do anything else that contradicts the wholesome teaching ¹¹that comes from the glorious Good News entrusted to me by our blessed God.

Paul's Gratitude for God's Mercy

¹²I thank Christ Jesus our Lord, who has given me strength to do his work. He considered me trustworthy and appointed me to serve him, ¹³even though I used to blaspheme the name of Christ. In my insolence, I persecuted his people. But God had mercy on me because I did it in ignorance and unbelief. ¹⁴Oh, how generous and gracious our Lord was! He filled me with the faith and love that come from Christ Jesus.

¹⁵This is a trustworthy saying, and everyone should accept it: "Christ Jesus came into the world to save sinners"—and I am the worst of them all. ¹⁶But God had mercy on me so that Christ Jesus could use me as a prime example of his great patience with even the worst sinners. Then others will realize that they, too, can believe in him and receive eternal life. ¹⁷All honor and glory to God forever and ever! He is the eternal King, the unseen one who never dies; he alone is God. Amen.

Timothy's Responsibility

¹⁸Timothy, my son, here are my instructions for you, based on the prophetic words spoken about you earlier. May they help you fight well in the Lord's battles. ¹⁹Cling to your faith in Christ, and keep your conscience clear. For some people have deliberately violated their consciences; as a result, their faith has been shipwrecked. ²⁰Hymenaeus and Alexander are two examples. I threw them out and handed

1:4a Greek *in myths and endless genealogies, which cause speculation.* 1:4b Greek *a stewardship of God in faith.* 1:10 Or *kidnappers.*

cornerstones

RECOGNIZE SATAN'S STRATEGIES
Read 1 TIMOTHY 4:1-2

We must be on our guard against Satan's clever counterfeits, because, as this passage tells us, he will be at work in the last days (which we are in). In fact, we are warned that some in the church will fall prey to these aberrant ideas and teachings. Therefore, as you listen to various teachers and pastors today, remember this:

- Any so-called gospel that distorts the message of Jesus as found in the Bible by adding to it or taking away from it . . .
- Any so-called gospel that offers Christianity without Christ or the Cross . . .
- Any so-called gospel that promises forgiveness without repentance . . .
- Any so-called gospel that presents the hope of heaven without the reality of hell . . .

. . . is not the gospel, but a "watered-down" version that will give you a false assurance. Such teachings are extremely hazardous to your spiritual health. Stay away from them at all costs.

For the next note on "Discernment," turn to p. 308.

---

them over to Satan so they might learn not to blaspheme God.

CHAPTER 2
Instructions about Worship

I urge you, first of all, to pray for all people. Ask God to help them; intercede on their behalf, and give thanks for them. [2] Pray this way for kings and all who are in authority so that we can live peaceful and quiet lives marked by godliness and dignity. [3] This is good and pleases God our Savior, [4] who wants everyone to be saved and to understand the truth. [5] For there is only one God and one Mediator who can reconcile God and humanity—the man Christ Jesus. [6] He gave his life to purchase freedom for everyone. This is the message God gave to the world at just the right time. [7] And I have been chosen as a preacher and apostle to teach the Gentiles this message about faith and truth. I'm not exaggerating—just telling the truth.

[8] In every place of worship, I want men to pray with holy hands lifted up to God, free from anger and controversy.

[9] And I want women to be modest in their appearance.* They should wear decent and appropriate clothing and not draw attention to themselves by the way they fix their hair or by wearing gold or pearls or expensive clothes. [10] For women who claim to be devoted to God should make themselves attractive by the good things they do.

[11] Women should learn quietly and submissively. [12] I do not let women teach men or have authority over them.* Let them listen quietly. [13] For God made Adam first, and afterward he made Eve. [14] And it was not Adam who was deceived by Satan. The woman was deceived, and sin was the result. [15] But women will be saved through childbearing,* assuming they continue to live in faith, love, holiness, and modesty.

CHAPTER 3
Leaders in the Church

This is a trustworthy saying: "If someone aspires to be an elder,* he desires an honorable position." [2] So an elder must be a man whose life is above reproach. He must be faithful to his wife.* He must exercise self-control, live wisely, and have a good reputation. He must enjoy having guests in his home, and he must be able to teach. [3] He must not be a heavy drinker* or be violent. He must be gentle, not quarrelsome, and not love money. [4] He must manage his own family well, having children who respect and obey him. [5] For if a man cannot manage his own household, how can he take care of God's church?

[6] An elder must not be a new believer, because he might become proud, and the devil would cause him to fall.* [7] Also, people outside the church must speak well of him so that he will not be disgraced and fall into the devil's trap.

[8] In the same way, deacons must be well re-

2:9 Or *to pray in modest apparel.*   2:12 Or *teach men or usurp their authority.*   2:15 Or *will be saved by accepting their role as mothers,* or *will be saved by the birth of the Child.*   3:1 Or *an overseer,* or *a bishop;* also in 3:2, 6.   3:2 Or *must have only one wife,* or *must be married only once;* Greek reads *must be the husband of one wife;* also in 3:12.   3:3 Greek *must not drink too much wine;* similarly in 3:8.   3:6 Or *he might fall into the same judgment as the devil.*

spected and have integrity. They must not be heavy drinkers or dishonest with money. ⁹They must be committed to the mystery of the faith now revealed and must live with a clear conscience. ¹⁰Before they are appointed as deacons, let them be closely examined. If they pass the test, then let them serve as deacons.

¹¹In the same way, their wives* must be respected and must not slander others. They must exercise self-control and be faithful in everything they do.

¹²A deacon must be faithful to his wife, and he must manage his children and household well. ¹³Those who do well as deacons will be rewarded with respect from others and will have increased confidence in their faith in Christ Jesus.

The Truths of Our Faith

¹⁴I am writing these things to you now, even though I hope to be with you soon, ¹⁵so that if I am delayed, you will know how people must conduct themselves in the household of God. This is the church of the living God, which is the pillar and foundation of the truth.

¹⁶Without question, this is the great mystery of our faith*:

Christ* was revealed in a human body
   and vindicated by the Spirit.*
He was seen by angels
   and announced to the nations.
He was believed in throughout the world
   and taken to heaven in glory.

CHAPTER 4

Warnings against False Teachers

Now the Holy Spirit tells us clearly that in the last times some will turn away from the true faith; they will follow deceptive spirits and teachings that come from demons. ²These people are hypocrites and liars, and their consciences are dead.*

³They will say it is wrong to be married and wrong to eat certain foods. But God created those foods to be eaten with thanks by faithful people who know the truth. ⁴Since everything God created is good, we should not reject any of it but receive it with thanks. ⁵For we know it is made acceptable* by the word of God and prayer.

A Good Servant of Christ Jesus

⁶If you explain these things to the brothers and sisters,* Timothy, you will be a worthy servant

3:11 Or the women deacons. The Greek word can be translated women or wives.   3:16a Or of godliness.
3:16b Greek He who; other manuscripts read God.
3:16c Or in his spirit.   4:2 Greek are seared.   4:5 Or made holy.   4:6 Greek brothers.

first steps

CAN YOU ENJOY WEALTH?

Read 1 TIMOTHY 6:17-19

The Lord can and will bless you with riches of some kind. They may not necessarily be material possessions. As verse 6 of this chapter says, "true godliness with contentment is itself great wealth." Still, if God does bless you with material riches, he requires three things of you:

1. Do Not Be Arrogant or Put Your Ultimate Hope in Your Wealth. As verse 10 of this chapter says, "For the love of money is the root of all kinds of evil. And some people, craving money, have wandered from the true faith and pierced themselves with many sorrows." Wealth is not sinful. Wealth is not godly. It all depends on the heart of the wealthy person. There are godly people who are wealthy, and there are ungodly people who are poor—and vice versa. The question you must always ask yourself is, "Do I possess my possessions, or do my possessions possess me?"

2. Enjoy What God Has Given You. If God blesses you materially, don't feel guilty about it. Be thankful, realizing that he wants you to enjoy what you have.

3. Be Generous, Do Good, and Share Your Wealth with Others. With wealth comes responsibility. Recognize that you are a steward of what God has given you, and invest what you have in his work.

If you follow these three principles, they will help you be content with whatever you have. When you give God total control of this area of your life, you will never be controlled by your wealth—or by the wealth you wish you had.

To begin the next topic, turn to p. A44.

of Christ Jesus, one who is nourished by the message of faith and the good teaching you have followed. [7] Do not waste time arguing over godless ideas and old wives' tales. Instead, train yourself to be godly. [8] "Physical training is good, but training for godliness is much better, promising benefits in this life and in the life to come." [9] This is a trustworthy saying, and everyone should accept it. [10] This is why we work hard and continue to struggle,* for our hope is in the living God, who is the Savior of all people and particularly of all believers.

[11] Teach these things and insist that everyone learn them. [12] Don't let anyone think less of you because you are young. Be an example to all believers in what you say, in the way you live, in your love, your faith, and your purity. [13] Until I get there, focus on reading the Scriptures to the church, encouraging the believers, and teaching them.

[14] Do not neglect the spiritual gift you received through the prophecy spoken over you when the elders of the church laid their hands on you. [15] Give your complete attention to these matters. Throw yourself into your tasks so that everyone will see your progress. [16] Keep a close watch on how you live and on your teaching. Stay true to what is right for the sake of your own salvation and the salvation of those who hear you.

CHAPTER **5**

Advice about Widows, Elders, and Slaves

Never speak harshly to an older man,* but appeal to him respectfully as you would to your own father. Talk to younger men as you would to your own brothers. [2] Treat older women as you would your mother, and treat younger women with all purity as you would your own sisters.

[3] Take care of* any widow who has no one else to care for her. [4] But if she has children or grandchildren, their first responsibility is to show godliness at home and repay their parents by taking care of them. This is something that pleases God.

[5] Now a true widow, a woman who is truly alone in this world, has placed her hope in God. She prays night and day, asking God for his help. [6] But the widow who lives only for pleasure is spiritually dead even while she lives. [7] Give these instructions to the church so that no one will be open to criticism.

[8] But those who won't care for their relatives, especially those in their own household, have denied the true faith. Such people are worse than unbelievers.

[9] A widow who is put on the list for support must be a woman who is at least sixty years old and was faithful to her husband.* [10] She must be well respected by everyone because of the good she has done. Has she brought up her children well? Has she been kind to strangers and served other believers humbly?* Has she helped those who are in trouble? Has she always been ready to do good?

[11] The younger widows should not be on the list, because their physical desires will overpower their devotion to Christ and they will want to remarry. [12] Then they would be guilty of breaking their previous pledge. [13] And if they are on the list, they will learn to be lazy and will spend their time gossiping from house to house, meddling in other people's business and talking about things they shouldn't. [14] So I advise these younger widows to marry again, have children, and take care of their own homes. Then the enemy will not be able to say anything against them. [15] For I am afraid that some of them have already gone astray and now follow Satan.

[16] If a woman who is a believer has relatives who are widows, she must take care of them and not put the responsibility on the church. Then the church can care for the widows who are truly alone.

[17] Elders who do their work well should be respected and paid well,* especially those who work hard at both preaching and teaching. [18] For the Scripture says, "You must not muzzle an ox to keep it from eating as it treads out the grain." And in another place, "Those who work deserve their pay!"*

[19] Do not listen to an accusation against an elder unless it is confirmed by two or three witnesses. [20] Those who sin should be reprimanded in front of the whole church; this will serve as a strong warning to others.

[21] I solemnly command you in the presence of God and Christ Jesus and the highest angels to obey these instructions without taking sides or showing favoritism to anyone.

[22] Never be in a hurry about appointing a church leader.* Do not share in the sins of others. Keep yourself pure.

[23] Don't drink only water. You ought to drink a little wine for the sake of your stomach because you are sick so often.

[24] Remember, the sins of some people are obvious, leading them to certain judgment. But there are others whose sins will not be revealed until later. [25] In the same way, the good deeds of some people are obvious. And the good deeds done in secret will someday come to light.

4:10 Some manuscripts read *continue to suffer.*   5:1 Or *an elder.*   5:3 Or *Honor.*   5:9 Greek *was the wife of one husband.*
5:10 Greek *and washed the feet of God's holy people?*   5:17 Greek *should be worthy of double honor.*   5:18 Deut 25:4; Luke
10:7.   5:22 Greek *about the laying on of hands.*

CHAPTER **6**

All slaves should show full respect for their masters so they will not bring shame on the name of God and his teaching. [2] If the masters are believers, that is no excuse for being disrespectful. Those slaves should work all the harder because their efforts are helping other believers* who are well loved.

False Teaching and True Riches

Teach these things, Timothy, and encourage everyone to obey them. [3] Some people may contradict our teaching, but these are the wholesome teachings of the Lord Jesus Christ. These teachings promote a godly life. [4] Anyone who teaches something different is arrogant and lacks understanding. Such a person has an unhealthy desire to quibble over the meaning of words. This stirs up arguments ending in jealousy, division, slander, and evil suspicions. [5] These people always cause trouble. Their minds are corrupt, and they have turned their backs on the truth. To them, a show of godliness is just a way to become wealthy.

[6] Yet true godliness with contentment is itself great wealth. [7] After all, we brought nothing with us when we came into the world, and we can't take anything with us when we leave it. [8] So if we have enough food and clothing, let us be content.

[9] But people who long to be rich fall into temptation and are trapped by many foolish and harmful desires that plunge them into ruin and destruction. [10] For the love of money is the root of all kinds of evil. And some people, craving money, have wandered from the true faith and pierced themselves with many sorrows.

6:2 Greek *brothers.*

Paul's Final Instructions

[11] But you, Timothy, are a man of God; so run from all these evil things. Pursue righteousness and a godly life, along with faith, love, perseverance, and gentleness. [12] Fight the good fight for the true faith. Hold tightly to the eternal life to which God has called you, which you have confessed so well before many witnesses. [13] And I charge you before God, who gives life to all, and before Christ Jesus, who gave a good testimony before Pontius Pilate, [14] that you obey this command without wavering. Then no one can find fault with you from now until our Lord Jesus Christ comes again. [15] For at just the right time Christ will be revealed from heaven by the blessed and only almighty God, the King of all kings and Lord of all lords. [16] He alone can never die, and he lives in light so brilliant that no human can approach him. No human eye has ever seen him, nor ever will. All honor and power to him forever! Amen.

[17] Teach those who are rich in this world not to be proud and not to trust in their money, which is so unreliable. Their trust should be in God, who richly gives us all we need for our enjoyment. [18] Tell them to use their money to do good. They should be rich in good works and generous to those in need, always being ready to share with others. [19] By doing this they will be storing up their treasure as a good foundation for the future so that they may experience true life.

[20] Timothy, guard what God has entrusted to you. Avoid godless, foolish discussions with those who oppose you with their so-called knowledge. [21] Some people have wandered from the faith by following such foolishness.

May God's grace be with you all.

2 Timothy

AUTHOR: **PAUL** | DATE WRITTEN: **A.D. 67** | GENRE: **EPISTLE**

Paul wrote this second letter to Timothy to encourage him to be faithful to Christ.
Paul also included a glimpse of what the last days would look like.

CHAPTER 1

Greetings from Paul

This letter is from Paul, chosen by the will of God to be an apostle of Christ Jesus. I have been sent out to tell others about the life he has promised through faith in Christ Jesus.

² I am writing to Timothy, my dear son.

May God the Father and Christ Jesus our Lord give you grace, mercy, and peace.

Encouragement to Be Faithful

³ Timothy, I thank God for you—the God I serve with a clear conscience, just as my ancestors did. Night and day I constantly remember you in my prayers. ⁴ I long to see you again, for I remember your tears as we parted. And I will be filled with joy when we are together again.

⁵ I remember your genuine faith, for you share the faith that first filled your grandmother Lois and your mother, Eunice. And I know that same faith continues strong in you. ⁶ This is why I remind you to fan into flames the spiritual gift God gave you when I laid my hands on you. ⁷ For God has not given us a spirit of fear and timidity, but of power, love, and self-discipline.

⁸ So never be ashamed to tell others about our Lord. And don't be ashamed of me, either, even though I'm in prison for him. With the strength God gives you, be ready to suffer with me for the sake of the Good News. ⁹ For God saved us and called us to live a holy life. He did this, not because we deserved it, but because that was his plan from before the beginning of time—to show us his grace through Christ Jesus. ¹⁰ And now he has made all of this plain to us by the appearing of Christ Jesus, our Savior. He broke the power of death and illumi-

nated the way to life and immortality through the Good News. ¹¹ And God chose me to be a preacher, an apostle, and a teacher of this Good News.

¹² That is why I am suffering here in prison. But I am not ashamed of it, for I know the one in whom I trust, and I am sure that he is able to guard what I have entrusted to him* until the day of his return.

¹³ Hold on to the pattern of wholesome teaching you learned from me—a pattern shaped by the faith and love that you have in Christ Jesus. ¹⁴ Through the power of the Holy Spirit who lives within us, carefully guard the precious truth that has been entrusted to you.

¹⁵ As you know, everyone from the province of Asia has deserted me—even Phygelus and Hermogenes.

¹⁶ May the Lord show special kindness to Onesiphorus and all his family because he often visited and encouraged me. He was never ashamed of me because I was in chains. ¹⁷ When he came to Rome, he searched everywhere until he found me. ¹⁸ May the Lord show him special kindness on the day of Christ's return. And you know very well how helpful he was in Ephesus.

CHAPTER 2

A Good Soldier of Christ Jesus

Timothy, my dear son, be strong through the grace that God gives you in Christ Jesus. ² You have heard me teach things that have been confirmed by many reliable witnesses. Now teach these truths to other trustworthy people who will be able to pass them on to others.

³ Endure suffering along with me, as a good soldier of Christ Jesus. ⁴ Soldiers don't get tied

1:12 Or *what has been entrusted to me.*

cornerstones

GUARD THE CONTENT OF YOUR THOUGHTS

Read 2 TIMOTHY 2:22

In Paul's second letter to Timothy, he gave Timothy helpful advice on how to live a pure life. This advice included: (1) recognizing his potential to sin; (2) avoiding influences that could inspire youthful lust; (3) pursuing faith, love, and peace; and (4) spending time with other believers whose hearts are pure.

One of the more difficult challenges of living a pure life is guarding the content of our thoughts. It has been said, "You can't stop a bird from flying over your head, but you can stop it from building a nest in your hair." In the same way, we cannot stop an impure or wicked thought from "knocking" on the door of our imagination, but we certainly can keep that door closed and locked.

If we don't, and we allow tempting thoughts to infiltrate our mind, we may fall, allowing our old nature to prevail.

The good news is that even though each one of us is still capable of falling, we don't have to. If we stay close to the Lord and follow Paul's advice in this verse, we will be building a strong "fortress" around our life—including our thoughts—and it will be harder for Satan's arrows of temptation to get through.

For the next note on "Purity," turn to p. 6.

---

up in the affairs of civilian life, for then they cannot please the officer who enlisted them. ⁵And athletes cannot win the prize unless they follow the rules. ⁶And hardworking farmers should be the first to enjoy the fruit of their labor. ⁷Think about what I am saying. The Lord will help you understand all these things.

⁸Always remember that Jesus Christ, a descendant of King David, was raised from the dead. This is the Good News I preach. ⁹And because I preach this Good News, I am suffering and have been chained like a criminal. But the word of God cannot be chained. ¹⁰So I am willing to endure anything if it will bring salvation and eternal glory in Christ Jesus to those God has chosen.

¹¹This is a trustworthy saying:

If we die with him,
    we will also live with him.
¹² If we endure hardship,
    we will reign with him.
If we deny him,
    he will deny us.
¹³ If we are unfaithful,
    he remains faithful,
    for he cannot deny who he is.

¹⁴Remind everyone about these things, and command them in God's presence to stop fighting over words. Such arguments are useless, and they can ruin those who hear them.

An Approved Worker

¹⁵Work hard so you can present yourself to God and receive his approval. Be a good worker, one who does not need to be ashamed and who correctly explains the word of truth. ¹⁶Avoid worthless, foolish talk that only leads to more godless behavior. ¹⁷This kind of talk spreads like cancer,* as in the case of Hymenaeus and Philetus. ¹⁸They have left the path of truth, claiming that the resurrection of the dead has already occurred; in this way, they have turned some people away from the faith.

¹⁹But God's truth stands firm like a foundation stone with this inscription: "The LORD knows those who are his,"* and "All who belong to the LORD must turn away from evil."*

²⁰In a wealthy home some utensils are made of gold and silver, and some are made of wood and clay. The expensive utensils are used for special occasions, and the cheap ones are for everyday use. ²¹If you keep yourself pure, you will be a special utensil for honorable use. Your life will be clean, and you will be ready for the Master to use you for every good work.

²²Run from anything that stimulates youthful lusts. Instead, pursue righteous living, faithfulness, love, and peace. Enjoy the companionship of those who call on the Lord with pure hearts.

²³Again I say, don't get involved in foolish, ignorant arguments that only start fights. ²⁴A servant of the Lord must not quarrel but must

2:17 Greek *gangrene.*   2:19a Num 16:5.   2:19b See Isa 52:11.

be kind to everyone, be able to teach, and be patient with difficult people. ²⁵Gently instruct those who oppose the truth. Perhaps God will change those people's hearts, and they will learn the truth. ²⁶Then they will come to their senses and escape from the devil's trap. For they have been held captive by him to do whatever he wants.

CHAPTER 3
The Dangers of the Last Days

You should know this, Timothy, that in the last days there will be very difficult times. ²For people will love only themselves and their money. They will be boastful and proud, scoffing at God, disobedient to their parents, and ungrateful. They will consider nothing sacred. ³They will be unloving and unforgiving; they will slander others and have no self-control. They will be cruel and hate what is good. ⁴They will betray their friends, be reckless, be puffed up with pride, and love pleasure rather than God. ⁵They will act religious, but they will reject the power that could make them godly. Stay away from people like that!

⁶They are the kind who work their way into people's homes and win the confidence of* vulnerable women who are burdened with the guilt of sin and controlled by various desires. ⁷(Such women are forever following new teachings, but they are never able to understand the truth.) ⁸These teachers oppose the truth just as Jannes and Jambres opposed Moses. They have depraved minds and a counterfeit faith. ⁹But they won't get away with this for long. Someday everyone will recognize what fools they are, just as with Jannes and Jambres.

Paul's Charge to Timothy

¹⁰But you, Timothy, certainly know what I teach, and how I live, and what my purpose in life is. You know my faith, my patience, my love, and my endurance. ¹¹You know how much persecution and suffering I have endured. You know all about how I was persecuted in Antioch, Iconium, and Lystra—but the Lord rescued me from all of it. ¹²Yes, and everyone who wants to live a godly life in Christ Jesus will suffer persecution. ¹³But evil people and impostors will flourish. They will deceive others and will themselves be deceived.

¹⁴But you must remain faithful to the things you have been taught. You know they are true, for you know you can trust those who taught you. ¹⁵You have been taught the holy Scriptures from childhood, and they have given you the wisdom to receive the salvation that comes by trusting in Christ Jesus. ¹⁶All Scripture is in-

3:6 Greek *and take captive.*

first steps
STUDYING THE BIBLE IS NECESSARY FOR OUR SPIRITUAL GROWTH
Read 2 TIMOTHY 3:16-17

The primary reason we should study the Bible is because it was inspired by the Creator of the universe to guide us through this adventure called life. This passage of Scripture gives us three more reasons why we should make the Bible part of our day-to-day life:

1. The Bible Teaches Us What Is True. The Bible is the only book we need to discover the foundational truths of how to know and walk with God. Some aberrant religious groups or cults insist we need another book to help us interpret what the Bible says. But the Bible needs no outside interpretation. It speaks for itself. In fact, the best commentary on the Bible is the Bible itself.

2. The Bible Shows Us What Is Wrong in Our Lives. God's Word serves to reprove us or to make us aware when we are headed in the wrong direction.

3. The Bible Helps Us Do What Is Right. If we read and meditate on God's Word, we will be molded into the man or woman God wants us to be.

When we allow the Bible to teach us in these three areas, we are told that we will be prepared and equipped to do good to everyone (see 2 Timothy 3:14-16). Our foundation will be solid, our motives pure, and our character more refined. What better reasons are there to make a commitment to stick with Bible study!

To begin the next topic, turn to p. A38.

spired by God and is useful to teach us what is true and to make us realize what is wrong in our lives. It corrects us when we are wrong and teaches us to do what is right. ¹⁷God uses it to prepare and equip his people to do every good work.

CHAPTER 4

I solemnly urge you in the presence of God and Christ Jesus, who will someday judge the living and the dead when he appears to set up his Kingdom: [2] Preach the word of God. Be prepared, whether the time is favorable or not. Patiently correct, rebuke, and encourage your people with good teaching.

[3] For a time is coming when people will no longer listen to sound and wholesome teaching. They will follow their own desires and will look for teachers who will tell them whatever their itching ears want to hear. [4] They will reject the truth and chase after myths.

[5] But you should keep a clear mind in every situation. Don't be afraid of suffering for the Lord. Work at telling others the Good News, and fully carry out the ministry God has given you.

[6] As for me, my life has already been poured out as an offering to God. The time of my death is near. [7] I have fought the good fight, I have finished the race, and I have remained faithful. [8] And now the prize awaits me—the crown of righteousness, which the Lord, the righteous Judge, will give me on the day of his return. And the prize is not just for me but for all who eagerly look forward to his appearing.

Paul's Final Words

[9] Timothy, please come as soon as you can. [10] Demas has deserted me because he loves the things of this life and has gone to Thessalonica. Crescens has gone to Galatia, and Titus has gone to Dalmatia. [11] Only Luke is with me. Bring Mark with you when you come, for he will be helpful to me in my ministry. [12] I sent Tychicus to Ephesus. [13] When you come, be sure to bring the coat I left with Carpus at Troas. Also bring my books, and especially my papers.*

[14] Alexander the coppersmith did me much harm, but the Lord will judge him for what he has done. [15] Be careful of him, for he fought against everything we said.

[16] The first time I was brought before the judge, no one came with me. Everyone abandoned me. May it not be counted against them. [17] But the Lord stood with me and gave me strength so that I might preach the Good News in its entirety for all the Gentiles to hear. And he rescued me from certain death.* [18] Yes, and the Lord will deliver me from every evil attack and will bring me safely into his heavenly Kingdom. All glory to God forever and ever! Amen.

Paul's Final Greetings

[19] Give my greetings to Priscilla and Aquila and those living in the household of Onesiphorus. [20] Erastus stayed at Corinth, and I left Trophimus sick at Miletus.

[21] Do your best to get here before winter. Eubulus sends you greetings, and so do Pudens, Linus, Claudia, and all the brothers and sisters.*

[22] May the Lord be with your spirit. And may his grace be with all of you.

4:13 Greek *especially the parchments.*   4:17 Greek *from the mouth of a lion.*   4:21 Greek *brothers.*

Titus

AUTHOR: **PAUL** | DATE WRITTEN: **A.D. 65** | GENRE: **EPISTLE**

Paul wrote this letter to address the challenges facing Titus as an overseer of the churches on the island of Crete. He included criteria for qualifications of leadership, sound teaching, and good works.

CHAPTER 1
Greetings from Paul

This letter is from Paul, a slave of God and an apostle of Jesus Christ. I have been sent to proclaim faith to* those God has chosen and to teach them to know the truth that shows them how to live godly lives. ²This truth gives them confidence that they have eternal life, which God—who does not lie—promised them before the world began. ³And now at just the right time he has revealed this message, which we announce to everyone. It is by the command of God our Savior that I have been entrusted with this work for him.

⁴I am writing to Titus, my true son in the faith that we share.

May God the Father and Christ Jesus our Savior give you grace and peace.

Titus's Work in Crete

⁵I left you on the island of Crete so you could complete our work there and appoint elders in each town as I instructed you. ⁶An elder must live a blameless life. He must be faithful to his wife,* and his children must be believers who don't have a reputation for being wild or rebellious. ⁷An elder* is a manager of God's household, so he must live a blameless life. He must not be arrogant or quick-tempered; he must not be a heavy drinker,* violent, or dishonest with money.

⁸Rather, he must enjoy having guests in his home, and he must love what is good. He must live wisely and be just. He must live a devout and disciplined life. ⁹He must have a strong belief in the trustworthy message he was taught; then he will be able to encourage others with wholesome teaching and show those who oppose it where they are wrong.

¹⁰For there are many rebellious people who engage in useless talk and deceive others. This is especially true of those who insist on circumcision for salvation. ¹¹They must be silenced, because they are turning whole families away from the truth by their false teaching. And they do it only for money. ¹²Even one of their own men, a prophet from Crete, has said about them, "The people of Crete are all liars, cruel animals, and lazy gluttons."* ¹³This is true. So reprimand them sternly to make them strong in the faith. ¹⁴They must stop listening to Jewish myths and the commands of people who have turned away from the truth.

¹⁵Everything is pure to those whose hearts are pure. But nothing is pure to those who are corrupt and unbelieving, because their minds and consciences are corrupted. ¹⁶Such people claim they know God, but they deny him by the way they live. They are detestable and disobedient, worthless for doing anything good.

CHAPTER 2
Promote Right Teaching

As for you, Titus, promote the kind of living that reflects wholesome teaching. ²Teach the older men to exercise self-control, to be worthy of respect, and to live wisely. They must have sound faith and be filled with love and patience.

³Similarly, teach the older women to live in a way that honors God. They must not slander others or be heavy drinkers.* Instead, they should

---

1:1 Or *to strengthen the faith of.* 1:6 Or *must have only one wife,* or *must be married only once;* Greek reads *must be the husband of one wife.* 1:7a Or *An overseer,* or *A bishop.* 1:7b Greek *must not drink too much wine.* 1:12 This quotation is from Epimenides of Knossos. 2:3 Greek *be enslaved to much wine.*

cornerstones

WE NEED TO SET AN EXAMPLE FOR OTHERS

Read TITUS 2:6-8

This passage gives some practical reasons and ways to live out your faith. Though these words were written to Titus, a leader in the early church, they apply to anyone whose life influences the lives of others. That is, the passage speaks to all of us! Take a moment to ponder these simple, yet useful, thoughts:

How Should We Behave?

- We need to be self-controlled and serious about life.
- We should do good deeds often as an example to others.
- We should love the truth.
- We should be earnest and serious in our pursuit of truth.
- We should think before we speak, making sure that our conversation is sound and sensible.

Why Should We Live Godly Lives?

- We represent God, who is holy.
- We are an example to others, particularly young people and new believers.
- Our behavior will silence our critics.

To begin the next topic, turn to p. A32.

---

teach others what is good. [4]These older women must train the younger women to love their husbands and their children, [5]to live wisely and be pure, to work in their homes,* to do good, and to be submissive to their husbands. Then they will not bring shame on the word of God.

[6]In the same way, encourage the young men to live wisely. [7]And you yourself must be an example to them by doing good works of every kind. Let everything you do reflect the integrity and seriousness of your teaching. [8]Teach the truth so that your teaching can't

2:5 Some manuscripts read *to care for their homes.*

---

off and running

CREATE A SPIRITUAL HUNGER IN THOSE AROUND YOU

Read TITUS 2:9-10

While we are not slaves, this verse could easily apply to workers and employees today—or to anyone who is asked to do something for someone else. Jesus gave a unique example of how this works when he told his disciples, "If a soldier demands that you carry his gear for a mile, carry it two miles" (Matthew 5:41). At that time, Roman law gave soldiers the right to retain private citizens to carry their pack for a mile. Yet Jesus told his disciples to go above and beyond that request. In so doing, they would have a captive audience for presenting the gospel. Today, when everyone seems to be demanding his or her rights, this verse is a direct contradiction to the current wave of thinking. But it all comes back to our frame of reference as Christians: Our goal on earth is not to win our own rights, but to win people to our Lord. Your work may be difficult. You may even think it is mundane and insignificant. But it is not. God has placed you in your place of employment for a reason—to let your light shine. Your dedicated work may be just the thing that wins your employer or supervisor to Christ. So look for opportunities to "go the extra mile."

For the next note on "Job Performance," turn to p. 252.

be criticized. Then those who oppose us will be ashamed and have nothing bad to say about us.

⁹Slaves must always obey their masters and do their best to please them. They must not talk back ¹⁰or steal, but must show themselves to be entirely trustworthy and good. Then they will make the teaching about God our Savior attractive in every way.

¹¹For the grace of God has been revealed, bringing salvation to all people. ¹²And we are instructed to turn from godless living and sinful pleasures. We should live in this evil world with wisdom, righteousness, and devotion to God, ¹³while we look forward with hope to that wonderful day when the glory of our great God and Savior, Jesus Christ, will be revealed. ¹⁴He gave his life to free us from every kind of sin, to cleanse us, and to make us his very own people, totally committed to doing good deeds.

¹⁵You must teach these things and encourage the believers to do them. You have the authority to correct them when necessary, so don't let anyone disregard what you say.

CHAPTER **3**
Do What Is Good
Remind the believers to submit to the government and its officers. They should be obedient, always ready to do what is good. ²They must not slander anyone and must avoid quarreling. Instead, they should be gentle and show true humility to everyone.

³Once we, too, were foolish and disobedient. We were misled and became slaves to many lusts and pleasures. Our lives were full of evil and envy, and we hated each other.

⁴But—"When God our Savior revealed his kindness and love, ⁵he saved us, not because of the righteous things we had done, but because of his mercy. He washed away our sins, giving us a new birth and new life through the Holy Spirit.* ⁶He generously poured out the Spirit upon us through Jesus Christ our Savior. ⁷Because of his grace he declared us righteous and gave us confidence that we will inherit eternal life." ⁸This is a trustworthy saying, and I want you to insist on these teachings so that all who trust in God will devote themselves to doing good. These teachings are good and beneficial for everyone.

⁹Do not get involved in foolish discussions about spiritual pedigrees* or in quarrels and fights about obedience to Jewish laws. These things are useless and a waste of time. ¹⁰If people are causing divisions among you, give a first and second warning. After that, have nothing more to do with them. ¹¹For people like that have turned away from the truth, and their own sins condemn them.

Paul's Final Remarks and Greetings
¹²I am planning to send either Artemas or Tychicus to you. As soon as one of them arrives, do your best to meet me at Nicopolis, for I have decided to stay there for the winter. ¹³Do everything you can to help Zenas the lawyer and Apollos with their trip. See that they are given everything they need. ¹⁴Our people must learn to do good by meeting the urgent needs of others; then they will not be unproductive.

¹⁵Everybody here sends greetings. Please give my greetings to the believers—all who love us.

May God's grace be with you all.

3:5 Greek *He saved us through the washing of regeneration and renewing of the Holy Spirit.*   3:9 Or *spiritual genealogies.*

Philemon

AUTHOR: **PAUL** | DATE WRITTEN: **A.D. 60** | GENRE: **EPISTLE**

This short but profound epistle contains a wonderful story of the importance of forgiveness among Christians.

Greetings from Paul

This letter is from Paul, a prisoner for preaching the Good News about Christ Jesus, and from our brother Timothy.

I am writing to Philemon, our beloved co-worker, [2] and to our sister Apphia, and to our fellow soldier Archippus, and to the church that meets in your* house.

[3] May God our Father and the Lord Jesus Christ give you grace and peace.

Paul's Thanksgiving and Prayer

[4] I always thank my God when I pray for you, Philemon, [5] because I keep hearing about your faith in the Lord Jesus and your love for all of God's people. [6] And I am praying that you will put into action the generosity that comes from your faith as you understand and experience all the good things we have in Christ. [7] Your love has given me much joy and comfort, my brother, for your kindness has often refreshed the hearts of God's people.

Paul's Appeal for Onesimus

[8] That is why I am boldly asking a favor of you. I could demand it in the name of Christ because it is the right thing for you to do. [9] But because of our love, I prefer simply to ask you. Consider this as a request from me—Paul, an old man and now also a prisoner for the sake of Christ Jesus.*

[10] I appeal to you to show kindness to my child, Onesimus. I became his father in the faith while here in prison. [11] Onesimus* hasn't been of much use to you in the past, but now he is very useful to both of us. [12] I am sending him back to you, and with him comes my own heart.

[13] I wanted to keep him here with me while I am in these chains for preaching the Good News, and he would have helped me on your behalf. [14] But I didn't want to do anything without your consent. I wanted you to help because you were willing, not because you were forced. [15] It seems you lost Onesimus for a little while so that you could have him back forever. [16] He is no longer like a slave to you. He is more than a slave, for he is a beloved brother, especially to me. Now he will mean much more to you, both as a man and as a brother in the Lord.

[17] So if you consider me your partner, welcome him as you would welcome me. [18] If he has wronged you in any way or owes you anything, charge it to me. [19] I, PAUL, WRITE THIS WITH MY OWN HAND: I WILL REPAY IT. AND I WON'T MENTION THAT YOU OWE ME YOUR VERY SOUL!

[20] Yes, my brother, please do me this favor* for the Lord's sake. Give me this encouragement in Christ.

[21] I am confident as I write this letter that you will do what I ask and even more! [22] One more thing—please prepare a guest room for me, for I am hoping that God will answer your prayers and let me return to you soon.

Paul's Final Greetings

[23] Epaphras, my fellow prisoner in Christ Jesus, sends you his greetings. [24] So do Mark, Aristarchus, Demas, and Luke, my co-workers.

[25] May the grace of the Lord Jesus Christ be with your spirit.

---

2 Throughout this letter, *you* and *your* are singular except in verses 3, 22, and 25.   9 Or *a prisoner of Christ Jesus.*
11 *Onesimus* means "useful."   20 Greek *onaimen,* a play on the name Onesimus.

The book of Hebrews was written for the Jews who had accepted Jesus as their Messiah. *They were in danger of slipping back into the traditions of Judaism because they had not put their roots down in the soil of Christianity.*

CHAPTER **1**

Jesus Christ Is God's Son

Long ago God spoke many times and in many ways to our ancestors through the prophets. ²And now in these final days, he has spoken to us through his Son. God promised everything to the Son as an inheritance, and through the Son he created the universe. ³The Son radiates God's own glory and expresses the very character of God, and he sustains everything by the mighty power of his command. When he had cleansed us from our sins, he sat down in the place of honor at the right hand of the majestic God in heaven. ⁴This shows that the Son is far greater than the angels, just as the name God gave him is greater than their names.

The Son Is Greater Than the Angels

⁵For God never said to any angel what he said to Jesus:

"You are my Son.
 Today I have become
  your Father.*"

God also said,

"I will be his Father,
 and he will be my Son."*

⁶And when he brought his supreme* Son into the world, God said,*

"Let all of God's angels worship him."*

⁷Regarding the angels, he says,

"He sends his angels like the winds,
 his servants like flames of fire."*

⁸But to the Son he says,

"Your throne, O God, endures forever and
  ever.
 You rule with a scepter of justice.
⁹ You love justice and hate evil.
 Therefore, O God, your God has anointed
  you,
 pouring out the oil of joy on you more
  than on anyone else."*

¹⁰He also says to the Son,

"In the beginning, Lord, you laid the
  foundation of the earth
 and made the heavens with your hands.
¹¹ They will perish, but you remain forever.
 They will wear out like old clothing.
¹² You will fold them up like a cloak
 and discard them like old clothing.
But you are always the same;
 you will live forever."*

¹³And God never said to any of the angels,

"Sit in the place of honor at my right hand
 until I humble your enemies,
 making them a footstool under your
  feet."*

¹⁴Therefore, angels are only servants—spirits sent to care for people who will inherit salvation.

CHAPTER **2**

A Warning against Drifting Away

So we must listen very carefully to the truth we have heard, or we may drift away from it. ²For the message God delivered through angels has

---

1:5a Or *Today I reveal you as my Son.* Ps 2:7. **1:5b** 2 Sam 7:14. **1:6a** Or *firstborn.* **1:6b** Or *when he again brings his supreme Son* (or *firstborn Son*) *into the world, God will say.* **1:6c** Deut 32:43. **1:7** Ps 104:4 (Greek version). **1:8-9** Ps 45:6-7. **1:10-12** Ps 102:25-27. **1:13** Ps 110:1.

cornerstones

WHY DID GOD CREATE ANGELS?
Read HEBREWS 1:4-14

Throughout the ages, people have been fascinated with and awed by angels. Some have even tried to worship them. But it is important to understand that angels are distinctly different from God's Son, Jesus Christ. One significant area of distinction is creation. Angels are created beings, while Jesus is not. Because angels are created, it is wrong to worship them.

If they are not to be worshiped, then what did God create angels for? God created angels for several reasons, three of which are the following:

1. Angels Worship God. As verse 6 attests, one of the reasons God created angels was to worship him. Some people may think this is egotistical, but consider how many people worship professional athletes and other celebrities. These people by comparison have done nothing to earn or be worthy of the worship they receive. God, on the other hand, has created angels and humans and given them life. In addition, God is majestic beyond our understanding, so worshiping him is simply the natural response of being in his presence. For it is an incredible privilege to be in the presence of God. Only God is worthy of worship, and his creation, which includes angels, should worship him.

2. Angels Serve as God's Messengers. God uses angels to deliver messages to his followers on earth (verse 7). The Bible records a few instances of this. In Daniel 10 God sent an angel to give Daniel an answer to his prayer. An angel was also sent to Jesus' tomb to tell his followers that he had risen from the dead (Matthew 28).

3. Angels Minister to God's Followers. God also created angels to minister to his followers (verse 14). In Genesis 19, two angels rescued Lot and his family from God's wrath on Sodom and Gomorrah. In Acts 12, an angel freed Peter from prison before he was to be tried in public for being a follower of Christ.

While angels play a significant role in the lives of believers, we must be careful that we do not give them the honor and praise that should be reserved for Jesus Christ alone.

For the next note on "What Are Angels?" turn to p. 330.

---

always stood firm, and every violation of the law and every act of disobedience was punished. [3] So what makes us think we can escape if we ignore this great salvation that was first announced by the Lord Jesus himself and then delivered to us by those who heard him speak? [4] And God confirmed the message by giving signs and wonders and various miracles and gifts of the Holy Spirit whenever he chose.

Jesus, the Man

[5] And furthermore, it is not angels who will control the future world we are talking about. [6] For in one place the Scriptures say,

"What are mere mortals that you should think about them,
   or a son of man* that you should care for him?
[7] Yet you made them only a little lower than the angels

and crowned them with glory and honor.*
[8] You gave them authority over all things."*

Now when it says "all things," it means nothing is left out. But we have not yet seen all things put under their authority. [9] What we do see is Jesus, who was given a position "a little lower than the angels"; and because he suffered death for us, he is now "crowned with glory and honor." Yes, by God's grace, Jesus tasted death for everyone. [10] God, for whom and through whom everything was made, chose to bring many children into glory. And it was only right that he should make Jesus, through his suffering, a perfect leader, fit to bring them into their salvation.

[11] So now Jesus and the ones he makes holy have the same Father. That is why Jesus is not ashamed to call them his brothers and sisters.* [12] For he said to God,

2:6 Or *the Son of Man.*   2:7 Some manuscripts add *You gave them charge of everything you made.*   2:6-8 Ps 8:4-6 (Greek version).   2:11 Greek *brothers;* also in 2:12.

BIG QUESTIONS

Why Would a Good God Send Anyone to Hell?

Read HEBREWS 2:2-3

If God loves people, why doesn't he just save everyone? Perhaps you have asked this question or know someone who has. While the question is good, it places the blame for people's damnation on the wrong person: God. God does not want anyone to spend eternity in hell. In fact, he earnestly desires that everyone spend all eternity with him in heaven. Scripture tells us, "The Lord . . . does not want anyone to be destroyed, but wants everyone to repent" (2 Peter 3:9). Throughout the Bible we see God's loving and patient invitation for us to come to him:

- "Come to me, all of you who are weary and carry heavy burdens, and I will give you rest." (Matthew 11:28)
- "'Come.' Let anyone who is thirsty come. Let anyone who desires drink freely from the water of life." (Revelation 22:17)

The truth is that there are some things only God can do—such as cleanse us of our sin, forgive us, and justify us. At the same time, there are some things only we can do—such as answer his call to come to him, believe in him, and repent of our sins. While God does indeed love everyone (see John 3:16, p. 103; Romans 5:8, p. 173), he has given us a wonderful but dangerous gift. That gift is called "free will." It is the ability to choose between right and wrong, good and evil, God and Satan, and heaven and hell. God will not force his salvation and forgiveness upon our lives. It is our choice to say yes or no.

Anyone who ends up in hell is there because of his or her willful and deliberate decision to reject God's offer of forgiveness. As the famous British author C. S. Lewis put it, "The gates of hell are locked from the inside."

For the next "Big Question" note, turn to p. 309.

"I will proclaim your name to my brothers and sisters.
I will praise you among your assembled people."*

[13] He also said,

"I will put my trust in him,"
that is, "I and the children God has given me."*

[14] Because God's children are human beings—made of flesh and blood—the Son also became flesh and blood. For only as a human being could he die, and only by dying could he break the power of the devil, who had* the power of death. [15] Only in this way could he set free all who have lived their lives as slaves to the fear of dying.

[16] We also know that the Son did not come to help angels; he came to help the descendants of Abraham. [17] Therefore, it was necessary for him to be made in every respect like us, his brothers and sisters,* so that he could be our merciful and faithful High Priest before God. Then he could offer a sacrifice that would take away the sins of the people. [18] Since he himself has gone through suffering and testing, he is able to help us when we are being tested.

CHAPTER 3
Jesus Is Greater Than Moses

And so, dear brothers and sisters who belong to God and* are partners with those called to heaven, think carefully about this Jesus whom

2:12 Ps 22:22. **2:13** Isa 8:17-18. **2:14** Or *has.* **2:17** Greek *like the brothers.* **3:1a** Greek *And so, holy brothers who.*

we declare to be God's messenger* and High Priest. ²For he was faithful to God, who appointed him, just as Moses served faithfully when he was entrusted with God's entire* house.

³But Jesus deserves far more glory than Moses, just as a person who builds a house deserves more praise than the house itself. ⁴For every house has a builder, but the one who built everything is God.

⁵Moses was certainly faithful in God's house as a servant. His work was an illustration of the truths God would reveal later. ⁶But Christ, as the Son, is in charge of God's entire house. And we are God's house, if we keep our courage and remain confident in our hope in Christ.*

⁷That is why the Holy Spirit says,

"Today when you hear his voice,
⁸   don't harden your hearts
as Israel did when they rebelled,
    when they tested me in the wilderness.
⁹ There your ancestors tested and tried my
        patience,
    even though they saw my miracles for
        forty years.
¹⁰ So I was angry with them, and I said,
    'Their hearts always turn away from me.
    They refuse to do what I tell them.'
¹¹ So in my anger I took an oath:
    'They will never enter my place of rest.'"*

¹²Be careful then, dear brothers and sisters.* Make sure that your own hearts are not evil and unbelieving, turning you away from the living God. ¹³You must warn each other every day, while it is still "today," so that none of you will be deceived by sin and hardened against God. ¹⁴For if we are faithful to the end, trusting God just as firmly as when we first believed, we will share in all that belongs to Christ. ¹⁵Remember what it says:

"Today when you hear his voice,
    don't harden your hearts
    as Israel did when they rebelled."*

¹⁶And who was it who rebelled against God, even though they heard his voice? Wasn't it the people Moses led out of Egypt? ¹⁷And who made God angry for forty years? Wasn't it the people who sinned, whose corpses lay in the wilderness? ¹⁸And to whom was God speaking when he took an oath that they would never enter his rest? Wasn't it the people who disobeyed him? ¹⁹So we see that because of their unbelief they were not able to enter his rest.

CHAPTER 4

Promised Rest for God's People

God's promise of entering his rest still stands, so we ought to tremble with fear that some of you might fail to experience it. ²For this good news—that God has prepared this rest—has been announced to us just as it was to them. But it did them no good because they didn't share the faith of those who listened to God.* ³For only we who believe can enter his rest. As for the others, God said,

"In my anger I took an oath:
    'They will never enter my place of rest,'"*

even though this rest has been ready since he made the world. ⁴We know it is ready because of the place in the Scriptures where it mentions the seventh day: "On the seventh day God rested from all his work."* ⁵But in the other passage God said, "They will never enter my place of rest."*

⁶So God's rest is there for people to enter, but those who first heard this good news failed to enter because they disobeyed God. ⁷So God set another time for entering his rest, and that time is today. God announced this through David much later in the words already quoted:

"Today when you hear his voice,
    don't harden your hearts."*

⁸Now if Joshua had succeeded in giving them this rest, God would not have spoken about another day of rest still to come. ⁹So there is a special rest* still waiting for the people of God. ¹⁰For all who have entered into God's rest have rested from their labors, just as God did after creating the world. ¹¹So let us do our best to enter that rest. But if we disobey God, as the people of Israel did, we will fall.

¹²For the word of God is alive and powerful. It is sharper than the sharpest two-edged sword, cutting between soul and spirit, between joint and marrow. It exposes our innermost thoughts and desires. ¹³Nothing in all creation is hidden from God. Everything is naked and exposed before his eyes, and he is the one to whom we are accountable.

Christ Is Our High Priest

¹⁴So then, since we have a great High Priest who has entered heaven, Jesus the Son of God, let us hold firmly to what we believe. ¹⁵This High Priest of ours understands our weaknesses, for he faced all of the same testings we do, yet he did not sin. ¹⁶So let us come boldly to

---

3:1b Greek *God's apostle.*   3:2 Some manuscripts do not include *entire.*   3:6 Some manuscripts add *faithful to the end.* 3:7-11 Ps 95:7-11.   3:12 Greek *brothers.*   3:15 Ps 95:7-8.   4:2 Some manuscripts read *they didn't combine what they heard with faith.*   4:3 Ps 95:11.   4:4 Gen 2:2.   4:5 Ps 95:11.   4:7 Ps 95:7-8.   4:9 Or *a Sabbath rest.*

the throne of our gracious God. There we will receive his mercy, and we will find grace to help us when we need it most.

CHAPTER 5

Every high priest is a man chosen to represent other people in their dealings with God. He presents their gifts to God and offers sacrifices for their sins. ²And he is able to deal gently with ignorant and wayward people because he himself is subject to the same weaknesses. ³That is why he must offer sacrifices for his own sins as well as theirs.

⁴And no one can become a high priest simply because he wants such an honor. He must be called by God for this work, just as Aaron was. ⁵That is why Christ did not honor himself by assuming he could become High Priest. No, he was chosen by God, who said to him,

"You are my Son.
    Today I have become your Father.*"

⁶And in another passage God said to him,

"You are a priest forever in the order of
    Melchizedek."*

⁷While Jesus was here on earth, he offered prayers and pleadings, with a loud cry and tears, to the one who could rescue him from death. And God heard his prayers because of his deep reverence for God. ⁸Even though Jesus was God's Son, he learned obedience from the things he suffered. ⁹In this way, God qualified him as a perfect High Priest, and he became the source of eternal salvation for all those who obey him. ¹⁰And God designated him to be a High Priest in the order of Melchizedek.

A Call to Spiritual Growth

¹¹There is much more we would like to say about this, but it is difficult to explain, especially since you are spiritually dull and don't seem to listen. ¹²You have been believers so long now that you ought to be teaching others. Instead, you need someone to teach you again the basic things about God's word.* You are like babies who need milk and cannot eat solid food. ¹³For someone who lives on milk is still an infant and doesn't know how to do what is right. ¹⁴Solid food is for those who are mature, who through training have the skill to recognize the difference between right and wrong.

CHAPTER 6

So let us stop going over the basic teachings about Christ again and again. Let us go on instead and become mature in our understanding. Surely we don't need to start again with the fundamental importance of repenting from evil deeds* and placing our faith in God. ²You don't need further instruction about baptisms, the laying on of hands, the resurrection of the dead, and eternal judgment. ³And so, God willing, we will move forward to further understanding.

⁴For it is impossible to bring back to repentance those who were once enlightened—those who have experienced the good things of heaven and shared in the Holy Spirit, ⁵who have tasted the goodness of the word of God and the power of the age to come—⁶and who then turn away from God. It is impossible to bring such people back to repentance; by rejecting the Son of God, they themselves are nailing him to the cross once again and holding him up to public shame.

⁷When the ground soaks up the falling rain and bears a good crop for the farmer, it has God's blessing. ⁸But if a field bears thorns and thistles, it is useless. The farmer will soon condemn that field and burn it.

⁹Dear friends, even though we are talking this way, we really don't believe it applies to you. We are confident that you are meant for better things, things that come with salvation. ¹⁰For God is not unjust. He will not forget how hard you have worked for him and how you have shown your love to him by caring for other believers,* as you still do. ¹¹Our great desire is that you will keep on loving others as long as life lasts, in order to make certain that what you hope for will come true. ¹²Then you will not become spiritually dull and indifferent. Instead, you will follow the example of those who are going to inherit God's promises because of their faith and endurance.

God's Promises Bring Hope

¹³For example, there was God's promise to Abraham. Since there was no one greater to swear by, God took an oath in his own name, saying:

¹⁴ "I will certainly bless you,
    and I will multiply your descendants
        beyond number."*

¹⁵Then Abraham waited patiently, and he received what God had promised.

¹⁶Now when people take an oath, they call on someone greater than themselves to hold them to it. And without any question that oath is binding. ¹⁷God also bound himself with an oath, so that those who received the promise could be perfectly sure that he would never

5:5 Or *Today I reveal you as my Son.* Ps 2:7.   5:6 Ps 110:4.   5:12 Or *about the oracles of God.*   6:1 Greek *from dead works.*
6:10 Greek *for God's holy people.*   6:14 Gen 22:17.

change his mind. [18]So God has given both his promise and his oath. These two things are unchangeable because it is impossible for God to lie. Therefore, we who have fled to him for refuge can have great confidence as we hold to the hope that lies before us. [19]This hope is a strong and trustworthy anchor for our souls. It leads us through the curtain into God's inner sanctuary. [20]Jesus has already gone in there for us. He has become our eternal High Priest in the order of Melchizedek.

CHAPTER **7**

Melchizedek Is Greater Than Abraham

This Melchizedek was king of the city of Salem and also a priest of God Most High. When Abraham was returning home after winning a great battle against the kings, Melchizedek met him and blessed him. [2]Then Abraham took a tenth of all he had captured in battle and gave it to Melchizedek. The name Melchizedek means "king of justice," and king of Salem means "king of peace." [3]There is no record of his father or mother or any of his ancestors— no beginning or end to his life. He remains a priest forever, resembling the Son of God.

[4]Consider then how great this Melchizedek was. Even Abraham, the great patriarch of Israel, recognized this by giving him a tenth of what he had taken in battle. [5]Now the law of Moses required that the priests, who are descendants of Levi, must collect a tithe from the rest of the people of Israel,* who are also descendants of Abraham. [6]But Melchizedek, who was not a descendant of Levi, collected a tenth from Abraham. And Melchizedek placed a blessing upon Abraham, the one who had already received the promises of God. [7]And without question, the person who has the power to give a blessing is greater than the one who is blessed.

[8]The priests who collect tithes are men who die, so Melchizedek is greater than they are, because we are told that he lives on. [9]In addition, we might even say that these Levites—the ones who collect the tithe—paid a tithe to Melchizedek when their ancestor Abraham paid a tithe to him. [10]For although Levi wasn't born yet, the seed from which he came was in Abraham's body when Melchizedek collected the tithe from him.

[11]So if the priesthood of Levi, on which the law was based, could have achieved the perfection God intended, why did God need to establish a different priesthood, with a priest in the order of Melchizedek instead of the order of Levi and Aaron?*

[12]And if the priesthood is changed, the law must also be changed to permit it. [13]For the priest we are talking about belongs to a different tribe, whose members have never served at the altar as priests. [14]What I mean is, our Lord came from the tribe of Judah, and Moses never mentioned priests coming from that tribe.

Jesus Is like Melchizedek

[15]This change has been made very clear since a different priest, who is like Melchizedek, has appeared. [16]Jesus became a priest, not by meeting the physical requirement of belonging to the tribe of Levi, but by the power of a life that cannot be destroyed. [17]And the psalmist pointed this out when he prophesied,

"You are a priest forever in the order of
    Melchizedek."*

[18]Yes, the old requirement about the priesthood was set aside because it was weak and useless. [19]For the law never made anything perfect. But now we have confidence in a better hope, through which we draw near to God.

[20]This new system was established with a solemn oath. Aaron's descendants became priests without such an oath, [21]but there was an oath regarding Jesus. For God said to him,

"The LORD has taken an oath and will not
    break his vow:
   'You are a priest forever.'"*

[22]Because of this oath, Jesus is the one who guarantees this better covenant with God.

[23]There were many priests under the old system, for death prevented them from remaining in office. [24]But because Jesus lives forever, his priesthood lasts forever. [25]Therefore he is able, once and forever, to save* those who come to God through him. He lives forever to intercede with God on their behalf.

[26]He is the kind of high priest we need because he is holy and blameless, unstained by sin. He has been set apart from sinners and has been given the highest place of honor in heaven.* [27]Unlike those other high priests, he does not need to offer sacrifices every day. They did this for their own sins first and then for the sins of the people. But Jesus did this once for all when he offered himself as the sacrifice for the people's sins. [28]The law appointed high priests who were limited by human weakness. But after the law was given, God appointed his Son with an oath, and his Son has been made the perfect High Priest forever.

7:5 Greek *from their brothers.*   **7:11** Greek *the order of Aaron?*   **7:17** Ps 110:4.   **7:21** Ps 110:4.   **7:25** Or *is able to save completely.*   **7:26** Or *has been exalted higher than the heavens.*

CHAPTER 8
Christ Is Our High Priest

Here is the main point: We have a High Priest who sat down in the place of honor beside the throne of the majestic God in heaven. [2] There he ministers in the heavenly Tabernacle,* the true place of worship that was built by the Lord and not by human hands.

[3] And since every high priest is required to offer gifts and sacrifices, our High Priest must make an offering, too. [4] If he were here on earth, he would not even be a priest, since there already are priests who offer the gifts required by the law. [5] They serve in a system of worship that is only a copy, a shadow of the real one in heaven. For when Moses was getting ready to build the Tabernacle, God gave him this warning: "Be sure that you make everything according to the pattern I have shown you here on the mountain."*

[6] But now Jesus, our High Priest, has been given a ministry that is far superior to the old priesthood, for he is the one who mediates for us a far better covenant with God, based on better promises.

[7] If the first covenant had been faultless, there would have been no need for a second covenant to replace it. [8] But when God found fault with the people, he said:

"The day is coming, says the LORD,
   when I will make a new covenant
   with the people of Israel and Judah.
[9] This covenant will not be like the one
   I made with their ancestors
when I took them by the hand
   and led them out of the land of Egypt.
They did not remain faithful to my
      covenant,
   so I turned my back on them, says the
      LORD.
[10] But this is the new covenant I will make
   with the people of Israel on that day,*
      says the LORD:
I will put my laws in their minds,
   and I will write them on their hearts.
I will be their God,
   and they will be my people.
[11] And they will not need to teach their
      neighbors,
   nor will they need to teach their relatives,*
   saying, 'You should know the LORD.'
For everyone, from the least to the greatest,
   will know me already.
[12] And I will forgive their wickedness,
   and I will never again remember their
      sins."*

[13] When God speaks of a "new" covenant, it means he has made the first one obsolete. It is now out of date and will soon disappear.

CHAPTER 9
Old Rules about Worship

That first covenant between God and Israel had regulations for worship and a place of worship here on earth. [2] There were two rooms in that Tabernacle.* In the first room were a lampstand, a table, and sacred loaves of bread on the table. This room was called the Holy Place. [3] Then there was a curtain, and behind the curtain was the second room* called the Most Holy Place. [4] In that room were a gold incense altar and a wooden chest called the Ark of the Covenant, which was covered with gold on all sides. Inside the Ark were a gold jar containing manna, Aaron's staff that sprouted leaves, and the stone tablets of the covenant. [5] Above the Ark were the cherubim of divine glory, whose wings stretched out over the Ark's cover, the place of atonement. But we cannot explain these things in detail now.

[6] When these things were all in place, the priests regularly entered the first room* as they performed their religious duties. [7] But only the high priest ever entered the Most Holy Place, and only once a year. And he always offered blood for his own sins and for the sins the people had committed in ignorance. [8] By these regulations the Holy Spirit revealed that the entrance to the Most Holy Place was not freely open as long as the Tabernacle* and the system it represented were still in use.

[9] This is an illustration pointing to the present time. For the gifts and sacrifices that the priests offer are not able to cleanse the consciences of the people who bring them. [10] For that old system deals only with food and drink and various cleansing ceremonies—physical regulations that were in effect only until a better system could be established.

Christ Is the Perfect Sacrifice

[11] So Christ has now become the High Priest over all the good things that have come.* He has entered that greater, more perfect Tabernacle in heaven, which was not made by human hands and is not part of this created world. [12] With his own blood—not the blood of goats and calves—he entered the Most Holy Place once for all time and secured our redemption forever.

[13] Under the old system, the blood of goats and bulls and the ashes of a young cow could

---

8:2 Or *tent;* also in 8:5.   **8:5** Exod 25:40; 26:30.   **8:10** Greek *after those days.*   **8:11** Greek *their brother.*   **8:8-12** Jer 31:31-34.   **9:2** Or *tent;* also in 9:11, 21.   **9:3** Greek *second tent.*   **9:6** Greek *first tent.*   **9:8** Or *the first room;* Greek reads *the first tent.*   **9:11** Some manuscripts read *that are about to come.*

cleanse people's bodies from ceremonial impurity. [14]Just think how much more the blood of Christ will purify our consciences from sinful deeds* so that we can worship the living God. For by the power of the eternal Spirit, Christ offered himself to God as a perfect sacrifice for our sins. [15]That is why he is the one who mediates a new covenant between God and people, so that all who are called can receive the eternal inheritance God has promised them. For Christ died to set them free from the penalty of the sins they had committed under that first covenant.

[16]Now when someone leaves a will,* it is necessary to prove that the person who made it is dead.* [17]The will goes into effect only after the person's death. While the person who made it is still alive, the will cannot be put into effect.

[18]That is why even the first covenant was put into effect with the blood of an animal. [19]For after Moses had read each of God's commandments to all the people, he took the blood of calves and goats,* along with water, and sprinkled both the book of God's law and all the people, using hyssop branches and scarlet wool. [20]Then he said, "This blood confirms the covenant God has made with you."* [21]And in the same way, he sprinkled blood on the Tabernacle and on everything used for worship. [22]In fact, according to the law of Moses, nearly everything was purified with blood. For without the shedding of blood, there is no forgiveness.

[23]That is why the Tabernacle and everything in it, which were copies of things in heaven, had to be purified by the blood of animals. But the real things in heaven had to be purified with far better sacrifices than the blood of animals.

[24]For Christ did not enter into a holy place made with human hands, which was only a copy of the true one in heaven. He entered into heaven itself to appear now before God on our behalf. [25]And he did not enter heaven to offer himself again and again, like the high priest here on earth who enters the Most Holy Place year after year with the blood of an animal. [26]If that had been necessary, Christ would have had to die again and again, ever since the world began. But now, once for all time, he has appeared at the end of the age* to remove sin by his own death as a sacrifice.

[27]And just as each person is destined to die once and after that comes judgment, [28]so also Christ died once for all time as a sacrifice to

take away the sins of many people. He will come again, not to deal with our sins, but to bring salvation to all who are eagerly waiting for him.

CHAPTER **10**

Christ's Sacrifice Once for All

The old system under the law of Moses was only a shadow, a dim preview of the good things to come, not the good things themselves. The sacrifices under that system were repeated again and again, year after year, but they were never able to provide perfect cleansing for those who came to worship. [2]If they could have provided perfect cleansing, the sacrifices would have stopped, for the worshipers would have been purified once for all time, and their feelings of guilt would have disappeared.

[3]But instead, those sacrifices actually reminded them of their sins year after year. [4]For it is not possible for the blood of bulls and goats to take away sins. [5]That is why, when Christ* came into the world, he said to God,

"You did not want animal sacrifices or sin
    offerings.
    But you have given me a body to offer.
[6] You were not pleased with burnt offerings
    or other offerings for sin.
[7] Then I said, 'Look, I have come to do your
    will, O God—
    as is written about me in the
    Scriptures.'"*

[8]First, Christ said, "You did not want animal sacrifices or sin offerings or burnt offerings or other offerings for sin, nor were you pleased with them" (though they are required by the law of Moses). [9]Then he said, "Look, I have come to do your will." He cancels the first covenant in order to put the second into effect. [10]For God's will was for us to be made holy by the sacrifice of the body of Jesus Christ, once for all time.

[11]Under the old covenant, the priest stands and ministers before the altar day after day, offering the same sacrifices again and again, which can never take away sins. [12]But our High Priest offered himself to God as a single sacrifice for sins, good for all time. Then he sat down in the place of honor at God's right hand. [13]There he waits until his enemies are humbled and made a footstool under his feet. [14]For by that one offering he forever made perfect those who are being made holy.

[15]And the Holy Spirit also testifies that this is so. For he says,

---

9:14 Greek *from dead works.*   **9:16a** Or *covenant;* also in 9:17.   **9:16b** Or *Now when someone makes a covenant, it is necessary to ratify it with the death of a sacrifice.*   **9:19** Some manuscripts do not include *and goats.*   **9:20** Exod 24:8.   **9:26** Greek *the ages.*   **10:5** Greek *he;* also in 10:8.   **10:5-7** Ps 40:6-8 (Greek version).

16 "This is the new covenant I will make
   with my people on that day,* says the
   Lord:
I will put my laws in their hearts,
   and I will write them on their
   minds."*

17 Then he says,

"I will never again remember
   their sins and lawless deeds."*

18 And when sins have been forgiven, there is no
need to offer any more sacrifices.

A Call to Persevere

19 And so, dear brothers and sisters,* we can
boldly enter heaven's Most Holy Place because
of the blood of Jesus. 20 By his death,* Jesus
opened a new and life-giving way through the
curtain into the Most Holy Place. 21 And since
we have a great High Priest who rules over
God's house, 22 let us go right into the presence
of God with sincere hearts fully trusting him.
For our guilty consciences have been sprinkled
with Christ's blood to make us clean, and our
bodies have been washed with pure water.
   23 Let us hold tightly without wavering to the
hope we affirm, for God can be trusted to keep
his promise. 24 Let us think of ways to motivate
one another to acts of love and good works.
25 And let us not neglect our meeting together,
as some people do, but encourage one another,
especially now that the day of his return is
drawing near.
   26 Dear friends, if we deliberately continue
sinning after we have received knowledge of
the truth, there is no longer any sacrifice that
will cover these sins. 27 There is only the terrible expectation of God's judgment and the raging fire that will consume his enemies. 28 For
anyone who refused to obey the law of Moses
was put to death without mercy on the testimony of two or three witnesses. 29 Just think
how much worse the punishment will be for
those who have trampled on the Son of God,
and have treated the blood of the covenant,
which made us holy, as if it were common and
unholy, and have insulted and disdained the
Holy Spirit who brings God's mercy to us. 30 For
we know the one who said,

"I will take revenge.
   I will pay them back."*

He also said,

"The Lord will judge his own people."*

10:16a Greek *after those days.*   10:16b Jer 31:33a.
10:17 Jer 31:34b.   10:19 Greek *brothers.*   10:20 Greek
Through his flesh.   10:30a Deut 32:35.   10:30b Deut
32:36.

Read HEBREWS 10:25

first steps

WHY WE NEED FELLOWSHIP WITH OTHER BELIEVERS

Involvement in a local church is necessary for
the spiritual growth of all Christians, and it is
something we never outgrow. For the new
believer, moreover, such interaction is critical
for four reasons:

**1. Fellowship Provides Us with Encourage-
ment and Love.** As Christians, we need a place
where we can be encouraged in our faith and
be reminded that we are a member of God's
family. When we go to church, we are surrounded by others who share our love for
Christ. Being in the presence of other believers
can encourage us to live for Christ, as well as
give us a sense of belonging and acceptance
that we don't receive from the world.

**2. Fellowship Allows Us to Learn from
Spiritually Mature Christians.** In the biblical
account of the early church, we are told how
the apostle Paul's friends, Priscilla and Aquila,
took time to help another believer learn more
about Jesus (see Acts 18:26, p. 154). Likewise,
younger Christians in the church today will
have the opportunity to gain spiritual wisdom
and insight from more mature Christians.

**3. Fellowship Helps Us Discern False
Teachings.** The Bible warns of false teachers
and teachings, to which the young believer is
especially susceptible because he or she lacks
basic Bible understanding. A healthy, Bible-
teaching church will encourage young believers
in their growth and help them discern truth
from error.

**4. Fellowship Prepares Us for Christ's
Return.** As the day for Christ's return comes
closer, we need to help each other through difficult times and keep our problems in perspective. We also need to encourage each other to
live holy lives and to share God's Good News
with others in the time that remains. God
wants the body of Christ to stand out and be a
light in these ever darkening days.

*For the next note on "Look for and Attend
the Right Church," turn to p. 229.*

cornerstones

CHRIST ENDURED GREAT PAIN FOR US
Read HEBREWS 12:1-3

Throughout the New Testament, the Christian life is compared to a race. With that in mind, we need to realize that it is not a short sprint, but a long-distance run. Sometimes, as we are participating in this race, we can grow discouraged by circumstances or by what others say to us. But just as a successful runner must "keep his eyes on the prize," we, too, must remember what this race is all about. We must bear in mind for whom and to whom we are running: Jesus Christ. In essence, we need to "[keep] our eyes on Jesus."

Corrie ten Boom, a Dutch Christian who survived the horrors of Hitler's concentration camps during World War II, often said, "Look within and be depressed. Look without and be distressed. Look at Jesus and be at rest."

God will see us through to the end. He has given us his word: "And I am certain that God, who began the good work within you, will continue his work until it is finally finished on the day when Christ Jesus returns" (Philippians 1:6).

To begin the next topic, turn to p. A31.

---

³¹ It is a terrible thing to fall into the hands of the living God.

³² Think back on those early days when you first learned about Christ.* Remember how you remained faithful even though it meant terrible suffering. ³³ Sometimes you were exposed to public ridicule and were beaten, and sometimes you helped others who were suffering the same things. ³⁴ You suffered along with those who were thrown into jail, and when all you owned was taken from you, you accepted it with joy. You knew there were better things waiting for you that will last forever.

³⁵ So do not throw away this confident trust in the Lord. Remember the great reward it brings you! ³⁶ Patient endurance is what you need now, so that you will continue to do God's will. Then you will receive all that he has promised.

³⁷ "For in just a little while,
    the Coming One will come and not delay.
³⁸ And my righteous ones will live by faith.*
    But I will take no pleasure in anyone who
        turns away."*

³⁹ But we are not like those who turn away from God to their own destruction. We are the faithful ones, whose souls will be saved.

CHAPTER 11
Great Examples of Faith
Faith is the confidence that what we hope for will actually happen; it gives us assurance about things we cannot see. ² Through their faith, the people in days of old earned a good reputation.

³ By faith we understand that the entire universe was formed at God's command, that what we now see did not come from anything that can be seen.

⁴ It was by faith that Abel brought a more acceptable offering to God than Cain did. Abel's offering gave evidence that he was a righteous man, and God showed his approval of his gifts. Although Abel is long dead, he still speaks to us by his example of faith.

⁵ It was by faith that Enoch was taken up to heaven without dying—"he disappeared, because God took him."* For before he was taken up, he was known as a person who pleased God. ⁶ And it is impossible to please God without faith. Anyone who wants to come to him must believe that God exists and that he rewards those who sincerely seek him.

⁷ It was by faith that Noah built a large boat to save his family from the flood. He obeyed God, who warned him about things that had never happened before. By his faith Noah condemned the rest of the world, and he received the righteousness that comes by faith.

⁸ It was by faith that Abraham obeyed when God called him to leave home and go to another land that God would give him as his inheritance. He went without knowing where he was going. ⁹ And even when he reached the land God promised him, he lived there by faith—for he was like a foreigner, living in tents. And so

10:32 Greek *when you were first enlightened.*   **10:38** Or *my righteous ones will live by their faithfulness;* Greek reads *my righteous one will live by faith.*   **10:37-38** Hab 2:3-4.   **11:5** Gen 5:24.

did Isaac and Jacob, who inherited the same promise. [10]Abraham was confidently looking forward to a city with eternal foundations, a city designed and built by God.

[11]It was by faith that even Sarah was able to have a child, though she was barren and was too old. She believed* that God would keep his promise. [12]And so a whole nation came from this one man who was as good as dead—a nation with so many people that, like the stars in the sky and the sand on the seashore, there is no way to count them.

[13]All these people died still believing what God had promised them. They did not receive what was promised, but they saw it all from a distance and welcomed it. They agreed that they were foreigners and nomads here on earth. [14]Obviously people who say such things are looking forward to a country they can call their own. [15]If they had longed for the country they came from, they could have gone back. [16]But they were looking for a better place, a heavenly homeland. That is why God is not ashamed to be called their God, for he has prepared a city for them.

[17]It was by faith that Abraham offered Isaac as a sacrifice when God was testing him. Abraham, who had received God's promises, was ready to sacrifice his only son, Isaac, [18]even though God had told him, "Isaac is the son through whom your descendants will be counted."* [19]Abraham reasoned that if Isaac died, God was able to bring him back to life again. And in a sense, Abraham did receive his son back from the dead.

[20]It was by faith that Isaac promised blessings for the future to his sons, Jacob and Esau.

[21]It was by faith that Jacob, when he was old and dying, blessed each of Joseph's sons and bowed in worship as he leaned on his staff.

[22]It was by faith that Joseph, when he was about to die, said confidently that the people of Israel would leave Egypt. He even commanded them to take his bones with them when they left.

[23]It was by faith that Moses' parents hid him for three months when he was born. They saw that God had given them an unusual child, and they were not afraid to disobey the king's command.

[24]It was by faith that Moses, when he grew up, refused to be called the son of Pharaoh's daughter. [25]He chose to share the oppression of God's people instead of enjoying the fleeting pleasures of sin. [26]He thought it was better to suffer for the sake of Christ than to own the treasures of Egypt, for he was looking ahead to

his great reward. [27]It was by faith that Moses left the land of Egypt, not fearing the king's anger. He kept right on going because he kept his eyes on the one who is invisible. [28]It was by faith that Moses commanded the people of Israel to keep the Passover and to sprinkle blood on the doorposts so that the angel of death would not kill their firstborn sons.

[29]It was by faith that the people of Israel went right through the Red Sea as though they were on dry ground. But when the Egyptians tried to follow, they were all drowned.

[30]It was by faith that the people of Israel marched around Jericho for seven days, and the walls came crashing down.

[31]It was by faith that Rahab the prostitute was not destroyed with the people in her city who refused to obey God. For she had given a friendly welcome to the spies.

[32]How much more do I need to say? It would take too long to recount the stories of the faith of Gideon, Barak, Samson, Jephthah, David, Samuel, and all the prophets. [33]By faith these people overthrew kingdoms, ruled with justice, and received what God had promised them. They shut the mouths of lions, [34]quenched the flames of fire, and escaped death by the edge of the sword. Their weakness was turned to strength. They became strong in battle and put whole armies to flight. [35]Women received their loved ones back again from death.

But others were tortured, refusing to turn from God in order to be set free. They placed their hope in a better life after the resurrection. [36]Some were jeered at, and their backs were cut open with whips. Others were chained in prisons. [37]Some died by stoning, some were sawed in half,* and others were killed with the sword. Some went about wearing skins of sheep and goats, destitute and oppressed and mistreated. [38]They were too good for this world, wandering over deserts and mountains, hiding in caves and holes in the ground.

[39]All these people earned a good reputation because of their faith, yet none of them received all that God had promised. [40]For God had something better in mind for us, so that they would not reach perfection without us.

CHAPTER 12

God's Discipline Proves His Love

Therefore, since we are surrounded by such a huge crowd of witnesses to the life of faith, let us strip off every weight that slows us down, especially the sin that so easily trips us up. And let us run with endurance the race God has set before us. [2]We do this by keeping our eyes on

11:11 Or *It was by faith that he [Abraham] was able to have a child, even though Sarah was barren and he was too old. He believed.*   11:18 Gen 21:12.   11:37 Some manuscripts add *some were tested.*

Jesus, the champion who initiates and perfects our faith.* Because of the joy* awaiting him, he endured the cross, disregarding its shame. Now he is seated in the place of honor beside God's throne. ³Think of all the hostility he endured from sinful people;* then you won't become weary and give up. ⁴After all, you have not yet given your lives in your struggle against sin.

⁵And have you forgotten the encouraging words God spoke to you as his children?* He said,

"My child,* don't make light of the LORD's discipline,
    and don't give up when he corrects you.
⁶ For the LORD disciplines those he loves,
    and he punishes each one he accepts as his child."*

⁷As you endure this divine discipline, remember that God is treating you as his own children. Who ever heard of a child who is never disciplined by its father? ⁸If God doesn't discipline you as he does all of his children, it means that you are illegitimate and are not really his children at all. ⁹Since we respected our earthly fathers who disciplined us, shouldn't we submit even more to the discipline of the Father of our spirits, and live forever?*

¹⁰For our earthly fathers disciplined us for a few years, doing the best they knew how. But God's discipline is always good for us, so that we might share in his holiness. ¹¹No discipline is enjoyable while it is happening—it's painful! But afterward there will be a peaceful harvest of right living for those who are trained in this way.

¹²So take a new grip with your tired hands and strengthen your weak knees. ¹³Mark out a straight path for your feet so that those who are weak and lame will not fall but become strong.

A Call to Listen to God

¹⁴Work at living in peace with everyone, and work at living a holy life, for those who are not holy will not see the Lord. ¹⁵Look after each other so that none of you fails to receive the grace of God. Watch out that no poisonous root of bitterness grows up to trouble you, corrupting many. ¹⁶Make sure that no one is immoral or godless like Esau, who traded his birthright as the firstborn son for a single meal. ¹⁷You know that afterward, when he wanted his father's blessing, he was rejected. It was too late for repentance, even though he begged with bitter tears.

¹⁸You have not come to a physical mountain,* to a place of flaming fire, darkness, gloom, and whirlwind, as the Israelites did at Mount Sinai. ¹⁹For they heard an awesome trumpet blast and a voice so terrible that they begged God to stop speaking. ²⁰They staggered back under God's command: "If even an animal touches the mountain, it must be stoned to death."* ²¹Moses himself was so frightened at the sight that he said, "I am terrified and trembling."*

²²No, you have come to Mount Zion, to the city of the living God, the heavenly Jerusalem, and to countless thousands of angels in a joyful gathering. ²³You have come to the assembly of God's firstborn children, whose names are written in heaven. You have come to God him-

---

12:2a Or *Jesus, the originator and perfecter of our faith.*   **12:2b** Or *Instead of the joy.*   **12:3** Some manuscripts read *Think of how people hurt themselves by opposing him.*   **12:5a** Greek *sons;* also in 12:7, 8.   **12:5b** Greek *son;* also in 12:6, 7.
12:5-6 Prov 3:11-12 (Greek version).   **12:9** Or *and really live?*   **12:18** Greek *to something that can be touched.*
12:20 Exod 19:13.   **12:21** Deut 9:19.

---

off and running

KEEPING YOUR MARRIAGE STRONG
Read HEBREWS 13:4

Tragically, many people do not take marriage seriously today. They forget that their vows are made before God and include the words "till death do us part." So what steps can you take to keep from becoming another marriage "casualty"? Here are four principles that will help you to maintain a strong and flourishing marriage:

1. Walk with God. As you cultivate and deepen your fellowship with God, you will have the power, the will, and the resources to stand when temptation comes knocking.

2. Walk with Your Spouse. Keep the friendship and romance alive in your marriage. Remember what you did when you first started courting your spouse. Compliment one another. Spend time together. Be genuinely interested in one

self, who is the judge over all things. You have come to the spirits of the righteous ones in heaven who have now been made perfect. ²⁴You have come to Jesus, the one who mediates the new covenant between God and people, and to the sprinkled blood, which speaks of forgiveness instead of crying out for vengeance like the blood of Abel.

²⁵Be careful that you do not refuse to listen to the One who is speaking. For if the people of Israel did not escape when they refused to listen to Moses, the earthly messenger, we will certainly not escape if we reject the One who speaks to us from heaven! ²⁶When God spoke from Mount Sinai his voice shook the earth, but now he makes another promise: "Once again I will shake not only the earth but the heavens also."* ²⁷This means that all of creation will be shaken and removed, so that only unshakable things will remain.

²⁸Since we are receiving a Kingdom that is unshakable, let us be thankful and please God by worshiping him with holy fear and awe. ²⁹For our God is a devouring fire.

CHAPTER **13**

Concluding Words

Keep on loving each other as brothers and sisters.* ²Don't forget to show hospitality to strangers, for some who have done this have entertained angels without realizing it! ³Remember those in prison, as if you were there yourself. Remember also those being mistreated, as if you felt their pain in your own bodies.

⁴Give honor to marriage, and remain faithful to one another in marriage. God will surely judge people who are immoral and those who commit adultery.

⁵Don't love money; be satisfied with what you have. For God has said,

"I will never fail you.
    I will never abandon you."*

⁶So we can say with confidence,

"The LORD is my helper,
    so I will have no fear.
What can mere people do to me?"*

⁷Remember your leaders who taught you the word of God. Think of all the good that has come from their lives, and follow the example of their faith.

⁸Jesus Christ is the same yesterday, today, and forever. ⁹So do not be attracted by strange, new ideas. Your strength comes from God's grace, not from rules about food, which don't help those who follow them.

¹⁰We have an altar from which the priests in the Tabernacle* have no right to eat. ¹¹Under the old system, the high priest brought the blood of animals into the Holy Place as a sacrifice for sin, and the bodies of the animals were burned outside the camp. ¹²So also Jesus suffered and died outside the city gates to make his people holy by means of his own blood. ¹³So let us go out to him, outside the camp, and bear the disgrace he bore. ¹⁴For this world is not our permanent home; we are looking forward to a home yet to come.

¹⁵Therefore, let us offer through Jesus a continual sacrifice of praise to God, proclaiming our allegiance to his name. ¹⁶And don't forget

12:26 Hag 2:6.   13:1 Greek *Continue in brotherly love.*   13:5 Deut 31:6, 8.   13:6 Ps 118:6.   13:10 Or *tent.*

---

another's lives. Try your best to look attractive for each other. Treat your partner with respect. Take practical steps to keep that fire of love burning.

3. Don't Walk on Thin Ice. Psalm 1 warns of the dangers of close relationships with those who do not love God as you do. You must avoid potentially dangerous and flirtatious relationships at all costs. Find Christian friends (of the same sex) who can be honest with you if they think you are heading into dangerous territory.

4. Count the Cost. Remember the price that comes with adultery and immorality. Are you ready to face the shame? Are you prepared for the disgrace and distrust you will bring upon your spouse and children—as well as the cause of Christ? A few moments of pleasure will result in a lifetime of regret.

An intense love for God and for your husband or wife will see you through the rough waters of sexual temptation. Don't be an easy target for Satan's arrows. Keep moving forward in your relationship with Christ and with your spouse.

For the next note on "Marriage," turn to p. 50.

to do good and to share with those in need. These are the sacrifices that please God.

¹⁷Obey your spiritual leaders, and do what they say. Their work is to watch over your souls, and they are accountable to God. Give them reason to do this with joy and not with sorrow. That would certainly not be for your benefit.

¹⁸Pray for us, for our conscience is clear and we want to live honorably in everything we do. ¹⁹And especially pray that I will be able to come back to you soon.

²⁰ Now may the God of peace—
who brought up from the dead our Lord Jesus,
the great Shepherd of the sheep,
and ratified an eternal covenant with his blood—

²¹ may he equip you with all you need
for doing his will.
May he produce in you,*
through the power of Jesus Christ,
every good thing that is pleasing to him.
All glory to him forever and ever!
Amen.

²²I urge you, dear brothers and sisters,* to pay attention to what I have written in this brief exhortation.

²³I want you to know that our brother Timothy has been released from jail. If he comes here soon, I will bring him with me to see you.

²⁴Greet all your leaders and all the believers there.* The believers from Italy send you their greetings.

²⁵May God's grace be with you all.

13:21 Some manuscripts read *in us.*   13:22 Greek *brothers.*   13:24 Greek *all of God's holy people.*

---

off and running
OUR NEEDS MUST COME LAST
Read HEBREWS 13:11-13

Jesus gave us the ultimate example to follow in meekness. Jesus, who is God, came to this earth and humbled himself in an incredible way by becoming a man. It is important to note that he never at any time ceased being God. But he did lay aside the privileges of deity to experience genuine human conditions, such as sorrow, anger, weariness, and pain (see Philippians 2:3-11, pp. 238-239). Yet the most dramatic act of his meekness came when he humbled himself to be crucified on a cross. Although he was led away to die, no one took his life. Jesus could have called down legions of angels to rescue him. But instead he "suffered and died" for us.

How should Christ's attitude affect the way we treat others? In short, we must put the needs of others before our own. During Jesus' earthly ministry, he always had time for others. We should follow his example. Here is a simple acrostic that will help you keep your priorities in order:

J is for Jesus.
O is for others.
Y is for yourself.

If you put the will of God first and the needs of others above your own, you will experience joy.

For the next note on "Attitude toward Self," turn to p. 32.

James

AUTHOR: JAMES, JESUS' HALF-BROTHER | DATE WRITTEN: A.D. 49 | GENRE: EPISTLE

James spoke about faith in his book, with an emphasis on results. He stressed the need to live a practical, working faith.

CHAPTER 1

Greetings from James

This letter is from James, a slave of God and of the Lord Jesus Christ.

I am writing to the "twelve tribes"—Jewish believers scattered abroad.

Greetings!

Faith and Endurance

²Dear brothers and sisters,* when troubles come your way, consider it an opportunity for great joy. ³For you know that when your faith is tested, your endurance has a chance to grow. ⁴So let it grow, for when your endurance is fully developed, you will be perfect and complete, needing nothing.

⁵If you need wisdom, ask our generous God, and he will give it to you. He will not rebuke you for asking. ⁶But when you ask him, be sure that your faith is in God alone. Do not waver, for a person with divided loyalty is as unsettled as a wave of the sea that is blown and tossed by the wind. ⁷Such people should not expect to receive anything from the Lord. ⁸Their loyalty is divided between God and the world, and they are unstable in everything they do.

⁹Believers who are* poor have something to boast about, for God has honored them. ¹⁰And those who are rich should boast that God has humbled them. They will fade away like a little flower in the field. ¹¹The hot sun rises and the grass withers; the little flower droops and falls, and its beauty fades away. In the same way, the rich will fade away with all of their achievements.

¹²God blesses those who patiently endure testing and temptation. Afterward they will receive the crown of life that God has promised to those who love him. ¹³And remember, when you are being tempted, do not say, "God is tempting me." God is never tempted to do wrong,* and he never tempts anyone else. ¹⁴Temptation comes from our own desires, which entice us and drag us away. ¹⁵These desires give birth to sinful actions. And when sin is allowed to grow, it gives birth to death.

¹⁶So don't be misled, my dear brothers and sisters. ¹⁷Whatever is good and perfect comes down to us from God our Father, who created all the lights in the heavens.* He never changes or casts a shifting shadow.* ¹⁸He chose to give birth to us by giving us his true word. And we, out of all creation, became his prized possession.*

Listening and Doing

¹⁹Understand this, my dear brothers and sisters: You must all be quick to listen, slow to speak, and slow to get angry. ²⁰Human anger* does not produce the righteousness* God desires. ²¹So get rid of all the filth and evil in your lives, and humbly accept the word God has planted in your hearts, for it has the power to save your souls.

²²But don't just listen to God's word. You must do what it says. Otherwise, you are only fooling yourselves. ²³For if you listen to the word and don't obey, it is like glancing at your face in a mirror. ²⁴You see yourself, walk away, and forget what you look like. ²⁵But if you look

---

1:2 Greek *brothers;* also in 1:16, 19.　1:9 Greek *The brother who is.*　1:13 Or *God should not be put to a test by evil people.*　1:17a Greek *from above, from the Father of lights.*　1:17b Some manuscripts read *He never changes, as a shifting shadow does.*　1:18 Greek *we became a kind of firstfruit of his creatures.*　1:20a Greek *A man's anger.*　1:20b Or *the justice.*

cornerstones

LIFE'S TRIALS WILL MAKE YOU STRONGER
Read JAMES 1:2-4

One of the keys to growing and being able to effectively continue in the Christian life is enduring. A key aspect of endurance is patience. The word used for "endurance" in verse 3 is the Greek word *hupomone,* which means "a patient enduring."

This cheerful, enduring patience, which helps us to continue in our Christian walk, actually comes—and develops—in times of testing and hardship. During these trials or "storms of life," our spiritual roots grow deeper, thus strengthening our faith. If we had our way, most of us would probably try to avoid these difficult times in our lives. Yet God promises that he will never give us more than we can handle (see 1 Corinthians 10:13, p. 200).

These times of trial and testing will make us either better or bitter. It really is up to us and the outlook we choose to take. If we can learn to walk in our relationship with God on the basis of faith as opposed to mere feeling, we will grow stronger and, as this passage says, "be perfect and complete, needing nothing."

For the next note on "Perseverance," turn to p. 284.

---

carefully into the perfect law that sets you free, and if you do what it says and don't forget what you heard, then God will bless you for doing it.

²⁶ If you claim to be religious but don't control your tongue, you are fooling yourself, and your religion is worthless. ²⁷ Pure and genuine religion in the sight of God the Father means caring for orphans and widows in their distress and refusing to let the world corrupt you.

CHAPTER 2
A Warning against Prejudice
My dear brothers and sisters,* how can you claim to have faith in our glorious Lord Jesus Christ if you favor some people over others?

² For example, suppose someone comes into your meeting* dressed in fancy clothes and expensive jewelry, and another comes in who is poor and dressed in dirty clothes. ³ If you give special attention and a good seat to the rich person, but you say to the poor one, "You can stand over there, or else sit on the floor"—well, ⁴ doesn't this discrimination show that your judgments are guided by evil motives?

⁵ Listen to me, dear brothers and sisters. Hasn't God chosen the poor in this world to be rich in faith? Aren't they the ones who will inherit the Kingdom he promised to those who love him? ⁶ But you dishonor the poor! Isn't it the rich who oppress you and drag you into court? ⁷ Aren't they the ones who slander Jesus Christ, whose noble name* you bear?

⁸ Yes indeed, it is good when you obey the royal law as found in the Scriptures: "Love your neighbor as yourself."* ⁹ But if you favor some people over others, you are committing a sin. You are guilty of breaking the law.

¹⁰ For the person who keeps all of the laws except one is as guilty as a person who has broken all of God's laws. ¹¹ For the same God who said, "You must not commit adultery," also said, "You must not murder."* So if you murder someone but do not commit adultery, you have still broken the law.

¹² So whatever you say or whatever you do, remember that you will be judged by the law that sets you free. ¹³ There will be no mercy for those who have not shown mercy to others. But if you have been merciful, God will be merciful when he judges you.

Faith without Good Deeds Is Dead
¹⁴ What good is it, dear brothers and sisters, if you say you have faith but don't show it by your actions? Can that kind of faith save anyone? ¹⁵ Suppose you see a brother or sister who has no food or clothing, ¹⁶ and you say, "Good-bye and have a good day; stay warm and eat well"— but then you don't give that person any food or clothing. What good does that do?

¹⁷ So you see, faith by itself isn't enough. Unless it produces good deeds, it is dead and useless.

¹⁸ Now someone may argue, "Some people have faith; others have good deeds." But I say, "How can you show me your faith if you don't have good deeds? I will show you my faith by my good deeds."

2:1 Greek *brothers;* also in 2:5, 14.   2:2 Greek *your synagogue.*   2:7 Greek *slander the noble name.*   2:8 Lev 19:18.
2:11 Exod 20:13-14; Deut 5:17-18.

¹⁹You say you have faith, for you believe that there is one God.* Good for you! Even the demons believe this, and they tremble in terror. ²⁰How foolish! Can't you see that faith without good deeds is useless?

²¹Don't you remember that our ancestor Abraham was shown to be right with God by his actions when he offered his son Isaac on the altar? ²²You see, his faith and his actions worked together. His actions made his faith complete. ²³And so it happened just as the Scriptures say: "Abraham believed God, and God counted him as righteous because of his faith."* He was even called the friend of God.* ²⁴So you see, we are shown to be right with God by what we do, not by faith alone.

²⁵Rahab the prostitute is another example. She was shown to be right with God by her actions when she hid those messengers and sent them safely away by a different road. ²⁶Just as the body is dead without breath,* so also faith is dead without good works.

CHAPTER **3**

Controlling the Tongue

Dear brothers and sisters,* not many of you should become teachers in the church, for we who teach will be judged more strictly. ²Indeed, we all make many mistakes. For if we could control our tongues, we would be perfect and could also control ourselves in every other way.

³We can make a large horse go wherever we want by means of a small bit in its mouth. ⁴And a small rudder makes a huge ship turn wherever the pilot chooses to go, even though the winds are strong. ⁵In the same way, the tongue is a small thing that makes grand speeches.

But a tiny spark can set a great forest on fire. ⁶And the tongue is a flame of fire. It is a whole world of wickedness, corrupting your entire body. It can set your whole life on fire, for it is set on fire by hell itself.*

⁷People can tame all kinds of animals, birds, reptiles, and fish, ⁸but no one can tame the tongue. It is restless and evil, full of deadly poison. ⁹Sometimes it praises our Lord and Father, and sometimes it curses those who have been made in the image of God. ¹⁰And so blessing and cursing come pouring out of the same mouth. Surely, my brothers and sisters, this is not right! ¹¹Does a spring of water bubble out with both fresh water and bitter water? ¹²Does a fig tree produce olives, or a grapevine produce figs? No, and you can't draw fresh water from a salty spring.*

first steps

PRAYER ALLOWS US TO VOICE OUR REQUESTS TO GOD
Read JAMES 4:2-3

There may come a time in your life when you wonder why you are not growing in your faith. Or you might wonder why you don't ever have the opportunity to lead others to Christ. When you ask yourself these kinds of questions, you may be able to answer them with another question: "Have I asked God to help me in this area?"

Understand that this passage does not advocate that you *demand* things from God as though he were some "cosmic butler," prepared to answer your every beck and call. Yet it is equally wrong to fail to ask him to help meet your needs or to bless your life and spiritually strengthen you. God wants to bless you because you are his child. Unfortunately, many of us fail to receive what God has for us because we don't pray.

Take a moment to look at your own spiritual progress. Do you want to have a better understanding of the Bible? Are you looking for some Christian friends? Do you want the Lord to show you what your gifts and talents are? God wants to bless you, but he may be just waiting for your invitation for him to do so.

For the next note on "Pray," turn to p. 241.

True Wisdom Comes from God

¹³If you are wise and understand God's ways, prove it by living an honorable life, doing good works with the humility that comes from wisdom. ¹⁴But if you are bitterly jealous and there is selfish ambition in your heart, don't cover up the truth with boasting and lying. ¹⁵For jealousy and selfishness are not God's kind of wisdom. Such things are earthly, unspiritual, and demonic. ¹⁶For wherever there is jealousy and selfish ambition, there you will find disorder and evil of every kind.

¹⁷But the wisdom from above is first of all pure. It is also peace loving, gentle at all times, and willing to yield to others. It is full of mercy and good deeds. It shows no favoritism and is always sincere. ¹⁸And those who are

---

2:19 Some manuscripts read *that God is one;* see Deut 6:4.   **2:23a** Gen 15:6.   **2:23b** See Isa 41:8.   **2:26** Or *without spirit.*
3:1 Greek *brothers;* also in 3:10.   **3:6** Or *for it will burn in hell* (Greek *Gehenna*).   **3:12** Greek *from salt.*

cornerstones

WE MUST LIVE OUT OUR FAITH
Read JAMES 2:14-17

While you do not need to change your lifestyle before you come to Christ, once you do come to Christ, your lifestyle should show tangible changes. If it does not, then one could doubt whether Christ has really come into your life. The way you live should reflect what you believe. As John the Baptist said, "Prove by the way you live that you have repented of your sins and turned to God" (Luke 3:8).

James brings out another important reason for backing up our faith with our actions in verses 15 and 16: It makes it easier to share our faith with others. When people see that we genuinely care about them as individuals, then they will be much more open to hearing about what motivates us.

Can people see Jesus in the way you live? If not, it is time to move Jesus into the "driver's seat" of your life.

For the next note on "Faith and Works," turn to p. 230.

---

peacemakers will plant seeds of peace and reap a harvest of righteousness.*

CHAPTER **4**
Drawing Close to God
What is causing the quarrels and fights among you? Don't they come from the evil desires at war within you? ² You want what you don't have, so you scheme and kill to get it. You are jealous of what others have, but you can't get it, so you fight and wage war to take it away from them. Yet you don't have what you want because you don't ask God for it. ³And even when you ask, you don't get it because your motives are all wrong—you want only what will give you pleasure.

⁴You adulterers!* Don't you realize that friendship with the world makes you an enemy

3:18 Or *of good things,* or *of justice.*   **4:4** Greek *You adulteresses!*

---

off and running

CONTROL YOUR TONGUE
Read JAMES 3:1-12

It has been said that "A lie is halfway around the world while truth is still putting its shoes on." This illustrates the power of malicious speech. One unfounded rumor, one careless remark, one morsel of gossip can cause the greatest devastation. How correct James was when he wrote that the tongue is a flame of fire and full of wickedness.

Unfortunately, it is the sins of the tongue—backbiting, gossip, and tearing down another person—that we often excuse. We think that because we do not murder, commit adultery, or steal we are basically good people. But James makes it clear that certain kinds of speech are wrong. The content of a Christian's conversation should reflect what has happened in his or her heart. After all, part of the fruit, or evidence, of the Holy Spirit's presence in our lives is self-control (see Galatians 5:22-23, p. 226). The person who has no control over his or her tongue is usually out of control in other areas of life. But the person who has discipline over this area of life has yielded to the control of the Holy Spirit and will undoubtedly be able to keep other areas of his or her life in check as well.

For the next note on "Conversation," turn to p. 16.

of God? I say it again: If you want to be a friend of the world, you make yourself an enemy of God. [5] What do you think the Scriptures mean when they say that the spirit God has placed within us is filled with envy?* [6] But he gives us even more grace to stand against such evil desires. As the Scriptures say,

> "God opposes the proud
> but favors the humble."*

[7] So humble yourselves before God. Resist the devil, and he will flee from you. [8] Come close to God, and God will come close to you. Wash your hands, you sinners; purify your hearts, for your loyalty is divided between God and the world. [9] Let there be tears for what you have done. Let there be sorrow and deep grief. Let there be sadness instead of laughter, and gloom instead of joy. [10] Humble yourselves before the Lord, and he will lift you up in honor.

Warning against Judging Others

[11] Don't speak evil against each other, dear brothers and sisters.* If you criticize and judge each other, then you are criticizing and judging God's law. But your job is to obey the law, not to judge whether it applies to you. [12] God alone, who gave the law, is the Judge. He alone has the power to save or to destroy. So what right do you have to judge your neighbor?

Warning about Self-Confidence

[13] Look here, you who say, "Today or tomorrow we are going to a certain town and will stay there a year. We will do business there and make a profit." [14] How do you know what your life will be like tomorrow? Your life is like the morning fog—it's here a little while, then it's gone. [15] What you ought to say is, "If the Lord wants us to, we will live and do this or that." [16] Otherwise you are boasting about your own plans, and all such boasting is evil.

[17] Remember, it is sin to know what you ought to do and then not do it.

CHAPTER 5

Warning to the Rich

Look here, you rich people: Weep and groan with anguish because of all the terrible troubles ahead of you. [2] Your wealth is rotting away, and your fine clothes are moth-eaten rags. [3] Your gold and silver have become worthless. The very wealth you were counting on will eat away your flesh like fire. This treasure you have

---

first steps

RESIST THE DEVIL

Read JAMES 4:7-8

Satan recognizes the value of getting a foothold in the realm of our thoughts. He knows that sin is not merely a matter of actions and deeds, but something within the heart and the mind that eventually leads to the sinful action. Here are four practical and effective ways to resist the Devil and his temptations:

1. Submit Yourself to God. When you submit yourself to God, you are acknowledging his authority in your life. Because God is holy, which means pure and without sin, he will help you live a life that is pleasing to him. But in order to do this, you must submit to his authority.

2. Resist the Devil. To resist the devil means to not give in to temptation when it presents itself. Giving in to temptation is an open invitation for the devil and his demons to continually tempt you. But if you resist giving in to sin, the devil will flee from you, meaning that he will give up tempting you for the time being.

3. Draw Close to God. The closer you get to God, the more you distance yourself from your old partner, the devil. And the more time you spend with the Lord, through Bible study and prayer, the less likely you will be to fall. As Psalm 16:8 says, "I know the LORD is always with me. I will not be shaken, for he is right beside me."

4. Wash Your Hands and Purify Your Hearts. This set of instructions is a call to repentance for all those who are harboring sin in their life. To harbor sin in your life is to give the devil an opportunity to work in you and through you. But God is the one who should work in your life, not the devil. If you are harboring sin in any area of your life, stop doing it, confess it to God, and ask him to forgive you and then work through you.

For the next note on "Resist Temptation," *turn to p. 201.*

4:5 Or *that God longs jealously for the human spirit he has placed within us?* or *that the Holy Spirit, whom God has placed within us, opposes our envy?* **4:6** Prov 3:34 (Greek version). **4:11** Greek *brothers.*

cornerstones

WHAT DO DEMONS BELIEVE?

Read JAMES 2:19

Believe it or not, in some ways demons are quite orthodox in their beliefs. They recognize that Jesus is indeed the Son of God. In Matthew's Gospel, the demons say to Jesus, "Why are you interfering with us, Son of God? Have you come here to torture us before God's appointed time?" (Matthew 8:29). Clearly the demons understand Jesus' awesome power—and they shudder in fear at the thought of him!

Interestingly enough, many people today do not even accept that Jesus is God's Son. Yet, even if you do believe in God, these verses show that it is not enough to keep you from going to hell. Belief without obedience is worthless. Those who settle for less than a total commitment to Christ may find themselves in the company of the demons at the time of judgment.

For the next note on "What Are Demons?" turn to p. 158.

---

accumulated will stand as evidence against you on the day of judgment. ⁴For listen! Hear the cries of the field workers whom you have cheated of their pay. The wages you held back cry out against you. The cries of those who harvest your fields have reached the ears of the LORD of Heaven's Armies.

⁵You have spent your years on earth in luxury, satisfying your every desire. You have fattened yourselves for the day of slaughter. ⁶You have condemned and killed innocent people,* who do not resist you.*

Patience and Endurance

⁷Dear brothers and sisters,* be patient as you wait for the Lord's return. Consider the farmers who patiently wait for the rains in the fall and in the spring. They eagerly look for the valuable harvest to ripen. ⁸You, too, must be patient. Take courage, for the coming of the Lord is near.

⁹Don't grumble about each other, brothers and sisters, or you will be judged. For look—the Judge is standing at the door!

¹⁰For examples of patience in suffering, dear brothers and sisters, look at the prophets who spoke in the name of the Lord. ¹¹We give great honor to those who endure under suffering. For instance, you know about Job, a man of great endurance. You can see how the Lord was kind to him at the end, for the Lord is full of tenderness and mercy.

¹²But most of all, my brothers and sisters, never take an oath, by heaven or earth or anything else. Just say a simple yes or no, so that you will not sin and be condemned.

The Power of Prayer

¹³Are any of you suffering hardships? You should pray. Are any of you happy? You should sing praises. ¹⁴Are any of you sick? You should call for the elders of the church to come and pray over you, anointing you with oil in the name of the Lord. ¹⁵Such a prayer offered in faith will heal the sick, and the Lord will make you well. And if you have committed any sins, you will be forgiven.

¹⁶Confess your sins to each other and pray for each other so that you may be healed. The earnest prayer of a righteous person has great power and produces wonderful results. ¹⁷Elijah was as human as we are, and yet when he prayed earnestly that no rain would fall, none fell for three and a half years! ¹⁸Then, when he prayed again, the sky sent down rain and the earth began to yield its crops.

Restore Wandering Believers

¹⁹My dear brothers and sisters, if someone among you wanders away from the truth and is brought back, ²⁰you can be sure that whoever brings the sinner back will save that person from death and bring about the forgiveness of many sins.

5:6a Or *killed the Righteous One.* **5:6b** Or *Don't they resist you?* or *Doesn't God oppose you?* or *Aren't they now accusing you before God?* **5:7** Greek *brothers;* also in 5:9, 10, 12, 19.

1 Peter

AUTHOR: PETER | DATE WRITTEN: A.D. 63 | GENRE: EPISTLE

The theme of Peter's first epistle is suffering. *He brought inspired words of comfort to those who suffered under persecution.*

CHAPTER **1**
Greetings from Peter

This letter is from Peter, an apostle of Jesus Christ.

I am writing to God's chosen people who are living as foreigners in the provinces of Pontus, Galatia, Cappadocia, Asia, and Bithynia.* ²God the Father knew you and chose you long ago, and his Spirit has made you holy. As a result, you have obeyed him and have been cleansed by the blood of Jesus Christ.

May God give you more and more grace and peace.

The Hope of Eternal Life

³All praise to God, the Father of our Lord Jesus Christ. It is by his great mercy that we have been born again, because God raised Jesus Christ from the dead. Now we live with great expectation, ⁴and we have a priceless inheritance—an inheritance that is kept in heaven for you, pure and undefiled, beyond the reach of change and decay. ⁵And through your faith, God is protecting you by his power until you receive this salvation, which is ready to be revealed on the last day for all to see.

⁶So be truly glad.* There is wonderful joy ahead, even though you have to endure many trials for a little while. ⁷These trials will show that your faith is genuine. It is being tested as fire tests and purifies gold—though your faith is far more precious than mere gold. So when your faith remains strong through many trials, it will bring you much praise and glory and honor on the day when Jesus Christ is revealed to the whole world.

⁸You love him even though you have never seen him. Though you do not see him now, you trust him; and you rejoice with a glorious, inexpressible joy. ⁹The reward for trusting him will be the salvation of your souls.

¹⁰This salvation was something even the prophets wanted to know more about when they prophesied about this gracious salvation prepared for you. ¹¹They wondered what time or situation the Spirit of Christ within them was talking about when he told them in advance about Christ's suffering and his great glory afterward.

¹²They were told that their messages were not for themselves, but for you. And now this Good News has been announced to you by those who preached in the power of the Holy Spirit sent from heaven. It is all so wonderful that even the angels are eagerly watching these things happen.

A Call to Holy Living

¹³So think clearly and exercise self-control. Look forward to the gracious salvation that will come to you when Jesus Christ is revealed to the world. ¹⁴So you must live as God's obedient children. Don't slip back into your old ways of living to satisfy your own desires. You didn't know any better then. ¹⁵But now you must be holy in everything you do, just as God who chose you is holy. ¹⁶For the Scriptures say, "You must be holy because I am holy."*

¹⁷And remember that the heavenly Father to whom you pray has no favorites. He will judge or reward you according to what you do. So you must live in reverent fear of him during your time as "foreigners in the land." ¹⁸For you know that God paid a ransom to save you from the

1:1 *Pontus, Galatia, Cappadocia, Asia,* and *Bithynia* were Roman provinces in what is now Turkey. 1:6 Or *So you are truly glad.* 1:16 Lev 11:44-45; 19:2; 20:7

cornerstones

HOW THE HOLY SPIRIT WORKS WITH THE FATHER AND THE SON
Read 1 PETER 1:2

The Holy Spirit has the distinct honor of being one of the three members of the Trinity—the other two members being God the Father and Jesus Christ, his Son. This particular verse shows how the Holy Spirit works with the Father and the Son in the life of a believer:

- The Father chooses us and makes us his children.
- Jesus redeems us, having died for us while we were still sinners.
- The Holy Spirit draws us to the Lord and continues to work in our lives to make us pleasing to God.

As you can see, all three members of the Trinity work in concert to bring us into a relationship with God. For that reason, we see that the Holy Spirit is indeed an integral part of what has been called "the Godhead."

For the next note on "Who Is the Holy Spirit?" turn to p. 228.

---

empty life you inherited from your ancestors. And the ransom he paid was not mere gold or silver. [19]It was the precious blood of Christ, the sinless, spotless Lamb of God. [20]God chose him as your ransom long before the world began, but he has now revealed him to you in these last days. [21]Through Christ you have come to trust in God. And you have placed your faith and hope in God because he raised Christ from the dead and gave him great glory.

[22]You were cleansed from your sins when you obeyed the truth, so now you must show sincere love to each other as brothers and sisters.* Love each other deeply with all your heart.*

[23]For you have been born again, but not to a life that will quickly end. Your new life will last forever because it comes from the eternal, living word of God. [24]As the Scriptures say,

"People are like grass;
     their beauty is like a flower in the field.
The grass withers and the flower fades.
[25]   But the word of the Lord remains
          forever."*

And that word is the Good News that was preached to you.

CHAPTER **2**
So get rid of all evil behavior. Be done with all deceit, hypocrisy, jealousy, and all unkind speech. [2]Like newborn babies, you must crave pure spiritual milk so that you will grow into a full experience of salvation. Cry out for this nourishment, [3]now that you have had a taste of the Lord's kindness.

Living Stones for God's House
[4]You are coming to Christ, who is the living cornerstone of God's temple. He was rejected by people, but he was chosen by God for great honor.

[5]And you are living stones that God is building into his spiritual temple. What's more, you are his holy priests.* Through the mediation of Jesus Christ, you offer spiritual sacrifices that please God. [6]As the Scriptures say,

"I am placing a cornerstone
     in Jerusalem,*
     chosen for great honor,
and anyone who trusts in him
     will never be disgraced."*

[7]Yes, you who trust him recognize the honor God has given him. But for those who reject him,

"The stone that the builders rejected
     has now become the cornerstone."*

[8]And,

"He is the stone that makes people stumble,
     the rock that makes them fall."*

They stumble because they do not obey God's word, and so they meet the fate that was planned for them.

[9]But you are not like that, for you are a chosen people. You are royal priests,* a holy nation, God's very own possession. As a result, you can show others the goodness of God, for he called you out of the darkness into his wonderful light.

[10]"Once you had no identity as a people;
     now you are God's people.

1:22a Greek *must have brotherly love.*   **1:22b** Some manuscripts read *with a pure heart.*   **1:24-25** Isa 40:6-8.   **2:5** Greek *holy priesthood.*   **2:6a** Greek *in Zion.*   **2:6b** Isa 28:16 (Greek version).   **2:7** Ps 118:22.   **2:8** Isa 8:14.   **2:9** Greek *a royal priesthood.*

Once you received no mercy;
  now you have received God's mercy."*

[11] Dear friends, I warn you as "temporary residents and foreigners" to keep away from worldly desires that wage war against your very souls. [12] Be careful to live properly among your unbelieving neighbors. Then even if they accuse you of doing wrong, they will see your honorable behavior, and they will give honor to God when he judges the world.*

Respecting People in Authority
[13] For the Lord's sake, respect all human authority—whether the king as head of state, [14] or the officials he has appointed. For the king has sent them to punish those who do wrong and to honor those who do right.

[15] It is God's will that your honorable lives should silence those ignorant people who make foolish accusations against you. [16] For you are free, yet you are God's slaves, so don't use your freedom as an excuse to do evil. [17] Respect everyone, and love your Christian brothers and sisters.* Fear God, and respect the king.

Slaves
[18] You who are slaves must accept the authority of your masters with all respect.* Do what they tell you—not only if they are kind and reasonable, but even if they are cruel. [19] For God is pleased with you when you do what you know is right and patiently endure unfair treatment. [20] Of course, you get no credit for being patient if you are beaten for doing wrong. But if you suffer for doing good and endure it patiently, God is pleased with you.

[21] For God called you to do good, even if it means suffering, just as Christ suffered* for you. He is your example, and you must follow in his steps.

[22] He never sinned,
    nor ever deceived anyone.*
[23] He did not retaliate when he was insulted,
    nor threaten revenge when he suffered.
  He left his case in the hands of God,
    who always judges fairly.
[24] He personally carried our sins
    in his body on the cross
  so that we can be dead to sin
    and live for what is right.
  By his wounds
    you are healed.
[25] Once you were like sheep
    who wandered away.
  But now you have turned to your Shepherd,
    the Guardian of your souls.

first steps
TRIALS SHARPEN OUR FAITH
Read 1 PETER 1:3-7

God has selected you for a choice work. But before he can use you, he must toughen the grain of your life. He does this by allowing you to go through difficulties so that your faith can be tested and purified. While this process may not be enjoyable, this passage of Scripture gives us four insights into what we should remember during the testing of our faith, so that our faith will be stronger in the end:

1. Remember *Whose* You Are. You are God's child (verse 3).

2. Remember *What* God Has Promised You. God has promised you the priceless gift of eternal life (verse 4).

3. Remember *Who* Will See You Through. God will protect you until you reach your final destination: heaven (verses 5-6).

4. Remember *Why* God Lets You Go through Trials. God wants to test the genuineness of your faith so that your life will result in praise and glory when Jesus returns (verse 7).

Although it is great to spend time on a "spiritual mountaintop," so to speak, we cannot stay there forever. More often than not, at the bottom of that mountain lies cold, hard reality. Yet fruit grows best in the "valleys" (the hard times of life), not on the mountaintops (when everything is going well). Our greatest character development takes place when we take what we have learned on the mountaintop and put it into practice in the valley.

For the next note on "Have Courage in Trials," turn to p. 211.

CHAPTER 3
Wives
In the same way, you wives must accept the authority of your husbands. Then, even if some refuse to obey the Good News, your godly lives will speak to them without any words. They will be won over [2] by observing your pure and reverent lives.

[3] Don't be concerned about the outward

2:10 Hos 1:6, 9; 2:23.   2:12 Or *on the day of visitation.*   2:17 Greek *love the brotherhood.*   2:18 Or *because you fear God.*
2:21 Some manuscripts read *died.*   2:22 Isa 53:9.

cornerstones

KNOWING AND TRUSTING GOD IS THE SOURCE OF INEXPRESSIBLE JOY
Read 1 PETER 1:8

Many people today are seeking joy and happiness but are not finding it. Perhaps they don't understand what happiness really is. At best, they will only find fleeting happiness from possessions, pleasures, or accomplishments. But the joy God gives is not merely some emotional feeling. It is not affected by our circumstances. In fact, it is an unchanging, natural by-product of our faith in Jesus Christ.

As you trust in Jesus and look forward to his return, you will be filled with an "inexpressible joy." It won't be just some sort of emotional high, but it will be a deep, supernatural experience of contentedness based upon the fact that your life is right with God. And this lasting joy and happiness will sustain you for the rest of your life.

For the next note on "Joy," turn to p. 190.

---

beauty of fancy hairstyles, expensive jewelry, or beautiful clothes. ⁴You should clothe yourselves instead with the beauty that comes from within, the unfading beauty of a gentle and quiet spirit, which is so precious to God. ⁵This is how the holy women of old made themselves beautiful. They trusted God and accepted the authority of their husbands. ⁶For instance, Sarah obeyed her husband, Abraham, and called him her master. You are her daughters when you do what is right without fear of what your husbands might do.

Husbands
⁷In the same way, you husbands must give honor to your wives. Treat your wife with understanding as you live together. She may be weaker than you are, but she is your equal partner in God's gift of new life. Treat her as you should so your prayers will not be hindered.

All Christians
⁸Finally, all of you should be of one mind. Sympathize with each other. Love each other as brothers and sisters.* Be tenderhearted, and keep a humble attitude. ⁹Don't repay evil for evil. Don't retaliate with insults when people insult you. Instead, pay them back with a blessing. That is what God has called you to do, and he will bless you for it. ¹⁰For the Scriptures say,

"If you want to enjoy life
    and see many happy days,
keep your tongue from speaking evil
    and your lips from telling lies.
¹¹ Turn away from evil and do good.
    Search for peace, and work to maintain it.
¹² The eyes of the Lord watch over those who
        do right,
    and his ears are open to their prayers.
But the Lord turns his face
    against those who do evil."*

Suffering for Doing Good
¹³Now, who will want to harm you if you are eager to do good? ¹⁴But even if you suffer for doing what is right, God will reward you for it. So don't worry or be afraid of their threats. ¹⁵Instead, you must worship Christ as Lord of your life. And if someone asks about your Christian hope, always be ready to explain it. ¹⁶But do this in a gentle and respectful way.* Keep your conscience clear. Then if people speak against you, they will be ashamed when they see what a

3:8 Greek *Show brotherly love.*   **3:10-12** Ps 34:12-16.   **3:16** Some English translations put this sentence in verse 15.

---

off and running

NEVER USE VULGAR SPEECH
Read 1 PETER 3:10

One thing that should certainly change when we come to Christ is the way we talk. If we continue using God's name in vain or keep telling dirty jokes, something is not right. Proverbs 8:13 says, "All who fear the LORD will hate evil." That includes vulgar speech. But when we become indifferent to the way we

good life you live because you belong to Christ. [17] Remember, it is better to suffer for doing good, if that is what God wants, than to suffer for doing wrong!

[18] Christ suffered* for our sins once for all time. He never sinned, but he died for sinners to bring you safely home to God. He suffered physical death, but he was raised to life in the Spirit.*

[19] So he went and preached to the spirits in prison—[20] those who disobeyed God long ago when God waited patiently while Noah was building his boat. Only eight people were saved from drowning in that terrible flood.* [21] And that water is a picture of baptism, which now saves you, not by removing dirt from your body, but as a response to God from* a clean conscience. It is effective because of the resurrection of Jesus Christ.

[22] Now Christ has gone to heaven. He is seated in the place of honor next to God, and all the angels and authorities and powers accept his authority.

CHAPTER **4**
Living for God

So then, since Christ suffered physical pain, you must arm yourselves with the same attitude he had, and be ready to suffer, too. For if you have suffered physically for Christ, you have finished with sin.* [2] You won't spend the rest of your lives chasing your own desires, but you will be anxious to do the will of God. [3] You have had enough in the past of the evil things that godless people enjoy—their immorality and lust, their feasting and drunkenness and wild parties, and their terrible worship of idols.

[4] Of course, your former friends are surprised when you no longer plunge into the flood of wild and destructive things they do. So they slander you. [5] But remember that they will have to face God, who will judge everyone, both the living and the dead. [6] That is why the Good News was preached to those who are now dead*—so although they were destined to die like all people,* they now live forever with God in the Spirit.*

[7] The end of the world is coming soon. Therefore, be earnest and disciplined in your prayers. [8] Most important of all, continue to show deep love for each other, for love covers a multitude of sins. [9] Cheerfully share your home with those who need a meal or a place to stay.

[10] God has given each of you a gift from his great variety of spiritual gifts. Use them well to serve one another. [11] Do you have the gift of speaking? Then speak as though God himself were speaking through you. Do you have the gift of helping others? Do it with all the strength and energy that God supplies. Then everything you do will bring glory to God through Jesus Christ. All glory and power to him forever and ever! Amen.

Suffering for Being a Christian

[12] Dear friends, don't be surprised at the fiery trials you are going through, as if something strange were happening to you. [13] Instead, be very glad—for these trials make you partners with Christ in his suffering, so that you will have the wonderful joy of seeing his glory when it is revealed to all the world.

[14] So be happy when you are insulted for being a Christian,* for then the glorious Spirit of God* rests upon you.* [15] If you suffer, however, it must not be for murder, stealing, making trouble, or prying into other people's affairs. [16] But it is no shame to suffer for being a Christian. Praise God for the privilege of being called by his name! [17] For the time has come for judgment, and it must begin with God's household. And if judgment begins with us, what terrible fate awaits those who have never obeyed God's Good News? [18] And also,

3:18a Some manuscripts read *died.*   **3:18b** Or *in spirit.*   **3:20** Greek *saved through water.*   **3:21** Or *as an appeal to God for.*   **4:1** Or *For the one* [or *One*] *who has suffered physically has finished with sin.*   **4:6a** Greek *preached even to the dead.*   **4:6b** Or *so although people had judged them worthy of death.*   **4:6c** Or *in spirit.*   **4:14a** Greek *for the name of Christ.*   **4:14b** Or *for the glory of God, which is his Spirit.*   **4:14c** Some manuscripts add *On their part he is blasphemed, but on your part he is glorified.*

---

speak (or the way others speak around us), we are downplaying the destructiveness of sin and doing a disservice to the Lord.

If you find that this area is a trouble spot for you, commit it to God, and he will begin by cleaning up your thoughts. Then consciously replace that coarse language with praise and thankfulness to God for his goodness. As you focus upon God's goodness, your mind will be less filled with the perverse and wicked thoughts of this world.

For the next note on "Conversation," turn to p. 254.

cornerstones

OUR CONDUCT SHOULD CAUSE OTHERS TO GLORIFY CHRIST

Read 1 PETER 2:9-12

Have you ever felt like your life wasn't really important in the grand scheme of things? Have you ever wondered if it was possible to make a difference in the world around you? These verses show that you can—and should—play a significant role in this world.

Remember Who You Are. First, think about who you are. Christians need to be different than those who do not know the Lord. Your godly lifestyle, priorities, and outlook should set you apart from nonbelievers.

Make a Difference. We are not to isolate ourselves from the world. God has placed us in this world so that our lives can have an impact on the people with whom we come into contact. Our Christian character and lifestyle will expose those who are living an ungodly life and confront them with the life-changing message of the gospel.

In many ways, the holiest moment of a church service is when God's people go out the doors of the church and into the world. That is when your godly living will cause people to ask, "What makes you different?"

Some people may criticize, ridicule, or persecute you for living a godly life. Others, however, may come to know Jesus as a result of your faithful obedience to God's Word. If they do, they will glorify God for your testimony and their newfound salvation.

For the next note on "Honesty and Integrity," turn to p. 270.

"If the righteous are barely saved,
  what will happen to godless
    sinners?"*

[19] So if you are suffering in a manner that pleases God, keep on doing what is right, and trust your lives to the God who created you, for he will never fail you.

CHAPTER 5

Advice for Elders and Young Men

And now, a word to you who are elders in the churches. I, too, am an elder and a witness to the sufferings of Christ. And I, too, will share in his glory when he is revealed to the whole world. As a fellow elder, I appeal to you: [2] Care for the flock that God has entrusted to you. Watch over it willingly, not grudgingly—not for what you will get out of it, but because you are eager to serve God. [3] Don't lord it over the people assigned to your care, but lead them by your own good example. [4] And when the Great Shepherd appears, you will receive a crown of never-ending glory and honor.

[5] In the same way, you younger men must accept the authority of the elders. And all of you, serve each other in humility, for

"God opposes the proud
  but favors the humble."*

[6] So humble yourselves under the mighty power of God, and at the right time he will lift you up in honor. [7] Give all your worries and cares to God, for he cares about you.

[8] Stay alert! Watch out for your great enemy, the devil. He prowls around like a roaring lion, looking for someone to devour. [9] Stand firm against him, and be strong in your faith. Remember that your Christian brothers and sisters* all over the world are going through the same kind of suffering you are.

[10] In his kindness God called you to share in his eternal glory by means of Christ Jesus. So after you have suffered a little while, he will restore, support, and strengthen you, and he will place you on a firm foundation. [11] All power to him forever! Amen.

Peter's Final Greetings

[12] I have written and sent this short letter to you with the help of Silas,* whom I commend to you as a faithful brother. My purpose in writing is to encourage you and assure you that what you are experiencing is truly part of God's grace for you. Stand firm in this grace.

[13] Your sister church here in Babylon* sends you greetings, and so does my son Mark. [14] Greet each other with Christian love.*

Peace be with all of you who are in Christ.

4:18 Prov 11:31 (Greek version). **5:5** Prov 3:34 (Greek version). **5:9** Greek *your brothers*. **5:12** Greek *Silvanus*. **5:13** Greek *The elect one in Babylon*. Babylon was probably symbolic for Rome. **5:14** Greek *with a kiss of love*.

2 Peter

AUTHOR: **PETER** | DATE WRITTEN: **A.D. 66** | GENRE: **EPISTLE**

In this epistle Peter wanted to remind the believers of certain important spiritual truths. Peter also warned of false teachers and spoke of the hope in the Lord's coming.

CHAPTER **1**

Greetings from Peter

This letter is from Simon* Peter, a slave and apostle of Jesus Christ.

I am writing to you who share the same precious faith we have. This faith was given to you because of the justice and fairness* of Jesus Christ, our God and Savior.

² May God give you more and more grace and peace as you grow in your knowledge of God and Jesus our Lord.

Growing in Faith

³ By his divine power, God has given us everything we need for living a godly life. We have received all of this by coming to know him, the one who called us to himself by means of his marvelous glory and excellence. ⁴ And because of his glory and excellence, he has given us great and precious promises that enable you to share his divine nature and escape the world's corruption caused by human desires.

⁵ In view of all this, make every effort to respond to God's promises. Supplement your faith with a generous provision of moral excellence, and moral excellence with knowledge, ⁶ and knowledge with self-control, and self-control with patient endurance, and patient endurance with godliness, ⁷ and godliness with brotherly affection, and brotherly affection with love for everyone.

⁸ The more you grow like this, the more productive and useful you will be in your knowledge of our Lord Jesus Christ. ⁹ But those who fail to develop in this way are shortsighted or blind, forgetting that they have been cleansed from their old sins.

¹⁰ So, dear brothers and sisters,* work hard to prove that you really are among those God has called and chosen. Do these things, and you will never fall away. ¹¹ Then God will give you a grand entrance into the eternal Kingdom of our Lord and Savior Jesus Christ.

Paying Attention to Scripture

¹² Therefore, I will always remind you about these things—even though you already know them and are standing firm in the truth you have been taught. ¹³ And it is only right that I should keep on reminding you as long as I live.* ¹⁴ For our Lord Jesus Christ has shown me that I must soon leave this earthly life,* ¹⁵ so I will work hard to make sure you always remember these things after I am gone.

¹⁶ For we were not making up clever stories when we told you about the powerful coming of our Lord Jesus Christ. We saw his majestic splendor with our own eyes ¹⁷ when he received honor and glory from God the Father. The voice from the majestic glory of God said to him, "This is my dearly loved Son, who brings me great joy."* ¹⁸ We ourselves heard that voice from heaven when we were with him on the holy mountain.

¹⁹ Because of that experience, we have even greater confidence in the message proclaimed by the prophets. You must pay close attention to what they wrote, for their words are like a lamp shining in a dark place—until the Day dawns,

1:1a Greek *Symeon*. **1:1b** Or *to you in the righteousness.* **1:10** Greek *brothers.* **1:13** Greek *as long as I am in this tent* [or *tabernacle*]. **1:14** Greek *I must soon put off my tent* [or *tabernacle*]. **1:17** Matt 17:5; Mark 9:7; Luke 9:35.

cornerstones

GOD IS LOVING AND JUST
Read 2 PETER 3:3-9

The scoffers described in this passage mistook Christ's delayed return to earth to mean that there would be no final judgment at all. Because "everything has remained the same since the world was first created," they not only doubted Christ's return but forgot about God's judgment in the past. More importantly, these scoffers overlooked God's love and mercy. It is for their sake that God is restraining his judgment because "He does not want anyone to be destroyed."

This passage shows two important and seemingly contradictory aspects of God's character: love and justice. The Bible tells us that God is love. In spite of his extensive knowledge of our sinfulness and unworthiness, he has declared, "I have loved you, my people, with an everlasting love. With unfailing love I have drawn you to myself" (Jeremiah 31:3). One of the clearest demonstrations of his love is found at the cross on which Jesus died for us: "But God showed his great love for us by sending Christ to die for us while we were still sinners" (Romans 5:8).

God's love, however, is often misunderstood. Many think that because he loves us, he won't judge us. But his love for us does not negate the fact that he is also just. Scripture clearly and repeatedly makes the point that only the godly will see his face (Psalm 11:7). Therefore, we can be certain that our sins must be dealt with. For those who have accepted God's gift of salvation—Jesus' death on the cross—their sins have been forgiven. For those who haven't accepted this gift, God's judgment is certain.

Every day is another opportunity for nonbelievers to come to faith in Jesus Christ. It is also evidence of the tremendous love God has for his creation. In his holiness God is unapproachable, but in his love he approaches us. The next time you are tempted to doubt God's tender love for you, just take a long, hard look at the cross, and remember that it was not the nails that held Jesus there, but his love for you and others!

For the next note on "Who Is God?" turn to p. 156.

---

and Christ the Morning Star shines* in your hearts. [20]Above all, you must realize that no prophecy in Scripture ever came from the prophet's own understanding,* [21]or from human initiative. No, those prophets were moved by the Holy Spirit, and they spoke from God.

CHAPTER **2**
The Danger of False Teachers
But there were also false prophets in Israel, just as there will be false teachers among you. They will cleverly teach destructive heresies and even deny the Master who bought them. In this way, they will bring sudden destruction on themselves. [2]Many will follow their evil teaching and shameful immorality. And because of these teachers, the way of truth will be slandered. [3]In their greed they will make up clever lies to get hold of your money. But God condemned them long ago, and their destruction will not be delayed.

[4]For God did not spare even the angels who sinned. He threw them into hell,* in gloomy pits of darkness,* where they are being held until the day of judgment. [5]And God did not spare the ancient world—except for Noah and the seven others in his family. Noah warned the world of God's righteous judgment. So God protected Noah when he destroyed the world of ungodly people with a vast flood. [6]Later, God condemned the cities of Sodom and Gomorrah and turned them into heaps of ashes. He made them an example of what will happen to ungodly people. [7]But God also rescued Lot out of Sodom because he was a righteous man who was sick of the shameful immorality of the wicked people around him. [8]Yes, Lot was a righteous man who was tormented in his soul by the wickedness he saw and heard day after day. [9]So you see, the Lord knows how to rescue godly people from their trials, even while keeping the wicked under

1:19 Or *rises.*   1:20 Or *is a matter of one's own interpretation.*   2:4a Greek *Tartarus.*   2:4b Some manuscripts read *in chains of gloom.*

punishment until the day of final judgment. [10]He is especially hard on those who follow their own twisted sexual desire, and who despise authority.

These people are proud and arrogant, daring even to scoff at supernatural beings* without so much as trembling. [11]But the angels, who are far greater in power and strength, do not dare to bring from the Lord* a charge of blasphemy against those supernatural beings.

[12]These false teachers are like unthinking animals, creatures of instinct, born to be caught and destroyed. They scoff at things they do not understand, and like animals, they will be destroyed. [13]Their destruction is their reward for the harm they have done. They love to indulge in evil pleasures in broad daylight. They are a disgrace and a stain among you. They delight in deception* even as they eat with you in your fellowship meals. [14]They commit adultery with their eyes, and their desire for sin is never satisfied. They lure unstable people into sin, and they are well trained in greed. They live under God's curse. [15]They have wandered off the right road and followed the footsteps of Balaam son of Beor,* who loved to earn money by doing wrong. [16]But Balaam was stopped from his mad course when his donkey rebuked him with a human voice.

[17]These people are as useless as dried-up springs or as mist blown away by the wind. They are doomed to blackest darkness. [18]They brag about themselves with empty, foolish boasting. With an appeal to twisted sexual desires, they lure back into sin those who have barely escaped from a lifestyle of deception. [19]They promise freedom, but they themselves are slaves of sin and corruption. For you are a slave to whatever controls you. [20]And when people escape from the wickedness of the world by knowing our Lord and Savior Jesus Christ and then get tangled up and enslaved by sin again, they are worse off than before. [21]It would be better if they had never known the way to righteousness than to know it and then reject the command they were given to live a holy life. [22]They prove the truth of this proverb: "A dog returns to its vomit."* And another says, "A washed pig returns to the mud."

CHAPTER **3**

The Day of the Lord Is Coming

This is my second letter to you, dear friends, and in both of them I have tried to stimulate your wholesome thinking and refresh your memory. [2]I want you to remember what the holy prophets said long ago and what our Lord and Savior commanded through your apostles.

[3]Most importantly, I want to remind you that in the last days scoffers will come, mocking the truth and following their own desires. [4]They will say, "What happened to the promise that Jesus is coming again? From before the times of our ancestors, everything has remained the same since the world was first created."

[5]They deliberately forget that God made the heavens by the word of his command, and he brought the earth out from the water and surrounded it with water. [6]Then he used the water to destroy the ancient world with a mighty flood. [7]And by the same word, the present heavens and earth have been stored up for fire. They are being kept for the day of judgment, when ungodly people will be destroyed.

[8]But you must not forget this one thing, dear friends: A day is like a thousand years to the Lord, and a thousand years is like a day. [9]The Lord isn't really being slow about his promise, as some people think. No, he is being patient for your sake. He does not want anyone to be destroyed, but wants everyone to repent. [10]But the day of the Lord will come as unexpectedly as a thief. Then the heavens will pass away with a terrible noise, and the very elements themselves will disappear in fire, and the earth and everything on it will be found to deserve judgment.*

[11]Since everything around us is going to be destroyed like this, what holy and godly lives you should live, [12]looking forward to the day of God and hurrying it along. On that day, he will set the heavens on fire, and the elements will melt away in the flames. [13]But we are looking forward to the new heavens and new earth he has promised, a world filled with God's righteousness.

[14]And so, dear friends, while you are waiting for these things to happen, make every effort to be found living peaceful lives that are pure and blameless in his sight.

[15]And remember, our Lord's patience gives people time to be saved. This is what our beloved brother Paul also wrote to you with the wisdom God gave him—[16]speaking of these things in all of his letters. Some of his comments are hard to understand, and those who are ignorant and unstable have twisted his letters to mean something quite different, just as

cornerstones

KEEP AN ETERNAL PERSPECTIVE
Read 2 PETER 3:10-11

If Jesus were to come today, would you be embarrassed by what you are doing? That is a good question to ask yourself each morning—and especially those times when immoral thoughts pop into your head. Jesus emphasized the importance of keeping a pure heart when he said, "God blesses those whose hearts are pure, for they will see God" (Matthew 5:8).

A literal definition of the word *pure* is "without hypocrisy," or "single." In other words, Jesus says that we must have a singular, sincere devotion to him in order to see God.

The Bible reminds us that the hope of the coming return of Jesus Christ can have a spiritually purifying effect on our lives: "And all who have this eager expectation will keep themselves pure, just as he is pure" (1 John 3:3). As we recognize the holiness of God and his imminent return, we should pray along with the psalmist, "Teach me your ways, O LORD, that I may live according to your truth! Grant me purity of heart, so that I may honor you" (Psalm 86:11).

For the next note on "Purity," turn to p. 174.

For the next note on "Purity," turn to p. 174.

they do with other parts of Scripture. And this will result in their destruction.

Peter's Final Words
17 I am warning you ahead of time, dear friends. Be on guard so that you will not be carried away by the errors of these wicked people and lose your own secure footing. 18 Rather, you must grow in the grace and knowledge of our Lord and Savior Jesus Christ.

All glory to him, both now and forever! Amen.

1 John

AUTHOR: JOHN | DATE WRITTEN: A.D. 85–90 | GENRE: EPISTLE

In this letter, John pointed out that a person either is or is not a child of God. *There is no middle ground. John clearly emphasized that if one is really a child of God, it will become evident in one's habitual behavior.*

CHAPTER 1

Introduction

We proclaim to you the one who existed from the beginning,* whom we have heard and seen. We saw him with our own eyes and touched him with our own hands. He is the Word of life. ²This one who is life itself was revealed to us, and we have seen him. And now we testify and proclaim to you that he is the one who is eternal life. He was with the Father, and then he was revealed to us. ³We proclaim to you what we ourselves have actually seen and heard so that you may have fellowship with us. And our fellowship is with the Father and with his Son, Jesus Christ. ⁴We are writing these things so that you may fully share our joy.*

Living in the Light

⁵This is the message we heard from Jesus* and now declare to you: God is light, and there is no darkness in him at all. ⁶So we are lying if we say we have fellowship with God but go on living in spiritual darkness; we are not practicing the truth. ⁷But if we are living in the light, as God is in the light, then we have fellowship with each other, and the blood of Jesus, his Son, cleanses us from all sin.

⁸If we claim we have no sin, we are only fooling ourselves and not living in the truth. ⁹But if we confess our sins to him, he is faithful and just to forgive us our sins and to cleanse us from all wickedness. ¹⁰If we claim we have not sinned, we are calling God a liar and showing that his word has no place in our hearts.

CHAPTER 2

My dear children, I am writing this to you so that you will not sin. But if anyone does sin, we have an advocate who pleads our case before the Father. He is Jesus Christ, the one who is truly righteous. ²He himself is the sacrifice that atones for our sins—and not only our sins but the sins of all the world.

³And we can be sure that we know him if we obey his commandments. ⁴If someone claims, "I know God," but doesn't obey God's commandments, that person is a liar and is not living in the truth. ⁵But those who obey God's word truly show how completely they love him. That is how we know we are living in him. ⁶Those who say they live in God should live their lives as Jesus did.

A New Commandment

⁷Dear friends, I am not writing a new commandment for you; rather it is an old one you have had from the very beginning. This old commandment—to love one another—is the same message you heard before. ⁸Yet it is also new. Jesus lived the truth of this commandment, and you also are living it. For the darkness is disappearing, and the true light is already shining.

⁹If anyone claims, "I am living in the light," but hates a Christian brother or sister,* that person is still living in darkness. ¹⁰Anyone who loves another brother or sister* is living in the light and does not cause others to stumble. ¹¹But anyone who hates another brother or

1:1 Greek *What was from the beginning.*   1:4 Or *so that our joy may be complete;* some manuscripts read *your joy.*
1:5 Greek *from him.*   2:9 Greek *hates his brother;* similarly in 2:11.   2:10 Greek *loves his brother.*

cornerstones
OUR LOVE FOR OTHERS MIRRORS THE CONDITION OF OUR HEART
Read 1 JOHN 2:9-11

Being a Christian involves more than just vocalizing our love to God. It also means demonstrating God's love to others. Humanly speaking, it is much easier to dislike someone than it is to love him or her. Grudges and resentment come easily. Yet bitterness toward others is a poison. Not only does it affect our relationships with other people, but it spiritually blinds us as well. Worse yet, harboring bitterness toward other people is a sin that can lead to other sins.

If you are having trouble loving others, then you need to learn how to walk "in the light." How do you do that? First John 2:6 says, "Those who say they live in God should live their lives as Jesus did." Take a look at the way you treat the people in your life; then compare your relationships with Jesus' relationships in the Gospels (Matthew, Mark, Luke, and John). Here is a sampling of what you will find:

- Jesus reached out to the unlovable (see Luke 19:1-10, p. 91).
- Jesus gave a second chance to a friend who had let him down (see John 18:25-27, p. 123; John 21:15-19, p. 127).
- Jesus showed patience toward those who questioned him (see John 20:24-28, pp. 126-127).
- Jesus cared for the sick (see Luke 5:12-16, p. 69).
- Jesus initiated conversations with those whom others despised (see John 4:4-42, pp. 104-105).
- Jesus wept with those who grieved (see John 11:1-44, pp. 113-114).

Ask God to help you love as Jesus loved, and you will see some radical changes in your heart and in your life.

For the next note on "Love," turn to p. 250.

---

sister is still living and walking in darkness. Such a person does not know the way to go, having been blinded by the darkness.

¹² I am writing to you who are God's children
  because your sins have been forgiven
    through Jesus.*
¹³ I am writing to you who are mature in the faith*
  because you know Christ, who existed
    from the beginning.
I am writing to you who are young in the faith

  because you have won your battle
    with the evil one.
¹⁴ I have written to you who are God's children
  because you know the Father.
I have written to you who are mature in the faith
  because you know Christ, who existed
    from the beginning.
I have written to you who are young in the faith
  because you are strong.
God's word lives in your hearts,

2:12 Greek *through his name.*   **2:13** Or *to you fathers;* also in 2:14.

---

off and running
MAKE SURE YOUR FRIENDSHIPS HONOR GOD
Read 1 JOHN 1:7

What is the key to having a friendship that honors God? First, make sure that you are walking in obedience to God, "living in the light" of God's presence. If you are not committed to obeying God, then you will probably make friends

and you have won your battle with the evil one.

Do Not Love This World

¹⁵Do not love this world nor the things it offers you, for when you love the world, you do not have the love of the Father in you. ¹⁶For the world offers only a craving for physical pleasure, a craving for everything we see, and pride in our achievements and possessions. These are not from the Father, but are from this world. ¹⁷And this world is fading away, along with everything that people crave. But anyone who does what pleases God will live forever.

Warning about Antichrists

¹⁸Dear children, the last hour is here. You have heard that the Antichrist is coming, and already many such antichrists have appeared. From this we know that the last hour has come. ¹⁹These people left our churches, but they never really belonged with us; otherwise they would have stayed with us. When they left, it proved that they did not belong with us.

²⁰But you are not like that, for the Holy One has given you his Spirit,* and all of you know the truth. ²¹So I am writing to you not because you don't know the truth but because you know the difference between truth and lies. ²²And who is a liar? Anyone who says that Jesus is not the Christ.* Anyone who denies the Father and the Son is an antichrist.* ²³Anyone who denies the Son doesn't have the Father, either. But anyone who acknowledges the Son has the Father also.

²⁴So you must remain faithful to what you have been taught from the beginning. If you do, you will remain in fellowship with the Son and with the Father. ²⁵And in this fellowship we enjoy the eternal life he promised us.

²⁶I am writing these things to warn you about those who want to lead you astray. ²⁷But you have received the Holy Spirit,* and he lives within you, so you don't need anyone to teach you what is true. For the Spirit* teaches you

first steps

A DISCIPLE WALKS AS JESUS WALKED

Read 1 JOHN 2:3-6

If you call yourself a disciple, you need to follow in Jesus' footsteps. As verse 6 says, you need to "live [your life] as Jesus did." Another translation says that you should "walk as he walked." Walking implies a steady motion— you put one foot in front of the other, and you keep moving. That is the way we should follow Christ. We need to stick with it and be consistent. How do you practically live as Christ did?

- Make time for God and his Word every single day.
- Spend time in prayer with the Lord throughout the day.
- Take time to be with God's people.

There is a tremendous benefit to the disciple who stays close to Christ. By walking as he walked, the Bible tells us we will have help to keep us from sinning (see 1 John 3:6, p. 308). For that reason, one of the greatest identifying marks of a disciple is that his or her walk resembles the Master's walk.

To begin the next topic, turn to p. A43.

everything you need to know, and what he teaches is true—it is not a lie. So just as he has taught you, remain in fellowship with Christ.

Living as Children of God

²⁸And now, dear children, remain in fellowship with Christ so that when he returns, you will be full of courage and not shrink back from him in shame.

2:20 Greek *But you have an anointing from the Holy One.*   2:22a Or *not the Messiah.*   2:22b Or *the antichrist.*
2:27a Greek *the anointing from him.*   2:27b Greek *the anointing.*

with those who also lack this commitment. Any relationship that does not encourage you to live obediently to God and entices you to sin dishonors God.

On the other hand, if you are committed to obeying God, you will seek out friends who are also committed to him. As you walk with those who share the same love for the Lord as you have, you will be filled with joy and have greater impetus to keep from sinning. And your friendships will honor God.

To begin the next topic, turn to p. A49.

cornerstones

UNDERSTAND THE DIFFERENCE BETWEEN THE TRUE GOSPEL AND A FALSE GOSPEL
Read 1 JOHN 4:1-3

False teachings are not unique to our times. They cropped up in the days of the early church as well. When John wrote this passage, a teaching called Gnosticism (which means "to know") had become popular. It taught that Jesus was a mere human being, born by natural procreation. It also claimed that "the Christ" came upon Jesus at his baptism and left him before his crucifixion. This, of course, was false and unscriptural. Yet it is important to note that this heresy is still taught by some today.

As this text says, we need to "test" these teachings to see if they really come from God. Since false teachers don't carry ID cards, here are three simple questions to ask of anyone you may suspect of being a false teacher:

1. What Is Their Ultimate Hope? Some hope to make a better world. Mormons expect to be equal with God. They also hope that each Mormon couple will be given their own planet to populate. Jehovah's Witnesses believe God will come back to earth at the end of time and establish a paradise here. They hope to live in this paradise on earth. But the hope for the Christian is to spend eternity with Jesus Christ in heaven.

2. What Is the Basis for This Hope? Do they teach that you can only get to heaven by living a good life? Do they say that you obtain salvation by faith in Jesus Christ and by performing certain things or rituals, like baptism, keeping the Sabbath, or other works? You must beware of the "and's." The Bible says, "God saved you by his grace when you believed. And you can't take credit for this; it is a gift from God. Salvation is not a reward for the good things we have done, so none of us can boast about it" (Ephesians 2:8-9).

3. How Do They View Jesus Christ? Another earmark of a false teacher preaching a false gospel is what he or she claims about the person of Jesus Christ. This is really the central and primary issue. Many cults seek to make their teachings more palatable to those in the church by including Jesus Christ in their teachings. They may even use terms like "saved" and "born again," and speak of Jesus dying on the cross. Interestingly enough, some teachings may pass the first two tests but fail this ultimate test, which is believing that Jesus was resurrected from the dead.

Any attempts to cast doubt upon the Bible's sufficiency should be rejected. Any "broadness" that would admit any other way to God outside of Christ is false. To say that Jesus is not the only way to God is to call Jesus a liar! Anytime Jesus, the unique Son of God, is reduced to merely a son of God or *one of many* prophets from God, it is erroneous. The best way to know the false is to be familiar with the true: God's Word, the Bible.

For the next note on "Discernment," turn to p. 154.

---

²⁹Since we know that Christ is righteous, we also know that all who do what is right are God's children.

CHAPTER **3**

See how very much our Father loves us, for he calls us his children, and that is what we are! But the people who belong to this world don't recognize that we are God's children because they don't know him. ²Dear friends, we are already God's children, but he has not yet shown us what we will be like when Christ appears. But we do know that we will be like him, for we will see him as he really is. ³And all who have this eager expectation will keep themselves pure, just as he is pure.

⁴Everyone who sins is breaking God's law, for all sin is contrary to the law of God. ⁵And you know that Jesus came to take away our sins, and there is no sin in him. ⁶Anyone who continues to live in him will not sin. But anyone who keeps on sinning does not know him or understand who he is.

⁷Dear children, don't let anyone deceive you about this: When people do what is right, it shows that they are righteous, even as Christ is

How Can I Tell the Difference between True and False Teachings about God?

Read 1 JOHN 4:1-2

The Bible tells us that we must be especially careful in these "last days," for the coming Antichrist and false prophet will perform signs and miracles and deceive many (see 2 Thessalonians 2:9-10, pp. 255-256). So how does one tell the true gospel from a counterfeit or false gospel? Here are four tests you can apply to make sure the teachings you hear really come from God:

1. Does the Teaching Recognize Jesus Christ as the Son of God and the Only Way of Salvation? Proper teaching must agree that Jesus Christ is God's unique Son, and that he "came in a real body" (verse 2). Most cults deny Christ's deity, recognizing him only as a great teacher or, as Jehovah's Witnesses claim, simply God's first created creature. So find out what this teaching has to say about Jesus.

2. Does the Teaching Agree with Scripture? The apostle Paul commended the Bereans because "they searched the Scriptures day after day to see if Paul and Silas were teaching the truth" (Acts 17:11). Don't simply take some pastor or teacher's word as gospel without examining it in the light of God's Word first.

3. If Miracles Are Involved, Do They Bring Glory to God or to Someone Else? Remember, God is not the only one who can do miracles. As mentioned above, the Antichrist will deceive many with his miraculous wonders. In the Old Testament, when God enabled Moses to perform miracles in front of Pharaoh to persuade him to release the Hebrews, Pharaoh's own sorcerers—working through the power of the occult—were able to duplicate a number of those miracles (Exodus 7:10-12, 22). While some miracles come from God, others may actually be performed by the devil himself. Satan is a great imitator. In the last days, "false messiahs and false prophets will

rise up and perform great signs and wonders so as to deceive, if possible, even God's chosen ones" (Matthew 24:24). Do not accept any miracle at face value. Make sure that the person who does the miracle has a strong personal relationship with Jesus Christ (see Matthew 7:21-23, p. 10). More important, be certain the miracle glorifies Jesus Christ and does not contradict what Scripture teaches.

4. Is the Teaching Widely Accepted by the World at Large? Contrary to conventional wisdom, the more popular a teaching is does not make it a more "correct" teaching. For instance, relativism, or the idea that each person can live the way he or she wants to as long as he or she is true to himself or herself, is a popular belief. However, we know that God's Word teaches differently. As shown in this passage, if the message is really from God, the world won't listen to it (1 John 4:6).

The more you study the "real thing"—God's Word—the more you will be able to quickly identify the counterfeits. And remember, "the Spirit who lives in you is greater than the spirit who lives in the world" (1 John 4:4).

---

righteous. [8] But when people keep on sinning, it shows that they belong to the devil, who has been sinning since the beginning. But the Son of God came to destroy the works of the devil. [9] Those who have been born into God's family do not make a practice of sinning, because

God's life* is in them. So they can't keep on sinning, because they are children of God. [10]So now we can tell who are children of God and who are children of the devil. Anyone who does not live righteously and does not love other believers* does not belong to God.

Love One Another

[11]This is the message you have heard from the beginning: We should love one another. [12]We must not be like Cain, who belonged to the evil one and killed his brother. And why did he kill him? Because Cain had been doing what was evil, and his brother had been doing what was righteous. [13]So don't be surprised, dear brothers and sisters,* if the world hates you.

[14]If we love our Christian brothers and sisters,* it proves that we have passed from death to life. But a person who has no love is still dead. [15]Anyone who hates another brother or sister* is really a murderer at heart. And you know that murderers don't have eternal life within them.

[16]We know what real love is because Jesus gave up his life for us. So we also ought to give up our lives for our brothers and sisters. [17]If someone has enough money to live well and sees a brother or sister* in need but shows no compassion—how can God's love be in that person?

[18]Dear children, let's not merely say that we love each other; let us show the truth by our actions. [19]Our actions will show that we belong to the truth, so we will be confident when we stand before God. [20]Even if we feel guilty, God is greater than our feelings, and he knows everything.

[21]Dear friends, if we don't feel guilty, we can come to God with bold confidence. [22]And we will receive from him whatever we ask because we obey him and do the things that please him. [23]And this is his commandment: We must believe in the name of his Son, Jesus Christ, and love one another, just as he commanded us.

[24]Those who obey God's commandments remain in fellowship with him, and he with them. And we know he lives in us because the Spirit he gave us lives in us.

CHAPTER **4**

Discerning False Prophets

Dear friends, do not believe everyone who claims to speak by the Spirit. You must test them to see if the spirit they have comes from God. For there are many false prophets in the world. [2]This is how we know if they have the Spirit of God: If a person claiming to be a prophet* acknowledges that Jesus Christ came in a real body, that person has the Spirit of God. [3]But if someone claims to be a prophet and does not acknowledge the truth about Jesus, that person is not from God. Such a person has the spirit of the Antichrist, which you heard is coming into the world and indeed is already here.

[4]But you belong to God, my dear children. You have already won a victory over those people, because the Spirit who lives in you is greater than the spirit who lives in the world. [5]Those people belong to this world, so they speak from the world's viewpoint, and the world listens to them. [6]But we belong to God, and those who know God listen to us. If they do not belong to God, they do not listen to us. That is how we know if someone has the Spirit of truth or the spirit of deception.

Loving One Another

[7]Dear friends, let us continue to love one another, for love comes from God. Anyone who loves is a child of God and knows God. [8]But anyone who does not love does not know God, for God is love.

[9]God showed how much he loved us by sending his one and only Son into the world so that we might have eternal life through him. [10]This is real love—not that we loved God, but that he loved us and sent his Son as a sacrifice to take away our sins.

3:9 Greek *because his seed.*   **3:10** Greek *does not love his brother.*   **3:13** Greek *brothers.*   **3:14** Greek *the brothers;* similarly in 3:16.   **3:15** Greek *hates his brother.*   **3:17** Greek *sees his brother.*   **4:2** Greek *If a spirit;* similarly in 4:3.

off and running

PRAY EXPECTING TO GET ANSWERS

Read 1 JOHN 5:14-15

Prayer is not getting your will in heaven. It is getting God's will on earth. Prayer is not an argument with God in which you try to persuade him to move things your way. Prayer is an exercise in which his Spirit enables you to move yourself his way. Prayer is not overcoming God's reluctance. It is laying hold of his willingness.

[11] Dear friends, since God loved us that much, we surely ought to love each other. [12] No one has ever seen God. But if we love each other, God lives in us, and his love is brought to full expression in us.

[13] And God has given us his Spirit as proof that we live in him and he in us. [14] Furthermore, we have seen with our own eyes and now testify that the Father sent his Son to be the Savior of the world. [15] All who confess that Jesus is the Son of God have God living in them, and they live in God. [16] We know how much God loves us, and we have put our trust in his love.

God is love, and all who live in love live in God, and God lives in them. [17] And as we live in God, our love grows more perfect. So we will not be afraid on the day of judgment, but we can face him with confidence because we live like Jesus here in this world.

[18] Such love has no fear, because perfect love expels all fear. If we are afraid, it is for fear of punishment, and this shows that we have not fully experienced his perfect love. [19] We love each other* because he loved us first.

[20] If someone says, "I love God," but hates a Christian brother or sister,* that person is a liar; for if we don't love people we can see, how can we love God, whom we cannot see? [21] And he has given us this command: Those who love God must also love their Christian brothers and sisters.*

CHAPTER 5
Faith in the Son of God

Everyone who believes that Jesus is the Christ* has become a child of God. And everyone who loves the Father loves his children, too. [2] We know we love God's children if we love God and obey his commandments. [3] Loving God means keeping his commandments, and his commandments are not burdensome. [4] For every child of God defeats this evil world, and we achieve this victory through our faith. [5] And who can win this battle against the world? Only those who believe that Jesus is the Son of God.

[6] And Jesus Christ was revealed as God's Son by his baptism in water and by shedding his blood on the cross*—not by water only, but by water and blood. And the Spirit, who is truth, confirms it with his testimony. [7] So we have these three witnesses*—[8] the Spirit, the water, and the blood—and all three agree. [9] Since we believe human testimony, surely we can believe the greater testimony that comes from God. And God has testified about his Son. [10] All who believe in the Son of God know in their hearts that this testimony is true. Those who don't believe this are actually calling God a liar because they don't believe what God has testified about his Son.

[11] And this is what God has testified: He has given us eternal life, and this life is in his Son. [12] Whoever has the Son has life; whoever does not have God's Son does not have life.

Conclusion

[13] I have written this to you who believe in the name of the Son of God, so that you may know you have eternal life. [14] And we are confident that he hears us whenever we ask for anything that pleases him. [15] And since we know he hears us when we make our requests, we also know that he will give us what we ask for.

[16] If you see a Christian brother or sister* sinning in a way that does not lead to death, you should pray, and God will give that person life. But there is a sin that leads to death, and I am not saying you should pray for those who commit it. [17] All wicked actions are sin, but not every sin leads to death.

[18] We know that God's children do not make a practice of sinning, for God's Son holds them securely, and the evil one cannot touch them. [19] We know that we are children of God and

---

4:19 Greek We love. Other manuscripts read We love God; still others read We love him.   4:20 Greek hates his brother.
4:21 Greek The one who loves God must also love his brother.   5:1 Or the Messiah.   5:6 Greek This is he who came by water and blood.   5:7 A few very late manuscripts add in heaven—the Father, the Word, and the Holy Spirit, and these three are one. And we have three witnesses on earth.   5:16 Greek a brother.

We like to gravitate toward the latter part of these verses. But don't forget the first part. You have to first stay in Christ by maintaining a healthy, ongoing relationship with him. When that happens, you will see your will coming in line with his, and your requests will begin to mirror what Christ wants to do in your life and in the lives of those around you. At that point, you can be assured that God is listening to you and will answer your prayers.

For the next note on "Prayer Time," turn to p. 146.

that the world around us is under the control of the evil one.

²⁰And we know that the Son of God has come, and he has given us understanding so that we can know the true God.* And now we live in fellowship with the true God because we live in fellowship with his Son, Jesus Christ. He is the only true God, and he is eternal life.

²¹Dear children, keep away from anything that might take God's place in your hearts.*

5:20 Greek *the one who is true.*   5:21 Greek *keep yourselves from idols.*

2 John

AUTHOR: **JOHN** | DATE WRITTEN: **A.D. 90** | GENRE: **EPISTLE**

In this letter John pointed out that true Christian love involves more than just an emotional feeling. It is grounded in what is true. John also warned of false teachers, urging the believers not to receive them.

Greetings

This letter is from John, the elder.*

I am writing to the chosen lady and to her children,* whom I love in the truth—as does everyone else who knows the truth—²because the truth lives in us and will be with us forever.

³Grace, mercy, and peace, which come from God the Father and from Jesus Christ—the Son of the Father—will continue to be with us who live in truth and love.

Live in the Truth

⁴How happy I was to meet some of your children and find them living according to the truth, just as the Father commanded.

⁵I am writing to remind you, dear friends,* that we should love one another. This is not a new commandment, but one we have had from the beginning. ⁶Love means doing what God has commanded us, and he has commanded us to love one another, just as you heard from the beginning.

⁷I say this because many deceivers have gone out into the world. They deny that Jesus Christ came* in a real body. Such a person is a deceiver and an antichrist. ⁸Watch out that you do not lose what we* have worked so hard to achieve. Be diligent so that you receive your full reward. ⁹Anyone who wanders away from this teaching has no relationship with God. But anyone who remains in the teaching of Christ has a relationship with both the Father and the Son.

¹⁰If anyone comes to your meeting and does not teach the truth about Christ, don't invite that person into your home or give any kind of encouragement. ¹¹Anyone who encourages such people becomes a partner in their evil work.

Conclusion

¹²I have much more to say to you, but I don't want to do it with paper and ink. For I hope to visit you soon and talk with you face to face. Then our joy will be complete.

¹³Greetings from the children of your sister,* chosen by God.

1a Greek *From the elder.* **1b** Or *the church God has chosen and its members.* **5** Greek *I urge you, lady.* **7** Or *will come.* **8** Some manuscripts read *you.* **13** Or *from the members of your sister church.*

3 John

AUTHOR: JOHN | DATE WRITTEN: A.D. 90 | GENRE: EPISTLE

John wrote this letter to commend Gaius, a fellow believer, for the hospitality he showed to traveling teachers of the gospel.

Greetings

This letter is from John, the elder.*

I am writing to Gaius, my dear friend, whom I love in the truth.

²Dear friend, I hope all is well with you and that you are as healthy in body as you are strong in spirit. ³Some of the traveling teachers* recently returned and made me very happy by telling me about your faithfulness and that you are living according to the truth. ⁴I could have no greater joy than to hear that my children are following the truth.

Caring for the Lord's Workers

⁵Dear friend, you are being faithful to God when you care for the traveling teachers who pass through, even though they are strangers to you. ⁶They have told the church here of your loving friendship. Please continue providing for such teachers in a manner that pleases God. ⁷For they are traveling for the Lord,* and they accept nothing from people who are not believers.* ⁸So we ourselves should support them so that we can be their partners as they teach the truth.

⁹I wrote to the church about this, but Diotrephes, who loves to be the leader, refuses to have anything to do with us. ¹⁰When I come, I will report some of the things he is doing and the evil accusations he is making against us. Not only does he refuse to welcome the traveling teachers, he also tells others not to help them. And when they do help, he puts them out of the church.

¹¹Dear friend, don't let this bad example influence you. Follow only what is good. Remember that those who do good prove that they are God's children, and those who do evil prove that they do not know God.*

¹²Everyone speaks highly of Demetrius, as does the truth itself. We ourselves can say the same for him, and you know we speak the truth.

Conclusion

¹³I have much more to say to you, but I don't want to write it with pen and ink. ¹⁴For I hope to see you soon, and then we will talk face to face.

¹⁵*Peace be with you.

Your friends here send you their greetings. Please give my personal greetings to each of our friends there.

1 Greek *From the elder.* 3 Greek *the brothers;* also in verses 5 and 10. 7a Greek *They went out on behalf of the Name.* 7b Greek *from Gentiles.* 11 Greek *they have not seen God.* 15 Some English translations combine verses 14 and 15 into verse 14.

Jude

AUTHOR: JUDE, JESUS' HALF-BROTHER | DATE WRITTEN: A.D. 65 | GENRE: EPISTLE

Jude centers around the great apostasy, or falling away from the faith, that will happen on earth before the return of Jesus Christ.

Greetings from Jude

This letter is from Jude, a slave of Jesus Christ and a brother of James.

I am writing to all who have been called by God the Father, who loves you and keeps you safe in the care of Jesus Christ.* ²May God give you more and more mercy, peace, and love.

The Danger of False Teachers

³Dear friends, I had been eagerly planning to write to you about the salvation we all share. But now I find that I must write about something else, urging you to defend the faith that God has entrusted once for all time to his holy people. ⁴I say this because some ungodly people have wormed their way into your churches, saying that God's marvelous grace allows us to live immoral lives. The condemnation of such people was recorded long ago, for they have denied our only Master and Lord, Jesus Christ.

⁵So I want to remind you, though you already know these things, that Jesus* first rescued the nation of Israel from Egypt, but later he destroyed those who did not remain faithful. ⁶And I remind you of the angels who did not stay within the limits of authority God gave them but left the place where they belonged. God has kept them securely chained in prisons of darkness, waiting for the great day of judgment. ⁷And don't forget Sodom and Gomorrah and their neighboring towns, which were filled with immorality and every kind of sexual perversion. Those cities were destroyed by fire and serve as a warning of the eternal fire of God's judgment.

⁸In the same way, these people—who claim authority from their dreams—live immoral lives, defy authority, and scoff at supernatural beings.* ⁹But even Michael, one of the mightiest of the angels,* did not dare accuse the devil of blasphemy, but simply said, "The Lord rebuke you!" (This took place when Michael was arguing with the devil about Moses' body.) ¹⁰But these people scoff at things they do not understand. Like unthinking animals, they do whatever their instincts tell them, and so they bring about their own destruction. ¹¹What sorrow awaits them! For they follow in the footsteps of Cain, who killed his brother. Like Balaam, they deceive people for money. And like Korah, they perish in their rebellion.

¹²When these people eat with you in your fellowship meals commemorating the Lord's love, they are like dangerous reefs that can shipwreck you.* They are like shameless shepherds who care only for themselves. They are like clouds blowing over the land without giving any rain. They are like trees in autumn that are doubly dead, for they bear no fruit and have been pulled up by the roots. ¹³They are like wild waves of the sea, churning up the foam of their shameful deeds. They are like wandering stars, doomed forever to blackest darkness.

¹⁴Enoch, who lived in the seventh generation after Adam, prophesied about these people. He said, "Listen! The Lord is coming with countless thousands of his holy ones ¹⁵to execute judgment on the people of the world. He will convict every person of all the ungodly things they have done and for all the insults that ungodly sinners have spoken against him."*

1 Or *keeps you for Jesus Christ.*   5 As in the best manuscripts; various other manuscripts read *[the] Lord,* or *God,* or *Christ;* one reads *God Christ.*   8 Greek *at glorious ones,* which are probably evil angels.   9 Greek *Michael, the archangel.*   12 Or *they are contaminants among you;* or *they are stains.*   14-15 The quotation comes from intertestamental literature: Enoch 1:9.

[16] These people are grumblers and complainers, living only to satisfy their desires. They brag loudly about themselves, and they flatter others to get what they want.

A Call to Remain Faithful

[17] But you, my dear friends, must remember what the apostles of our Lord Jesus Christ said. [18] They told you that in the last times there would be scoffers whose purpose in life is to satisfy their ungodly desires. [19] These people are the ones who are creating divisions among you. They follow their natural instincts because they do not have God's Spirit in them.

[20] But you, dear friends, must build each other up in your most holy faith, pray in the power of the Holy Spirit,* [21] and await the mercy of our Lord Jesus Christ, who will bring you eternal life. In this way, you will keep yourselves safe in God's love.

[22] And you must show mercy to* those whose faith is wavering. [23] Rescue others by snatching them from the flames of judgment. Show mercy to still others,* but do so with great caution, hating the sins that contaminate their lives.*

A Prayer of Praise

[24] Now all glory to God, who is able to keep you from falling away and will bring you with great joy into his glorious presence without a single fault. [25] All glory to him who alone is God, our Savior through Jesus Christ our Lord. All glory, majesty, power, and authority are his before all time, and in the present, and beyond all time! Amen.

20 Greek *pray in the Holy Spirit.*   **22** Some manuscripts read *must reprove.*   **22-23a** Some manuscripts have only two categories of people: (1) those whose faith is wavering and therefore need to be snatched from the flames of judgment, and (2) those who need to be shown mercy.   **23b** Greek *with fear, hating even the clothing stained by the flesh.*

Revelation

AUTHOR: JOHN | DATE WRITTEN: A.D. 95 | GENRE: APOCALYPTIC

In this great book, we learn of Jesus Christ's return to the earth, as well as the events preceding that climactic moment.

CHAPTER 1
Prologue

This is a revelation from* Jesus Christ, which God gave him to show his servants the events that must soon* take place. He sent an angel to present this revelation to his servant John, ²who faithfully reported everything he saw. This is his report of the word of God and the testimony of Jesus Christ.

³God blesses the one who reads the words of this prophecy to the church, and he blesses all who listen to its message and obey what it says, for the time is near.

John's Greeting to the Seven Churches

⁴This letter is from John to the seven churches in the province of Asia.*

Grace and peace to you from the one who is, who always was, and who is still to come; from the sevenfold Spirit* before his throne; ⁵and from Jesus Christ. He is the faithful witness to these things, the first to rise from the dead, and the ruler of all the kings of the world.

All glory to him who loves us and has freed us from our sins by shedding his blood for us. ⁶He has made us a Kingdom of priests for God his Father. All glory and power to him forever and ever! Amen.

⁷ Look! He comes with the clouds of heaven.
And everyone will see him—
even those who pierced him.
And all the nations of the world
will mourn for him.
Yes! Amen!

⁸"I am the Alpha and the Omega—the beginning and the end,"* says the Lord God. "I am the one who is, who always was, and who is still to come—the Almighty One."

Vision of the Son of Man

⁹I, John, am your brother and your partner in suffering and in God's Kingdom and in the patient endurance to which Jesus calls us. I was exiled to the island of Patmos for preaching the word of God and for my testimony about Jesus. ¹⁰It was the Lord's Day, and I was worshiping in the Spirit.* Suddenly, I heard behind me a loud voice like a trumpet blast. ¹¹It said, "Write in a book* everything you see, and send it to the seven churches in the cities of Ephesus, Smyrna, Pergamum, Thyatira, Sardis, Philadelphia, and Laodicea."

¹²When I turned to see who was speaking to me, I saw seven gold lampstands. ¹³And standing in the middle of the lampstands was someone like the Son of Man.* He was wearing a long robe with a gold sash across his chest. ¹⁴His head and his hair were white like wool, as white as snow. And his eyes were like flames of fire. ¹⁵His feet were like polished bronze refined in a furnace, and his voice thundered like mighty ocean waves. ¹⁶He held seven stars in his right hand, and a sharp two-edged sword came from his mouth. And his face was like the sun in all its brilliance.

¹⁷When I saw him, I fell at his feet as if I were dead. But he laid his right hand on me and said, "Don't be afraid! I am the First and the Last. ¹⁸I am the living one. I died, but look—I am alive forever and ever! And I hold the keys of death and the grave.*

1:1a Or *of.* 1:1b Or *suddenly,* or *quickly.* 1:4a *Asia* was a Roman province in what is now western Turkey. 1:4b Greek *the seven spirits.* 1:8 Greek *I am the Alpha and the Omega,* referring to the first and last letters of the Greek alphabet. 1:10 Or *in spirit.* 1:11 Or *on a scroll.* 1:13 Or *like a son of man.* See Dan 7:13. "Son of Man" is a title Jesus used for himself. 1:18 Greek *and Hades.*

cornerstones

JESUS HAS AN ETERNAL DOMINION

Read REVELATION 1:4-8

This passage of Scripture confirms two important aspects about Jesus Christ: his majesty and dominion. Yet Jesus is distinctly different than any type of royalty or government we are familiar with. The following six points show that difference:

1. He Is the First to Rise from Death and Die No More. Christ gives us a glimpse of what will happen after we die.

2. He Is Greater than Any King in All the Earth. He is Lord over all creation—no earthly leader can make that claim.

3. He Loves Us and Demonstrated His Love by His Death. Rarely has someone in authority over others offered to die in their place.

4. He Has Set Us Free from Our Sins and Given Us a Place of Honor in His Kingdom. For those of us who have received Jesus into our lives, he has given us a place of tremendous privilege and access to the throne of God.

5. He Will Return Again in Triumph. This king will draw the attention of the entire universe with his return.

6. He Is Eternal. He always has been and always will be. No one else but God could make that claim.

Some people have a rather stereotypical view of Jesus. They picture him as most artists have, with long, flowing hair—perhaps a staff in his hand and a lamb wrapped around his neck. Yet the Bible never does give us a description of Jesus' physical appearance. If it did, we would undoubtedly worship the image instead of the Lord. This description of Christ in Revelation—though it does not give us a physical picture—allows us to see the glorified Christ. And this Christ is full of power and majesty.

To begin the next topic, turn to p. A24.

---

[19]"Write down what you have seen—both the things that are now happening and the things that will happen.* [20]This is the meaning of the mystery of the seven stars you saw in my right hand and the seven gold lampstands: The seven stars are the angels* of the seven churches, and the seven lampstands are the seven churches.

CHAPTER 2

The Message to the Church in Ephesus

"Write this letter to the angel* of the church in Ephesus. This is the message from the one who holds the seven stars in his right hand, the one who walks among the seven gold lampstands:

[2]"I know all the things you do. I have seen your hard work and your patient endurance. I know you don't tolerate evil people. You have examined the claims of those who say they are apostles but are not. You have discovered they are liars. [3]You have patiently suffered for me without quitting.

[4]"But I have this complaint against you.

You don't love me or each other as you did at first!* [5]Look how far you have fallen! Turn back to me and do the works you did at first. If you don't repent, I will come and remove your lampstand from its place among the churches. [6]But this is in your favor: You hate the evil deeds of the Nicolaitans, just as I do.

[7]"Anyone with ears to hear must listen to the Spirit and understand what he is saying to the churches. To everyone who is victorious I will give fruit from the tree of life in the paradise of God.

The Message to the Church in Smyrna

[8]"Write this letter to the angel of the church in Smyrna. This is the message from the one who is the First and the Last, who was dead but is now alive:

[9]"I know about your suffering and your poverty—but you are rich! I know the blasphemy of those opposing you. They say they are Jews, but they are not, because their

---

1:19 Or *what you have seen and what they mean—the things that have already begun to happen.*   **1:20** Or *the messengers.* **2:1** Or *the messenger;* also in 2:8, 12, 18.   **2:4** Greek *You have lost your first love.*

synagogue belongs to Satan. ¹⁰Don't be afraid of what you are about to suffer. The devil will throw some of you into prison to test you. You will suffer for ten days. But if you remain faithful even when facing death, I will give you the crown of life.

¹¹"Anyone with ears to hear must listen to the Spirit and understand what he is saying to the churches. Whoever is victorious will not be harmed by the second death.

The Message to the Church in Pergamum
¹²"Write this letter to the angel of the church in Pergamum. This is the message from the one with the sharp two-edged sword:

¹³"I know that you live in the city where Satan has his throne, yet you have remained loyal to me. You refused to deny me even when Antipas, my faithful witness, was martyred among you there in Satan's city.

¹⁴"But I have a few complaints against you. You tolerate some among you whose teaching is like that of Balaam, who showed Balak how to trip up the people of Israel. He taught them to sin by eating food offered to idols and by committing sexual sin. ¹⁵In a similar way, you have some Nicolaitans among you who follow the same teaching. ¹⁶Repent of your sin, or I will come to you suddenly and fight against them with the sword of my mouth.

¹⁷"Anyone with ears to hear must listen to the Spirit and understand what he is saying to the churches. To everyone who is victorious I will give some of the manna that has been hidden away in heaven. And I will give to each one a white stone, and on the stone will be engraved a new name that no one understands except the one who receives it.

The Message to the Church in Thyatira
¹⁸"Write this letter to the angel of the church in Thyatira. This is the message from the Son of God, whose eyes are like flames of fire, whose feet are like polished bronze:

¹⁹"I know all the things you do. I have seen your love, your faith, your service, and your patient endurance. And I can see your constant improvement in all these things.

²⁰"But I have this complaint against you. You are permitting that woman—that Jezebel who calls herself a prophet—to lead my servants astray. She teaches them to commit sexual sin and to eat food offered to idols. ²¹I gave her time to repent, but she

does not want to turn away from her immorality.

²²"Therefore, I will throw her on a bed of suffering,* and those who commit adultery with her will suffer greatly unless they repent and turn away from her evil deeds. ²³I will strike her children dead. Then all the churches will know that I am the one who searches out the thoughts and intentions of every person. And I will give to each of you whatever you deserve.

²⁴"But I also have a message for the rest of you in Thyatira who have not followed this false teaching ('deeper truths,' as they call them—depths of Satan, actually). I will ask nothing more of you ²⁵except that you hold tightly to what you have until I come. ²⁶To all who are victorious, who obey me to the very end,

To them I will give authority over all the nations.
²⁷ They will rule the nations with an iron rod
and smash them like clay pots.*

²⁸They will have the same authority I received from my Father, and I will also give them the morning star!

²⁹"Anyone with ears to hear must listen to the Spirit and understand what he is saying to the churches.

CHAPTER **3**
The Message to the Church in Sardis
"Write this letter to the angel* of the church in Sardis. This is the message from the one who has the sevenfold Spirit* of God and the seven stars:

"I know all the things you do, and that you have a reputation for being alive—but you are dead. ²Wake up! Strengthen what little remains, for even what is left is almost dead. I find that your actions do not meet the requirements of my God. ³Go back to what you heard and believed at first; hold to it firmly. Repent and turn to me again. If you don't wake up, I will come to you suddenly, as unexpected as a thief.

⁴"Yet there are some in the church in Sardis who have not soiled their clothes with evil. They will walk with me in white, for they are worthy. ⁵All who are victorious will be clothed in white. I will never erase their names from the Book of Life, but I will announce before my Father and his angels that they are mine.

⁶"Anyone with ears to hear must listen to

the Spirit and understand what he is saying to the churches.

The Message to the Church in Philadelphia

7 "Write this letter to the angel of the church in Philadelphia.

This is the message from the one who is
holy and true,
the one who has the key of David.
What he opens, no one can close;
and what he closes, no one can open:*

8 "I know all the things you do, and I have opened a door for you that no one can close. You have little strength, yet you obeyed my word and did not deny me. 9 Look, I will force those who belong to Satan's synagogue—those liars who say they are Jews but are not—to come and bow down at your feet. They will acknowledge that you are the ones I love.

10 "Because you have obeyed my command to persevere, I will protect you from the great time of testing that will come upon the whole world to test those who belong to this world. 11 I am coming soon.* Hold on to what you have, so that no one will take away your crown. 12 All who are victorious will become pillars in the Temple of my God, and they will never have to leave it. And I will write on them the name of my God, and they will be citizens in the city of my God—the new Jerusalem that comes down from heaven from my God. And I will also write on them my new name.

13 "Anyone with ears to hear must listen to the Spirit and understand what he is saying to the churches.

The Message to the Church in Laodicea

14 "Write this letter to the angel of the church in Laodicea. This is the message from the one who is the Amen—the faithful and true witness, the beginning* of God's new creation:

15 "I know all the things you do, that you are neither hot nor cold. I wish that you were one or the other! 16 But since you are like lukewarm water, neither hot nor cold, I will spit you out of my mouth! 17 You say, 'I am rich. I have everything I want. I don't need a thing!' And you don't realize that you are wretched and miserable and poor and blind and naked. 18 So I advise you to buy gold from me—gold that has been purified by fire. Then you will be rich. Also buy white garments from me so you will not be shamed by your nakedness, and ointment for your eyes so you will be able to see. 19 I correct and discipline everyone I love. So be diligent and turn from your indifference.

20 "Look! I stand at the door and knock. If you hear my voice and open the door, I will come in, and we will share a meal together as friends. 21 Those who are victorious will sit with me on my throne, just as I was victorious and sat with my Father on his throne.

22 "Anyone with ears to hear must listen to the Spirit and understand what he is saying to the churches."

CHAPTER 4

Worship in Heaven

Then as I looked, I saw a door standing open in heaven, and the same voice I had heard before spoke to me like a trumpet blast. The voice said, "Come up here, and I will show you what must happen after this." 2 And instantly I was in the Spirit,* and I saw a throne in heaven and someone sitting on it. 3 The one sitting on the throne was as brilliant as gemstones—like jasper and carnelian. And the glow of an emerald circled his throne like a rainbow. 4 Twenty-four thrones surrounded him, and twenty-four elders sat on them. They were all clothed in white and had gold crowns on their heads. 5 From the throne came flashes of lightning and the rumble of thunder. And in front of the throne were seven torches with burning flames. This is the sevenfold Spirit* of God. 6 In front of the throne was a shiny sea of glass, sparkling like crystal.

In the center and around the throne were four living beings, each covered with eyes, front and back. 7 The first of these living beings was like a lion; the second was like an ox; the third had a human face; and the fourth was like an eagle in flight. 8 Each of these living beings had six wings, and their wings were covered all over with eyes, inside and out. Day after day and night after night they keep on saying,

"Holy, holy, holy is the Lord God, the
Almighty—
the one who always was, who is, and who
is still to come."

9 Whenever the living beings give glory and honor and thanks to the one sitting on the throne (the one who lives forever and ever), 10 the twenty-four elders fall down and worship the one sitting on the throne (the one who lives forever and ever). And they lay their crowns before the throne and say,

3:7 Isa 22:22. 3:11 Or *suddenly*, or *quickly*. 3:14 Or *the ruler*, or *the source*. 4:2 Or *in spirit*. 4:5 Greek *They are the seven spirits*.

[11] "You are worthy, O Lord our God,
  to receive glory and honor and power.
For you created all things,
  and they exist because you created what
    you pleased."

CHAPTER 5
The Lamb Opens the Scroll
Then I saw a scroll* in the right hand of the one who was sitting on the throne. There was writing on the inside and the outside of the scroll, and it was sealed with seven seals. [2]And I saw a strong angel, who shouted with a loud voice: "Who is worthy to break the seals on this scroll and open it?" [3]But no one in heaven or on earth or under the earth was able to open the scroll and read it.

[4]Then I began to weep bitterly because no one was found worthy to open the scroll and read it. [5]But one of the twenty-four elders said to me, "Stop weeping! Look, the Lion of the tribe of Judah, the heir to David's throne,* has won the victory. He is worthy to open the scroll and its seven seals."

[6]Then I saw a Lamb that looked as if it had been slaughtered, but it was now standing between the throne and the four living beings and among the twenty-four elders. He had seven horns and seven eyes, which represent the sevenfold Spirit* of God that is sent out into every part of the earth. [7]He stepped forward and took the scroll from the right hand of the one sitting on the throne. [8]And when he took the scroll, the four living beings and the twenty-four elders fell down before the Lamb. Each one had a harp, and they held gold bowls filled with incense, which are the prayers of God's people. [9]And they sang a new song with these words:

"You are worthy to take the scroll
  and break its seals and open it.
For you were slaughtered, and your blood
    has ransomed people for God
  from every tribe and language and
    people and nation.
[10] And you have caused them to become
  a Kingdom of priests for our God.
  And they will reign* on the earth."

[11]Then I looked again, and I heard the voices of thousands and millions of angels around the throne and of the living beings and the elders. [12]And they sang in a mighty chorus:

"Worthy is the Lamb who was
    slaughtered—
  to receive power and riches
and wisdom and strength
  and honor and glory and blessing."

[13]And then I heard every creature in heaven and on earth and under the earth and in the sea. They sang:

"Blessing and honor and glory and power
  belong to the one sitting on the throne
    and to the Lamb forever and ever."

[14]And the four living beings said, "Amen!" And the twenty-four elders fell down and worshiped the Lamb.

CHAPTER 6
The Lamb Breaks the First Six Seals
As I watched, the Lamb broke the first of the seven seals on the scroll.* Then I heard one of the four living beings say with a voice like thunder, "Come!" [2]I looked up and saw a white horse standing there. Its rider carried a bow, and a crown was placed on his head. He rode out to win many battles and gain the victory.

[3]When the Lamb broke the second seal, I heard the second living being say, "Come!" [4]Then another horse appeared, a red one. Its rider was given a mighty sword and the authority to take peace from the earth. And there was war and slaughter everywhere.

[5]When the Lamb broke the third seal, I heard the third living being say, "Come!" I looked up and saw a black horse, and its rider was holding a pair of scales in his hand. [6]And I heard a voice from among the four living beings say, "A loaf of wheat bread or three loaves of barley will cost a day's pay.* And don't waste* the olive oil and wine."

[7]When the Lamb broke the fourth seal, I heard the fourth living being say, "Come!" [8]I looked up and saw a horse whose color was pale green. Its rider was named Death, and his companion was the Grave.* These two were given authority over one-fourth of the earth, to kill with the sword and famine and disease* and wild animals.

[9]When the Lamb broke the fifth seal, I saw under the altar the souls of all who had been martyred for the word of God and for being faithful in their testimony. [10]They shouted to the Lord and said, "O Sovereign Lord, holy and true, how long before you judge the people who belong to this world and avenge our blood for what they have done to us?" [11]Then a white robe was given to each of them. And they were told to rest a little longer until the full number of their brothers and sisters*—their fellow

---

5:1 Or *book;* also in 5:2, 3, 4, 5, 7, 8, 9.   5:5 Greek *the root of David.* See Isa 11:10.   5:6 Greek *which are the seven spirits.*
5:10 Some manuscripts read *they are reigning.*   6:1 Or *book.*   6:6a Greek *A choinix* [1 quart or 1 liter] *of wheat for a denarius, and 3 choinix of barley for a denarius.* A denarius was equivalent to a laborer's full day's wage.   6:6b Or *harm.*
6:8a Greek *was Hades.*   6:8b Greek *death.*   6:11 Greek *their brothers.*

cornerstones

WHAT WILL LIFE IN HEAVEN BE LIKE?

Read REVELATION 7:13-17

The apostle Paul had a taste of heaven by means of a vision. He wrote about his experience in 2 Corinthians 12:2-4. Upon entering God's presence, he said, "I was caught up to paradise." The word *paradise* literally means "the royal garden of a king with all kinds of fruit and flowers." This passage of Scripture shows us four aspects of the life we will live in the wonderful place called paradise:

1. We Will Live a Life without Fear and Worry. Heaven is a place of protection (verse 15). We will have no reason to fear anything there. We won't find bars on windows, crime on the streets, or any other type of violence. God will be our shelter.

2. We Will Live a Life without Need. Heaven is a place of complete sufficiency (verse 16). Hunger and thirst will not be a part of our vocabulary there. That is because the Lord will feed us and quench our thirst.

3. We Will Live a Life without Pain. Heaven is a place of comfort (verse 16). Elsewhere, the Bible says that in heaven "there will be no more death or sorrow or crying or pain" (Revelation 21:4). Our heavenly bodies will not be subjected to the illnesses, aches, and pains that we know so well here on earth.

4. We Will Live a Life without Sorrow. Heaven is a place of joy (verse 17). Being in God's presence is a joyful and wonderful experience. Sorrow will not be found in heaven, and God will wipe away all of our tears.

While we can look forward to the glories of heaven, one thing far outweighs them all: the fact that we will be able to spend eternity with Jesus. Dwight L. Moody once wrote, "It is not the jeweled walls and pearly gates that are going to make heaven attractive. It is being with God." May that truth inspire you as you live out your life on this earth.

To begin the next topic, turn to p. A28.

---

servants of Jesus who were to be martyred—had joined them.

¹²I watched as the Lamb broke the sixth seal, and there was a great earthquake. The sun became as dark as black cloth, and the moon became as red as blood. ¹³Then the stars of the sky fell to the earth like green figs falling from a tree shaken by a strong wind. ¹⁴The sky was rolled up like a scroll, and all of the mountains and islands were moved from their places.

¹⁵Then everyone—the kings of the earth, the rulers, the generals, the wealthy, the powerful, and every slave and free person—all hid themselves in the caves and among the rocks of the mountains. ¹⁶And they cried to the mountains and the rocks, "Fall on us and hide us from the face of the one who sits on the throne and from the wrath of the Lamb. ¹⁷For the great day of their wrath has come, and who is able to survive?"

CHAPTER **7**

God's People Will Be Preserved

Then I saw four angels standing at the four corners of the earth, holding back the four winds so they did not blow on the earth or the sea, or even on any tree. ²And I saw another angel coming up from the east, carrying the seal of the living God. And he shouted to those four angels, who had been given power to harm land and sea, ³"Wait! Don't harm the land or the sea or the trees until we have placed the seal of God on the foreheads of his servants."

⁴And I heard how many were marked with the seal of God—144,000 were sealed from all the tribes of Israel:

5	from Judah	12,000
	from Reuben	12,000
	from Gad	12,000
6	from Asher	12,000
	from Naphtali	12,000
	from Manasseh	12,000
7	from Simeon	12,000
	from Levi	12,000
	from Issachar	12,000
8	from Zebulun	12,000
	from Joseph	12,000
	from Benjamin	12,000

Praise from the Great Crowd

9After this I saw a vast crowd, too great to count, from every nation and tribe and people and language, standing in front of the throne and before the Lamb. They were clothed in white robes and held palm branches in their hands. 10And they were shouting with a great roar,

"Salvation comes from our God who sits
    on the throne
    and from the Lamb!"

11And all the angels were standing around the throne and around the elders and the four living beings. And they fell before the throne with their faces to the ground and worshiped God. 12They sang,

"Amen! Blessing and glory and wisdom
    and thanksgiving and honor
and power and strength belong to our God
    forever and ever! Amen."

13Then one of the twenty-four elders asked me, "Who are these who are clothed in white? Where did they come from?"

14And I said to him, "Sir, you are the one who knows."

Then he said to me, "These are the ones who died in* the great tribulation.* They have washed their robes in the blood of the Lamb and made them white.

15 "That is why they stand in front of God's
    throne
    and serve him day and night in his
    Temple.
And he who sits on the throne
    will give them shelter.
16 They will never again be hungry or thirsty;
    they will never be scorched by the heat
    of the sun.
17 For the Lamb on the throne*
    will be their Shepherd.
He will lead them to springs of life-giving
    water.
And God will wipe every tear from their
    eyes."

CHAPTER 8

The Lamb Breaks the Seventh Seal

When the Lamb broke the seventh seal on the scroll,* there was silence throughout heaven for about half an hour. 2I saw the seven angels who stand before God, and they were given seven trumpets.

3Then another angel with a gold incense burner came and stood at the altar. And a great amount of incense was given to him to mix with the prayers of God's people as an offering on the gold altar before the throne. 4The smoke of the incense, mixed with the prayers of God's holy people, ascended up to God from the altar where the angel had poured them out. 5Then the angel filled the incense burner with fire from the altar and threw it down upon the earth; and thunder crashed, lightning flashed, and there was a terrible earthquake.

The First Four Trumpets

6Then the seven angels with the seven trumpets prepared to blow their mighty blasts.

7The first angel blew his trumpet, and hail and fire mixed with blood were thrown down on the earth. One-third of the earth was set on fire, one-third of the trees were burned, and all the green grass was burned.

8Then the second angel blew his trumpet, and a great mountain of fire was thrown into the sea. One-third of the water in the sea became blood, 9one-third of all things living in the sea died, and one-third of all the ships on the sea were destroyed.

10Then the third angel blew his trumpet, and a great star fell from the sky, burning like a torch. It fell on one-third of the rivers and on the springs of water. 11The name of the star was Bitterness.* It made one-third of the water bitter, and many people died from drinking the bitter water.

12Then the fourth angel blew his trumpet, and one-third of the sun was struck, and one-third of the moon, and one-third of the stars, and they became dark. And one-third of the day was dark, and also one-third of the night.

13Then I looked, and I heard a single eagle crying loudly as it flew through the air, "Terror, terror, terror to all who belong to this world because of what will happen when the last three angels blow their trumpets."

CHAPTER 9

The Fifth Trumpet Brings the First Terror

Then the fifth angel blew his trumpet, and I saw a star that had fallen to earth from the sky, and he was given the key to the shaft of the bottomless pit.* 2When he opened it, smoke poured out as though from a huge furnace, and the sunlight and air turned dark from the smoke.

3Then locusts came from the smoke and descended on the earth, and they were given power to sting like scorpions. 4They were told not to harm the grass or plants or trees, but only the people who did not have the seal of God on their foreheads. 5They were told not to

7:14a Greek *who came out of.* 7:14b Or *the great suffering.* 7:17 Greek *on the center of the throne.* 8:1 Or *book.*
8:11 Greek *Wormwood.* 9:1 Or *the abyss,* or *the underworld;* also in 9:11.

kill them but to torture them for five months with pain like the pain of a scorpion sting. [6] In those days people will seek death but will not find it. They will long to die, but death will flee from them!

[7] The locusts looked like horses prepared for battle. They had what looked like gold crowns on their heads, and their faces looked like human faces. [8] They had hair like women's hair and teeth like the teeth of a lion. [9] They wore armor made of iron, and their wings roared like an army of chariots rushing into battle. [10] They had tails that stung like scorpions, and for five months they had the power to torment people. [11] Their king is the angel from the bottomless pit; his name in Hebrew is *Abaddon,* and in Greek, *Apollyon*—the Destroyer.

[12] The first terror is past, but look, two more terrors are coming!

The Sixth Trumpet Brings the Second Terror

[13] Then the sixth angel blew his trumpet, and I heard a voice speaking from the four horns of the gold altar that stands in the presence of God. [14] And the voice said to the sixth angel who held the trumpet, "Release the four angels who are bound at the great Euphrates River." [15] Then the four angels who had been prepared for this hour and day and month and year were turned loose to kill one-third of all the people on earth. [16] I heard the size of their army, which was 200 million mounted troops.

[17] And in my vision, I saw the horses and the riders sitting on them. The riders wore armor that was fiery red and dark blue and yellow. The horses had heads like lions, and fire and smoke and burning sulfur billowed from their mouths. [18] One-third of all the people on earth were killed by these three plagues—by the fire and smoke and burning sulfur that came from the mouths of the horses. [19] Their power was in their mouths and in their tails. For their tails had heads like snakes, with the power to injure people.

[20] But the people who did not die in these plagues still refused to repent of their evil deeds and turn to God. They continued to worship demons and idols made of gold, silver, bronze, stone, and wood—idols that can neither see nor hear nor walk! [21] And they did not repent of their murders or their witchcraft or their sexual immorality or their thefts.

CHAPTER **10**
The Angel and the Small Scroll

Then I saw another mighty angel coming down from heaven, surrounded by a cloud, with a rainbow over his head. His face shone like the sun, and his feet were like pillars of fire. [2] And in his hand was a small scroll* that had been opened. He stood with his right foot on the sea and his left foot on the land. [3] And he gave a great shout like the roar of a lion. And when he shouted, the seven thunders answered.

[4] When the seven thunders spoke, I was about to write. But I heard a voice from heaven saying, "Keep secret* what the seven thunders said, and do not write it down."

[5] Then the angel I saw standing on the sea and on the land raised his right hand toward heaven. [6] He swore an oath in the name of the one who lives forever and ever, who created the heavens and everything in them, the earth and everything in it, and the sea and everything in it. He said, "There will be no more delay. [7] When the seventh angel blows his trumpet, God's mysterious plan will be fulfilled. It will happen just as he announced it to his servants the prophets."

[8] Then the voice from heaven spoke to me again: "Go and take the open scroll from the hand of the angel who is standing on the sea and on the land."

[9] So I went to the angel and told him to give me the small scroll. "Yes, take it and eat it," he said. "It will be sweet as honey in your mouth, but it will turn sour in your stomach!" [10] So I took the small scroll from the hand of the angel, and I ate it! It was sweet in my mouth, but when I swallowed it, it turned sour in my stomach.

[11] Then I was told, "You must prophesy again about many peoples, nations, languages, and kings."

CHAPTER **11**
The Two Witnesses

Then I was given a measuring stick, and I was told, "Go and measure the Temple of God and the altar, and count the number of worshipers. [2] But do not measure the outer courtyard, for it has been turned over to the nations. They will trample the holy city for 42 months. [3] And I will give power to my two witnesses, and they will be clothed in burlap and will prophesy during those 1,260 days."

[4] These two prophets are the two olive trees and the two lampstands that stand before the Lord of all the earth. [5] If anyone tries to harm them, fire flashes from their mouths and consumes their enemies. This is how anyone who tries to harm them must die. [6] They have power to shut the sky so that no rain will fall for as long as they prophesy. And they have the power to turn the rivers and oceans into blood, and to strike the earth with every kind of plague as often as they wish.

10:2 Or *book;* also in 10:8, 9, 10.   **10:4** Greek *Seal up.*

⁷When they complete their testimony, the beast that comes up out of the bottomless pit* will declare war against them, and he will conquer them and kill them. ⁸And their bodies will lie in the main street of Jerusalem,* the city that is figuratively called "Sodom" and "Egypt," the city where their Lord was crucified. ⁹And for three and a half days, all peoples, tribes, languages, and nations will stare at their bodies. No one will be allowed to bury them. ¹⁰All the people who belong to this world will gloat over them and give presents to each other to celebrate the death of the two prophets who had tormented them.

¹¹But after three and a half days, God breathed life into them, and they stood up! Terror struck all who were staring at them. ¹²Then a loud voice from heaven called to the two prophets, "Come up here!" And they rose to heaven in a cloud as their enemies watched.

¹³At the same time there was a terrible earthquake that destroyed a tenth of the city. Seven thousand people died in that earthquake, and everyone else was terrified and gave glory to the God of heaven.

¹⁴The second terror is past, but look, the third terror is coming quickly.

The Seventh Trumpet Brings the Third Terror

¹⁵Then the seventh angel blew his trumpet, and there were loud voices shouting in heaven:

"The world has now become the Kingdom
    of our Lord and of his Christ,*
and he will reign forever and ever."

¹⁶The twenty-four elders sitting on their thrones before God fell with their faces to the ground and worshiped him. ¹⁷And they said,

"We give thanks to you, Lord God, the
    Almighty,
    the one who is and who always was,
for now you have assumed your great power
    and have begun to reign.
¹⁸ The nations were filled with wrath,
    but now the time of your wrath has
        come.
It is time to judge the dead
    and reward your servants the prophets,
    as well as your holy people,
and all who fear your name,
    from the least to the greatest.
It is time to destroy
    all who have caused destruction on the
        earth."

¹⁹Then, in heaven, the Temple of God was opened and the Ark of his covenant could be seen inside the Temple. Lightning flashed, thunder crashed and roared, and there was an earthquake and a terrible hailstorm.

CHAPTER **12**

The Woman and the Dragon

Then I witnessed in heaven an event of great significance. I saw a woman clothed with the sun, with the moon beneath her feet, and a crown of twelve stars on her head. ²She was pregnant, and she cried out because of her labor pains and the agony of giving birth.

³Then I witnessed in heaven another significant event. I saw a large red dragon with seven heads and ten horns, with seven crowns on his heads. ⁴His tail swept away one-third of the stars in the sky, and he threw them to the earth. He stood in front of the woman as she was about to give birth, ready to devour her baby as soon as it was born.

⁵She gave birth to a son who was to rule all nations with an iron rod. And her child was snatched away from the dragon and was caught up to God and to his throne. ⁶And the woman fled into the wilderness, where God had prepared a place to care for her for 1,260 days.

⁷Then there was war in heaven. Michael and his angels fought against the dragon and his angels. ⁸And the dragon lost the battle, and he and his angels were forced out of heaven. ⁹This great dragon—the ancient serpent called the devil, or Satan, the one deceiving the whole world—was thrown down to the earth with all his angels.

¹⁰Then I heard a loud voice shouting across the heavens,

"It has come at last—
    salvation and power
and the Kingdom of our God,
    and the authority of his Christ.*
For the accuser of our brothers and sisters*
    has been thrown down to earth—
the one who accuses them
    before our God day and night.
¹¹ And they have defeated him by the blood
        of the Lamb
    and by their testimony.
And they did not love their lives so much
    that they were afraid to die.
¹² Therefore, rejoice, O heavens!
    And you who live in the heavens, rejoice!
But terror will come on the earth and the
        sea,
    for the devil has come down to you in
        great anger,
    knowing that he has little time."

11:7 Or *the abyss,* or *the underworld.*   11:8 Greek *the great city.*   11:15 Or *his Messiah.*   12:10a Or *his Messiah.*
12:10b Greek *brothers.*

cornerstones

WHO CAN THWART SATAN'S AGENDA?

Read REVELATION 12:10-12

God uses his faithful followers to undermine Satan's plans. In this passage three significant ways are revealed to us as to how these martyrs for the gospel stayed true to Jesus and overcame the devil's attacks:

1. They Overcame Him by the Blood of the Lamb. The Bible says, "Without the shedding of blood, there is no forgiveness" (Hebrews 9:22). It is only through what Jesus did for us on the cross that we can approach God. These people knew that they could never go to heaven or overcome Satan's accusations on their own merit or ability. They realized that they had fallen short of God's ideal, but they also knew that the blood of Jesus "cleanses us from all sin" (1 John 1:7).

2. They Overcame Him by Their Testimony. The believers described in these verses had come to understand what God had done for them and were proclaiming it to others. They not only realized that they had unconditional access to God, but they also sought to "invade enemy territory" by reaching out to others with the message of the gospel.

3. They Overcame Him by Their Attitude toward Life. These believers did not love their lives more than Christ. They endured execution for their faith because they realized that a better life was awaiting them in heaven with Christ. As the apostle Paul said, "For to me, living means living for Christ, and dying is even better" (Philippians 1:21).

History relates the story of a Christian who was persecuted by Rome for his faith. As he stood before the emperor, he was told, "Give up Christ. If you don't, I'll banish you."

The Christian replied, "You cannot banish me from Christ, for God says, 'I will never leave you or forsake you.'"

The ruler said, "I'll confiscate your property."

The Christian patiently responded, "My treasures are laid up in heaven. You can't touch them."

The emperor shot back, "I'll kill you!"

The Christian answered, "I've been dead to the world in Christ for forty years. My life is hid with Christ in God. You can't touch it."

The emperor turned to some of the members of his court and said in disgust, "What can you do with such a fanatic?"

May God give his church more men like this man.

To begin the next topic, turn to p. A26.

---

¹³When the dragon realized that he had been thrown down to the earth, he pursued the woman who had given birth to the male child. ¹⁴But she was given two wings like those of a great eagle so she could fly to the place prepared for her in the wilderness. There she would be cared for and protected from the dragon* for a time, times, and half a time. ¹⁵Then the dragon tried to drown the woman with a flood of water that flowed from his mouth. ¹⁶But the earth helped her by opening its mouth and swallowing the river that gushed out from the mouth of the dragon. ¹⁷And the dragon was angry at the woman and declared war against the rest of her children— all who keep God's commandments and maintain their testimony for Jesus.

¹⁸Then the dragon took his stand* on the shore beside the sea.

CHAPTER 13
The Beast out of the Sea

Then I saw a beast rising up out of the sea. It had seven heads and ten horns, with ten crowns on its horns. And written on each head were names that blasphemed God. ²This beast looked like a leopard, but it had the feet of a bear and the mouth of a lion! And the dragon

12:14 Greek *the serpent;* also in 12:15. See 12:9.   **12:18** Greek *Then he took his stand;* some manuscripts read *Then I took my stand.* Some translations put this entire sentence into 13:1.

gave the beast his own power and throne and great authority. [3] I saw that one of the heads of the beast seemed wounded beyond recovery—but the fatal wound was healed! The whole world marveled at this miracle and gave allegiance to the beast. [4] They worshiped the dragon for giving the beast such power, and they also worshiped the beast. "Who is as great as the beast?" they exclaimed. "Who is able to fight against him?" [5] Then the beast was allowed to speak great blasphemies against God. And he was given authority to do whatever he wanted for forty-two months. [6] And he spoke terrible words of blasphemy against God, slandering his name and his dwelling—that is, those who dwell in heaven.* [7] And the beast was allowed to wage war against God's holy people and to conquer them. And he was given authority to rule over every tribe and people and language and nation. [8] And all the people who belong to this world worshiped the beast. They are the ones whose names were not written in the Book of Life before the world was made—the Book that belongs to the Lamb who was slaughtered.*

[9] Anyone with ears to hear
    should listen and understand.
[10] Anyone who is destined for prison
    will be taken to prison.
Anyone destined to die by the sword
    will die by the sword.

This means that God's holy people must endure persecution patiently and remain faithful.

The Beast out of the Earth

[11] Then I saw another beast come up out of the earth. He had two horns like those of a lamb, but he spoke with the voice of a dragon. [12] He exercised all the authority of the first beast. And he required all the earth and its people to worship the first beast, whose fatal wound had been healed. [13] He did astounding miracles, even making fire flash down to earth from the sky while everyone was watching. [14] And with all the miracles he was allowed to perform on behalf of the first beast, he deceived all the people who belong to this world. He ordered the people to make a great statue of the first beast, who was fatally wounded and then came back to life. [15] He was then permitted to give life to this statue so that it could speak. Then the statue of the beast commanded that anyone refusing to worship it must die.

[16] He required everyone—small and great, rich and poor, free and slave—to be given a mark on the right hand or on the forehead. [17] And no one could buy or sell anything without that mark, which was either the name of the beast or the number representing his name. [18] Wisdom is needed here. Let the one with understanding solve the meaning of the number of the beast, for it is the number of a man.* His number is 666.*

CHAPTER 14
The Lamb and the 144,000

Then I saw the Lamb standing on Mount Zion, and with him were 144,000 who had his name and his Father's name written on their foreheads. [2] And I heard a sound from heaven like the roar of mighty ocean waves or the rolling of loud thunder. It was like the sound of many harpists playing together.

[3] This great choir sang a wonderful new song in front of the throne of God and before the four living beings and the twenty-four elders. No one could learn this song except the 144,000 who had been redeemed from the earth. [4] They have kept themselves as pure as virgins,* following the Lamb wherever he goes. They have been purchased from among the people on the earth as a special offering* to God and to the Lamb. [5] They have told no lies; they are without blame.

The Three Angels

[6] And I saw another angel flying through the sky, carrying the eternal Good News to proclaim to the people who belong to this world—to every nation, tribe, language, and people. [7] "Fear God," he shouted. "Give glory to him. For the time has come when he will sit as judge. Worship him who made the heavens, the earth, the sea, and all the springs of water."

[8] Then another angel followed him through the sky, shouting, "Babylon is fallen—that great city is fallen—because she made all the nations of the world drink the wine of her passionate immorality."

[9] Then a third angel followed them, shouting, "Anyone who worships the beast and his statue or who accepts his mark on the forehead or on the hand [10] must drink the wine of God's anger. It has been poured full strength into God's cup of wrath. And they will be tormented with fire and burning sulfur in the presence of the holy angels and the Lamb. [11] The smoke of their torment will rise forever and ever, and they will have no relief day or night, for they have worshiped the beast and his statue and have accepted the mark of his name."

13:6 Some manuscripts read *and his dwelling and all who dwell in heaven.*   13:8 Or *not written in the Book of Life that belongs to the Lamb who was slaughtered before the world was made.*   13:18a Or *of humanity.*   13:18b Some manuscripts read *616.*   14:4a Greek *They are virgins who have not defiled themselves with women.*   14:4b Greek *as firstfruits.*

cornerstones

WHAT ROLE WILL ANGELS PLAY IN THE END TIMES?
Read REVELATION 14:6-7

The Bible tells us that the last days are going to be spiritually dark. Many people will be deceived into believing "teachings that come from demons" (see 1 Timothy 4:1, p. 261), and people will become increasingly immoral, proud, and disobedient (see 2 Timothy 3:1-5, p. 267). We already see this beginning to happen. There is a fresh demand for psychics, an increasing amount of violent crime on the streets, and a blatant lack of values in much of entertainment today.

This text shows that during the Tribulation, which is generally recognized as the last seven years on earth before Christ's return, the demons will not be the only ones at work. The angels of God will fly through the heavens preaching the everlasting gospel to make sure that everyone throughout the world is aware of the upcoming judgment of God. In essence, it will be the final "wake-up call" for people to turn to Jesus Christ.

To begin the next topic, turn to p. A27.

---

[12]This means that God's holy people must endure persecution patiently, obeying his commands and maintaining their faith in Jesus.

[13]And I heard a voice from heaven saying, "Write this down: Blessed are those who die in the Lord from now on. Yes, says the Spirit, they are blessed indeed, for they will rest from their hard work; for their good deeds follow them!"

The Harvest of the Earth
[14]Then I saw a white cloud, and seated on the cloud was someone like the Son of Man.* He had a gold crown on his head and a sharp sickle in his hand.

[15]Then another angel came from the Temple and shouted to the one sitting on the cloud, "Swing the sickle, for the time of harvest has come; the crop on earth is ripe." [16]So the one sitting on the cloud swung his sickle over the earth, and the whole earth was harvested.

[17]After that, another angel came from the Temple in heaven, and he also had a sharp sickle. [18]Then another angel, who had power to destroy with fire, came from the altar. He shouted to the angel with the sharp sickle, "Swing your sickle now to gather the clusters of grapes from the vines of the earth, for they are ripe for judgment." [19]So the angel swung his sickle over the earth and loaded the grapes into the great winepress of God's wrath. [20]The grapes were trampled in the winepress outside the city, and blood flowed from the winepress in a stream about 180 miles* long and as high as a horse's bridle.

CHAPTER **15**
The Song of Moses and of the Lamb
Then I saw in heaven another marvelous event of great significance. Seven angels were holding the seven last plagues, which would bring God's wrath to completion. [2]I saw before me what seemed to be a glass sea mixed with fire. And on it stood all the people who had been victorious over the beast and his statue and the number representing his name. They were all holding harps that God had given them. [3]And they were singing the song of Moses, the servant of God, and the song of the Lamb:

"Great and marvelous are your works,
    O Lord God, the Almighty.
Just and true are your ways,
    O King of the nations.*
[4] Who will not fear you, Lord,
    and glorify your name?
For you alone are holy.
All nations will come and worship before
    you,
    for your righteous deeds have been
    revealed."

The Seven Bowls of the Seven Plagues
[5]Then I looked and saw that the Temple in heaven, God's Tabernacle, was thrown wide open. [6]The seven angels who were holding the seven plagues came out of the Temple. They were clothed in spotless white linen* with gold sashes across their chests. [7]Then one of the four living beings handed each of the seven angels a gold bowl filled with the wrath of God,

14:14 Or *like a son of man.* See Dan 7:13. "Son of Man" is a title Jesus used for himself.   **14:20** Greek *1,600 stadia* [296 kilometers].   **15:3** Some manuscripts read *King of the ages.*   **15:6** Other manuscripts read *white stone;* still others read *white [garments] made of linen.*

who lives forever and ever. [8] The Temple was filled with smoke from God's glory and power. No one could enter the Temple until the seven angels had completed pouring out the seven plagues.

CHAPTER 16

Then I heard a mighty voice from the Temple say to the seven angels, "Go your ways and pour out on the earth the seven bowls containing God's wrath."

[2] So the first angel left the Temple and poured out his bowl on the earth, and horrible, malignant sores broke out on everyone who had the mark of the beast and who worshiped his statue.

[3] Then the second angel poured out his bowl on the sea, and it became like the blood of a corpse. And everything in the sea died.

[4] Then the third angel poured out his bowl on the rivers and springs, and they became blood. [5] And I heard the angel who had authority over all water saying,

"You are just, O Holy One, who is and who always was,
    because you have sent these judgments.
[6] Since they shed the blood
    of your holy people and your prophets,
    you have given them blood to drink.
    It is their just reward."

[7] And I heard a voice from the altar,* saying,

"Yes, O Lord God, the Almighty,
    your judgments are true and just."

[8] Then the fourth angel poured out his bowl on the sun, causing it to scorch everyone with its fire. [9] Everyone was burned by this blast of heat, and they cursed the name of God, who had control over all these plagues. They did not repent of their sins and turn to God and give him glory.

[10] Then the fifth angel poured out his bowl on the throne of the beast, and his kingdom was plunged into darkness. His subjects ground their teeth in anguish, [11] and they cursed the God of heaven for their pains and sores. But they did not repent of their evil deeds and turn to God.

[12] Then the sixth angel poured out his bowl on the great Euphrates River, and it dried up so that the kings from the east could march their armies toward the west without hindrance. [13] And I saw three evil* spirits that looked like frogs leap from the mouths of the dragon, the beast, and the false prophet. [14] They are demonic spirits who work miracles and go out to all the rulers of the world to gather them for battle against the Lord on that great judgment day of God the Almighty.

[15] "Look, I will come as unexpectedly as a thief! Blessed are all who are watching for me, who keep their clothing ready so they will not have to walk around naked and ashamed."

[16] And the demonic spirits gathered all the rulers and their armies to a place with the Hebrew name *Armageddon*.*

[17] Then the seventh angel poured out his bowl into the air. And a mighty shout came from the throne in the Temple, saying, "It is finished!" [18] Then the thunder crashed and rolled, and lightning flashed. And a great earthquake struck—the worst since people were placed on the earth. [19] The great city of Babylon split into three sections, and the cities of many nations fell into heaps of rubble. So God remembered all of Babylon's sins, and he made her drink the cup that was filled with the wine of his fierce wrath. [20] And every island disappeared, and all the mountains were leveled. [21] There was a terrible hailstorm, and hailstones weighing as much as seventy-five pounds* fell from the sky onto the people below. They cursed God because of the terrible plague of the hailstorm.

CHAPTER 17

The Great Prostitute

One of the seven angels who had poured out the seven bowls came over and spoke to me. "Come with me," he said, "and I will show you the judgment that is going to come on the great prostitute, who rules over many waters. [2] The kings of the world have committed adultery with her, and the people who belong to this world have been made drunk by the wine of her immorality."

[3] So the angel took me in the Spirit* into the wilderness. There I saw a woman sitting on a scarlet beast that had seven heads and ten horns, and blasphemies against God were written all over it. [4] The woman wore purple and scarlet clothing and beautiful jewelry made of gold and precious gems and pearls. In her hand she held a gold goblet full of obscenities and the impurities of her immorality. [5] A mysterious name was written on her forehead: "Babylon the Great, Mother of All Prostitutes and Obscenities in the World." [6] I could see that she was drunk—drunk with the blood of God's holy people who were witnesses for Jesus. I stared at her in complete amazement.

[7] "Why are you so amazed?" the angel asked.

16:7 Greek *I heard the altar.*   16:13 Greek *unclean.*   16:16 Or *Harmagedon.*   16:21 Greek *1 talent* [34 kilograms].
17:3 Or *in spirit.*

"I will tell you the mystery of this woman and of the beast with seven heads and ten horns on which she sits. [8] The beast you saw was once alive but isn't now. And yet he will soon come up out of the bottomless pit* and go to eternal destruction. And the people who belong to this world, whose names were not written in the Book of Life before the world was made, will be amazed at the reappearance of this beast who had died.

[9] "This calls for a mind with understanding: The seven heads of the beast represent the seven hills where the woman rules. They also represent seven kings. [10] Five kings have already fallen, the sixth now reigns, and the seventh is yet to come, but his reign will be brief.

[11] "The scarlet beast that was, but is no longer, is the eighth king. He is like the other seven, and he, too, is headed for destruction. [12] The ten horns of the beast are ten kings who have not yet risen to power. They will be appointed to their kingdoms for one brief moment to reign with the beast. [13] They will all agree to give him their power and authority. [14] Together they will go to war against the Lamb, but the Lamb will defeat them because he is Lord of all lords and King of all kings. And his called and chosen and faithful ones will be with him."

[15] Then the angel said to me, "The waters where the prostitute is ruling represent masses of people of every nation and language. [16] The scarlet beast and his ten horns all hate the prostitute. They will strip her naked, eat her flesh, and burn her remains with fire. [17] For God has put a plan into their minds, a plan that will carry out his purposes. They will agree to give their authority to the scarlet beast, and so the words of God will be fulfilled. [18] And this woman you saw in your vision represents the great city that rules over the kings of the world."

CHAPTER **18**

The Fall of Babylon

After all this I saw another angel come down from heaven with great authority, and the earth grew bright with his splendor. [2] He gave a mighty shout:

"Babylon is fallen—that great city is fallen!
    She has become a home for demons.
She is a hideout for every foul* spirit,
    a hideout for every foul vulture
    and every foul and dreadful animal.*
[3] For all the nations have fallen*
    because of the wine of her passionate
        immorality.

The kings of the world
    have committed adultery with her.
Because of her desires for extravagant
        luxury,
    the merchants of the world have grown
        rich."

[4] Then I heard another voice calling from heaven,

"Come away from her, my people.
    Do not take part in her sins,
    or you will be punished with her.
[5] For her sins are piled as high as heaven,
    and God remembers her evil deeds.
[6] Do to her as she has done to others.
    Double her penalty* for all her evil
        deeds.
She brewed a cup of terror for others,
    so brew twice as much* for her.
[7] She glorified herself and lived in luxury,
    so match it now with torment and
        sorrow.
She boasted in her heart,
    'I am queen on my throne.
I am no helpless widow,
    and I have no reason to mourn.'
[8] Therefore, these plagues will overtake her
        in a single day—
    death and mourning and famine.
She will be completely consumed by fire,
    for the Lord God who judges her is
        mighty."

[9] And the kings of the world who committed adultery with her and enjoyed her great luxury will mourn for her as they see the smoke rising from her charred remains. [10] They will stand at a distance, terrified by her great torment. They will cry out,

"How terrible, how terrible for you,
    O Babylon, you great city!
In a single moment
    God's judgment came on you."

[11] The merchants of the world will weep and mourn for her, for there is no one left to buy their goods. [12] She bought great quantities of gold, silver, jewels, and pearls; fine linen, purple, silk, and scarlet cloth; things made of fragrant thyine wood, ivory goods, and objects made of expensive wood; and bronze, iron, and marble. [13] She also bought cinnamon, spice, incense, myrrh, frankincense, wine, olive oil, fine flour, wheat, cattle, sheep, horses, chariots, and bodies—that is, human slaves.

[14] "The fancy things you loved so much
    are gone," they cry.

17:8 Or *the abyss,* or *the underworld.*   18:2a Greek *unclean;* also in each of the two following phrases.   18:2b Some manuscripts condense the last two lines to read *a hideout for every foul [unclean] and dreadful vulture.*   18:3 Some manuscripts read *have drunk.*   18:6a Or *Give her an equal penalty.*   18:6b Or *brew just as much.*

"All your luxuries and splendor
    are gone forever,
    never to be yours again."

¹⁵The merchants who became wealthy by selling her these things will stand at a distance, terrified by her great torment. They will weep and cry out,

¹⁶ "How terrible, how terrible for that great
        city!
    She was clothed in finest purple and
        scarlet linens,
    decked out with gold and precious
        stones and pearls!
¹⁷ In a single moment
    all the wealth of the city is gone!"

And all the captains of the merchant ships and their passengers and sailors and crews will stand at a distance. ¹⁸They will cry out as they watch the smoke ascend, and they will say, "Where is there another city as great as this?" ¹⁹And they will weep and throw dust on their heads to show their grief. And they will cry out,

"How terrible, how terrible for that great
        city!
    The shipowners became wealthy
        by transporting her great wealth on the
        seas.
    In a single moment it is all gone."

²⁰ Rejoice over her fate, O heaven
        and people of God and apostles and
        prophets!
    For at last God has judged her
        for your sakes.

²¹ Then a mighty angel picked up a boulder the size of a huge millstone. He threw it into the ocean and shouted,

"Just like this, the great city Babylon
    will be thrown down with violence
    and will never be found again.
²² The sound of harps, singers, flutes, and
        trumpets
    will never be heard in you again.
    No craftsmen and no trades
        will ever be found in you again.
    The sound of the mill
        will never be heard in you again.
²³ The light of a lamp
        will never shine in you again.
    The happy voices of brides and grooms
        will never be heard in you again.
    For your merchants were the greatest in the
        world,
        and you deceived the nations with your
        sorceries.

²⁴ In your* streets flowed the blood of the
        prophets and of God's holy people
    and the blood of people slaughtered all
        over the world."

CHAPTER 19

Songs of Victory in Heaven

After this, I heard what sounded like a vast crowd in heaven shouting,

"Praise the Lord!*
    Salvation and glory and power belong
        to our God.
² His judgments are true and just.
    He has punished the great prostitute
who corrupted the earth with her
        immorality.
    He has avenged the murder of his
        servants."

³And again their voices rang out:

"Praise the Lord!
    The smoke from that city ascends forever
    and ever!"

⁴Then the twenty-four elders and the four living beings fell down and worshiped God, who was sitting on the throne. They cried out, "Amen! Praise the Lord!"
⁵And from the throne came a voice that said,

"Praise our God,
    all his servants,
all who fear him,
    from the least to the greatest."

⁶Then I heard again what sounded like the shout of a vast crowd or the roar of mighty ocean waves or the crash of loud thunder:

"Praise the Lord!
    For the Lord our God,* the Almighty,
    reigns.
⁷ Let us be glad and rejoice,
    and let us give honor to him.
    For the time has come for the wedding feast
        of the Lamb,
    and his bride has prepared herself.
⁸ She has been given the finest of pure white
        linen to wear."
    For the fine linen represents the good
        deeds of God's holy people.

⁹And the angel said to me, "Write this: Blessed are those who are invited to the wedding feast of the Lamb." And he added, "These are true words that come from God."
¹⁰Then I fell down at his feet to worship him, but he said, "No, don't worship me. I am a servant of God, just like you and your brothers and

---

18:24 Greek *her.*   19:1 Greek *Hallelujah;* also in 19:3, 4, 6. *Hallelujah* is the transliteration of a Hebrew term that means "Praise the Lord."   19:6 Some manuscripts read *the Lord God.*

cornerstones

WHO WILL GO TO HELL?

Read REVELATION 20:11-15

The event described in this passage is the final judgment of humankind, also known as the Great White Throne Judgment. The standard by which you will be judged is simple. If you have accepted God's wonderful gift of salvation through his Son, Jesus Christ, your name will be found in the Book of Life, and you will spend eternity in heaven with God. If you have chosen to reject Christ, then your final destination will be the lake of fire. No arguments. Case closed.

Sadly, many people will unwittingly choose the latter option. They do so, not because they want to spend their eternity in agony, but because they just "go with the flow." They do what everybody else does and don't think for themselves. Jesus called this choice the easy way. In describing the way to heaven and the way to hell, Jesus said, "You can enter God's Kingdom only through the narrow gate. The highway to hell is broad, and its gate is wide for the many who choose that way. But the gateway to life is very narrow and the road is difficult, and only a few ever find it" (Matthew 7:13-14). The only way to get off this broad road and "cancel" your reservation for hell is to make sure your name is entered into God's reservation book for heaven—the Book of Life.

For the next note on "What Is Hell?" turn to p. 256.

---

sisters* who testify about their faith in Jesus. Worship only God. For the essence of prophecy is to give a clear witness for Jesus.*"

The Rider on the White Horse

¹¹ Then I saw heaven opened, and a white horse was standing there. Its rider was named Faithful and True, for he judges fairly and wages a righteous war. ¹²His eyes were like flames of fire, and on his head were many crowns. A name was written on him that no one understood except himself. ¹³He wore a robe dipped in blood, and his title was the Word of God. ¹⁴The armies of heaven, dressed in the finest of pure white linen, followed him on white horses. ¹⁵From his mouth came a sharp sword to strike down the nations. He will rule them with an iron rod. He will release the fierce wrath of God, the Almighty, like juice flowing from a winepress. ¹⁶On his robe at his thigh* was written this title: King of all kings and Lord of all lords.

¹⁷Then I saw an angel standing in the sun, shouting to the vultures flying high in the sky: "Come! Gather together for the great banquet God has prepared. ¹⁸Come and eat the flesh of kings, generals, and strong warriors; of horses and their riders; and of all humanity, both free and slave, small and great."

¹⁹Then I saw the beast and the kings of the world and their armies gathered together to fight against the one sitting on the horse and his army. ²⁰And the beast was captured, and with him the false prophet who did mighty miracles on behalf of the beast—miracles that deceived all who had accepted the mark of the beast and who worshiped his statue. Both the beast and his false prophet were thrown alive into the fiery lake of burning sulfur. ²¹Their entire army was killed by the sharp sword that came from the mouth of the one riding the white horse. And the vultures all gorged themselves on the dead bodies.

CHAPTER 20

The Thousand Years

Then I saw an angel coming down from heaven with the key to the bottomless pit* and a heavy chain in his hand. ²He seized the dragon—that old serpent, who is the devil, Satan—and bound him in chains for a thousand years. ³The angel threw him into the bottomless pit, which he then shut and locked so Satan could not deceive the nations anymore until the thousand years were finished. Afterward he must be released for a little while.

⁴Then I saw thrones, and the people sitting on them had been given the authority to judge. And I saw the souls of those who had been beheaded for their testimony about Jesus and for proclaiming the word of God. They had not worshiped the beast or his statue, nor accepted

19:10a Greek *brothers.* **19:10b** Or *is the message confirmed by Jesus.* **19:16** Or *On his robe and thigh.* **20:1** Or *the abyss,* or *the underworld;* also in 20:3.

his mark on their foreheads or their hands. They all came to life again, and they reigned with Christ for a thousand years.

[5] This is the first resurrection. (The rest of the dead did not come back to life until the thousand years had ended.) [6] Blessed and holy are those who share in the first resurrection. For them the second death holds no power, but they will be priests of God and of Christ and will reign with him a thousand years.

The Defeat of Satan

[7] When the thousand years come to an end, Satan will be let out of his prison. [8] He will go out to deceive the nations—called Gog and Magog—in every corner of the earth. He will gather them together for battle—a mighty army, as numberless as sand along the seashore. [9] And I saw them as they went up on the broad plain of the earth and surrounded God's people and the beloved city. But fire from heaven came down on the attacking armies and consumed them.

[10] Then the devil, who had deceived them, was thrown into the fiery lake of burning sulfur, joining the beast and the false prophet. There they will be tormented day and night forever and ever.

The Final Judgment

[11] And I saw a great white throne and the one sitting on it. The earth and sky fled from his presence, but they found no place to hide. [12] I saw the dead, both great and small, standing before God's throne. And the books were opened, including the Book of Life. And the dead were judged according to what they had done, as recorded in the books. [13] The sea gave up its dead, and death and the grave* gave up their dead. And all were judged according to their deeds. [14] Then death and the grave were thrown into the lake of fire. This lake of fire is the second death. [15] And anyone whose name was not found recorded in the Book of Life was thrown into the lake of fire.

CHAPTER 21

The New Jerusalem

Then I saw a new heaven and a new earth, for the old heaven and the old earth had disappeared. And the sea was also gone. [2] And I saw the holy city, the new Jerusalem, coming down from God out of heaven like a bride beautifully dressed for her husband.

[3] I heard a loud shout from the throne, saying, "Look, God's home is now among his peo-

ple! He will live with them, and they will be his people. God himself will be with them.* [4] He will wipe every tear from their eyes, and there will be no more death or sorrow or crying or pain. All these things are gone forever."

[5] And the one sitting on the throne said, "Look, I am making everything new!" And then he said to me, "Write this down, for what I tell you is trustworthy and true." [6] And he also said, "It is finished! I am the Alpha and the Omega—the Beginning and the End. To all who are thirsty I will give freely from the springs of the water of life. [7] All who are victorious will inherit all these blessings, and I will be their God, and they will be my children.

[8] "But cowards, unbelievers, the corrupt, murderers, the immoral, those who practice witchcraft, idol worshipers, and all liars—their fate is in the fiery lake of burning sulfur. This is the second death."

[9] Then one of the seven angels who held the seven bowls containing the seven last plagues came and said to me, "Come with me! I will show you the bride, the wife of the Lamb."

[10] So he took me in the Spirit* to a great, high mountain, and he showed me the holy city, Jerusalem, descending out of heaven from God. [11] It shone with the glory of God and sparkled like a precious stone—like jasper as clear as crystal. [12] The city wall was broad and high, with twelve gates guarded by twelve angels. And the names of the twelve tribes of Israel were written on the gates. [13] There were three gates on each side—east, north, south, and west. [14] The wall of the city had twelve foundation stones, and on them were written the names of the twelve apostles of the Lamb.

[15] The angel who talked to me held in his hand a gold measuring stick to measure the city, its gates, and its wall. [16] When he measured it, he found it was a square, as wide as it was long. In fact, its length and width and height were each 1,400 miles.* [17] Then he measured the walls and found them to be 216 feet thick* (according to the human standard used by the angel).

[18] The wall was made of jasper, and the city was pure gold, as clear as glass. [19] The wall of the city was built on foundation stones inlaid with twelve precious stones:* the first was jasper, the second sapphire, the third agate, the fourth emerald, [20] the fifth onyx, the sixth carnelian, the seventh chrysolite, the eighth beryl, the ninth topaz, the tenth chrysoprase, the eleventh jacinth, the twelfth amethyst.

[21] The twelve gates were made of pearls—

20:13 Greek *and Hades;* also in 20:14.   21:3 Some manuscripts read *God himself will be with them, their God.*   21:10 Or *in spirit.*   21:16 Greek *12,000 stadia* [2,220 kilometers].   21:17 Greek *144 cubits* [65 meters].   21:19 The identification of some of these gemstones is uncertain.

each gate from a single pearl! And the main street was pure gold, as clear as glass.

²²I saw no temple in the city, for the Lord God Almighty and the Lamb are its temple. ²³And the city has no need of sun or moon, for the glory of God illuminates the city, and the Lamb is its light. ²⁴The nations will walk in its light, and the kings of the world will enter the city in all their glory. ²⁵Its gates will never be closed at the end of day because there is no night there. ²⁶And all the nations will bring their glory and honor into the city. ²⁷Nothing evil* will be allowed to enter, nor anyone who practices shameful idolatry and dishonesty— but only those whose names are written in the Lamb's Book of Life.

CHAPTER **22**

Then the angel showed me a river with the water of life, clear as crystal, flowing from the throne of God and of the Lamb. ²It flowed down the center of the main street. On each side of the river grew a tree of life, bearing twelve crops of fruit,* with a fresh crop each month. The leaves were used for medicine to heal the nations.

³No longer will there be a curse upon anything. For the throne of God and of the Lamb will be there, and his servants will worship him. ⁴And they will see his face, and his name will be written on their foreheads. ⁵And there will be no night there—no need for lamps or sun—for the Lord God will shine on them. And they will reign forever and ever.

⁶Then the angel said to me, "Everything you have heard and seen is trustworthy and true. The Lord God, who inspires his prophets,* has sent his angel to tell his servants what will happen soon.*"

Jesus Is Coming

⁷"Look, I am coming soon! Blessed are those who obey the words of prophecy written in this book.*"

⁸I, John, am the one who heard and saw all these things. And when I heard and saw them, I fell down to worship at the feet of the angel who showed them to me. ⁹But he said, "No, don't worship me. I am a servant of God, just like you and your brothers the prophets, as well as all who obey what is written in this book. Worship only God!"

¹⁰Then he instructed me, "Do not seal up the prophetic words in this book, for the time is near. ¹¹Let the one who is doing harm continue to do harm; let the one who is vile continue to be vile; let the one who is righteous continue to live righteously; let the one who is holy continue to be holy."

¹²"Look, I am coming soon, bringing my reward with me to repay all people according to their deeds. ¹³I am the Alpha and the Omega, the First and the Last, the Beginning and the End."

¹⁴Blessed are those who wash their robes. They will be permitted to enter through the gates of the city and eat the fruit from the tree of life. ¹⁵Outside the city are the dogs—the sorcerers, the sexually immoral, the murderers, the idol worshipers, and all who love to live a lie.

¹⁶"I, Jesus, have sent my angel to give you this message for the churches. I am both the source of David and the heir to his throne.* I am the bright morning star."

¹⁷The Spirit and the bride say, "Come." Let anyone who hears this say, "Come." Let anyone who is thirsty come. Let anyone who desires drink freely from the water of life. ¹⁸And I solemnly declare to everyone who hears the words of prophecy written in this book: If anyone adds anything to what is written here, God will add to that person the plagues described in this book. ¹⁹And if anyone removes any of the words from this book of prophecy, God will remove that person's share in the tree of life and in the holy city that are described in this book.

²⁰He who is the faithful witness to all these things says, "Yes, I am coming soon!"

Amen! Come, Lord Jesus!

²¹May the grace of the Lord Jesus be with God's holy people.*

21:27 Or *ceremonially unclean.*   22:2 Or *twelve kinds of fruit.*   22:6a Or *The Lord, the God of the spirits of the prophets.* 22:6b Or *suddenly,* or *quickly;* also in 22:7, 12, 20.   22:7 Or *scroll;* also in 22:9, 10, 18, 19.   22:16 Greek *I am the root and offspring of David.*   22:21 Other manuscripts read *be with all;* still others read *be with all of God's holy people.* Some manuscripts add *Amen.*

The *Holy Bible,* New Living Translation, was first published in 1996. It quickly became one of the most popular Bible translations in the English-speaking world. While the NLT's influence was rapidly growing, the Bible Translation Committee determined that an additional investment in scholarly review and text refinement could make it even better. So shortly after its initial publication, the committee began an eight-year process with the purpose of increasing the level of the NLT's precision without sacrificing its easy-to-understand quality. This second-generation text was completed in 2004, with minor changes subsequently introduced in 2007.

The goal of any Bible translation is to convey the meaning and content of the ancient Hebrew, Aramaic, and Greek texts as accurately as possible to contemporary readers. The challenge for our translators was to create a text that would communicate as clearly and powerfully to today's readers as the original texts did to readers and listeners in the ancient biblical world. The resulting translation is easy to read and understand, while also accurately communicating the meaning and content of the original biblical texts. The NLT is a general-purpose text especially good for study, devotional reading, and reading aloud in worship services.

We believe that the New Living Translation—which combines the latest biblical scholarship with a clear, dynamic writing style—will communicate God's word powerfully to all who read it. We publish it with the prayer that God will use it to speak his timeless truth to the church and the world in a fresh, new way.

The Publishers
October 2007

Translation Philosophy and Methodology. English Bible translations tend to be governed by one of two general translation theories. The first theory has been called "formal-equivalence," "literal," or "word-for-word" translation. According to this theory, the translator attempts to render each word of the original language into English and seeks to preserve the original syntax and sentence structure as much as possible in translation. The second theory has been called "dynamic-equivalence," "functional-equivalence," or "thought-for-thought" translation. The goal of this translation theory is to produce in English the closest natural equivalent of the message expressed by the original-language text, both in meaning and in style.

Both of these translation theories have their strengths. A formal-equivalence translation preserves aspects of the original text—including ancient idioms, term consistency, and original-language syntax—that are valuable for scholars and professional study. It allows a reader to trace formal elements of the original-language text through the English translation. A dynamic-equivalence translation, on the other hand, focuses on translating the message of the original-language text. It ensures that the meaning of the text is readily apparent to the contemporary reader. This allows the message to come through with immediacy, without requiring the reader to struggle with foreign idioms and awkward syntax. It also facilitates serious study of the text's message and clarity in both devotional and public reading.

The pure application of either of these translation philosophies would create translations at opposite ends of the translation spectrum. But in reality, all translations contain a mixture of these two philosophies. A purely formal-equivalence translation would be unintelligible in English, and a purely dynamic-equivalence translation would risk being unfaithful to the original. That is why translations shaped by dynamic-equivalence theory are usually quite literal when the original text is relatively clear, and the translations shaped by formal-equivalence theory are sometimes quite dynamic when the original text is obscure.

The translators of the New Living Translation set out to render the message of the original texts of Scripture into clear, contemporary English. As they did so, they kept the concerns of both formal-equivalence and dynamic-equivalence in mind. On the one hand, they translated as simply and literally as possible when that approach yielded an accurate, clear, and natural English text. Many words and phrases were rendered literally and consistently into English, preserving essential literary and rhetorical devices, ancient metaphors, and word choices that give structure to the text and provide echoes of meaning from one passage to the next.

On the other hand, the translators rendered the message more dynamically when the literal rendering was hard to understand, was misleading, or yielded archaic or foreign wording. They clarified difficult metaphors and terms to aid in the reader's understanding. The translators first struggled with the meaning of the words and phrases in the ancient context; then they rendered the message into clear, natural English. Their goal was to be both faithful to the ancient texts and eminently readable. The result is a translation that is both exegetically accurate and idiomatically powerful.

Translation Process and Team. To produce an accurate translation of the Bible into contemporary English, the translation team needed the skills necessary to enter into the thought patterns of the ancient authors and then to render their ideas, connotations, and effects into clear, contemporary English. To begin this process, qualified biblical scholars were needed to interpret the meaning of the original text and to check it against our base English translation. In order to guard against personal and theological biases, the scholars needed to represent a diverse group of Evangelicals who would employ the best exegetical tools. Then to work alongside the scholars, skilled English stylists were needed to shape the text into clear, contemporary English.

With these concerns in mind, the Bible Translation Committee recruited teams of scholars that represented a broad spectrum of denominations, theological perspectives, and backgrounds within the worldwide Evangelical community. (These scholars are listed at the end of this introduction.) Each book of the Bible was assigned to three different scholars with proven expertise in the book or group of books to be reviewed. Each of these scholars made a thorough review of a base translation and submitted suggested revisions to the appropriate Senior Translator. The Senior Translator then reviewed and summarized these suggestions and proposed a first-draft revision of the base text. This draft served as the basis for several additional phases of exegetical and stylistic committee review. Then the Bible Translation Committee jointly reviewed and approved every verse of the final translation.

Throughout the translation and editing process, the Senior Translators and their scholar teams were given a chance to review the editing done by the team of stylists. This ensured that exegetical errors would not be introduced late in the process and that the entire Bible Translation Committee was happy with the final result. By choosing a team of qualified scholars and skilled stylists and by setting up a process that allowed their interaction throughout the process, the New Living Translation has been refined to preserve the essential formal elements of the original biblical texts, while also creating a clear, understandable English text.

The New Living Translation was first published in 1996. Shortly after its initial publication, the Bible Translation Committee began a process of further committee review and translation refinement. The purpose of this continued revision was to increase the level of precision without sacrificing the text's easy-to-understand quality. This second-edition text was completed in 2004, and an additional update with minor changes was subsequently introduced in 2007. This printing of the New Living Translation reflects the updated 2007 text.

Written to Be Read Aloud. It is evident in Scripture that the biblical documents were written to be read aloud, often in public worship (see Nehemiah 8; Luke 4:16-20; 1 Timothy 4:13; Revelation 1:3). It is still the case today that more people will hear the Bible read aloud in church than are likely to read it for themselves. Therefore, a new translation must communicate with clarity and power when it is read publicly. Clarity was a primary goal for the NLT translators, not only to facilitate private reading and understanding, but also to ensure that it would be excellent for public reading and make an immediate and powerful impact on any listener.

The Texts behind the New Living Translation. The Old Testament translators used the Masoretic Text of the Hebrew Bible as represented in *Biblia Hebraica Stuttgartensia* (1977), with its extensive system of textual notes; this is an update of Rudolf Kittel's *Biblia Hebraica* (Stuttgart, 1937). The translators also further compared the Dead Sea Scrolls, the Septuagint and other Greek manuscripts, the Samaritan Pentateuch, the Syriac Peshitta, the Latin Vulgate, and any other versions or manuscripts that shed light on the meaning of difficult passages.

The New Testament translators used the two standard editions of the Greek New Testament: the *Greek New Testament*, published by the United Bible Societies (UBS, fourth revised edition, 1993), and *Novum Testamentum Graece*, edited by Nestle and Aland (NA, twenty-seventh edition, 1993). These two editions, which have the same text but differ in punctuation and textual notes, represent, for the most part, the best in modern textual scholarship. However, in cases where strong textual or other scholarly evidence supported the decision, the translators sometimes chose to differ from the UBS and NA Greek texts and followed variant readings found in other ancient witnesses. Significant textual variants of this sort are always noted in the textual notes of the New Living Translation.

Translation Issues. The translators have made a conscious effort to provide a text that can be easily understood by the typical reader of modern English. To this end, we sought to use only vocabulary and language structures in common use today. We avoided using language likely to become quickly dated or that reflects only a narrow subdialect of English, with the goal of making the New Living Translation as broadly useful and timeless as possible.

But our concern for readability goes beyond the concerns of vocabulary and sentence structure. We are also concerned about historical and cultural barriers to understanding the Bible, and we have sought to translate terms shrouded in history and culture in ways that can be immediately understood. To this end:

- We have converted ancient weights and measures (for example, "ephah" [a unit of dry volume] or "cubit" [a unit of length]) to modern English (American) equivalents, since the ancient measures are not generally meaningful to today's readers. Then in the textual footnotes we offer the literal Hebrew, Aramaic, or Greek measures, along with modern metric equivalents.

• Instead of translating ancient currency values literally, we have expressed them in common terms that communicate the message. For example, in the Old Testament, "ten shekels of silver" becomes "ten pieces of silver" to convey the intended message. In the New Testament, we have often translated the "denarius" as "the normal daily wage" to facilitate understanding. Then a footnote offers: "Greek *a denarius*, the payment for a full day's wage." In general, we give a clear English rendering and then state the literal Hebrew, Aramaic, or Greek in a textual footnote.

• Since the names of Hebrew months are unknown to most contemporary readers, and since the Hebrew lunar calendar fluctuates from year to year in relation to the solar calendar used today, we have looked for clear ways to communicate the time of year the Hebrew months (such as Abib) refer to. When an expanded or interpretive rendering is given in the text, a textual note gives the literal rendering. Where it is possible to define a specific ancient date in terms of our modern calendar, we use modern dates in the text. A textual footnote then gives the literal Hebrew date and states the rationale for our rendering. For example, Ezra 6:15 pinpoints the date when the postexilic Temple was completed in Jerusalem: "the third day of the month Adar." This was during the sixth year of King Darius's reign (that is, 515 B.C.). We have translated that date as March 12, with a footnote giving the Hebrew and identifying the year as 515 B.C.

• Since ancient references to the time of day differ from our modern methods of denoting time, we have used renderings that are instantly understandable to the modern reader. Accordingly, we have rendered specific times of day by using approximate equivalents in terms of our common "o'clock" system. On occasion, translations such as "at dawn the next morning" or "as the sun was setting" have been used when the biblical reference is more general.

• When the meaning of a proper name (or a wordplay inherent in a proper name) is relevant to the message of the text, its meaning is often illuminated with a textual footnote. For example, in Exodus 2:10 the text reads: "The princess named him Moses, for she explained, 'I lifted him out of the water.' " The accompanying footnote reads: "*Moses* sounds like a Hebrew term that means 'to lift out.' "

   Sometimes, when the actual meaning of a name is clear, that meaning is included in parentheses within the text itself. For example, the text at Genesis 16:11 reads: "You are to name him Ishmael (*which means 'God hears'*), for the LORD has heard your cry of distress." Since the original hearers and readers would have instantly understood the meaning of the name "Ishmael," we have provided modern readers with the same information so they can experience the text in a similar way.

• Many words and phrases carry a great deal of cultural meaning that was obvious to the original readers but needs explanation in our own culture. For example, the phrase "they beat their breasts" (Luke 23:48) in ancient times meant that people were very upset, often in mourning. In our translation we chose to translate this phrase dynamically for clarity: "They went home *in deep sorrow*." Then we included a footnote with the literal Greek, which reads: "Greek *went home beating their breasts*." In other similar cases, however, we have sometimes chosen to illuminate the existing literal expression to make it immediately understandable. For example, here we might have expanded the literal Greek phrase to read: "They went home beating their breasts *in sorrow*." If we had done this, we would not have included a textual footnote, since the literal Greek clearly appears in translation.

- Metaphorical language is sometimes difficult for contemporary readers to understand, so at times we have chosen to translate or illuminate the meaning of a metaphor. For example, the ancient poet writes, "Your neck is *like* the tower of David" (Song of Songs 4:4). We have rendered it "Your neck is *as beautiful as* the tower of David" to clarify the intended positive meaning of the simile. Another example comes in Ecclesiastes 12:3, which can be literally rendered: "Remember him . . . when the grinding women cease because they are few, and the women who look through the windows see dimly." We have rendered it: "Remember him before your teeth—your few remaining servants—stop grinding; and before your eyes—the women looking through the windows—see dimly." We clarified such metaphors only when we believed a typical reader might be confused by the literal text.

- When the content of the original language text is poetic in character, we have rendered it in English poetic form. We sought to break lines in ways that clarify and highlight the relationships between phrases of the text. Hebrew poetry often uses parallelism, a literary form where a second phrase (or in some instances a third or fourth) echoes the initial phrase in some way. In Hebrew parallelism, the subsequent parallel phrases continue, while also furthering and sharpening, the thought expressed in the initial line or phrase. Whenever possible, we sought to represent these parallel phrases in natural poetic English.

- The Greek term *hoi Ioudaioi* is literally translated "the Jews" in many English translations. In the Gospel of John, however, this term doesn't always refer to the Jewish people generally. In some contexts, it refers more particularly to the Jewish religious leaders. We have attempted to capture the meaning in these different contexts by using terms such as "the people" (with a footnote: Greek *the Jewish people*) or "the religious leaders," where appropriate.

- One challenge we faced was how to translate accurately the ancient biblical text that was originally written in a context where male-oriented terms were used to refer to humanity generally. We needed to respect the nature of the ancient context while also trying to make the translation clear to a modern audience that tends to read male-oriented language as applying only to males. Often the original text, though using masculine nouns and pronouns, clearly intends that the message be applied to both men and women. A typical example is found in the New Testament letters, where the believers are called "brothers" (*adelphoi*). Yet it is clear from the content of these letters that they were addressed to all the believers—male and female. Thus, we have usually translated this Greek word as "brothers and sisters" in order to represent the historical situation more accurately.

We have also been sensitive to passages where the text applies generally to human beings or to the human condition. In some instances we have used plural pronouns (they, them) in place of the masculine singular (he, him). For example, a traditional rendering of Proverbs 22:6 is: "Train up a child in the way he should go, and when he is old he will not turn from it." We have rendered it: "Direct your children onto the right path, and when they are older, they will not leave it." At times, we have also replaced third person pronouns with the second person to ensure clarity. A traditional rendering of Proverbs 26:27 is: "He who digs a pit will fall into it, and he who rolls a stone, it will come back on him." We have rendered it: "If you set a trap for others, you will get caught in it yourself. If you roll a boulder down on others, it will crush you instead."

We should emphasize, however, that all masculine nouns and pronouns used to represent God (for example, "Father") have been maintained without exception. All decisions of this kind have been driven by the concern to reflect accurately the intended meaning of the original texts of Scripture.

Lexical Consistency in Terminology. For the sake of clarity, we have translated certain original-language terms consistently, especially within synoptic passages and for commonly repeated rhetorical phrases, and within certain word categories such as divine names and non-theological technical terminology (e.g., liturgical, legal, cultural, zoological, and botanical terms). For theological terms, we have allowed a greater semantic range of acceptable English words or phrases for a single Hebrew or Greek word. We have avoided some theological terms that are not readily understood by many modern readers. For example, we avoided using words such as "justification" and "sanctification," which are carryovers from Latin translations. In place of these words, we have provided renderings such as "made right with God" and "made holy."

The Spelling of Proper Names. Many individuals in the Bible, especially the Old Testament, are known by more than one name (e.g., Uzziah/Azariah). For the sake of clarity, we have tried to use a single spelling for any one individual, footnoting the literal spelling whenever we differ from it. This is especially helpful in delineating the kings of Israel and Judah. King Joash/Jehoash of Israel has been consistently called Jehoash, while King Joash/Jehoash of Judah is called Joash. A similar distinction has been used to distinguish between Joram/Jehoram of Israel and Joram/Jehoram of Judah. All such decisions were made with the goal of clarifying the text for the reader. When the ancient biblical writers clearly had a theological purpose in their choice of a variant name (e.g., Esh-baal/Ishbosheth), the different names have been maintained with an explanatory footnote.

For the names Jacob and Israel, which are used interchangeably for both the individual patriarch and the nation, we generally render it "Israel" when it refers to the nation and "Jacob" when it refers to the individual. When our rendering of the name differs from the underlying Hebrew text, we provide a textual footnote, which includes this explanation:

"The names 'Jacob' and 'Israel' are often interchanged throughout the Old Testament, referring sometimes to the individual patriarch and sometimes to the nation."

The Rendering of Divine Names. All appearances of *'el, 'elohim,* or *'eloah* have been translated "God," except where the context demands the translation "god(s)." We have generally rendered the tetragrammaton (*YHWH*) consistently as "the Lord," utilizing a form with small capitals that is common among English translations. This will distinguish it from the name *'adonai,* which we render "Lord." When *'adonai* and *YHWH* appear together, we have rendered it "Sovereign Lord." This also distinguishes *'adonai YHWH* from cases where *YHWH* appears with *'elohim,* which is rendered "Lord God." When *YH* (the short form of *YHWH*) and *YHWH* appear together, we have rendered it "Lord God." When *YHWH* appears with the term *tseba'oth,* we have rendered it "Lord of Heaven's Armies" to translate the meaning of the name. In a few cases, we have utilized the transliteration, *Yahweh,* when the personal character of the name is being invoked in contrast to another divine name or the name of some other god (for example, see Exodus 3:15; 6:2-3).

In the New Testament, the Greek word *christos* has been translated as "Messiah" when the context assumes a Jewish audience. When a Gentile audience can be assumed, *christos* has been translated as "Christ." The Greek word *kurios* is consistently translated "Lord," except that it is translated "Lord" wherever the New Testament text explicitly quotes from the Old Testament, and the text there has it in small capitals.

Textual Footnotes. The New Living Translation provides several kinds of textual footnotes, all designated in the text with an asterisk:

- When for the sake of clarity the NLT renders a difficult or potentially confusing phrase dynamically, we generally give the literal rendering in a textual footnote. This allows the reader to see the literal source of our dynamic rendering and how our translation relates to other more literal translations. These notes are prefaced with "Hebrew," "Aramaic," or "Greek," identifying the language of the underlying source text. For example, in Acts 2:42 we translated the literal "breaking of bread" (from the Greek) as "the Lord's Supper" to clarify that this verse refers to the ceremonial practice of the church rather than just an ordinary meal. Then we attached a footnote to "the Lord's Supper," which reads: "Greek *the breaking of bread.*"

- Textual footnotes are also used to show alternative renderings, prefaced with the word "Or." These normally occur for passages where an aspect of the meaning is debated. On occasion, we also provide notes on words or phrases that represent a departure from long-standing tradition. These notes are prefaced with "Traditionally rendered." For example, the footnote to the translation "serious skin disease" at Leviticus 13:2 says: "Traditionally rendered *leprosy.* The Hebrew word used throughout this passage is used to describe various skin diseases."

- When our translators follow a textual variant that differs significantly from our standard Hebrew or Greek texts (listed earlier), we document that difference with a footnote. We also footnote cases when the NLT excludes a passage that is included in the Greek text known as the *Textus Receptus* (and familiar to readers through its translation in the King James Version). In such cases, we offer a translation of the excluded text in a footnote, even though it is generally recognized as a later addition to the Greek text and not part of the original Greek New Testament.

- All Old Testament passages that are quoted in the New Testament are identified by a textual footnote at the New Testament location. When the New Testament clearly quotes from the Greek translation of the Old Testament, and when it differs significantly in wording from the Hebrew text, we also place a textual footnote at the Old Testament location. This note includes a rendering of the Greek version, along with a cross-reference to the New Testament passage(s) where it is cited (for example, see notes on Psalms 8:2; 53:3; Proverbs 3:12).

- Some textual footnotes provide cultural and historical information on places, things, and people in the Bible that are probably obscure to modern readers. Such notes should aid the reader in understanding the message of the text. For example, in Acts 12:1, "King Herod" is named in this translation as "King Herod Agrippa" and is identified in a footnote as being "the nephew of Herod Antipas and a grandson of Herod the Great."

- When the meaning of a proper name (or a wordplay inherent in a proper name) is relevant to the meaning of the text, it is either illuminated with a textual footnote or included within parentheses in the text itself. For example, the footnote concerning the name "Eve" at Genesis 3:20 reads: "*Eve* sounds like a Hebrew term that means 'to give life.' " This wordplay in the Hebrew illuminates the meaning of the text, which goes on to say that Eve "would be the mother of all who live."

As WE SUBMIT this translation for publication, we recognize that any translation of the Scriptures is subject to limitations and imperfections. Anyone who has attempted to communicate the richness of God's Word into another language will realize it is impossible to make a perfect translation. Recognizing these limitations, we sought God's guidance and wisdom throughout this project. Now we pray that he will accept our efforts and use this translation for the benefit of the church and of all people.

We pray that the New Living Translation will overcome some of the barriers of history, culture, and language that have kept people from reading and understanding God's Word. We hope that readers unfamiliar with the Bible will find the words clear and easy to understand and that readers well versed in the Scriptures will gain a fresh perspective. We pray that readers will gain insight and wisdom for living, but most of all that they will meet the God of the Bible and be forever changed by knowing him.

The Bible Translation Committee
October 2007

ECCLESIASTES, SONG OF SONGS
Daniel C. Fredericks, *Belhaven College*
David Hubbard (deceased), *Fuller Theological Seminary*
Tremper Longman III, *Westmont College*

PROPHETS
John N. Oswalt, Senior Translator
Asbury Theological Seminary

ISAIAH
John N. Oswalt, *Asbury Theological Seminary*
Gary Smith, *Union University*
John Walton, *Wheaton College*

JEREMIAH, LAMENTATIONS
G. Herbert Livingston, *Asbury Theological Seminary*
Elmer A. Martens, *Mennonite Brethren Biblical Seminary*

EZEKIEL
Daniel I. Block, *Wheaton College*
David H. Engelhard, *Calvin Theological Seminary*
David Thompson, *Asbury Theological Seminary*

DANIEL, HAGGAI—MALACHI
Joyce Baldwin Caine (deceased), *Trinity College, Bristol*
Douglas Gropp, *Catholic University of America*
Roy Hayden, *Oral Roberts School of Theology*
Andrew Hill, *Wheaton College*
Tremper Longman III, *Westmont College*

HOSEA—ZEPHANIAH
Joseph Coleson, *Nazarene Theological Seminary*
Roy Hayden, *Oral Roberts School of Theology*
Andrew Hill, *Wheaton College*
Richard Patterson, *Liberty University*

GOSPELS AND ACTS
Grant R. Osborne, Senior Translator
Trinity Evangelical Divinity School

MATTHEW
Craig Blomberg, *Denver Seminary*
Donald A. Hagner, *Fuller Theological Seminary*
David Turner, *Grand Rapids Baptist Seminary*

MARK
Robert Guelich (deceased), *Fuller Theological Seminary*
George Guthrie, *Union University*
Grant R. Osborne, *Trinity Evangelical Divinity School*

LUKE
Darrell Bock, *Dallas Theological Seminary*
Scot McKnight, *North Park University*
Robert Stein, *The Southern Baptist Theological Seminary*

JOHN
Gary M. Burge, *Wheaton College*
Philip W. Comfort, *Coastal Carolina University*
Marianne Meye Thompson, *Fuller Theological Seminary*

ACTS
D. A. Carson, *Trinity Evangelical Divinity School*
William J. Larkin, *Columbia International University*
Roger Mohrlang, *Whitworth University*

LETTERS AND REVELATION
Norman R. Ericson, Senior Translator
Wheaton College

ROMANS, GALATIANS
Gerald Borchert, *Northern Baptist Theological Seminary*
Douglas J. Moo, *Wheaton College*
Thomas R. Schreiner, *The Southern Baptist Theological Seminary*

1 & 2 CORINTHIANS
Joseph Alexanian, *Trinity International University*
Linda Belleville, *Bethel College, Mishawaka, Indiana*
Douglas A. Oss, *Central Bible College*
Robert Sloan, *Houston Baptist University*

EPHESIANS—PHILEMON
Harold W. Hoehner (deceased), *Dallas Theological Seminary*
Moises Silva, *Gordon-Conwell Theological Seminary*
Klyne Snodgrass, *North Park Theological Seminary*

HEBREWS, JAMES, 1 & 2 PETER, JUDE
Peter Davids, *St. Stephen's University*
Norman R. Ericson, *Wheaton University*
William Lane (deceased), *Seattle Pacific University*
J. Ramsey Michaels, *S. W. Missouri State University*

1–3 JOHN, REVELATION
Greg Beale, *Westminster Theological Seminary*
Robert Mounce, *Whitworth University*
M. Robert Mulholland, Jr., *Asbury Theological Seminary*

SPECIAL REVIEWERS
F. F. Bruce (deceased), *University of Manchester*
Kenneth N. Taylor (deceased), *Translator*, The Living Bible

COORDINATING TEAM
Mark D. Taylor, *Director and Chief Stylist*
Ronald A. Beers, *Executive Director and Stylist*
Mark R. Norton, *Managing Editor and O.T. Coordinating Editor*
Philip W. Comfort, *N.T. Coordinating Editor*
Daniel W. Taylor, *Bethel University, Senior Stylist*

Now that you are a Christian, one thing you will want to do on a daily basis is study the Bible. You may, however, have some questions about this. For example, you may ask yourself, *How do I study the Bible?* Or, *Where do I begin reading?* This feature will answer those questions and give you the information you need to develop the basic techniques necessary for effective Bible study.

Pray for Wisdom and Understanding. The most often overlooked and undervalued aspect of Bible study is prayer. Yet prayer is essential to gaining wisdom and understanding when you read God's Word. Through prayer, you can approach God and acknowledge your incomplete knowledge of his Word, as well as your need for him to open your heart to his instruction. Therefore, determine to begin each study with prayer. Only God can give you the wisdom to understand his Word.

Read in an Orderly Manner. If you received a letter and read only a few sentences here and there, the letter would not make much sense to you. But if you read the letter in order, you would understand it. The same holds true when you read the New Testament.

Sadly, many Christians do not realize the shallowness of the skipping-around approach. They read a portion of Matthew, a story from Acts, a verse or two from James, and then a chapter or so from Revelation and wonder why they do not have a good understanding of God's Word. Furthermore, they end up misinterpreting the meaning of these passages because they have failed to grasp the context from which they came.

To avoid developing this poor habit, you need to discipline yourself to read in an orderly manner. One way to do this is to use an established reading plan. A reading plan lists Scripture passages to be read in a certain order. Many of the existing plans were created with a goal in mind. Some plans break the whole Bible down into 365 daily readings. Others help you read through the Bible in the order that the events actually happened. For now, you may want to use the following plan as your reading guide. Start with the Gospel of John. This Gospel was written so that we might believe that Jesus is the Son of God. Then, after you have finished reading John, read the rest of the New Testament. Once you have finished the New Testament, you should get a full Bible and read the books of the Old Testament. There you will see the coming of Jesus foreshadowed.

Finish What You Start. In life, the benefits of doing anything are often not realized until the task is completed. The same is true when reading a book from the Bible. Once you choose a book to read, read it from beginning to end. Although you may benefit spiritually by reading a verse from one book or a story from another, you will benefit more by reading the entire book from which the verse or story came. Reading the entire book puts each verse and story in its proper context. Thus, you will have a better understanding of what each verse and story means. In addition, by reading books from beginning to end you will become more familiar with the Bible as a whole. You may even discover passages that will one day become your favorites.

Meditate on God's Word and Ask Questions. Thinking about what you have read cannot be overemphasized. Meditating on what you have read helps you discover the importance of the passage. It also helps you to examine your life in light of what God reveals in his Word.

One of the best ways to begin meditating on God's Word is to ask questions. Here are a few questions to help you get started:

- What is the main subject of the passage?
- To whom is this passage addressed?
- Who is speaking?
- About what or whom is the person speaking?
- What is the key verse?
- What does this passage teach me about God?

To see how the text might apply to you personally, ask yourself these questions:

- Is there any sin mentioned in the passage that I need to confess or forsake?
- Is there a command given that I should obey?
- Is there a promise made that I can apply to my current circumstances?
- Is there a prayer given that I could pray?

Invest in a Few Good Resource Books. The Bible alludes to many ancient customs that are completely unfamiliar to us today. Much of the subtle meaning behind these allusions that would give us greater insight into and appreciation for God's Word is therefore lost. To understand the culture in which the Bible was written, you may want to purchase a few good biblical resource books.

There are two types of resource books you should look into purchasing: (1) a one- or two-volume commentary on the whole Bible and (2) a Bible dictionary. Most one- or two-volume commentaries are concise. They give you the necessary information on important words, phrases, and verses from the Bible. They will not give you commentary on each verse, and they will not go into detailed explanations on any one verse. But they are good resources to help you begin to understand God's Word. The price for such a commentary can range from twenty-five to forty dollars per volume.

Bible dictionaries contain short articles (in alphabetical order) on people, places, and objects found in the Bible. Some Bible dictionaries also contain maps, diagrams, and pictures of biblical cities, regions, and artifacts. Bible dictionaries cost between twenty-five and thirty-five dollars. You can find these resources wherever Christian books are sold.

If you apply these practices to your daily personal Bible study, you are bound to develop habits that will help you grow in your faith.

TO INVESTIGATE

Abuse

Jesus was abused (Matthew 26:67-68)

Abuse has no place in family relationships (Ephesians 5:21–6:4)

Accountability

We are accountable for every word that we speak (Matthew 12:36)

We are accountable for what we believe (John 3:18)

God will examine our actions (2 Corinthians 5:10)

Accusations

Christians' sins are forgiven (Colossians 1:22)

Adoption, Spiritual

Christians are God's children (John 1:12)

All of God's children are equal in God's eyes (Galatians 3:28)

God chose us to be his children (Ephesians 1:4-5)

Jesus is our spiritual brother (Hebrews 2:11)

Alcohol

Becoming drunk is a sin (Romans 13:13-14)

God hates drunkenness (Galatians 5:19-21)

Anger

Anger can give Satan a place in your life (Ephesians 4:26-27)

Christians should get rid of anger (Colossians 3:8)

Be slow to become angry (James 1:19)

Appearance

Christians should care more for spiritual status than physical appearance
(1 Timothy 2:9-10)

Do not judge others by their appearance (James 2:2-4)

Inner beauty is more important than physical beauty (1 Peter 3:1-6)

Arguments
We should avoid arguments (Philippians 2:14)

Armor
Spiritual armor prepares us for life (Romans 13:12)
The armor of God (Ephesians 6:11-18)

Assurance
We can be assured of eternal life (John 5:24)
Nothing can separate God's children from God (Romans 8:35-39)

Atonement
Jesus provided the atonement for sins (Romans 3:23-25)
Our atonement allows us to know God (Ephesians 2:13)
Sin requires that a sacrifice be made (Hebrews 9:22)
Jesus' sacrifice was perfect (1 Peter 1:18-19)
We cannot improve Jesus' sacrifice (1 Peter 3:18)

Attitude
God will reward the meek (Matthew 5:5)
We should imitate Jesus' attitude (Philippians 2:5)

Authority (see also Respect)
Jesus is the highest authority (Matthew 28:18)
God gave government its authority (John 19:11)
Christians should obey the government (Romans 13:1-2)
Parents are authorities to their children (Ephesians 6:1)
The Bible is our authority (2 Timothy 3:16)
Church leaders are authoritative (Hebrews 13:17)

Bad Language
Use good language (Ephesians 4:29)
Foul language is not fitting for a Christian (Ephesians 5:4)
Our speech reflects our relationship with God (Colossians 4:6)
Our speech should be an example to others (1 Timothy 4:12)

Baptism
Baptism signifies repentance (Matthew 3:11)
All followers of Jesus should be baptized (Matthew 28:19)
Baptism is closely linked with a changed life (Acts 2:38)
Entire families of the early church were baptized (Acts 16:33-34)

Belief
Belief affects the way we live (Mark 1:15)
Beliefs should reflect the heart (Romans 10:9)
Believing is more than acknowledging (James 2:21)

Bible

The Bible is inspired by God (2 Timothy 3:16)

The Bible helps us grow spiritually (1 Peter 2:2)

Birth

Jesus' birth (Luke 2:7)

God's children are reborn spiritually (John 1:12-13)

People must be reborn spiritually to enter heaven (John 3:3)

Blessing

God blesses those who follow Jesus (Matthew 5:3-11)

Blood

Jesus' blood seals God's relationship with his people (Matthew 26:28)

Jesus' blood allows us to have access to God (Romans 5:8-9)

Christians are redeemed by Jesus' blood (Ephesians 1:5-7)

Blood is required for forgiveness (Hebrews 9:22)

Body of Christ

There are many parts, but one body (1 Corinthians 12:12-13)

Christians make up the body of Christ (1 Corinthians 12:27)

Different members of the body help each other grow (Ephesians 4:11-12)

Jesus is the head of the body (Colossians 1:18)

Book of Life

The names of Christians are in the Book of Life (Philippians 4:3)

Our names cannot be removed from the Book of Life (Revelation 3:5)

Only those whose names are in God's Book will enter heaven
    (Revelation 20:15)

Caring

Care for your enemies (Luke 6:27)

God cares for his children (Romans 1:6-7)

Treat parents with care (Ephesians 6:2)

Care for the elderly (1 Timothy 5:1-4)

Christians need to care for the needy (James 1:27)

Children

Children must obey their parents (Colossians 3:20)

Church (see also Worship)

Satan works against the church (Matthew 16:18)

The church sends out missionaries (Acts 13:2)

The church is a family of Christians (Galatians 6:10)

Christ is the head of the church (Colossians 1:18)

The church is made up of God's children (1 John 3:1)

Comfort

God promises to comfort those who mourn (Matthew 5:4)
God comforts those who are hurting (2 Corinthians 1:3-11)
All pain will end (Revelation 21:3-4)

Complain

Christians should not complain to each other (Philippians 2:14)

Confession of Sin

God purifies those who confess their sin (1 John 1:8-9)

Conscience (see also Repentance)

Keep your conscience clear (1 Timothy 1:18-19)
Jesus' forgiveness clears your conscience (Hebrews 9:14)
A clear conscience helps you live a God-honoring life (1 Peter 3:16)

Courage

Jesus' strength gives us courage (John 16:33)
Courage helps us boldly represent Christ (Acts 4:31)
Christians should be courageous (1 Corinthians 16:13)
Pray for courage (Ephesians 6:19-20)

Covenant

Jesus established a new covenant (Luke 22:20)
God's covenant brings life (2 Corinthians 3:6)
The new covenant is superior to the old covenant (Hebrews 8:6)
The old covenant foreshadowed the new covenant (Hebrews 10:1)

Criticism

Take care of your own problems before criticizing others
　(Matthew 7:3-5)
Harsh criticism can destroy rather than help (Galatians 5:15)

Cross

Jesus was crucified (Matthew 27:31-35)
Christians should pick up their own crosses (Mark 8:34-38)
Jesus' death was a sacrifice (Colossians 1:20-22)
Jesus' cross is an example for us (Hebrews 12:2)

Cult

Only Jesus brings salvation (John 14:6)
Members of the occult will never enter God's Kingdom
　(Galatians 5:19-21)
Be careful in your spiritual life (1 Thessalonians 5:21)

Darkness, Spiritual

Jesus brings light to darkened lives (John 1:5)

Living without God is living in spiritual darkness (Acts 26:17-18)

God rescued us from eternal darkness (Colossians 1:13)

Sinners' eternal punishment will be in darkness (Jude 1:4-13)

Death

The death of Christians brings fellowship with Jesus (Acts 7:59)

God provides eternal life (Romans 6:23)

Jesus will raise everyone who has died (1 Corinthians 15:20-23)

Death is not the end of a person (1 Thessalonians 4:13-14)

Prepare your spiritual life before death (Hebrews 9:27-28)

Decisions

Ask God for wisdom before making decisions (James 1:2-8)

Demons (see also Satan)

Demons are no match for Jesus (Mark 1:34)

Demons want to destroy people (Mark 5:5)

Demons submit to the name of Jesus (Luke 10:17)

Demons are powerful (Acts 19:16)

Demons cannot separate people from God's love (Romans 8:38-39)

Demons want to mislead people (1 Timothy 4:1-2)

Desires

Desire to do God's will (1 Peter 4:2)

God's children desire to obey God (1 John 2:3-6)

Devotion

Let your life be devoted to God (Romans 12:1-2)

Discipline

Punishment should lead to repentance (2 Corinthians 7:8-9)

Sometimes God punishes us to bring us back to himself
(Hebrews 12:5-11)

Discrimination

God does not discriminate among his people (Acts 10:34)

All Christians are equal in God's eyes (Galatians 3:28)

God will judge those who discriminate (Colossians 3:25)

Do not discriminate against the poor (James 2:1-9)

Earth

Jesus sustains the earth (Hebrews 1:3)

Education

Christians should always learn more about God (Ephesians 4:14-15)

Embarrassment

We should not be embarrassed about the gospel (Romans 1:16)

We should not be embarrassed by Jesus (Galatians 1:10)

Emotions

Jesus experienced emotions (John 11:35)

Encouragement

Encourage your neighbor (Romans 15:2)

We should encourage each other (Hebrews 10:24-25)

Envy

Envy has no place in a Christian's life (Titus 3:3)

Eternal life

Belief in Jesus is required for eternal life (John 3:15-16)

Jesus came to give life (John 10:10)

Jesus gives eternal life (John 11:25)

Jesus is eternal life (John 14:6)

Faith

Faith is needed for salvation (Romans 3:28)

Christianity is the only true faith (Ephesians 4:5)

Faith is hoping in what is not seen (Hebrews 11:1)

Faith accompanies obedience to God (Hebrews 11:7-12)

Family

Christians are members of God's family (Ephesians 2:19)

Children should obey their parents (Ephesians 6:1)

Families should take care of each other (1 Timothy 5:3-5)

Fear

Love drives fear away (1 John 4:18)

Following Jesus

Jesus wants our highest love (Luke 14:26-27)

Forgiveness

We must forgive others (Matthew 6:14-15)

Don't keep track of how many times you forgive (Matthew 18:21-35)

Freely forgive others as God has forgiven you (Colossians 3:13)

God will forgive our sins if we confess them (1 John 1:8-9)

Friendship

Friendship is marked by sacrifice (John 15:13-15)
We can be friends with God (James 2:23)

Giving

God will reward us for giving to others (Mark 9:41)
Giving helps others live (Acts 2:44-45)
We should support Christian workers (Acts 28:10)
God loves a cheerful giver (2 Corinthians 9:7)
God is pleased with our gifts (Hebrews 13:16)
Giving reflects God's love (1 John 3:17)

God

God is our father (Matthew 6:9)
God is all-powerful (Luke 1:37)
God is spirit (John 4:24)
God is all-knowing (Romans 11:33)
God is knowable (Ephesians 1:17)
God is approachable (James 4:8)
God is love (1 John 4:16)

God's Will

God directs events in our lives (Acts 16:6-7)

God's Word

God's Word shows us what we are really like (Hebrews 4:12)

Gospel

The gospel's message is for everyone (Luke 24:46-47)
People should respond to the gospel with faith (John 1:12)
The gospel of Jesus (1 Corinthians 15:1-5)
Believing the gospel brings a change to life (1 Thessalonians 1:4-5)

Grace

God's grace makes salvation possible (Ephesians 1:7-8)
God accepts us by his grace (Ephesians 2:8-9)
We can confidently come to God to receive grace (Hebrews 4:16)

Grief (see also Sorrow)

God promises to comfort those who grieve (Matthew 5:4)
God comforts those who grieve (2 Corinthians 1:3-11)
All grief will end (Revelation 21:3-4)

Guilt

All people are guilty of sin (Romans 3:9-12)
Jesus Christ takes away all guilt (Romans 3:23-24)

Hate

People need to get rid of their own hatred (Colossians 3:8)

Heart

Those who have pure hearts will see God (Matthew 5:8)

Words and actions begin in the heart (Luke 6:45)

Heaven

Few people will enter heaven (Matthew 7:13-14)

Jesus is preparing heaven for his followers (John 14:2-3)

Heaven is much better than earth (Philippians 1:23)

There will not be any sadness in heaven (Revelation 21:4)

People in heaven will walk with God (Revelation 22:5)

Hell

Hell is a place of weeping (Matthew 8:12)

God will punish those who do not turn from their sin (2 Peter 2:4-9)

God will send to hell those who do not believe in him (Revelation 21:8)

Holy Spirit

The Holy Spirit teaches us (John 14:26)

The Holy Spirit guides us (John 16:13)

The Holy Spirit lives within us (Romans 8:11)

The Holy Spirit opens our spiritual eyes (1 Corinthians 2:10)

Hope

Jesus' resurrection gives us hope (1 Corinthians 6:14)

We have hope in Jesus (1 Corinthians 15:19)

Humility

Be humble in dealing with others (Philippians 2:1-11)

Humble yourself before God (James 4:7-10)

Hypocrisy

Beware of hypocrisy in your own life (Luke 12:1-2)

Get rid of hypocrisy (1 Peter 2:1)

Insult

Do not insult others (1 Peter 3:9)

Jesus Christ

Jesus is the Son of God (Luke 1:35)

Jesus is God (John 1:1-5)

Jesus gives life (John 10:10)

Jesus is the Good Shepherd (John 10:11)

Jesus rose from the dead (Romans 1:4)
Jesus is the Creator (Colossians 1:15-17)
Jesus is faithful (2 Timothy 2:13)
Jesus is coming again (Titus 2:13)

Judgment

God will judge the words we speak (Matthew 12:36)
People whose names are in God's Book of Life will enter heaven
   (Revelation 20:11-15)

Kindness

Be kind to people who treat you wrongly (1 Thessalonians 5:15)
Choose to be kind rather than to argue (2 Timothy 2:24)
Being kind takes effort (2 Peter 1:5-7)

Kingdom of God

God's Kingdom is open to those who do his will (Matthew 7:21)
Entering God's Kingdom costs someone everything (Matthew 13:44-45)
No one deserves God's Kingdom (Matthew 18:23-35)
God's Kingdom is within our hearts (Luke 17:20-21)
Only those who are spiritually reborn can enter God's Kingdom (John 3:3)
God calls people into his Kingdom (1 Thessalonians 2:12)
God's Kingdom cannot be shaken (Hebrews 12:28)

Leadership

Leaders must be servants (Matthew 20:25-28)

Life

Jesus came to give abundant life (John 10:10)
Jesus is life (John 14:6)
Christ is the reason for life (Philippians 1:21)
Our lives should honor God (Colossians 3:17)

Light

Jesus is the Light of the World (John 8:12)

Loneliness

God remains with us (Matthew 28:20)

Love

Love your enemies (Matthew 5:43-44)
Loving God is the most important command (Mark 12:29-30)
We cannot be separated from Jesus' love (Romans 8:35-39)
God's love for us is beyond our understanding (Ephesians 3:18)
God is love (1 John 4:16)

Marriage
Two people become one through marriage (Mark 10:2-12)
Married partners are united to each other for life (1 Corinthians 7:39)

Mercy
We should imitate God's mercy (Luke 6:36)
Jesus is merciful (1 Timothy 1:2)
Mercy is from God (2 Timothy 1:2)

Messiah
The Messiah will come again (Mark 14:61-62)
Jesus claimed to be the Messiah (John 4:25-42)
The Messiah brings salvation (Hebrews 2:10)

Money
Do not make money the most important part of your life (Matthew 6:19)
Money can distract people from God (Mark 10:17-24)
Christians should share their resources with those in need (Acts 2:42-45)
Do not love money (Hebrews 13:5)

Murder
Hateful anger is the same in God's eyes as murder (Matthew 5:21-22)

Music
We should make music for God's glory (Colossians 3:16)

Needs
God will take care of our needs (Philippians 4:19)

Obedience (see also Submission)
People who obey God's Word will be blessed (Luke 11:28)
Children should obey their parents (Ephesians 6:1)
God's children obey him (1 John 2:3)

Pain
All pain will end (Revelation 21:3-4)

Patience
Patience demonstrates love (1 Corinthians 13:4)
Be patient with each other (Ephesians 4:2)

Peace
Jesus gives us peace (Romans 5:1)
We can have peace through prayer (Philippians 4:4-7)

Power

God's power works in those who believe (Ephesians 3:20)
Jesus is the greatest power (Hebrews 1:1-4)
Prayer can be powerful (James 5:16)

Praise (see Worship)

Prayer

Jesus taught his disciples how to pray (Matthew 6:9-13)
Pray in Jesus' name (John 16:23-24)
Pray with the right motives (James 4:3)
Pray according to God's will (1 John 5:14-15)

Pride (see also Self-esteem)

God opposes the proud (James 4:6)

Problems (see Suffering, Trials)

Prophecy

We should listen to God's message (1 Thessalonians 5:20)
True prophets speak God's words (2 Peter 1:20-21)

Purity

Purity begins in the heart (Matthew 5:27-30)

Questions

God welcomes our sincere questions (Luke 7:18-23)

Rapture (see Second Coming of Christ)

Repentance (see also Confession of Sin)

Without repenting of our sin, we would perish (Luke 13:3-5)
Angels rejoice when a sinner repents (Luke 15:7)
God wants everyone to repent and believe (2 Peter 3:9)

Reputation

Guard your reputation (2 Corinthians 8:18-24)

Respect (see also Authority)

Husbands and wives should respect each other (Ephesians 5:33)
Those in leadership should have respectful children (1 Timothy 3:4)
Show respect to all people (1 Peter 2:17)

Responsibility

Responsible people are faithful with what they have been given
(Matthew 25:14-30)
Responsible people know their abilities and limitations (Acts 6:1-7)
Being responsible is rewarding (Galatians 6:4)

Rest

Jesus promises to give us rest from our burdens (Matthew 11:28-30)

Rest is a gift from God (Hebrews 4:9-11)

Resurrection

Christ's resurrection is a historical fact (Matthew 28:5-10)

All people will be resurrected (John 5:24-30)

We will experience resurrection (Romans 6:3-11)

Our resurrected bodies will be eternal bodies (1 Corinthians 15:51-53)

Revenge

Jesus is our example when we are tempted to take revenge (1 Peter 2:21-23)

Righteous/Righteousness

Righteousness is not attained by works (Romans 4:18-25)

We become righteous through faith in Christ (Philippians 3:9)

Sacrifice

We should sacrifice ourselves for God (Romans 12:1)

Sadness (see Grief, Sorrow)

Salvation

Those who receive salvation become God's children (John 1:12-13)

Belief and trust in Jesus Christ are the only way to be saved (John 14:6)

Receiving salvation means we must turn from our sins (Acts 2:37-38)

Salvation cannot be earned; it is a gift of God (Romans 6:23)

Salvation is by God's grace alone (Ephesians 2:1-9)

God wants to give us salvation (Revelation 3:20)

Satan (see also Demons)

Satan will tempt Jesus' followers (Matthew 4:1-11)

Satan is completely evil (John 8:44)

Satan is the temporary ruler over this world (Ephesians 2:1-2)

Believers have the authority to resist Satan (James 4:1-10)

Jesus destroyed Satan's work with his death (1 John 3:7-8)

Satan is a defeated enemy (Revelation 20:10)

Second Coming of Christ

We do not know when Jesus will return (Matthew 24:36)

Christ's return will be joyous for believers (Luke 12:35-40)

The Second Coming will be a time of judgment on unbelievers (John 12:37-50)

The promise of Christ's return (Acts 1:10-11)

Christ's return will be visible and glorious (1 Thessalonians 4:16)

Jesus is coming soon (Revelation 22:20-21)

Self-esteem (see also Pride)

We are of great value to God (Luke 12:4-12)

Sickness

Jesus can heal sicknesses (Matthew 4:23-25)

Believers ought to have compassion on the sick (Matthew 25:34-40)

Sin

All people have sinned (Romans 3:23)

Sin leads to eternal death (Romans 6:23)

Jesus takes the penalty of our sin on himself (Romans 8:1-2)

Sin begins with temptation (James 1:15)

We can sin by avoiding something we should do (James 4:17)

God is willing to forgive our sins (1 John 1:8-9)

Sorrow (see also Grief)

God promises comfort to those who experience sorrow (Matthew 5:4)

We are sorrowful over believers who die, but one day we will meet again
(1 Thessalonians 4:13-18)

Sorrow will not exist in God's Kingdom (Revelation 21:3-4)

Speech

Our speech should be kind and gentle (2 Timothy 2:24-25)

Submission (see also Obedience)

Christ is our example of submission to the Father's will
(Matthew 26:39, 42)

Following Christ requires submission to him (Luke 14:27)

God created lines of authority for harmonious relationships
(1 Corinthians 11:2-16)

Submit to God (James 4:7-10)

Suffering (see also Trials)

Christ's followers will suffer (Matthew 16:21-26)

Jesus can help us through suffering (Hebrews 2:11-18)

Christ showed how to handle suffering (1 Peter 2:21-24)

There will be no suffering in Christ's Kingdom (Revelation 21:4)

Temptation

How to respond when tempted (Matthew 4:1-11)

God will provide a way of escape from every temptation (1 Corinthians 10:13)

Run from temptation (2 Timothy 2:22)

Christ can help us, for he, too, has faced temptation (Hebrews 2:18; 4:15-16)

Thankfulness

Be thankful for salvation (Ephesians 2:4-10)

We are called to give thanks in all circumstances (1 Thessalonians 5:16-18)

Trials (see also Suffering)

Jesus understands our struggles (John 15:18)

God knows what he is doing with our lives (Romans 8:28)

God expects us to grow through our trials (James 1:2-4)

Trust (see Faith)

Truth

Truth is found in Jesus Christ (John 14:6)

God's Word is truth (John 17:17)

We should speak truthfully (Ephesians 4:25)

We must not only believe the truth but also live in it (1 John 1:5-7)

Unbelievers

We must share the gospel with unbelievers (John 17:14-19)

Unbelievers do not belong to Christ (Romans 8:9)

We should avoid situations that force us to compromise our beliefs
(2 Corinthians 6:14-18)

Unbelievers will not enter heaven (1 John 5:10-12)

Wisdom

Wise people build on the solid foundation of God and his Word
(Matthew 7:24-27)

God will give us wisdom if we ask for it (James 1:5)

Work

Our work for God is never wasted (1 Corinthians 15:58)

All work should be done as though we are working for God (Ephesians 6:5-9)

Worry

We do not need to worry (Luke 12:27-32)

We can give our worries to God (1 Peter 1:5-7)

Worship (see also Church)

We can worship because of Christ's sacrifice on our behalf (Hebrews 10:1-10)

We should worship with reverence for God (Hebrews 12:28)

When we draw near to God, he draws near to us (James 4:8)

prophecies about JESUS

For the Gospel writers, one of the main reasons for believing in Jesus was the way his life fulfilled the Old Testament prophecies about the Messiah. Following is a list of some of the main prophecies and their fulfillments.

PROPHECY	Old Testament Reference	New Testament Fulfillment
Messiah was to be born in Bethlehem	Micah 5:2	Matthew 2:1-6; Luke 2:1-20
Messiah was to be born of a virgin	Isaiah 7:14	Matthew 1:18-25; Luke 1:26-38
Messiah was to be a prophet like Moses	Deuteronomy 18:15, 18-19	John 7:40
Messiah was to enter Jerusalem in triumph	Zechariah 9:9	Matthew 21:1-9; John 12:12-16
Messiah was to be rejected by his own people	Isaiah 53:1-3 Psalm 118:22	Matthew 26:3-4; John 12:37-43; Acts 4:1-12
Messiah was to be betrayed by one of his followers	Psalm 41:9	Matthew 26:14-16, 47-50; Luke 22:16, 47-48
Messiah was to be tried and condemned	Isaiah 53:8	Luke 23:1-25; Matthew 27:1-2

Messiah was to be silent before his accusers	Isaiah 53:7	Matthew 26:62-63; 27:12-14; Mark 15:3-5; Luke 23:8-10
Messiah was to be struck and spit upon by his enemies	Isaiah 50:6	Matthew 26:67; 27:30; Mark 14:65
Messiah was to be mocked and taunted	Psalm 22:7-8	Matthew 27:39-44; Luke 23:11, 35-36
Messiah was to die by crucifixion	Psalm 22:14, 16-17	Matthew 27:31; Mark 15:20, 25
Messiah was to suffer with criminals and pray for his enemies	Isaiah 53:12	Matthew 27:38; Mark 15:27-28; Luke 23:32-34
Messiah was to be given vinegar and gall	Psalm 69:21	Matthew 27:34; John 19:28-30
Others were to cast lots for Messiah's garments	Psalm 22:18	Matthew 27:35; John 19:23-24
Messiah's bones were not to be broken	Exodus 12:46	John 19:31-36
Messiah was to die as a sacrifice for sin	Isaiah 53:5-6, 8, 10-12	John 1:29; 11:49-52; Acts 10:43; 13:38-39
Messiah was to be raised from the dead	Psalm 16:10	Matthew 28:1-10; Mark 16:1-8; Luke 24:1-12; John 20:1-9; Acts 2:22-32
Messiah is now at God's right hand	Psalm 110:1	Mark 16:19; Luke 24:50-51

What does it mean when someone refers to "the flesh"? What is the significance of the phrase "the blood"? And why is it important to "disciple" others? Whether you have just become a Christian or are simply interested in learning more about Christianity, you will soon discover that Christians sometimes seem to speak their own language. This basic glossary of commonly used Christian terms and phrases will help you uncover some of the mystery behind the Christian vocabulary. In addition, some entries will point you to areas of further study so that you can see how these expressions apply to your life. If for some reason you still have trouble comprehending what a Christian term means (or if it is not listed here), do not hesitate to ask a more mature Christian, a Bible study leader, or your pastor. As the saying goes, "There is only one bad question: the question you never ask." The more you learn about your Christian faith and the God you now serve, the deeper and more meaningful your spiritual walk will be.

Abide: To remain consistently in fellowship with God by maintaining a close relationship with Jesus Christ. Most commonly used in the phrase "abide in Christ." (For further study, turn to "Live as a Disciple," page A42.)

Accepting Christ: To receive God's gift of salvation by believing in Jesus Christ, asking God to forgive you of your sin that you have repented of, inviting Christ to take up residence in your heart, and allowing the Holy Spirit to change your life. (For further study, turn to How You Can Know God, page A11.) See also *Repent*.

Accountability: To be held responsible for your actions. For example, we are accountable to God for what we do with the talents and abilities he gives us. (For further study, turn to "Accountability," page A35.)

Altar Call: See *Invitation*.

Angels: Spirit messengers who worship God and care for believers. (For further study, turn to "What Are Angels?" page A26.)

Antichrist: Literally means "false Christ" or "instead of Christ." The Bible says that one great Antichrist, or "false Christ," will appear in the final days before Christ's return to earth and will deceive many (see Revelation 13:1-7, pages 328-329). This term is also used to describe anyone who opposes Jesus Christ and his teachings (see 1 John 2:18, page 307; 1 John 4:3, page 310; 2 John 1:7, page 313).

Atonement: The removal of God's punishment for sin through the perfect sacrifice of Jesus Christ (see Romans 3:25, page 170). (For further study, turn to "The Solution: Jesus Christ," page A13.)

Backslide: To stop moving forward in the Christian walk; to spiritually regress. (For further study, turn to "What Is Backsliding?" page 97.)

Baptism: 1. Water baptism is an outward display of what has happened in the life of the believer: the death of the old nature (when one is placed under the water), and the birth of a new nature (when one is raised up) (see Colossians 2:12, page 245). While it is not necessary for salvation, it demonstrates a person's submission to Christ. Baptism is also a demonstration of that person's willingness to live God's way. Jesus himself stressed its importance (see Matthew 28:19, page 38). 2. Spirit baptism occurs when the Holy Spirit enters a person's life. This baptism occurs only after he or she has received Jesus Christ as Lord and Savior. See also *Filling of the Holy Spirit.*

Burdens: Refers to helping other believers by sharing in their trials, sorrows, and concerns so that they will not feel alone (see Galatians 6:1-3, page 226).

Believer: Someone who has accepted Jesus Christ as Savior and Lord.

Blood (the): Refers to the blood Christ shed on the cross of Calvary, where he essentially became the sacrifice for our sins.

Body of Christ (the): Another term for the church—all those who call Jesus Christ their Lord. Throughout the New Testament Jesus Christ is often referred to as the "head" of this body (see Ephesians 1:22-23, page 228). See also *Church.*

Book of Life (the): A record found in heaven that lists the names of every individual who has committed his or her life to Jesus Christ and can be called a follower of God (Daniel 12:1; see Luke 10:20, page 78; Revelation 3:5, page 321; Revelation 21:27, page 336).

Born Again: Describes what takes place when a person accepts Jesus Christ as his or her personal Savior. Essentially, one becomes spiritually "reborn" at that point, escaping spiritual death and receiving eternal life (see John 3:3-7, page 103).

Bride of Christ (the): Another term for the church or Christian believers as a whole (see 2 Corinthians 11:2, page 218). See also *Church.*

Calling: 1. (Noun) God's invitation to men and women to receive the gift and benefits of salvation (see Ephesians 1:18, page 227; 1 Thessalonians 2:12, page 250;

2 Thessalonians 2:14, page 256). 2. (Noun) God's divinely appointed plan or purpose for a believer, as in "He believes that God's calling is for him to . . ." (see Ephesians 4:1, page 230; 2 Timothy 1:9, page 265). 3. (Verb) When God directs an individual toward a particular vocation or area of service (e.g., "He believes that God is calling him to be a pastor").

Carnal: To be controlled and motivated by one's sinful, human nature rather than the Holy Spirit; a failure to live the Christian life as Jesus meant it to be lived.

Christ: Shortened form of the name "Jesus Christ," the Son of God and Savior of the world; not a name as much as a title. The word *Christ* (or *Christos*) is Greek for "anointed one," which was often used in the description of Jewish kings and high priests. (For further study, turn to "The Solution: Jesus Christ," page A13.)

Church (the): 1. The collective body of Christian believers around the world and throughout the ages. 2. A place where people come together to fellowship with other believers, learn more about the Christian faith through the leadership of a pastor, and use their God-given talents and abilities to glorify God. (For further study, turn to "Look for and Attend the Right Church," page A38.)

Commitment: 1. The decision to accept Jesus Christ as one's Savior and Lord (e.g., "The young woman made a commitment to Christ after the pastor's message"). 2. A person's willingness to stay true to Christ regardless of the cost.

Communion: 1. A time when fellow believers come together to remember the effects of Jesus' sacrifice on the cross for them by receiving and eating the elements Jesus used in the Lord's Supper (also known as the "Last Supper"). The bread symbolizes Jesus' body, broken for us on the cross, while the wine (or juice) represents Jesus' blood, shed on the cross for our sins (see 1 Corinthians 10:16-17, page 200). See also *Lord's Supper.* 2. The deep closeness and fellowship a person can experience with God as a result of entering into a personal relationship with him (see 1 Corinthians 1:9, page 189).

Confess: 1. To agree with, as in agreeing with God about our sins and sinful condition. To admit your sins to God and ask for his forgiveness (see 1 John 1:9, page 305). 2. To publicly acknowledge your relationship with and commitment to Jesus Christ (see Romans 10:9-10, page 180).

Consecration: A dedication to serve God wholeheartedly and to be used for his glory (1 Chronicles 29:5; see Romans 12:1, page 183; 2 Corinthians 8:5, page 215).

Conversion: When a person makes a decision to receive Jesus Christ as Savior and Lord, turning from the darkness and futility of this world to the light and hope found in Christ (see Acts 26:18, page 163).

Conviction: 1. To feel guilt and remorse after committing some wrongdoing. 2. To feel genuine sorrow and concern over one's sinful condition and unworthiness before God. The Holy Spirit is responsible for this conviction in the life of the unbeliever (see John 16:8, page 120).

Cross: 1. Reference to Jesus' death on the cross of Calvary and to what his death represents. (For further study, turn to "The Solution: Jesus Christ," page A13.) 2. Reference to our identification with Jesus Christ; setting aside our personal ambition to follow and serve God (see Matthew 16:24, page 22). See also *Denying Self.*

Demons: Spirit beings who serve Satan. They are essentially fallen angels (approximately one-third of the original angel population), who lost their former position in heaven along with Satan for their rebellion against God (see Revelation 12:4, page 327). (For further study, turn to "What Are Demons?" page A27.)

Denying Self: To place God's will and desires above your own (see Matthew 16:24, page 22).

Devil: See *Satan.*

Devotions: A personal time of fellowship and communion with God that includes Bible study, prayer, and worship. (For further study, turn to "Study the Bible," page A37 and "Pray," page A38.)

Disciple: 1. One of the twelve original close followers of Jesus Christ during his earthly ministry. 2. One who learns, follows, and lives by the teachings of Jesus Christ; one who imitates Christ. (For further study, turn to "Live as a Disciple," page A42.)

Discipleship: The process of making other disciples; the practice of introducing people to Jesus Christ and then encouraging them to grow in their faith by teaching them about the Lord and showing them how to live as a follower of Christ (see Matthew 28:19-20, page 38).

Divinity: Connotes the self-contained power and holy nature of God.

Doctrine: The fundamental tenets, or cornerstones, of a belief system (in this case, Christianity).

Election: God's choice of an individual or group for a specific purpose or destiny (see Ephesians 1:4-5, page 227).

End Times: The final days on this earth before the return of Jesus Christ.

Evangelism: Literally means the sharing of the "Good News," or the gospel of Jesus Christ, with others. (For further study, turn to "Share Your Faith," page A41.)

Faith: 1. A firm conviction that produces a full acknowledgment of God's truth; a belief and hope in God and his Word in response to the message of salvation (see John 1:12, page 101). 2. Having a certainty in what you hope for even though you may not be able to see it (see Hebrews 11:1-40, pages 284-285).

Fall (the): Refers to the first act of disobedience against God, when Adam and Eve ate fruit from the tree that God had forbidden them to touch in the Garden of Eden (Genesis 3:1-24; see Romans 5:12, page 173). (For further study, turn to "The Problem: Sin," page A11.)

Family of God: Those individuals throughout history who have accepted God's free gift of salvation, which has entitled them to be God's children (see John 1:12, page 101). (For further study, turn to "Adopted and Assured," page A20.)

Fasting: When a person voluntarily abstains from food for a given time to devote himself or herself to prayer for a specific need, responsibility, or request (see Matthew 6:17-18, page 7; Acts 14:23, page 149).

Father (the): 1. Reference to God, the Father—the source and giver of life, wisdom, and salvation (see Ephesians 1:17, page 227; Hebrews 12:9, page 286; James 1:17, page 289). 2. Used when speaking of God as the Father of Jesus Christ (see 2 Corinthians 1:3, page 209). 3. Used to describe God's relationship to a believer after conversion (see John 1:12-13, page 101). See also *Trinity*.

Fellowship: 1. (Noun) A communion or partnership with other believers. 2. (Verb) To communicate and meet with fellow believers to encourage one another in the Christian faith and to assist those who have special needs (see Acts 2:42, page 131; Romans 1:12, page 167; Hebrews 10:25, page 283). (For further study, turn to "Look For and Attend the Right Church," page A38.)

Filling of the Holy Spirit: 1. The entrance of the Holy Spirit into a person's life after he or she has accepted Jesus Christ as personal Savior (see Acts 2:38, page 131; Galatians 4:6, page 224). 2. The empowerment of the Holy Spirit in one's life to perform a certain task (see Acts 1:8, page 129; Acts 4:31, page 135). (For further study, turn to "Live in God's Power," page A40.) See also *Baptism*.

Flesh (the): Speaks of our human, or sinful, nature and tendencies; the weaker element in human nature (see Matthew 26:41, page 35; Romans 6:19, page 175; Romans 7:5-6, page 175).

Foundation: The basis upon which we build our lives. According to the Bible, a strong foundation for living is based upon God and his Word (Isaiah 28:6; see Matthew 7:24, page 10; 2 Timothy 2:19, page 266).

Freedom in Christ: Describes the spiritual liberty, or freedom, we have as followers of Jesus Christ. We are freed from the controlling power of sin and released from the obligation of meeting God's righteous requirements on our own through the death and resurrection of Jesus Christ. This freedom does not give us the right to disregard God's laws. It simply allows us to obey God out of love rather than obligation (see Romans 6:7, pages 174-175; Romans 8:2, page 176; Galatians 5:13, page 226; Galatians 6:1, page 226; 1 Peter 2:16, page 297). (For further study, turn to "Faith and Works," page A32.)

Fruit (of the Spirit): 1. Evidence of the presence of the Holy Spirit at work in our lives. This is often displayed through our attitudes and our actions (see Matthew 7:16, page 9). 2. The character traits the Holy Spirit produces in our lives—love, joy, peace, patience, kindness, goodness, faithfulness, gentleness, and self-control (see Galatians 5:22-23, page 226).

Gifts: See *Spiritual Gifts.*

Gifts of the Spirit: See *Spiritual Gifts.*

Glorification: The ultimate state of the believer after death, when he or she becomes like Christ (see Romans 8:17, page 176; Philippians 3:21, page 240).

Godhead: All that God is (i.e., his person, character, abilities, etc.).

Gospel: 1. The "Good News" of salvation; the explanation of how one can be saved from the eternal punishment of hell and receive forgiveness and eternal life through Jesus Christ (see 1 Corinthians 15:1-5, page 205). 2. This term in the plural refers to the first four books of the New Testament.

Grace: The undeserved favor, forgiveness, and acceptance we receive from God through our acceptance of Jesus Christ as our Lord and Savior (see Ephesians 2:8-9, page 228).

Great Commission: Signifies Christ's command to us to go out into all the world—whether that is across the street or across the ocean—and win people to the Lord so they, too, can become dedicated followers of Jesus Christ (see Matthew 28:19-20, page 38). (For further study, turn to "Share Your Faith," page A41.)

Hardness of Heart: The dulling of one's spiritual perception; a built-up stubbornness or animosity toward the will and ways of God (see 2 Corinthians 4:4, page 211; Ephesians 4:18, pages 230-231).

Harvest (the): Describes the "reaping" of souls through the process of sharing the message of the gospel with others and leading them to Jesus Christ (see John 4:35-36, page 105; Galatians 6:9, page 226).

Holiness: 1. A description of the flawless, sinless character of God. 2. To reflect a devotion to God and his ways in your life; a singlehearted pursuit to become more Christlike in character.

Holy Ghost: See *Holy Spirit.*

Holy Spirit: One of the distinctive, powerful Persons of the threefold Godhead. His responsibilities include convicting us of our sin, leading us to Christ, and helping us grow in character, faith, and knowledge after conversion. (For further study, turn to "Who Is the Holy Spirit?" page A24.)

Intercession or Interceding: To pray for someone; to make a petition to God on behalf of another (Psalm 106:23; see Romans 8:26, page 177; Ephesians 1:16-17, page 227). (For further study, turn to "Pray," page A38.)

Invitation: The moment (usually at the end of a gospel presentation) when a pastor or evangelist invites people to accept Jesus Christ into their lives. This is also referred to as an "altar call," since people are sometimes asked to come forward to a specified location to make a public stand of their newfound faith.

Jesus: Refers to Jesus Christ, the Son of God and Savior of the world. See also *Christ.*

Judgment: A reference to God's divine judgment, reserved for the end of the age. At that time, each person will stand before God and will be found "guilty" or "innocent" based upon his or her rejection or acceptance of Jesus Christ (see Matthew 25:32, page 34; Hebrews 9:27, page 282; Revelation 20:12, page 335).

Justification: Being cleansed of our sins. (For a more in-depth description of justification, see "What God Has Done for You," page A19.)

Laborers: Those who are actively serving the Lord and sharing their faith with others (see Matthew 9:37-38, page 12; 1 Corinthians 3:8-9, page 192). (For further study, turn to "Share Your Faith," page A41.)

Lamb (the): A reference to Jesus Christ, who became the "sacrificial lamb" by his death for our sins on the cross of Calvary (Isaiah 53:7-8; see John 1:29, page 102; 1 Peter 1:19, page 296).

Last Days: A reference to the last days on earth prior to the return of Jesus Christ. See also *End Times.*

Lord's Supper: Jesus' last supper with his disciples. This is also when fellow believers come together to remember Jesus' sacrifice on the cross for them by receiving and eating the elements Jesus used in the Lord's Supper (also known as the "Last Supper"). The bread symbolizes Jesus' body, broken for us on the cross, while the wine (or juice) represents Jesus' blood, shed on the cross for our sins (see 1 Corinthians 10:16-17, page 200). See also *Communion.*

Lordship: Signifies the supremacy and authority of the Lord Jesus Christ in the life of the believer and over all the earth (see 1 Corinthians 8:6, page 198).

Lucifer: Another name for Satan. See *Satan*.

Meditate: To contemplate and reflect upon something. As believers, we are told to ponder such things as the meaning of a passage of Scripture or truths we learn about the Lord through our pastors and teachers (Joshua 1:8; Psalms 43:5; 63:6). (For further study, turn to "Study the Bible," page A37.)

Messiah: The Hebrew word for God's "anointed one" (Jesus Christ) who came to save the world by taking the punishment for our sins. See also *Christ*.

Millennium: Refers to the thousand-year reign of Jesus Christ on the earth during which there will be no more war (Isaiah 2:4; see Revelation 20:1-6, pages 334-335).

New Creation: A description of what we become once we allow Jesus Christ to take residence in our lives (see 2 Corinthians 5:17, pages 212-213). (For further study, turn to "Adopted and Assured," page A20.)

New Nature: That which enables us to live godly lives through the power of the Holy Spirit. It replaces our "old nature" when we accept Jesus Christ into our lives (see Romans 6:8, page 175). See also *New Creation*.

Old Nature: That which follows our basic, sinful instincts. Before we came to Christ, we were under this nature's control (see Ephesians 4:22, page 231; 2 Peter 1:9, page 301).

Original Sin: Refers to the first transgression humankind ever committed, when Adam and Eve took fruit from the tree that God had forbidden them to touch. See also *the Fall*.

Prayer: Conversation with God in which we express praise, needs, thanks, and concerns. (For further study, turn to "Pray," page A38.)

Predestination: The idea that God knew before the beginning of time those who would follow him (see Romans 8:29, page 177; Ephesians 1:4, page 227). See also *Election*.

Propitiation: See *Atonement*.

Purify: To cleanse or rid oneself of those things that are not pleasing to God (see 2 Corinthians 7:1, page 214; James 4:8, page 293; 1 John 3:3, page 308). (For further study, turn to "Purity," page A30.)

Quiet Time: Time spent alone in prayer and in the study of God's Word. (For further study, turn to "Study the Bible," page A37, and "Pray," page A38.)

Rapture: When Christ takes his followers from earth to be with him (1 Thessalonians 4:17, page 253).

Rebirth: See *Born Again*.

Receiving Christ: See *Accepting Christ*.

Recommitment: When a person returns to the Lord after having abandoned his or her relationship with Christ and gone back to his or her former life. (For further study, turn to "What Is Backsliding?" page 97.)

Redemption: The price Jesus paid for the sins of the world. (For a more in-depth description of redemption, see "The Problem: Sin," page A11, and "The Solution: Jesus Christ," page A13.)

Regeneration: See *New Creation*.

Renewal: A time of soul-searching, confession of sin, and spiritual reawakening that leads one to a deeper walk with God (Psalm 51:10; see 2 Corinthians 4:16, page 211; James 4:8-10, page 293). See also *Revival*.

Repent: Literally means "to change your direction." To turn away from those things or activities that displease God and start doing the things that please him. (For further study, turn to "The Response: Accept God's Offer," page A16.)

Resurrection: 1. When Christ rose from the dead the third day after his crucifixion, breaking the power of death and completing the work of salvation (see Acts 2:23-24, page 130; Romans 1:4, page 167; Romans 4:25, page 173). 2. When all will rise again at the appearance of Jesus Christ (Daniel 12:2; see John 5:29, page 106; John 6:40, page 107; Acts 24:15, page 161; 1 Thessalonians 4:16, page 253).

Revival: Literally "to flourish anew." A time of spiritual renewal when many come to a committed relationship with Jesus Christ; a time of returning to God (Psalm 51:12-13). See also *Renewal*.

Righteousness: Right standing before God; being right before God.

Salvation: The means by which a person can receive eternal life through accepting Jesus Christ as his or her Lord and Savior (see John 3:16, page 103). See also *Gospel*.

Sanctification: Becoming more and more like Jesus Christ through the work of the Holy Spirit (see Philippians 1:6, page 237; 2 Thessalonians 2:13, page 256). (For further study, turn to "Live as a Disciple," page A42.)

Satan: A fallen angel who lost his former position as a high-ranking angel in heaven because of his pride; his chief aim is to foster rebellion against God in the hearts of men and women. (For further study, turn to "Who Is the Devil?" page A25.)

Savior: A reference to Jesus that signifies his role in bringing us the gift of salvation and freedom from the punishment we deserve.

Second Coming: A reference to Jesus Christ's return to earth to establish his kingdom (see Matthew 26:64, page 36; Acts 1:11, page 129; Hebrews 9:28, page 282).

Servanthood: 1. A level of commitment that involves a willingness to serve and honor God with your life (Deuteronomy 10:12). 2. The act of following Jesus' humble example toward others by treating them better than yourself and helping to care for their needs (see Philippians 2:3-8, pages 238-239).

Sin: 1. (verb) To "miss the mark," or fall short of God's level of perfection; to break God's commands. 2. (noun) The one thing that separates us from a relationship with God. (For further study, turn to "The Problem: Sin," page A11).

Sinful Nature: See *Old Nature.*

Sinner: Word used to describe what we are by nature. We are not sinners because we sin; rather, we sin because we are sinners.

Son (the): See *Son of God.*

Son of God: Another reference for Jesus Christ, signifying Jesus' relationship to God the Father (see Matthew 3:17, page 3; Hebrews 10:29, page 283; 1 John 4:15, page 311).

Soul: The vital existence of a human being; the immaterial essence of an individual through which he or she perceives, reflects, feels, and desires.

Soul Winner: A person who actively shares his or her faith with others in order to lead them to Christ. See also *Laborers.*

Sovereignty: A description of God's supreme power and authority.

Spirit (the): See *Holy Spirit.*

Spiritual Gifts: Certain supernatural gifts and abilities given to you by the Holy Spirit in order to build up, edify, and encourage the church (see Romans 12:6, page 183; Ephesians 4:11, page 230). (For further study, turn to "What Are Spiritual Gifts?" page 231.)

Stumble: To spiritually regress, or to commit some sin against God, thus hindering your Christian growth. See also *Backslide.*

Surrender: To yield your personal rights and will to the Lord; to fully give your life to the Lord for his service (see Romans 12:1, page 183).

Testimony: 1. The story of how you came into a relationship with Jesus Christ. 2. An account of what God has been doing in your life.

Tithe: A portion of your earnings (often considered to be 10 percent of gross income) that you set aside to give to the Lord (Genesis 28:22; Malachi 3:10). (For further study, turn to "Give to God," page A43.)

Trials: Difficult times and circumstances that test your faith. (For further study, turn to "Have Courage in Trials," page A44.)

Tribulation: 1. A time of intense difficulty. 2. A description of the time just prior to the Second Coming of Jesus Christ when the world will go through unprecedented turmoil (see Matthew 24:6-13, page 31).

Trinity: The three persons who make up the Godhead: God the Father, God the Son (Jesus), and God the Holy Spirit (see Matthew 28:19, page 38; John 14:26, page 118; 1 Peter 1:2, page 295).

Walk: 1. A description of your spiritual growth or progress. 2. Your daily relationship with God.

Witness: 1. (Verb) To tell others about the message of salvation through Jesus Christ. (For further study, turn to "Share Your Faith," page A41.) 2. (Noun) The demonstration of God's presence in your life.

Works: Your deeds and actions. (For further study, turn to "Faith and Works," page A32.)

World (the): 1. Signifies the present condition of human affairs on this earth that are in opposition to God and his ways (see Ephesians 2:2, page 228; James 4:4, pages 292-293). 2. The temporal possessions of this earth (see Matthew 16:26, page 22; Colossians 3:2, page 246).

Worldly: See *Carnal.*

Worship: A sincere expression of reverence and devotion toward God. Worship can take place through singing songs of praise, praying, and meditating upon God's Word.

Yield: See *Surrender.*

Bibles At Cost

To order additional copies call

USA:
1(800)778-8865
www.biblesatcost.com

Canada:
1(888)888-4548
www.biblesatcostcanada.com

New Believer's New Testament

Become Involved in an Outreach Ministry — USA

To help or join a ministry	Contact
Harvest Crusade — Greg Laurie — USA	(800)821-3300
Silver Ring Thing (Teen Abstinence)	(412)424-2400
Fellowship of Christian Athletes	(800)289-0909
Child Evangelism Fellowship	(636)456-4321
Youth for Christ	(800)843-9000
Crisis Pregnancy Care Net	(800)395-HELP

Find a Bible-Teaching Church! — USA

To Find a Church	National Phone Number
Assembly of God	(417)862-2781
Calvary Chapel	(714)979-4422
Evangelical Free	(800)745-2202
Lutheran Church	(773)380-2700
Church of the Nazarene	(816)333-7000
Presbyterian Church	(502)569-5000
Southern Baptist	(615)244-2355
United Methodist Church	(800)251-8140

www.biblesatcost.com   A Bible Distribution Ministry

CP0606